MW00563916

Serving Military Families

This text introduces readers to the unique culture of military families, their resilience, and the challenges of military life. Personal stories from nearly 70 active duty, reservists, veterans, and their families from all branches and ranks of the military, practitioners, and researchers bring their experiences to life. A review of the latest research, theories, policies, and programs better prepares readers for understanding and working with military families. Objectives, key terms, tables, figures, summaries, and exercises, including web-based exercises, serve as a chapter review. The book concludes with a glossary. Readers learn about diverse careers within which they can make important differences for families.

Engaging vignettes are featured throughout:

Voices From the Frontline offer personal accounts of issues faced by actual program leaders, practitioners, researchers, policy makers, service members, veterans, and their families.
Spotlight on Research highlights the latest studies on dealing with combat-related issues.
Best Practices review the optimal strategies used in the field.
Tips from the Frontline offer suggestions from experienced personnel.

Updated throughout including the latest demographic data, the new edition also features:

- *New chapter (9) on women service members* that addresses the accomplishments and challenges faced by this population, including sexual bias and assault, and combat-related psychological disorders.
- *New chapter (10) on veterans and families* looks at veterans by era (e.g., World War II), each era's signature issues and how those impact programs and policies, and challenges veterans may face, such as employment, education, and mental and physical health issues.
- Two new, more comprehensive and cohesive chapters (11 and 12) review military and civilian programs, policies, and organizations that support military and veteran families.
- Additional information on traumatic brain injury and Post-traumatic Stress Disorder, the deployment cycle, stress and resilience, the possible negative effects of military life on families, same-sex couples and their children, and the recent increase in suicides in the military.
- More applied cases and exercises that focus on providing services to military families.

Intended as a text for advanced undergraduate or graduate courses on military families or as a supplement for courses on the family, marriage and family, stress and coping, or family systems taught in family science, human development, clinical or counseling psychology, sociology, social work, and nursing, this book also appeals to helping professionals who work with military and veteran families.

Karen Rose Blaisure is a Professor at Western Michigan University where she teaches a course on Family Life and the Military. **Tara Saathoff-Wells** is a Research and Evaluation Scientist for the Clearinghouse for Military Family Readiness at the Pennsylvania State University. **Angela Pereira** is a retired U.S. Army Colonel and a consultant and educator on psychological health and military life issues. **Shelley MacDermid Wadsworth** is Professor of Human Development and Family Studies and Director of the Military Family Research Institute at Purdue University. **Amy Laura Dombro** is a writer who develops resources for teachers, family support professionals, and community leaders to assist military and veteran families and children.

Textbooks in Family Studies Series

The *Textbooks in Family Studies Series* is an interdisciplinary series that offers cutting edge textbooks in family studies and family psychology. Volumes can be complete textbooks and/or supplementary texts for the undergraduate and/or graduate markets. Both authored and edited volumes are welcome. Please contact the series editor, Robert Milardo at rhd360@maine.edu, for details in preparing a proposal that should include the goal of the book, table of contents, an overview of competing texts, the intended market including course name(s) and level, and suggested reviewers.

These are the books currently in the series:

Father-Daughter Relationships: Contemporary Research and Issues written by Linda Nielsen (2012)

Stepfamilies: A Global Perspective on Research, Policy and Practice written by Jan Pryor (2014)

Serving Military Families: Theories, Research, and Application, Second Edition written by Karen Rose Blaisure, Tara Saathoff-Wells, Angela Pereira, Shelley MacDermid Wadsworth, and Amy Laura Dombro (2016)

Evidence-based Approaches to Relationship and Marriage Education edited by James J. Ponzetti, Jr. (2016)

Evidence-based Parenting Education: A Global Perspective edited by James J. Ponzetti, Jr. (2016)

Evidence-based Approaches to Sexuality Education: A Global Perspective edited by James J. Ponzetti, Jr. (2016)

Serving Military Families

Theories, Research, and Application

Second Edition

Karen Rose Blaisure
Western Michigan University

Tara Saathoff-Wells
Clearinghouse for Military Family Readiness at Penn State

Angela Pereira
Colonel, U.S. Army, Retired

Shelley MacDermid Wadsworth
Military Family Research Institute at Purdue University

Amy Laura Dombro

Routledge
Taylor & Francis Group

NEW YORK AND LONDON

First published 2016
by Routledge
711 Third Avenue, New York, NY 10017

and by Routledge
27 Church Road, Hove, East Sussex BN3 2FA

Routledge is an imprint of the Taylor & Francis Group, an informa business

© 2016 Taylor & Francis

The right of Karen Rose Blaisure, Tara Saathoff-Wells, Angela Pereira, Shelley MacDermid Wadsworth, and Amy Laura Dombro to be identified as the authors of this work has been asserted by them in accordance with sections 77 and 78 of the Copyright, Designs and Patents Act 1988.

All rights reserved. No part of this book may be reprinted or reproduced or utilised in any form or by any electronic, mechanical, or other means, now known or hereafter invented, including photocopying and recording, or in any information storage or retrieval system, without permission in writing from the publishers.

First edition published by Routledge © 2012

Trademark notice: Product or corporate names may be trademarks or registered trademarks, and are used only for identification and explanation without intent to infringe.

Library of Congress Cataloging-in-Publication Data
Blaisure, Karen.
    [Serving military families in the 21st century.]
    Serving military families : theories, research, and application / authored by Karen Rose Blaisure, Tara Saathoff-Wells, Angela Pereira, Shelley MacDermid Wadsworth, and Amy Laura Dombro.— Second edition.
        pages cm — (Services in the family series)
    Includes bibliographical references and index.
    1. Families of military personnel—Services for—United States.   2. Families of military personnel—United States.   3. United States—Armed Forces—Military life.   I. Title.
    UB403.S52 2015
    355.1'20973—dc23
    2015004175

ISBN: 978-1-138-84124-6 (hbk)
ISBN: 978-1-138-84125-3 (pbk)
ISBN: 978-1-315-73234-3 (ebk)

Typeset in New Caledonia
by Apex CoVantage, LLC

To all members and veterans of the U.S. military and their families for their personal sacrifices, their dedication to duty, and their patriotism.

Contents

Figures

Tables

Foreword

An extraordinary team of talented scholars and practitioners authored the first edition, *Serving Military Families in the 21st Century*. This second edition comprises 14 chapters including a new chapter on women in the military and women veterans, and a new chapter on veterans and their families. The remaining chapters include updated demographics on service members and their families, expanded descriptions of mental health programs available to military families, and new interviews with an array of active military, family members, researchers and service providers.

This book serves as an introduction to military families and the effects of military service on adults, their relationships, and their children. Relatively few individuals served on active duty in the last decade, in fact much less than 1% of the U.S. population.[1] And perhaps not surprisingly, about eight-in-ten veterans say the American public doesn't understand the problems faced by those in the military or their families. By and large the public agrees; they don't understand. This book aims to correct the gap in understanding families with active military members as well as families with recent veterans. There is good reason to do so.

The experience of veterans commands our attention as many, but not all, report challenges in readjusting to civilian life following service. Nearly half of veterans report experiencing strains in family life after leaving the military, 47% say they have frequent outbursts of anger, and nearly a third (32%) report there are times when they didn't care about anything. For those who experience combat, the appearance of psychological and relational problems is disconcerting with over half reporting emotional trauma and many reporting reliving distressing experiences in the form of flashbacks or sleep disturbances. About one-in-six recent veterans report experiencing serious injuries while serving in the military and most of those injuries are combat related. Nearly half report knowing someone who was killed while in the military.

Coupled with these statistics is the changing face of the military over recent decades. Service members are far more likely to be married (about 53%) than was the case in the past (about 41% in 1973), and they are more likely to be married than civilians of comparable ages.[2] These are sobering statistics and they challenge students of families to enrich our understanding of those who serve and their relationships with intimate partners, children, and extended kin. Recent work in the field, and a new chapter in this book, evidences the changing roles of women in the military and the core challenges they face.

The 14 chapters in this volume provide an extensive primer on military culture and family life, essential background for chapters that address a variety of issues including detailed descriptions of the many programs developed for individuals and families. The presentation spans an array of ordinary challenges facing all families in their development and maintenance, as well as challenges that are unique to military families. The

---

[1] Taylor, P. (ed.). (2011). *The military-civilian gap: War and sacrifice in the post-9/11 era*. Washington, DC: Pew Social & Demographic Trends.

[2] Lundquist, J., & Xu, Z. (2014). Reinstitutionalizing families: Life course policy and marriage in the military. *Journal of Marriage & Family, 76*, 1063–1081.

unique challenges of military families include frequent relocations, separations and long deployments in difficult conditions, combat injury, and violent death all of which can have profound effects on children, spouses, parents, and extended kin. And while many current and former soldiers experience difficulties, many do not and clearly demonstrate resilience in their personal and family lives. Recent veterans, for instance, report levels of personal happiness and satisfaction in their family lives comparable to the general public. In this volume, the authors wisely present a balanced perspective that neither omits addressing the challenges of military life, nor fails to appreciate resiliency and the benefits of participation in a culture of service.

Robert M. Milardo, PhD
Professor of Family Relations,
University of Maine
Series Editor

Preface

We are proud to have the opportunity to write a second edition of *Serving Military Families*. It allows us to update information about service members and families. It also allows us to bring veterans and their families into the conversation.

Serving in the military is not just a job. There is a sense of calling, a depth of feeling that service and family members have, often for generations. As Lieutenant Colonel Jessica Milam, Deputy Chief, Air Force Diversity Operations explains, "The military culture has a core value of service before self. When the nation calls, we understand it is an honor to serve. This shared value creates a strong bond and culture within the military and places a unique responsibility on military families. Understanding these and other realities of military life and acknowledging them to service members and their families are essential in supporting military families in your personal life and professional life."

Given this sense of calling and the strong bond and culture within the military, it follows that the transition from military to civilian life is a major life event full of promise for the future yet full of loss—of a mission, culture, and strong bonds. According to the National Center of Veterans Analysis and Statistics, approximately 21.3 million Americans are veterans. Veterans alive today have served during five conflict eras beginning with World War II up until the present time. Lieutenant Colonel Milam's comments about supporting service members holds true for supporting veterans and for their families. If we are going to support veterans and veteran families in our personal and professional lives, we have to understand the realities of becoming and being a veteran and a veteran family.

If you are reading this book, you are likely supporting or hope to support service members and their families or veterans and their families in your career. You and others who do this work often share a sense of calling. You may be a college student preparing to work with military families. Or you may already be established in your career as a social worker, teacher, child-care provider, nurse or physician, lawyer, counselor, law enforcement officer, writer, or researcher. You may work in a university setting or a civilian social service agency where you sometimes meet and work with military and veteran family members, perhaps more often than you used to. Or you may work in an organization that has as its mission to serve military and/or veteran families. Perhaps you are a member of a military or veteran family. When we consider the 21.3 million veterans and 2.2 million service members in the U.S. and their families, the chances are that whatever you do or will do, and wherever you do it, you will end up serving members of military and veteran families. That means each day you have an opportunity to make a difference in the lives of those who have sacrificed or are currently sacrificing so much for the rest of us.

In this book you will find information and research about military and veteran families that you can use to build your knowledge base about their lives and the military culture. You will learn about how much military and veteran families have in common with civilian families as well as issues specific to military and veteran families.

You will have the chance to meet people who study and work with military and veteran families, as well as those who make policy and design programs and those who are family members themselves. As so many of them have said to us, "No one can ever know it all when it comes to military and veteran families, but if you can listen and ask questions with genuine curiosity and respect and with the intent to serve, families will help fill in the gaps of what you need to know." You will learn how service members share commonalities and how they differ in their experiences of military service. You will learn how military life may impact families differently. You will learn how veterans from different eras, fighting different wars understand one another. You will learn how the implications of serving in the military can vary across the life span.

In addition, you will learn about services available to military and veteran families from both the military and civilian sectors. There comes a time when every family needs support of one kind or another. Yet, just because services exist and individuals and organizations are committed to supporting families, it doesn't necessarily mean that families are being served or that they are receiving the support they need when they do connect with a program or service provider. To take advantage of the support offered, a person must know about and understand the services being offered and be able to negotiate the method by which to access those services. Yet, the wide array of services offered by the military, federal, state, and local governments, and the community—both in–person or online—can be overwhelming to negotiate at the best of times. When a family is experiencing stress, no matter the reason, it can be even more of a challenge.

If and how one begins to search for support can depend on a variety of factors including one's culture, personal style, mental health, access to a computer and/or transportation, and past experiences with seeking support. In military and veteran families, stigma may be an obstacle, as seeking help can be viewed as a weakness and, in the case of a current service member, as a potential threat to their career.

Creating positive change for military and veteran families means building bridges between families and the support they need. It means building bridges between what we know and what we do. To these ends, throughout this book you will find a series of features filled with information you can tailor to the unique strengths and needs of the diverse families you work with. These include:

- **Spotlight on Research:** Here you will find the work of researchers who are working to learn more about military and veteran families with the goal of informing and enriching the work of practitioners like you. As you will see, there are many areas in regards to military families—such as how families deal with a service member's death due to combat—that we still have much to learn about. Our knowledge of veteran families is largely based on what we know about veterans and their experiences as they transition into and experience civilian life. If you are a researcher or planning to go into research, there is plenty of work to be done.
- **Best Practices:** This feature includes accepted strategies from the field.
- **Voices From the Frontline:** In this feature you will find stories of support program leaders, practitioners, researchers, policy makers, and most importantly service members and veterans and their families. Each has generously shared their personal experiences, successes, challenges, and insights from a moment in time. By the time you are reading this book, their stories will have taken new paths. Like the family members you will (or already do) work with—and members of your family and ours—each is a unique individual in a unique family constellation.
- **Tips from the Frontline:** In these sections, you will find concrete, hands-on suggestions based on the experiences and wisdom of people you met in this book.

As you read, we predict that you will not only learn about military families but, like some of the people you meet in the following pages (including some of the authors), you will learn something about yourself, your assumptions and stereotypes about the military and our country. Being open to learning, not only about others but about yourself as well, is a key ingredient to being an effective provider of family support, no matter your role.

We think you will be inspired too by the families you meet as Shelley, one of the authors of this book, was the day she walked into a small office at the Pentagon: *"The walls were covered with sheets filled with writing. I asked a senior-level person what was going on. The Secretary of Defense had given a small team three weeks to figure out how to get every child in Iraq back to school. They were busy solving a problem no one had ever tackled before."* Like these professionals, every day military and veteran family members are faced with problems they may never have tackled before.

DoD needs a workforce of people to support military families and veterans. As a country, we need a sustainable support network for military and veteran families long after our troops come home.

To help you meet your goal of making a positive difference in the lives of military and veteran families, this second edition includes the following updates and additions:

- A new chapter on women in the military and women veterans.
- A new chapter on veterans and veteran families.
- The three chapters on programs and services in the first edition have been integrated into two chapters to make it easier to obtain a sense of the landscape of possibilities and support families in making connections.
- Updated demographics and descriptions of service members, veterans, and their families.
- Expanded descriptions of mental health treatment approaches with a focus on including family members.
- Twenty-two new interviews with family members, researchers, and clinicians to bring the new topics above to life.
- Updated exercises focused on providing services to military and veteran families.

In Chapter 1, you will be introduced to the military culture and military families. You will meet Colonel Angela Pereira, U.S. Army, Retired, one of the co-authors of this book who grew up in a military family and provided psychological health care to troops in Iraq before retiring. This chapter discusses the role of the military in our country and the strengths and challenge of military families.

Chapter 2 describes requirements to join the military and factors that lead people to do so. It will paint pictures for you of service personnel, active duty and selected reserve by branch and discuss what we know and do not know about military families.

Chapter 3 describes features of military life, including a sense of community; the priority of the military mission; relocation; spouse employment and education; and separation due to temporary duty, deployment, or death of the service member.

In Chapter 4, we take a closer look at children and youth in military families. Among the people you will meet is Connery Otto, a high school senior, who talks about "growing up military." This chapter looks at young peoples' experiences of moving and going to child care and school. Randy Ott, now an adult, shares his perspective looking back on his childhood in a military family. This chapter then turns its focus to the impact of parental deployment on children's behavior and psychological wellbeing and ways to support children with parental deployment, injury, and death.

Chapter 5 will ground you in theories about stress and resilience, providing you with a framework to shape your attitudes and approach to your work with military and veteran families. You will see that, at times, families are suffering and may need specialized intervention. But you will also see that dealing with challenging times can be an opportunity for families to recognize and draw upon their strengths and to grow. In the words of Froma Walsh, PhD, who you will meet: *"What is remarkable is the potential for individual and family resilience—the capacity to rebound, and even grow stronger—when family members pull together as a team to master their challenges. Families hold the keys to resilience."*

Chapter 6 focuses on common individual and family milestones that service members experience during their careers and how the military, as an organization, has developed support structures and programs to help service members through significant life transitions, including separation from the military. There is also discussion of the limits of the military to meet every individual and family need.

In Chapter 7 you will learn about the effects of war on service members. You will meet Colonel Rick L. Campise who describes his work as a psychologist in a combat zone supporting service members with issues that range from trauma over the horrors of war to everyday life issues, including finances and relationships with their significant others and their children. A discussion of the physical and psychological effects of war including discussions of traumatic brain injuries and moral injuries ends with good news: exposure to stress and involvement in traumatic events can lead to positive changes in relationships, and to philosophical, physical, and spiritual growth.

Chapter 8 discusses research focused on risk and resilience experienced in family systems and familial roles in relation to war and deployment experiences. There is a particular focus on marital relationships, combat injured families, and emerging research with parents of service members. You will hear voices of service members and their spouses and meet researchers who focus on military family relationships. Each of these areas of research addresses assumptions and clarifies strengths and concerns for military family well-being. In turn, these findings inform policies that are directed toward these families.

Chapter 9 considers women in the military and women veterans. In this chapter you will meet Captain Emily Spencer, U.S. Army, who shares insights into the many roles of her life including serving as an active duty Explosives Ordinances Disposal Specialist and being the mother of two young children. You will learn about the changing role of women in our country's Armed Forces and gain insight into some of their concerns including sexual assault, homelessness, combat-related psychological disorders, and the evolving relationship between women veterans and the Department of Veterans Affairs.

Chapter 10 focuses on veteran families. In this chapter you will meet four members of the Yeary family, each of whom shares their perspective on their family's transition from military to civilian life. You will also learn about the current veteran population and veteran family experiences within and between generations of combat. Finally this chapter will discuss the services offered and challenges facing the Department of Veteran Affairs and how a range of veteran organizations advocate for and support military families.

Chapter 11 discusses policies and programs that support military families. You will learn about the different ways that the Department of Defense supports Active and Reserve Component families and laws and policies that respond to unique situations faced by military members and their families. The chapter closes with a discussion about how the Department of Defense is working to change the view of psychological health in the military and programs that the Department has developed to respond to the increased challenges and stresses that military families experience as a result of recent sustained military operations around the world.

In Chapter 12, we discuss civilian organizations that support military families and how these organizations advocate for, assist, and increase our knowledge about military families. Insights about how collaborative efforts can improve life for military families may inspire your thinking and practice around collaboration.

Chapter 13 discusses innovations in family-focused systems of care; direction for working with those who have experienced traumatic events and injuries, such as TBI and PTSD, and their families; and information pertaining to caregivers and to families who have experienced the death of their service member.

Finally, Chapter 14 looks ahead with you to serving military families. We invite you to examine your stance as a family support professional. Then examine some of the obvious and not-so-obvious careers that offer a way to serve military families, either directly or indirectly. These career paths are illustrated through stories shared by working professionals. This chapter concludes with a discussion about compassion satisfaction and its role in providing highly competent and compassionate support to military families.

Acknowledgments

We owe thanks to the many individuals and organizations who made this textbook possible. We would like to recognize the pivotal role of the Military Family Research Institute (MFRI) at Purdue University in the development of this book. MFRI staff and students helped with this effort in a myriad of ways, including answering many questions, designing the cover, and providing many materials in addition to doing the high-quality work they complete every day.

Stories form the heart of this book. These stories come from nearly 70 military family members, service members, veterans, researchers, clinicians, writers, film producers, students, university staff, and experts from military and civilian family support organizations who agreed to share their experiences and reflections. We are grateful, as we know readers will be, for their generosity.

We would like to recognize the following persons for their assistance in locating or confirming the status of public information: Captain Lori Laraway, Nurse Corps, U.S. Navy; Lieutenant Colonel Laurel Devine, U.S. Army; Aggie Byers; Marianne Coates; and Kirsten Woodward, MSW, LCSW.

Many thanks to Pat Chandler for insight into the Reserve Component; Jackie Chandler for reading and responding to early versions of the chapters; students enrolled in *Military Family Life* and *Family Life and the Military* courses taught during fall 2010 for their feedback on selected chapters; Nicole Eckerson and Diana Boulin for preparing figures and tables; Ashley Machacek and Andreza Mancuso Schaden for assistance with the reference list, figures, and tables; Karley Jonkman and Daphne Bland for assistance with proof-reading; the Department of Family and Consumer Sciences and the College of Education and Human Development at Western Michigan University for administrative and travel support; Cheryl Wellman for her assistance in manuscript preparation; Richard J. Westphal, RN, PhD, Captain (Retired), Nurse Corps, U.S. Navy for guidance on the use of the Stress Continuum; Sandra K. Dye, PhD, Chief Master Sergeant, U.S. Air Force Reserve for loaning her boots to be photographed; and our colleagues, friends, and family for their encouragement.

We want to thank the following reviewers for their useful feedback on the revision plan for the second edition: Karen Allen (Arkansas State University, USA), Nancy Anderson (Warner University, USA), Josephine G. Pryce (University of Alabama, USA), Heidi Radunovich (University of Florida, USA), and Ross Wadey (University of Roehampton, UK). We are also grateful for the editorial expertise and guidance of Debra Riegert and the rest of the Routledge team, including Angela Halliday, Lindsay Murray and Natalie Larkin.

Finally, for sustaining us through multiple weeklong writing sessions we would like to recognize Tony Vargas for his generous hospitality, Jerry Strouse and Ed Silverman for their homemade treats, and Patch (otherwise known as the Perfect Army Trained Canine Helper) for being sweet and playing fetch.

Authors

Karen Rose Blaisure, PhD, a licensed marriage and family therapist and a certified family life educator, is a professor of family science in the Department of Family and Consumer Sciences at Western Michigan University in Kalamazoo. Her research focuses on education and policy initiatives for families experiencing separation and divorce. She regularly teaches a graduate course, *Family Life and the Military*, for students in the helping professions. From 1986 through 1989, she worked as a program specialist and an education services supervisor and, in 1992, as a special project consultant at the Navy Family Services Center in Norfolk, Virginia (renamed the Naval Station Norfolk Fleet and Family Support Center). In these roles, she regularly facilitated programs on deployment, reunion, and parenting. She has presented on military families to many professional groups and has written about the Navy's Return and Reunion program.

Tara Saathoff-Wells, PhD, a certified family life educator, is a research and evaluation scientist at the Clearinghouse for Military Family Readiness at Penn State. From 1989 through 1994, she worked in Kenya and Mozambique with both indigenous and U.S. expatriate populations. As a doctoral student, she completed an internship with the U.S. Department of State in the Family Liaison Office, the primary family and child resource and support office for U.S. diplomatic families. Her research focuses on high needs military families who are eligible for family services, including home visitation, early intervention, and prevention of child maltreatment through parent education.

Colonel Angela Pereira, PhD, U.S. Army, Retired, is a consultant and an educator on psychological health and military life issues, having completed a distinguished career in the military. She is a member of the External Advisory Council of the Military Family Research Institute at Purdue University in West Lafayette, Indiana. She previously served as the U.S. Army's regional mental health consultant and director of the U.S. Army Europe Regional Medical Command's Solider and Family Support Services in Heidelberg, Germany; as a member of the Department of Defense Task Force on Mental Health; as the director of the Combat Stress Control/Mental Health Clinic in Abu Ghraib, Iraq; as the director of education and training on health and wellness at the U.S. Army Center for Health Promotion and Preventive Medicine; and as a division social worker for the Third Armored Division during Operations Desert Shield/Storm. Board certified in clinical social work, she earned her PhD from the University of South Carolina in Columbia and her master's and bachelor's degrees from the University of California, Berkeley. Dr. Pereira's many honors include the Legion of Merit, the Bronze Star Medal, and the Order of Military Medical Merit.

Shelley M. MacDermid Wadsworth, PhD, is a professor in the Department of Human Development and Family Studies at Purdue University in West Lafayette, Indiana, where she also directs the Military Family Research Institute and the Center for Families. Her research focuses on relationships between job conditions and family life, with special focus on military families and organizational policies, programs, and practices. Dr. MacDermid Wadsworth is a fellow of the National Council on Family Relations and a recipient of the Work Life Legacy Award from the Families and Work Institute. Dr. MacDermid Wadsworth served as a civilian co-chair of the Department of Defense Task Force on Mental Health and also served on the Psychological Health External Advisory Committee of the Defense Health Board and the Returning Veterans Committee of the Institute of Medicine.

Amy Laura Dombro, MS, develops resources to assist teachers, family support professionals, and community leaders in making positive change for children and families. As former head of the Bank Street Infant and Family Center, Amy works with and for organizations including the Military Family Research Institute, ZERO TO THREE, The What to Expect Foundation, and Families and Work Institute to translate information so that it is engaging and easy to use. In addition, she often documents stories of successes, challenges, and lessons learned so that readers can benefit from the experiences of others. Her recent publications include *Honoring Our Babies and Toddlers: Supporting Young Children Affected by a Military Parent's Deployment, Injury or Death* (ZERO TO THREE, 2009) and *Powerful Interactions: How to Connect with Children to Extend Their Learning* (NAEYC, 2011).

1

An Introduction to Military Culture and Military Families

In Chapter 1, you will

- Meet retired Army Colonel Angela Pereira, one of the coauthors of this book.
- Review the role of the military in the United States.
- Gain insights into military culture.
- Learn basic military terms.
- Consider the strengths and challenges faced by military families.
- Understand why helping professionals should learn about military families.

Meet

Coauthor Angela Pereira, Colonel, U.S. Army, Retired

People join the military for many different reasons: education benefits, the camaraderie and sense of belonging, the travel, the challenge, following a family member's footsteps. My father was in the Army for 27 years. When I was growing up, we moved every three years in the United States and Germany. I went to eight different schools between the first and twelfth grade. After graduating college, I realized how much I wanted to join those doing the important work of watching over our nation.

Recently retired, I was an Army social worker for 25 years. I did just about every kind of job a social worker can do in the Army. I worked in community mental health and in the exceptional family member program with families who have children with special needs. I worked in corrections. I provided services on the ground to soldiers of an armored division during the Gulf War. I've been a policymaker and worked on program development. And I've been in management roles—first serving as a regional chief of domestic violence for one-third of the Army family advocacy programs in Europe and later as the consultant and program director for mental health services for Army soldiers and families in Europe. During my Army career, I served in Fort Riley, Kansas; San Antonio, Texas; Frankfurt, Germany; Saudi Arabia; Iraq (twice); Kuwait; Fort Jackson, South Carolina; Aberdeen Proving Ground, Maryland; and Heidelberg, Germany (twice). In 15 years of marriage, my husband, who also served in the Army, and I were apart for a total of 6 years due to our work.

INTRODUCTION

Like Colonel Pereira, you may have grown up in a military family. Perhaps you are a service member, planning to become one, or a veteran. Or you may have never thought much about the military and could never see yourself signing up. Perhaps someone very dear to you is serving in the military or has served. You may be a student considering entering a helping profession. Perhaps you are already out in the field working with children and families. You may be a first responder, a law enforcement agent, or a public health worker. You may be working with military or veteran families. This book is for you.

We, the authors, bring to this book a wide range of experience and knowledge about the military. As you will see, some of us were born into the military and made it our life's work. Some of us worked as civilians with a branch of the military or have family members who are serving. Others of us are relatively new to the military and have had to confront and lay aside misperceptions as we got to know service members and their families and learned more about military life. Throughout this book, we look forward to sharing some of our experiences, questions, and lessons learned about the military and military families.

WHY FOCUS ON MILITARY AND VETERAN FAMILIES?

Military service members and veterans are members of your families and neighborhoods. They are your work colleagues and schoolmates, little league coaches, teachers, firefighters, bank tellers, and insurance agents. They are parents, children, uncles, aunts, and grandparents—people you have known all your lives as well as people you have never met. Relationships with service members, veterans, and their loved ones are embedded into your communities in many different ways, as noted in Box 1.1.

Military and veteran families offer you, as a current or future human service professional, a unique opportunity to learn about and work with individual and family capacities, strengths, and challenges within distinctive cultural and sociohistorical contexts. The military is often described as having a culture of its own, "a military culture." As a workplace organization, it has no rival among other career paths in terms of the number of individuals and families who are systematically affected by U.S. international diplomatic relations and policy.

For over two decades, U.S. military engagements have been conducted with a volunteer military. Major engagements during this time have been **Gulf War I** (1990–1991), **Operation Enduring Freedom** (OEF; the name given to the U.S. military actions in

---

BOX 1.1   TIPS FROM THE FRONTLINE

Military families want what every family wants. Just as all Americans are concerned about quality education for their children and work and career opportunities for both spouses, so are military families. Families bring issues from the civilian world with them, such as issues around money, parenting, caring for elderly parents, and raising children.

Today many military families are living out in their communities and may never live or work on a military installation. They are learning what a military family is while their service member is serving in a war zone. They need a targeted support system that includes support from their families, friends, and community. We are all in this together.

Joyce Wessel Raezer
Executive Director, National Military Family Association

Afghanistan that began in October 2001), **Operation Iraqi Freedom** (OIF; the name given to the U.S. military actions in Iraq that began in March 2003 and ended in August 2010), **Operation New Dawn** (OND; the name given to the U.S. military action in Iraq that began in September 2010), and operations in various African countries (Taylor, 2014). At this time in our history, operations in both Afghanistan and Iraq have been underway for over a decade. If you, the reader, are within the typical age range of today's college student (18–24 years old), this current effort has been ongoing for more than half of your life. If you are older, you may remember other conflicts and/or peacekeeping missions involving U.S. military personnel. Regardless of your age, however, you, your friends, family, colleagues, and clients will be affected directly or indirectly by these military engagements and the impact of them for the foreseeable future.

UNDERSTANDING THE ROLE OF THE MILITARY

This section addresses the historical roots of the U.S. Armed Forces, the civilian control of the military, the relatively new use of an all-volunteer force, the concept of total—both active and reserve—force, and the branches of the military. The information below will help to clarify misconceptions and promote greater understanding of the structure and function of the military.

History

The roots of today's U.S. Armed Forces extend from 1636 when the English colonists brought the tradition of militias, where citizens organized themselves into military units for the purpose of defense. This tradition of the "citizen-soldier" is now called the National Guard (National Guard, 2009). Then, nearly 150 years later, in 1775, the Continental Congress established the Continental Army (initially formed from militia members), the Continental Navy, and the Continental Marines in order to defend the colonies and fight for their independence from Great Britain. When the War of American Independence ended with the signing of the Treaty of Paris in 1783 and its ratification the following year, Congress disbanded the Continental Navy, the Continental Marines, and the Continental Army although it did maintain a small number of soldiers at a few critical forts. In a few years, however, Congress established the War Department in 1789 and the Department of the Navy in 1798 to defend the country and protect the merchant fleet at sea (Cooper, 1999; Goodspeed, 2003).

Central to democracy is the civilian control of the military, in contrast to a **military dictatorship** in which a leader, who may be from the military or who assumes military rank once in power, or a **military junta** (a group of military leaders) rules a country without the consent of the people and often through oppressive means. In countries where the military is in control of the nation, it is free to take any action it deems appropriate, without input from the citizens of that nation, and that is, in effect, an authoritarian government instead of a democracy.

In the United States, civilian control of the military is established in the U.S. Constitution and is divided between the U.S. President (see Article II of the U.S. Constitution) and members of Congress who are elected by U.S. citizens (see Article 1 of the U.S. Constitution). In the United States, the military follows civilian leadership and carries out the policies of the United States as directed by the President. The military is one of many tools used to carry out U.S. policy. Another tool is the U.S. State Department's Diplomatic Corps.

The current Armed Forces reflect changes that occurred following the end of World War II. Today, the **Department of Defense** (DoD; the federal department tasked with national security and supervising the U.S. Armed Forces) is led by the **Secretary of Defense**, a cabinet post, who oversees national security agencies and the Department of the Army, the Department of the Air Force (created from the World War II Army Air Forces), and the Department of the Navy (which includes the Marine Corps).

Each service has a **Chief of Staff**, the most senior ranking officer, who is responsible for the readiness of personnel, among numerous other responsibilities, and who serves on the **Joint Chiefs of Staff** (JCS), an advisory body to the President and the Secretary of Defense. The operational **chain of command** (the highly structured line of authority and responsibility that designates who is in charge of what and whom and along which orders are passed) begins with the President of the United States and continues down to the Secretary of Defense and then to the commanders of the unified combatant commands (DoD, 2009).

Between the War of American Independence and 1973, the United States relied periodically on conscription or a draft to acquire the service personnel needed to engage in wars or conflicts. In 1973, however, the military became an all-volunteer force. The following list summarizes the history of conscription in the United States, ending with the current policy of registration of males 18–25 years of age with the Selective Service (Chambers, 1999; Hansen, 2000; Perri, 2008).

- 1792—Congress passed an act requiring all able-bodied male citizens to have a gun and join the state militia. There was no penalty for noncompliance.
- War of 1812—The war ended before conscription was enacted.
- 1862—The government of the Confederate South initiated a compulsory military draft.
- 1863—The first wartime conscription passed by the U.S. Congress required male citizens, ages 20–45, and aliens seeking citizenship to enroll. Exemptions were made for only sons and some occupations. Enrollment quotas for each congressional district were filled first by selectees from Class 1 (all men 20–35 and single men 35–45) and then by Class 2 (married men 35–45). Conscription was controversial because substitutions and exemptions that could be bought for $300.
- 1898 (Spanish–American War)—Congress declared that men 18–45 years of age were subject to military service.
- 1917–1918 (World War I)—The Selective Service Act of 1917 prohibited substitutions; allowed for conscientious objectors due to religion; and established boards to register, induct, or defer men 21–30. Opposition to conscription was strong.
- 1940–1946 (World War II)—The Selective Training and Service Act was passed by Congress in 1940. Males 21–35 were required to register and a lottery was held. As the war progressed, the age was lowered to 18 and the selection was changed from lottery to age, with the oldest called up first.
- 1950–1953 (Korea)—Men between 18½ and 35 were drafted for an average of 2 years. World War II veterans were exempted from the draft. The Universal Military Training and Service Act of 1951 required males 18–26 to register.
- 1964–1973 (Vietnam)—The first lottery since 1942 was held in 1969 for men born between 1944 and 1950, replacing the "oldest first" practice. Exemptions and deferments for college students were established. Some joined Reserve or National Guard units that were less likely to be deployed.
- 1973—The draft ended with the expiration of the 1967 Selective Service Act (extended by Congress in 1971); registration with the Selective Service continued until 1975. The all-volunteer force began.
- 1980 to present—Congress reinstated registration with the Selective Service System for most male U.S. citizens and male aliens living in the United States between 18 and 25.

Registration with the Selective Service does not mean a man will be inducted into the military. If a draft were instituted "men would be called in sequence determined by random lottery number and year of birth [and] examined for mental, physical and moral fitness by the military before being deferred or exempted from military service or inducted into the Armed Forces" (Selective Service System, 2009, para. 1).

Along with an all-volunteer force, another important shift emerged in the 1970s with the implementation of the "total force" policy. With this policy, the total force is considered to be the combination of **Active Component** members (who work full time in the Army, Navy, Marine Corps, and Air Force), and **Reserve Component** members (comprised of the Ready Reserve, Standby Reserve, and Retired Reserve, which are defined and described below), and key government civilian employees. However, it was not until the beginning of the Gulf War in 1990 when Americans began to feel the practical implications of a total force policy. At this time, the total force policy, coupled with the downsizing of the Active Component, meant large numbers of reservists and members of the National Guard were called to active service (Knox & Price, 1999). More recently, the total force policy has guided the mobilization of service personnel for OEF, OIF, and OND.

Downsize in Active Force and Increase in Military Operational Tempo

At the end of the 1980s, after the fall of the communist system in the Soviet Union and its satellite Eastern European nations, the Union of Soviet Socialist Republics (the USSR or Soviet Union, for short) was no longer seen as a threat to the United States. By 1991, the Soviet Union had collapsed into independent nations. The **Cold War**—the ongoing political, military, and economic tension between the Soviet Union and its satellites and the United States and other powers of the western world that had existed since the end of World War II—was over. Because the largest threat against the United States no longer existed, military planners and Congress reduced the size of the U.S. military. The number of military combat divisions and the total number of active duty military were significantly reduced. The downsizing continued after the Persian Gulf War. Combat forces were reduced from 18 to 13 active duty divisions (self-sustaining Army and Marine military units consisting of 10,000–30,000 combat and support service members) by 1993 (Bruner, 2005; Global Security, 2005).

In 5 years, the active duty force decreased 27%, from 2,065,597 members in 1990 to 1,505,283 in 1995 (Office of the Deputy Assistant Secretary of Defense, Military Community and Family Policy [DASD], 2014; Office of the Deputy Under Secretary of Defense, Military Community and Family Policy [DUSD], 2010).

Throughout the Cold War, U.S. active duty forces alone numbered over 2 million personnel, with over 3.5 million serving during the Korean and Vietnam Wars (Bruner, 2005). Today, the size of the military is one-third smaller than in 1990. In 2014, active duty and selected reserve totaled just over 2.2 million service members, compared with 3.2 million in 1990 and 2.45 million in 1995. Since 1995, the Marine Corps and the Army have increased by approximately 5% and 12% respectively, while the Navy and Air Force have decreased by approximately 26% and 18% respectively. The **Selected Reserve** (reservists in the Army, Navy, Marine Corps, Air Force, and Coast Guard; and members of each state's Army and Air National Guard) decreased nearly 12% from 953,192 members in 1995 to 842,510 in 2013 (DASD, 2014).

While the size of the U.S. military has decreased, the military **operational tempo** or **optempo** (i.e., the frequency and intensity of military operations or missions) has greatly increased since September 11, 2001. In addition to combat **deployments** (moving people and material to an area of military operation), thousands of U.S. military personnel continue to be deployed in peacekeeping operations throughout the world, although the number of U.S. military members serving in United Nations peacekeeping missions has decreased dramatically since the mid-1990s (Serafino, 2004). Recent peacekeeping missions have included those in Kuwait, Bosnia, the Balkans, Kosovo, South Korea, the Sinai, Haiti, Georgia, Ethiopia/Eritrea, and Liberia.

The right size and structure for the military depends primarily on the kinds of missions that it will be given. Since the early 1990s, many defense analysts, military leaders, and policymakers have debated the appropriate size and structure of the military and whether the United States should continue to participate in so many peacekeeping missions, especially during periods when it is also heavily involved in armed conflicts (Bruner, 2005). More than two decades after the end of the Cold War, U.S. policymakers are still trying to determine how best to configure the U.S. military force.

The term **Armed Forces of the United States** refers to all of the components of the Army, Navy, Air Force, Marine Corps, and Coast Guard, when it augments the Navy. The Coast Guard's main missions are maritime law enforcement and safety, maritime homeland security, and search and rescue (U.S. Coast Guard, 2010). It normally operates under the Department of Homeland Security but can be transferred to the Department of the Navy during time of war or national emergencies to provide naval support.

Uniformed Services include the Army, Navy, Air Force, Marine Corps, Coast Guard, Public Health Service Commissioned Corps, and the National Oceanic and Atmospheric Administration Commissioned Officer Corps. The first five are Armed Forces and the last two are Noncombatant Uniformed Services.

Department of Defense's Budget and Privatization

The Department of Defense's annual budget request is included in the President's comprehensive budget that is submitted to Congress. In response, the Congress passes a budget resolution itself (i.e., a revenue and spending plan) and appropriation bills to authorize funding of discretionary programs, including defense, under the jurisdiction of Congressional Appropriation Committees. The DoD's requested budget for fiscal year (FY) 2015 was $601 billion: $495.6 billion for the base budget (e.g., operations and maintenance, personnel, procurement, civilian workers, research and development); $26.6 billion to fund the defense portion of the President's Opportunity, Growth, and Security Initiative, an economic initiative with designated spending in defense and non-defense categories; and $79 billion in Overseas Contingency Operations for OEF, Iraq activities, counterterrorism, and work with NATO allies (Office of the Under Secretary of Defense, 2014). The FY 2015 DoD budget request represented a decrease in defense spending since the end of the Iraq War and reflects deductions to discretionary spending as required by the Budget Control Act of 2011 (commonly referred to as sequestration) and the Bipartisan Budget Act of 2013 (DoD, 2014b). The requested FY 2015 DoD budget was 39% larger after correcting for the effects of inflation than in FY 2000 (Kolb et al., 2014) and was approximately 16% of the expected federal budget for FY 2015.

The DoD budget covers programs and services for military families. The DoD's FY 2015 budget included funding requests for Military Family Support programs: child care and youth ($1.1 billion); Morale, Welfare and Recreation (MWR; $1.4 billion); family services ($1.9 billion); commissaries ($1.1 billion); DoD Education Activity Schools ($2.3 billion); and military spouse employment ($100 million). The DoD awards contracts to private companies that provide the professionals for staff services and programs in **CONUS** (within the continental United States). Some of these companies are listed in the last chapter of this book for those who are interested in applying for jobs in child care or youth programming, MWR, family services, and spouse employment programs.

Private companies also construct housing on military installations and build most military equipment such as aircraft, submarines, ships, drones, and communications equipment (Kolb et al., 2014). The U.S. is the world's largest exporter of arms (e.g., missiles, bombers, fighter jets, tanks), and, in 2010, accounted for 53% of the arms trade (Astore, 2012).

Private contractors or private military firms (PMF) provide the military with services such as transport, security, tactical combat operations, logistical support, and construction. Singer (2005) noted that while using private contractors allows military service members to focus on fighting and reduces the need to deploy more military service members, the privatization of the military also poses dilemmas. Dilemmas include private companies profiting from war and falling outside the military's chain of command. For example, they can leave the area of conflict when they deem the risk too great. Additionally, many who work in PMF are former military personnel, which can raise the question about companies that "exploit skills learned at public expense for private profit" (p. 128). In addition, contractors can earn more pay, but perhaps reap fewer benefits, than military service members for similar work.

Branches of the U.S. Armed Forces

The branches of the Armed Forces depend upon one another, yet their missions and traditions make each unique. The Army, Navy, Marine Corps, and Air Force each has a long military history and distinct customs that differ from its sister services. Each branch of the military has its own language, character, and terminology. For example, the Navy and Air Force call their **military installations** (i.e., facilities owned or leased and operated by the military) "**bases**," the Army refers to them as "**posts**," and the Marine Corps uses the term "**camps**." Even rank structures are not completely consistent from branch to branch. The differences in character, customs, and language are often the basis of much banter and competition between the services. However, what stays constant across the services is a commitment to the country and to the other members of the greater military community, as illustrated by their core values (U.S. Army, n.d.; U.S. Air Force, n.d.; U.S. Navy, n.d.-b; U.S. Marine Corps, n.d.-b).

Army—loyalty, duty, respect, selfless service, honor, integrity, and personal courage
Air Force—integrity first, service before self, excellence in all we do
Navy—honor, courage, and commitment
Marine Corps—honor, courage, and commitment

Collectively the U.S. Armed Forces, under the direction of the Commander-in-Chief, engage in fighting wars, humanitarian efforts, peacekeeping, evacuations, and protecting the security of the United States. Each force has its specific mission. The Army defends the United States, its territories, commonwealths, and possessions. Army units are deployed to combat zones and to locations such as South Korea to help secure borders or to Kosovo to participate in peacekeeping. The Navy provides combat-ready naval forces. Navy carrier groups and vessels are stationed around the world to provide a deterrent and a quick response to crises and humanitarian emergencies. The Marine Corps, under the authority of the Navy, maintains a ready expeditionary force. Along with the Army, the Marine Corps provides ground troops in combat and humanitarian efforts. The Air Force provides air and space defense and is involved in peacekeeping, humanitarian, and aeromedical evacuation missions. It provides air cover for ground troops.

Generally, we think of the services in terms of their missions to defend separate domains: air space by the Air Force, ground by the Army and Marine Corps, and seas by the Navy. Despite the distinct missions of each of the services, however, they may use similar processes or use similar equipment to accomplish their missions. Both the Army and the Marine Corps are equipped with tanks; the Air Force, Navy, Army, and Marine Corps all use aircraft to accomplish their missions; and both the Army and the Marine Corps are trained in close-range and hand-to-hand combat.

Each branch of the Armed Forces has a Special Operations Command (SOC) that can deploy highly trained members rapidly for special operations missions such as reconnaissance, rescue, infiltration, and raids. Such forces are often the first sent into

TABLE 1.1   Reserve Component Categories

Ready Reserve	Active status	Selected Reserve	Selected reserve units Individual mobilization augmentees Active guard or reserve members of the selected reserve
	May be called to active duty	Individual Ready Reserve	Completing military service obligation Officer training programs/health scholarship programs
		Inactive National Guard	Inactive ready reserve Muster once a year, do not need to train
Standby Reserve	May be mobilized involuntarily	Active status list	Maintain affiliation with military Key employees (e.g., removed from ready reserve because critical to national security in their civilian job) Other active status members place here due to hardship/physical disability
		Inactive status list	Retain reserve affiliation in a nonparticipating status May have skills which may be useful to armed forces
Retired Reserve	May be called to active duty	Reserve officers and enlisted retired and drawing or not drawing pay Reserve officers/enlisted eligible for retired pay but have not reached 60 Reserve physical disability retirees Other reserve retirees	

Source: Information compiled from Office of the Assistant Secretary of Defense for Reserve Affairs (2005). *Reserve component categories of the reserve components of the Armed Forces.* Washington, DC: Author. Retrieved from http://ra.defense.gov/documents/publications/RC101%20Handbook-updated%2020%20Sep%2005.pdf.

combat situations and work behind enemy lines. Each branch has units that might sound familiar: Army Special Forces and the 75th Ranger Regiment, Air Force Special Tactics Squadrons, Navy SEALS, and Marine Corps Reconnaissance. Special operation units undergo the most demanding training offered by the Armed Forces. Although training is limited to the most highly qualified candidates, attrition rates are high.

The Reserve Component contains three categories: the Standby Reserve, the Retired Reserve, and the Ready Reserve (see Table 1.1). The **Standby Reserve** personnel are temporarily not in the Ready Reserves due to a hardship or disability, or due to being designated as having civilian employment critical to national security. The **Retired Reserve** personnel are those reserve officers and enlisted who receive retired pay or are eligible for retired pay but are not 60 years old or over, not members of the Ready or Standby Reserves, and have not chosen to be discharged. The **Ready Reserve** consists of the selected reserve, the **Individual Ready Reserve** (personnel who have served as active duty or in the selected reserve and still have time remaining on their military service obligation), and the **Inactive National Guard** (required only to muster once a year with their unit) (Office of the Assistant Secretary of Defense for Reserve Affairs, 2005).

The selected reserve consists primarily of the following: the Army, Navy, Marine Corps, and Air Force Reserves, a federal force that is under the control of the President; and the Army and Air National Guard, which is a state force under the control of a state's Governor unless released by the Governor to the President at the latter's request. The National Guard has limited law enforcement power during crises. Reservists and National Guard members of the selected reserve typically drill one weekend a month and two weeks or more a year.

For decades, individuals in the selected reserve were known as "weekend warriors," typically responding to natural disasters within the United States. Many families needed to know very little about the military culture in order to support their loved one as a member of the National Guard or Reserves. Also, families usually did not worry about their loved ones being activated to full-time service and sent to combat zones. However, with the advent of the Gulf War (1990–1991), reliance on the Reserve Component rose sharply. The total force concept emphasized the increased reliance on reservists for combat and peacekeeping missions (Knox & Price, 1999). As operational tempo has increased, reservists have continued to be vital to U.S. military capabilities. Nearly 30% of deployed forces for OEF and OIF have come from the Reserve Component (Institute of Medicine, 2010), requiring many family members, with little or no prior identity as a military family, to quickly learn a new culture and respond to new stressors.

THE CULTURE OF THE MILITARY

Successfully working and living within the military culture requires fluency in a new language; knowledge of the chain of command; comfort on military installations; respect for those who serve; appreciation of the strengths of and challenges faced by military families; and knowledge of the steps taken by the DoD and each branch of the military to make military life more family-friendly. Each branch has developed its own subculture based on its specializations and missions. The cultural nuances can be as simple as the difference between the Army battle cry "Hooah!" (which has come to stand for "heard, understood and acknowledged" or HUA, but is more often use to show motivation or to motivate other soldiers), the Marine Corps battle cry, "Oorah!" (also used to show spirit or enthusiasm), and the Marine Corps motto, "Semper Fi," which is short for the Latin *Semper Fidelis* or "Always Faithful."

As you learn about the military as a culture, consider the following questions: What are its rituals and what meaning do these rituals hold? What are the rules for social interaction in this culture? What expectations do you have of yourself and others? Anthropologist and scholar Ward Goodenough (1981) defines culture as "a system of standards or rules for perceiving, believing, evaluating, and acting" (p. 110). For many of you, the military is a new culture to get to know. If you are part of the military, this book is an opportunity for you to step back and gain new insights into a familiar culture and perhaps yourself. As you study the military in the weeks to come, here are a few tips to keep in mind:

- Be aware of what you bring to your classroom or workplace. We each have expectations, values, biases, and prejudices that often are based in past experiences. These are part of being human. They may assist or interfere with knowing and understanding others. Being aware of them can help you remain open to learning more about another culture.
- Adopt the stance of being a learner. Listen. Observe. Ask questions of yourself, your classmates and colleagues, and military families.
- Be open. Try to withhold judgment. If something you hear stirs up feelings, ask yourself "why?" Continue to listen, observe, and ask questions.
- Remember, every family, every parent and child, is both unique and part of multiple cultures.

Language

Every occupation has specialized terminology, and the military is no different. Military language is replete with acronyms and abbreviations that can overwhelm civilian workers and family members new to military service. For example, what does an "E-5" refer to?

What does an E-5 mean when he tells his family "In today's brief, my CO said even though my MOS is needed downrange, I'll probably be TDY to another post first. Tomorrow I'm going to the PX for an ACU. Remember my Navy buddy who was sent as an IA? Well, he went outside the wire and was injured by an IED but his IBA protected him pretty well. He was MEDEVAC'd to an OCONUS base and is expected to be fine." The translation: "In our meeting today, my boss said that even though people who do my job are needed in the combat zone, I'll probably be temporarily sent to another location first. Tomorrow I'm going to the store for a combat uniform. Remember my friend who is in the Navy who was the only one sent from his ship to the combat zone? Well, he was outside of his work group's camp and was injured by a homemade terrorist bomb, but his body armor protected him pretty well. He was flown to a military base somewhere outside of the United States and is expected to be fine."

Most people pick up military language quickly when they are exposed to it in daily life. It helps to have a patient interpreter or a military-civilian "dictionary." Box 1.2 lists a few

---

BOX 1.2   TIPS FROM THE FRONTLINE

A "POCKET" MILITARY-CIVILIAN DICTIONARY

OIF—Operation Iraqi Freedom; the war in Iraq that began in 2003

OEF—Operation Enduring Freedom; the term used to refer to the conflict that began in Afghanistan in 2001 and includes operations in other countries (e.g., Pakistan, Uzbekistan, Djibouti, Turkey and Tajikistan)

FOB—Forward Operating Base; a stand-alone military camp in a combat location where service members live and work

IA—Individual Augmentee(s); a service member or small group of service members who are assigned to a unit going to combat during or just prior to the unit's deployment to a combat zone

PX or BX—Post Exchange or Base Exchange; a tax-free department store on a military installation and reserved for use by military beneficiaries

Commissary—a tax-free grocery store located on a military installation and reserved for use by military beneficiaries

CO—Commanding Officer; the officer responsible for the welfare of the service members assigned to his/her unit and for the accomplishment of that unit's missions

MOS—Military Occupational Specialty; a job title and code used by the Army and Marines; similarly the Air Force uses Air Force Specialty Codes (AFSC) and the Navy uses a Navy Enlisted Classification (NEC) system

TDY or TAD—Temporary Duty; a short-term assignment to another installation or unit

ACU—Army Combat Uniform

IED—Improvised Explosive Device; an unconventional bomb often used in terrorist attacks

Battle Rattle—military slang for protective armor used in combat; also referred to as IBA or Interceptor Body Armor

MEDEVAC or MEDIVAC—Medical evacuation; the quick transfer of wounded service members from the battlefield to the medical facility that can provide the specialized care needed, while providing professional medical care en route

OCONUS—Outside of the continental or contiguous United States (CONUS)

common terms and their definitions. The glossary at the end of this book includes military terms used in this textbook. Throughout this book, we will define many terms that you can use to build your military vocabulary. To continue building a military vocabulary, visit the DoD Dictionary of Military Terms (http://www.dtic.mil/doctrine/dod_dictionary).

As in civilian life, a word may have multiple meanings in the military depending upon the context. For example, family members typically use the term **separation** to refer to time apart from their service member (although spouses may also use the word to indicate a break in a romantic relationship). However, **separation from the military** can refer to being released from active duty, discharged from military obligations, and transferred to the reserves or retired list (Naval Inspector General, n.d.). The word separation also appears in the term **family separation allowance** that may be paid to service members when required to be away from their permanent duty station for more than 30 continuous days.

Chain of Command

We live within a society that recognizes authority, such as the authority of employers, experts, and the legal system. The military's authority and structure permeates the daily lives of service members and their families. While civilians can quit their jobs, service members cannot. They must serve out their contracts. For active duty service members, contracts include a set number of years of "24-7-365" (24 hours a day, 7 days a week, for 365 days a year) active duty service, and additional years in the individual ready reserve during which time they could be called back to active service. The contracts of members who join the Reserve Component (i.e., the Air or Army National Guard or the Reserves) stipulate they can be called to active service at the direction of the state's Governor (National Guard) or the President (the Reserves and National Guard).

The military chain of command is highly structured and begins with a civilian: the President of the United States who serves as the Commander in Chief of the U.S. Armed Forces. As noted earlier, civilian control of a nation's military is a significant feature of a democracy, and the U.S. Constitution divides responsibility for the military between the President and Congress. The chain of command designates who is in charge of what and whom at each link in the chain and ensures an efficient means of carrying out orders. Service members know who is in their chain of command, up to the President. Each service member must follow the orders given by those of higher rank in their chain of command unless the order is unlawful; military personnel have an obligation to disobey orders that do not comply with the U.S. Constitution or the Uniformed Code of Military Justice, the judicial code that pertains to members of the United States military.

As Figure 1.1 illustrates, the President directs the Secretary of Defense who, under the direction of the President, directs and has authority and control over the JCS; the unified commands; and the departments of the Army, Navy (including the Marine Corps), and Air Force. The President chairs the National Security Council (NSC), which advises and assists the President on national security issues and foreign policy. The core NSC meeting attendees include the Vice President, the Secretary of State, the Secretary of the Treasury, the Secretary of Defense, the Assistant to the President for National Security Affairs, the Chairman of the JCS, and the Director of National Intelligence (National Security Council, n.d.; Department of Defense, 2012b).

The JCS are the senior officers of their respective services, who are military advisors to the President, the Secretary of Defense, and the NSC. Through the Chairman of the JCS, they respond to requests for and may voluntarily offer advice or opinions. Members of the JCS are the Chairman of the JCS, the Vice Chairman of the JCS, the Army Chief of Staff, the Marine Corps Commandant, the Chief of Naval Operations, and the Air Force Chief of Staff (Department of Defense 2012b; Joint Chiefs of Staff, n.d.).

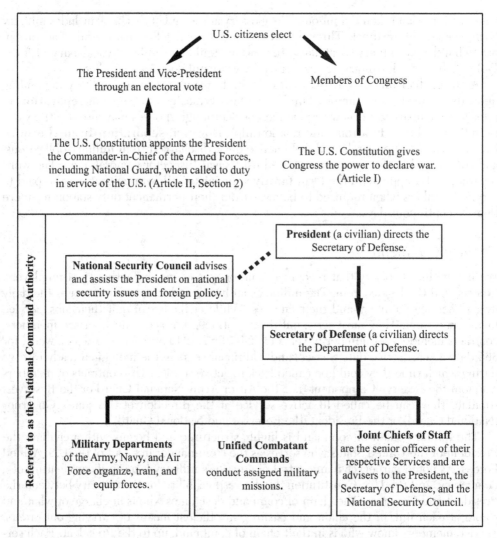

Figure 1.1   The chain of command. (Information compiled from Joint Chiefs of Staff (n.d.). *Joint Chiefs of Staff*. Retrieved from http://www.jcs.mil/; National Security Council (n.d.). Retrieved November 27, 2014 from http://www.whitehouse.gov/administration/eop/nsc; Department of Defense. (2012b) Organization of the Department of Defense (DoD). Retrieved from http://www.defense.gov/orgchart.)

The JCS transmit orders of the President or Secretary to Commanders (either an Admiral or four-star General) of the Unified Commands. **Unified Commands** are composed of units from two or more military departments working under a single commander to conduct operations in support of a continuing defense or combat mission in a region (e.g., U.S. European Command or USEUCOM) or an ongoing functional mission (e.g., U.S. Special Operations Command or USSOCOM). The Unified Commands are established by the President, with input from the JCS, and report to the Chairman of the JCS.

On April 6, 2011, President Obama signed a new **Unified Command Plan** (an annual review with possible modification of the Unified Commands) designating six unified combatant commands (DoD, 2011a). They are listed here along with their acronyms: U.S. Pacific Command (USPACOM), U.S. European Command (USEUCOM), U.S. Northern Command (USNORTHCOM), U.S. Southern Command (USSOUTHCOM), U.S. Central Command (USCENTCOM), and U.S. Africa Command (USAFRICOM). The

USCENTCOM, or CENTCOM as it is usually referred to in the media, oversees many of the OEF, OIF, and OND and related operations. It consists of 20 countries, including Afghanistan and Iraq. The four unified functional commands are U.S. Transportation Command (USTRANSCOM), U.S. Special Operations Command (USSOCOM), U.S. Strategic Command (USSTRATCOM), and the Joint Forces Command (USJFCOM) approved for dissolution (DoD, 2011b).

The Department of the Army, the Department of the Navy (which includes the Marine Corps), and the Department of the Air Force are **military departments**. Each department is responsible for organizing, training, and equipping its personnel.

A service member's **rank** is an achieved status, representing a level of responsibility and attainment of knowledge, expertise, and leadership skills. Rank is displayed on military uniforms through insignias to facilitate identification of rank. Those with higher rank have greater responsibilities and can issue orders to those of lower rank in their chain of command. If you are unfamiliar with how rank is displayed on uniforms, visit one of the numerous websites that show ranks for enlisted personnel and officers by branches of the military.

"E" refers to enlisted service members (i.e., pay grades or ranks E-1 to E-9). They typically join (i.e., enlist) in the military after high school and sign the enlisted document DoD Form 4/1 that states the required number of years in active duty and the required number of years in the Reserve Component. In total, these years equal the Military Service Obligation, typically 8 years for the initial enlistment (e.g., 3 years on active duty and 5 years in the inactive ready reserve). Enlisted service members first go through basic training (Army and Air Force) or boot camp (Navy and Marine Corps) and then to advanced training (called Military Occupational Speciality, or MOS, in the Army and Marine Corps). The service obligation is the length of time that must be served before the service member can voluntarily separate (leave) the military or retire if 20 or more years were served.

"O" refers to officers (i.e., pay grades or ranks O-1 to O-10). They join the military by attending one of the military academies, after college by being accepted into the officer's candidate school, or by participating in the Reserve Officers' Training Corps (ROTC) during college. Upon successful completion of their training, they are issued their commission, that is, their appointment as an officer, in the name of the President of the United States. Commissioned officers must complete 8 years of military service obligation, either in Active or Reserve Components or a combination of both. The length of the active duty service obligation varies by branch and by whether the officer attended ROTC, a military academy, or Officer Candidate School.

"W" refers to **warrant officers** (i.e., pay grades W-1 to W-5). They are designated an officer through a warrant (a specific authorization) as opposed to an officer who is designated through a commission. Warrant officers usually are technical experts or specialists with a specific set of skills. The Navy, Marines Corps, and Army have warrant officers while the Air Force does not. Active duty service members authorized as a warrant officer must complete 6 years of active duty service obligation.

Pay grades are equivalent across the military and are used to determine basic pay and allowances due to a service member. While titles of ranks may differ across branches of the military, pay grades do not and thus offer the way to tell who is the higher-ranking service member. For example, a Private First Class in the Army, a Seaman in the Navy, a Lance Corporal in the Marine Corps, and an Airman First Class in the Air Force are all E-3s, even though they have different titles. Also, while an O-3 in the Army, Marine Corps, and Air Force has the rank of Captain, in the Navy an O-3 is a Lieutenant, and a Navy Captain is an O-6.

The title associated with a rank may differ from branch to branch. Recognizing and addressing service members by the correct rank are important skills for civilians working with the military. The service member's last name is typically found above the right breast pocket of the uniform. It is best to address someone with the rank and last name, such as Private First Class Smith, Master Sergeant Mancuso, or Commander Rodriguez. However, last names are not found on dress uniforms, so it is also polite to refer only to the rank if the person's name is unknown, such as "Hello, Private," "Good evening, Master Sergeant," or "Thank you, Commander." Even though chaplains hold officer rank, it is common to address them as "Chaplain" rather than by their rank.

Rank structure and the use of military rank when addressing service members is very important to most military members, who would rather that you ask them how they should be addressed than to be addressed by a civilian title (e.g., "Mr." or "Ms."). In fact, if you inadvertently address an enlisted service member by an officer's rank or address them as "Sir," or "Ma'am," you may receive a response similar to, "I work for a living!" This quip is a reference to a long-standing military joke that officers do little work and that enlisted service members really run the military. Conversely, since officers of all branches are typically addressed as "Sir" and "Ma'am," using these honorifics is appropriate when speaking to officers.

The average military career lasts less than 10 years; most military service members do not serve the 20 years necessary for retirement. Retirement with less than 20 years is possible if a service member, with a 30% or greater disability rating, is placed on a temporary or permanent disability list by the military or is eligible for the Temporary Early Retirement Program (TERA). TERA was offered to service members with at least 15 years of service but less than 20 from 1993 to 2001 as a way to reduce the size of the military. TERA was reauthorized in 2011 and is in effect between 2012 and 2018 unless extended by Congress (Defense Finance and Accounting Service, 2012). Fewer than a third of separations from the military each year are due to retirements. The "up or out" policy in which service members must earn promotion within a specified time or exit active duty service is designed to maintain a force that is young and avoid too many personnel at higher ranks. For example, most service members in the Marine Corps leave after fulfilling one 4-year enlistment contract. Still, a greater percent of personnel remain in the military until retirement now as part of an all-volunteer force than during the era of conscription (Segal & Segal, 2004). Given most service members join as young adults, return to civilian life typically occurs when they are in their 20s, and those who retire from the military could be as young as 38.

Retirement benefits and compensation while serving are, of course, of great interest to service members and their families. The National Defense Authorization Act of Fiscal Year 2013 established the Military Compensation and Retirement Modernization Commission (2014) to review and make recommendations about compensation and retirement to the President and Congress.

Military Installations

The DoD operates more than 30 million acres of property in over 5000 locations around the world and operates or controls hundreds of military installations (DoD, 2009). Installations include the National Guard armories found in local communities across the United States and the forts, bases, camps, or other installations in approximately 63 countries. The DoD operates Naval Station Norfolk in Virginia, the world's largest naval base, and the National Training Center in Fort Irwin, California, a world-class training center that specializes in desert combat, counterinsurgency operations, and urban terrain training (DoD, 2009).

American military installations overseas differ significantly from those in the continental United States in several ways that impact the military unit, service members, and their families. Installations located in the United States can include schools, recreational and health-care facilities, and department and grocery stores for use only by military beneficiaries. (A **beneficiary** is someone who is eligible for a military-related benefit, in this case, shopping at the stores on military installations.) Commonly, installations overseas are broken up into smaller areas of land with fewer services and organizations on each installation. Other agencies and services are often located on one installation some distance from the installation on which the service or family member works or lives. This distance can be inconvenient for service and family members who tend to rely on these services and facilities even more overseas than at installations located in the United States. There may be fewer options for some services in the local community requiring the service member or family member to travel to the more distant installation for services. This situation requires coordinating time and travel, both of which may be limited. Cultural differences, language barriers, and unfavorable local currency exchange rates might provide additional obstacles to getting services (Burrell, 2006).

Just as laws, regulations, and customs differ from country to country, they differ from civilian communities to military installations. Working or living on a military installation requires knowing and following regulations about appropriate conduct. Regulations and laws on military installations are strictly enforced and are often more stringent than those in civilian communities. For example, although wearing a helmet while riding bicycles or motorcycles is not required by law in all states, all military installations mandate that helmets be worn. Similarly, not all states require the use of a "hands-free" device while driving and using a mobile phone, but they are required when driving and telephoning on military installations. Traffic regulations and laws, such as speed limits and the use of seat belts, are generally much more strictly enforced. In addition, service members who live on military installations are required to maintain their residences to a certain standard and can lose their "on base" or "on post" housing privileges if they fail to do so or if they or a family member conduct themselves inappropriately. Standards of politeness may also be higher than civilians are accustomed to. Courteous and respectful language (e.g., "please," "thank you," "pardon me," "excuse me," "Ma'am," and "Sir") and polite behavior (e.g., holding a door for someone, placing trash in correct receptacles) are expected.

Respect for Those Who Serve

Respecting those who serve in the military includes acknowledging the ramifications of service and of having an all-volunteer force: some citizens must voluntarily decide to allow their country to determine what job they will do, where they will live, and if they will go into combat. Joining the military also means conducting oneself according to the values noted above. These values require "service before self," that is, a commitment to serve the country even to the point of sacrificing one's own life.

Voices From the Frontline

GOING TO IRAQ

When I put on the uniform, I made the decision I would do whatever my country decided was appropriate for me to do. My last deployment before retiring was to Iraq. How could I not go? It was my turn to hold the baton. To say to those who were there, "Let me take it now. You need a rest." I knew I was putting my life at risk and it was scary. I got my life in order at home—preparing for the worst—and headed off for a year.

It was a horrible year. We were under daily mortar attacks and experienced three very major coordinated attacks by insurgents. Sometimes people are afraid to ask me about my experience, and it's not easy for me to talk about. But I had a job to do, and I did it.

Angela Pereira
Colonel, U.S. Army, Retired

Many **military operational specialties** (MOS; jobs or occupations) place personnel in danger not only during operations but also during training. Military personnel often work with highly specialized equipment that costs millions of dollars and in environments in which a mistake can cost one's own life or the lives of others. Military members often advance more quickly in their military career path than their age counterparts in their civilian career path (Duckworth, 2003). With this acceleration comes responsibility for the well-being of others in the unit and their families that extends well beyond an eight-to-five workday. Active duty means that service members are available 24 hours a day, 7 days a week, for 365 days a year. For example, they can be called into work early or kept late; they can be sent on temporary or extended assignments with only a few hours notice; and even though service members are granted leave (i.e., time off), it can be revoked regardless of the plans made or family members disappointed.

Personal Sacrifice and Discipline

When civilians join the military, they voluntarily give up many privileges, much of their autonomy, and many rights that they had as civilians. As an example, one of the rights that they are relinquishing is their right to privacy. A military supervisor can enter a service member's quarters (residence) at any time to monitor the service member's behavior or inspect his or her living conditions when he or she lives on a military installation (e.g., U.S. Army Garrison Baumholder, 2008). The supervisor can look for contraband items, ensure that the quarters are clean, or check if the service member is conducting himself or herself in a manner that represents the U.S. military positively. As another example, a supervisor can forbid a service member from taking a second job.

Military members also give up some political rights. The political election ballots of military voters are very often not counted because the mail delivery system delivers them to election officials after the deadline required for those ballots to be counted, or they vote absentee in states that routinely do not count absentee ballots unless election results are very close (Roff, 2009). Military members serving overseas are also not able to participate in the voting process for presidential delegates in any state that requires that participants appear in person to have their votes counted.

There are also military regulations that restrict how service members can participate in political activities (Office of the Law Revision Counsel, 2008). Military members are allowed to vote for and support any political party or candidate they choose but cannot do so in uniform. They cannot attend political rallies in uniform either because that might suggest that the military or one of its branches endorses that particular candidate or party. Service members cannot use their workplaces or any other government facility to engage in political activities, such as gathering votes and gaining support for a candidate or political party. Service members are also not permitted to strike for higher wages.

Service members can be required to spend weeks or months of training away from their homes and families to ensure that they can perform their jobs well in spite of intense pressure. Military units often conduct grueling military training in extreme, sometimes very uncomfortable, conditions that approximate war and require that service members perform their jobs flawlessly.

The military services place the accomplishments of their assigned missions before everything else, including individual needs and family concerns. Service members are required to accept and comply with this priority. They know that they can be sent to new locations, either temporarily or permanently, to work or train with no advance notice to them or to their families. The instability they live with can be very disruptive to their or their family members' activities or personal goals. For example, the military services will not ask a service member if there is a reason that he or she cannot be sent to a new unit, such as a daughter's involvement in an upcoming soccer tournament or the service member's own enrollment in a college course.

Accomplishing the tasks and living the lifestyle required of the military demands a focus on the mission and a personal discipline to keep physically, emotionally, and mentally fit. To be certain that service members are physically fit, each service has a periodic physical fitness test that the service member must pass. This physical fitness test usually includes a weigh-in, to ensure that a member's weight falls within what is considered appropriate limits for someone who may have to run, jump, and carry heavy equipment in combat. In addition, the physical fitness test includes a demonstration by each member that he or she is in good physical condition. In the Army, for example, every 6 months a soldier must complete a 2-mile run within a certain time and complete a specified minimum number of push-ups and sit-ups within 2 minutes. Failing to pass the weigh-in or the fitness test results in administrative actions against the service member and can result in disciplinary action or the end of his or her military career. To avoid this, service members are required to participate in unit physical fitness training, often early in the morning while it is still dark and most civilians are still in their beds, or to conduct regular physical training on their own before or after work. Not all persons who seek to enter the military are accepted. In Chapter 2, we will address the entrance standards.

Military Laws and Discipline   Service members are subject to the **Uniform Code of Military Justice** (UCMJ; part of the U.S. Code of law that regulates the conduct of the Uniformed Services) and to the *Manual for Courts-Martial* (MCM), an executive order that contains detailed instructions for implementing military law for the U.S. military. Under the UCMJ (Office of the Law Revision Counsel, 2008), service members can be charged, tried, and convicted of a range of crimes, including assault or robbery and military-specific crimes like desertion. The MCM (Joint Service Committee on Military Justice, 2008) specifies the procedures used in courts-martial. These documents are designed to balance the need for individual rights with the need for a system of justice that accommodates the discipline requirements of the military.

Under the UCMJ, military commanders have the authority to administer disciplinary actions or punishment for minor offenses, which can be addressed through nonjudicial punishment. Examples of these offenses are disobeying an order, showing up late for a formation (i.e., a gathering of military members for an inspection, physical training, or some other purpose), improperly wearing a military uniform, and showing disrespect to a higher-ranking service member. These kinds of offenses do not require a formal hearing with judicial due process protection that a regular civilian court must provide. The kinds of punishments commanders are able to administer are based on the rank of the commander. These usually include restriction, extra duty, and forfeiture of up to half the service member's pay. A court-martial usually takes place when there is a more serious crime that requires that the service member receives **judicial due process**. Judicial due process, or due process of law, is the principle that the government must respect all of the legal rights that are owed to a person, including witnesses, a jury, a pre-trial hearing, formal notification of the charges, free legal representation, and a speedy trial. These processes are necessary in order to protect the service member when the punishment could potentially be severe, such as involuntary separation from the military or imprisonment (Library of Congress, 2009).

APPRECIATION FOR THE STRENGTHS OF AND CHALLENGES FACED BY MILITARY FAMILIES

Most military families adjust well to the challenges that come with military life. They demonstrate numerous strengths while responding to frequent moves, separations from extended family, deployments, and living in other counties (Wiens & Boss, 2006). The resilience of military families is highlighted throughout this book.

Research on military families has moved beyond **deficits models** (i.e., identifying the factors families lack that are associated with unhealthy development) to **strengths-based models** that identify and build on families' existing strengths to encourage healthy development (MacDermid, Samper, Schwarz, Nishida, & Nyaronga, 2008). Military families share with civilian families the **normative stressors** of family life, that is, stressors that occur for most families and at expected times, such as life cycle transitions (e.g., birth of a child, death of an aged grandparent) and developmental changes (e.g., children going to school). However, military families experience additional stressors that are normative for them: lengthy work hours, frequent moves, separations, deployments, **unaccompanied tours** (i.e., assignments to overseas locations where the family is not authorized to travel with and remain with the service member), dangerous work settings, and combat-related activities. Active duty and selected reserve members differ somewhat in the types of stressors they experience. For example, while active duty members move many times throughout their careers as they are assigned to different military installations, members of the National Guard and Reserves could serve their whole careers at one installation. National Guard and Reserve members work at and advance in their civilian job or career and their military career, while active duty members typically focus on their military career.

Families, military and civilian, also experience **nonnormative stressors**. Nonnormative stressors are ones that do not occur to most families and are unexpected (e.g., a child with a terminal illness). Examples of nonnormative stressors unique to military families would be injury or death of their service member by friendly fire or their service member missing in action. However, worry about service members' safety during deployment would be considered normative (Blaisure & Arnold-Mann, 1992; MacDermid et al., 2008).

Research on military families has identified many strengths associated with positive adjustment to the challenges of military life (e.g., flexibility, strong family relationships, social support) (Wiens & Boss, 2006). This research and lessons learned from those who work with military families will be shared in upcoming chapters.

STEPS TAKEN TO MAKE MILITARY LIFE MORE FAMILY-FRIENDLY

The welfare and success of military families are crucial to the accomplishment of the mission of the DoD. Therefore, the DoD has developed and funded numerous programs and services to help military families adapt to and thrive within the military community and to assist them in dealing with challenges that come with a military life. However, this approach has not always been the case. Until the advent of the all-volunteer force, only the service member himself or herself was of concern to the DoD. Basic needs such as schools, housing, recreation, health care, and shopping facilities have historically been provided for military families, but the specialized programs that have been developed and funded to meet many needs that military families may have were instituted within the past 30 years (MacDermid Wadsworth & Southwell, 2011). In fact, until recently a standing military joke was that, "If the military wanted you to have a spouse, it would have issued one to you!"

In recent decades, the DoD has begun to view spouses and other family members as vital to the success of an all-volunteer force (MacDermid Wadsworth & Southwell, 2011). If family members are well cared for and doing well in the military community, the service member is more likely to consider staying in the military; and civilians who know that spouses and children will be supported are more likely to join the military. The DoD also realizes that service members who know that their families are taken care of will not need to spend as much time and energy worrying about them, especially during times when they cannot physically be with their families, such as during combat deployments.

Most civilians do not know that the DoD manages the largest school and child development center systems in the United States. The Department of Defense Education Activity operates 179 schools in 12 foreign countries, seven states, Guam, and Puerto Rico. The DoDEA enrolls more than 77,000 students who are children of active duty and DoD civilian employees (DoDEA, 2014b). The DoD Child Development System operates over 750 Child Development Centers located on 300 military installations worldwide and caring for approximately 200,000 military and DoD civilian children each day (DoD, 2014C).

There are numerous other examples of the ways in which the DoD has tried to improve family life for the military. For example, the Departments of the Air Force and Army now have a dual-military program that tries, when possible, to assign service members who are married to service members to the same location so that they can live together (Department of the Army, 2006a, 2009). The Army also has an assignment stabilization program for keeping service members from having to change assignments during the child's senior year in high school because changing high schools, especially during the final year, is a significant stressor for teenage family members. Each branch of the military has extensive family support that sponsors programs affecting almost every aspect of family life. These range from social services programs, such as domestic abuse and violence programs that work to prevent, identify, and treat child and spouse abuse and neglect; to medical programs, such as those identifying family members with special medical and/or educational requirements and then ensuring that those families are assigned to locations where the services they require are available; to programs that encourage mutual support of families, such as family social support and recreation groups that help service members and their families offer each other social and emotional support and exchange information.

While the service branches have different titles for their programs and may manage and deliver the services differently, each places great emphasis on the successful and appropriate delivery of all of its family services and programs. All of the programs for military families are regulated extensively, and they are overseen and enforced by the very top leadership of each of the services. These programs are monitored very closely and constantly evaluated and modified, as part of the DoD's effort to ensure that military families thrive. These programs and services will be introduced and discussed at length in later chapters of this textbook.

APPLYING WHAT YOU LEARN

There are both civilian and military career paths where people can work with members of the military community. In upcoming chapters, you will become familiar with programs and services for military families. In Chapter 14, you will learn where to apply for jobs working in the military community. There is also a possibility that you may choose a career path where interaction with military families is only occasional or unexpected. No matter where your choices may lead you in life, having a better understanding of military families and the contexts that shape their lives, give them strength, and challenge them will help you become a better neighbor, family member, and community member.

SUMMARY

- Service members and their loved ones live in communities throughout the United States.
- Civilian control of the military is a central feature of democracy in the United States.
- The military has a distinctive culture and a history that begins prior to the formation of the country. The military culture is exhibited through language, a chain

of command, location (e.g., military installations), respect for service, personal sacrifice and discipline, and military laws.

- The Active and Reserve Components combined total approximately 2.2 million service members, a 33% decline in numbers since the end of the Cold War.
- The branches of the U.S. Armed Forces depend upon one another, yet their missions and traditions make each unique. Under the direction of the Commander in Chief, the Armed Forces engage in fighting wars, humanitarian efforts, peacekeeping, evacuations, and protecting the security of the United States.
- The total force concept emphasizes reliance on the Reserve Component for combat and peacekeeping missions. Families of Reserve Component service members, with little or no prior identification as a military family, suddenly have been required to learn a new culture and respond to new stressors.
- Most military families demonstrate numerous family strengths while responding to frequent moves, separations from extended family, deployments, and living in other countries. The resilience of military families is highlighted throughout this book.
- The DoD has developed and funded programs and services to help military families adapt to and thrive within the military community and to assist them in dealing with challenges that come with a military life.

EXERCISES

To become aware of military links in your own community and your own preconceptions and depth of knowledge, answer the following questions:

1. Go to the Department of Defense website (http://www.defense.gov). Find the links to the military branches and explore their websites to learn more. How do they each contribute to national security and how do they coordinate with one another?
2. Learn about the military links and relationships in your local community:
   a. Campus—is there a military science program (often a Reserve Officer Training Corps or ROTC) at your university or college? If so, what branches are represented and how many students are involved? Who are the instructors for this program? How many students of your university have served in or been wounded or killed in recent conflicts?
   b. Is there a military installation near you? If so, what kind of installation is it? How many service members and civilians are part of the installation?
   c. Is there an Armory in your town or county?
   d. Is there a Veterans Affairs (VA) health-care facility in your community? If so, what services do they provide?
   e. Is there a Veterans of Foreign Wars (VFW) and/or American Legion hall in your community? What purpose do these organizations serve?
3. Consider the history of military service in the United States. From the beginning of the country, arguments have been made that those with more money and more power have been able to sidestep military service, even when there has been conscription. Respond to these questions:
   a. The current law in the United States requires its male citizens and aliens living in the United States to register with the Selective Service. Do you agree with this policy? Should female citizens and aliens living in the United States be required to register?

    b. Should the United States require its citizens, upon reaching the age of 18, to engage in military service? Public service? Would you prefer the United States to require military service of everyone, use a lottery and only draft some persons, or continue with an all-volunteer policy? What are the possible consequences of each option?

    c. Do you prefer that the country continue with the practice of the all-volunteer force even if it means multiple deployments for the same individuals and families?

4. Think about your experience with the military.

    a. Are you part of a military family? Do you know anyone serving in the military? Are you or have you been a member of the military? Have you ever considered joining? Why or why not?

    b. How many service members or military family members do you think you encounter in an average week or average day and where in your school or community, maybe even without being aware they are in the military?

    c. What are your views about war? About the wars in Iraq and Afghanistan?

    d. If you could ask a service member who just returned home from war a question what would it be? How would you feel asking the question? How do you think he or she would feel about your question?

    e. If you could ask a family member a question, what would it be? How do you think you would each feel?

    f. How might your political or religious views influence your thoughts and feelings about the military, service members, or family members you might meet in your work?

    g. Do you know someone who has been injured or killed while serving in the military?

    h. How do you think the military impacts your everyday life?

    i. What else do you want to learn about the military? How will you go about learning it?

2

An Overview of Military Personnel and Their Families

In Chapter 2, you will

- Meet Lisa Drew and her husband, Captain PC Drew, who discuss the decision to become a military family.
- Examine demographic characteristics of recruits and service members and how they compare to civilians.
- Understand the variety of family structures found in the military.
- Identify limitations in the data about military family demographics.
- Gain insights into how military families do–and do not–reflect the larger population.
- Consider how this information will be useful to working with military families.

Meet

Captain PC Drew, U.S. Marine Corps, and Lisa Drew

Captain Drew begins: *I grew up in a military family but my wife, Lisa, did not. After Lisa and I married, I was working in the financial services industry where people were totally focused on money. Lisa and I wondered if this was the environment we wanted to raise our children in. Then came 9/11. We asked ourselves: What do we need to do for ourselves and our kids? We started talking about joining the military for real.*

Lisa continues: *But no way was I going to do the military: too scary, too much worry, too little pay, moving around all the time and the biggest one for me—being by myself if and when he deployed.*

We visited PC's sister, Campbell, then in the military too, and her husband, an Air Force Captain at the time. I envied what they had: they were living overseas, Sam had a guaranteed paycheck, a secure job, 30 days vacation, and health insurance. Of course "The Question" loomed in my mind: What if PC gets sent to war and killed? PC's sister helped me get my arms around all the unknowns and worry. They are something every military family experiences.

We did it. We took a big pay cut. PC joined. It was the best decision for our family at the time; we couldn't have been happier. Since then we've lived in Japan for 5 years, spent a lot of time apart while PC was deployed, and now we're back in the States.

Here's what I've learned about the military: I'm lucky to be surrounded by such brave, amazing, selfless people. There is always someone to help if you need it. I think about my friend who took our toddler for the whole day when I caught his stomach bug (while PC was deployed and I was pregnant!). She brought him back at night, bathed, fed, and with his jammies on. We're lucky our kids are growing up surrounded by these people.

Our family is just like any other family. We want the best for our kids. I'm not sure how much they will remember as they grow up, but I hope being surrounded by so many diverse people in the military and our travels around Asia have at least shown them different cultures and different ways of doing things. As for whether or not they choose to join the military, that's up to them, but thankfully it's a long way down the road.

INTRODUCTION

Lisa Drew and her husband Captain PC Drew describe a process shared by many who consider joining the military: the decision is a family one, influenced by experiences and reactions of family and friends (Laurence, 2006). Across the country individuals and couples weigh the benefits of a secure income against raising children with regular separations from a parent; adults who have worked in the civilian sector reassess their career goals; parents and teenagers discuss the pros and cons of enlisting; and older siblings join and introduce brothers and sisters to the possibility of serving. In some families, military service is passed along from one generation to the next; military service is the largest parental occupational pool from which recruits come (Ender, 2006).

This chapter provides a demographic overview of military recruits, military service personnel, and their families. As you read the descriptions of military personnel and their family members, consider how civilian and military families share many characteristics. As Lisa says, her family is like any family. She and PC make decisions about what is a rewarding life, they rely on the support of family members and friends, and they wonder about their children's future.

The DoD gathers data about several characteristics of active duty and reserve component service members to better understand their needs and strengths. Data are also gathered about family members—spouses, children, and other dependents—in order to better understand the needs that stem from having one or more service members within a family system. These data inform the policies and programs that are intended to enhance quality of life for both service members and their families.

Four main sources of publicly available data and reports describe military service members and their families. Each source contributes to our understanding of the larger military family community. At times numbers presented for the same year that come from different sources may vary because of slight differences in definitions used by services. Yet, the overall picture each creates is similar.

The first source of public data comes from the Defense Manpower Data Center (DMDC), which publishes tables monthly and yearly that show the number of active duty personnel by rank and location. Data specifically highlighting female service members are published each September, and data on casualties are updated periodically (web addresses for casualty tables found in the reference list of this book link to the most recent data). A second source of public data is the annual *Demographics: Profile of the Military Community* (DASD, 2014). Third, DoD publishes the *Population Representation in the Military Services: Fiscal Year Report* (Office of the Under Secretary of Defense, Personnel and Readiness, n.d.) annually as required by the Senate Committee on Armed Services (Report 93–884, May 1974). Finally, the *Quadrennial Quality of Life Review* (DUSD, 2009b) reports the programming for and identified needs of military families. Some data are reported by fiscal year (FY) rather than by calendar year. The military's FY is the same as the U.S. federal government's: October 1 through September 30. For example, FY 2011 began October 1, 2010, and ended September 30, 2011.

This chapter continues building your foundational knowledge of military families and their service members. It may be tempting to skim through paragraphs with statistics and skip looking at tables and figures. To make it easier to think about the significance of the data, we include comparisons with civilian populations when possible. For example, how many military service personnel are there? Do you think it is the same, less than, or greater than the number of employees of Walmart, the largest retailer and private employer in the U.S.? Moreover, we expect that you are curious about a number of details, such as who joins the military and why, which branch of the service is the largest, what percentage of service members have children, or if more military couples are divorcing. These and other details are highlighted in this chapter. We encourage you to take time to think about the numbers, because they provide a picture of the military community. Knowing more about the larger community will help you better understand military families that you meet.

JOINING, STAYING IN, AND SEPARATING FROM THE MILITARY

While we commonly say that individuals joined the military, actually they must apply and be accepted into one of the branches of service. The DoD uses the terms **applicants** (those who apply to enter the military) and **accessions** (those accepted into the military, also called recruits) to differentiate between these groups. For example, in 2011, of the 283,108 active duty enlisted applicants with no prior service, only 54% became active duty enlisted accessions. You may also encounter the term **endstrength**, which refers to the total number of military personnel required by the Armed Forces or a branch of the Armed Forces, taking into account recruitment, retention, death, and retirements and other separations (Office of the Under Secretary of Defense, Personnel and Readiness, n.d.).

Of the 315,684 individuals who joined the U.S. military in FY 2011, 54% joined the Active Component, and 46% joined the Reserve Component. Ninety percent became enlisted personnel, 10% were commissioned as officers, and 1% became warrant officers (Office of the Under Secretary of Defense, Personnel and Readiness, n.d.).

Every year some individuals who have left the military decide to rejoin. Veterans with prior service may apply to either the Active or Reserve Component and to another service branch. A majority of accessions are individuals who never were in the military prior to joining, referred to as nonprior service. However, a larger percent of accessions in the Reserve Component are prior service than in the Active Component. In FY 2011, 44% of enlisted reserve accessions were prior service compared with only 1.6% of active duty enlisted accessions (Office of the Under Secretary of Defense, Personnel and Readiness, n.d.).

Who joins the military and why became very important questions to answer when conscription ended and the all-volunteer force began in the 1970s. Given that the average stay in the military is just under 10 years, the DoD must continually attract and accept into its ranks the best candidates possible. The following sections address the requirements for joining, demographic descriptions of recruits, reasons for joining and remaining in military service, and factors that may lead to ineligibility to serve.

Aptitude and Education Requirements

Critical thinking and analytical abilities are both important characteristics to consider when reviewing qualifications of applicants for a job or a profession. The DoD uses two measures for these characteristics: the Armed Forces Qualifying Test (AFQT), and educational credentials (i.e., high school diploma, adult education, college credit, General Education Certificate). Among recent nonprior service enlisted accessions, 77% scored above the 50th percentile on the AFQT and 98% had earned a high school diploma. (Office of the Under Secretary of Defense, Personnel and Readiness, n.d.).

Race, Ethnicity, Geographic Region, Median Household Income, and Gender

To examine the extent to which racial or ethnic groups are represented in new military recruits, we can compare the number of active duty, nonprior service recruits identifying with a race or an ethnicity with the percent of 18–24-year-old civilians who also identify with the same group. This comparison results in a recruit/civilian comparison ratio. For example, a 1.0 ratio means that the percent is the same in the military and civilian population. A 1.1 ratio means that for every one person in the military there are 1.1 persons in the 18–24-year-old population, or a 10% overrepresentation. A 0.95 ratio means there is a 5% underrepresentation.

Table 2.1 shows that in FY 2011, four racial groups were overrepresented and two racial groups were underrepresented in recruitment numbers. Regarding ethnicity, Hispanics were underrepresented and non-Hispanics were represented nearly proportionally (Office of the Under Secretary of Defense, Personnel and Readiness, n.d.).

The same recruit/civilian comparison ratio can be used to consider the proportional representation of regions of the country. In FY 2011, the South (1.18) was overrepresented, and the West (0.97) was represented proportionally. The Northeast (0.68) and the North Central regions (0.90) of the United States were underrepresented (Office of the Under Secretary of Defense, Personnel and Readiness, n.d.).

Using data on 2006 and 2007 recruits, Watkins and Sherk (2008) examined the median household income of the census tract in which recruits lived, in order to estimate

TABLE 2.1 Comparison of the Percent and Proportion of Recruits and 18–24 Year-Old Civilians by Race and Ethnicity FY 2011

Racial and Ethnic Groups	Recruit/Civilian Comparison Ratio[a]	Percent of Military Nonprior Service Active Component Enlisted Accessions	Percent of 18–24 Year-Old Civilians
Native Hawaiian or other Pacific Islander	2.51	0.93	0.37
American Indian/Alaska Native	1.73	1.9	1.1
Combination of two or more races	2.14	4.7	2.2
Black or African American	1.08	16.3	15.0
White	0.92	70.8	77.0
Asian	0.72	3.1	4.3
Unknown	NA	2.3	0.00
Hispanic	0.87	16.9	19.4
Non-Hispanic	1.01	81.6	80.6
Unknown	NA	1.5	0

Source: Data compiled from Office of the Under Secretary of Defense, Personnel and Readiness (n.d.). *Population representation in the military services: Fiscal year 2011 report*. Retrieved from http://prhome.defense.gov/RFM/MPP/AP/POPREP.

[a] Ratio calculated by authors.

the economic status of the recruits' parents. Recruits were overrepresented from areas in which the median income was more than $42,000 and underrepresented from lower income areas.

Of the active component, nonprior service accessions in 2011, 17% were women. Women continue to be underrepresented in the military services (Office of the Under Secretary of Defense, Personnel and Readiness, n.d.).

Propensity to Serve and Motivation to Join

Voices From the Frontline

ON JOINING THE MILITARY

I always ask the people under my command: Why did you join the military? Everyone has a crazy and entertaining story, but they all seem to fall into one of the categories below:

- It's a chance to protect and serve my country.
- It's what my family does.
- It's a steady paycheck.
- The educational benefits are amazing.
- I needed to get away from my family, town, or circumstances.
- I wanted to see the world.

Captain PC Drew
U.S. Marine Corps

Throughout the history of the United States, many considered military service to be a duty of citizenship. That perspective changed for many during the Vietnam era when mistakes and misinformation by government and high-ranking military leaders led to a mistrust of the military. More recently, however, the American public has shown an increase in its confidence in the military and in support for those in uniform (Laurence, 2006).

Researchers studying those who join the military typically examine **propensity to serve** (interest or plans to serve) and **motivation to serve** (reasons for serving). These concepts become important for predicting who will join and remain in an all-volunteer military. The propensity to serve increased in the first years of the all-volunteer force but has been declining for 30 years. This decline is assumed to reflect economic conditions, educational opportunities, and combat deployments (Woodruff, Kelty, & Segal, 2006). Regarding motivation for joining, as Captain Drew noted, military service members vary. Woodruff et al. (2006) have categorized these reasons as

- Institutional (i.e., patriotism, desire to serve, adventure/challenge, desire to be a soldier, "After 9/11, I wanted to serve my country.")
- Future-oriented (i.e., desire military career, money for college, "Being in the military gives me something I can be proud of for my whole life.")
- Occupational (i.e., support of one's family, crisis, lack of better options, best available option, "I got laid off from the factory where I was working. Signing up for the military meant I'd have a job and could support my girls.")
- Pecuniary (i.e., financial incentives such as enlistment bonuses, steady income, health care, "The money looked good.")

Voices From the Frontline

WHO IS THE NATIONAL GUARD?

The National Guard is made up of an amazing array of people, each with his or her own reasons for serving. Most of our National Guard are civilian soldiers and airmen who have other jobs. They are teachers, mechanics, ministers, contractors, policemen and women, emergency medical technicians, nurses, physician assistants, artists, and students. They are moms and dads, (sometimes single moms and dads), grandparents, sisters, and brothers. They may leave elderly parents and young children when they deploy. They have chosen to serve because they want to give back to our country; they like the camaraderie of those they train with; and they appreciate the extra job, training, and achievement they can obtain. They are all ages: close to retirement, in the middle of their careers, and young men and women still in college or just out of high school.

Barbara Purinton
Vermont Family Readiness Support Assistant

To examine motivating factors for joining and staying in the Army National Guard, Griffith (2009) examined survey data about recruitment and retention gathered from over 22,000 first-time junior-ranking soldiers (E-1 to E-4) during three time periods occurring between 2002 and 2006. Because units could choose whether to administer the surveys, results cannot be generalized to all Army National Guard service personnel. Educational benefits and service to country were the top two reasons for *joining* the Army National Guard across the three time periods. The top reason for *remaining* in the military across all time periods was education benefits (e.g., tuition assistance while on active duty, GI bills for veterans). While in the first time period, money and a sense of fulfillment were tied for second as reasons for remaining, by the third time period in 2006, money dropped to sixth, replaced by belongingness/camaraderie.

This study also noted that demands of serving during wartime influenced junior enlisted personnel's reported intentions of serving. Those who planned on leaving the Army National Guard after completing their current obligation increased from 40% prior to OIF to 57% in 2006. However, the percentage of respondents indicating they wanted to leave the Army National Guard prior to the end of their current obligation dropped from 8% prior to OIF to 2% in 2006, reflecting higher levels of belongingness, camaraderie, and wanting to serve the country. These results are consistent with another study of E-1 to E-6 Army reservists from a reserve combat division, 23% of whom had deployed in the past year. This study also noted that institutionally oriented soldiers reported stronger intentions to stay in the reserves than occupationally oriented soldiers (Griffith, 2008).

As well as the factors noted above, service members' decisions to remain in the military are influenced by a sense of job satisfaction (Griffith, 2008). Those with greater job satisfaction are more likely to remain or indicate intentions to remain in the military. In a study of nearly 25,000 military members in the 1990s, Reserve Component respondents reported higher levels of military job satisfaction than Active Component respondents, perhaps reflecting differing work experiences (Sanchez, Bray, Vincus, & Bann, 2004). However, both active duty and reserve respondents who indicated higher job pressure and who saw their biggest life problem resulting from job issues rather than nonjob issues such as family or individual stressors reported lower job satisfaction. Greater job satisfaction was reported by older members and by officers. Older members were probably satisfied enough to continue to serve past their initial time period. Higher job satisfaction among officers may be explained by the varying duties, responsibilities, and privileges associated with a higher rank and pay grade. Married respondents also reported greater job satisfaction than nonmarried. Active duty Black respondents and reserve Black and Hispanic respondents reported lower job satisfaction than White respondents. Finally, a greater number of pleasant life changes (e.g., marriage, birth of a child, promotion) were associated with lower levels of job satisfaction, perhaps reflecting that even positive life changes may add to work-family stress (Sanchez et al., 2004).

Factors That May Lead to Ineligibility

Multiple situations may make a potential recruit ineligible for service: medical or physical conditions (e.g., obesity, asthma); illegal substance use; failure of the AFQT; prior felony or serious misdemeanor convictions; and too many dependents under the age of 18 (Bicksler & Nolan, 2009; Christenson, Taggart, & Messner-Zidell, 2009). Depending upon their needs, the military services may provide waivers for certain conditions or situations. In 2009, however, both active duty and reserve components met or exceeded recruiting goals with respect to numbers and high quality of recruits, an achievement attributed to challenging economic conditions in the country, increasing bonuses for enlistment, spending more on recruiting, and declining violence in Iraq (Bicksler & Nolan, 2009).

DESCRIPTION OF SERVICE PERSONNEL

The United States has 1.37 million active duty and nearly 843,000 selected reserve personnel, totaling more than 2.2 million members (Deputy Assistant Secretary of Defense, Military Community and Family Policy [DASD], 2014). When the nearly 260,000 Individual Ready Reserve and Inactive National Guard are added, the total is approximately 2.5 million military personnel. In comparison, Walmart has nearly the same number of employees worldwide: 2.1 million (*Corporate Facts: Walmart by the Numbers*, 2010). In this section, Description of Service Personnel, we will consider the number of service personnel by branch of service, age, education, gender, and ethnicity.

Active Duty and Selected Reserve by Branch of Service

Based on Defense Manpower Data Center information, Table 2.2 shows numbers of active duty personnel as of the end of FY 2014. The Army has the largest percentage and the Marine Corps and Coast Guard the smallest. As noted earlier in the chapter, the DMDC issues monthly strength reports. However, to gain a more in-depth description of active duty and selected reserve personnel and their families, we need to rely on the

TABLE 2.2   Number and Percent of Active Duty Personnel by Branch of Service as of September 30, 2014

Service	Cadets/Midshipmen	Enlisted	Officer[a]	Total	Percent[b]
Army	4,394	406,519	97,297	508,210	36.9
Air Force	3,879	250,104	62,349	316,332	22.9
Navy	4,455	267,159	54,440	326,054	23.6
Marine Corps	NA	166,977	20,914	187,891	13.6
Coast Guard	874	31,126	8,347	40,347	2.9
Total	*13,602*	*1,121,885*	*243,347*	*1,378,834*	*100%*

Source: Compiled from Defense Manpower Data Center (2014a). *Active duty military strength report for September 30, 2014.* Retrieved November 23, 2014. from https://www.dmdc.osd.mil/appj/dwp/dwp_reports.jsp.

[a] Includes warrant officers.
[b] Percents rounded and calculated by authors.

TABLE 2.3   Number and Percent of Active Duty and Selected Reserve Personnel by Branch FY 2013

Service	Enlisted	Officer[a]	Total	Percent[b]
Army	429,103	98,967	528,070	39
Air Force	261,775	64,798	326,573	24
Navy	265,977	53,861	319,838	23
Marine Corps	174,610	21,238	195,848	14
Total Active Duty	*1,131,465*	*238,864*	*1,370,329*	*100*
Army National Guard	312,670	45,065	357,735	42
Army Reserve	162,959	35,250	198,209	24
Air National Guard	90,977	14,731	105,708	13
Air Force Reserve	56,853	14,060	70,913	8
Navy Reserve	48,124	14,320	62,444	7
Marine Corps Reserve	35,401	4,100	39,501	5
Coast Guard Reserve	6,695	1,305	8,000	1
Total Selected Reserve	*713,679*	*128,831*	*842,510*	*100*

Source: Office of the Deputy Assistant Secretary of Defense, Military Community and Family Policy (2014). *2013 demographics. Profile of the military community.* Exhibits 2.03 (p. 12), 2.04 (p. 13), 3.02 (p. 57). Washington, DC: Author. Retrieved from http://www.militaryonesource.mil/footer?content_id=279104.

[a]   Includes warrant officers.
[b]   Percents are rounded.

Demographics Report, published annually in December. A comparison of Tables 2.2 and 2.3 notes a slight increase in the number of active duty personnel from 2013 to 2014.

Table 2.3 shows the distribution of active duty and selected reserve personnel across branches of the service for FY 2013. Recall that the selected reserve includes both federal reservists and state Army and Air National Guard personnel. The Army has the majority of active duty (39%) and selected reserve members (66%), followed by the Air Force. For every officer, there are approximately five enlisted service members (DASD, 2014).

When compared with the overall civilian population in the United States, service personnel on average are younger. The difference is because the maximum age in the military is much lower than in the civilian work force. Enlisted service members and officers in the selected reserve are on average older than their active duty counterparts. In FY 2013, the average age of active duty enlisted personnel was 27 and officers was 35; the average age of selected reserve enlisted personnel was 30 and officers was 39 (DASD, 2014).

Education

Voices From the Frontline

A COLLEGE STUDENT AND MEMBER OF ROTC

I always wanted to have the military and college life together. ROTC allows me to do both and helps pay for college. When I graduate, I will have my B.S. and be commissioned as a junior officer. Then I'll start specialized training.

I did it a little differently than most. When I got out of high school, I went into the Army Reserves and found that the military is a good fit for me. I contracted with the ROTC for 4 years of active duty or reserves because I enjoyed it.

To be a student and a cadet, I have to be organized. I get up each day at 6:00 AM for PT, then go to classes. Like everyone else, I take courses for my major but I also take an additional two or three ROTC credits. Our classes cover various military topics like running a mission and first aid. In my program, every now and then we have a formal dinner in our dress uniforms. Once a semester we have a two-to-three day field training exercise where we set up a base and learn skills like **land navigation** (using a map and compass to travel from one place to another) and **squad tactics** (strategies used by a small unit of service members to achieve a goal). I will also have a month of training during the summer after my junior year.

Being in the military is like being part of a family. We have about 317 cadets in our battalion. These are the people I mostly hang out with. There are no respect issues with other students when we wear our uniforms to class once a week. I tend to get questions from my professors about the military perspective. Other students seem to pretty much ignore the uniform. I look forward to being a leader and making a difference in the military.

Kendra Beth Klinger
College student and member of ROTC

Compared with the civilian population aged 25 and older, the active duty population (enlisted and officer) has a higher level of formal education. In FY 2013, 88% of the civilian population aged 25 and over had a high school diploma or more education, while 99% of active duty and 93% of selected reserve enlisted did so. In addition, over 80% of active duty and selected reserve officers had a bachelor's or an advanced degree compared to 32% of the civilian population aged 25 and over. The Air Force had the highest percentage of active duty members with a bachelor's or an advanced degree (DASD, 2014).

Gender

While 54% of the U.S. civilian workforce is made up of women aged 16 and over, women make up only one-seventh of the active duty military. As noted in Table 2.4, in FY 2013, 15% of active duty and 18% of the selected reserve were women.

The Air Force had the greatest *percentage* of women of the active duty branches, and the Army had the largest *number* of women. Likewise, among the branches in the selected reserve, the Air Force Reserve had the greatest *percentage* of women, and the Army National Guard had the largest *number* of women (DASD, 2014).

TABLE 2.4   Percent of Active Duty and Selected Reserve Who Are Women FY 2013[a]

Percent of Active Duty				Percent of Selected Reserve			
	Enlisted	Officer	Total		Enlisted	Officer	Total
Air Force	19	20	19	Air Force Reserve	26	27	26
Navy	18	17	18	Army Reserve	22	25	23
Army	13	16	14	Navy Reserve	22	18	21
Marine Corps	7	6	7	Air National Guard	19	18	19
				Army National Guard	16	13	15
				Marine Corps Reserve	4	7	4
				Coast Guard	16	22	17
Total Across Branches	*14*	*16*	*15*		*18*	*19*	*18*

Source: Office of the Deputy Assistant Secretary of Defense, Military Community and Family Policy (2014). *2013 demographics: Profile of the military community.* Exhibits 2.13 (p. 18) and 3.17 (p. 67). Washington, DC: Author. Retrieved from http://www.militaryonesource.mil/footer?content_id=279104.

[a] Percents are rounded.

Ethnicity and Race

In 1948, President Harry S. Truman signed Executive Order 998 requiring racial equality among service members. Today, the DoD understands that ethnic and racial diversity of the services creates a force with broader skills and experiences and a stronger force.

The military shows a trend of increasing diversity over the past 20 years. Table 2.5 shows that 31% of active duty and 25% of selected reserve are racially diverse. The Navy and the Army are the most diverse in both active duty and selected reserve personnel. Enlisted personnel are more racially diverse than officers (DASD, 2014).

Table 2.6 shows the percentage of service members on active duty and in the selected reserve by race in FY 2013. In addition, 12% of active duty and 10% of selected reserve members reported Hispanic ethnicity in FY 2013 (DADS, 2014).

As Dr. Jennifer Lundquist explains in Voices From the Frontline, the military provides a location to study the impact of policies and practices that integrate work and housing, enforce equal employment opportunities, and reflect a social hierarchy built on rank and not class or race. As a result, service personnel report much better race relations in the military than in the civilian world, and Black and Latino service personnel report high

TABLE 2.5 Percent of Military Members who Identify as a Racial Minority by Branch FY 2013

	Percent of Active Duty Racial Minority				Percent of Selected Reserve Racial Minority		
	Enlisted	Officer	Total		Enlisted	Officer	Total[a]
Navy	43	20	39	Navy Reserve	40	21	36
Army	33	27	32	Army Reserve	34	29	33
Air Force	29	19	27	Air Force Reserve	32	17	29
Marine Corps	21	19	21	Marine Corps Reserve	20	20	20
				Army National Guard	22	15	21
				Air National Guard	19	12	18
				Coast Guard	28	32	28
Total Across Branches	32	22	31	Total	26	20	25

Source: Office of the Deputy Assistant Secretary of Defense, Military Community and Family Policy (2014). *2013 demographics: Profile of the military community*. Exhibits 2.03 (p. 12), 2.24 (p. 23), 2.26 (p. 24), 3.11 (p. 63), 3.30 (p. 76), and 3.33 (p. 79). Washington, DC: Author. Retrieved from http://www.militaryonesource.mil/footer?content_id=279104.
[a] Percents calculated by authors.

TABLE 2.6 Percent of Active Duty and Selected Reserve Personnel by Race FY 2013

	Active Duty	Selected Reserve
White	69.3	74.9
Black or African American	17.0	15.6
Asian	3.8	3.3
American Indian or Alaska Native	1.4	0.9
Multi-racial	3.1	1.1
Native Hawaiian or other Pacific Islander	1.0	0.6
Other or Unknown	4.3	3.6

Source: Office of the Deputy Assistant Secretary of Defense, Military Community and Family Policy (2014). *2013 demographics: Profile of the military community*. Exhibits 2.19 (p. 21) and 3.23 (p. 71). Washington, DC: Author. Retrieved from http://www.militaryonesource.mil/footer?content_id=279104.

satisfaction with the quality of life and employment opportunities afforded by the military (Lundquist, 2008).

Voices From the Frontline

RACE AND THE MILITARY

I grew up in Annapolis, Maryland, home to the U.S. Naval Academy, curious about what happened behind the Academy gates. When working on my PhD in Sociology and Demography, I became interested in understanding how the economic, social, and cultural conditions experienced by military families differ from those faced by civilian families and have pursued this line of research. In doing so, I discovered that racial differences found in U.S. society are not evident in the military. Why? The military is one of the few places in U.S. society where interracial contact is high and where full racial equality comes closest to realization. It was among the first U.S. institutions to become racially integrated. There is a notably greater degree of African American job mobility and superior opportunities for advancement in the military relative to the civilian labor force. On-base housing is explicitly racially integrated, and there is evidence that off-base housing is also highly racially integrated. The high prevalence of interracial marriage in the military (at more than twice that of civilian rates) could be interpreted as an indicator of the quality of Black–White relations. Moreover, African American soldiers and their spouses report overall higher quality of life than any other group in the service, civilian race differences in divorce and marriage rates (e.g., lower rate of marriage and higher rate of divorce in the African American community) do not apply to those in the military service, and the racial gap in preterm birth is substantially reduced in the military setting.

Jennifer Lundquist, PhD
Associate Professor, University of Massachusetts, Department of Sociology
Associate Director, Social and Demographic Research Institute, University of
Massachusetts

DESCRIPTION OF MILITARY FAMILIES

This section summarizes demographic data about those whom the DoD has traditionally recognized as family members and dependents of service members. Knowing the target population is necessary for creating or updating programs designed to build strengths, meet particular needs, and improve overall quality of life. For example, what decisions would you make about designing or funding parenting programs if you know that children under the age of five represent a large proportion of active duty military children? While reading this section, consider the gaps in our knowledge of characteristics and categories of family members and how these gaps might affect our understanding of the familial support systems and their connections to programming available for these service members.

Voices From the Frontline

BEING A FORMER SPOUSE OF A SERVICE MEMBER

I think it is so great that service members and their families are being supported. But when you are no longer an "official family member," you are out there floating around. As a former spouse, I have this different perspective on life, and it's hard to find a place to fit in.

I'm 23 but I am so different than other 23 year olds. I know the value of money and hard work. My former husband was in the infantry. I was preparing for his possible death since I was 17. Most people my age never think about such a thing, but you can't help whom you fall in love with.

In some ways, being a military family member is like being a service member, even if you never saw combat. You come home and your family expects you to be the same but you are changed. Marines give 110%. The mission always has to be completed. And now here I am in college where people slack off and I ask myself, "Is it worth it?" But I'm going to stick with it, work hard and do it for me. The military is still part of who I am.

Sonia Santamaria
College student, former spouse of a Marine

Data about families are not gathered the same way across the service branches even though the DoD works to learn more about the total force under its command. In terms of data about families, several limitations impact the state of our knowledge about family diversity, support systems, needs, and strengths.

As an organization, the military focuses on the **family of creation** (the family system created through partnering and/or parenting). These are the relationships that have implications for legal responsibilities of service members and are most commonly reported in DoD publications. However, these reports do not include data on adopted children. Likewise, most reports do not address service members' **family-of-origin relationships** (e.g., relationships with parents or siblings or others one grew up with) unless they are identified as an adult dependent of a service member. As a result, little is known about the extended families of service members, including cohabiting relationships.

The service branches offer slightly different responses in reporting marital status, in that the Navy only offers "Married" or "Never Married" as choices while other branches include "Divorced" and "Other" as choices (DASD, 2013). The married category includes first-time marriages as well as remarriages. These data allow for a very broad categorization of marital status but may frustrate both research and policy/program professionals who would like to better understand marital relationship development, strengths and challenges, as well as marital programming within the larger military community.

DoD-Recognized Family Members

In FY 2013, there were 2.2 million military service personnel with nearly 3 million associated family members. The DoD defines a family member as a spouse, child, or another person who meets certain legal definitions (e.g., guardianship of sibling). Given the definition, 57% of active duty personnel and 55% of selected reserve personnel had family responsibilities. Approximately 63% of family members were children, 37% were spouses, and less than 1% were other dependents (DASD, 2014).

The DoD keeps a record of all dependents of a service member through the **Defense Enrollment and Eligibility Reporting System** (DEERS; a system that verifies those who are eligible for military-based services and benefits). Each eligible person is enrolled into this system so that he/she can be identified as a family member or legal dependent when interacting with the military community. In addition to spouses and children, service members may be the primary or legal caregiver for children who are not their own and who are under the age of 22. To qualify as an eligible family member, children who are 21 or 22 must be full-time students. Additionally, service members may care for one or more adult dependents, including disabled older children, siblings, former spouses, parents, or grandparents. Each of these persons, if claimed as a family member by the service member, will be enrolled in and acknowledged through DEERS (DASD, 2014).

It is important to recognize that service members may likely feel emotionally or financially responsible for unmarried partners, parents, siblings, grandparents, aunts, uncles, cousins, and others who do not meet the DoD's definition of family member. As a human service professional, it is important to acknowledge all who play important roles in the lives of service members.

Number of Family Members

As noted in Chapter 1, the number of military members decreased once the Cold War ended. Most of the decrease in both the active duty and the selected reserve occurred between 1990 and 2000. In just the past 25 years, the number of active duty members decreased by a third from 2 million in 1990 to 1.3 million in 2013. However, even though the number of family members decreased approximately 30% from 2.6 million in 1990 to 1.8 million in 2013, they still outnumber active duty personnel; for every one active duty member, there are 1.4 family members. The same trend is seen in the selected reserve, which decreased approximately 30% during the same time period, from 1.2 million in 1990 to 842,510 in 2013. Selected reserve families decreased approximately 28%, from 1.5 million in 1990 to 1.1 million in 2013. For every selected reserve member, there are 1.3 family members (DASD, 2014).

The active duty Army is the largest branch of the armed services, both in number of service personnel and family members. In FY 2013, the Navy had slightly more active duty members than the Air Force, but the Air Force had more family members than the Navy. The Marine Corps had the fewest service personnel and family members. Across the branches in the selected reserves in FY 2013, the Army National Guard and Army Reserve had the greatest number of personnel and family members. The Air National Guard and Air Force Reserve were next in size, followed by the Navy and the Marine Corps (DUSD, 2010).

A Snapshot of Family Composition

This section provides a snapshot of the types of military families. Details about parenthood, marriage, divorce, children, ethnicity, race, and geographic location follow.

Across both Active and Reserve Components, junior enlisted members (E-1 to E-4) and junior officers (O-1 to O-3) are most likely to be single with no children; senior enlisted members, senior officers, and senior warrant officers are most likely to be married with children. This difference in family status is largely due to age differences as junior military personnel are younger on average than senior personnel. The military includes in the "single/never-married" category military personnel who have never married, who are divorced or widowed, or whose marriage was annulled (DASD, 2014).

Figure 2.1 shows that in 2013, 40% of active duty members and 45% of selected reserve members were single with no children. The remaining members were married or had children or both. Among active duty personnel, 56% were married (with or without children) compared with 47% of selected reserve personnel. Forty-three percent of active duty and selected reserve had children.

Marital Status

Fifty-five percent of active duty members and 46% of selected reserve members were married in FY 2013. In general, older and higher-ranking enlisted members and officers are

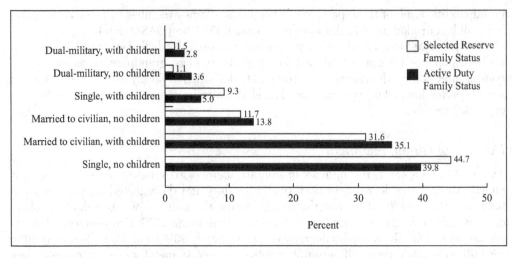

Figure 2.1   Active duty and selected reserve military family status FY 2013. (Data compiled from Office of the Deputy Assistant Secretary of Defense, Military Community and Family Policy. (2014). *2013 demographics: Profile of the military community.* Exhibits 5.08 (p. 120) and 6.08 (p. 142). Washington, DC: Author: Retrieved from http://www.militaryonesource.mil/footer?content_id=267470)

TABLE 2.7   Percent of Married Active Duty and Selected Reserve by Sex in 2013

	Active Duty Married				Selected Reserve Married		
	Men	Women	Total		Men	Women	Total
Army	61	47	59	Army National Guard	44	27	42
Navy	55	36	52	Army Reserve	48	35	45
Marine Corps	47	37	46	Navy Reserve	60	42	56
Air Force	60	50	58	Marine Corps Reserve	28	36	29
				Air National Guard	59	45	56
				Air Force Reserve	58	46	55
				Coast Guard	56	49	55
Total Across Branches	57	44	55		48	36	46

Source: Office of the Deputy Assistant Secretary of Defense, Military Community and Family Policy. (2014) *2013 Demographics report. Profile of the military community.* Exhibits 2.56 (p. 42) and 3.60 (p. 95). Washington, DC: Author. Retrieved from http://www.militaryonesource.mil/footer?content_id=279104.

more likely to be married than younger and entry-level personnel. This trend holds true across all branches for both active duty and selected reserve members (DASD, 2014). It is not known what percent of married personnel are in remarriages; however, in 2008, 16% of military spouses reported that they were currently in a stepfamily (DMDC, 2009).

Table 2.7 shows the percent of women and men in the active duty and selected reserve components who were married in 2013; the Army and the Air Force had the highest percentage of married service personnel. Across all branches, men on active duty were more likely than women to be married. Likewise in the selected reserve, male service personnel were more likely than women to be married, across all branches except for the Marine Corps Reserve (DASD, 2014).

Dual-military marriages are those in which a military member in one branch of service is married to a military member in the same or different branch of service. For example, active duty male and female Army sergeants could be married to one another, or an Air Force active duty officer could be married to a Marine Corps Reserve officer (DASD, 2014).

Of all active duty members in FY 2013, 6% were in dual-military marriages, as were 3% of all selected reserve members. Of married members 12% of married active duty and 6% of married selected reserve personnel were in dual-military marriages, while 88% and 94%, respectively, were in military–civilian marriages (DASD, 2014).

Active duty and selected reserve female service members are more likely to be in dual-military marriages than their male counterparts. In 2013, 46% of married active duty females were in dual-military marriages: 59% of married active duty Marine Corps women, 56% of married Air Force women, 39% of married Army women, and 38% of married Navy women. The percentage of their married male counterparts who were in dual-military marriages ranged from 13% of married Air Force men to 5% of married Army, Navy, and Marine Corps men (DASD, 2014).

In FY 2013, 24% of married selected reserve women compared with 3% of married selected reserve men were in dual-military marriages. Specifically, 52% of married Marine Corps Reserve women, 38% of Air Force Reserve and Air National Guard women, 30% of married Army Reserve women, and 20% of married Navy Reserve women were in dual-military marriages (data on dual-military marriages in the Army National Guard were not available). The percent of their married male counterparts who were in dual-military marriages ranged from about 7% of married Air Force Reserve men to 2% of married Navy Reserve men (DASD, 2014).

Divorce

Comparing divorce rates for those in the military to overall divorce rates in the United States is difficult as calculations are done differently and in both cases are done imperfectly. The U.S. divorce rate does not include data from six states (i.e., California, Georgia, Hawaii, Indiana, Louisiana, and Minnesota). Additionally, the U.S. divorce rate is reported as the number of divorces per 1000 total population, which is misleading because it includes children who cannot marry and, thus, cannot divorce. The 2009 U.S. divorce rate was 3.4 divorces per 1000 people, a decline from 3.5 in 2008 and 3.6 in 2007 (Tejada-Vera & Sutton, 2010).

Meanwhile, the DoD estimates the percentage of divorces each year by counting the number of service personnel who indicated that they were married 1 year but did not indicate that they were married a year later. This method can overlook those who divorce and remarry within the year because they would be listed as married at both data collection points. Also, the divorce figures include cases of those who were widowed although the DoD states the number of widowed cases is small and unlikely to affect the percent reported. Finally, the numbers and percents presented here indicate only those who divorced in 2013, not those who divorced in prior years. According to this method, 3.4% of active duty personnel and 2.6% of the selected reserve personnel divorced in 2013.

Figures 2.2 and 2.3 show the percent of active duty and reserve component enlisted members and officers who divorced in FY 2000 and the percent who divorced in FY 2013. Across each branch of the service and in both years, the percent of enlisted members who divorced was higher than the percent of officers who divorced. Overall, increases occurred for both enlisted and officer service members in the Active and Reserve Components. However, the percentage of active duty enlisted who divorced in 2013 was lower than in the three prior years (DASD, 2013).

Parenthood

In FY 2013, 43% of active duty and 43% of selected reserve service members had children, and of those who were parents, they had an average of two children per member. There are differences between the branches and between active duty and selected reserve

Figure 2.2 Estimated percent of active duty who divorced in 2000 and 2013. (Data compiled from Office of the Deputy Assistant Secretary of Defense, Military Community and Family Policy. (2014). 2013 *demographics: Profile of the military community*. Exhibit 2.71 (p. 49). Washington, DC.: Author. Retrieved from http://www.militaryonesoule.mil/footer?content_id=267470)

Figure 2.3 Estimated percent of selected reserve who divorced in 2000 and 2013. (Data compiled from Office of the Deputy Assistant Secretary of Defense, Military Community and Family Policy. 2014. 2013 demographics: Profile of the military community. Exhibit 3.75 (p.102). Washington, D.C.: Author. Retrieved from http://www.militaryonesource.mil/footer?content_id=267470)

in the average age of the service member at the time of their first child's birth. In general, active duty members in each branch become parents earlier than their corresponding selected reserve colleagues (DASD, 2013).

Compared to civilians, military members are more likely to have their first child during their 20s and less likely to have them in their teens or 30s (MacDermid Wadsworth, 2010). In FY 2013, 51% of active duty members and 37% of selected reserve members were between the ages of 20 and 25 when their first child was born, and their average age was 25.6 and 27.4, respectively (DASD, 2013).

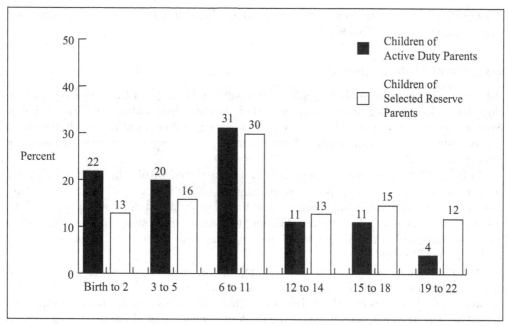

Figure 2.4   Percent of children by age groups FY 2013. (Data compiled from Office of the Deputy Assistant Secretary of Defense, Military Community and Family Policy. (2014). 2013 *demographics: profile of the military community.* Exhibits 5.32, 5.33, 5.34 (p.156). Washington, D.C.: Author. Retrieved from http://www.militaryonesource.mil/footer?content_id=267470)

Children

As a group, children of active duty members are younger than children of reserve component members. As Figure 2.4 illustrates, 42% of active duty component children in 2013 were age birth to 5 years, while only 29% of selected reserve component children were in this category in 2014.

Spouses

Spouses of active duty members are younger on average than spouses of selected reserve members, reflecting the older average age of those in the reserves. Fifty-three percent of active duty spouses and 33% of selected reserve spouses are 30 years old or younger. Likewise, spouses married to enlisted personnel are younger than spouses of officers in both active duty and selected reserve (DASD, 2014).

Information about race and ethnicity of dependents appears limited to survey information collected from active duty spouses. The following information on race and ethnicity of active spouses comes from the *2012 Survey of Active Duty Spouses* (DMDC, 2013a) that used random sampling procedures. Service member pay grades represented in this study range from E-1 to E-9 and O-1 to O-6. Pay grades of the most senior officers (O-7 to O-9) were not included. Fifty-one percent of the sample was 30 years old or younger.

In this survey, 14% of the spouses indicated they were Hispanic. A greater percentage of spouses married to enlisted personnel (13%) than to officers (8%) were Hispanic (DMDC, 2009). When responding to the question asking their race, spouses could choose more than one category, which 4% did. Percentages were: White (78%), Black or African American (14%), Asian (9%), American Indian or Alaska Native (2%), and Native Hawaiian or other Pacific Islander (2%). Greater diversity was reported from Army and Navy than

Air Force and Marine spouses, from enlisted than officer spouses, and from older spouses than younger spouses (DMDC, 2013a).

Location of Military Families

Although military personnel are deployed to countries throughout the world, most active duty and selected reserve personnel and their families live within the United States. Spouses and children tend to live where their service member is stationed although there are exceptions (e.g., unaccompanied tours, choose to live apart to pursue a career or education).

In FY 2013, 87% of active duty personnel were assigned within the United States and its territories, and approximately 12% were assigned within Europe and in East Asia. Fifty percent of the active duty component were stationed in six U.S. states: California, Virginia, Texas, North Carolina, Georgia, and Washington. Another six states had no active duty members stationed in them. The remaining 38 states had .1% to 5.1% of the active duty members (DASD, 2014).

As with the active duty component, the majority of the selected reserve was located in the U.S. or its territories in FY 2013. Only about 1% of the selected reserve were located at permanent duty stations outside of the United States, including North Africa, Europe, and East Asia. The Marine Corps Reserve had the largest contingent of internationally located personnel (DASD, 2014).

In FY 2013, 52% of the selected reserve lived in 13 states: California, Texas, Florida, Pennsylvania, New York, Ohio, Georgia, Virginia, Illinois, North Carolina, Alabama, Louisiana, Missouri, and Indiana (DUSD, 2010).

In approximately 30 local labor markets, the military plays a significant role in the regional economy. For example, in Virginia Beach, Virginia, Jacksonville, North Carolina, and Killeen, Texas, more than 15% of employed people are active duty service personnel. Moreover, communities with significant military presence are among the least residentially and racially segregated in the United States (Segal & Segal, 2004).

Both active duty and reserve service members may be stationed outside the United States and its territories. Whether the DoD infrastructure at the military facility is sufficient to support families usually determines whether a tour is accompanied or unaccompanied.

An **accompanied tour** is an assignment to an overseas location that includes the service member's family. This type of tour is "command sponsored," meaning that the service member's new command is responsible for the support and welfare of the service member's family. Transportation of family members and household goods, housing, commissary and exchange privileges, medical care, child care, and schools are some of the services provided to command-sponsored families.

For families with Army or Air Force active duty members, the most common stations outside the United States currently are in Europe, with the most populous installations in Germany, Italy, the United Kingdom, Turkey, Spain, and Belgium. For Navy families, the most common stations outside the United States are in Italy, Greece, and Japan. The Marine Corps has a large, accompanied installation in Japan. Germany is usually an accompanied tour of 3 years but Army personnel can choose to go unaccompanied for 2 years.

Unaccompanied tours overseas occur when areas are deemed to be politically unstable, dangerous, or lacking in support services for families. No services are provided to families through the DoD in these locations; however, service members might elect to bring their families at their own expense and request support services.

South Korea may be accompanied or unaccompanied. For single service members, the length of military assignments to South Korea is generally 12 months although service members can request an extension of their overseas assignments. Married service members have the option of accepting a 1-year unaccompanied assignment or bringing their family members for a 2- or 3-year tour. Married military members assigned to installations in the northern part of South Korea, near the **Demilitarized Zone** (a buffer zone between North Korea and South Korea), can opt to accept a 2-year accompanied tour or a 1-year unaccompanied tour (McMichael, 2008).

FAMILIES OF LESBIAN, GAY, AND BISEXUAL MILITARY SERVICE MEMBERS

Our knowledge about the families of lesbian, gay, and bisexual (LGB) military service members is limited. The DoD Directive 1304.26, commonly referred to as **Don't Ask, Don't Tell** (DADT), was issued by President Clinton in 1993 in response to the passage of federal law prohibiting gays and lesbians from serving in the U.S. Armed Forces. Under this directive the military could not ask recruits about their sexual orientation and military members were not to disclose that they were gay or lesbian because they would be discharged from the military. As a result, DoD data about family structures with same-sex partners, with or without children, were not collected. However, with the repeal of DADT in 2011 and the 2013 Supreme Court decision finding section 3 of the federal Defense of Marriage Act (DOMA) unconstitutional, LGB service members can serve openly in the military and their dependents can receive the same benefits as dependents of heterosexual service members (United States v. Windsor, 2013). As a result, we should learn more about LGB service members and their families in the coming years.

Meanwhile, using data from the American Community Survey and the General Social Survey, Gates (2010) estimated that LGB service members constituted 0.9% of the active duty force and 3.4% of the National Guard and Reserve (including the ready reserve, the standby reserve, and the retired reserve), or nearly 71,000 service personnel. It was estimated that 37% of active duty and 20% National Guard and Reserve LGB personnel live with minor children (Gates, 2011, personal communication, in Oswald & Sternberg, 2014).

On December 22, 2010, President Barack Obama signed legislation to repeal "Don't Ask, Don't Tell" (Parrish, 2010), and the DoD began a certification process that included reviewing regulations, policies, and eligibility for benefits (e.g., designated beneficiary for benefits); preparing training materials for use by family support staff, military chaplains, personnel specialists, commands, and others; and carrying out training (Pellerin, 2011). Repeal of DADT went into effect September 20, 2011, after completion of the certification process and a required 60-day waiting period (Marshall, 2011). The U.S. was the 23rd country in NATO to allow LGB service personnel to serve, openly, in the military (Oswald & Sternberg, 2014).

As part of the required certification process leading up to the repeal, the DoD, through an independent research agency, Westat, conducted surveys with random samples of 200,000 military members and 150,000 spouses. The purpose was to obtain opinions about the impact of repealing the law restricting lesbians, gay men, and bisexuals from serving openly on a variety of aspects of military life. Results indicated that the majority of military personnel and spouses believed repeal of DADT would have a neutral effect on unit cohesion, readiness, effectiveness, morale, family readiness, retention, referral, and attendance at social events and family and deployment support programs (Westat, 2010).

Before the repeal of DADT, the National Defense Research Institute (2010) issued a report that included focus groups with service members and an online survey of LGB service members. Although results cannot be generalized due to nonprobability sampling, they do suggest that repeal of DADT would result in LGB service members being more visible and their families participating in military family events and military ceremonies. Data do not exist to indicate the percent of LGB military families participating in events and ceremonies, but antidotal reports from family readiness groups and information offered by military family organizations indicate that many are identifying as military families and participating in unit functions, registering in DEERs and obtaining ID cards, and using services for military families. Family support centers and family readiness programs have and continue to work on making their language, materials, and services inclusive of LGB military families (see militaryonesource.mil).

However, as Ariana Bostian-Kentes, the President of the Military Partners and Families Coalition (MPFC), and her partner Captain Stephanie Boltrick note, some LGB service members remain concerned about possible negative repercussions of disclosing their sexual orientation. Clearly more work is needed. As the RAND (2010) report indicated, to implement the repeal of DADT clear commitment from leadership, clear standards of conduct for all, and zero tolerance for harassment will be necessary.

Voices From the Frontline

PRACTICE INCLUSIVITY. . . . ALLOW PEOPLE TO TELL THEIR STORIES

Don't Ask, Don't Tell (DADT) was the law and policy that came into effect in 1993 prohibiting lesbian, gay, and bisexual service members from disclosing their sexual orientation or from speaking about their same-sex relationships while serving in the Armed Forces. On December 22, 2010, the DADT Repeal Act of 2010 became law. The Army began educating Army personnel on the process and policies associated with the repeal of DADT on February 17, 2011, in order to prepare the force for implementation. The repeal occurred September 20, 2011.

Stephanie: My military career began in December of 2002. I was a senior in high school, with just 5 months remaining until graduation. I enlisted in the Army Reserve as a military police officer. Three days after graduation from high school, I left home to attend basic training at Fort Leonard Wood, Missouri. It was the first time that I was away from home for longer than a week. To say the least, the experience was dramatic and incredibly challenging.

I arrived at Michigan State University (MSU) in the fall of 2003, just three weeks after completing basic training. I began my academic career at MSU with the intent of graduating with a degree in criminal justice and receiving my commission as an officer in the Army from the Army Reserve Officer Training Corps (ROTC) program, with an active duty assignment as a military police officer. What I realized after my first semester at MSU was that helping people as a law enforcement officer was not what I actually wanted to do. I discovered after self-reflection and exploration that I wanted to work in the mental health field, and serve my community in a way that assisted people in becoming healthy, productive members of society.

It was wonderful to be able to identify my career goals and professional aspirations so early on in my life. What wasn't so wonderful, however, was my internal struggle with my sexuality, and being forced to hide my true identity. I knew I was a lesbian. I also knew that if I were to come out of the closet, my career in the military would end before it really began. Not only would my career be over, but it would end in a terrible way: under the DADT policy, "homosexual conduct" warranted a dishonorable discharge. This was a terrifying reality for me.

With the support of my family and friends, I was able to, well, push through my ROTC experience. What I mean by that is, I would do the bare minimum of standards, isolate myself from my fellow cadets, and keep as far of a distance as possible from anyone in the military when I was anywhere on campus other than the ROTC building. The reason for this hyper-vigilant approach was because I was completely paranoid that I would be outed as a lesbian and kicked out of the military. For someone who wants to serve their country more than anything else in the world, this is the worst thing that could happen.

During the fall of our last year in the ROTC program, we were required to submit our duty assignment and job requests. I knew that doing active duty was something that I would not be able to do, because it would be far too psychologically stressful on me to live within an active duty community where I would have to hide every aspect of my personal life every single day. After taking this into consideration, I decided that it would be best for me to elect to take a commission within one of the reserve component branches (Army Reserves and Army National Guard). My thought was that being in the National Guard would be less stressful, and I wouldn't have to worry as much about hiding my personal life. I found this to be completely inaccurate, as many of my fellow Soldiers would ask me questions about my personal life in an attempt to build rapport and connect with me. I was in the closet all over again.

The repeal of DADT was announced in December of 2010. I anxiously waited for September 20, 2011, the date that the repeal would go into effect. I imagined my first drill weekend post-repeal as a celebration with rainbows and confetti dropping from the ceiling. I was disappointed to realize that weekend that the majority of the Soldiers didn't even realize that the repeal of DADT had gone into effect.

Organization climate post-repeal varies from state to state, unit to unit, and command to command. While the policy clearly states that it is now legal for lesbian, gay, bisexual, and (LGB) service members to serve openly and authentically, they are not in any way protected under federal law or equal opportunity (EO) laws. In addition, the lack of cultural competency and understanding of the LGB population has a negative impact on mission effectiveness; when leaders and organization members lack the education and understanding of a particular minority group, they will not be able to make responsible and intentionally inclusive efforts within their ranks. Until the LGB population is a protected class that is viewed as a valued aspect of diversity, the military will not be able to progress forward and improve mission effectiveness.

Another important component of this topic is the fact that the repeal did not include our transgender brothers and sisters. Developing a policy and passing legislation that allows for all people to serve openly is something that still needs to be addressed. This is a very important piece of the puzzle that has been left behind.

Ariana: Stephanie and I met through my work with Military Partners and Families Coalition (MPFC), an organization that I co-founded to provide support, resources, education, and advocacy for LGBT military families. I was inspired to start MPFC after experiencing the stress and anxiety of being closeted while in a previous relationship with someone who was Active Duty Army. During the last three years of that relationship, we lived in different states and I always felt so alone and isolated—even more so when I received news that she was deploying to Afghanistan. I worried about basic things, like how to discreetly send her a care package, what to write on the customs form, whether or not I should put a man's name or picture in my cards to her, all in an effort to conceal our relationship. Talking on Skype while she was deployed was risky and incredibly stressful. We had to be conscious of our display of emotions and the visibility of our relationship. I felt bad for her having to hide who she was and bad for myself that I couldn't be a part of the military community that creates such a groundswell of support when someone is deployed. Each hour of each day that she was gone I worried that something would happen and I'd be left in the dark with no way to get information or support, because in the eyes of the Army, I was nobody to her.

A cultural shift

Stephanie: The education to ready us for the repeal of DADT came in the form of a PowerPoint emailed to us along with a note giving us the name of someone to contact if we had questions. In the military, time is money. It was incredibly disappointing and disconcerting that the military didn't see this as a learning opportunity and a chance to secure success through education on the topic and what the expectations would be in a post-DADT military environment.

It continues to be a difficult decision for people to make regarding coming out to their units. I myself did not feel comfortable being open about my personal life until April of 2014, when I was promoted to the rank of Captain. It was important for me to be able to feel like I had a sense of security in some way – obtaining the rank of Captain provided me with that. I came out to my unit by introducing my best friend, partner, and hero to my unit before she pinned the rank of Captain on me.

It would be beneficial in terms of mission effectiveness and promoting diversity and inclusion within the military to incorporate LGBT cultural competency/diversity training into the curriculum of military courses. This would ensure that all individuals enlisting in the military are exposed to consistent messages throughout their military career, from start to finish, regarding the LGBT population. People come from all sorts of backgrounds to the military. Diversity is something that is viewed as valuable from all demographics, with the exception of the LGBT community. Action from the Department of Defense (DoD) and key leaders is necessary. Until guidance is formally released, Soldiers in the ranks may not fully understand why inclusivity is essential to mission effectiveness. Such action must take place in order for a major cultural shift to occur.

Many of us from the LGBT community have been the boots-on-the-ground for changes in the military. The help and advocacy of our straight allies is also necessary to ensure that the process continues, and progress advances. With the efforts of allies like Patrick Murphy and Leon Panetta in collaboration with the efforts of the LGBT community, the repeal of DADT was able to become a reality.

Ariana: After years of having to be vigilant about hiding our families and identities, it is impossible for LGB military families to be automatically welcomed with open arms, or included alongside the greater military community. When people have experienced repeated oppression based on who they are, they aren't conditioned to expect acceptance. This is especially important to keep in mind for providers of services and support for the military community. It's incumbent upon them to do the work, to do the outreach, to receive the education, and to be explicit about being inclusive with their services and supportive of LGBT people.

Whether you are a new or experienced provider, it is important to be able to step back and reflect on how you are conducting your practice. For example, are you using inclusive language? The minute you ask a woman who you don't know, "Do you have a husband?" you have created an obstacle to being able to build strong rapport by automatically assuming that the individual is heterosexual. It's exhausting to continually have to come out, to be vulnerable and to educate people on your behalf. Doing things like using gender-neutral language removes those obstacles to building rapport. Simply changing the question to, "Are you in a relationship?" or "Do you have a partner?" opens up the conversation so that your client doesn't have to correct and educate you, or flat out lie to you because they don't feel comfortable coming out. Paying attention to how your words and actions impact others should be an ongoing part of any practice – no matter how experienced or new to the field of social and mental health services you are. Practice inclusivity. Continually broaden your awareness. Allow people to tell their stories and listen rather than assume you know their experience or what is best.

It is popular sentiment to respond, "Oh, that doesn't matter to me," when someone comes out to you. People with the best intent say harmful things like, "I don't see race or gender or sexuality. People are people. Love is love." These statements are dismissive of identities and experiences. It should matter to you that someone trusts you enough to come out to you. Some ideas of better responses are, "Thank you for telling me" or "I'm glad you feel comfortable enough to share about yourself with me." Imagining what it is like on the other side can be very valuable. It is the responsibility of providers who are serving service members and their families to be the most aware and educated.

Today, recently enlisted service members may not fully understand the history of DADT and that it did and still does affect countless service members, veterans, and their families. The policy may be history, but it doesn't mean everything is better now—it doesn't mean that service members feel comfortable serving our country and living their life freely and genuinely. Furthermore, transgender service members still cannot serve openly. DADT was about sexual orientation. However, one stroke of a pen and implementation of an inclusive policy would make that change. If mission effectiveness is the military's stated goal at the end of the day, then why would it deny the service of so many highly skilled, motivated, creative, and dedicated people?

There were many sinister effects of DADT. The stress of the policy negatively affected entire families. People were taught to lie about their relationships, children had to learn to lie at school and to their friends. Families today are still struggling to grow and move forward from these traumatic experiences. Who knows how many people took their lives not being able to live authentically as who they were?

The military has much room for improvement. I care about the well-being of ALL service members.

The military is an institution with high standards. I have the utmost respect and a profound appreciation for people who are serving and who have served our country. At the present time, the military is not performing to standard regarding the support provided to its diverse team. There is much room for improvement. It is critical that this institution promotes a healthy and productive work environment that sets the standard for workplace environment and inclusivity for our country as a whole. That is why I am so passionate about this work.

Captain Stephanie Boltrick, LLMSW
Medical Service Corps Officer, United States Army

Ariana Bostian-Kentes
President, Military Partners and Families Coalition (MPFC)
Program Manager for Inclusive Leadership Education,
University of Michigan Spectrum Center

SUMMARY

- This chapter provided a demographic picture of military recruits, military service personnel, and their families.
- Four main sources of publicly available data and reports describe military service members and their families: DMDC's monthly and yearly reports on the number of active duty personnel; the annual publication, *Demographics: Profile of the Military Community*; the annual *Population Representation in the Military Services* report; and the *Quadrennial Quality of Life Review*.
- As a group, Active and Reserve Component recruits typically exceed the performance of their civilian counterparts on measures of aptitude in math and reading, educational attainment, and health.
- Those who join the military report various reasons for joining: institutional, occupational, future-oriented, and financial.
- Military personnel as a group are younger than the civilian population. They reflect ethnic and racial diversity found in the United States. However, the military is largely male and does not reflect the U.S. workforce that is just over half female.
- In 2013, there were 3 million family members of service personnel, and a majority of these family members were children. Approximately 43% have children. Active duty (55%) are more likely to be married than reservists (46%).
- More research on military families is needed, particularly in the areas of divorce, remarriage, stepfamilies, families of LGB service members, and extended families of service personnel.

EXERCISES

1. Of those motivating factors discussed in this chapter (institutional, occupational, future-oriented, and pecuniary), which ones would most likely motivate you to join the military? Why? Which ones are most likely to motivate you to seek another career path? Why?
2. If possible, ask an active duty member and a member of the Reserve Component what motivated them to join the military and what has motivated them to remain.

You may wish to share the four motivating factors with the service members and ask them to reflect on how much each factor played into their decision to join and into their decision to remain in the military.

3. Estimate the number of family members a service member might have. Write down the family members you are including in your estimate (e.g., parents, children, grandparents, cousins, nieces, nephews, aunts, uncles).

4. If you were designing family life education (e.g., workshops, web-based information, social networking sites) or recreational services, how would you use the demographics shared in this chapter to guide your work for active duty service personnel and their family members? For reserve component service members and their family members? What additional demographic information would you like to have about military families in order to better design programs and services?

5. Locate current military strength reports at the Defense Manpower Data Center site (https://www.dmdc.osd.mil/appj/dwp/dwp_reports.jsp). Compare the totals by branch of service with the totals reported in this chapter.

6. Examine the website for the Office of the Assistant Secretary of Defense for Reserve Affairs at http://ra.defense.gov/. Describe what you learned about families of those service personnel in the reserve component.

7. Examine one of the many reports found on Military OneSource (http://www.militaryonesource.mil/footer?content_id=267470). What additional information about military families did you learn?

3

Defining Features of Military Family Life

In Chapter 3, you will

- Meet Rhonda Thomlinson, spouse of a Navy Chaplain.
- Discover normative stressors in the lives of military families.
- Consider the importance of spouse education and employment.
- Understand how moving, separations, and deployments influence family life.
- Gain insights into the factors that promote resilience in military families.

Meet

Rhonda Thomlinson, Spouse of a Navy Chaplain

My husband and I were married for a good 20 years before he joined the Navy as a chaplain. A lot of spouses are 18 to early 20s and I really respect them. My husband had the advantage that his father was retired Air Force, so he understood the military environment. However, it was quite the shock for me. I knew nothing coming to it outside of a few times way back in college going to a PX. That was my total experience. I was surprised at how much I didn't know.

I meet new people and do new things, from making new friends to living on a beautiful island. I'm not saying there aren't days I don't think, "What did I get into?" especially at the beginning. But with a positive attitude there are many new and amazing opportunities.

I was surprised at how unique and strong the ties are between people. In the military, we can share things with one another; we have common experiences.

It's not always easy. When our spouses are deployed, there are times we may be out of communication, and there's a lot to handle at home. I've become a firm believer that anything that can go wrong will go wrong during a deployment. Once the water heater started leaking right over my electric dryer and my husband's ship still hadn't left the harbor.

There are times it is virtually impossible to continue a career path. Sometimes spouses may not be able to work or need special qualifications depending on where they are. A friend of mine has started a career online doing medical transcription.

You have to keep your mind open. I couldn't find a good job that paid me enough to make it worth my while. Luckily with the cost of living where my husband is stationed now, we're okay. I'm hoping to become a Family Readiness Officer, hired by the command as a liaison with families to coordinate communication.

They say you can't understand someone until you walk a mile in their shoes. Sometimes service members and families have experiences and civilians can't follow in their footsteps, no matter whose shoes are worn. But we can be open and respectful, listen, and begin to understand the culture.

INTRODUCTION

Military life includes many defining characteristics, such as those noted by Rhonda Thomlinson above and those highlighted in Chapter 1 (e.g., living within a chain of command, placing service to others before self, being part of a community). It may also bring periodic separation from family, geographic mobility and residence in foreign countries, and risk of injury and death (Segal, 1986). With the advent of the all-volunteer force, the numbers of spouses and children have increased and so has the importance of spouse employment and raising children. This chapter will address characteristics of military life that affect many families: a sense of community; the priority of the mission (i.e., "duty first"); relocation, including mobility and living outside of the United States; spouse employment challenges; separation, including deployment; and risk of injury or death. Issues specific to military children are addressed in Chapter 4. First, however, we'll examine the military, and the family, as "greedy" institutions, and the norms and roles that accompany each.

The military and families have both been called "greedy institutions" because they demand an individual's loyalty, commitment, time, and energy (Segal, 1986). Institutions influence and structure, in varying degrees, social life through sets of norms and roles (Parsons & Bales, 1956). **Norms** are expectations about how to act in a situation. Norms can be explicitly stated or implicitly understood. For example, an **explicit norm**, or overtly stated expectation, in the military is wearing a uniform on duty, while in a family an explicit norm may be a set bedtime for children. An **implicit norm**, or implied expectation, in the military is showing respect for all military service members and veterans, while in a family an implicit norm is how affection is shown. **Roles** consist of a group of norms that govern a situation. These are similar to "parts" played by actors who assume characters to play on stage or in a movie (Goffman, 1959). The military has numerous roles, such as noncommissioned officers, commanders, platoon leaders, and command financial specialists. Likewise, families are comprised of numerous roles, such as parents, daughters, sons, cousins, grandparents, aunts, and uncles. Whether in the military or in families, each role carries expectations about how to act.

Both families and the military exert normative pressures on their members. Families feel the pressure of *military* norms and roles through the demands made on the service member's loyalty (e.g., service before self even when in danger), commitment (e.g., signing a contract to work for the military for 4, 6, or 8 years), time (e.g., always available), and energy (e.g., focus on the mission). Spouses and children may feel pressure to regulate their behavior so it does not negatively affect the service member's career. Likewise, service members may worry a superior in their unit will see family problems as an indication of their inability to lead others competently.

In turn, however, the military feels the pressure of *families'* norms and roles through the demands made on service members' loyalty, commitment, time, and energy to be with and care for family members. As a result of this pressure, the military in recent years has responded to the importance of families in the lives of its members by improving access to and quality of services, such as child development centers and online information (e.g., http://militaryonesource.mil/), to support families.

Military families, as all families, face stressors that may be developmental (e.g., birth of a child, aging, death of a parent) or related to a family member's occupation. Occupations usually bring normative stressors that are experienced by most workers in that occupation. The normative stressors of military life such as relocation, separation, and risk of injury or

BOX 3.1   TIPS FROM THE FRONTLINE

ON NORMALIZING STRESS

We can support military families by recognizing their strengths and celebrating their resilience.

There's a lot of stress in our country experienced by everyone. Not just our military families. Look at the Gulf Coast. Fishing is a dangerous, unpredictable, stressful occupation, and in most cases not lucrative. Think about the families of firefighters and police officers. People who choose these occupations risk their lives everyday. Is this any different than the military? How do we support these families?

I would suggest that one way is to normalize stress, that is, to recognize that military families, and other families, face challenges everyday, yet they have strengths as individuals, families, and a community to cope with these challenges. We can support military families by recognizing their strengths and celebrating their resilience.

Evonne Carawan, Director
*Personnel Readiness and Community Support Office of the
Deputy Assistant Secretary of the Navy (Military Personnel Policy)*

death are shared by families with members in some other occupations (Orthner & Rose, 2009). For example, many dual-earner couples in business or the diplomatic corps move to support the job or career advancement of one spouse while the job or career of the "trailing spouse" is secondary. Migrant workers move regularly for work, and their children change schools accordingly; if parents and children are separated, they may use technology to stay involved in each other's lives. Commercial fishermen, who often describe their occupation as central to their identity, engage in a dangerous and unpredictable occupation (Zvonkovic, Solomon, Humble, & Manoogian, 2005). As you read about the characteristics of military families, imagine other occupations that may place similar demands on civilian family life. Think about the strengths individuals, families, and communities have to cope with these demands (see Box 3.1).

THE SENSE OF COMMUNITY

Many military family members comment on the sense of belonging to a community that comes from living among others who share similar challenges and experiences. Throughout this book you will find firsthand accounts of the importance of this sense of community to the well-being of families. They rely on each other to understand what it is like to relocate, worry about a loved one's safety, and keep a home functioning and children cared for when the military parent is frequently away.

Sharing in a sense of community bolsters positive family adaptation (Bowen, Mancini, Martin, Ware, & Nelson, 2003). We can think of families experiencing support within the military community in three ways: informal, formal, and unit level (Rosen, Durand, & Martin, 2000). As with civilian families, military families are likely to seek interpersonal connection and assistance from informal support systems, such as community groups (e.g., church, work, clubs), friends, neighbors, and family (Martin & McClure, 2000). Military families take care of one another through such acts as giving and receiving emotional support (e.g., listening, understanding) and practical help (e.g., child care, help around the house and yard, car rides). Such support and help are important in adjusting well to challenges such as deployments and relocations (Bowen et al., 2003).

Formal support can be considered the family programs and services available to service members and their families by each branch of the military. For example, Chaplains provide spiritual guidance, religious services, counseling, and workshops for military and family members. In upcoming chapters, you will read more about military family support centers, Military OneSource, and programs such as the Exceptional Family Member Program, the Family Advocacy Program, the New Parent Support Program, Spouse Employment Assistance, and financial literacy programs. These programs and services have expanded since the introduction of the all-volunteer force in 1973 and reflect the DoD's recognition that recruitment, retention, and mission readiness are affected by the quality of life offered in the military (MacDermid Wadsworth & Southwell, 2011).

Unit-level support is offered through the unit commander and unit leaders, including a family readiness group or key volunteer network. Each branch of the military emphasizes "we take care of our own," and this attitude is perhaps most keenly put into action at the unit level. Unit support includes information and social–emotional support (e.g., social events, deployment programming) through which families can strengthen their informal networks of support. Units that support families positively influence their sense of community and thereby affect their adaptation to military life (Bowen et al., 2003).

Spouses and children of active duty service members are likely to live near or on military installations and have opportunities to interact with other military families on a daily basis as they shop, go to the movies, exercise, attend religious activities, and attend school and community events. A built-in support system arises when a group of people who live close to one another experience similar day-to-day lives. They can empathize and share their insights and advice. A sense of community is more difficult to cultivate if military families are not located near one another. For example, National Guard or Reserve unit's families are spread across a state or region, and family members do not necessarily identify with being a military family when their loved one joins.

DUTY FIRST

From the first day when a loved one puts on a uniform, families experience the consequences of "duty first," that is, the priority of a mission over family events or needs. Military service is an obligation—an obligation to fulfill regardless of other competing demands. The mission may include deploying, training, standing watch, or just staying late to complete a task. To accomplish the mission of the military, its leaders must be able to send its members *wherever* they are needed, *whenever* they are needed. As a result, service members may miss the birth of a baby, a significant birthday, significant milestones in a child's life, funerals of close loved ones, and the list goes on.

Duty first means more workload for family members at home as they pick up the roles and tasks the service member would perform if at home. They can also feel under scrutiny within a military community as they are expected to follow codes of conduct when on base doing everyday tasks (e.g., shopping, going to school), when living in military housing, and when their loved one has leadership responsibilities (MacDermid Wadsworth & Southwell, 2011). At the same time that the mission takes priority, many military families find pride in also "serving" the country through their daily support of their loved one and the sacrifice of family time.

Many military leaders recognize that the more reasonable and predictable the demands, the more likely they are to retain families (Martin & McClure, 2000). For example, service members have access to types of leave not "charged" against their paid leave time. Leaders may authorize a leave for morale or rest and recuperation, or emergency unpaid leave; they can also grant special liberty of a short period of time to an individual or unit in recognition of their superior work. They can also let a service member off to attend a program or special event (MacDermid Wadsworth & Southwell, 2011).

RELOCATIONS

Issues related to moving differ for Active and Reserve Components. Moving is a hallmark of military life for many active duty members (Burrell, 2006). If the new duty station is of significant distance from the old one, family members typically move. However, members of the Reserve Component who wish to move a great distance from their current unit because of personal or professional reasons (e.g., taking a job elsewhere to advance their civilian career) cannot assume that they will find a new unit with which to drill. They will need to return to the initial unit to drill in order to meet their obligation to the National Guard until they serve out their contract or locate a unit closer to their new residence that will accept them.

Active Duty

The active duty military lifestyle is a mobile lifestyle. Often for those who join the military, the adventure of "seeing the world" is part of the motivation. Family members, too, can appreciate the allure of living in a variety of locations, learning to adapt to new cultures, picking up another language, acquiring a larger vision of the world and its inhabitants, and becoming more culturally competent through living daily life in another country. Successfully navigating these challenges can help to develop self-confidence and maturity among service members, spouses, and children. A move can also provide adults and children the opportunity to start over at school or work, to shed negative behaviors, and to apply new coping skills (Burrell, Adams, Durand, & Castro, 2006).

When the military directs the active duty service member to change duty location, it issues a **Permanent Change of Station (PCS)** order that relocates the member's work affiliation from one duty station to another. Service members may submit a duty preference form, indicating where they would prefer to be stationed. However, the PCS order may or may not assign the member to any of the preferred stations. In the end, where a service member is assigned is determined by the needs of the Army, Air Force, Navy, or Marine Corps. In the Army, junior enlisted and command level officers are the most frequent movers (Burrell et al., 2006).

Whether it is called PCSing, moving, or relocating, active duty military families do so often. For example, Army families average a move every 2–3 years (Burrell, 2006). Military families move more often than their civilian counterparts and move longer distances, including outside of the United States (Booth, Segal, & Bell, 2007). In 2009, approximately 13% of military members were stationed overseas (DASD, 2014).

If a new duty station is close to the former one, families may choose to stay in their current residence, if they live off base, and may be able to stay in the current on-base housing. For example, numerous ships, submarines, air commands, and shore commands are located in the Hampton Roads area of Virginia. A service member completing a rotation on a ship whose homeport is Naval Station Norfolk could receive PCS orders to another ship there or to a command located at a nearby base, allowing the member and her or his family to remain where they are living. However, if the new installation is a significant distance away from the current one, perhaps in another state or country, then the PCS orders will often result in a move for the whole family. At times, spouses and children may remain near the old duty station while the service member relocates because of schooling for the children or a delay in selling a house. In other situations, families have a multiple-hop move during which they relocate first to temporary housing and then to permanent housing on the installation when it becomes available or to housing in the local civilian community. In these cases, children may attend a temporary school before moving to the permanent one.

Although studies on military families and relocation are limited, they suggest that a majority of military families adjust well to relocation. However, the preparation for the move, the actual move, and the first year following a move can include challenges and stresses for both adults and children. Relocation can be considered a process rather than an event, beginning with the anticipation of moving and ending months after the physical move, only to be reexperienced when the anticipation begins again with the expected next PCS (MacDermid, Weiss, Green, & Schwarz, 2007).

There are many challenges inherent in a move. On the practical side, families must decide whether to request a government move or a **Personally Procured Transportation Move** (i.e., a "do it yourself" move) and then proceed with the corresponding tasks. Other practical matters include understanding qualifications for moving allowances (i.e., money for a special need, in this case, relocation) and ensuring the total weight of household goods does not exceed the amount allowed. Parents must arrange for schooling at the new location and obtain or update copies of school and health records.

Meanwhile, adults and children are saying good-bye to friends and family and perhaps beginning to grieve over the loss of daily connection to these important people or to worry about making friends in the new location. An employed spouse may be ending a favorite job and despairing over finding another at the next duty station as frequent relocations can hinder the ability to build a career (Booth et al., 2007).

Families must accomplish many tasks before moving day arrives. To facilitate the process of moving, families are encouraged to use online tools and to visit the installation's relocation office, transportation office, and housing office. The online Relocation Assistance Program, including the Plan My Move tool found at http://www.militaryone source.mil/moving enables service members and their families to prepare a customized calendar of tasks to accomplish, to learn about allowances associated with the move, and to obtain information about the new installation and its surrounding community. The website contains tip sheets on many topics associated with moving such as helping children cope,creating an inventory of belongings, and shipping a vehicle overseas.

In addition to online resources, each service branch has a Relocation Program located in the respective family center: Army Community Services (ACS), Marine Corps Community Services (MCCS), Navy Fleet and Family Support Services (FFSP), and the Airman and Family Readiness Centers (A&FRC). A relocation office can assist in determining PCS allowances, using Plan My Move, connecting with resources at the new installation, and accessing a loan closet (i.e., basic household goods to use until a shipment of personal belongings arrive). Many military installations have a housing office where service and family members can receive assistance to determine housing allowances and the availability of family, unaccompanied, and off-base housing and to arrange for temporary lodging.

In quality of life studies, Army soldiers have reported between moderate to very large problems with relocation, decreasing their satisfaction with military life. In a 2003 Army study, 36% of those surveyed had to wait for permanent housing to become available after they had arrived at the new duty station; 47% perceived they did not have enough preparation time before the move; 43% had delays in and 40% had problems with the accuracy of reimbursements for costs incurred while traveling from the old duty station to the new one; 46% experienced a reduction in spouse income; and 38% encountered problems changing dependents' schools (Booth et al., 2007).

Personal, social, and financial supports are central to adjusting positively to relocations (Orthner, 2002). A conceptual model of resilience and risk provides some insight into how adults and children can cope with relocation challenges (MacDermid et al., 2008). In this model, resilience and risk are measured at the level of the individual (e.g., social skills, coping style), the family (e.g., parental warmth), and community (e.g., social supports). This model guided researchers at the Military Family Research Institute who conducted a study of 608 randomly selected premove and postmove married families with one or more children from the Army and Air Force in 2004–05 (MacDermid et al., 2007). The service member, spouse, and one child between the ages of 10 and 17 completed a survey for a total number of 1083 participants.

Families reported an average of 4.9 changes in duty station prior to their current one and received an average of 83 days notice of the move. Less than half (48%) received a PCS order similar to what they had requested, and 13% experienced a change in PCS orders after receiving an earlier set of orders. Parents considered moving more difficult when it occurred during the summer, when they experienced more severe daily hassles (i.e., general household stress), when service members lacked confidence in their ability to handle the move and found adjustment to new work situations more difficult, and when spouses were dissatisfied with services on the military installation. Those persons who reported an **external locus of control** (i.e., assuming they have little or no control over events that are affecting them) or high negative emotion appeared at risk for experiencing negative events and evaluating events more negatively.

In this study, multiple resilience factors were associated with positive coping and enhanced psychological well-being, resulting in the expectation of and the actual experience of easier moves. Human capital factors included "positive self-evaluations, sense of mastery, optimism, good physical and psychological health … [and] skills acquired from education, training, and experiences, high role balance, [and] life satisfaction." Social capital factors included "marital satisfaction, better family functioning, responsive and effective parenting, social competence and involvement in group activities" (MacDermid et al., 2008, pp. 16–17). For the adults and children in this study, important positive coping strategies included positivity, balancing family and work, and using formal (e.g., religious organizations) and informal (e.g., support from friends, family, coworkers, unit leaders, children's teachers) support.

Reserve Component

Air and Army National Guard
As you will recall from Chapter 1, the Air National Guard and Army National Guard are state forces under the control of the Governor unless released to the U.S. President. Members of the Guard typically serve their service obligation with units close to where they live. However, they may accept assignment at a unit within the state that requires significant travel. Reasons for doing so may be prompted by an opportunity for promotion or a change in MOS. For Guard members who wish to move out of state, they must fulfill their contract either by (1) returning to drill with their unit, or (2) identifying a Guard unit in the new state that will accept them and obtaining the agreement of the first unit to release them to the new unit. Finding a new unit may be a challenge as it is up to the Guard members to locate a new unit in need of their occupational specialty or willing to accept them and send them to a school to learn a new one. The same tasks are required of those who wish to transfer to another unit within a state. An interstate transfer refers to changing units across state lines, whereas an intrastate transfer refers to changing units within a state.

For those who remain with a unit that is far away from their home, the time away from family will be increased. They have to allow for substantial travel time to and from their drill weekend. To remain in the Guard and in their specialty, some members may choose not to move their households as it would be too difficult to return for drill once a month or to find a new unit. Also, some specialties are only found in a few units across the country. In these cases, for example explosive ordinance disposal units, members may need to fly in from multiple states.

Army, Navy, Air Force, and Marine Corps Reserves
As a federal force, the Army, Air Force, Navy, and Marine Force Reserves may be reassigned to another duty station but

typically only within a region. Regions may encompass many states, so PCS orders may mean having significant travel demands in order to drill or may prompt reserve members to move their households to be nearer to their new unit.

SPOUSE EDUCATION AND EMPLOYMENT

Education

Education is important to military spouses. Of those responding to the 2012 Survey of Active Duty Spouses, over 89% had at least some college education, and over a third had earned a bachelor's or graduate degree (DMDC, 2013a). While 31% of spouses had achieved their educational goals, a majority were or wanted to be enrolled in higher education. Those who were not in school but wished to be cited cost, family responsibilities, and child care needs as barriers (DMDC, 2013a). Experiencing frequent moves and deployments also hinder enrolment (Office of the Deputy Assistant Secretary of Defense, Military Community and Family policy [PASD], (2015).)

Guidance and support are available to military spouses who wish to pursue education. Spouses may use the services of the Education Center found on most military installations but may not know they can. Spouses can access assistance finding educational opportunities, financial aid, on-base courses, distance education courses, career counseling, and testing services (National Military Family Association, 2007). In addition, the DoD Spouse Education and Career Opportunities (SECO) program gives military spouses access to career counselors who, among other services, provide information on funding education (see http://www.militaryonesource.mil/seco).

A number of federal laws, DoD policies, and regulations apply to education and military family members. Three examples follow: Signed into law in 2008, the Higher Education Opportunity Act (HR 4137) makes service members on active duty for more than 30 days and their spouses and children eligible for instate tuition at state colleges and universities where they reside or are permanently stationed. Once instate tuition rates are being paid, they will continue to apply even if service members are reassigned outside the state, so long as they or their family members remain continuously enrolled. Second, the Veterans' Access, Choice, and Accountability Act of 2014 extends eligibility for the Marine Gunnery Sergeant John David Fry Scholarship to spouses as well as children of service members who die in the line of duty on or since September 11, 2001. Third, service members who qualify for the Post 9/11 GI Bill may transfer some or all of the benefits to dependent children or a spouse. Certain criteria must be met and the VA must approve the transfer. (U.S. Department of Veterans Affair 2013c).

The Military Spouse Career Advancement Accounts (MyCAA) program funds education for an associate's degree or training leading to certifications and licensure. This program is open to spouses of active duty personnel or activated personnel in the Reserve Component in the following pay grades: E1-E5, W1-W2, or O1-O2. The maximum benefit is $4,000 with a $2,000 cap per fiscal year. A spouse has 3 years to complete the education or training (see http://www.militaryfamily.org/get-info/spouse-education/financial-assistance/mycaa-accounts.html).

Employment

Employment is important for the wellbeing of many spouses their satisfaction with the military, and the financial health of many military families (DASD, 2015). However, accessing reliable and affordable child care, needing recertification or licensing when relocating to a new state, and living in difficult labor markets are significant sources of stress and frustration in achieving steady employment. Frequent relocations, deployments, and being the primary caregiver to children owing to the long and/or unpredictable hours worked by the military member also affect spouses' success in finding employment (Castaneda & Harrell, 2008; DoD, 2014).

Data on spouse employment and education are available for spouses of active duty members but not for spouses of reservists. Comparing military spouses to civilian spouses has focused primarily on wives (Harrell, Lim, Castaneda, & Golinelle, 2005) as the vast majority of active duty spouses across all branches are female. The number of male spouses has been increasing so future analyses will be able to include comparisons of male civilian and military spouse employment (Little & Hisnanick, 2007).

Compared with civilian spouses, military spouses have a lower rate of employment, earn less, work fewer weeks in a year, and are more likely to be looking for a job (Harrell et al., 2005). A PCS move or a deployment decreases the odds of spouses being in employment (Dorvil & Pflieger, 2014). Spouses were 3% less likely to work if their husbands had been deployed over 30 days in the past year, and almost 5% less likely to work if they had children under the age of 6 years (Hosek & MacDermid Wadsworth, 2013).

Recent data indicate 25% of female spouses in the labor force are unemployed (DoD, 2014c). Those employed fulltime earn 14 to 25% less than comparable civilian spouses (DoD, 2014; Hosek & MacDermid Wadsworth, 2013). Only 57% of military spouses responding to the 2012 Survey of Active Duty Spouses were employed in the area of their training or education (Dorvil & Pflieger, 2014; DoD, 2014c). A majority of female spouses responding to the 2013 Military Spouse Employment Survey reported being overqualified (having more education and/or experience than needed) for their current or most recent position. The economic downturn beginning in 2008 may be a partial explanation for their underemployment (Blue Star Families, 2014).

The pursuit of employment or a career is a major component of military spouses' assessment of their quality of life (Castaneda & Harrell, 2008), and they experience factors that both help and hinder securing employment. In comparison to civilian counterparts, military spouses are more likely to reside in metropolitan areas, have graduated from high school, and have some college education—factors that enhance the possibility of obtaining employment. They also are more likely to be younger and have young children at home— factors that are barriers to employment (Harrell et al., 2005). For example, in FY 2013, 54% of active duty spouses were 30 years old or younger, and an additional 20% were between ages 31 and 35 (DASD, 2014).

Military spouses come from a society in which dual incomes are often needed, expected, and prepared for through education. For example, studies have found that a majority of spouses report a second income to pay bills and cover basic living expenses as an important or a very important reason to be employed. Spouses with less education, married to junior enlisted service members, and experiencing financial challenges were more likely to report working because of financial necessity (DMDC, 2013a; Harrell et al., 2005). A better financial status translates in higher spouse satisfaction with military life (DASD, 2015).

The desire for employment goes beyond financial needs. While 85% of spouses responding to the *2008 Survey of Active Duty Spouses* were intensely proud of being married to a service member, only 25% consider that being a military spouse fulfills their personal needs. Regardless of their employment status, a majority considered a career as an important or very important reason to work (DMDC, 2009).

Military spouses have access to supports to offset disrupted employment and underemployment. Military spouses who must leave their employment due to a PCS move are eligible for unemployment compensation in 44 states and the District of Columbia. Typically employers' individual unemployment compensation premiums are not raised when military spouses claim unemployment compensation because the compensations come from a state's unemployment fund (see www.nmfa.org).

The Spouse Education and Career Opportunities program (see https:myseco.militaryonesource.mil) has two goals: to reduce the 25% unemployment rate for military spouses and the 25% gap in female spouse wages. In FY 2013, the SECO Career Center, where spouses receive careercounseling services, averaged 12,000 calls per month. The SECO

Military Spouse Employment Partnership Career Portal allows employers to list jobs directly to military spouses. Since 2011, employers have listed more than 1.3 million jobs on the portal and hired more than 55,000 military spouses (Military OneSource, 2014).

Spouses are also eligible to use the Employment Assistance Program available in each service branch: the Army Employment Readiness Program, the Navy Family Employment Readiness Program, the Air Force Employment Assistance Program, and the Marine Corps Family Member Employment Assistance Program. These programs offer inperson assistance such as career counseling, guidance on resumé and cover letter preparation, local job leads, and encouragement.

SEPARATION

In addition to frequent relocations, another normative stressor for military families is separation from the military member. Families report such separations as one of the most stressful parts of military life, particularly when the service member is deployed in dangerous situations. Separations occur when service members are ordered to go on temporary duty (TDY) to a temporary duty station (TDS) or on an unaccompanied tour (i.e., families are not allowed to accompany the service member). They can also be sent for schooling and on training exercises. However, the most well-known type of separation from family is deployment.

Regardless of the reason for separation, family members typically want to know the expected length of a separation. Deployment lengths are different among the services. Historically, Air Force personnel generally deployed for 4 months, Marine and Navy personnel for 6–7 months, and Army personnel for 1 year. Because the Marine Corps is dependent upon the Navy for transportation and logistical support while deployed, it uses the same deployment length as the Navy. Deployment lengths are the same for activated reserve units as for the respective active duty branch. Deployment lengths have generally remained the same during OEF/OIF, with a few exceptions. In 2007, the length of an Army deployment was increased to 15 months, with some units being extended up to 18 months. The Army deployment length was reduced back to 12 months in 2008. In addition, service members who are not deployed with their units but as individual augmentees (IAs) can find themselves deploying with a unit from a different branch; they then may be subject to the same length of deployment as that branch (i.e., an airman deploying with an Army unit may be sent home after the usual 4-month deployment or might be deployed with that unit for the entire 12-month period). IAs are most often Army personnel deploying with another Army unit; however, many Air Force and Navy personnel have deployed with Army units.

Temporary Duty or TDY

Military life is known for separating active duty service members from their families for periods of time. They are separated when they go to boot camp, join officer's candidate school, attend one of the military academies, or begin college where they might participate in ROTC. They are separated when they go to additional schools to learn their MOS. Once assigned to a duty station and for the rest of their career, service members may still be sent for a brief amount of time to another duty station. TDY orders reassign military members to another station where they will undergo additional training or attend an advanced school in their MOS. TDY can range in length from one week to several months. During this time, the service member may or may not be able to return home because of the type of duty required, the location, or the cost of transportation.

Although TDYs typically are shorter than 4–18-month combat deployments, they can disrupt family life. Schedules are reorganized and family members readjust each time the service member leaves and returns, which could be multiple times in the span of a few months or one year.

Deployments

According to the Deployment Health Clinical Center (n.d.), "military members meet deployment criteria anytime they leave the physical locale of the parent command and enter an environment for operational deployment or are stationed in a hostile territory" (para. 2). Service members may be deployed to established military installations in the United States or in another country, to an urban or a rural "field setting" in another country, or on a ship. Deployment typically refers to being sent to engage in military action that includes combat, peacekeeping, or humanitarian missions. Navy families may refer to a ship or submarine that is out to sea on a 2-week training exercise as being deployed or being on a cruise.

Deployments span all branches of the military and both the Active and Reserve Components. Deployments may be for a week (e.g., operational exercises) to 12 or 18 months or longer. Deployments may be planned for months (e.g., troop rotations to serve in war zones) or may be ordered with only the briefest of notification, as in conducting a mission of humanitarian assistance in response to a natural disaster (Deployment Health Clinical Center, n.d.). For example, multiple units from the Air Force, Army, Marines, and Navy were deployed in Humanitarian Assistance/Disaster Response (HA/DR) missions in response to the 2014 Ebola virus outbreak in West Africa, the 2013 typhoon in the Philippines, the 2011 earthquake and tsunami in Japan, and the 2010 earthquake in Haiti.

Voices From the Frontline

A military spouse never exactly knows what to expect before the first deployment. I thought it was going to be a piece of cake. Families don't realize the stress on a partner when your Soldier, Marine, Airman, or Seaman is deployed. Not only are you mother and father, you are the fix-it person. I've changed a tire, fixed a garage door, while worrying about my husband. Where is he? Is he safe?

As each deployment progresses, it can wear you down. We spouses help each other a lot. Family Readiness Groups made up of volunteers keep families informed, provide resources, and help guide new military families. Yes, it's hard when my husband has to be away from our family for so long. Then he tells me about little girls in Afghanistan who are going to school now or how we helped to build a new school or hospital over there, and it makes me proud. He told me about the locals who come on base to sell things to the U.S. service members. I ended up sending boxes of clothes to an Afghani man who runs the bazaar. You realize the difference you are making. It really is worth it to be a part—if you can help someone.

Sabrina Beharie
Military spouse and mom

Military families have helped one another for centuries by sharing experiences and coping strategies. Emerging from experiences and studies of Navy families is the **emotional cycle of deployment model** that was first introduced by Logan (1987), a former Navy officer and spouse of a career Navy officer. This model, used by the United Nations as well as those working with Navy families (United Nations, 1995), identified six stages as noted in Table 3.1.

TABLE 3.1   Logan's (1987) Proposed Emotional Cycle of Deployment

Adjustment Stages		Possible Feelings and Actions
Predeployment	Anticipation of loss	Sadness, anger, irritability, worry, bickering, restlessness, focused on completing the "to do" list
	Detachment and withdrawal	Discomfort, distancing from one another, wanting the departure day to arrive so the deployment can begin
During deployment	Emotional disorganization	Pain from saying good-bye, guilt for feeling relief the deployment has started, routines disrupted, withdrawal from family and friends, sleep disturbances, restless, indecisive
	Recovery and stabilization	New patterns established, adapted to new roles and responsibilities, increased confidence, may feel stressed
	Anticipation of homecoming	Excited, nervous, tense, apprehensive, making emotional room for the returning spouse
Postdeployment	Renegotiation of relationships	Joy, relief, annoyance, adapt to changes in roles and responsibilities
	Reintegration and stabilization	Relaxed, comfortable with one another, enjoyment, new routines established

Source: Adapted from Logan, K. V. (1987). The emotional cycle of deployment. *U.S. Naval Proceedings, 113*, 43–47, Copyright © (1987) U.S. Naval Institute / http://www.usni.org.

Although this model and its more recent versions are used extensively throughout the military (Morse, 2006; Pincus, House, Christenson, & Adler, 2001), we lack validation studies of it and so cannot claim it as evidence-based practice. The model does highlight structural issues that families typically encounter during predeployment (e.g., preparing financially and legally), deployment (e.g., redistributing responsibilities), and postdeployment (e.g., family roles). However, the emotional and stress reactions listed in the model may differ from family to family. Only a few studies have examined the cycle of deployment models to know whether they approximate the experiences of families.

Researchers surveyed 216 National Guard soldiers and partners 30 to 60 days prior to a combat deployment to determine levels of distress. Spouses and partners scored higher on PTSD symptoms, depression, and social impairment than soldiers and levels reported in the general population surveys. The researchers concluded that the results of the study supported partners' experience of predeployment distress as suggested by the Emotional Cycle of Deployment. The researchers also noted that of the 40 partners who screened positive for mental health problems, 15% reported receiving individual counseling and 28% reported receiving psychiatric medication, while 38% reported attending family readiness groups (Erbes, Meis, Polusny, & Arbisi, 2012). Researchers from the Military Family Research Institute at Purdue University examined the reintegration phase. In this study of reservists, three reintegration patterns were identified. Some families adapted well, some experienced a decrease in well-being and then recovered, and some experienced variations in well-being throughout the reintegration period (MacDermid Wadsworth, Pagnan, & Seidel, 2010).

A more recent study of 50 wives of Army or Army National Guard personnel noted variations in marital satisfaction postdeployment. Although perception of marital satisfaction level was typically higher postdeployment than before or during deployment, 29% of wives experienced a dip and then a rebound of marital satisfaction and another 29% reported a decrease in marital satisfaction (Parcell & Maguire, 2014).

Researchers are investigating why reintegration can be a time of turmoil. In another recent study, service members and romantic partners described the turbulence that can accompany reintegration. While some couples grew stronger, others experienced greater upheaval, due in part to relationship uncertainty and interfering in one another's completion of daily activities. This relationship turbulence was greater for couples who had been reunited longer, suggesting an initial honeymoon phase upon the service member's return from deployment (Theiss & Knobloch, 2014).

The predeployment, during deployment, and postdeployment timeline resonates with families and is easy to present during briefing and educational programs and through written materials. Although initially developed during a time when female sailors did not deploy, staff at Navy Fleet and Family Support Centers have found the module useful for male and female service members, their partners, and children (Navy Personnel Command, n.d.). Sharing one or more models of a deployment cycle with families may provide them information they can use to develop their own meaning of their separation and reintegration experience, according to their own timelines (Wiens & Boss, 2006).

The emotional cycle of deployment model was developed during a time of relative predictability of deployments. With the downsizing of the military in the 1990s and the advent of OEF and OIF, the tempo of rotations significantly changed. The time between deployments shortened at the same time that deployments lengthened and return dates became less certain (Lincoln, Swift, & Shorteno-Fraser, 2008). This accelerated optempo has meant that for many military families the stage of "reintegration and stabilization" quickly is overtaken by the "anticipation of loss" stage. In recognition of this optempo and multiple deployments, the National Military Family Association suggested that "cycle of deployment" should be replaced by "spiral of deployment." A spiral suggests not returning back to the beginning, but carrying experiences, feelings, attitudes, and lessons learned forward to the next separation (National Military Family Association, 2006).

A feature of a cycle, or a spiral, of deployment, particularly an extended one, is **boundary ambiguity**, that is, having a family member "present" physically but not psychologically or present psychologically but not physically (Faber, Willerton, Clymer, MacDermid, & Weiss, 2008). Under great stress, such boundary ambiguity may be experienced as an **ambiguous loss** (Boss, 2006). As you read more about the stages of deployment below, consider conditions under which boundary ambiguity may result in families experiencing an ambiguous loss. Read Ginny Wescott's description of what she says to families preparing for deployment in Box 3.2.

BOX 3.2   VOICES FROM THE FRONTLINE

DEPLOYMENT CHANGES EVERYONE

As military families we face lots of challenges: a child seeing a neighbor getting notice of her husband's death downrange while standing at the corner waiting for the school bus, or parents and children and couples being separated for a year.

Deployment changes everyone. I am honest when I help families prepare. I say, "This isn't going to be easy." Every person, every family, every deployment is different. I tell family members, "Even though I have been through multiple deployments as a spouse, I don't know what you are feeling right now, but here are some things you might want to think about."

We have to help people think about what will work for them. I encourage family members to talk together, for example, about communication. People think things are so much easier now because family members can be connected so easily thanks to technology. I remember the days of writing letters to my husband when he was on a ship and they never arrived. Sometimes Skype can create bigger problems than that. For example, say you decide to Skype every day at 4:00. Then one day your service member isn't there or doesn't answer. A spouse might worry: Is he having an affair? Has he been injured or killed? Is he on an unexpected mission? Maybe he's just stuck in traffic. The service member worries too when the spouse misses a call. For some families talking face-to-face once a week might be better. They need to talk about these things and set some family rules before the deployment.

The transition home can be difficult. People are not only having to reintegrate back into their daily lives at home after being in a war zone, they have to become part of a family again. In World War II it would take service members a week or two to get home by ship. They'd have that time to process and be with their buddies. Today, service members board a plane and go from one world to another in 10–12 hours. Sometimes they are sitting next to civilians. They're on their own, without the bond and understanding of people they served with.

Ginny Wescott, Certified Family Life Educator
Family Advocacy Program Prevention & Education Specialist for Marine Corps
and Army as well as long time military spouse

Predeployment   Reservists and active duty members may spend months and perhaps a year **gearing up** for the deployment during which time their unit is focused on preparing personnel and accompanying gear (the type of gear depends upon the mission of the unit, e.g., civil engineering, infantry, medical). Small subgroups or an individual from the unit may be selected to deploy. Regardless if it is one person or the whole unit, military members need to acquire gear, obtain and prepare uniforms, go to medical appointments, complete legal and financial paperwork, and, if they have leadership responsibilities, ensure others in their unit are prepared. During this gear-up time, individuals or whole units often spend weeks, if not months, away from home obtaining additional training.

This preparation is vital to the conduct of the mission, including the safety of everyone in the unit. The focus on preparation often means service members have less time than they would like with their family, just when family members want extra time with them. Families count all of this preparation and training time as separation, that is as "boots away from home" time, rather than counting as separation just the "boots on the ground" time once the unit has reached its deployment location (Castaneda et al., 2008, p. 251). Even when at home, however, service members may be thinking and worrying about unit preparations. When service members are physically present yet psychologically absent from family life, families can experience increased stress (Boss, 2006).

At times, individuals or units are given only a week or as little as 6 hours to pack and report at the designated area for deployment. These short-notice deployments emphasize the need for military families always to be prepared for separation, a lesson learned quickly by families of service members in special forces units.

National Guard and Reserve families have additional steps to take when preparing for deployment when the service member also has a civilian job. Service members must continue to meet the obligations of their civilian employment and may even be asked to train another employee to do the job they have been doing (Griffith, 2005). Families need to prepare for a possible period of time when income from the civilian job has ended and income from the military has yet to begin. For a first deployment, families of a member of the National Guard or Reserves may find themselves quickly becoming a "military family" as they obtain ID cards, learn about military benefits, and seek information on services on installations.

Active and Reserve Component families who are well-prepared for deployment are more likely to "weather deployments more successfully" than those who are less prepared (Booth et al., 2007, p. 31). As noted above, units follow a general deployment schedule, but they or individual service members may be called to deploy with only hours or a few days notice. Given the likelihood of emergencies requiring deployment with little warning, the military's goal is for families to be prepared, that is, to "think about deployments as a condition of [military] life rather than as atypical events" (Booth et al., 2007, p. 31).

One major step in preparation for military parents is making arrangements for the care of their children during deployment. Most service members who are parents know the civilian parent will care for their children during deployment. Other service members who are in dual-military marriages, are single parents with custody or joint custody, or are legally responsible for a child or an adult member unable to care for themselves in the absences of the service member are required to submit a **Family Care Plan** to their command. A Family Care Plan must indicate: who will care for the member's child or children during deployment and other absences (e.g., training, temporary duty); arrangements to provide financial, medical, and logistical support (e.g., housing, transportation, food, clothing) for the children's well-being; name and consent to the plan of any noncustodial parent who will not be the caregiver during the service member's absence; and who will be the temporary caregiver in case of incapacity or death of the service member while permanent custody is established. The caregiver must be nonmilitary, and the service member must indicate that the caregiver has agreed to the arrangements and has received copies of relevant documents (e.g., power of attorney). Typically extended family members (e.g., the service member's parent or parents, a sibling, an aunt or an uncle) are appointed caregivers or guardians, but friends and the spouse of another military member have fulfilled these roles. Caregivers will need to show a power of attorney and the children's ID card to use military medical treatment facilities and a letter from the commanding officer of a military installation to use the commissaries and exchanges on behalf of the children (DoD, 2011b).

Military families need to prepare financially, legally, psychologically, and relationally. The increased stress that occurs during this phase is fueled by anticipation of a separation—a separation that has inherent risks and dangers. In response to the stress, family members may find themselves arguing more or feeling more tense. Some report they wish the deployment would "just begin" and then may feel guilty about having such thoughts. However, these reactions are common and families benefit from anticipating stages of deployment and from avoiding becoming overly worried about the significance of these reactions (Wiens & Boss, 2006). Meanwhile, couples experiencing more severe relationship conflict may try to ignore it before deployment and hope that disagreements will be resolved by the imposed separation (Drummet, Coleman, & Cable, 2003).

During Deployment   Multiple factors related to deployment can result in stress for military families. Renegotiation of boundaries is one of them. Military families often spend great effort maintaining their loved one's psychological presence in the family when the physical presence is not possible. Additional stressors include maintaining a relationship while apart and caring for children (Drummet et al., 2003).

Deployments call for family reorganization and adaptation as roles and responsibilities in the family are redistributed (Faber et al., 2008). As a stone thrown into a pond produces ripples, so does the deployment of a spouse, romantic partner, parent, adult child, sibling, niece, or nephew produce ripples throughout a family. For example, imagine the shifts and changes in roles and responsibilities among family members when the parent who helps with homework, the spouse who maintains connections with the extended family, the daughter who assists parents with investments, or the older brother who guides younger siblings is now deployed. This reorganization and adaptation may be challenging as family members unfamiliar with certain tasks become responsible for them but may be unclear if they will remain responsible for them when the deployed family member returns (Boss, 2006).

Postdeployment   During World War II and immediately following the end of the war, Reuben Hill (1949) conducted one of the first studies of military families, focusing on their adaptation during deployment and when service members returned. He noted that adjustment to both deployment and reintegration included a process of disorganization, recovery, and achievement of reorganization. The families who "closed ranks" during deployment faced more difficulty adjusting during reintegration even though they had functioned well while separated from the service member. By closing ranks, the family left the returning family member with a limited or even no role to assume. However, those families who adapted roles to accommodate the absence and then return of the member adjusted well to separation and reunion (MacDermid Wadsworth, 2010).

Adaptability continues to be a key component of family adjustment during reintegration. Upon return from deployment, the service member may again be physically but not psychologically present. It takes time to adjust to coming back from days spent inside and outside the wire, days spent inside a ship or submarine, or days flying missions. Service members may do highly dangerous jobs and may have experienced frightening and sad events and situations. While happy to be home and with their families, they may be thinking about the deployment, their buddies, and their shared experiences. Returned service members may spend significant time with buddies and talking with them because they know "what it was like." Service members may worry civilians, even family members, will be judgmental or repelled by their stories, or may wish not to burden their family members with vivid images and horrific situations. Family members who consider these buddies as support systems may find it easier to accept the time needed to transition psychologically from a combat, humanitarian, or routine deployment to daily life at home.

While active duty service members who deploy as a unit will have access to buddies in their unit during the months following return from deployment, reservists and Individual Augmentees do not have such ready access. National Guard and Federal Reservists likely live far from one another and by definition Individual Augmentees did not deploy with their home unit. These service personnel may report the lack of someone they can confide in who "knows what it is like." Sometimes they have friends or other family members who have deployed and with whom they can talk, helping the process of emotionally coming home.

Returning from deployment also brings another reorganization of family roles and responsibilities. Family members may have grown comfortable and confident in their roles and may not wish to relinquish their responsibilities. Service members may or may not want to assume their old roles.

Active duty spouses have reported changes in their husband or wife after returning from deployment. Positive changes, reported by more than 50% of the spouses completing the 2012 *Survey of Active Duty Spouses*, included appreciating family, friends, and life more; having more confidence; and showing positive personality changes. Problematic changes reported by more than 50% of responding spouses included the returning partner having trouble sleeping, getting angry faster, and being more emotionally distant. Some of the changes in returning partners noted by less than 50% of spouses were having difficulty adjusting (48%), showing negative personality changes (46%), having mental health concerns (40%), drinking more alcohol (31%), and taking more risks with personal safety (24%; Dorvil & Pflieger, 2014).

One study of reservists and their families suggest that returning to civilian work assisted in dissipating perceived boundary ambiguity as routines were established. However, life events such as health problems or job changes were added stressors that prolonged the boundary ambiguity and made adjustment more difficult (Faber et al., 2008). During reintegration families must establish what many military families call "a new normal." Family life will not be the same as it was prior to deployment. People grow and change, especially children, and the goal is to mesh this growth and these changes into a mutually satisfactory and supportive family life.

Coping with Deployments   *Active duty families.* Service members and their spouses realize that separations are part of military life, as data from the *2012 Survey of Active Duty Spouses* illustrate. Approximately 81% reported their military spouse had deployed at least once for 30 days or more. Sixteen percent reported their spouse was currently deployed, 44% reported their spouse had been deployed in the last three years although not currently, and 21% reported their spouse had been deployed at some point but not during the last three years. Seventy-two percent reported their spouse's most recent deployment was to a combat zone (Dorvil & Pfieger, 2014).

If married or in a significant relationship other than marriage, service members and their partners face maintaining their relationship during challenging circumstances, including multiple deployments. One analysis of research on Army families concluded, "family members ... expect their Soldiers to be deployed but become increasingly dissatisfied as the length, frequency, and unpredictability of deployments increase" (Booth et al., 2007, p. 30). Military spouses find deployments stressful, particularly combat, longer, and extended deployments. Being pregnant and having children increases spouses' risk of stress and depression, as does having a returning military spouse who is experiencing posttraumatic stress disorder (PTSD) (de Burgh, White, Fear, & Iversen, 2011). Extensions of deployments often spark anger and stress, particularly when they occur just before the expected time of return (Hosek, Kavanagh, & Miller, 2006).

Multiple deployments are associated with symptoms of depression and anxiety for spouses (DASD, 2015). Experiencing one deployment appeals not to facilitate coping with subsequent deployments for many spouses. For example, in 2008, 44% of spouses found coping more difficult with multiple deployments, 39% found it neither more nor less difficult, and 18% found it less difficult (DMDC, 2009).

As Table 3.2 illustrates, spouses reported experiencing problems during deployments. The most common were loneliness, being a "single" parent, and emotionally connecting with their spouse. Reflecting on readjusting to having the spouse home after deployment, 51% of active duty spouses reported it was easy or very easy, and 21% reported it difficult or very difficult (DMDC, 2013a).

The military responds to situations that are dynamic, meaning that deployment schedules can and sometimes are expected to change. Family members are called upon to be flexible and to adapt personal and family plans to changes in military schedules. For example, imagine the changes in personal schedules that would occur if a reunion date was moved 1 week earlier or later than expected. Family members who had arranged time off

TABLE 3.2   Percentage of Spouses at Home Reporting Problems Experienced to a Large or a Very Large Extent During the Most Recent Deployment

Percentage of Spouses Reporting this Problem to a Large or a Very Large Extent			
Loneliness	38%	Managing child care	17%
Being a "single" parent	25%	Job demands	16%
Emotionally connecting with deployer	24%	Lack of/problems with military offered support	16%
Dealing with issues/decisions alone	24%	Managing expenses and bills	15%
Technical difficulties communicating with deployer	23%	Education demands	13%
Serious emotional problems in the family	22%	Safety of family in the community	11%
House/car repairs, yard	22%	Serious health problems in the family	13%
No time for recreation, fitness, or entertainment	19%	Marital problems	13%
		Other	8%

Source: Data compiled from Tables 81a–9 (pp. 448–81) of the Defense Manpower Data Center (2013a). *2012 Survey of active duty spouses: Tabulation of responses.* Retrieved from http://www.militaryonesource.mil/footer?content_id=279101.

from work would need to renegotiate time off, if possible, and revise transportation plans, perhaps at great expense.

Throughout the deployment cycle, it is common for family members to want and to request information. Prior to deployment, families want to know such information as deployment and return dates, the status of communication options down range, and where their loved one will be. During deployment families want reliable and timely information about their service member's well-being and safety (Faber et al., 2008). After reunion, families want to know that their service member is adjusting well and, if not, how to obtain help. Knowing the facts of a situation, the availability of help, and how to obtain help can reduce the experience of stress (Boss, 2006). However, some information cannot be told to family members or shared over the phone or in e-mail with family members who live at a distance. Sometimes service members withhold information from families out of the mistaken belief that the less families know the easier it will be for them.

Irregular communication and long separations stress relationships. Spouses report access to means of communication with a deployed service member as important or very important as a way to cope with a deployment (DMDC, 2009). Table 3.3 lists other items that spouses at home report as helping them cope with a deployment.

National Guard and Reserve familes. The research on deployment and families has primarily focused on active duty. Due to demographic (e.g, age and sex) and geographical differences between the Active and Reserve Components, more research on National Guard and Reserve families is necessary. In a 2006 study of deployment experiences of National Guard and Reserve members and their families, researchers interviewed military family experts from each of the six Reserve Components (i.e., Army National Guard, Air National Guard, Army Reserve, Air Force Reserve, Navy Reserve, and Marine Forces Reserve) and interviewed by telephone service members and family members from 653 families from four of the Reserve Components (i.e., Army National Guard, Army Reserve, Air Force Reserve, and Marine Forces Reserve) (Castaneda et al., 2008).

Most families in this study indicated their families were *ready* or *very ready* for deployment. Approximately 17% of service members and family members indicated their families were *somewhat ready*, and the same percentage indicated their families were *not ready at all*. Approximately 40% of respondents indicated readiness referred to financial matters, household responsibilities, and emotional or mental preparation. A quarter indicated readiness referred to legal preparation. Ten percent indicated readiness referred

TABLE 3.3 Percentage of Spouses at Home Reporting Item as Important or Very Important to Coping with the Most Recent Deployment

E-mail to and from deployer	95%	Understanding why deployment is important/necessary	66%
Telephone calls	93%	Support from civilian community	60%
Knowing length of deployment	93%	Contact with someone in deployer's unit	60%
No changes in length of deployment	84%	Family readiness/support group	57%
Temporary reunions with spouse	83%	Instant/text messaging with deployer	55%
Deployment pay	82%	Reunion planning information or classes	50%
Predeployment information	76%	Local counseling/support services	50%
Recreation, fitness, and entertainment activities	71%	Telephonic counseling/support services (i.e., Military OneSource)	42%
Support from the military community	69%		

Source: Data compiled from Defense Manpower Data Center (2009). *2008 Survey of active duty spouses: Tabulation of responses (Report No. 2008-041).* Tables 22a–22q (p. 138–171). Arlington, VA: DMDC. Retrieved from http://prhome.defense.gov/MCFP/docs/2008%20Military%20Spouse%20Survey.pdf.

to learning about military programs and benefits; addressing employment-related issues; finding information about the deployment; determining how to communicate during deployment; canceling classes or vacation plans; and preparing the service member to deploy. Almost two-thirds of service members and spouses indicated they coped well or very well with deployment, and 16% of service members and 20% of spouses indicated they coped moderately well. Less than 10% of service members and spouses indicated they coped poorly. The remaining respondents indicated they did not know how well they coped or did not answer (Castaneda et al., 2008).

A majority of service members and spouses reported at least one problem faced by their families because of the deployment or activation. Over a third of spouses reported emotional and household problems, and a quarter reported children's issues. In comparison, fewer service members than spouses reported their families experiencing these problems although more service members than spouses reported problems related to employment. Service members and their spouses were more in agreement on whether the family experienced financial or legal problems, and education. Approximately 10% of service members and spouses reported marital and health-care problems (Castaneda et al., 2008).

Those service members and spouses reporting *no* problems were more financially comfortable, felt they had received sufficient notice, and believed their families were ready or very ready for the deployment. Army reservists were *least likely* to report *no* problems. Husbands of service members, spouses with no children, and spouses married to Air Force reservists were *most likely* to report *no* problems (Castaneda et al., 2008).

The top three formal military supports service members and spouses reported using during deployment were Tricare, Family Readiness Groups or Key Volunteers, and MilitaryOneSource.com. The top three informal resources reported used were family, religious institutions, and friends and neighbors (Castaneda et al., 2008).

Positives of Deployment. Perhaps startling to those not connected to the military, service members and military families may speak of the benefits and positive outcomes of deployments. Benefits of deployments for service members include using their skills and training, gaining experience vital to advancing in their career, additional money, assisting the nation, and time to think (Booth et al., 2007; Newby, McCarroll, et al., 2005). Partners may also derive benefits from deployments: having time to focus on career advancement or educational goals, gaining confidence and independence, and developing new interests.

A majority of service members and spouses in the 2006 study of National Guard and Reserves reported at least one positive development in their lives as a result of the deployment or activation. For service members, these positives included financial gain; family closeness; patriotism, pride, or civic responsibility; independence, confidence, or resilience; and employment and education. Spouses reported the following positives: family closeness; patriotism, pride, or civic responsibility; financial gain and independence, confidence, or resilience; and employment or education. Service members who were likely to report no positives reported receiving less or insufficient notice, and spouses who were likely to report no positives were male spouses, Army Reserve spouses, prior military, and those who described employers as not supportive (Castaneda et al., 2008).

RISK OF INJURY OR DEATH

The military calls on its personnel to engage in training, conduct operations, and deploy on missions that are inherently dangerous during both peacetime and time of war. Military work is physical work even during peacetime, and workplace injuries and deaths occur. During times of war, going outside the wire on patrol, landing and guiding in an F-18 on the deck of an aircraft carrier, diving into deep waters in a submarine, loading bombs and missiles, and flying helicopters during a firefight to pick up the wounded are only a few examples of the dangers.

Injury and death of a service member are realities faced by military families. Since 9/11 and the beginning of OEF/OIF, military families have faced even greater possibility of their service member risking injury and death. Since September 2001, approximately 2.6 million service personnel have deployed (Institute of Medicine, 2014). During this time, a majority of deployers went to a combat zone, and family members worried about their loved one's safety (DMDC, 2009).

Research is limited on what helps family members cope with the fear that injury and death may occur. As noted in the section on deployment, communicating with the military member helps. Other coping strategies include contact with family, friends, and support groups; involvement with work or volunteer activities to provide social contact and benefits from positively contributing to society; self-awareness of stress levels and seeking assistance when appropriate; engaging in healthy behaviors (e.g., exercise, nutritional eating, adequate sleep); limiting time spent listening to or watching media accounts about the military; and recognizing that daily life may feel overwhelming at times (Wright, Burrell, Schroeder, & Thomas, 2006).

The military refers collectively to those who have died or have been wounded while serving as **casualties**. As of May 2015, over 52,000 service members had been wounded in action and over 6,800 have died during OEF, OIF, OND, and OIR (DOD, 2015). Improvised explosive devices (IEDs) attacks and direct combat have produced the majority of casualties. Other reasons include noncombat helicopter/aircraft accidents, medical (e.g., heart attack), and vehicle accidents. *The Washington Post* newspaper publishes data based on military press releases and hosts an interactive website, "Faces of the Fallen" (http://projects.washingtonpost.com/fallen), where service members are listed by name, branch of service, state of residence, and date of death.

Combat and operational stress injuries include such wounds as **traumatic brain injury** (TBI; a blow or jolt to or penetration of the head), amputations, spinal cord injuries, chronic pain associated with musculoskeletal conditions, depression, anxiety, and **post-traumatic stress disorder** (an anxiety disorder that may occur following a traumatic event). An injury can disrupt family functioning. Lives are changed, not only for those wounded but also for families and loved ones. Changes can include short-term disruptions in routine until the service member recovers or major reorganizations of roles so family members can provide daily care for a son, daughter, spouse, mother, father, niece, or nephew. As we will see in other chapters, a constellation of protective factors available within and for the family can promote resilience in the service member and family.

With injuries come many challenges for military families. Upon notification of their service member being wounded, families are thrown into uncertainty as initial communication can be brief and lack the details family members want to know: how bad is the injury, where is the service member, can we talk to her or him? Sometimes service members find a way to call home before the official notification occurs in an attempt to reassure their families. If the service member is being transported to the United States, family members usually will travel to the military hospital and remain for weeks and even months as treatment and recovery progress. Longer-term challenges include ongoing health decisions, financial concerns, whether the service member can continue in the military, employment decisions for a spouse or parents providing care, and disruptions in children's lives (Cozza, 2009b).

When there is a death, the military notifies the next of kin in person. The Army sends a **Casualty Notification Officer** (CNO), often accompanied by a military chaplain and/or organization commander to notify a service member's designated next of kin. In cases of a death by a hostile action (e.g., combat) or terrorist attack, the secondary next of kin will also be notified in person. The Army assigns a **Casualty Assistance Officer** (CAO) to be with the family through the transition to provide information and assistance with funeral or memorial services, filing paperwork for benefits and entitlements, and relocation. If the next of kin lives geographically far from an Army installation or an Army National Guard or Reserve unit, the CNO and CAO may be the same soldier (U.S. Army Human Resources Command, 2010).

The Navy and Marine Corps **Casualty Assistance Calls Officer** (CACO) and the Air Force **Casualty Assistance Representative** (CAR) serve both functions: to notify next of kin and to be with the family through the transition to provide information and assistance. Service members assigned as a CNO, CAO, CACO, or CAR are senior enlisted personnel or commissioned officers who receive initial and ongoing training specifically for this position. When assigned a family, the CAO, CACO, and CAR serve as the official liaison between the family and the Army, Air Force, Marine Corps, or Navy and assist the family until benefit and entitlement processing is completed (DoD, 2014a).

Family members enrolled in the military sponsorship system (i.e., DEERS) may remain in military housing for up to 365 days after the death of a service member and retain some privileges until remarriage, such as shopping on the base or post exchange. They also may use Morale, Welfare, and Recreation programs. Children in the Department of Defense Domestic Dependent Elementary and Secondary Schools (DDESS) may remain enrolled until graduation unless they move to another school system. Additional benefits, entitlements, resources, and a description of the casualty assistance process are described in the DoD (2014a) publication, A Survivor's Guide to Benefits: Taking Care of Our Families, which is updated semiannually. Families, including families of National Guard or Reserve personnel killed on active duty, may live in a state that provides benefits and support to survivors. They should check with the state's Department of Military and Veterans Affairs (DoD, 2014a).

Military families face challenges associated with frequent relocation and separation and with the risk of injury and death. Knowing about these normative stressors of military life can sensitize you to how stressors may pile up and to strengths of military families such as family role flexibility, active coping strategies, and sense of community that bolsters positive family adaptation (Wiens & Boss, 2006). As you continue learning more about military life, consider how this knowledge and sensitivity can guide you in interactions with individual military families who are both unique from and similar to other military families.

SUMMARY

- The normative stressors associated with the military lifestyle (e.g., relocation, separation, risk of injury or death) are shared by other occupations.
- Sharing in a sense of community encourages positive adaptation to military family life. Military families benefit from informal, formal, and unit-level support.
- The mission of a military unit takes priority over family events or needs. This "duty first" means more workload for family members at home as they pick up the roles and tasks the service member would perform if at home.
- Moving every few years is a hallmark of military life for active duty members, as they are relocated many times during a career.
- A majority of military spouses are seeking additional education and are or wish to be employed. Employment or a career is a major factor for military spouses' assessment of their quality of life.
- Families report separation as one of the most stressful parts of military life, even more so when the service member is deployed in dangerous situations. A feature of a deployment cycle is boundary ambiguity, that is, having a family member "present" physically but not psychologically or present psychologically but not physically.

- Adaptability is a key component of family adjustment during deployment and afterwards.
- Military work is physical work even during peacetime, and workplace injuries and deaths occur.
- The military refers collectively to those who have died or have been wounded while serving as "casualties."
- When there is a death, a military representative notifies the next of kin in person. The representative stays with the family through the transition to provide information and assistance with funeral or memorial services, filing paperwork for benefits and entitlements, and relocation.

EXERCISES

To gain insight into the characteristics of military family life, answer the following questions:

1. If you knew you had to move your entire household every 2–3 years, how would you live your life differently than you do now? How do you think this might impact your relationships with your family members? Friends? New people you meet?
2. Imagine you had 90 days to move your entire household to another country. What steps would be involved in not only moving items but also ending a job, and saying good-bye to friends and extended family? What steps would you also have to take to ensure a place to stay in the new location, daycare or a school for children, and a new job? What other steps would you need to take to facilitate a positive adjustment? What would you look forward to the most? The least?

3. Imagine you are working as a child and youth specialist in a community program. A father, with a two-year old in his arms, comes to pick up his 8 year-old from the after-school program. He seems distressed. While his daughter continues to play with friends, you talk briefly with him and discover his wife, a nurse in the Army Reserves, was just notified that she will be deployed as an Individual Augmentee and must report in two weeks. The father says that while he knew a deployment was possible, he never really thought it would happen to them. He wonders what kind of support the Army has for families who live in a state with no large military installation. He seems calmer after talking with you. His daughter runs up and after a hug, she puts on her jacket and the three of them leave. The next day the 8 year-old arrives at the after-school program looking sad. Over the course of 2 hours she reveals that her mom will be going to another country to help soldiers and other people who get hurt. Her friends suggest that her mom could tell her boss that she needs to stay home because she has children. The father arrives looking worried. He says he has to figure out how he is going to manage taking care of two children without his wife and family close by. He says he doesn't know where to start. How can you assist this family? Think about the challenges they are facing and the strengths they can apply to coping now and in the coming months. As an Individual Augmentee going to another Army unit, how long may the service member be gone? What should the father and service member be doing in the coming weeks and months to help their children? To help themselves as a couple? What resources do you recommend to them?
4. What assistance could you give the family described in the prior exercise if instead of a wife, the father had a male partner serving as a nurse in the Army reserves? What assistance could you provide if the wife or male partner was serving as a nurse in the Navy Reserves? What would change if instead of deploying as an

Individual Augmentee, the service member deployed as part of an Air National Guard unit? As part of an Army National Guard unit?

5. Put together a welcome kit for military families moving into your hometown. Include in this kit the information a family would need to know and the community resources that might be of interest to military families.

6. In a farming region of a state, the local religious and social service agencies decided to pool their resources and offer a support group for parents and other family members of service members. Because of your training in family life education, you have been asked to design this group so that it is part education and part facilitation. Develop a program plan for this group. Indicate the topics and resources you will cover and how you will facilitate discussions.

7. Now imagine after 3 months of leading this support group, a couple calls you and frantically reports that their 22 year-old child has been hurt in an explosion. They are about to leave to go to the military hospital in another state but wanted to let you know they will email you when they know more but at this point is seems a leg has been severely damaged and there is a possible mild traumatic brain injury. They give you permission to let the other group members know what has happened. You have 2 days before the group meets again. Outline how you will structure the group meeting and why. Consider looking for resources that might be useful to the group members.

4

Children and Youth in Military Families

In Chapter 4, you will

- Meet Connery, a high school senior, who has been raised in a military family.
- Learn about military children's experiences of moving and going to school.
- Discover the impact of parental deployments on children's adjustment.
- Consider how to support children during parental deployment, injury, or death.

Meet

Connery, A High School Senior

"We've had it good for us."

A military family is different from civilian families. Being an active-duty son, I had to get used to moving around every 4 years. That's good because you are going to have to move anyway when you go to college or get a job. If you aren't the coolest guy in one state, you can have a fresh start. Here a lot of people know me. I call it home. I was 10 when we moved here and now I'm 18. It's the longest I've lived anywhere.

When I was born, we moved to Germany. I just remember my grandmother coming, and mom and I traveled around with her. I have experienced different cultures and know lots of people not like me. I'm open to new ideas.

The benefits are a huge plus. I am under my dad's health insurance, auto insurance, and dental insurance while I'm living with him.

As a military kid, you have more respect for authority. Having a commanding officer for a dad, I feel you have to say, "Sir, yes, sir" and get on with it. It helps when you have procrastination issues like me.

You see and do neat things. I got to sit in the cockpit of an A-10. My dad flies it. The A-10 is a close air support for troops on the ground that sticks with the soldiers and keeps our guys alive. There's a lot of buttons. It's a safe plane. You can take a hit and go back in.

When my dad goes off to missions, he's fulfilling a commitment he has made. I've experienced his leaving many times. Maybe his discipline has rubbed off on me. I want to go into the Air Force Reserve or Air National Guard. The benefits are good. I want to follow my dad's footsteps and serve my country. I'd like to fly a helicopter. I hear stories that being a pilot is all it is cracked up to be. It's like being on a roller coaster all the time. I want to have a civilian job, too, in architecture. My parents are behind it as long as I finish college first, but I always planned to do that. I'm aware of the danger, and I still want to do my part.

I don't recommend military life for everyone. It was hard to leave my really good friends when we moved. We talk on Facebook sometimes, but now my life has moved on. You can have friends but not a huge bond.

The most important thing is to be on good terms with your family. Talk. Hang out together. My brothers and I are good friends. We always had each other every time we moved. We hold a lot of respect for our parents. They put us first. If you don't have a close-knit family, you kick yourself in the butt. We've had it good for us.

INTRODUCTION

Nearly 2 million children in the United States have at least one parent serving in the military. In 2013, there were approximately 1.2 million children of active duty personnel and over 700,000 children of selected reserve personnel (DASD, 2014). Many of these children have only known military family life, while some recall a prior civilian life. Others transitioned through a parent leaving active duty and joining the National Guard or Reserve, or vice versa. Still more children are military-connected when a sibling joins either the Active Duty or Reserve Component.

In addition to those children with a parent currently in the military, there are another 2 million children who experience military family life while at least one parent is active duty or a Reservist for some years, but now are living a civilian life because their parent separated from the military (Lester & Flake, 2013). Finally, there are adults who, as military children, grew up in the military culture. We are learning more about their perspectives of life as they share their stories with the media and researchers (Martin, Rosen, & Sparacino, 2000). Later in this chapter Randy Ott, an adult raised in the military, looks back on the impact the military culture has had on his life.

Of course not all children with a parent in the military experience the same type of "military family life." For example, those children whose parents are active duty may experience separations, relocations including overseas, and life on or near a major military installation. These children usually are familiar and comfortable with military culture and being on military bases or posts. They typically attend either DoDEA schools or civilian schools with a high population of military children. However, children of parents who are in the Air or Army National Guard or the Reserves may never experience relocating to a new community or know many children like themselves. Although they may visit an Armory or an Air National Guard base, their daily lives are lived in the civilian rather than a military world.

In this chapter, we examine the influence of military culture, relocation, child care, education, and deployment on children. Connery, the 18-year-old high school senior you met at the beginning of this chapter, shares some of his perceptions of life in a military family. He emphasizes being close to his brothers and parents as a key component of living in a military family. As you read, notice how many of Connery's and Randy's points are highlighted in what we know about military children. The experiences of military children vary, and not all may have such positive responses as Connery and Randy.

Military children face relocations, separations, and risks of parental injury. The studies we have of military children suggest that most adapt well to military life (Chandra et al., 2011; MacDermid et al., 2008). However, some military children experience more extensive and intensive stressors when parents deploy multiple times over the course of a few years, are injured, or die. These events and a pile-up of stressors (e.g., combat deployment followed by a PCS move and extended work hours at the new duty station and another combat deployment) can immobilize individual family members, including children, and wear away or overwhelm families' coping skills. Even then we know that protective factors such as positive family dynamics, social support, and finding meaning from such adversities can make a difference in the resilience of children and families (Boss, 2006; Park,

2011; Walsh, 2002; Wiens & Boss, 2006). While research on military children has been increasing, more studies are needed that are based on representative, rather than convenience, samples and designed to examine strengths in military children. In addition, studies that apply a life course perspective can help us understand the link between children's and parents' development and, for example, the trajectories of children whose military parent was wounded or died (Cozza & Lerner, 2013).

RELOCATION

As noted in Chapter 3, relocation is a well-known feature of active duty military life. If raised their whole life in an active duty family, military children will have moved an average of six to nine times between kindergarten and graduating from high school (Department of Defense-State Liaison Office, 2010), or every 2–3 years (Finkel, Kelley, & Ashby, 2003). Military children have reported traveling and meeting new people as benefits of military life. Yet, both of these benefits occur because of one of the "toughest" parts of military life for children: moving (Ender, 2002, 2006; National Military Family Association, 2010).

Moving can seem to be a perpetual process for some active duty military children and teens. They are preparing to move, physically moving, settling in, or wondering where the next move will be. Prior to the physical move, they are saying good-bye to friends and family and perhaps beginning to grieve over the loss of daily connection to these important people. Little is known about military children under the age of 5 and relocation. However, as with any move or transition, infants, toddlers, and preschoolers are greatly influenced by the prevalent emotions of their caregivers and consistency in routine.

For school-age children and teens, a move usually means changing schools, rejoining sports teams and interest groups, and finding new friends. They may be concerned about whether they will be "behind" or "ahead" others in their grade. However, they also report liking the opportunity to start over at a new school that a relocation offers (Finkel et al., 2003).

The website *Military Youth on the Move* includes information for children, teens, and parents on transitioning to a new location and school. Some military installations have a youth sponsorship program that will match a new child to a child approximately of the same age who is living in the new location in order to assist with integration into the new installation, surrounding community, and school.

Although research has given us some insight into the experiences of military children with moves, our knowledge is still limited. For example, few studies have followed children longitudinally as they go through the process of a move or followed up with them for a period of time afterward to determine the longer-term consequences. Most studies ask children about their experiences only after the fact. Most studies are relatively small, and as noted above, there is little information about preschool children (Weber & Weber, 2005). To better understand how relocation affects military children, we need representative samples across age ranges and branches of service and more focus on what factors are associated with positive adjustment.

Relocation often means changing schools for military children. The *Military Families on the Move* study (MacDermid et al., 2007) introduced in Chapter 3 offers some insight into what can make transitioning to a new school easier or more difficult for youth. The study included collecting data from one child, age 10–17; the service member; and the spouse from 608 Army and Air Force families. The average number of schools attended by these youth since the age of 5 was 4.08. Children reported experiencing school transitions as more difficult when they were female, had social anxiety (i.e., fear of negative evaluation), had negative attitudes about moving, and had negative perceptions of their own academic competence. They also indicated moves during the school year as more difficult. However, summer moves may also result in challenges for teens who, without the interaction with peers that comes with attending school, may not be able to identify potential friends and create friendships (Tyler, 2002).

Evidence suggests that the number of moves is not what predicts children's adjustment (Finkel et al., 2003). Although teens report loss of friends, maneuvering in new surroundings, and changing schools as stressful, factors such as maternal functioning (or the functioning of the major caregiver), family cohesiveness, and time at a current residence appear to be more important than the rate of mobility (i.e., dividing the number of moves a child experiences by the child's age) in predicting children's psychosocial adjustment (Finkel et al., 2003). In a nonrepresentative sample of 86 mother–child pairs, children, whose average age was 12, reported less loneliness and more positive relationships with peers when they lived longer at the current residence. Trusting relationships with mothers, cohesive family ties, and longer time at the current residence reduced children's concern about others evaluating them negatively and predicted children's self-esteem. Mothers' self-reports of depressive symptoms were associated with children's sadness, anxiety, and withdrawal. The number of moves did not predict children's adjustment in these areas (Finkel et al., 2003).

Military children may learn positive coping skills when faced with multiple relocations. A study examined 179 military parents' perceptions of teens' adjustment to multiple relocations. The average number of moves was 4.89, with a range of 1–18 moves. Military parents, from the four military branches, were recruited from four secondary schools with a large proportion of military teens. Seventy-five percent of parents considered relocations to have positively influenced their children's development, and parental perception of this positive influence increased as the number of moves increased. Also, parents perceived improved behavior as the frequency of moves (i.e., number of relocations per year of life) increased (Weber & Weber, 2005).

The education of children can affect whether and when military families move to a new location. If service members are scheduled to deploy soon after arriving at a new duty station, families may choose to remain where they are currently living or move to be close to extended family. If the date for the permanent change of duty station occurs after the beginning of the school year, families may choose to remain in their current location to allow children to complete the academic year at the same school. Finally, if the quality of education is better at the current location, families may remain in order not to negatively affect the education of their children (DOD, 2011c).

Military teens perceive themselves as adaptable and comfortable talking with others because of frequent relocations, including moves outside of the United States (National Military Family Association, 2010). In some ways, military children share these and other characteristics with children of missionaries, business executives, and diplomats who live years in cultures outside of their "passport country" (Ender, 2002). They are often identified as "third culture kids" because they spend a significant number of their developmental years outside of their parents' culture(s) (Pollock & Van Reken, 2001).

Raised within the military community on self-sufficient bases and posts, whether the installations are in or outside of the United States, military children can feel in a world apart from their civilian cousins and peers. Then, upon adulthood or when their parent leaves the military, they are no longer officially part of the military community (unless they join themselves as an adult) and may not feel in synch with the larger civilian population. As a result, they can feel between cultures and may enter adulthood feeling in "a world between worlds" (Pollock & Van Reken, 2001, p. 29).

The Internet has facilitated the connection of military children, including those who are now adults, with others who have shared experiences. A quick search of the Internet for the term **military brat** (or Air Force brat, Army brat, Navy brat, or Marine Corps brat), a positive and affectionate term claimed by military children to refer to themselves and others growing up in the military (Wertsch, 1991), will show social networking and informational sites. Some military brats hold reunions based on the DoDEA school attended (Martin et al., 2000). Although the origin of the term is disputed, military children use "backronyms" including "'brave, resilient, adaptable, and trustworthy'" to describe the meaning of BRAT (Park, 2011, p. 67).

Voices From the Frontline

I WOULD NOT TRADE MY UPBRINGING FOR ANYTHING.

My dad was in the U.S. Army. We lived anywhere and everywhere. I remember Christmas in Florida, Georgia, North Carolina, and Germany. In the first grade, I went to five, maybe six, different schools. It was hard on me. My parents decided that I should repeat the year. I remember thinking, "Am I dumb?" Then we were in the same place from the time I was 10 to 15. I was able to skip the 8th grade to put me back on track with my peers and graduated with people my age. It gave me a huge confidence boost.

I look very positively on the experience of moving so often. It gave me more strength. I think we underestimate military kids when we assume moving is hard on them. It teaches perseverance and grit, and how to adjust to new places and people.

When I was 10, my parents divorced. My dad was my parent. The Army raised me. The military gave us structure and stability. My dad never had to worry about missing his job. My sister and I had the beauty and the benefit of walking to school with our friends and going to the Youth Center after school to do our homework and play games until our parents picked us up. (I can still shoot a pretty mean game of pool.) We were always around soldiers. I saw the culture, the structure. I would see men and women in uniform. There were people of different cultures. There was a sense of community, a commonality, and I felt it.

We moved to a new base just before I started the 4th grade. My dad's work was in a big building near our house. My school was maybe a mile away. The first day of school I followed the other kids but got lost on my way home. I found the big building where my dad worked, I remembered the color, and I waited there for an hour while my dad was out looking for me. Eventually some of the people he worked with found him and we connected up. I don't remember feeling scared or lost even though this was a brand new place. It speaks to the trust and security of living on a base.

The way I live my life, I learned from my dad and others around him. He and the military influenced who I am today in many ways. For example, when you live on a base, you have the responsibility to help care for the grounds around your house. Today, I mow the lawn every week. That's what you do.

I'm never late. To me on time is late so I am always early. I don't know any different. (My wife is not that way but we work it out.) When I sit in the living room and take my shoes off, I get up and put them into the closet. Habits that I learned then still stick with me and I like who I am and what I learned from military culture.

My dad was a good athlete and today I stay in good shape. I remember going to watch my dad in competitions. He'd get an award sometimes. People from different units and services would compete with respect and become a community. I see the importance now. It is a true community of force and protection for all of us civilians. One day these soldiers might be fighting together and some may not come back so I see the importance now of them being together in all walks of life and serving.

I almost joined the military two times. I'd say, "Why go to college? It's for the birds." I wanted to be like my dad, who did not go to college. When I was a senior I worked at the Army bowling alley during Desert Storm. It was 1991. Every now and then I'd see officers. They were respectful and would keep others in line. I wanted to be like them and so realized I needed to go to college. Even though from high school teachers I'd been told I should go to college, I had to figure it out myself. I was influenced by the military culture and all its differences.

I currently work in higher education where I teach courses on leadership and direct the Center for Academic Success Programs. A university is like an Army base. We have buildings, roads, a structure. There are expectations in terms of conduct and my colleagues and I each serve something bigger than ourselves.

I have one mind and one body and I want to use them to the fullest. I finished my doctoral work in 2011 and a year later, I started what turned out to be a two-year-long process to join the military. I was turned down at first and had to redo everything including my physical to reapply. Two weeks ago, at age 40, I was accepted into the Navy Reserve. The Navy is the only branch that would take me because of my age. I think there is wisdom in taking someone my age. I may not be as fit as I was at 30 but I have years of knowledge and experience. I will continue to work at the university and serve my weekend a month and two weeks a year.

My joining was a family decision. I could be deployed overseas. I could be killed. I definitely will be away from home more often. My wife and I talked. She doesn't know the military culture except for what my dad tells her and what she sees in the news and movies. But she knows this decision is very important to me.

I know what I experienced growing up and what the military culture taught me as a person. I want to give that to my son. Right now he spends time with my dad and learns from him. We are lucky for that. I want him to learn from my service, too. I want him to have an appreciation of the country we have. Cliché or not, freedom isn't free. I want him to know what that means. I want him to learn discipline, timeliness, and the importance of ongoing education, fitness, and exercise. I want him to gain appreciation for different cultures. The military still has more work to do in this area but it is a beginning.

I hope I can serve for 20 years. It means a lot for me. I will learn something new and have the opportunity to be in a culture that means so much to me. I have the opportunity to serve my country and be with people I respect. I am looking forward to it.

I look in the mirror and I am happy with myself. I am not nearly perfect, but feel I can influence and help others. The military helped me start on this never-ending journey of learning, self-improvement, and helping others. I would not trade my upbringing for anything.

Randy Ott, PhD
Director, Center for Academic Success Programs
Western Michigan University

CHILD CARE

Provision of child care is an important daily issue that affects a large number of military families with children. In FY 2013, 42% of children of active duty parents and 29% of children of selected reserve parents were age 5 or under (DASD, 2014).

In particular, dual-military, single parents, and those with children under the age of 6 have indicated that the availability of child care that is responsive to a parent's work schedule (e.g., overnight duty, early morning hours, evening hours) influences their decision to remain in the military. Child care is also important to military families with a civilian spouse who is or wants to be employed (Zellman, Gates, Moini, & Suttorp, 2009). Box 4.1 highlights how child care providers play an important role in supporting military families.

BOX 4.1   BEST PRACTICES

Military parents have a wide array of strengths and skills and want the best for their children. However, corrosive stress, the experience of combat, and injuries (visible and invisible) can make it difficult for parents to function as they did before. Service members and spouses may feel overwhelmed or distracted. A parent may become depressed—unable to access feelings of competence or hope. Family life may become disorganized.

All these are natural responses to difficult situations. However, these changes can disrupt family relationships and a baby or toddler's sense of safety, security, and self.

For children under age 3, whose brains are literally being wired cognitively and emotionally, early relationships with parents and other caregivers are laying the foundation for the future. This is where you come in.

You may provide child care, health care, mental health services, or family support. This guide will support you in building respectful, responsive relationships with family members.

As you will see, the little things you say and do matter. When you genuinely listen, family members are less alone. When you reflect back their strengths, there is hope. When you play a game of peek-a-boo or sing a silly song with a child, you remind families (and yourself) of the joy babies and toddlers feel and give. As you build trust with family members, they are more likely to get the support and information they need to be more available to their babies and toddlers. The positive cycle continues. (ZERO TO THREE, 2009, p. 6)

Found on most military installations, **child development centers (CDCs)** serve infants to 5-year-olds, and **family child care (FCC) providers** (called child development providers in the Navy) serve children from infancy to 12 years of age. CDC hours of operation are typically 6:00 AM to 6:30 PM (or 0600 to 1830 in military time). FCC homes may offer even longer hours as well as evening, nighttime, and weekend hours. Both CDCs and FCC providers may offer care on an hourly basis (Zellman et al., 2009). **School-age care (SAC) programs**, along with resource and referral services, are also available to families. A military installation's website typically includes information about local CDCs, FCC providers, and SAC programs.

The military's systematic and multipronged approach to delivering child care has been lauded as a model for the nation, although that was not always the case (Pomper, Blank, Duff Campbell, & Schulman, 2005). The Military Child Care Act of 1989 is credited for drastically improving the quality of child care and its affordability (Zellman et al., 2009). As a result, all child care that comes under the purview of the DoD is subject to DoD and national accreditation standards. Ninety-eight percent of military CDCs have earned accreditation by the National Academy of Early Childhood Programs, a division of the National Association for the Education of Young Children, compared with 8–10% of community child care centers (Graham, 2010). It is estimated that military parents pay 25% less in child care fees than civilian parents (Castaneda & Harrell, 2008).

FCC providers also must meet DoD guidelines for certification (e.g., background check; certification in CPR and First Aid; an initial training that includes child abuse protection; fire, medicine, and program inspection; health screening), participate in ongoing training, and meet recertification requirements. In addition, home visits are conducted to ensure the safety and well-being of children. FCCs may be required to meet state licensing requirements and accreditation with the National Association for Family Child Care (Commander, Navy Region Mid Atlantic. n.d.). Nationally, only 1% of civilian FCC homes are accredited (Smith & Sarkar, 2008).

Care for school-age children is offered through before- and after-school school-age and youth programs (Zellman et al., 2009). Children can participate in physical activities and sports, complete homework, do arts and crafts, or access computers. Programs may be accredited through the National After School Association.

Single parents and dual-military parents have priority in accessing care by DoD policy. Most CDCs have waiting lists, and these families are given priority on them. Care for infants is the longest wait list, and infant care is the most expensive for centers although not for families. Fees are based on income, not on the cost of care, and so benefit mostly those in the junior ranks with the youngest children (Zellman et al., 2009). As of fall 2014, fees ranged from $50 to $148 per week (Assistant Secretary of Defense, 2014).

Military spouses have raised concern about the limited capacity, limited hours, high costs of child care, and use of multiple types of child care (Castaneda & Harrell, 2008; Smith & Sarkar, 2008; Zellman et al., 2009). A study with a random, stratified sample of active duty, single parent, dual-military, and civilian-spouse families with children from infancy to age 12 found that parents of children under the age of 5 face a number of difficulties related to child care (Zellman et al., 2009). In this sample, more than 50% of parents had irregular work hours, forcing them to rely on multiple arrangements to meet their child care needs. Although single parents and dual-military parents received priority at CDCs, with their lack of evening, overnight, holiday, and weekend care, these facilities were the option least likely to fit military schedules. Military parents in this and other studies found child care too expensive (Castaneda & Harrell, 2008). Most parents did not know that their child care was subsidized, and some believed CDCs make a profit for the DoD, which they do not (Zellman et al., 2009).

FCC homes may provide longer hours of care and more flexible scheduling than CDCs. However, these benefits may be unstable. If the provider becomes ill or has a family emergency, child care may be compromised. Even a provider's back-up plan can be uncertain as it usually involves other FCC providers who may be at capacity and cannot accommodate an additional child (Zellman et al., 2009).

The DoD has initiated two programs, *Operation: Military Child Care* and *Military Child Care in Your Neighborhood*, to assist active duty, Reserve, and National Guard parents in locating child care when they live at a distance from military installations. In addition, the Air Force Reserve and Air National Guard members drilling at specific installations can use the Air Force Home Community Care program. The DoD partnered with the National Association of Child Care Resources and Referral Agencies (NACCRRA), a national organization for agencies that offer child care resources and referrals (http://www.naccrra.org), to offer these programs. Continued attention is needed, however, to examine more policy alternatives to meet the needs of families. Suggestions include offering subsidized slots at community centers, developing wraparound care, and partnering with community after-school programs (Zellman et al., 2009).

EDUCATION

In addition to child care, other concerns of military families are access to a quality education for their children and availability of regular after-school and summer activities.

A majority of school-age military children attend private or public civilian schools in the communities where they live or are home-schooled (DoDEA, 2015). Many attend school with other military children in a community near a military installation. However, a family may move in order to be closer to extended families during deployment. Going back home to be near grandparents or other extended family may result in a military child attending a school with students and staff unfamiliar with military life. Likewise, children of Reserve Component personnel typically attend civilian schools, many of which are located far from major military installations. They too may feel isolated from other children who do not have a parent serving in the military.

Military children may experience physical disruptions in their formal education, reflecting the high mobility of these military families. A parent's change of duty station may mean a change of schools for military children. Relocations can take families to military installations across the country. International moves may take children to countries where they do not speak the language and/or are unfamiliar with the local customs and culture.

More than 78,000 or nearly 7% of the 1.2 million student-age military children attend schools established specifically for DoD family members (DoDEA, 2014b). The DoDEA, a DoD organization that falls under the direction of the Under Secretary of Defense for Personnel and Readiness, operates 181 schools in 12 foreign countries, seven U.S. states, Guam and Puerto Rico for family members of U.S. military personnel and civilian DoD employees.

The DoDEA schools provide students with a standardized curriculum that makes it easier for students of military families to move from school to school, particularly from a domestic school to an overseas school or vice versa. The DoDEA schools provide resources and support to help students cope with the stress of frequent moves and other stressors that come with being a military family member.

The DoD also provides resources to civilian schools relied on by military families so students not in a location with a DoD school can receive support coping with the challenges associated with military life. In recent years, the DoDEA has granted public schools throughout the nation grants for improving the education for military students and for providing professional development for educators in schools that serve military students (DOD, 2011c).

Military children show academic strengths. In 2010, children in DoDEA schools, grades 3–11, exceeded national averages on standardized testing in math, science, language arts, social studies, and reading (DoDEA, 2010a, 2010c). In 2014, 75% of DoDEA students in graduating classes took the SAT test (a college admissions test), compared with a national rate of 52%. DoDEA students' average critical reading score exceeded and writing scores were slightly above or at the national average scores although the DoDEA math score was lower than the national average. African American and Hispanic DoDEA students continued to score higher in each section of the SAT than their stateside civilian peers in 2014, continuing a multiyear trend (DoDEA, 2014a). Reasons for this difference in performance are not clear but may reflect the fact that military children avoid some of the hardships that disproportionately affect ethnic minority families in the civilian population: parental unemployment, limited parental education, extreme poverty, lack of access to health care, poor-quality schools, discrimination, and/or disadvantaged or dangerous neighborhoods.

In addition to the process of saying good-bye to friends and making new ones because of relocation, children and their parents have had to contend with differences in education policy across states. However, the recent Interstate Compact on Educational Opportunities for Military Children is establishing continuity in many education policies and practices across the 50 states (Military Interstate Children's Compact Commission, 2014; see Chapter 12 for more information on this compact).

Teachers and other school staff members play an important role in the lives of children. Learning provides a positive focus, and the school day provides a structure and a routine that can benefit children. School teachers, counselors, and administrators may find the following recommendations (Chandra et al., 2010; DoDEA, 2011; "Educator's Guide to the Military Child During Deployment," n.d.; Harrison & Vannest, 2008) helpful in creating a school environment that supports military children and their families:

- Know which students have a parent or parents serving in the military.
- Talk with parents to learn about past, current, or future deployments and relocations. Let parents know you appreciate their service and are there to support their children during any transitions.
- Recognize that adjusting to transitions throughout the cycle of deployment takes time and patience.
- Recognize signs when students are having difficulty adjusting.
  - Extensive clinginess.
  - Disruptions in eating and sleeping patterns.
  - Misbehavior.
  - Headaches, stomachaches, other unexplained pains.
  - Difficulties in speech.
  - Withdrawn or aggressive behavior.
  - Excessively active.
- Recognize more serious signs of difficulty coping.
  - Not resuming typical levels of academic engagement.
  - Continuing intense emotional responses.
  - Continuing depression, withdrawal, noncommunication.
  - Disturbing drawings or writings.
  - Hurting themselves intentionally or appearing likely to hurt others.
  - Significant weight loss or gain.
  - Poor hygiene or personal care.
  - Symptoms of alcohol or drug use.
  - Anxious or aggressive.
- Act.
  - Speak with parents about observations.
  - Consult with administrators and knowledgeable community supports.
  - Be sensitive to students' needs.
  - Provide structure in the classroom and offer time to listen to students.
  - Use objectivity about war and conflict, setting aside personal beliefs in order to help students.
  - Focus on safety and security of students and parents.
  - Use patience, consider briefly reducing workload for students, and offer tutoring or mentoring support.
  - Be approachable, attentive, and knowledgeable about children, relocation, and deployment; acknowledge and normalize their feelings.
  - Be culturally sensitive.
  - Encourage appropriate ways to handle feelings such as anger.
  - Weave deployments into subjects (e.g., geography, social studies, cultures).
- Ensure school is a safe place for military children: maintain routines, be sensitive, and encourage all staff to be aware of needs of military children.
- Encourage parents to visit the classroom. Military parents could discuss their jobs or their knowledge of another culture.
- If feasible, invite the deployed parent to communicate with the class. If not possible, encourage the class to write a letter to the parent.
- Maintain communication, to the extent possible, with the nondeployed parent about the student's class work.

BOX 4.2   BEST PRACTICES

RESOURCES FOR SCHOOL STAFF

Learn More about Military Families

Access the DoDEA's *Educational Partnership* website for information and resources for school leaders, military families, and military leaders: http://www.dodea.edu/Partnership/eferencesAndGuides.cfm.

Building Resilient Kids, developed and offered through the Military Child Initiative at Johns Hopkins School of Public Health: http://www.jhsph.edu/research/centers-and-institutes/military-child-initiative/

Stay Updated

Military Child Education Coalition: http://www.militarychild.org

Military Impacted Schools Association: http://militaryimpactedschoolsassociation.org/

Department of Defense Education Activity: http://www.dodea.edu

Direct Students and Families to Resources

Military OneSource: http://www.militaryonesource.com

Military Youth on the Move: http://apps.militaryonesource.mil/MOS/f?p=MYOM:HOME2:0

Student Online Achievement Resources: http://www.soarathome.org

Tutor.com for U.S. military families: http://www.tutor.com/military

- If concerned about the nondeployed parent's adjustment to the deployment, encourage his or her use of resources.
- Encourage parents to attend school activities and parent–teacher conferences.

Box 4.2 lists resources for school staff about military children and support for military families.

DEPLOYMENT

Since 9/11, the optempo of the military has increased significantly compared with the prior decade, particularly for the National Guard and Reserves. As a result, the number of children affected is larger than in prior conflicts since World War II (Committee on the Initial Assessment of Readjustment Needs of Military Personnel, Veterans, and Their Families; Board on the Health of Selected Populations; Institute of Medicine [Committee on the Initial Assessment of Readjustment Needs], 2010).

Over 1 million U.S. military children have experienced separation from their parents because of wars since 2001 (MacDermid Wadsworth, 2010). Combat deployment and the possibility of multiple deployments have been continuous factors in the lives of many military children, complicated by uncertainty of length and by parental injury or death or the threat of them (Cozza, 2009b). Box 4.3 illustrates that deployed parents, and grandparents, worry about maintaining their relationships with their children and their grandchildren.

Research prior to and since 9/11 suggests that deployments influence children's academic functioning, behavior, and psychological well-being (Sheppard, Malatras, & Israel, 2010).

> ### BOX 4.3   VOICES FROM THE FRONTLINE
> **REFLECTIONS OF A MILITARY GRANDPARENT**
>
> When I was in Iraq I held a monthly parent forum. Parents were worried their kids didn't know them. For some it's true. When a child is 5 and his mom or dad has been deployed three times that doesn't leave much time to spend together. Our grandchildren were ages 10, 4, and 2 when I deployed. I went from being active in their lives to talking with them during occasional calls and the mail. I worried, too.
>
> **Colonel Rick Campise, Col, USAF, BSC**
> *Commander, 559th Medical Group*

Studies on children and deployment undertaken in the 1990s suggested that symptoms of distress exhibited by children did not meet clinical significance (Committee on the Initial Assessment of Readjustment Needs, 2010). In many studies, the impact of deployment was small on the variables measured, yet statistically significant. Results of studies conducted in past 14 years are noting possible effects on children of multiple parental deployments and total number of months of deployment. Woven throughout studies is the recognition of the important role parental adjustment and relational processes such as parenting and communication has on children's well-being (MacDermid Wadsworth, Lester, Marini, Cozza, Sornborger, Strouse, & Beardslee, 2013).

Academics

Prior to OEF/OIF, studies of the effect of deployment on children's academic functioning either showed no effect or a slight decrease (Sheppard et al., 2010). For example, the math scores of children of deployed Army enlisted and officers showed a small 1–2 point decrease compared to scores of children whose military parent had not deployed. The largest decrease occurred for children who experience parental deployments over 3 months, total parental deployment of 7 or more months within the last 4 years, maternal deployment, and total maternal deployment of 7 or more months (Lyle, 2006).

More recent research suggests parental deployment has a modest negative affect on some children's and teen's academic functioning (Lester & Flake, 2013). A study of academic achievement of children in DoD schools from 2002 to 2006 whose active duty parent was in the Army (Engel, Gallagher, & Lyle, 2010) found similar effects as the study noted above (Lyle, 2006). The decreases in academic achievement were small, from less than 1% to 1.5% points, but significant. Decreases in test scores in math and science were greater than those for language, arts, social studies, and reading.

Of the military spouses responding to the 2012 Active Duty Spouse Survey who had a child in the household, 19% reported their child having academic problems and 16% reported their child exhibiting behavior problems at school (Dorvil & Pfieger, 2014). Similar results were found in a survey of 101 Army spouses. Fourteen percent reported one or more children having problems in school that included conflict with teachers, losing interest in school, and lower grades during a deployment (Flake, et al., 2009). A study sponsored by the National Military Family Association considered the academic engagement (e.g., arrive at school on time, complete homework) of 11- to 17-year-olds. Academic engagement was more problematic as children aged, when there was poorer quality of communication between the caregiver and youth, and when the caregiver reported poorer mental health (Chandra et al., 2011).

Chandra and colleagues conducted 24 focus groups of teachers, counselors, and administrative staff at 12 schools that served a high concentration of Army families assigned to one of two installations with high deployment rates (Chandra, Martin, Hawkins, & Richardson, 2010). They also conducted telephone interviews with 16 school staff members (i.e., teachers, counselors, and administrative staff) who worked in areas with higher numbers of National Guard and Reservists. What follows are themes from the interviews, although not every focus group or interviewee mentioned each theme.

Overall, school personnel noted that many military children were able to handle the stress of deployment well, yet some children had difficulty with functioning well at school. School personnel thought three points contributed to military children experiencing difficulty with deployment: when they were unsure of the length of the deployment, when they experienced increased stress at home, and when they perceived the parent at home had difficulty adjusting (Chandra et al., 2010). Moreover, school personnel concluded that parental deployment isolates children of National Guard and Reservists who may know few, if any, other children in their school with a deployed military parent. Some children's sadness and anger were apparent in classroom and peer interactions. Increased number of chores at home (e.g., helping with younger siblings more) and taking care of the nondeployed parent emotionally at times interfered with children's functioning at school. School personnel noted that depressed adult caregivers at home did not attend school activities, did not assist children with homework, and at times kept children at home "as a source of comfort" rather than sending them to school (p. 221). Although school personnel recognized the resilience of some children to do well in school after an initial adjustment period, they noted the toll multiple and extended deployments were having even on these children. In subsequent deployments children who demonstrated resilience during the first deployment became "less engaged in school work" and engaged in more risk-taking behaviors (p. 221). During the reintegration phase when the deployed parent returned, school personnel noticed that some children had difficulties in adjusting. Finally, school personnel saw school as a safe haven for those military children who experienced instability at home (Chandra et al., 2010).

Behavior and Psychological Well-Being

Studies of military children and deployment conducted during OEF/OIF have focused on preschool children (Chartrand, Frank, White, & Shope, 2008), school-age children, and teens (Chandra et al., 2011; Huebner & Mancini, 2005; Huebner, Mancini, Wilcox, Grass, & Grass, 2007) but not on infants and toddlers (Cozza, 2009a). The following sections address children's worry about parental safety during deployment, psychological distress and behavioral problems, parental factors influencing child adjustment during deployment, child maltreatment, and evidence of resilience and maturity.

Children's Worry about Parental Safety   Children under the age of 14 in the United States have lived during an era in which their country has been responding to terrorism and using its military on extended combat operations. Likewise, youth, who now are between the ages of 14 and 21, were toddlers, preschoolers, or first and second graders when the World Trade Center was attacked and the United States launched OEF and OIF. These events prompted, and may continue to prompt, civilian and military children to worry about their own and their loved ones' safety.

Military children worry about their parent's well-being when they are apart. Worry can be evident even during the predeployment phase. Very young children may show their stress by clinging more to parents, crying more, and resisting engaging in their daily eating and sleeping routines. Preschoolers often are concerned about practical matters such as where will mommy sleep or what will daddy eat and may become confused, angry, or sad when they ask their parent to stay home but their parent leaves on deployment anyway. Their stress is manifested in regression to earlier behaviors, becoming aggressive or demanding, and behaving in attention-seeking ways (Lincoln, Swift, & Shorteno-Fraser, 2008).

School-age children can become very concerned about their parent's physical safety when "going to war." They may express volatile emotions, have trouble sleeping, be distracted by worry, and have difficulty focusing on school work (Lincoln et al., 2008).

Teens are clearly knowledgeable about the possible injury and death of a parent deployed to a combat zone and media accounts of combat and danger in theater sustain this awareness (Huebner & Mancini, 2005). They may act out, play "cool," and stop activities they once enjoyed (Lincoln et al., 2008). Although phone calls, e-mails, and face-to-face video calls can momentarily reassure children, once contact ends, uncertainty can reappear (Huebner et al., 2007).

How worries about parental safety can influence adolescents' psychological well-being and behaviors is illustrated in two studies. One study engaged teens in focus groups (Huebner et al., 2007), and the other used a telephone interview design (Chandra et al., 2011).

In the first study, 107 adolescents between the ages 12 and 18, attending a free camp for military children experiencing parental deployment, participated in focus groups to discuss their experiences. About a third of the teens described signs consistent with depression (e.g., losing interest in activities, isolation, changes in eating and sleeping) and higher anxiety (e.g., ruminating on the deployed parent's safety and daily life). These signs, along with changes in roles and responsibilities and increased emotionality in the family added up to stressful situations for these youth. The 27 youth who described getting angry and lashing out often also described trying to hide their emotions in order to protect the nondeployed parent, siblings, or friends (Huebner et al., 2007).

The second study likewise found evidence of increased anxiety among 1507 military adolescents who were between 11 and 17 years old. Of these adolescents 30% reported symptoms of anxiety, a higher percent than what has been found in another, albeit somewhat younger, youth sample (Chandra et al., 2011).

In Box 4.4, Dr. Patricia Lester notes the importance of parents being tuned into the concerns and worries of their children. Rather than diminishing children's fears, avoiding discussions of children's possible worries and questions can actually magnify fear and feed anxiety. For example, one of the authors of this textbook recalls a situation during peacetime in which a mother sought guidance because her 6-year-old sobbed and would

---

BOX 4.4   BEST PRACTICES

SUPPORTING CHILDREN BY SUPPORTING THEIR FAMILIES

Creating a shared story about deployment experiences and having that story to share builds resilience of families and their children.

Today's military families are experiencing understandable reactions to the challenges they face. The stress of wartime and multiple deployments reverberates within families.

We created FOCUS to support children and teens by enhancing the strengths of families in areas of emotional regulation (identifying and understanding emotions, communication, problem solving, goal setting, and managing reminders of deployment and combat stress). Families talk, play, and work with resiliency trainers to create their family's unique story of deployment experiences, challenges, and successes.

One of our challenges is always how to make concepts concrete and specific that children at different ages can understand. For example, there is a lot of discussion in sessions about how to use a calendar so deployment isn't one big overwhelming chunk of time for children. It's complicated because there is often uncertainty about return dates. So our resiliency trainers work together with families to come up with ideas that are not linked to a specific day.

A little boy with a Marine Corps dad liked to wear his dad's boots. At one session, the family brought in Dad's boots and outlined them. They then made a map from their home to Iraq. Each month the little boy put down the outline of his dad's boots on a path showing Dad coming home. It allowed him to mark time and see it pass concretely.

Children have questions about danger and risk. When a child asks, "Will my dad (or mom) die?" it can be hard to know what to say. Many parents—like most of us—try to avoid questions like this. So we do lots of talking together with families to help parents know what to say. A family with a younger child (age 3–7) might bring in their service member's flak vest and helmet and talk about training and how the deployed parents' buddies will help keep him safe.

As a child gets to be older, the conversation shifts. The parent who is at home might acknowledge, "I get worried, too," then share ideas of what helps them when they are worried and suggest, "Let's make a plan together about what we can do when we get worried."

Over the years, we've learned a lot about resilience from military families. One of my favorite stories is about a family in Okinawa who came in with a 4-year-old. When the child was 2, his dad deployed. It was a tough time, in part because Dad had always given him his "special good-night kiss." Mom couldn't do it right. This time the family came in advance of Dad's next deployment saying, "We want to make this transition smoother."

Dr. Patricia Lester
Director of Family Resiliency Training for Military Families (FOCUS)

not be consoled whenever the family discussed the upcoming, routine deployment. She was encouraged to ask her son what he thought deployment meant. After listening to their son, the mother and father realized that he had heard the family and neighbors talk about a recent accident a board a deployed ship in which dozens of sailors had died. As a result, their son equated deployment with ships exploding and sailors dying. Given this understanding of deployment, his reactions were justified and warranted, particularly when the adults around him seemed nonchalant about what he perceived to be a clear possibility of his father dying at sea. Once the parents realized what their son thought and feared, they explained what deployment was, that the explosion on the other ship was atypical, and the ways in which the ship's Captain and crew made sure everyone aboard was safe during deployment. The parents reported that after this conversation their son no longer displayed signs of panic when discussing the upcoming deployment and, when the deployment began, displayed an appropriate level of sadness.

Psychological Distress and Behavioral Problems   Studies of children who experienced parental deployment in peacetime and wartime prior to OEF/OIF indicated that children exhibited increases in externalizing and internalizing symptoms, including depression and anxiety, but that they typically did not need clinical assistance (Cozza,

Chun, & Polo, 2005). Studies of military children since 9/11 indicate parental deployment is associated with emotional and behavioral stress and risk-taking as well as struggles at school (MacDermid Wadsworth et al., 2013). Multiple parental deployments are associated with problematic behaviors in children (DASD, 2015).

Young children, who could be separated from a deployed parent for a length of time that represents one-third or half of their lives, may exhibit confusion, fear, anxiety, and clinginess (Barker & Berry, 2009). In a study focused on the adjustment of preschoolers (Chartrand et al., 2008), researchers examined parent and teacher reports about children, ages 1.5–5, enrolled in Marine Corps CDC. They found that 3- to 5-year-olds with a deployed parent (but not 1.5- to 3-year-olds) displayed more behavioral problems than those of the same age whose parent was not deployed. In another study of 57 Army families with children under the age of 4, parents reported an increase in behavioral problems during deployment. Although young children showed confusion and distress when the deployed parent returned home, the majority of parents indicated that problematic behaviors disappeared within 3 weeks; however, 31% of children showed continuing attachment problems past this time. Parents of these children listed one or two behaviors that persisted, such as children not staying in their own bed, not wanting comfort from the returning parent, not wanting the returning parent to leave the home, or preferring the other parent or caregiver in lieu of the returning parent (Barker & Berry, 2009). It may be that young children are developmentally more vulnerable to parental separation because they are establishing an internal working model of attachment (MacDermid Wadsworth, 2013).

Deployment is associated with an increase in the number of outpatient medical visits for mental and behavioral health care for military children. An examination of over 642,000 medical records of 3- to 8-year-old children of active duty personnel during fiscal years 2006 and 2007 indicated that there was an 11% increase in outpatient medical visits during a parental deployment. Diagnoses of behavioral disorders increased 18% and stress disorders increased 19% with a deployed parent. During the same time, however, there was an 11% decrease in outpatient visits for routine care or for physical complaints such as colds. Rates were increased for children of male service members compared with children of female service members, for children of married parents compared with children of single parents, and for older than younger children. Researchers suggest that these results may be explained by mothers being more familiar with children's typical behaviors versus fathers or extended family members in the case of single parents, and by older children having a greater range of emotional and behavioral responses. Girls and boys did not differ in the number of visits (Gorman, Eide, & Hisle-Gorman, 2010). A second study of healthcare records of more than 300,000 5 to 17 year olds of Active Duty Army personnel showed increases in diagnoses related to stress and adjustment, depression, and pediatric behavioral problems for children who experienced parental deployment. The effects were larger for children experiencing longer parental deployments (12 months or more) compared to shorter parental deployments (1-11 months), boys than girls, and older than younger children (Mansfield, Kaufman, Engle, & Gaynes, 2011).

Voices From the Frontline

DISENTANGLING THE IMPACT OF DEPLOYMENT

I've been a youth and family researcher for years. I started studying military youth and families 5 years ago. Lots of what I'd learned over the years about children and families was transferrable. Although military youth have some unique experiences, it is also important to remember that they are children and youth first and follow the same developmental milestones. That information can help any researcher or provider in working with these families.

Visiting military families on installations and talking with them by phone gave me insight into their experiences. Aside from deployment and reintegration, these include frequent moves and transitions to new homes, schools, and communities that can be a source of difficulty but also a source of strength.

We still have relatively little information on the experiences of military families. Our first project at RAND [a nonprofit institution focused on research and analysis] was Children on the Home Front. The National Military Family Association funded us to explore the lives of military youth. In the summer and fall of 2007, we did a pilot study in which we surveyed youth attending the association's Operation Purple summer camps and their parent or primary caregiver at home. The next year, we conducted a larger study, with 1500 families, to assess the impact of parental deployment and reintegration and followed youth and families over a year.

We've also worked with the U.S. Army to learn what teachers and other school staff see in the many hours they spend each day with military and other youth. Recently, the Department of Defense has funded us to look at how families from all services and components fare before, during, and after a specific period of deployment. Unlike studies before, this research will allow us to disentangle the specific effect of deployment from other life experiences and to surface the factors that contribute to family resilience.

As we've been studying the functioning and well-being of military youth and teens, we have learned a lot about how they are handling deployment. We assessed youth anxiety symptom levels and found that one-third reported symptoms in the moderate or elevated range as opposed to 15% of civilian kids. Colleagues working with younger children have found the same thing. The more months a parent was deployed, the more symptoms of anxiety were reported.

We've also found a strong relationship between the mental health of the nondeployed parent and child. This is true in the literature about civilian families, too. In military families, we see that parents (or other caregivers) at home often put themselves last. The fact that the challenges of the parents impact children has led us to recommend that the at-home parent also receive support throughout deployment. We also recommend that we continue to study military families as systems and examine how the experiences of each family member influence others in the family.

If you are going to work with military families:

- Bring the principles and knowledge you have gained working with other families.
- Consider the strengths that each family brings and try to build on these assets to help families confront the stress of deployment.
- Get a little smart about resources available to families. If you work in a community with an installation, don't be intimidated. Make a connection and learn what resources are available. And remember that most families don't live on installations—they live in the community. They are your neighbors, and your support means a lot.

To work with or study military youth and families you don't have to know the entire lexicon or military structure. You do have to listen, learn about, and understand their experience.

Anita Chandra, Dr.PH, Behavioral Scientist
Manager, Behavioral and Social Sciences Group, RAND Corporation

Chandra and colleagues, who conducted the telephone interview study of military adolescents referred to earlier, asked both adolescents and their nondeployed caregivers questions about challenges, behaviors, and emotional responses. The researchers found more reported difficulties and problematic behavior during deployment and reintegration among the middle and older adolescence groups compared to the younger youth and among girls (Chandra et al., 2011). According to caregivers, youth experienced more challenges during deployment and reintegration as the total number of parental deployments increased; however, data provided by the youth did not show this outcome. Caregivers who reported poorer mental health also indicated more child emotional difficulties and family functioning problems; youth of these caregivers reported greater anxiety and emotional difficulties. Finally, compared with a 2001 national sample of children in the United States, military children in this sample exhibited significantly more emotional and behavioral difficulties. Results of a survey of seventh, ninth, and eleventh graders in California school district showed having a military parent decreased the odds of positive well-being. Experiencing the deployment or multiple deployments of a parent or sibling increased the likelihood of feeling sad or hopeless and the likelihood of depressive symptoms for ninth and eleventh graders. Experiencing two or more deployments was associated with increased odds of suicidal ideation for students in these two grades (Cederbaum, et al., 2014).

A study of Army and Marine Corps families explored the link between parent combat deployment and parental distress on the behavioral and emotional adjustment of their school-aged children who were between 6 and 12 years old (Lester et al., 2010). The children either had a currently deployed parent or a recently returned parent. The military children in this sample did not differ from community norms for girls and boys in depression scores or in internalizing or externalizing symptoms. They did, however, show significantly higher levels of anxiety; 32% of children with a recently returned parent and 25% of children with a currently deployed parent had anxiety symptoms in the clinical range. Girls whose active duty parent was currently deployed had a higher externalizing score than girls with a recently returned parent, whereas boys were opposite. Boys with a recently returned parent showed higher externalizing scores than boys with a currently deployed parent. The total number of combat months predicted depression and externalizing behaviors, but not internalizing behaviors, in children.

Sixty-five youths from grades 4–8 who attended a charter school for military children located near a Naval Air Stations-Joint Reserve Base and their parents participated in a study on adjustment and coping strategies (Morris & Age, 2009). Better adjustment was associated with higher levels of effortful control (i.e., being able to pay attention and inhibit or use behavioral responses as strategies to regulate emotions and behavior) and perceived maternal support. The study also indicated that compared to a community sample, military youth, at least during an extended period of wartime, are at risk for conduct problems (Morris & Age, 2009). In the study of 101 Army spouses noted earlier, 32% percent reported children exhibiting enough symptoms to place them in a high-risk category. High levels of parenting stress and perceived lack of military support predicted parental reports of increased problems in psychosocial functioning. Perceived support by the military, community, or religious organizations was associated with less parenting stress and fewer children in a high-risk category (Flake et al., 2009).

Military spouses who responded to the 2012 Active Duty Spouse Survey were asked to answer questions about the child in their household whose birthday month was closest to their own. Fifty-two percent of the children selected were male and the average age of child selected was 6.5 years. Children who showed greater insecurity than the overall average had experienced a parental deployment in the past 12 months. Thirteen percent of spouses indicated their child coped poorly, 60% coped well, and 26% coped neither poorly or well to the deployment. Twenty-eight percent reported their child was angry about military requirements and 24% reported that their child exhibited behavioral problems at

BOX 4.5   TIPS FROM THE FRONTLINE

MAINTAINING THE PSYCHOLOGICAL PRESENCE OF THE MILITARY PARENT FOR CHILDREN

- Phone calls, webcams, e-mails, and letters are important in maintaining psychological presence and emotional connection among family members. However, they are not always possible, particularly according to a child's schedule. So, children need other ways to maintain connection that they can access when they feel a need to be close to the deployed parent.
- Children benefit from concrete items such as photographs, videos, and audio messages that can be prepared before the deployment. Some children like deployment dolls that have a clear plastic cover on the head where a photo of a parent can be placed, a life-sized poster board photo of a parent, or a stuffed toy replica of their deployed parent.
- Younger children can watch a video, DVD, or digital movie of the deployed parent reading their favorite books and doing everyday tasks such as shaving, putting on makeup, washing dishes, helping to pick up toys, and mowing the yard.
- Smell can also bring a person to mind; service members can give their child a T-shirt, hat, or scarf that "smells like" mom or dad. This article of clothing could be placed on a stuffed animal for younger children to cuddle.
- Family and service members can share an activity while apart, such as reading the same book or doing the same puzzle book.
- The deployed parent can leave "surprises" for children to find throughout the deployment.

home. However, approximately 60% reported their child becoming closer to family members, accepting responsibilities, and being proud of having a military parent. Having a parent deployed at the time of the survey or in the past year increased the likelihood of the spouse reporting that the child exhibited anger or behavioral problems and decreased the likelihood of the spouse reporting that the child accepted responsibility (Dorvil & Pflieger, 2014).

Parental Factors   Family and parental factors influence children's lives and how they cope with the stress of deployment (Sheppard et al., 2010). How well children adjust to the stressor of deployment and to many other stressors depends to a great extent upon the responses of their parents. Parents who respond with an attitude that conveys a sense of security and confidence and with effective coping strategies serve as "a powerful protective factor" in the lives of their children. Parents who cope with the stressor and feel able to cope transmit to their children a repertoire of effective coping behaviors (MacDermid et al., 2008; Walsh, 2007).

Voices From the Frontline

FACILITATING A PREDEPLOYMENT PROGRAM FOR FAMILIES

"I love you."

When I worked at a Navy Family Services Center (now called a Fleet and Family Support Center), predeployment programs for families often occurred aboard ships so children would know where their mother or father was going to live during the deployment. The families toured the ship to see where the deploying parent would sleep, eat, and work. They often had dinner aboard ship for children to feel reassured that their parent would be cared for while they were separated. Afterward, while parents remained on the mess deck (i.e., the cafeteria) to discuss typical reactions of children to deployment and ways to support children during deployment, we divided the children and teens into small groups by ages and took them to different areas of the ship for their own age-appropriate program centered around normalizing feelings and identifying positive steps to take when feeling sad or lonely during deployment.

I remember facilitating a group of 6- and 7-year-olds. During one activity in which the children were drawing pictures of feelings we asked them, "What would you like your dad to know or do with you before he leaves on deployment?" (At this time, this ship only accommodated male service members.) Children often said play a game, go to an amusement park, go swimming, or see a movie as did these children, except one. One 7-year-old boy said nothing. About 20 minutes later after the group was involved in another activity, he motioned to me with his finger to lean over to him. He whispered in my ear, "I want my daddy to tell me he loves me."

During the final part of the program, the children and children's group facilitators returned to the mess deck. The children sat with their parents and the facilitators reported back to the large group of parents, in general and using no names, what the children did and said during their group time. When we reported that the 6- and 7-year-olds wanted to hear their fathers say, "I love you" to them, the mess deck went silent. The wisdom and the need of a Navy child for his daddy to "tell me that he loves me," educated all of us. From then on, "say 'I love you'" became my first message from children to deploying parents.

Karen Blaisure
Coauthor of this textbook and Professor of Family Studies at Western Michigan University

Positive parent–child relationships and family adjustment influence child adjustment (Lincoln et al., 2008). Studies conducted during OEF and OIF have demonstrated the close association between maternal or caregiver adjustment and children and youth adjustment to deployment (Chandra et al., 2011).

The study of Army and Marine Corps children and parents described earlier found that parental distress and children's level of distress were linked. The at-home mothers and the active duty parents (primarily fathers) had clinically significant differences in global distress, anxiety, and depression compared with community norms. At-home civilian mother distress predicted depression and externalizing and internalizing behaviors in children. PTSD symptoms in active duty parents predicted depression and internalizing and externalizing symptoms in children; and the greater the symptoms in the parent, the greater the symptoms in the child. Depression and anxiety symptoms in active duty parents predicted internalizing symptoms in children (Lester et al., 2010).

Multiple and dangerous deployments and the stress associated with them can result in the reduction of **parental efficacy**, that is parents' availability and effectiveness in caring for their children. One way this stress can be exhibited in some military families is in child maltreatment (Cozza, 2009a).

Since 2001, studies have found an increase in child maltreatment of military children during deployment. A state-level study of military families in Texas where there are numerous military installations showed an increased rate of child maltreatment before and after the first large-scale deployment after 9/11 (Rentz et al., 2007). Research on Army families with one or more instances of substantiated child maltreatment found the overall rate of child maltreatment was 42% greater during combat deployments compared to periods of time when soldiers were not deployed (Gibbs, Martin, Kupper, & Johnson, 2007). Of the types of substantiated child maltreatment, child neglect was the most common (Gibbs et al., 2007; McCarroll, Fan, Newby, & Ursano, 2008). In the 1990s, Army families experienced a decline in substantiated child neglect; however, the rate in 2004, after the initiation of OEF/OIF, approximated 1991 rates (McCarroll et al., 2008). Although researchers have not reached a consensus on how rates of child maltreatment in military families compare with nonmilitary families, the study of military families in Texas from 2000 to 2003 showed the rate of child maltreatment was higher for nonmilitary families (Rentz et al., 2007).

A major way to promote children's positive adjustment to deployment then is to support parents in acquisition and use of positive coping strategies themselves (DASD, 2015). Given the knowledge that deployment and reintegration are stressful times for families, additional prevention efforts should be focused on increasing positive parent–child relationships and family adjustment all along the deployment cycle (Chandra et al., 2011).

Results of focus groups with 71 military fathers from 14 military installations across the world suggest multiple messages to share with military families about father involvement. Leaving most of the parenting to wives, some military fathers become visitors in their children's lives by pulling back and having a "softened" role as a parent (Willerton, Schwarz, MacDermid Wadsworth, & Oglesby, 2011). Others, feeling guilty over not being the ideal involved father, may use permissive parenting practices. However, fathers can expand their ideas on involvement in their children's lives by not equating "good fathering" only with a physical presence but by focusing on quality time and managing their time well to facilitate involvement with children when home; planning and thinking creatively before deployment about ways to be psychologically present when deployed; and considering how to best reunite and resume day-to-day parenting with their children after deployment (Willerton, Schwarz, et al., 2011). Better connections between deployed parents and their children result in fewer child behavioral and attachment problems, and better reconnection once reunited (DASD, 2015).

Overall   The research on deployment and children suggests that as a group military children are resilient; studies are not finding a majority of them having academic, behavioral problems, or psychological symptoms rising to clinical levels. However, for some military children, parental deployments, particularly combat deployment and multiple deployments, appear to be taking a toll in terms of academic outcomes, worry, internalizing and externalizing symptoms, anxiety, and depression. In summary, risk factors for problematic adjustment to deployment include combat deployments; multiple deployments; total number of deployed months (Chandra et al., 2011; Engel et al., 2010; and Lester et al., 2010; Lyle, 2006); nondeployed caregiver distress (Chandra et al., 2011); deployed parent post-traumatic stress symptoms, PTSD, and other mental health problems (Lester, Leskin, et al., 2011; Lester, Mogil, et al., 2011); and caregiver–youth communication (Chandra et al., 2011). Factors that promote resilience include positive parent–child relationships and communication, social support, overall family adjustment, parental emotional well-being, and effective parental coping skills (Lester et al., 2010; MacDermid et al., 2008).

It is important to note that multiple contexts beyond the family system affect military children and may contribute, or diminish, their coping skills. As noted earlier, schools and teachers play important roles in the lives of military children. Likewise, other interlocking systems including school, health and mental health care, spiritual/religious, and community affect children's wellbeing and functioning (Lester & Flake, 2013; MacDermid Wadsworth et al., 2013). To better understand military children and family outcomes and trajectories, researchers recommend applying theories and frameworks built on systemic thinking, such as ecological and attachment theories, risk and resilience perspectives, and life course perspectives (Lester & Flake, 2013; MacDermid Wadsworth, 2013; MacDermid et al., 2013; Riggs & Riggs, 2012).

Leaders and service providers within these systems can be aware of the impact of multiple and long deployments, the deployment spiral, and the interconnection within and among systems on children's wellbeing in order to encourage development of capabilities and processes associated with resilience (Lester, Leskin, et al., 2011; Lester, Mogil, et al., 2011; Walsh, 2002). For example, providers can and do offer online, group education, family support groups, and one-on-one counseling to families in order for them to prepare for both the emotional side of deployment and reintegration and the practical side (e.g., financial and legal documents, communication plans, budgets); gain information and guidance on parenting; address family stress and find help for overwhelming emotions such as sadness, depression, anxiety, or anger; develop a shared meaning of deployments; promote close family relationships, goal setting, and problem solving; enhance family communication and address family conflict; and develop strong social support systems for all family members, including children and adolescents (Chandra et al., 2011; Gewirtz, Erbes, Polusny, Forgatch, & DeGarmo, 2011; Lester, Leskin, et al., 2011; MacDermid et al., 2008; Morris & Age, 2009). Service providers can identify and encourage parents to provide social support for one another. Those who work with children can notice changes in their appearance, attitude, or behaviors and then talk with parents to determine if they need assistance with self-care or with obtaining help for their children.

PARENTAL INJURY AND DEATH

As noted earlier, reintegration with a parent returning from deployment can be stressful for children. Combat-related injuries, both physical and psychological, pose additional challenges for family members, including children who must adapt to a new understanding of their parent (Gorman, Fitzgerald, & Blow, 2010).

Although few studies exist that examine children's adjustment to parental injury, medical and social service professionals who work with families of injured service members indicate that children will take their cue from their parents (Cozza, Chun, & Polo, 2005). Children benefit from developmentally appropriate information about the injury whether visible or invisible, reassurance of the parent's love for the child, encouragement to ask questions, and guidance on how to interact with the parent (e.g., "Mommy cannot give you a piggyback ride because she hurt her back, but she can play frisbee with you," or "sometimes Daddy forgets things so we write down what we will do tomorrow to help Daddy remember"). Parents may benefit from learning how to communicate with their children about injuries, particularly if the injury has interfered with the ability to interact sensitively. Resources for families can be found in Chapters 11 and 12.

Nonvisible injuries such as depression, anxiety, and posttraumatic stress symptoms may be particularly challenging for children. For example, a study of National Guard fathers demonstrated a link between increases in postdeployment PTSD symptoms and lower levels of effective parenting as reported by the service members (Gewirtz, Polusny, DeGarmo, Khaylis, & Erbes, 2010). Evidence points to PTSD negatively affecting parent–child relationship parenting through emotional numbing/avoidance (Ruscio, Weathers, King, & King, 2002). The symptom of hyperarousal may also play a factor. For example, service members or veterans with PTSD symptoms may withdraw from family interactions, do less monitoring of children, be less involved with children, and exhibit volatile emotions when stressed and when in conflict with children members (Gewirtz et al., 2010).

When a parent is first injured, the parent–child attachment, with either parent or both, may be challenged by separations due to hospitalizations perhaps at great distances from the child's home, medical treatments, doctor and therapy visits, and rehabilitation. The child's developmental needs may be overlooked to a small or large degree, perhaps placing the child at risk for psychological distress, and problems with attachment, regulation of emotions, behavior, health, and well-being. Social support for the family improves the quality of life for its members and supports child development. Training, resources, and support can increase rehabilitation professionals' ability to involve children in the rehabilitation process (Gorman, Fitzgerald, & Blow, 2010). More information about children in combat-wounded families is presented in Chapter 8 and ideas for helping their families is presented in Chapter 13.

Approximately 7000 service members have died while serving in OEF, OIF, OND, and OIR since 9/11 (DoD, 2015). Yet we know very little about how children adjust to the death of a military parent (Holmes, Rauch, & Cozza, 2013). In general, however, bereavement is a risk factor for children developing emotional or behavior problems (Cozza et al., 2005).

The National Child Traumatic Stress Network (2008a, 2008b) has published a series of manuals for medical providers, educators, and parents on traumatic grief in children. These publications remind us that children may show grief in different and multiple ways. They may regress in behaviors, show sadness, become fearful, develop problems in school, notice "aches and pains," be moody, show anger and irritation, withdraw, and/or isolate themselves. They may "not be themselves" as they do uncharacteristic behaviors.

Young children whose parents die while deployed may not initially understand the permanence of death. They often seek the comfort of their closest caregivers and need extra attention and reassurance. School-age children may ask lots of questions about their parent's death and about death in general. Teens may try to hide their emotions (National Child Traumatic Stress Network, 2008a, 2008b).

Some children may develop traumatic grief, that is, exhibiting symptoms of posttraumatic stress whether initially or months following a parent's death, given it is unexpected, sudden, or traumatic. These symptoms can include children experiencing intrusive thoughts about the death or reliving the details of the death, if known; avoiding conversation, activities, or reminders of the parent or the parent's death; and startling easily, being "on alert," and becoming nervous, jumpy, distracted, and angry. If symptoms persist, appear after an initial stable period, or they disrupt daily life (e.g., attending school, playing with friends, participating in or enjoying activities), counseling may be appropriate (National Child Traumatic Stress Network, 2008a, 2008b).

Given the public nature of a military death during wartime, children and other family members may experience unexpected or unwanted intrusions while they are mourning. Families have a right to as much privacy as they wish, including privacy from the media. Children who hear someone say that their "parent died 'needlessly' in an 'unnecessary' war may find it much harder to accept and integrate that death than [children] whose parent's death is considered 'noble' or 'heroic.'...[O]lder teenagers may have their own opinions and feelings about the war, and these may either ease or complicate their grief" (National Child Traumatic Stress Network, 2008b, p. 4).

Following the death of a loved one, parents can assist their children by providing a sense of security by being physically and emotionally close and predictable; being patient; "listening" to what children's behaviors are saying they need; encouraging expression of feelings; knowing that grief and other feelings can get mixed up; and being aware of possible reminders of the death at unexpected times. Parents can also promote positive adjustment by supporting children's connection to the person who has died by talking and looking at photographs and videos; providing age-appropriate explanations; spending time with each child and considering their individual needs; and informing other adults about the children's experiences. Parents may need to advocate for children at school; encourage children's involvement in a project or organization, possibly one related to the interests of the person who died; and encourage bonds with other children by attending camps or support groups for children who are grieving (National Child Traumatic Stress Network, 2008a).

Death of a service member brings other changes in military children's lives. If living on a military installation, the family will need to move within a year and the move may also bring a change in schools. With a death of a parent comes a possibility of losing touch with that parent's side of the family. Finally, the remaining parent will need to support and guide children as they realize the loved one will not be there for small and major milestones in life (National Child Traumatic Stress Network, 2008a).

Adults are also encouraged to care for themselves by seeking social support; exercising, eating healthy foods, and sleeping adequately; showing feelings; and modeling healthy coping (e.g., "I miss Daddy right now, that's why I'm crying. Let's take a walk together because I like being with you."). They are also encouraged to seek professional support if necessary (National Child Traumatic Stress Network, 2008a).

The risk of injury and death of a parent is a stressor known by many military children. They may also experience changes brought about by relocation and separation from a parent due to long duty hours, TDYs, or deployments. Positive family dynamics, social support, and finding meaning from such adversities can make a difference in the resilience of children. If you work with children directly, you know the importance of acceptance, listening, and guidance in supporting them through life's minor and major stressors. Likewise, by building trusting, responsive relationships with adult family members, you may have a positive influence on their ability to support their children. As a helping professional, what you know and what you say and do matters to families.

SUMMARY

- Nearly 2 million children in the United States have a parent who is serving in the Active or Reserve Component of the military.
- Even in the face of relocations, separations, and risks of injury and death, the majority of military families adapt, and their resilience is evident.
- Studies are needed to identify the particular strengths families use to overcome stressful situations.
- Children who grow up in the military culture on average move every 2–3 years. Evidence suggests that children's adjustment to moving is influenced by family cohesiveness and time at a current residence.
- Military child care includes CDCs, FCC providers, SAC programs, and resource and referral services.
- Military children attend civilian schools with a small or large presence of other military children, and DoDEA schools. Overall, military children attending DoDEA schools compare very favorably to civilian children.
- Teachers and other school staff members play important roles in supporting military children during relocation and parental deployments.
- Combat deployment and multiple deployments have been continuous factors in the lives of many military children, complicated by uncertainty of length and by parental injury or death or the threat of them.
- Evidence exists of children's positive adjustment to deployment as well as evidence of the "wear and tear" of multiple deployments, complicated deployments, and compromised parenting.
- When a parent is injured, the parent–child attachment may be challenged and a child's developmental needs may be overlooked. Social support for the family can promote attachment and positive child development.
- A parent and close adults can provide important emotional support and guidance to children whose parent or other loved one has died.
- Professionals who work with military families can focus interventions and supports toward decreasing identified risk factors and enhancing protective factors related to children's adjustment.

EXERCISES

1. Investigate academic databases and websites for more information about third culture kids. For example, the U.S. Department of State's Family Liaison Office has a webpage on third culture kids, at http://www.state.gov/m/dghr/flo/c21995.htm.

2. If you live near a school district with a high percentage of military children or near a DoDEA school, interview two elementary or secondary teachers about their experiences with military children in their classes. How do their experiences compare or contrast with those described in this chapter? What tips do they have for supporting military children?

3. Prepare tip sheets for extended family members about children and deployment and how to support children of different ages when their parent or another loved one deploys. Be sure to include tips on how to support a child who lives at a distance from grandparents, aunts, uncles, and cousins.

4. Identify local programs and support systems for children whose parents serve in the Reserve Component (i.e., National Guard and Reserve).

5. Talk with a teenager who has grown up in the military culture. Prepare topics to discuss based on information presented in this chapter. For example, "many military teens will have attended multiple schools by your age. Tell me your experiences about attending school." Compare what you learned from this teenager with what you have studied.

5

Ways of Thinking About Family Stress and Resilience

In Chapter 5, you will

- Meet Froma Walsh, a clinical researcher and practitioner, who draws on stress and resilience theories in working with families.
- Learn how individual and family stress, coping, and resilience are conceptualized.
- Discover how stress theories and applied models of stress and resilience help us better understand and support military families.
- Practice applying concepts to a case study example of a military family.
- Gain insights into how the military is using a focus on resilience to guide prevention and treatment of combat and operational stress in service members and families.

Meet

Froma Walsh, MSW, PhD, Codirector,
Chicago Center for Family Health, University of Chicago

All of my work has been directed to understand how families best support each other in overcoming adversity. My family resilience approach expands the mental health field's focus on symptomatic individuals to facilitate the family's powerful role in their recovery. In military families, like all families, serious crises or an overload of stress can break down their functioning. It can happen to any family in situations of trauma, tragic loss, disruptive transitions, or chronic disabling conditions. Although some individual lives and bonds are shattered, what is remarkable is the potential for individual and family resilience—the capacity to rebound—and even grow stronger—when family members pull together as a team to master their challenges. Families hold the keys to resilience.

My conviction in the potential for family resilience goes back to my own childhood experience. My parents faced devastating losses and ongoing financial hardship, yet they supported each other and loved me well, encouraging me always to reach for the best. My father had a disability and experienced crushing disappointments, yet he didn't lose his "can-do" spirit. When a fire destroyed our apartment building, we lost everything and were homeless for a time. The kindness and generosity of others were "lifelines" in our recovery. Our adversity taught us valuable lessons: that we may not be able to control bad things that happen in life, but our resilient response is what matters. And that resilience is nurtured by caring relationships—with our loved ones and with our communities.

As I grew up, people commented on my resilience, but assumed I was strong despite my troubled family situation. Our society has a myth of "the rugged individual." We tend to credit individuals for success and blame families for problems. Early resilience research focused on individual character traits for hardiness and assumed that distressed families were hopelessly dysfunctional. But my own resilience was due to the strength my family rallied through hard times. And as resilience research advanced, it became clear that a systemic perspective is required, recognizing family influences in resilience.

The family is the primary resource in the recovery when someone has suffered trauma, with physical and/or psychological wounds. By strengthening the family, we build "lifelines"—supportive bonds for healing and resilience. We tap positive resources in the kinship network, including children and grandparents, aunts and uncles, and godparents. We recruit positive role models and mentors, draw out stories of resilience in overcoming past adversity to inspire best efforts, and we encourage important family members to support each other. More than coping, or just surviving trauma or stressful conditions, gaining resilience enables families and their members to thrive. And they become more resourceful in meeting future challenges.

Most research funding is directed at problems—we need to redirect attention from how families fail to how they can succeed. It is important to see families not as damaged, but as challenged by adversity, with the potential to repair and rebuild their lives. We have much to learn from families that overcome adversity to inform our efforts to help those who are struggling. To understand military families—and all families—it takes both large-scale quantitative studies and small case studies in a mixed-methods approach. My research-informed Family Resilience Framework identifies nine key processes that practitioners can facilitate for family resilience. They can be applied to help families rebound from serious crises, to navigate disruptive transitions, and to cope effectively with prolonged hardship or disabling conditions. Our Center has developed a range of programs and modalities from brief counseling to multifamily groups.

I've learned the most in my career from the families I have worked with—seeing the extraordinary resilience of ordinary families when faced with adversity. This practice is about tapping into families' own potential for healing and positive growth. Through appreciative inquiry, we draw out their sparks of resilience. This approach doesn't ignore or minimize difficulties or simply tell a family "don't worry; be happy." We start by listening to their stories to understand their struggle and bring out their best efforts and strengthen their bonds. When hopes and dreams have been shattered, we help them to envision new possibilities for personal and relational fulfillment. Helping professionals can benefit from this approach, too. Hernandez found that therapists who work this way gain "vicarious resilience" and are less likely to suffer burnout. Clients' stories and efforts, their hope, courage, endurance, and triumph of the human spirit can restore our spirit in our work and in our own lives.

INTRODUCTION

The goal of this chapter is to help students and new professionals in human services form a strong grounding in theories about stress and resilience that have clear connections to practice with military families and their individual members in multiple settings. As Dr. Walsh stated, the theories that guide our practice determine whether we look for and see only damage or if we see those "sparks of resilience" that propel families to overcome challenges.

You may have heard the descriptive proverb "Sometimes one can't see the forest for the trees," meaning that people sometimes get bogged down in details and lose sight of the larger picture that shapes, supports, and constrains those details. This chapter is designed to give you a good foundation of the quickly growing "forest" of stress and resilience research and to reinforce this knowledge through practice exercises where you can apply concepts of stress, coping, and resilience to examples of individuals and their families.

The field of stress and resilience research and theory spans multiple disciplines and has a strong connection to reflections on human reactions in war contexts during the nineteenth and twentieth centuries (Hobfoll, 1998). Indeed, two of the more familiar concepts derived from this connection are battle/combat fatigue and shell shock, which have, in turn, framed much of the present-day study of PTSD. But there is much more to the study of stress and resilience than a focus on psychosocial outcomes to traumatic events. Events and circumstances do not have to be traumatic to be stressful. As readers interested in gaining a deeper understanding of military family life, theories about stress and resilience are valuable tools for a variety of human service professions. These theories help us understand stress and resilience processes, assess individuals' or families' strengths and challenges in the face of adverse circumstances, and give us guidance as to best practices for intervention and prevention.

You can think of the forest as being the wide-ranging and multidisciplinary study of stress and resilience. Each discipline occupies space within the forest and may be thought of as groves or particular stands of trees that share a common focus in particular aspects of stress and resilience that help differentiate one discipline from the next. Yet, there is also shared ground where the borders of one discipline blend to some degree with neighboring disciplines and the opportunity to shape and be shaped by another discipline creates growth and change in our communal understanding of the larger forest. The study of stress and resilience is experiencing a time of interdisciplinary growth and change brought on, in part, by the continuing connection with the contexts of war and other human conflicts (Haglund, Nedstadt, Cooper, Southwick, & Charney, 2007; Hobfoll, Horsey, & Lamoureux, 2009; MacDermid Wadsworth, 2010; Walsh, 2003c), and we benefit from starting with a strong, basic foundation that draws from multiple sources.

This chapter first focuses on characteristics of "the forest" of stress and resilience literature. This section highlights common terms used in this area of research and how they are defined when applied to individuals and when applied to families, as well as their underlying assumptions about care and keys to well-being. A case study example of a military family is presented so that you can begin applying the concepts and then refer back to the case study as the chapter continues to present different theories and models that are useful in interpreting the needs, strengths, and challenges present in this family system.

The second section of this chapter explores a few of the "groves" of discipline-based stress theories and their usefulness in working with military families and their members. All the theories and models presented in this chapter have been selected due to a shared commitment to understanding how context shapes experiences of stress and resilience, but some focus primarily on individuals, while others focus primarily on family systems or particular relationships. We organize these theories by their primary focus and level of analysis. At the individual level, we review three lines of theory and research development. The first line of research focuses on learning how individuals think about and perceive stressful events (cognitions), how certain cognitive responses and patterns indicate types of coping strategies, and the circumstances (i.e., contexts) in which some strategies may be more or less effective for individuals trying to resolve their stress (Folkman & Moskowitz, 2007; Lazarus & Folkman, 1984). A second line of research brings together the rapidly expanding field of neurobiology with psychosocial research to better understand how hormonal and chemical influences on brain and body functioning are linked with both positive and negative psychosocial outcomes (Charney, 2004; Haglund et al., 2007; Sussman, 2006). The third line of individually focused research centers on the individual in context (Hobfoll, 1998) and concentrates on understanding the roles that resources (such as personal skills/abilities, social support, health, money, and community) play in coping with stressors and gaining/losing or maintaining one's optimal level of well-being.

As helpful as it is to gain a foundation in understanding individual stress, we realize that most people are connected to other people in meaningful ways as Dr. Walsh so eloquently stated at the beginning of this chapter. Military families are, after all, the focus of this text and much attention has been focused on the families—spouses, children, parents, and siblings—of the military personnel who are currently serving or have served in the theatres of the Global War on Terror, as well as ongoing humanitarian and peace-keeping missions where our troops are or have been called upon to provide help. At the family level, we also review three different branches of family stress theory. As mentioned earlier, there is a longstanding connection between the study of stress and military action. Reuben Hill's book, *Families Under Stress* (1949), is considered a landmark work that focused on deployment cycle issues of World War II veterans and their families. Hill's work established the basis of studying stress at the family level, and several researchers continue to refine and expand on his initial model of family stress (Malia, 2006; McCubbin et al., 1980). Each of the family stress theories reviewed in this chapter builds upon this and other writings as the researchers work to expand our understanding of families and the stress process.

We first review the contributions of McCubbin and Patterson (1983a, 1983b) who offered a significant expansion of Hill's model of family stress and explicated ways for researchers and practitioners to identify and measure adaptation processes and adjustment levels in family systems. The second line of family level work focuses on two particular circumstances that are stressful for families: ambiguous loss (not knowing what has happened to a family member or experiencing significant change in a family member, such as brain trauma) and boundary ambiguity (uncertainty in knowing if a person is psychologically and/or physically present in a family system, such as in different phases of deployment and reunion) (Boss, 1987, 2006, 2007; Wiens & Boss, 2003). The third branch of family level theory offers a practical framework for understanding and fostering family resilience and takes care to attend to the contextual details that both help and hinder family resilience (Walsh, 2003a, 2003c, 2007).

Each of these lines of research is part of the larger field of stress and resilience. Yet, because they focus on different concerns and questions, they offer unique pieces of information that can help human service professionals tailor their approaches to a variety of individual and family stress issues. At the end of this chapter, we developed exercises where you can practice the concepts and each theoretical focus with the example of the military family in this chapter's case study. You may find it useful to take short reading breaks between each theory and go to the exercises to practice what you just read. By applying each theoretical lens to the same case study, you will be able to see how having a solid grounding in the wide-ranging field of stress and resilience gives therapists and practitioners a flexible toolkit when working with a wide variety of family members and challenges.

CASE STUDY 5.1   Example of a Military Family

Joe Smith is the oldest of three boys raised by a single parent mom and her parents near Atlanta, GA. Joe enlisted in the U.S. Marine Corps after graduating from high school in 2001 and has supported his younger siblings as they have finished high school and entered into the workforce. Joe's youngest brother followed in Joe's footsteps and just enlisted in the Marines. Joe was deployed to Afghanistan soon after the terrorist attacks on the World Trade Center towers. This first deployment was 13 months long, after which he returned with his unit to Camp Legeune, NC. Joe met and married his wife, Jane, in 2004 and was deployed for a second time shortly thereafter. Jane was pregnant with their first child, and she moved back to her hometown and lived with her parents during her pregnancy and until Joe returned. Joe returned from his second deployment to his wife and 6-month-old baby daughter. Joe and Jane had applied for base housing during this separation and were able to move into housing within a week of Joe's return.

Jane has been working toward a college degree in nursing and is planning to transfer to a local college to finish her degree. Their baby girl is healthy, but developed colic and still cries from mid-afternoon through the evening several nights a week. She is also not sleeping through the night yet. The pediatrician assures them that colic will resolve itself by 8–9 months. Joe has been experiencing trouble sleeping since his return and when the baby wakes up crying in the middle of the night, Joe often experiences a startle reaction and has trouble getting back to sleep. He often goes for a run to help handle his hyperreaction, which worries Jane and has created a sense that he is not able to be a parenting partner.

In addition, Joe has received notification that he has been accepted into the Infantry Unit Leaders Course, a positive move in his career in the Marine Corps where he can become an Anti-Tank Section Leader. His orders state that he will be temporarily assigned to a station several states away to complete 5 months of advanced training. He leaves in 1 week.

Although this family is new on base, neighbors have welcomed them into the neighborhood and several wives of Joe's colleagues have made a point to contact Jane and give her information on groups and resources available on base.

THE STUDY OF STRESS AND RESILIENCE

One of the first things to keep in mind about this area of study is that the most common terms of stress, coping, and resilience can be used to describe individuals or families. For example, you are likely to read original studies and reports that vary in their focus on (1) individual characteristics (e.g., "I am going to have to find a new job once we relocate to Fort Bragg for my spouse's new PCS"), or (2) family characteristics (e.g., "The medical social worker and physical and occupational therapists are helping us work through issues in our daily caregiving challenges once our son is discharged from Walter Reed Medical Center"). Writers and readers both must be careful to remember the level of focus that is being reported so that we maintain clarity in the state of our knowledge about different level phenomena. Additionally, children, adolescents, and adults have been studied differently (MacDermid et al., 2008), which leads to different emphases on factors involved in resilience. This all means that comparing studies across age groups and from individuals to families can become difficult. So, how are stress, coping, and resilience conceptualized and how are definitions both similar and different when shifting from an individual focus to a family focus?

Individual Stress

The major definitions of **stress** emphasize that it is both a process and a state of being (Hobfoll, 1998; Malia, 2006). Considering stress as a process is useful because it focuses our attention on the interaction of a person with his/her larger environment. The process view highlights a person's cognitive and emotional reactions to a situation and affords us the opportunity to understand what happens when a person's appraisal of a situation or context results in a judgment of a *mismatch* in one's abilities and/or resources to meet the demands of the situation. The state of **being stressed** is due to the tension created by the mismatch. In the discussion on specific theories later in this chapter, you will begin to see some variations in what is included in the researchers' working definitions of stress. Some of these definitions focus solely on psychological aspects of stress (Lazarus & Folkman, 1984), while others include physiological and neurobiological characteristics in their working definitions (Aldwin, 1994; Charney, 2004; Haglund et al., 2007).

Family Stress

Family stress is conceptualized as "an upset in the steady state of the family [system]" (Malia, 2006, p. 143), which requires that the family make adjustments in order to maintain or regain a sense of coherence. Researchers who study the family level of stress look at ways in which the individual members contribute to the family's responses to the stressor and interact with each other and the outcomes they achieve as a family system as a result of these dynamics. Complicating the study of family stress is the reality that families rarely face only one stressor at a time, and it is unlikely that all previous stressors are resolved before a new one presents itself in the family's life. Theorists call the occurrence of overlapping demands **pileup of stressors** (Lavee, McCubbin, & Olsen, 1987; McCubbin & Patterson, 1983b), which itself can increase the sense of stress in the family. Walker (1985) cautions family stress researchers against assuming an idea that a "no stress" standard exists for any family's typical pattern.

Stressors

If individuals and family systems both can experience stress, how are stressors defined and identified? The main elements of a stressor include that it is a life event or occurrence (Boss, 1987) or an environmental context (McCubbin & Patterson, 1983), which either generates or has the potential to generate change as a person or family works to address the identified event or situation. McCubbin and Patterson describe stressors as aligning into two basic categories of normative (expectable) and nonnormative (often not expected or anticipated, sometimes catastrophic) stressors. Boss (as cited in Malia, 2006) expands this classification system to identify whether stressors are "normative or catastrophic, developmental or situational, predictable or unexpected, ambiguous or clear, and volitional or nonvolitional" (p. 145). You will read more about Boss's taxonomy a little later in this chapter and have an opportunity to practice applying it. Researchers also believe that it is important to know other information about the stressor, such as where the stressor originates (internal or external), as well as the duration of exposure to the stressor and whether or not the stressor occurs in tandem with other stressors (Boss, 2001; Lavee et al., 1987; Luthar, 2006; McCubbin & Patterson, 1983a, 1983b).

Chapter 3 identified several stressors that are normative for military families, and MacDermid et al. (2008) name several experiences of life as a military child that are normative, particularly for children in active duty families. But these same stressors may not be normative for Reserve and National Guard families. Military-related stressors include deployment and extended separation of families from their service member, frequent relocations to new stations, spousal employment and education opportunities, risk of injury or death of the service member, and exposure to combat-related activities. Other stressors are similar across both military and civilian families and, depending on their particular characteristics, may be normative or nonnormative. These include family life transitions of marriage, divorce, parenthood, high school graduation, and job advancement/loss/retirement; daily hassles such as a flat tire or sick pet, cranky teenagers who do not want to do their household chores, or surprise visits from family members; and events over which there may be very little control, like an unclear health diagnosis, a natural or human-made disaster, or loss of a family member or close friend.

Resilience

Resilience is studied hand-in-hand with stress and is viewed as a process of positive adaptation and growth after experiencing an adverse event/circumstance. The term "resilience" has been used in much of the literature focused on children and adolescents who are living in or exposed to adverse environments (Luthar, 2006), while the term "hardiness" is used more often in research with adults. **Hardiness** is usually described more as a personality trait and thus more fixed (one is a hardy individual or not), while resilience is conceptualized as more dynamic (one can gain or lose resiliency in the interplay between the person and environment). MacDermid et al. (2008) note that while there is no universally agreed upon definition of resilience, "most definitions include two key elements: 1) exposure to adverse or traumatic circumstances; and 2) successful adaptation following exposure" (p. 1). As such, resilience cannot be assessed in the absence of an undesirable event. These elements apply to studies of individuals in multiple age groups (child, youth, adult) and at individual, family, and community levels.

MacDermid et al. (2008) identify several characteristics that are useful in understanding how resilience can be identified within military families as well as limits and/or threats to attaining successful adaptation after adversity. These characteristics include:

1. Resilience is dynamic and includes both environmental and psychobiological components, similar to the way a child development professional would explain that early brain development is influenced by both genetics and the environments that support or put healthy development at risk.
2. Resilience is a process and develops over time.
3. Resilience is strength-based, and programs that use a strengths-based model build upon identifying existing strengths to support healthy outcomes for individuals and families.
   a. Resilience is situation-specific. Individuals and families have different traits and abilities and develop particular skill sets through their experiences. Not every person or family has identical strengths or abilities.
   b. Resilience can be enhanced through the dynamic interactions of the environmental and psychobiological systems.
4. There are multiple pathways to resilience.
5. When multiple risk factors co-occur, the likelihood of exhibiting resilience decreases.

This all means that resilience can be measured by several different outcome indicators and is influenced by several risk and protective factors. A family's unique mixture of risk and protective factors include the outcome, that is, the family's resilience. So how can we know if an individual or family is exhibiting resilience? Both researchers and human service professionals use psychological health, physical health, quality of life and relationship indicators, a sense of **self-efficacy** (the extent to which persons believe that they can meet a goal or expectation), as well as **family coherence** (satisfaction with interpersonal connections and dynamics among family members), to gain a sense of a person's or family's resiliency (Walsh, 2002).

Coping

Coping is used to describe a variety of efforts to overcome challenges or difficulties. Some researchers (Folkman & Moskowitz, 2007; Lazarus & Folkman, 1984) focus on different individual cognitive and behavioral strategies: (1) to regulate one's distress (**emotion-focused coping**), such as when the evening news reports injuries and casualties of American personnel in the area where a service member is stationed; (2) to address the problem creating the stress event (**problem-solving coping**), such as making alternative caregiving arrangements for children when a single parent is deployed; or (3) to reframe and give different meaning to an event (**meaning-focused coping**), such as when a civilian neighbor tries to give comfort to a National Guard family whose service member just got orders by saying "This is for our country."

Factors including flexibility in family roles and rules, family belief systems, connections to community and other social support, as well as communication and problem-solving strategies are all pieces to understanding family-level resilience (Boss, 2001; Malia, 2006; Walsh, 2003c). Family researchers focus on abilities, behaviors, and strategies available within the family system to meet challenges presented by a stressor. For example, role flexibility (the ability to take on a different role or responsibility when a service member deploys and returns) and family organization and communication patterns are important elements of family-level coping. When studying coping, researchers across disciplines are asking questions such as "How did you think/feel about the stressor event?" (i.e., a cognitive effort), "What did you do?" (i.e., a behavioral effort), and "How well did these thoughts, feelings, and strategies work as you addressed the challenge?".

Context and Resources

As the field of stress and resilience continues to be refined through therapeutic practice, theorists are able to explicate ways in which contextual specifics shape stress, coping, and resilience experiences. Researchers in the fields of psychology and health traditionally have not focused on context beyond immediate conditions, but rather concentrated on learning as much as possible about individual thought processes and coping behaviors (Lazarus & Folkman, 1984) and psychobiological responses and treatments (Ozbay et al., 2007). An exception in the psychological field is Hobfoll and associates, who used an ecological model of **individuals-nested in families-nested in social settings** (e.g., Hobfoll, 1998; Hobfoll, Dunahoo, & Monnier, 1995; Hobfoll et al., 2009). This model centers individuals within their family and larger social settings (neighborhood, religious setting, school/work) and highlights how individuals need meaningful connections with others in order to access and build resources for healthy living. Research using this model centered on interactions between the different levels of their model and how these connections (or lack thereof), particularly to resources, affect an individual's ability to be resilient in the face of stressors.

Access to and utility of resources are part of the overall context of a stressor experience. Most folks could identify a sizable list of potential resources that could be helpful in meeting a challenge: money, doctors, insurance, medical facilities, therapists, and being able to take medical leave from a job are all potential sources of support (i.e., resources) for an individual or family with a health crisis. Being able to access and use these resources can make a huge difference for both the individual directly affected by the health issue and for his/her family members, who are also affected by the challenge. Resources are not just defined by their existence, they are also defined by their utility (usefulness) to the people affected by the stressor event. Other elements of context can shape perceptions of usefulness and the applicability of a given resource.

To illustrate how perceptions of a potential resource of support can be shaped, think about how religious beliefs lead to different assumptions about health, both physical and psychological. A person with a religious belief system that shuns medical intervention in favor of allowing the will of God to prevail will likely not seek out or value resources that are part of the formal medical system. Likewise, a company may have a very good maternity leave policy for female employees when they become mothers, but not have any corollary policies for male employees who become fathers. Thus resources can exist, but not be perceived as useful (as in the case of religious belief) or not be available to a person because of their definition (maternal leave) or status (males). The contextually based work of Hobfoll and associates (Hobfoll, 1998; Hobfoll et al., 1995, 2009) puts the individual at the center of attention while also emphasizing that we need to examine availability and utility of individual, family, and community resources in order to better comprehend individual resiliency. This body of work provides a bridge to contextually based family stress and resilience research.

The disciplines of family science, marriage and family therapy, and social work focus their research on understanding collective coping strategies and resource management utilized by family systems when facing challenges (Boss, 2001; Malia, 2006). One of the central premises in the study of family stress is that context is important (Boss, 1987, 2006, 2007; McCubbin & Patterson, 1983b; Walker, 1985; Walsh, 2003c, 2007). In order to understand the family's responses to a stressor event, one needs to understand the family's condition (strength, health, and resilience) prior to the stressful event. Additionally, helping professionals need to gain an understanding of how the event is stress inducing for a particular family system. Context provides at least a partial glimpse into the effects of a stressor. Context also shapes the stressor event and a person's/family's responses to it. Boss's classification of family stressors (Boss, 2001) mentioned earlier in this chapter, helped define important elements of context that are useful for helping professionals and the people with whom they are working. This taxonomy lends itself well to asking questions that will help both a client and a helping professional gain a clearer sense of the stressor and identify coping strategies and resources for individuals and families. These questions include, but are not limited to

1. *What is the source of the stressor?* Does it originate from within the family system (internal) or outside the family system (external)? Both addiction and tornadoes are stressors, but they have different effects on individuals and families.
2. *What type of stressor is being presented?*
   a. Is this a normative, developmental, or predictable event, such as transitions to parenthood, the "terrible twos" or death of an elderly family member? Or, is it catastrophic, situational, or otherwise unexpected, such as a car accident?
   b. Is the stressor one in which the facts surrounding the event are clear and knowable (clear) or are there limits to knowing what happened and/or what the outcomes might be (**ambiguous**), such as a missing child?
   c. Is the stressor one that was wanted or chosen (**volitional**), such as taking steps to change one's marital status or is this stressor event imposed upon the person/family (**nonvolitional**), such as being laid off of work or having to relocate in order to keep a job?
3. *How long is this stressor expected to last (duration)?* Is the event short-term (**acute**), such as a child having difficulties with a friend, or longer-term (**chronic**), such as an ongoing health issue?
4. *What else is going on that may impact the relative effects of this stressor (density)?* It may be that the event is the only big thing going on at the time and is easily identified (isolated) or there may be a pileup of stressor events, including the identified event (**cumulative**), occurring that contribute to the current situation. For example, deployment may be the stressor of the moment in a family's life where other issues such as caring for young children, spousal health issues, and isolation from other military families are also present.

Thus, it is important for a helping professional to work with clients to identify the nature and context of the stressor event and to facilitate identification of resources that will support resilience in the face of the challenge. In doing so, helping professionals are guided by theory. Tara Saathoff-Wells, one of the coauthors of this textbook, explains and illustrates in Box 5.1 how theory can guide our everyday practices.

BOX 5.1   BEST PRACTICES

USING THEORY TO GUIDE OUR PRACTICE

Theory helps me understand life. I love theory. It uncovers assumptions I make about myself, about other people, and the way things are "supposed to be." It helps me be thoughtful about the way things are and how to improve them.

All my life I've been trying to understand people, their relationships, and how organizations and cultures work. My family lived in Ethiopia where my dad worked for the United States Agency for International Development (USAID). After high school, I started traveling on my own. I spent a lot of time exploring what I wanted to do with my life (learn about cultures and family life by seeking out international experiences as a young adult) and learning what I did NOT want to do (work in child care at minimum wage). My mom had to buy a new address book every few years. There were so many cross-outs and new addresses, the pages with my contact information were like archaeological digs. Between 1989 and 1994, I spent a lot of time in Africa including working to help reunite children with their families in displacement camps in Mozambique as their civil war was ending and teaching school for American children in Kenya.

I can be easily upset or outraged by things that don't seem "right" or well thought out. I taught my first university level *Military Family Life* Class in 2008. Our college football team invited a nearby unit of the National Guard, ROTC students, and staff to come to Military Appreciation Night. A ceremony was planned for halftime. No one from the university came over and visited with families and service members except for me and some of my students.

The weather that night was tough—bone chilling cold with dense, dripping fog. The vapor lights from the stadium created a halo effect, and the tent where service members and their families were gathered was on the backside of the stadium with auxiliary lights. The National Guard had set up examples of their artillery, including a couple of cannons, as well as big inflatables for children to play on during the pregame tailgate, and personnel were stationed around them as dusk and darkness set in. The fog further limited visibility to about 100 yards outside the stadium.

One of the typical pregame activities for football games is the firing of the cannon to get the fans excited for the game. It is also fired when the team scores a touchdown and other points. About a half hour before the game, university staff started firing the cannon for the game, but no one had warned the service members, many of whom had just returned home from a tour in Baghdad.

One of my students who was with me is a Retired First Sergeant and former ROTC instructor. He, his wife, and I were talking with the service members near the inflatables when the first blast from the cannon came. It was startling for all of us, but the service members hit the ground with immediate self-protection behavior—it was a cold, dark, and foggy night in an unfamiliar place with bad lighting and they knew it was not their cannon that had been shot. They automatically used their training for survival in response to an unknown threat, while we (civilians) thought, "Woah—it is getting close to game time!" As the service members realized they were safe, they had to also handle their adrenaline reactions and a couple felt embarrassed about their actions in front of civilians. All three of us responded by reassuring them that their response was normal. The "First Sarge" stayed with them to help them "walk it off" and process their emotional and survival reactions, which was really meaningful to the service members. His wife and I went back to the tent with the families and reassured them about the cannon blast. Later, my student talked with the event coordinators to explain that setting off a cannon at night without warning is not the best way to welcome and honor service members.

At first, I was upset at the lack of preparation, understanding, and connection between the event people and service members. Then, I realized the event planners and staff needed help to make the connections. Good intentions simply are not enough to ensure that a community creates a truly supportive and appropriate event for military families. It is an example of where knowing the theory of stress and coping and individual stress reactions, as well as the basics of deployment experiences, would have been helpful. When planning an event for returning service members and their families, you need to consider the experiences they've had and how they may interpret events differently than the planning committee or general audience.

Another example where application of theory could positively influence how we organize events for military families is on the media and Internet portrayal of surprise reunions between young children and service members who have come home on leave for a holiday or family event. As a child development person who has some understanding of all the feelings and stressors involved around issues of separation, reuniting, and connecting, I think families should be able to reunite in private. It bothers me that it has become acceptable for the public to be there, too. It may feel like I'm crashing the party, but this is something we need to reconsider. How much of a family's life—any family—should be "out there" for everyone to see and take part in? The focus of the video may be on this very emotional reunion, but why should we assume that we should be an audience to this family event? Thinking about the larger ripple effects, when these are recorded in a classroom, are there other children present who also have a deployed parent? What might this mean to them? Military families and children experience enough uncertainty in the deployment cycle. Dates for return are delayed, missions can be dangerous, a service member may opt to stay longer so a buddy can go back. Is there really a good enough reason to promote the public consumption of a family's reunion moment? This is a case where applying theory leads to at least questioning the assumption that this is OK and perhaps modifying our behavior.

Tara Saathoff-Wells
Coauthor of this textbook and Research and Evaluation Scientist,
Clearinghouse for Military Family Readiness at Penn State

THEORIES AND MODELS OF STRESS AND RESILIENCE

Clinicians, therapists, and other human service professionals need to have a strong repertoire of theories and models to use as they work with military families and individual members. Theories that can be applied to real life situations and that can be evaluated for their accuracy and usefulness are extremely important in developing high-quality intervention and prevention programs. Now that you have started building your knowledge regarding concepts in stress and resilience, we present a short review of theories and models that have strong applied components.

Theories and Models of Individual Stress, Coping, and Resilience

General stress and coping theory, as detailed by Lazarus and Folkman (1984), centers on understanding internal aspects of coping, that is, cognitions and emotions. This branch of theory is based in cognitive behaviorism and leads much of the discussion on the different aspects of coping strategies that we defined earlier: emotion-focused, problem-focused, and meaning-focused strategies. Recent theory development has begun to include a study of how specific effects and emotions impact coping strategies and effectiveness, with some support for linking positive effect with healthier adaptations to stress and as an important tool for restoring resources that may be depleted as the result of a stressful event (Folkman & Moskowitz, 2007). This theory also indicates that contextual factors will influence which coping strategies are more or less useful to a person trying to resolve or manage a stressful event.

For example, school-aged children may deal better with a parent's deployment if shown how to use emotion-focused coping actions (e.g., regulating feelings of distress) and meaning-focused coping (e.g., reframing the deployment as the parent helping others live safer lives) rather than a problem-focused perspective (e.g., trying to change deployment orders). In a situation where a service member is returning with a significant injury, members of his extended family system may vary in their individual coping actions. Family members may be similar in their initial attempts to regulate their levels of emotional distress that their son/brother/husband/father has been injured and has survived. As the injury treatment continues over time and family members have different daily life demands and interpersonal connections to their injured family member, coping actions and involvement may vary significantly. Family members who are more distant (physically, psychologically) may turn to more meaning-focused coping to try to make sense of why this happened, while family members who are more immediately connected to and affected by the service member's injury may continue with active emotion-focused coping for the daily distress as well as problem-solving coping. Problem solving may include coordinating child and work schedules around visits to the service member and medical appointments and learning to administer to short-term and/or long-term caregiving needs that may result from the injury. Human service professionals can use the different concepts of stress and coping theory to help clients identify multiple facets of their reactions to a stressing event and process information for addressing their needs.

Psychobiological stress research is useful for clinicians and therapists. This line of research integrates neurobiological research with psychosocial research to include physiological measures of stress, such as cortisol, serotonin, and dopamine levels; autonomic response systems, including respiration and perspiration rates and eye dilation; and magnetic resonance imaging (MRI) brain scans (see Haglund et al., 2007 for a comprehensive overview), as well as self-reports on stressful events and circumstances. Interventions and recommendations focus on teaching a person experiencing stress to recognize physiological messages, such as tensed muscles, shallow breathing, clenched jaws and then to use such coping strategies as deep breathing, muscle relaxation, guided imagery, and exercise to release the physical experience of stress. In addition, a helping professional drawing on this line of applied research would integrate psychosocial bases of distress, coping, and resilience to help the client explore issues such as irrational thoughts about what is/was possible to do during a stressful event. In clinical and therapeutic settings, this research opens up opportunities to prevent and treat stress-related psychopathology by addressing the hormonal and chemical factors involved in stress, coping, and resilience.

Psychobiological research also contributes to our understanding of lifespan development and change with regard to a variety of stressful experiences. Such understanding may be particularly useful for working with children and youth in military families. Research on early brain development shows that there is a high level of **neural plasticity** (flexibility in development of neural connections) that responds to early experiences and deprivations, in effect starting the lifelong process of "tailoring" the brain to the person with all his/her personal, social, and environmental experiences. This process includes early stressful experiences.

Data show that there are hormonal and chemical processes in the human experience of stress. These experiences create pathways in the neural circuitry for response patterns to develop when facing a new potential stressor. Developmentalists often describe two such pathways that early experiences help forge: learned helplessness and strong self-efficacy, both of which are aspects of a sense of self. It is important to note that individuals can and do experience both positive and negative perceptions of self. Research shows that individuals who experience positive outcomes to early stress experiences may be able to incorporate these early experiences to build a foundation for resilient responses to later stress-inducing events (Boyce & Chesterman, 1990), described by Walsh (2003c) as "struggling well." Persons may be more at risk of future negative stress reactions due to development of neurobiological responses if they have early experiences that result in chronic distress or that are not manageable or responsive to coping attempts (Khoshaba & Maddi, 1999). One of the Best Practices segments in Chapter 4 gives insight into how knowing the ways that stress affects both the brain and coping skills in young children can be used to develop programs that support young children who experience parental deployment, injury, or loss.

Conservation of resources (Hobfoll, 1989) is another useful theory in understanding ways that people seek out, invest, and protect resources they find valuable in coping with stressful events. Hobfoll, who was introduced as a researcher who views the person in the context of family and community, posits several assumptions about the roles resources play in facilitating or inhibiting resilience (Hobfoll, 1998; Hobfoll et al., 1995). In general, people invest in resources that they perceive to be valuable and useful, which are in turn shaped by family, community, and culture. When those resources are lost or threatened, stress results and people will try to conserve (maintain) the resources they have. Resource losses are proportionally more powerful than resource gains and some resources, when lost, are always a negative experience. Finally, when resource loss occurs across levels (individual, family, community), successful coping and adaptation may be hindered. To bring this model to a practical level, consider the following two examples.

A school counselor can use Hobfoll's model to work with a child and his family when a mother is called up for active duty in her National Guard unit. The counselor can work with the child to help him identify his resources for support, such as having a sense of humor (individual: enjoying telling and listening to jokes with friends and family, saving a few jokes for video contact with his mom while she is deployed), being able to adjust with his remaining family members by helping with tasks that his mom would normally do (family: adding certain chores such as keeping track of breakfast items for the grocery list, feeding pets), and having friends with whom he can talk and spend time (community: scouts, sports, free time with buddies).

Hobfoll's model could be applied to a very different situation, as well. A medical social worker in a VA hospital can use the model to help map changes in resources and support for a soldier who has returned from theatre with physical and/or psychological trauma. There may be changes in personal resources and abilities (including health issues such as mobility and limb function, traumatic brain injury that can affect a myriad of executive functions), changes in family resources (stresses in a romantic relationship, needing help from parents, not being able to fulfill roles as a parent to his/her children), and changes in community resources (needing to identify specialized therapists, not being able to go back to a job/career due to the injury, strain in friendships, and loss of close connections with fellow unit members). Hobfoll's model facilitates thinking about the ripple effects of a variety of potential events military families and their members face.

The models of individual risk and resilience in this chapter provide a good starting point in building your theoretical map of stress and coping. General stress and coping theory gives insight into how individuals process stressful events, cognitively and emotionally, and different intrapersonal skills and strategies a person may use to try and resolve his or her distress. Psychobiological research contributes to our understanding of the intricate interactions between our physical and psychosocial experiences of stress and the ways in which our physical bodies respond to and try to regulate stress responses of which we may not be consciously aware. The conservation of resources model brings to the forefront how individuals are embedded in a larger social system in which they strive to gain and maintain resources and connections that support continued positive well-being. It also addresses consequences of losing resources for well-being and takes into account how resource loss can have ripple effects beyond a single individual.

Using Theory to Understand Military Experiences

Service members specialize into particular jobs and skill sets (MOS) as part of their training. These specializations can often be translated into a variety of settings and meet multiple needs within a mission. For example, an Air Force medic who provides care in a post-operative care unit in a Naval Hospital CONUS may be deployed to work at a MEDEVAC station in theatre and be tasked to work in the morgue, identifying and caring for the remains of those who died, whether military or civilian. A Marine Corps diesel mechanic may take care of fleet vehicles at her duty station, but be sent downrange when on deployment to maintain vehicles that are targets. It is important to go beyond a service member's or veteran's MOS and learn more about their daily working and living conditions to better understand the kinds of stressors and environments to which they were exposed. Dr. Susanne Gibbons reminds us that we need to consider what kinds of questions to ask and how to understand our military and veteran population.

Spotlight on Research

HEALTH-CARE PROVIDERS AND FINDING PURPOSE

My work involves deployed military health care providers (HCPs) and their stress and coping. Other than nurses who served in Vietnam, HCPs in the military and their war/ combat experiences are poorly understood despite their growing numbers. We need to learn more.

I work with students who are active duty nurses. Many have been deployed more than once. Some were deployed in the 1990s and then again to Iraq or Afghanistan. These men and women have experiences as nurses and as warriors.

My colleagues, Edward Hickling PhD at the University of Florida, Scott Barnett, PhD at the Veterans Administration Hospital in Tampa Florida, and Dorraine Watts, PhD at St. Petersburg College, and I did a secondary analysis of data from the 2005 and the 2008 *Department of Defense (DoD) Surveys of Health Related Behaviors Among Active Duty Military Personnel* to learn about gender differences in how active duty HCPs react to operational stress.

We found HCPs to be a resilient group. But we have to be careful about the term resilience. Bruce McEwen's allostatic load model is probably the best way to consider stress and coping in the military. This model looks at the weight of stressors for an individual that may include moving, deployment, being in combat. The path of recovery from these stressors depends on an array of factors: biology, genetics, early life experiences, age, how established one is in a career, finances, and the presence or not of a support system. When you are thinking about working to support HCPs and other service members, you have to look at the whole picture to begin to understand coping with stress.

People mistakenly believe because HCPs are not in combat they are not at risk for psychological consequences. But HCPs are in intense war situations, trying to put people back together and having to decide who to save and who to let go. They are exhausted and work long hours. Some people thrive during deployment. Many carry on during and afterwards but it doesn't mean they haven't been harmed and aren't somehow changed. These experiences are life changing. War is war. People describe their trauma memories are often in Technicolor. These memories stick. They change who you are.

Our findings suggest that similar to those in combat, exposure to life-threatening situations increase the probability of an adverse psychological response. We also found that finding purpose in what you do within a supportive environment appears to help mediate the impact of these experiences.

It is important for all of us in a community to recognize the stressors people are under. If you are a child care provider or teacher, a social worker or primary health-care provider, you have to figure out the right questions to ask to find out what someone may be experiencing. For example: How are things at home? Are they different than before deployment? How's the family doing? Is anything new or unusual going on?

We are now looking at military HCPs and their families. You can't separate one from the other. There's much we as researchers and the public still have to learn.

Susanne Gibbons, PhD, C-ANP, C-GNP,
Uniformed Services University of the Health Sciences

Daniel K. Inouye Graduate School of Nursing

Theories and Models of Family Stress, Resilience, and Coping

Family stress theory has generated scholarly and applied interest since just after World War II. One of the earliest scholars was Reuben Hill (1949, 1958) who developed a model of family stress that he called the ABCx Model and is considered to be the father of family stress theory. Hill's work, as mentioned earlier in this chapter, centered on deployment issues faced by World War II veterans and their families. Several scholars have worked to refine and strengthen family stress theory, and several model variations are in use today (see Malia, 2006 for an overview). It would be overwhelming to try to cover each iteration of family stress theory in this chapter, so we have limited it to a group of researchers who proposed one of the more significant expansions of Hill's ABCx Model, called the Double ABCx Model of Family Stress and Adaptation (McCubbin & Patterson, 1983). The value of this refinement is that it tried to account for the passage of time in understanding how stress and adaptation work in a family's life, from precrisis to postcrisis and adaptation.

According to family stress theory, the individual and the family make up the family system, and the family system's adaptation is predicted, in part, from the combination of stressors that occur (A), the resources accessed to address the stressors (B), and the perception (C) of the resulting crisis (x) (McCubbin & Patterson, 1983). Basic assumptions of family stress theory and the Double ABCx Model include a developmental view of the human life cycle. Thus, developmental change (growth, transitions in capabilities and relationships) is seen as a natural and integral part in the family system's growth over time. Stress is part of this developmental process (Figley & McCubbin, 1983). A second key element of family stress theory is that not all stressors are equal. There are important differences between family transitions and experiences that are due to normative and nonnormative stressors. You can review the more detailed definitions of each type in the earlier section of this chapter that defined the major terms, but in general, normative transitions are ones that are expectable and that a person and family may anticipate and look forward to (or at least be aware that it is coming!) while nonnormative transitions are due to experiences that are not expected or typical and may range from being a short-term stressor (such as a health scare) to being a catastrophic event (such as a tornado). Boss's taxonomy (2001), detailed earlier in this chapter, helps us better define the characteristics of stressors and transitions, which can help families understand their circumstances and make choices about resources and coping strategies. You can practice applying Boss's taxonomy of stressor characteristics in one of the exercises at the end of this chapter.

Applying Family Stress and Other Theories to Deployment-Affected Families

Figure 5.1 uses deployment as the initial stressor to illustrate several factors that may influence stress, coping, and resilience in military families. When a service member receives orders for deployment, several tasks have been identified that both the service member and his/her family must address in order for everyone to meet the needs of both work and family (see the "Deployments" section of Chapter 3). Deployment is just one of the stressors (a) that a family may be experiencing at that point in time. Drawing on the case study presented earlier in this chapter, what other stressors are evident in the family of Joe and Jane Smith when Joe received notice to deploy for the second time?

Individuals and families in the military may have a variety of resources (b) to respond to the demands of military life including a deployment cycle. The service member has been trained to do his/her job under demanding circumstances, is part of a unit with a clear mission, and will have to be cleared with a good bill of health in order to deploy. In addition to a service member's job skills, connections, and health, several skills are useful for all members of the family. These include communication and problem-solving skills, connections to family and community, flexibility and stability, and the ability to maintain family rituals and traditions even when members may be physically separated. Other resources may be more directly instrumental, such as receiving an increase in income due to the special pay linked with hazardous duty or special training. What other interpersonal and community-based resources do you think would be helpful for a family facing deployment? What potential resources are mentioned in the case study?

In the Double ABCx Model, perceptions of the stressor event (c) can influence behaviors and beliefs about an individual's and family's ability to cope with the stressor. Previous chapters have described how a sense of patriotism and participating in something larger than oneself can be an integral part of military service. Service members may look forward to a deployment because they know that they are bringing needed skills and knowledge to address an urgent issue in the field (such as water treatment in Haiti after the earthquake in January 2010) or to give relief to their fellow service members (such as Col. Pereira's work with soldiers under fire in Baghdad). Military spouses and significant others may be simultaneously proud of their partner, yet worried for their safety. If children are involved, there may be a sense of loss for both the parenting partner and the children. The ways in which the service member and the family system perceive the deployment event can influence the ways that resources are accessed and the type of coping strategies used to alleviate the distress associated with deployment. In reviewing the case study, what details give insight into the resources Jane drew upon for the first deployment of her husband? Are these resources that you think she could draw upon for the second deployment? Why or why not?

Families do not simply enact their individual and collective coping strategies at just one point in time, but rather over time. Deployment can range from 4 months to more than a year and predeployment preparations may add several additional months to a family's experience of deployment-related tensions. Family stress theorists emphasize that time is an important factor in understanding responses to stressful events. Over time new normative and nonnormative stressors may be introduced into a family system (health

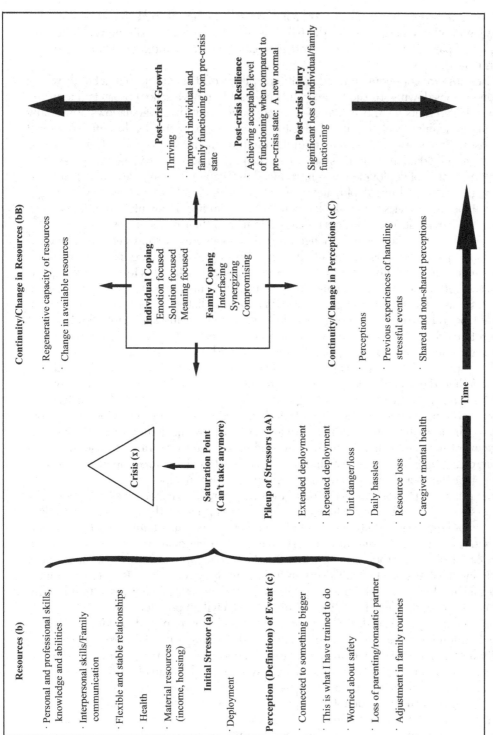

Figure 5.1 Adaptation of the Double ABCx Model to military families and deployment.

Source: (Adapted with permission. From McCubbin, H. I., & Patterson, J. M. (1983a). The family stress process: The Double ABCx Model of adjustment and adaptation. In H. L. McCubbin, M. B. Sussman, & J. M. Patterson (Eds.), *Advances and development in family stress theory and research* (pp. 7–37). New York: Haworth.)

issues of a family member, graduation of a high school senior, a tornado hits the local community), and others may dissipate (the baby's colic resolves itself, a sibling is able to care for an aging parent, a reliable and honest mechanic can be counted on when the family car has issues).

Crises (aA) are commonly framed as either a pileup of stressors, such as a family where everyone comes down with the flu and all three children have school projects due in the same week as tryouts for sports teams, or a traumatic event that overshadows other daily needs and schedules, such as natural disasters, loss of a job, or the death/injury of a loved one. Crises give a sense that there is saturation in the amount and/or magnitude of stressors that an individual and family system can accommodate with existing resources. The concept of a spiral of deployment was introduced in Chapter 3 to help describe what families may face with multiple deployments. Framed within family stress theory, what might precipitate a sense of crisis for a deployment-affected family? How might multiple and/or extended deployments tax a family's coping systems and their resilience over time?

In accounting for the possible changes over time in a family system, the second part of the model expands the original list of stressors, resources, and perceptions. Just as there can be change in the number and significance of stressors in a family's life, it is also expectable to see both continuity and change in both resources and perceptions of events. Some resources may have stable or regenerative qualities so that they remain viable over an extended period of time. Examples include interpersonal skills and stable familial and friend relationships. Other resources may not be as stable or have an infinite capacity to serve as a resource. For example, in a family faced with the injury of a service member, a working spouse may use all his/her available sick days in order to be with their injured partner. When those paid sick days (a finite resource) are used, the family member may have to choose other avenues such as going back to work, taking an informal leave of absence, invoking the federal Family and Medical Leave Act, or even leaving his/her job. Similarly, the availability and stability of close friendships and family relationships may change over time due to changes in their lives (children entering different stages of development, changing jobs) or due to a change in their emotional resource capacity to "always be there" for the spouse/children of their deployed service member.

Perceptions of stressors can also change over time. Previous experiences of deployment and other stressful events may change a family's perception of their ability to handle a continued or new crisis. Additionally, not all members of the same family may have shared perceptions of the same event or stressors. What is "no big deal" to one person may be a "very big deal" to another. As you will see below, being able to coordinate differences while being flexible is a set of skills very useful to family systems. This is true for military families facing deployment, families experiencing other normative changes in military life (such as relocation to a new PCS), and families in the civilian population.

The model is useful in describing the context and factors of a deployment-affected family. Yet, family stress theory is not limited to describing a family's stress experience. Practitioners can use this model to help a family find **adaptive coping strategies** for stabilizing and maintaining "balance in the family system which [in turn] facilitates organization and unity and promotes individual growth and development" (Figley & McCubbin, 1983, p. 24). In turn, these adaptive coping strategies influence individual's abilities to meet personal and relational demands. Whereas general stress and coping theory has drawn attention to individual coping strategies, family stress theory focuses on coordination and flexibility of coping skills between family members and their larger community to help meet the challenges presented by the stressor event.

These adaptive strategies, to some extent, involve **restructuring** the family's current operating system and **consolidating** afterward (McCubbin & Patterson, 1983, pp. 22–23). That is, modifications may need to be made within the family system in the areas of roles, family rules, patterns of interaction and communication, and goals. In addition to modifications, the family unit and its individual members are also called upon to consolidate and support individual and group efforts toward implementing these changes. These strategies also include highlighting changes in individual and family needs in areas of support and resources for maintaining or improving quality of life. According to family stress theory, the family's and individual members' efforts at restructuring and consolidation are facilitated by three adaptive coping strategies of interfacing with the larger community, synergizing efforts between family members, and compromising within the family system and between the family system and the larger environment to settle into a satisfying way of life (McCubbin & Patterson, 1983). So what might these coping strategies look like in practice with military families?

Let's take an example of an active duty military family relocating from a large military installation in the Southeastern United States to a university town in the Midwest, where the service member's new assignment is as a military science instructor in the university's ROTC program. This family has one service member parent, a second parent who works as a dental hygienist, and two school-age children. They have been living on a large U.S. military installation for the past 3 years, and the children attend a school on base. Life in the university town will be vastly different. There is no large military installation nearby and no significant group of military families in the area. Several changes are on the horizon for this family.

- **Interfacing**: A family and its individual members operate within the larger social contexts of work, community, and school groups. An active duty military family that receives PCS orders has to interface (i.e., develop relationships) at several levels with a new community that may or may not be similar in culture and sociohistorical contexts. The service member has orders, which specify his/her job duties and place in the ROTC program, while the spouse may be making choices about finding a new job (or not), locating civilian shopping venues because there is no PX or commissary nearby, and finding medical professionals who accept TRICARE (i.e., the military health insurance program). Children will be looking for new playmates, wondering about their new school and teachers, and figuring out a new home and neighborhood. The entire family will be interfacing with a new community across several dimensions.
- **Synergizing**: Synergizing is composed of coordinating all family system and individual members' efforts and is focused on consolidating the various change efforts within the family system. Ideally, the family works in a coordinated fashion addressing issues of change concerning both individual members and the family as a whole. Cooperation and effective communication among family members are key to this coping strategy and families who are able to coordinate their efforts tend to experience lower levels of chaos and anxiety. For the family in the example, the parents work to find effective ways to organize information and tasks about moving requirements, finding housing and schools, keeping track of important family papers (marriage and birth certificates, school and medical records, pet records), and working with their children to help them with transitions in schools and friends and activities, as well as changes in roles they may have as family members.
- **Compromising**: Compromising entails family and individual efforts of achieving balance within the new community. Relocating from a large military installation in the Southeastern United States to a university town in the Midwest may present quite a few cultural challenges for this family. Developing friendships with other children and adjusting to new schools that are not full of military kids and that don't have teachers familiar with military life may take time. There may be a relatively low level of community support for the military, complete with strong

ideological stances that are part of the public face of the community. Adjusting to life as a military spouse living far from an installation may mean that the spouse has to expend quite a bit of energy maintaining long-distance social support networks and feel very cautious in developing local friendships and ties outside the other families in the ROTC program. The service member may not be able to help with some key family transitions due to his/her job requirements and expectations. Thus, there are several opportunities for compromising that the family has to negotiate in adjusting to a new community.

Consequently, family stress theory views the family's and individual members' attempts to achieve a good "fit" with the new community as requiring the coping strategies of *interfacing* with the new environment at numerous levels, *synergizing* change efforts within the family system, and addressing family and individual-level issues of *compromise* with differences in community and lifestyle. Family stress theory and the Double ABCx Model provide helping professionals with a practical way to map and identify family stressors, supports, perceptions of events, and coping behaviors that help or hinder the family's adaptation to changes in their lives.

Finding Resilience in the Face of Ambiguity

Other clinical researchers have helped refine elements of family stress theory, such as Boss's (2001) taxonomy of stressor characteristics and Walsh's (2003c, 2007) family resilience framework, in order to strengthen its usefulness in clinical intervention. In particular, Boss contributed to a deeper understanding of when a person experiences unclear losses and unclear shifts in relationships. **Ambiguous loss theory** (Boss, 2002, 2007) represents her work to better help clients experiencing ambiguous loss (a stressor) and boundary ambiguity (a perceptual response), examples of which follow below. This work focuses on stress and resilience when a person or family experiences losses that are not clear in nature and may not be resolvable and a key assumption of this theory is that there are both physical and psychological structures that shape every family system. Walsh's focus on family resilience has shaped clinical work to help families identify and strengthen shared sources of support within their family systems that can help them manage stressors and gain/maintain a sense of well-being in spite of adversity.

The term "ambiguous loss" refers to an unclear loss and the loss may be physical or psychological. For example, a person/family may experience an ambiguous physical loss of a family member, such as when a child goes missing or a parent has migrated for work but his/her whereabouts and safety are unknown. The person may be physically absent but is still psychologically present in the family system. Families may also experience an ambiguous psychological loss when a family elder experiences age-related dementia or when a teenager survives a car wreck with serious brain trauma that permanently alters his abilities and future. These persons are still physically present, but their psychological presence and roles within the family system are changed. In this line of research and clinical application, ambiguous loss is viewed as a relational disorder rather than a psychological disorder as it is a relationship (or series of relationships) that are ruptured (Boss, 2007).

Those military families who have experienced an unclear physical loss of a service member include those listed as Prisoners of War (POWs), Missing in Action (MIA), Killed in Action (KIA), as well as service members who are/were listed as Away Without Leave (AWOL) and have not been in contact with family members. Although the details differ in each of these experiences, families are faced with an unclear loss and one where information may never provide clarity or resolution. The common challenge these families face is to find meaning in their circumstances and to be able to live and grow despite ongoing ambiguity, to be resilient in the face of uncertainty. For helping professionals, it becomes important to work with families so that they can recognize their individual and collective abilities to tolerate ambiguity. Individuals and family systems differ in their abilities to tolerate the unknown and to be able to create meaning when information is not forthcoming (Boss, 2007). Factors that have been identified as influencing tolerance of ambiguity include cultural values and religious belief systems, as well as perceptions of the ambiguous loss experience.

One possible perception of such an experience can be boundary ambiguity or a sense of blurred boundaries as to who is in or out of the family system or relationship. It may not be clear to family members, or there may be disagreement among family members as to whether a person is part of the psychological or physical family system. In military families, examples can stem from deployment issues. For example, when a parent is deployed, is s/he still expected to be an active parent? How do romantic couples maintain a sense of intimacy when they are separated for 13 months and each are experiencing vastly different daily life experiences? What if a service member receives a "Dear John/Jane" e-mail from a spouse while deployed and there are children in the relationship? There can be uncertainties in knowing if a person is still part of the family or not. Both ambiguous loss and boundary ambiguity may result in feeling "stuck" at a particular moment in family development and individual development. The ambiguity of the situation can make decision-making difficult, families may not have access to rituals to help acknowledge changes in relationships, and communities may not know or acknowledge this loss, either due to cultural or religious norms. Human service professionals using information from ambiguous loss research may be able to help families and individuals process their distress that stems from ambiguous circumstances surrounding a loss in relationship so that they find their path(s) to resiliency in spite of challenges, creating meaning out of their experiences and acknowledging their losses and emotions about the experiences.

A third avenue of expansion in family stress theory is a **family resilience framework**. Froma Walsh, a clinical social worker and researcher, expanded our understanding of key processes involved in family resiliency. Walsh identified (2003c, 2007) several different resources that families may draw upon to help manage and reduce stress and cultivate resiliency and positive growth. These resources are categorized in three different domains of family functioning: family belief systems, family organizational patterns, and family communication processes.

Family systems are powerful transmitters of shared values, norms, and interaction patterns to their members and across generations. This characteristic of families does not mean that everyone in the system shares an identical view of the world and how to interact with others, but that there is a semblance of common ground that can be recognized within the family. Family belief systems shape how members make meaning of their world and when faced by a crisis, it is possible that this worldview could be challenged.

Walsh (2003c) identified several ways in which belief systems can provide a foundation for resilience in families. A family's belief system becomes apparent through a number of avenues. One avenue is through a process family members undertake to construct meaning out of a crisis. For example, they see the crisis as a meaningful challenge to unite rather than to divide and resulting distress and other reactions as understandable given the event and circumstances. Infusing a crisis with such meanings can result in less judgment and more compassion being exchanged among family members. In addition, a positive outlook in which family members exhibit perseverance or a "can-do" attitude, tackle what can be changed and acknowledge what cannot, emphasize each other's strengths, and voice hope can overcome debilitating despair. Finally, spirituality and religious expression and supports provide a larger vision beyond the immediate crisis and offer the possibility of transformative growth.

Family organizational patterns is a second domain in which family processes can cultivate resiliency and positive growth. Such processes include family members demonstrating flexibility in their attitudes, thoughts, and behaviors as they respond to the challenges presented by the crisis while also maintaining necessary stability (e.g., being dependable). Additionally, family members grow or maintain strong connections through mutual support coupled with respecting differences and each member's needs. Leadership by one or more family members offers guidance and protection, and members seek to heal distressed relationships among themselves. Finally, family members utilize social and economic resources by having strong community networks, mentors and extended family, and financial security.

The third and final domain of Walsh's (2002) key processes of family resilience is communication. Communication processes include family members presenting and seeking clarity in messages and information; open emotional sharing of a variety of feelings, including empathy, assuming responsibility for one's own feelings and behaviors, tolerating differences, and engaging in positive interactions and using humor when appropriate; and collaborating together to solve the problems that can be solved and to prevent additional ones when possible.

TRANSLATING THEORY INTO PRACTICE

This section explores recent innovations in promoting a culture of resilience within the military and their families. As Pauline Boss has stated, "Good theory is useful theory" (2007, p. 110). This means that we need to be able to test, apply, and translate our theories into real world settings. We need to be able to refine our theories when a position or hypothesis is not supported and gain a better understanding of how, why, when, and for whom our theories and evidence-based programs work. We first consider the models of resilience developed specifically to recognize the strengths of individuals and families while also acknowledging the challenges of military life. We then give a short description of the ways in which the DoD has incorporated evaluation into family readiness and resilience programs. Chapters 8 and 11 identify evidence-based programs that either have been developed specifically for military families or adapted to a military population. These programs are designed to foster healthy and resilient families and reduce the potential negative effects of adverse experiences that may be particular to military life.

Models of Resilience For Service Members

As Kathleen Marin and Dee Geise emphasized earlier, the military is moving beyond a medical treatment model to prevention by enhancing psychosocial strengths of service members and their families (Casey, 2011). Such an approach recognizes the strengths of individuals and families while also acknowledging the challenges of the military life. The Stress Continuum, the Comprehensive Soldier Fitness (CSF) program, and the Composite Life Cycle Model direct attention to early signs of stress reactions, emphasize ways to recognize and respond to stress in order to build and nurture resilience, and acknowledge the possibility of a pileup of stressors in the lives of service members and their families. As a result, the models offer guidance about the timing of support services and programs to those who work with military families.

Stress Reactions and the Stress Continuum

Combat operational stress reactions refer to the physical, cognitive, emotional, and/ or behavioral stress symptoms as a result of combat or as a result of other operations such as humanitarian assistance missions or peace support operations (Moore & Reger, 2007). Individuals may experience stress reactions because of a life threat (experiencing an event or events that provoke horror, terror, helplessness), wear and tear (result of accumulated stress, the daily grind of a job, or unpredictable events that do not provide time to adjust), loss (grieving loss of people, relationships, dreams), and inner conflict (doing something inconsistent with personal moral code, loss of faith in leaders, guilt about what one did or did not do to try to change a bad circumstance or event). (Nash, Westphal, Watson, & Litz, 2011). Stress reactions are common in humans, whether military or civilian. For example, imagine seeing a car accident, losing a close friend or family member, or carrying a full load of college courses while working full time. Exposure to these stressors is likely to result in stress reactions. While reactions may be experienced for just a few hours or days, or persist for weeks, months, or longer, they do not disrupt functioning. However, while also beginning with exposure to one or more stressors, a stress injury does disrupt functioning; and the more stressors experienced, the greater the risk of a stress injury. Stress injuries include traumatic, fatigue, grief, and moral injuries (Nash et al., 2011).

Combat Operational Stress Control (COSC) is a **core concept** (a principle that guides military leaders as they develop regulations and policies and that sets standards and expectations that leaders are to support) initiated by DoD for implementation by each of the services and coordinated by the DCoE for Psychological Health and Traumatic Brain Injury. According to the Army's *COSC Field Manual*, "the word control is used with combat and operational stress, rather than the word management, to emphasize the active steps that leaders, supporting BH [Behavioral Health] personnel, and individual Soldiers must take to keep stress within an acceptable range" (Headquarters, Department of the Army, 2006, p. 1-1).

COSC policies and programs emphasize enhancing resilience and performance through prevention and early interventions with individuals and families who experience psychological injury. COSC policies guide leaders' responses to and treatment of injuries and illnesses that are often called "invisible" when compared to "visible" physical injuries and illness (Nash et al., 2011).

In the past decade, each branch of the service has developed models and programs to improve, protect, and conserve the emotional health and resilience of their service members in order for them to perform their mission (Vythilingam, 2010). Toward the goal of early intervention, services are training their members to recognize the signs and symptoms of impaired psychological health that are often visible in behaviors, cognitive functioning, and affect; learn that seeking help for such an injury is as wise as seeking help for a physical wound; and know how to seek help for themselves, a buddy, or someone in their command when signs and symptoms are present. To augment the efforts at command levels to reduce the stigma of seeking help for combat and operational stress reactions and injury, the Real Warriors Campaign, launched in 2009 by the DCoE for Psychological Health and Traumatic Brain Injury, provides educational information about and video examples of service members seeking care for psychological health issues and continuing successful military and civilian careers.

The Navy and Marine Corps developed the Stress Continuum, an evidence-based model, for their COSC doctrine. The model was then adopted by DCoE for Psychological Health and Traumatic Brain Injury (n.d.) and other services. The Stress Continuum replaces a medical-illness model in which a service member was considered either ready for duty and not, that is, considered "a go" or a "no go" (Bureau of Medicine & Surgery and Deployment Health Directorate, 2008). Table 5.1 is an adapted version of the Stress Continuum that includes examples of indicators of stress reactions, injury, and illness for individuals and families (Department of the Navy, 2010; U.S. Marine Corps, n.d.-a; Westphal & Woodward, 2010).

In the prior medical-illness culture, a service member not ready for duty was turned over to medical caregivers for "fixing" and turned back to the unit when command leadership would again take over responsibility. Reflecting a major change in

TABLE 5.1 An Adapted Version of the Stress Continuum

Ready	Reacting	Injured	Ill
Individuals	Individuals	Individuals	Individuals
• Optimal performance • Prepared for deployment • Functioning well emotionally, socially, academically, vocationally • Optimistic outlook	• Feeling overwhelmed • Irritable, anxious • Mild or temporary distress or impairment • Sleep disturbances • Problems with concentration	• Guilt, anxiety • Decreased energy • Social isolation • Panic attacks • Addictive behaviors	• Severe stress injuries impacting daily life • Anger, rage • Depression, anxiety, addictive disorders, PTSD • Danger to self/others
Families	Families	Families	Families
• Communicate productively • Children secure, well-adjusted • Positive routines • Emotionally close	• Communication difficulties • Children insecure, acting out • Loss of routines • Reduced emotional closeness	• Silence/fighting • Behavioral problems • Chaotic • Loss of emotional closeness • Verbal/physical abuse	• Persistent problems • Trouble functioning

Self-help useful ⟵————————⟶ *Professional help needed*

Source: Adapted from Department of the Navy. (2010). *Combat and operational stress control (NTTP 1-15M, MCRP 6-11C)*. Washington, DC: Author; U.S. Marine Corps (n.d.-a). *Combat operational stress continuum for families*. Retrieved from http://www.usmc-mccs.org/cosc/coscContMatrixFamily.cfm?sid=ml&smid=6&ss mid=2.

approach, the Stress Continuum describes indicators of psychological health for individuals, families, and commands and refocuses responsibility for promoting psychosocial health on everyone in the system. Therefore, the common goal becomes building a culture that promotes resilience for service members and for families (Westphal & Woodward, 2010).

Recognized in the continuum is the knowledge that stress and trauma may be so overwhelming that individuals, families, or units experience stress reactions, injury, and illness. Prevention of stress reactions occurs through training and education of service members, noncommissioned and commissioned officers, and families about developing and maintaining resilience, including seeking help early when experiencing stress responses as a means to prevent injury and illness. For service members who are injured or ill, treatment is assumed to lead to reintegration with their units. The goal of reintegration is for service members to incorporate their traumatic experiences to establish a productive "new normal" in which they attain or exceed pretrauma levels of functioning (DCoE, 2010b).

The Department of the Navy Stress Continuum information includes guidance about actions individuals and families can take to maintain or regain adaptive coping and positive functioning while stress is present. The Continuum includes a "decision matrix" for determining when to intervene and what to do (U.S. Marine Corps, n.d.-a). Such information educates individuals and families about what signs warrant concern and intervention both for themselves and for others. Applying this guidance, individuals and families are considered "ready" when they are taking good care of themselves, engaging in productive family processes (e.g., clear communication about a stressor, productive conflict resolution, stressors seen as meaningful challenges), and using appropriate community and social resources (e.g., using the free YMCA membership available to families experiencing deployment in order to exercise when feeling tense, seeking out other military families for social and emotional support). The ongoing goal is to continue these positive coping strategies regardless of stressors.

An important expectation in the Stress Continuum model is the responsibility of family, friends, and colleagues and leaders in the military community for promoting and supporting positive coping and for intervening early. When an individual shows initial signs of distress (e.g., sleep disturbances, excessive worry, or anger), family, friends, or colleagues and supervisors at work can encourage the person under stress to engage in healthy behaviors (e.g., adequate sleep, good nutrition, exercise), obtain social support, and seek assistance if distress worsens. Of course, individuals and families can also identify that they need to begin or return to these positive coping strategies. If distress worsens and individuals have loss of functioning (e.g., isolation, outbursts, panic attacks) or a family experiences major disruptions in communication or verbal or physical abuse, families, friends, and others are to provide social support, remain calm, and encourage the person to seek help. If distress or diminished functioning persists (e.g. problems persist and worsen, the person becomes suicidal), they are to obtain medical help for the person, support resulting treatment, and provide social support (COSC, 2007). Coping effectively with challenges includes being aware of one's own stress reactions and personal stressors and using strategies, including seeking assistance, that promote and maintain physical, psychological, social (e.g., family relationships, friendships, work relationships), and spiritual health (Nash et al., 2011; Westphal & Woodward, 2010). In doing so, an individual or family is more likely to be resilient, that is, adapt successfully to exposure to an adverse or traumatic circumstance (MacDermid et al., 2008).

The Army's CSF Program

Comprehensive Soldier Fitness is a strength-based program rooted in positive psychology and designed to enhance soldier, family, and civilian worker resilience and performance. It combines a confidential personal assessment, online training, and unit training (Casey, 2011; Cornum, Matthews, & Seligman, 2011). Individuals assess themselves periodically in four psychosocial domains by taking the Global Assessment Tool (GAT), an online and confidential self-report questionnaire. The results of the GAT in turn direct individuals to relevant training tailored to their individual profile of strengths and assets. The four psychosocial dimensions of fitness are social (e.g, trust in others, feeling respected and valued), emotional (e.g., positive mood, life satisfaction, optimism, active coping style), spiritual (e.g., sustaining beliefs and values), and family (e.g., close relationships, safe and loving home life) (Peterson, Park, & Castro, 2011). In addition to the GAT and tailored training, master resilience trainers conduct unit-level trainings in these psychosocial areas (Reivich, Seligman, & McBride, 2011). Family members can take the GAT and access resilience materials for managing deployment and reintegration by going to the CSF website (http://csf.army.mil).

The Army's Composite Life Cycle Model

The Army's **Composite Life Cycle Model** illustrates how events and transitions in three areas of a soldier's life (i.e., unit, personal work, and family) can pile up across time and areas, potentially overwhelming a service member. The model is part of the Army's Health Promotion and Risk Reduction Campaign (U.S. Army, 2010). A greatly simplified rendition of this model is shown in Figure 5.2.

The stressors associated with the unit level in Figure 5.2 are predeployment, deployment, and reintegration home. Personal work stressors shown include basic and initial training, transitioning to duty assignments (which probably include relocating to another state or overseas), testing for promotion, being promoted, experiencing a death of another soldier, and injury. Stressors that may occur within family life include marriages, birth of a child, financial challenges, relationship difficulties, birth of a second child, divorce, remarriage, co-parenting challenges, and parental illness. Such a visual rendition of the ongoing transitions faced by soldiers and their families emphasizes the importance of readiness in each life cycle strand and the targeting of preventive interventions (e.g., predeployment programs, parenting education, financial literacy skills) at unit, service member, and family transition points (U.S. Army, 2010).

Resilience programming may be targeted toward all military families (i.e., **universal preventive interventions**), toward those who may be at higher risk for developing distress or loss of functioning (i.e., **selected preventive intervention**), or toward individuals who are exhibiting early signs of distress or loss of functioning (i.e., **indicated preventive interventions**) (Mrazek & Haggerty, 1994). As noted earlier, resilience building for military families includes a focus on preventing distress or loss of positive functioning and a focus on providing resources and additional support if family members experience distress, or severe or persistent distress or loss of functioning (Westphal & Woodward, 2010).

Predeployment programs and reintegration programs following return from deployment are examples of universal preventive interventions because almost all military families will experience a deployment. Predeployment programming for families of individual augmentees might be considered selected prevention intervention because these families experience separation from the service member when other families in the same unit do not and thus may be expected to experience greater stress. Many family programs (e.g., New Parent Support Program, FOCUS, Strong Bonds, Yellow Ribbon Reintegration events, financial readiness workshops) and services (e.g., child care, DoD schools, transition assistance program, spouse employment) reviewed in other chapters may be considered universal, selected, and indicated preventive interventions because they can simultaneously serve families experiencing no, some, or a great deal of stress. If distress is too great or functioning too impaired, indicated preventive interventions such as family therapy, substance abuse counseling, or family advocacy may be needed.

The DoD Annual Report to the Congressional Defense Committees (DoD, 2014c) includes a complete list of military family readiness programs and activities currently provided by the DoD and Departments of the Army, Navy, Marine Corps, and Air Force. Since the 2009 report, there has been significant emphasis and support to assess programs for overlap in service delivery and focus and to evaluate programs for their efficacy in strengthening families. One of the civilian partners you will learn about in Chapter 12, the Clearinghouse for Military Family Readiness at Penn State, was specifically tasked with developing evaluation plans and logic models for a set of five family readiness programs. Three of the programs focused on financial readiness for service members, with the remaining two focused on emergency preparedness and couple reintegration after deployment. Now that the evaluations plans and logic models are complete, the Services are partnering with the Military Family Research Institute at Purdue University to conduct a pilot implementation of each plan.

Life Cycle Strands

Passage of Time →

Life Cycle Strands	Join the Military	Year 1	Year 2	Year 3	Year 4	Year 5	Year 6	Year 7
Unit		Predeployment	Deployment	Re-integration	Predeployment	Deployment	Re-integration	Predeployment
Service Member	Basic and Individual Specialty Training	· First duty assignment · Promotion	· Death of a unit member	· Test for promotion · Promotion · Leadership position · Re-enlisting	· New duty assignment	· Injury · Test for promotion · Promotion	· Leadership training	· New duty assignment · Re-enlisting
Family	· Separation from family · Dating · Purchase vehicle	· Marriage · Spouse seeking employment · Major purchases	· Financial challenges	· Birth of first child · Credit counseling	· Relationship problems	· Birth of second child	· Divorce	· Remarriage · Co-parenting and blended family challenges · Parental illness

Figure 5.2 Simplified composite life cycle model. (Adapted from U.S. Army (2010). *Health promotion, risk reduction and suicide prevention report 2010*.

Source: Retrieved from http://www.army.mil/~news/2010/07/28/42934-army-health-promotion-risk-reduction-and-suicide-prevention-report/index.html.)

BOX 5.2 BEST PRACTICES

A MORE HOLISTIC VIEW OF FAMILY SUPPORT AND BUILDING RESILIENCE.

Ms. Geise begins: Prior to 9/11, we had done a lot of work with family support providing programs to help address needs of soldiers and their families such as providing child care and assistance with handling finances. It wasn't always that way. The Wickham white paper, "The Army Family," published in 1983 by Army Chief of Staff General John A. Wickham Jr., changed how the Army provided for soldiers and their families. "The Army Family" recognized the integral support role of soldiers' families and the initiative marked the first systemic effort to design programs and policies comprehensive enough to address Army family concerns as a whole.

The last 10 years with multiple deployments has been a game changer. A service member may be unmarried on a first deployment, married on the second, and a parent by the third. Families are experiencing stresses we never imagined, and these stresses reverberate within a family, affecting everyone.

In 2007, General Casey (36th Chief of Staff of the Army) and Mrs. Casey went out to talk with and, most importantly, listen to families. The Caseys found that service members and families felt they were being left to handle extraordinary demands on their own. We were not focusing on the important things like what happens when a service member returns home.

The Army Family Covenant signed by General Casey in 2007 recognizes the link between readiness and the well-being of families and a new level of commitment from Army leaders to families. It was saying to families, "The Army is behind you."

Ms. Marin continues: Today we have a more holistic view of family support and building resilience. We want to go beyond just reacting and helping families when they are hurting to help them not hurt as much when bad things happen. We want to help build on the strengths they develop in the military and mitigate experiences of combat.

The composite life cycle model has pinpointed stress points so that we can all see and talk about them. The resiliency continuum shows how resilience is built in the individual, family, and society. It is a visual representation of a spectrum of care that says everyone has a responsibility for promoting resilience. These research-based models are helpful at both a content and conceptual level.

We can deconstruct them to be sure we are providing needed services. For example, we can develop a memorandum of agreement (MOA) so that a child of a military family entering her senior year in a new high school doesn't have to take a course in the history of that state to graduate when she already did so in the state where she used to live.

The models add to our understanding of stress and resilience. They are wonderful training tools and have led us to develop our Comprehensive Soldier Fitness and Family Members Program. This path of lifelong learning begins by providing individuals a chance to assess their strengths and weaknesses in four dimensions: emotional, social, spiritual, and family. It then links them to tailored self-development training around thinking skills and coping strategies. They can track their growth over time to enhance performance and build resilience skills.

They can work at a holistic level allowing everyone to see how they can contribute to creating a culture of resiliency. Service providers can see themselves as part of the bigger effort to build resiliency as they realize that any and every contact with a family can make a difference. Think, for example, about clerks at the lending closet who give out pots and pans to new families on an installation. If clerks are schooled as to stress points and ways to promote resilience, they might take an extra minute to smile or ask an open-ended question that could lead a family member to a resource on the base and help them feel welcome.

Kathleen Marin
Director of Installation Services, U.S. Army Office of the Assistant Chief of Staff for Installation Management, and Dee Geise, Chief, Soldier & Family Readiness, U.S. Army `Office of the Assistant Chief of Staff for Installation Management

Voices From the Frontline

REFLECTIONS OF A CHAPLAIN

People do recover and gain strength from difficult times. When I'm with an individual or family who is affected by grief and loss, I try to help people find the opportunity that every feeling and experience brings. I don't want to make it sound simple. It isn't. Helping people see possibilities and hope is part and parcel of healing. If I can avoid judgment and stupid questions—if I can "be there"—stories will be told more easily and people will see they are not alone in their grief, shame, guilt, despair, or whatever they are feeling and that there is hope.

Chaplain Charles Purinton
Army National Guard Chaplain

Each of the branches of family stress theory contributes to our overall understanding of how families meet both normative and nonnormative stressors in the course of their development. The Double ABCx Model provides professionals with a way to map multiple aspects of a stressor event and a family system's response(s) to it over time, including family resiliency. Ambiguous loss theory facilitates a deeper understanding of ways individuals and families may experience living with unknown, unclear, and/or irresolvable losses in their family systems and what supports and resources are helpful in those circumstances. The family resilience framework helps families and practitioners identify key resources families need in order to foster resiliency in the face of struggles. Each of the models and branches of theory presented in this chapter, whether individually or family focused, contributes to the larger field of stress and resilience research and practice.

SUMMARY

- Professionals working with military families will see a broad range of normative and nonnormative stressors that affect individuals of all ages and in varied family relationships. To reiterate Pauline Boss (2007), "Good theory is useful theory" (p. 110).
- Theories and their models must be useful and testable in both research and practice. It is through the interaction of research and practice that we refine, amend, and strengthen our knowledge of human development, human relationships, and human stress and resilience.

EXERCISES

1. We have identified several key concepts used in studying individual and family stress and resilience and started making connections to how these concepts are important to helping professionals. To better see the connection between

theory and practice, divide your group into teams. Each team practices applying at least five concepts to the fictional case study presented in this chapter. When ready, each team presents the description of the case study using the chosen concepts.

2. Continue the theory-to-practice journey by applying one individually focused and one family-focused theoretical model to the case study. What do your models emphasize? Where do you find their greatest utility in providing you with important information? Where do you find their limitations in addressing issues faced by this service member and his family?

3. The Public Broadcasting System (PBS) has documentaries on its website profiling military men and women available. Choose one of the documentaries and follow the story of at least one of the soldiers profiled. To gain a fuller picture, stay with the same soldier for this practice. By doing so, you can begin to see both the characteristics of their stress and their sources of resilience. Films to consider:

A Soldier's Heart (2005)
http://www.pbs.org/wgbh/pages/frontline/shows/heart/etc/credits.html

Lioness (2008)
http://www.pbs.org/independentlens/lioness/film.html

Where Soldiers Come From (2011)
http://www.pbs.org/pov/wheresoldierscomefrom/

First, as you watch one of the programs, determine the following dimensions of the stressor experiences by a soldier and her or his family, using the classification of family stress (Boss, 2001):
    Source of stressor: internal or external?
    Type of stressor: normative or catastrophic, developmental/predictable or situational/unexpected, clear or ambiguous, volitional or nonvolitional?
    Duration: acute or chronic?
    Density: isolated or cumulative?
Second, apply the nine key processes of family resilience (Walsh, 2002, 2003c) by finding examples of family members engaging in a key process of family resilience:
    Belief systems: meaning making, positive outlook, transcendence and spirituality
    Organizational structure: flexibility, connectedness, social and economic resources
    Communication processes: clarity, open emotional sharing, collaborative problem solving
Third, what do you wish was included in the storyline of your soldier to give you more insight into her or his challenges and efforts to be resilient?

6

Individual and Family Development in the Military

In Chapter 6, you will

- Meet Patrick Chandler, SPC (retired) and Graduate Student.
- Learn about basic institutional sources of support designed to help service members meet job-related milestones in early and middle adulthood and handle challenges inherent in a military career.
- Gain insights about typical young adult milestones of marriage and becoming a parent in the military population.
- Learn about specific stress and resilience mechanisms in service members and how they relate to personal and family well-being.

Meet

Patrick Chandler, SFC (Retired), Going To School: Living A Dream

I appreciate school. Education is my goal.

I often hear people say they are going back to school when they get out of the military. But life doesn't always happen that way. By the time you retire, you might have a family, a house, and bills to pay.

After 17 years in the military, I was medically discharged. I'm a wood carver and aspiring artist and always wanted to go to art school. My wife Jackie encouraged me to "live my dream." Thanks to her encouragement and support, I am. I am forever grateful.

At 40, I'm older than three of my teachers. I've been told I look like I'm 24–26, so I don't think my fellow students see me as an icon of days gone by. They know I've been working. I think as we get to know each other and they realize I'm older and have been in the military that they will have some questions.

I think I appreciate school in a different way than many of my younger classmates. Some see education as a means to the end. For me, education is my goal. I know I text more slowly. The other day some of them texted me and didn't think I was answering because I was so slow typing out my response.

I entered school this year as a sophomore. I received credit for five classes based on my military equivalency paperwork. I've received a lot of support from the Military and Veterans Affairs Office. I was surprised at the length they go to. For example, at my university, if you are coming off active duty, tuition is covered for the first semester. That saves a lot of money and will make my GI Bill money go further. I'd like to get my master's degree so I can teach art history and that will take a lot of schooling.

I know my wife is behind me, and my kids are, too. While they don't come up to me and say, "I'm proud of you," they don't get mad when I have to do my homework and they want to play Pictionary. The other day I heard my daughter tell a friend, "My dad is in art school." I hope living in a family where parents are living their dreams teaches our kids that doing so is doable. I certainly hope the path to turning their dreams into reality is shorter and easier than mine.

INTRODUCTION

The previous chapters have drawn your attention to important aspects of military culture, key data about the military family population in both the Active and Reserve Components, common life experiences military families face in times of peace and conflict, and ways that helping professionals frame stress and resilience in their work in order to facilitate healthy coping with military families facing difficult times. By identifying typical and common life course milestones in young and middle adulthood that often co-occur with military service, the goal of the first portion of this chapter is to help you develop a coherent picture of military personnel and their families as they live in our larger society, making comparisons (when possible) to their civilian family counterparts.

Additionally, this chapter focuses on how current research, program, and policy development are being shaped by resilience perspectives both to meet immediate needs of service members and their families and to develop more effective programming that enhances and supports resilience capacities in families. Theory-guided policy and practice help us be more strategic in focusing on important risk and protective factors and developing programs that support individuals and families who may vary greatly in their current stress and resilience processes. However, the amount of research about service members is more extensive than research about their families. The Department of Defense (DoD) initiates a vast array of research about their personnel, tracking, and reporting information to Congress such as the yearly Demographic Profiles. A wide array of information is tracked on installations to assess the utilization of resources and the health and performance of personnel at least in part because personnel (and resources) are funded through the federal government. Military personnel may be expected to participate in surveys and other research by their superiors. Direct information about spouses, children, and other dependents cannot be compelled by unit command, so information about family members relies upon volunteering information and participation in surveys and assessments.

Willerton, MacDermid Wadsworth, and Riggs (2011) note that the scholarship on U.S. military families generally increases during times of military engagement and gradually decreases after actions come to a close. One effect of this cyclical pattern is that researchers draw from current concerns about families in general and can compare and contrast military families with civilian families. This research reveals which issues (e.g., spousal relationships, risk-taking behaviors, trauma/injury, reintegration), organizational factors (e.g., Active or Reserve Component, deployments, combat exposure, unit cohesion), and family characteristics (e.g., marital status, parenting/caregiving responsibilities) are of primary concern during the current military action.

A second potential effect of the rise and fall in research about military families is that most research may be generated when these families are experiencing nonnormative stressors of extended combat deployments. Thus, the body of literature on these families may reflect that we generally know less about everyday resilience and much more when military families face extreme stressors. Researchers and practitioners remind us that it is essential to understand everyday resilience mechanisms in order to better understand how they operate when pileup of stressors occurs (even if stressors are considered typical or short-term) and what happens when the unexpected and/or traumatic events must be addressed while everyday life continues (Davis, Luecken, & Lemery-Chalfant, 2009). A closer examination of the mechanisms of resilience in everyday military life, as well as during times of war, is important in moving beyond crisis management to a focus on resilience and strengths. Such a shift in practice will help us better understand both the daily and extraordinary life events for military families.

Current research trends and program initiatives reflect, in varying degrees, an understanding that stress and resilience are best understood in tandem (Office of the President of the United States, 2011). Since the transition to the all-volunteer force, programs and policies have been implemented that reflect an increased understanding in the importance of strengthening all family systems (not just those identified as high risk), supportive relationships, and community ties (Heubner, Mancini, Bowen, & Orthner, 2009) for enhanced military readiness and family well-being. Yet, there is still a lag in current publications that focus on what we are learning about resilience, particularly with families who may not reach a level of distress that leads to seeking treatment or other interventions designed to help members manage and enhance their resilience strategies.

The next few pages illustrate what we know about common developmental milestones of service members and the material supports that have been developed within the military institution to facilitate these experiences. As you read this chapter and the ones that follow, think about patterns evident in current research about service members and their family systems. Which issues and organizational and familial characteristics have received attention? Which are identified as gaps in our collective knowledge that are important to learn about?

YOUNG ADULTHOOD AND WORK-BASED SUPPORTS IN MILITARY LIFE

As described in Chapter 2, almost half of active duty service members are age 25 or younger and within the Reserve Component one-third are 25 and younger with one-half age 30 and under. Is this also your age group? When you think about the process of becoming an adult in contemporary U.S. society, what are important milestones for young adults in the United States? What are some of the challenges that young adults face today in their efforts to gain expertise for employment, become financially independent, establish a stable residence, form adult friendships and romantic relationships, and make choices about parenthood?

Pursuing work and establishing a career are closely tied to many of these markers of adulthood. When you think about the benefits of employment, what do you list as important or necessary? Perhaps health insurance is a priority, or summers off to spend with children. Maybe the adventures of being highly mobile and traveling to different parts of the United States or other countries is important. Maybe you want to go into a field that has a really good starting salary to help pay off student loans, to help finance your education if you want to go back to school, or to be able to enjoy a certain lifestyle or hobby.

Young adults, whether they are military service members or civilians, face these same questions and challenges both as products of our culture's expectations for this age group and of our current economic, social, and geopolitical circumstances. Take a few moments to reflect on your current financial status. Do you know the average income for full-time employment in your age and education bracket? Does your current (or future) job/career provide a wide array of benefits such as on-the-job training; opportunities for advancement; and help with expenses such as housing, food, child care, and health insurance? Do you know if your chosen field has supportive family policies? The following section reviews many of these material supports for both military and civilian populations in relation to understanding models of stress and resilience.

The military as a major social institution has made significant shifts in both material and social supports for service members since the transition to an all-volunteer force in 1973 (Kelty, Kleykamp, & Segal, 2010). These supports affect many decisions young adults make about entering military service and extending service or transitioning back to civilian life. Under the all-volunteer system, the U.S. military is subject to market forces just as any other business organization and has had to adjust in order to recruit and retain quality personnel. Traditional investment in training and supporting service members expanded after 1973 to include family support in order to provide a viable career pathway that extended beyond the typical 2–4 years' service in the former conscription system.

As Kelty and colleagues (2010) point out, military service functions differently in the transition to adulthood under the all-volunteer system than it did in the earlier conscription era. Conscription led to a force that was primarily young, single, and male with a low likelihood of career service, and these young persons were more likely to delay milestones that are markers of adulthood, such as marriage and parenthood. Additionally, conscripted service was more likely to interrupt progress in education and career development until the advent of the first GI Bill, which specifically funded higher education opportunities for returning service members after World War II. Kelty and colleagues posit that young adults entering military service today are more likely to view this move as either a transformative step to adult roles and responsibilities associated with a career or an investment in gaining knowledge, skills, and abilities to better meet future life goals after military service.

Other than the GI Bill, and the expanded versions that have been implemented since 2001, what types of material and social supports are offered to service members that would be helpful in transitioning into adult roles and responsibilities? Take a moment to review Figure 5.1 and its descriptive text in Chapter 5 that describes sources of support at the individual and family levels. As you make connections between resources of support and well-being, can you identify resources that might be available for one deployment but not always available for multiple deployments? What challenges do military personnel and their families face in finding or accessing resources when there is a combat injury, a move to a new duty station, a child is completing college applications, or a parent has a health crisis? The next few paragraphs highlight ways in which the organizational structure of the military addresses multiple needs of service members and their families, enhancing resources for support and well-being, particularly for the young adult, Active Component population. More detailed information on specific policies and programs that provide support to military families are detailed in Chapters 11 and 12.

Job Training and Unit Cohesion

Each branch within the military provides training for every occupation (MOS) needed to function in its organization and connects individual service members through the hierarchical structures of unit and rank. Entering service members complete both basic and advanced training and continue skill development throughout their time in service by attending both technical and leadership schools. Additionally, each branch utilizes a buddy system that begins in basic training as part of a way to help the new recruit transition from civilian to service member and learn how to work as part of a team with responsibility for the well-being of one's colleagues that extends from work to life (Ramsberger, LeGree, & Mills, 2003). Service members are paired with a colleague who may be at the same level/rank or with a more experienced service member, depending on the overall purpose. This system is called Battle Buddies in the Army, Shipmates in the Navy, and Wingmen in the Air Force. Thus, job skill training, job advancement opportunities, and structured connections to one's work and social community are integrated into military life and culture for the service member.

Compensation, Benefits, and Allowances

All training is "on the job," such that service members are employed (paid with access to benefits) during their training. In terms of pay compensation, there are more than 70 unique types of pay and allowances for which a service member may be eligible in addition to basic monthly pay (http://www.military.com/benefits/military-pay/military-pay-overview). Salary is based on rank, longevity, and annual pay raises or cost of living adjustments (COLA). Service members also receive special pay beyond salary for work such as foreign language learning, hardship or hazardous duty, special duty assignments, combat-related injury and rehabilitation, and overseas extensions, among other work and skill acquisition assignments. Military members are usually paid twice per month and receive a Leave and Earnings Statement (LES; a military "paycheck"). The LES gives monthly information about entitlements (pay, allowances, incentive pay), deductions (e.g., taxes and allotments which are money sent to banks, pay for TRICARE), and status of leave used and available.

Table 6.1 shows the 2013 rates of pay for the general U.S. population by age and education level. This is the latest year for which data about the U.S. civilian population is currently available. A recent report by the Congressional Budget Office (CBO, 2011) specifically compared federal civilian employee salaries with military personnel cash compensation rates. When educational attainment, years on the job, and gender (male federal civilian workers only) are matched, both enlisted and officer rank military personnel earn more than their federal civilian counterparts. The average enlisted person earns more cash compensation than 75% of the average civilian employee; compared to median officer cash compensation, that margin increases after 2 years of service and grows at a greater rate than the enlisted median. Rates for military personnel in 2014 are available at the following Secretary of Defense website: http://militarypay. defense.gov/pay/bp/index.html. Table 6.2 shows the average basic pay compensation for service members at the most commonly achieved ranks in their first 4 years in the

TABLE 6.1   Civilian Full-Time, Year-Round Mean Earnings by Age and Educational Attainment in FY 2013

Age	High School Graduate or GED	Bachelor's Degree	Master's Degree	Professional Degree
	Educational Level			
18–24 years	$17,638	$28,149	$29,936	–
25–29 years	$29,128	$44,161	$52,188	$51,306

Source: Data compiled from the U.S. Census Bureau, Current Population Survey (2013). Annual Social and Economic Supplement. Table PINC-04. Retrieved from http://www.census.gov/hhes/www/cpstables/032014/perinc/pinc04_000.htm

TABLE 6.2   Examples of Mean Monthly and Yearly Basic Pay by Rank and Years of Service in FY 2014 (Most Common Young Adult Ranks Shown)

Years of Service	E-1 to E-4 Monthly	E-1 to E-4 Annual	E-5 to E-7 Monthly	E-5 to E-7 Annual	O-1 to O-4 Monthly	O-1 to O-4 Annual
2 or fewer years	$1,693.92	$20,327.04	$2,488.10	$29,857.20	$3,645.50	$43,746.00
3–4 years	$1,888.80	$22,665.60	$2,824.76	$33,897.12	$4,613.11	$55,357.32

Source: Data compiled from Office of the Assistant Secretary of Defense, Personnel and Readiness (2014). Monthly basic pay table for 2014. Retrieved from http://militarypay.defense.gov/pay/BASIC/docs/Active%20Duty%20Tables/2014 BasicPayTableActiveUncapped.pdf military. Generally speaking, basic pay comprises about 55% of an active duty service member's total compensation package (Hogan & Seifert, 2010) with special pay and allowances constituting the remaining 45%. So what types of allowances are included in the remaining 45% of the compensation?

Basic needs such as housing, medical care, grocery/other shopping, and outlets for recreation are often met through multiple services on a military installation and the costs associated with many of these services are offset by specific **allowances** (a set dollar amount that is designed to at least partially compensate for the costs of items considered necessary for the service member). Active duty service members and their families primarily live on or close to the installation where the service member is stationed. In fact, the majority of single service members are required to live on their installation. Married service members may live on the installation or the neighboring civilian community, and all active duty service members are allotted a Basic Allowance for Housing (BAH). The BAH rate is based on whether the service member has dependents (spouse, children, other dependents) and where the service member is stationed. You can view current and past BAH rates at http://www.military.com/benefits/military-pay/basic-allowance-for-housing-rates. Service members are also provided with a Basic Allowance for Subsistence (BAS), which is intended to offset the monthly cost of meals, but only for the service member. Additionally, all service members and their dependents are covered by the DoD's healthcare system, TRICARE. Just as with health insurance in the civilian market, there are different plans and options within TRICARE and these vary in terms of their deductibles, co-pays, and health issues covered. Consequently, military personnel and their families have to research these options to choose what best meets their needs and fits their budget.

Larger installations typically offer several amenities where goods can be purchased tax free, including a **commissary** (grocery store), an **exchange** (a series of stores where durable goods and merchandise, as well as restaurants, postal services, and businesses such as hair salons are available), and **shoppettes** (convenience stores). Additional amenities include health-care facilities and various recreation facilities (e.g., bowling alleys, recreational centers, golf courses). Child Development Centers and schools overseen by the DoDEA are also located on military installations. Large installations within the United States and outside the United States offer these amenities to help meet the needs of daily life for service members, civilian employees, and their families. For both new and established service members and newly activated Reserve Component members, the amenities provided within the installation can help ease the hassles of finding similar facilities in the neighboring civilian community, particularly when new to an installation and community. The establishment of these services on installations indicates a significant commitment by the military to supply a comprehensive infrastructure for community-level material and social supports. These services continue to be available to family members during off-site training and deployments that service members expect as part of their work. By developing this social infrastructure, the military has transitioned to an organization that is both more family and career military oriented than in the conscription era.

FAMILY DEVELOPMENT IN EARLY AND MIDDLE ADULTHOOD AND WORK-BASED SUPPORTS IN MILITARY LIFE

Two significant life milestones often associated with early and middle adulthood are finding a long-term romantic partner and having children and, within the military, each of these milestones can impact recruitment and retention. Both of these milestones are affected by several factors in the U.S. civilian population, including geographic location, age, race/ethnicity, and education level. Research in the active duty military population also indicates that some of these factors influence timing of marriage, such as sex (Lundquist & Smith, 2005) and educational status (Segal & Segal, 2004), while recent research on the links between race, military service, and marriage indicates a significant departure from civilian norms (Lundquist, 2004; Teachman & Tedrow, 2008). How may active duty military status impact the likelihood of marrying in young adulthood? And, are Active Component personnel and Reserve Component personnel similar in marital patterns?

Transitions to Marriage

In Chapter 2, you learned the basics of how many service members in the Active and Reserve Components are married as related to their rank and gender and by branch of service. Generally speaking, as personnel progress in rank, they are more likely to be married. This is due, at least in part, to another important factor: age. The marriage rate is one demographic variable where there are some significant differences between the Active and Reserve Component (National Healthy Marriage Resource Center, 2010). Active duty personnel are more likely to be married than both their Reserve Component counterparts and the civilian population. In Fiscal Year (FY) 2013, over half of all active duty personnel were married with just over one-third of active duty personnel married at the lowest enlisted levels (E-1 to E-4) and over one-half of the entry level officer ranks (O-1 to O-3) married across all branches (DASD, 2014). Percentages of those married increase at each level in both the enlisted and officer groups of the Active Component with married status rates of 84% for those at the highest enlisted ranks of E-7 to E-9 and warrant officers (W-1 to W-5) and 97% of the highest ranking officers (O-7 to O-10) married across all branches in FY 2013. Within the selected reserve, fewer personnel were likely to be married at all enlisted levels as compared to their active duty counterparts (fewer than one-quarter in the youngest reserve ranks of E-1 to E-4 versus just over one-third of active duty at similar ranks) and this trend holds true between active duty and selected reserve and in comparing enlisted and officer categories in the two components in all but one group. Junior officers (O-1 to O-3) in the selected reserve were equally likely to be married as their active duty colleagues.

There are several factors that may increase the likelihood that active duty members will marry and may influence marrying at an earlier age than in the civilian population (see Box 6.1). The current payout structure of living allowances and other in-kind benefits

---

BOX 6.1   VOICES FROM THE FRONTLINE

SUPPORTING MARRIAGE

If you look at students on a college campus, the expectation is that you are single. In the military we bring young, enlisted troops into a campus culture and in subtle and not so subtle ways encourage them to marry young for the benefits.

It's common for a new recruit to think, "If I got married, I'd have a home, kitchen, more space, more income. It beats sharing a room in the barracks."

Wanting to be accepted and loved is a human need, especially when you are on an installation away from your family, your friends are deploying, and some of them may be getting injured or killed. You know you will soon be deploying too and who knows what may happen.

This is a big difference between young people of the same age who have taken different paths in life. It's one that can influence their relationships and families in the years to come.

Evonne Carawan
Director, Personnel Readiness and Community Support, Office of the Deputy Assistant Secretary of the Navy (Military Personnel Policy)

result in a pay increase for a service member who marries, regardless of rank and time in service (Hogan & Seifert, 2010). Additionally, single service members may want to improve their living quarters by moving out of the single member barracks and into married housing on base or off-base housing in the local community. Both of these options are typically restricted to married service members. Other research has also noted that individuals who choose the military are more likely to adhere to traditional values, one of which is placing a high regard on marriage (Hogan & Seifert, 2010; Karney & Crown, 2007; Lundquist, 2006). The military has also instituted family programming that is focused on strengthening marital relationships, such as *Strong Bonds*, and helping the single and dating population make healthy choices in romantic relationships. *Strong Bonds* and other programs geared toward strengthening family and important social relationships are detailed in Chapters 8, 11, and 12.

Other interesting differences in marriage rates between the Active Component and civilian populations are identified in research that focuses on race/ethnicity and military service. In particular, Lundquist (2004, 2006) and Teachman and Tedrow (2008) have highlighted how military service may act as a factor in promoting marriage for African American personnel and sustaining these marriages at significantly higher rates than their civilian counterparts. Lundquist argues that the military offers a structural context that minimizes differences for both racial and economic factors, which are often cited as contributing to significant differences in marriages rates between Black and White populations in the United States (Goldstein & Kenney, 2001; Sampson, 1995). As an integrated, merit-based, and **"total" institution** (one that rewards and promotes based on performance and that has 24/7 influence in an individual's daily experiences on and off the job), Lundquist contends that the military provides an environment in which African American men and women have access to equal employment opportunities and daily living supports that are more difficult to access in the civilian population. Further, as an institution that implemented a highly structured, racial desegregation plan in the mid-twentieth century, military installations and military connected communities that surround installations rank among the least racially segregated communities in the United States (Lundquist, 2004). Racially segregated workplaces and communities are associated with stronger perceptions of racial discrimination and higher reports of minority stress, thus the military context may serve to lessen the effects of both institutional and daily experiences of discrimination based on race for African American service personnel and their families in ways that are supportive of healthier family and relational outcomes.

Transitions to Parenthood

Earlier chapters have highlighted information about military families, such that you already know that in FY 2013 the birth to age 7 group of children constituted over half (54%) of the total number of children in active duty families and 43% of active duty members had children (DASD, 2014). In the selected reserve the trend of having slightly older personnel translates into a smaller percentage of children in the birth to age 7 group (40%). Table 6.3 gives the average ages at which members across active and selected reserve became parents for the first time in FY 2013. In that year, the average age of the active duty service member at the time of his/her first child's birth ranged from 24.1 years in the Marine Corps to 26.4 in the Air Force, and over half (50.8%) of members were between 20 and 25 years old at the time of their first child's birth. Within the selected reserve the age at first birth ranged from 25.7 years in the Marine Corps Reserve to 29.1 years in the Air Force Reserve. Forty percent of all first-time parents in the selected reserve in FY 2013 were between 20 and 25 years of age.

TABLE 6.3   Average Age at Birth of First Child in FY 2013 by Service Branch and Component

Active Duty		Selected Reserve	
	Average Age		Average Age
Marine Corps	24.1	Marine Corps Reserve	25.7
Army	25.4	Army National Guard	26.3
Navy	26.2	Army Reserve	27.3
Air Force	26.4	Air National Guard	29.0
		Navy Reserve	29.9
		Air Force Reserve	29.1
Total DoD	25.6	Total Select Reserve	27.3

Source: Data compiled from Office of the Deputy Assistant Secretary of Defense (Military Community and Family Policy) (2014). Exhibits 5.24 (p. 129) and 6.19 (p. 150). *2013 demographics: Profile of the military community.* Washington, DC: Author.

Average age at the onset of parenthood among active duty service members is slightly earlier as compared to the civilian population in the United States, which has seen a gradual rise in age at first birth for women (Mathews & Hamilton, 2009). Additionally, service members are most likely to be in their 20s and less likely to be in their teens or 30s when they become parents, which means that the range of typical ages at first birth is more restricted in the service member population as compared to the civilian population (MacDermid Wadsworth, 2010). Within the civilian population in 2006, age at first birth for women ranged from 22.6 years in Mississippi to 27.7 years in Massachusetts, with an average across the United States of 25 years. According to the 2002 National Survey of Family Growth, for males between ages 14 and 44 years, the average age at first child's birth was 25.1 years (Martinez, Chandra, Abma, Jones, & Mosher, 2002).

The most common age at which active duty males became a parent in FY 2013 was 22 years, while the most common age at birth of their first child for active duty females was 21 years. Within the Reserve Component, the most common age for male service members at birth of their first child was 27 years; it was 22 years for female service members. These average and most common ages at first birth held steady for Demographics Reports from FY 2003 through FY 2009 (DUSD, 2004, 2005, 2006, 2007, 2008, 2009a, 2009b, 2010). However, the most common age at birth of first child increased for active duty females and both males and females in the Reserve Component between 2010 and 2013 (DUSD 2011, 2012, 2013, 2014).

Researchers consistently point to the compensation system of allowances and the economic stability (relative to work in the civilian workforce) of military service, as well as strong support structures for family needs as factors that may lead to higher rates of earlier marriage and childbearing within the active duty service population (Hogan & Seifert, 2010; Kelty et al., 2010; Lundquist, 2004). The additional allowances that cover medical care and child care, in addition to the previously mentioned housing allowance, are part of the material supports to which these military families have access.

The DoD has also developed extensive family support programs that extend from spousal hiring initiatives to organized child and youth activities and strong school-community collaborations that may be perceived as family friendly, particularly to a service member who knows that their occupation may demand long and/or frequent separations from family, as well as put them in harm's way. There are also more specialized programs to help families address unique needs that members may have. For example, families who have a special needs family member, such as a child with a developmental delay or a medically fragile parent who is identified as a dependent in the DEERS system, have access to programs including the Exceptional Family Member Program (see Chapter 11 for more details). This combination of allowances and material and social supports creates an institution that encourages family development in young and middle adulthood, in spite of the stressors and dangers that were identified in Chapter 3 as expectable and normative in military life.

Military Connected Communities

The combination of military-based supports may also be viewed as community friendly. In military-affected communities, the local economy and resources are influenced by the presence of a military installation. Families may live off base; spouses may work in the local economy; civilians may work on base; and schools, religious communities, and businesses may provide resources of support and community building for all local persons. One very practical example of the military–community connection is in working with schools. Not all installations, particularly within the United States, have schools on base, and those that do are most likely to have elementary level only, with secondary students attending schools in the community.

School districts are funded by a variety of sources and often receive some funding on a *per student* basis. Thus, it is important to have a very close approximation of the number of students in a school district in order to have an accurate budget for operating costs and be ready to hire or release instructors and other personnel based on these changes. In a community that is connected to a military installation, the student count can vary based on restructuring, deployments, periodic turnover of personnel, and the addition or deletion of services (and thus personnel) at an installation. The DoD is required to coordinate with Local Educational Agencies (LEAs) to identify specific installations that are scheduled to experience population shifts that will affect the local school systems (DoDEA, 2015). This coordination is viewed as an important aspect of both family and operational readiness and is designed to meet several needs: school districts can plan ahead for changes in student population and prepare staff for changes that students may experience while in attendance (such as relocation and parental deployment/reunification) and families can rely on the coordination of the military and community to help accomplish the multiple tasks of helping children change school systems.

One initiative of this mandate is the Interstate Compact on Educational Opportunity for Military Children. In Chapter 4, you learned that this initiative is designed to help streamline multiple aspects of paperwork involved in enrolling a child into a new school system. Children in active duty families attend an average of eight different schools between kindergarten and high school graduation. Each change is an exercise in tracking paperwork and learning a new school district's requirements. Families receive a direct benefit from the military–local community connection through the establishment of the Interstate Compact. By working with local communities and school systems, this Compact simplifies the school transition process and supports children who experience high mobility in their school age years.

Connections between the military and the local community can come in other forms, too. As you read below about Chaplin Purinton's experiences and his perspective on his role in the military and the community, what other connections do you think would be useful and promote healthy relationships and interactions in military connected communities? Do you know of any connections in your communities that try to improve connections between military families and the larger community?

ON BRIDGING THE INFORMATION GAP BETWEEN MILITARY AND CIVILIAN COMMUNITIES

One of the chaplain's roles is that of pastor, to provide religious leadership. We are also trained to various degrees in counseling. As clergy in uniform, our job is supporting people as they experience the cycle of life while moving through the cycle of deployment.

Some states have developed initiatives such as the Military, Family and Community Network (MFCNetwork) of Vermont. Its mission is, "To develop and maintain a multi-group network among community, military, government and private sectors that creates awareness of challenges, identifies resources and provides services to all service members and their families throughout the deployment cycle" (http://www.vtmfen. org). I am a member of this group and I spoke to the state Chiefs of Police organization as a member of the network. Weeks after a 15-minute presentation, I began to hear from law enforcement professionals and members of our community that something had changed. When stopped for speeding, people were being asked: "Are you a member of a military family?" and if yes, "Have you recently returned home from deployment?" There are many small things all of us can do that when added together make a difference for military families.

Chaplain Charles Purinton
Army National Guard Chaplain

Several sources of military-based support, developed since the transition to the all volunteer force, support significant developmental milestones expected in early and middle adulthood, namely marriage and parenthood. In order for these support systems to flourish and improve, reviews of their effectiveness and value to both the service member and his/her family are conducted. As you learned in Chapter 5, most theories on stress and resilience acknowledge that individuals and families may perceive potential resources very differently and, based on their perceptions of need, they may or may not choose to access or rely on particular resources. Additionally, some resources may only be useful in the short-term, and the family may have to make adjustments as to which resources are tapped when confronted with a stressor or a series of stressors. The next section focuses on what we have learned about resilience and capacity building in military families and, when possible, makes connections to the supports that have been identified in the first part of this chapter.

UNDERSTANDING RESEARCH ABOUT RISK AND RESILIENCE

This section presents a growing body of research that has focused on identifying protective and risk factors in relation to resilience in service members and military families. Chapters 7 and 8 review current research specifically focused on how service members and their families are affected by war. For those of you who may not have taken a research class recently, some basic elements that define who/what is studied, how the group/topic is studied, and the strengths and limitations of different kinds of research are briefly reviewed.

Both the DoD and military family scholars have adopted **longitudinal** approaches to research on service members and their families. Longitudinal studies allow us *to follow people over time*, gathering data at multiple points, noting changes, and identifying factors that predict both vulnerability and resilience. For example, Karney and Crown (2011) report on the likelihood that deployment (deployed status, multiple or extended deployments) increases or decreases the risk of marital dissolution over time. Their data-set included all personnel (active duty and selected reserve) who were active between FY 2002 and FY 2005.

Perhaps the most significant undertaking in longitudinal research with service members is the Millennium Cohort Study. In 2001, the DoD began a 22-year longitu-dinal cohort study on the effects of military service, including deployments, on service member health and well-being while serving and after separation from military service. This study is the most comprehensive ever undertaken in U.S. military history to study the long-term effects of military service (http://www.millenniumcohort.org/index.php), and data are being collected every 3 years until 2022. The intent is to follow respon-dents even if they separate from service in order to learn about the development of any patterns related to their service experiences and physical and psychological health out-comes. The data collection process identifies each new set of respondents as **cohorts**. A cohort consists of new enrollees who join the study at the same time and the research design calls for multiple points of new enrollments. In 2011 the study was expanded to include a fourth cohort. The 2011 cohort will be the first to include both service mem-bers ($n = 50,000$) and spouses ($n = 10,000$), which will create opportunities for learning about couple dynamics and family level health.

Cross-sectional studies are also useful in learning about service members and their families. This type of study can provide us with rich information about events, incidents, and perceptions by *collecting data from a group at a single point in time*. Flake, Davis, Johnson, and Middleton (2009) offer an example of a cross-sectional study that relied on self-reports of Army spouses to report about their school age children's well-being during a deployment that affected a large Army base community. Cross-sectional studies often are referred to as "snapshots" that capture information at a specific point in time. Cross-sectional research can be helpful in assessing current moods, conditions, and needs of a population or com-munity and provide information that can be used for longer-term planning and research.

Both types of studies are useful in their application to military personnel and families, although there are differences in **scope** (how broad the research question is and how widely it can be generalized) and application. Helping professionals can use findings from Karney and Crown (2011) to develop marital support programs for groups that are at higher risk of marital dissolution, such as women service members in the Active Component and in the Army National Guard and Navy Reservists who do not have children. This study also dis-putes the conventional wisdom that families who experience deployment are automatically or commonly at risk for divorce, particularly if they have children. Programs for marriage enrichment can identify positive aspects of deployment for both the service member and his/her family while offering skills and resources to help families attain positive growth despite the stressors of deployment.

Professionals working on particular installations can use the findings from Flake et al. (2009) to identify and address current issues deployed families are facing at a particular installation or in a community and tailor support programs to better meet the specific needs that those family members are facing. For example, if a unit has experienced a high injury rate, there are likely several families who now need to navigate the health-care system; make decisions about travel to medical facilities, care of children and time off of work; and face the possibilities of death or long-term injury care of their service member. Although there are multiple resources to address these demands, the ways that family support professionals help families navigate these demands may differ in what it "looks like" at an active duty installation versus a four-county National Guard community affected by the same events. Critical skills for helping professionals include being able to take into consideration details about the unique experiences in the family system, their local military and civilian communities, and the in-theatre experiences of deployed service members.

Other aspects of research that scholars must address include defining how in-depth the study will be, how broadly one can **generalize** what is learned from the study (Does it apply to everyone all the time? Or to specific groups at a specific point in time?), and the best ways to communicate the findings to different **constituents** (people and organizations that can benefit from the knowledge gained, as well as any sponsors of the research). As you read the next section, keep these questions in mind to help you understand how much each study can tell us about service members and family life and where gaps in our knowledge still exist.

RECENT RESEARCH ON RISK AND RESILIENCE IN SERVICE MEMBERS

There is no shortage of research within the military community. In fact, research informs almost every facet of military life and organization. As an organization, the DoD relies on healthy and highly trained individuals who will remain in service for time spans ranging from a few years to a lifelong career. Thus, organizational research primarily focuses on issues that create risks to maintaining a physically and psychologically healthy unit ready to answer the call of service. Overarching questions include what experiences/issues pose threats to or promote strength and health in service members, what kinds of prevention and intervention policies and programs address these threats or strengths effectively, and what improvements in services (physical, psychological, medical, familial) are needed. Although most of the research about service members reviewed here has been since 2001, a large body of research on service members predating 2001 exists and some of it will be included.

Several behaviors and experiences have been identified, many in the years prior to OIE/OIF, as contributing to either heightened risks for or protection against negative effects of trauma. **Risky behaviors** include, but are not limited to alcohol and other drug misuse, disordered eating, increased risk-taking, and both sexual and nonsexual aggression. Life experiences that may put a service member at increased risk for negative physical, emotional, and/or relational well-being include combat and trauma exposure, traumatic injury, family history of violence and previous experiences as a victim of personal violence (familial, interpersonal, sexual), and family history of mental health risks (e.g. depression, anxiety, PTSD) (Solomon, Zur-Noah, Horesh, Zerach, & Keinan, 2008). **Protective factors** are those skills and resources that individuals and families can draw upon to help them cope with adversity. Protective factors can include staying connected with family and friends, being part of a unit with high trust and cohesion and strong leadership, maintaining or implementing behaviors such as getting enough rest and eating healthy, and having a positive sense of one's ability to persevere in tough times.

Interestingly, many of these risky behaviors, experiences, and protective factors are also a focus for screening within adolescent medicine (Hutchinson, Greene, & Hansen, 2008), which refers to health care for persons between the ages of 10 and 25 years. Hutchinson and colleagues advocate using and/or modifying two psychosocial evaluation tools common to this branch of medicine with service members, as 45% of the active duty and 33% of the selected reserve are ages 25 and under. The HEADSSS (Home, Education, Activity, Drugs, Sex, Suicide, and Safety) interview, with a few modifications to address military life, is designed to screen both for risky behaviors and contexts, as well as potential protective factors while framing the assessment in a strengths model that helps the adolescent become more aware of their behaviors and motivations, as well as sources of stress and support (Duncan et al., 2007; Goldenring & Cohen, 1988). Hutchinson and colleagues also recommend the CRAFFT (Car, Relax, Alone, Forget, Family, and Trouble) screening instrument, which focuses specifically on behaviors associated with substance abuse (Werner, Walker, & Greene, 1994). Both tools can augment other behavioral screenings and have validity in nonmilitary populations. Screening instruments such as these can give insight into the health and safety of a young military population, both of which may impact readiness.

Baseline Data from the Millennium Cohort Study

As mentioned earlier, the Millennium Cohort Study is longitudinal and is expected to have a wide variety of implications on the physical and psychological effects of military service for both service members and their families, across Active and Reserve Components, extending to life after service (veteran status). Data from the first cohort ($n = 77,000$ participants from 2001 to 2003) provided a baseline of information about rates of mental disorders and health issues found in this representative sample. **Baseline data** is the first data gathered in a longitudinal study, and it provides a comparison point for all future data. An important aspect of baseline data of the Millennium Cohort Study is that it was collected *prior to* our current involvement in OIE/OIF. Thus, the data reflect information about service member's health and wellness during peacetime and will allow researchers to assess the effects of multiple military service experiences, such as deployments and types of deployment exposures on both physical and mental health outcomes.

Physical and psychological health. What has the Millennium Cohort Study Team learned so far? Baseline data from the first cohort indicates that this cohort was as healthy or healthier when compared to the civilian population with the exception of alcohol use. This baseline data also established the prevalence rates of key mental disorders and risk-taking behaviors that can be followed over time for specific subgroups within the military population. These preconflict data allowed the study team to design **prospective** studies or studies that start in the present and continue into the future to see what experiences are linked to physical and psychological health outcomes late in life. To date, the publications generated from the early waves of data collection have begun to identify prevalence of risk factors and threats to both physical and psychological well-being for service members.

Health risk factors, including changes in risky behaviors and the development of health problems, are being tracked with this data set in relation to deployment experiences. Recent reports about these data find that negative behavioral changes include disrupted sleep patterns (Seelig et al., 2010), disordered eating patterns (Jacobson et al., 2009), cigarette smoking (Smith, Ryan, et al., 2008), and alcohol use (Jacobson et al., 2008). Health problems diagnosed since deployment include the development of diabetes (Boyko et al., 2010), high blood pressure (Granado et al., 2009), and respiratory problems (Smith, Wong, et al., 2009).

Psychological risk factors are also under consideration by the study team, and links between protective and risk factors to PTSD, depression, and anxiety are beginning to come into focus. Recent research from the Millennium Cohort research team indicates that predeployment experiences of both physical injury and psychological distress (Sandweiss et al., 2011) and prior trauma exposure (Smith, Wingard, et al., 2008) are linked with higher risk for postdeployment PTSD.

Continuing research of the Millennium Cohort participants is now beginning to identify common and less common trajectories of trauma and resilience of single and multiple deployers. Bonnano and colleagues (2012) focused on a sample of active duty, Reserve, and National Guard, who had deployed a single time ($n = 3,393$) or multiple times ($n = 4,394$). Data from this study are encouraging in that overwhelmingly, both single deployers and multiple deployers showed a low and stable pattern in their pre-deployment to post-deployment post-traumatic stress reports (83.1% and 84.9%, respectively, with an average of 2.7 years between assessments). The next most common trajectory was a moderate to improving post-traumatic stress across the deployment cycle (8% single and 8.5% multiple deployers). There was also a small group that was high in their reports of post-traumatic stress pre-deployment who were stable at post-deployment (2.2% each deployment group). The fourth trajectory represented by both single and multiple deployer groups was described as worsening-chronic. This trajectory started with lower pre-deployment levels of post-traumatic stress, but that stress increased significantly post-deployment. Army personnel with more combat exposure were more likely than any other service branch to be in the worsening-chronic group, whether they were in the single or multiple deployer group.

This study has some important findings for understanding deployment(s) and post-traumatic stress. First, the vast majority of personnel had low stress across the deployment cycle, indicating that resilience is the norm, whether one has experienced a single deployment or has deployed multiple times. Second, the next most common trajectories that started with elevated stress either maintained or lowered their stress levels across the deployment cycle. Third, for those who experienced more combat were also more likely to have chronic and worsening stress, a finding supported by other combat and trauma research. As the study progresses through to 2022, researchers will be able to identify patterns that contribute to well-being and resilience when service members face adverse events, repeated or multiple types of military-based stressors, and the roles that spouses and other social relationships play in affecting overall resilience.

There are several other studies, not tied to the Millennium data set, currently underway and recently completed that augment our knowledge about risk and protective factors for service members. Each study helps fill in gaps in our knowledge, improve measurement of risk and resilience, and gives better direction for program and policy development in supporting healthy outcomes for service members. A closer examination of three specific risk-taking behaviors follows below. From a helping professional's perspective, engaging in risk-taking behaviors may be important indicators of psychological distress and may be the ways in which the service member is trying to manage his/her distress.

Problem drinking. Alcohol misuse is a significant area of concern within the Armed Forces and is a topic also widely studied in the general U.S. population. Several recent studies have examined alcohol use in different military populations: women (Wallace, Sheehan, & Young-Zu, 2009), junior personnel (Williams, et al., 2010), active duty personnel (Stahre, Brewer, Fonseca, & Naimi, 2009), and National Guard (Ferrier-Aurbach et al., 2009). Additional research has also focused on alcohol use in relation to combat deployment experiences (Jacobson, et al., 2008).

Gender and age are consistently associated with increased risk of alcohol misuse in the military context. Women, representing approximately 15% of the military (DUSD, 2010), and junior enlisted personnel, those between the ages of 18 and 25, are considered to be at higher risk for problem drinking, similar to their same age civilian counterparts. Previous research indicates that women in traditionally male occupations (Wilsnack & Wilsnack, 1995) and women in the military (Ames & Cunradi, 2004) have higher rates of problem drinking than women in traditionally female occupations and men in the military, respectively. Junior personnel in both the Navy and Air Force have also been found to be at higher risk for problem drinking, such as binge drinking, than their older counterparts, both when compared to their respective branch and to other service branches in the recent baseline report from the Millennium Cohort Study (Riddle et al., 2007).

Binge drinking rates in the Active component, across all branches and ranks, were very common in anonymously reported behaviors on the 2005 Department of Defense Survey of Health Related Behaviors ($n = 12,197$ reported at least one episode out of 16,037 total respondents). Two-thirds reported at least one binge-drinking episode occurring between the ages of 17 and 25 (Stahre et al., 2009). Marines reported the greatest prevalence of binge drinking within 30 days of completing the survey (51.4%) and over the past year

(28.2%). Men, across all branches, averaged just under 42 episodes per year, while women (again across all branches) averaged just under 19 episodes of binge drinking per year. As a point of comparison, binge-drinking rates in the civilian population gradually increased from 1995 to 2001 (Naimi et al., 2003), and the 2001 rates of binge drinking were estimated at 12.5 episodes per year for men and 2.7 episodes per for women.

Binge drinkers were more likely to experience negative health and social and job outcomes than their peers who consumed alcohol without bingeing (Stahre et al., 2009). These negative outcomes included job performance issues, alcohol-induced injury/risky behaviors, interpersonal relationship issues (although no domestic violence data was gathered as part of this study), and both civilian and military legal issues. Although the highest risk group was composed of younger (17–25 years), less educated (high school or less), and single persons living on base or stationed onboard ships, there were also substantial numbers of older, higher ranking, married service members reporting binge drinking patterns as well. Thus, interventions for alcohol misuse need to be tailored to the local unit, and Naimi and colleagues recommend that programming go beyond common screening/treatment for alcoholism, include local community partnerships, and address the role of alcohol within the military culture.

Current alcohol research is also focused on understanding the relationship between deployment and changes in drinking behaviors (Jacobson et al., 2008) and in identifying alcohol usage patterns of National Guard and Reserve service members (Ferrier-Auerbach et al, 2009). Jacobsen and colleagues, using data from the first and second panel of the Millennium Cohort Study, were able to identify predeployment and postdeployment data on drinking behaviors for active duty, Reserve, and National Guard participants, as well as identify those who experienced combat exposure during deployment and those who did not and compare information with a group of participants who did not deploy between the two data collection periods. Overall, they found that combat-experience deployment for Reserve/Guard personnel increased the likelihood of new onset drinking, continued heavy weekly drinking as well as binge drinking, and the number of alcohol-related problems. Combat experience was linked to new onset binge drinking for active duty personnel across all branches. Personnel across both components, who also reported mental health symptoms including PTSD and depression in addition to combat exposure, were at significantly increased odds for escalation in problem drinking behaviors.

Ferrier-Auerbach and colleagues, in a cross-sectional study, tested predictors of *predeployment drinking behaviors* in a National Guard Brigade Combat Team (National Guard, 2009) and found, similar to other studies, that age (being younger) and marital status (being single) were linked with greater risk of various problematic drinking behaviors. Additionally, personality traits of negative internalizing and externalizing behaviors, such as high negative emotionality and disinhibition, respectively, were significantly predictive of problem drinking.

Problem drinking patterns that are identified predeployment are of significant concern to unit leaders, as the negative effects can compromise not just the individual but also the entire unit and the mission. Further research is recommended to learn if these patterns were temporary, typical, or a result of learning about their upcoming deployment. Within the Reserve Component context, changing status from civilian to active military status and all the significant life changes and stressors that entails may put these service members at higher risk than their active duty counterparts. They may also have less access to useful resources to lower this risk, such as base and unit tailored programs and proximity to a community of Guard/Reserve colleagues.

Other drug usage (both legal [i.e., energy drinks] and illegal [i.e., barbiturates, methamphetamines]), with the exception of tobacco, is not as well studied in the military population. Tobacco reduction education efforts within the active duty population and changes in smoking policies at installations have significantly decreased overall tobacco use (Klesges, Haddock, Lando, & Talcott, 1999; Woodruff, Conway, & Edwards, 2000). Jacobson and colleagues (2008) found links between increased risk in negative outcomes for new onset drinking and increased heavy drinking after deployment when both alcohol and tobacco use were co-occurring.

Alcohol use and misuse are of primary concern to the military community. Its links to individual negative personal, social, and career outcomes pose a threat to health, well-being, and readiness for both the individual and the unit they serve. Additionally, problem drinking is linked with negative interpersonal relationship outcomes, including relationships with family members and work colleagues. Interventions and policies are recommended by researchers to address a wider spectrum of maladaptive drinking behaviors and tailor programs to better meet the needs of military personnel at different ages and stages in both their life and career development.

Disordered eating. Weight control is one aspect of maintaining physical fitness to serve, and both active duty and selected reserve personnel must routinely go though fitness testing, including weighing-in. Military weight and percentage of body fat (%BF) standards are part of the physical fitness criteria and play a role in assessing job performance and consideration for promotion. Personnel who exceed established %BF standards are required to participate in a weight control program and may face disciplinary action if they fail to meet standards (Bathalon et al., 2006). Interestingly, one study found that being mandated to enter a prescribed weight loss program increased the risk of engaging in disordered eating patterns for military women (McNulty, 2008). Military standards for ideal weight and %BF are lower than standards set for the general population (Garber, Boyer, Pollack, Chang, & Shafer, 2008), thus personnel may meet criteria for the general population, yet still be considered overweight by the military. This conflict may increase body image dissatisfaction and the risk for disordered eating. Changes in assessing %BF are underway to try to minimize this conflict while increasing the effectiveness in identifying personnel at increased risk for weight-related health issues (Bathalon et al., 2006).

Disordered eating patterns have been identified in multiple military personnel surveys (Beekley et al., 2009; Carlton, Manos, & Van Slyke, 2005; Garber et al., 2008; Lauder & Campbell, 2001; McNulty, 2008) and in the baseline data of the Millennium Cohort Study (Riddle et al., 2007). Data from these studies indicate that disordered eating practices, including clinical diagnoses of anorexia nervosa and bulimia nervosa, occur more frequently in female personnel than male personnel and are more prevalent in the 17–25 age group, for those who have 14 or more years of service in their military career, and for those serving in the Navy.

Prevalence rates of disordered eating in a sample of military academy cadets were comparable to civilian college reports (Beekley et al., 2009), indicating that there is no identified significant difference between military and civilian populations in young adult populations. Although most studies have focused on the overweight aspect of physical fitness in the military, Beekley and colleagues also identify risks associated with severely underweight individuals. They noted that an eating disorder multidisciplinary team, including clinical psychologists, a registered dietitian, and a physician, had been established for intervention efforts with cadets. One treatment avenue available for cadets who were severely underweight was involuntary treatment in a clinical program, which showed at least short-term success.

Other research noted that temporary or "situational" disordered eating patterns spiked within the 2 months immediately prior to fitness testing and weigh-in (Lauder et al., 1999), as personnel felt the pressure to "make weight" —a bit like cramming for an exam. The behaviors identified in situational patterns included crash dieting, binging, purging, using laxatives and other pills, and fasting. Recommendations to reduce both situational and pervasive disordered eating included creation of preventative programming to instill healthier behaviors for new recruits and expansion of supportive interventions year round for all personnel. Interventions included individual nutritional education/counseling and healthier menu options on base (Garber et al., 2008) to mitigate both risky behaviors focused on passing the fitness tests and the development of lifelong patterns of disordered eating. Recent research with female veterans has also linked specific disordered eating behaviors with exposure to trauma and seeking treatment for mental health (Rowe, Gradus, Pineles, Batten, & Davison, 2009). Specifically, women veterans who indicated that they were survivors of **military sexual trauma** (MST: sexual trauma experienced while in active service) were at increased risk of both bingeing and starving behaviors. Women veterans who did not indicate MST, but did indicate exposure to other traumatic events also were at increased risk of bingeing behaviors.

Increased risk-taking. The current study of other types of risk-taking behaviors focuses almost exclusively on postdeployment behaviors. Although some research has employed a longitudinal, pretest/posttest design, many studies have relied on cross-sectional studies, which limits the ability to clarify the predictive connections between deployment and increased risk-taking. Additionally, this topic is overshadowed by a very strong research presence on PTSD and other mental health problems that may have more "clinical presence" (Killgore et al., 2008). Killgore and colleagues view increased risk-taking behaviors as an unaddressed public health concern and one that may be able to be linked to combat exposure and prolonged deployment. Although not explicitly tested in their study, they raise the possibility of being able to measure combat and deployment stressor changes in the limbic system (neurochemical and functional adaptive responses to stress in the human body) as an indicator that adjustment postdeployment is not simply a matter of setting aside service and survival skills once home, but requires a reorganizing of the stress response system.

Within the military population, the most commonly studied postdeployment risky behavior beside alcohol use is that of aggressive driving (Bell, Amoroso, Yore, Smith, & Jones, 2000; Hooper et al., 2006). Motor vehicle accidents are a major cause of death for both nondeployed (Bell et al., 2006) and recently returned soldiers (Hooper et al., 2006). The majority of these service member deaths occur within the youngest age group, 17–25 years. Fatal motor vehicle accidents are a leading cause of death within the civilian population in this age group as well (National Highway Traffic Safety Association [NHTSA], 2010). Earlier in this chapter, Chaplin Purinton described how communicating this known fact of aggressive driving with the Vermont State Police made a difference in how traffic stops were handled. Can you think of other ways information about risk-taking behaviors in military service members could have a practical impact for human service and public servant professionals in a community?

Killgore and colleagues expanded our understanding of other risky behaviors in their 2008 study of postcombat invincibility and risk-taking practices. One of the unique contributions of this study was the ability to identify specific combat experiences that confer either increased risk for or protective factors against engaging in risky behaviors after deployment. The risky behaviors in this study were alcohol use and aggressive behavior toward others and property. Three of the combat experiences were significantly and uniquely associated with increased use of alcohol, drinking in greater quantities, and drinking more than they meant to, respectively. Five of the combat experience categories were significantly associated with an increased risk of a variety of aggressive behaviors and with different levels of aggressive actions:

1. Violent combat exposure—more likely to get angry with unit member and yell/shout.
2. Human trauma exposure—increased angry verbal outbursts, likelihood of destroying property, and threaten unit member with physical violence.

3. Surviving a close call—increased destruction of property and threatening of others.
4. Killed enemy—more yelling/shouting, destruction of property, threats of physical violence, and actual physical violence against someone.
5. Killed friendly/nonhostiles—same increased risks as category 4.

This study also highlighted a few protective factors. Specifically, the combat experience of surviving a close call reduced alcohol consumption on a typical day of drinking, and experience with the death/injury of a buddy reduced the likelihood of driving while under the influence of alcohol or riding with a person who had been drinking. The authors caution that the magnitude (strength) of the associations for both risks and protection were modest, but that they were statistically reliable (not a fluke or accident). Killgore and colleagues recommend that the Veteran's Administration and civilian health-care systems need to be informed of increased risk-taking behaviors as service members return from deployments and transition out of the service. The VA and civilian health-care systems become the frontline primary care settings for veterans once they separate from military service, but their service experiences, particularly combat experiences, may have a profound effect on their later health and risk-taking behaviors.

Work-Based Supports and Risk and Resilience

At the beginning of this chapter, job training and unit cohesion were identified as important material supports for service members. Recent research has identified limitations and opportunities of these material supports to enhance resilience in service members and their families.

Job training. Each service member trains for a particular MOS in order to gain specialized technical and operational skills, in addition to maintaining good physical health. Although developing a high level of technical proficiency and the ability to perform one's work under pressure are primary goals of job training, there has been a recent increase in attention to enhancing psychological resilience that is tied to MOS training (Adler & Dolan, 2006; Maddi, Kahn, & Maddi, 1998; Thomas, Adler, Wittels, Enne, & Johannes, 2004). Previous research has shown that service members report faster physiological recovery than psychological recovery from intense mission training (Thomas et al., 2004) and that occupational stressors unique to particular jobs create specific types of occupational stress (Dobreva-Martinova, Villeneuve, Strickland, & Matheson, 2002; Pflanz & Sonnek, 2002).

An increased focus on psychological resilience in concert with physiological health and training in technical skills may be particularly relevant for specializations with a higher likelihood of exposure to danger (such as combat arms, combat support, and medical care) and the need to manage distressing situations for others (such as casualty assistance notification, unit leadership, and combat stress prevention). In one study of personnel completing combat medic training (Robinson et al., 2009), several mental health symptoms worsened from the beginning to the completion of the training, including increases in depression, anxiety, and suicidal ideation. The majority of personnel in this study had been enlisted for less than 1 year (84%) another 9% enlisted for 1–3 years, and just over half (53%) had attained college or more education. Additionally, over half of the sample participants were active duty personnel (59%), while the remaining personnel were serving in the Reserve Component.

The prevalence rates for all three mental health concerns were indistinguishable from the general entry level enlisted population at the time of entry into the program but increased by the end of training. Risk factors for this increase were associated with gender (women at much higher risk), age (younger at higher risk than older personnel), education (those with lower education at higher risk), status (active duty at higher risk than Reserve Component), and previous service history (those with no experience at higher risk). The general increase in symptoms from the beginning to completion of training argues against the idea that technical training offers protection against psychological distress within this particular study and indicates that service members may benefit from a training approach that incorporates both the technical and psychological aspects of an occupational specialization as part of a mission.

Unit Leadership and Cohesion

A growing body of research has linked leadership behaviors and organizational climate to the morale and well-being of service members. In a highly structured organization such as the military, leadership style and attitudes are linked to psychological outcomes for personnel (Hardy et al., 2010) and perceptions of stigma in needing and accessing mental health services (Wright et al., 2009). In the field of public health, targeted interventions that address both the public stigma (cultural attitudes about characteristics of persons with mental health needs that lead to biased assessments) and self-stigma (internalization of cultural attitudes and biases) have been created to reduce stigma as a potential barrier to treatment (Corrigan, 2004; Rosen, Walter, Casey, & Hocking, 2000). Positive ratings of unit leadership and unit cohesion, both as independent factors and in concert with one another, are related to lower perceptions of stigma about and help-seeking behaviors related to depression (Britt, Davison, Bliese, & Castro, 2004; Pietrzak et al., 2010), PTSD (Pietrzak et al., 2010), and general mental health (Wright et al., 2009). Recommendations from this line of research include targeting military leaders as change agents for their units, relaying more positive organizational attitudes toward mental health issues, and stressing the role of buddy care as part of military leadership training. One program that implemented this approach is Resilience Training (U.S. Army Medical Department, 2010b). This and other programs are detailed in Chapters 9 and 11.

Social Support

Several studies have noted that positive social support plays a key role as a protective factor for service members. Social support is broadly conceptualized to include relationships with family, friends, coworkers, employers, and community members and the extent to which these relationships are characterized by helpfulness and emotional care. Pietrzak and colleagues included measures of social support in their recent resilience studies, which indicated that higher levels of social support were linked with better mental health outcomes for Reserve Component personnel after deployment (Pietrzak et al., 2010) and OIF/OEF veterans up to 2 years after service (Pietrzak, Johnson, Goldstein, Malley, & Southwick, 2009).

A longitudinal study with a small National Guard population found that prior life stressors, perceptions of readiness for the mission, and concern about life/family disruption were important predeployment risk factors for experiencing postdeployment PTSD while both social support and experiencing fewer life stressors after deployment served as protective factors against the development of PTSD (Polusny et al., 2011). This builds on a body of research that acknowledges that the transition of Reserve Component personnel from citizen to service member and back to citizen is comprised of both events that are similar to their active duty counterparts (deployment experiences, training) and life events that are potentially very different from Active Component personnel (disruption in education, work, unfamiliar and extended separations from friends and family, lack of community support resources tailored to military experiences). More research on the ways that social support contributes to service member resilience is needed in both the Reserve and Active Components. In particular, learning more about the types of connections (family, friends, community members/organizations) and the use of both informal (personally chosen) and formal (program/organizational based) connections would facilitate our understanding of service member resilience in different contexts and access to support systems that are valued. Additional research should also consider how connections may result in negative effects. For example, if a unit develops a strong connection that establishes that risky behaviors are part of its "identity" and leadership develops in such a way that seeking help is discouraged, these social connections with coworkers and employers may have serious negative consequences for members of the unit.

TRANSITIONING OUT OF THE MILITARY

Retiring and Separating from the Military

Service members leave the military by retiring or "separating." As noted in Chapter 1, service members qualify for regular retirement and its associated benefits after 20 years of active service or due to a medical retirement before 20 years of active service are completed. They may qualify for retirement with at least 15 but less than 20 years of active service through the Temporary Early Retirement Authority (TERA). Regular military retirement eligibility for Reservists is slightly different in that personnel in the Reserve and National Guard need to have accrued 20 years of qualifying service and be age 60 in order to be eligible. In FY 2012, 23% of active component and 15% of reserve component separations consisted of personnel transitioning to retired status.

If a service member leaves the military prior to meeting eligibility requirements for retirement benefits, then the term **separation** is used to describe the process. According to the DoD, separation from the military is "a general term that includes discharge, release from active duty, release from custody and control of the Military Services, transfer to the IRR, and similar changes in active or Reserve status" (DoD, 2014a, p. 55).

When service members have separated, or been discharged from the military, they are veterans. The U.S. Department of Veterans Affairs defines veterans as:

> Veterans are individuals who have served in one of the seven uniformed services who meet the length of service and character of discharge requirements prescribed by law. This includes the Army, Navy, Marine Corps, Air Force, Coast Guard, Public Health Service, and Commissioned Officer Corps of the National Oceanic and Atmospheric Administration as well as eligible members of the Reserve and National Guard components, World War II Merchant Mariners, and certain members of the Philippine Armed Forces" (U.S. Department of Veterans Affairs, 2014c, p. 6).

The length of service and character of discharge requirements are important factors in determining eligibility for VA health benefits. For active duty personnel to be eligible for health-care benefits from the VA, they must serve 24 continuous months or the period they were called to duty. Service members of the National Guard or Reserves must be ordered to active duty and serve for the period of time they are activated. Initial training and yearly two-week training do not count toward the active duty requirement for reservists. If service members incur an injury or illness while serving, then they qualify for benefits immediately. The VA encourages all veterans to apply as there are other exceptions to the minimum duty requirement.

Enlisted   Enlisted military service members are separated when:

- They have met their service obligations (if they wish to remain in the military and the military wants them to stay, they re-enlist).

- The service obligation changes (e.g., the DoD issues a reduction in the number of service members, transfer to the inactive reserves).
- At the convenience of the government (e.g., early release to further education, accept public office).
- Disability.
- Defective enlistments and induction.
- Unsatisfactory entry-level performance and conduct.
- Unsatisfactory performance.
- Failure of drug or alcohol abuse rehabilitation or of weight control.
- Misconduct, in lieu of trial by court-martial.
- For reasons of security.
- Unsatisfactory participation in the Ready Reserve.
- Secretarial plenary authority.
- Reasons established by the military departments (DoD, 2014a).

Commissioned Officers   Commissioned officers resign their commission as part of their separation or retirement process, including transitioning from active duty to the reserves and vice versa. Each service has its own specific eligibility requirements and these requirements differ for Active and Reserve Components within each service. In general, eligibility to resign one's commission includes factors of meeting minimum (time in) service requirements and obligations that are defined by job specialization and any additional training (typically ranging from 4 to 10 years, initially); the types of deployments and PCSs incurred as part of service, and the anticipated short-term and long-term personnel needs of one's branch. If these eligibility criteria are not met, but an officer needs to separate for personal reasons, he or she may be financially obligated to repay the federal government for training, as the contract for commissioning an officer is interpreted as an exchange of education and training for a set number of years in service. In addition to voluntary resignation of commission, officers are also subject to involuntary separation due to substandard performance of duty; legal issues, such as violating standards of conduct that may also be punishable by military or civilian authorities; not making a necessary promotion in rank for continued service; attaining the mandatory retirement age (usually 60) or the maximum number of years of service (28 to 35, depending on rank; or force size reduction or budgetary requirements indicate a need to reduce the number of officers (DoD, 2013c).

SEPARATION DUE TO DISABILITY EVALUATION AND RATING

Service members, like everyone else, can be injured or contract an illness that potentially alters their ability to continue in military service. These injuries or illnesses may be the result of the dangers of their specialty but can also occur outside of the military workplace. The Integrated Disability Evaluation System (IDES) is utilized when a service member is identified as incurring an injury or illness that threatens continued duty (Office of Warrior Care Policy, 2014). Generally, the following steps are implemented to conduct an evaluation for both fitness for duty and determining level of disability:

- Allow recovery time for the service member.
- Evaluate service member's fitness for duty.
- Authorize return to duty for those who are found fit.
- Approve disability separations or retirements, including making benefits determinations, for those found unfit (p. 18).

The IDES consists of an integrated process across both the DOD and the VA, where one set of medical examinations is shared for both determination of fitness or need for assigning a disability rating. Because different MOSs require different physical and cognitive abilities, the examination process is detailed, involving a team of health-care and case-management specialists. Recovery from the injury or illness may also have an extended trajectory; thus the recovery and evaluation process may take up to 12 months to complete. Service members who need extended time to recuperate may be placed into their respective Service's Warrior Transition Unit during their recovery and evaluation process. This evaluation process is complex and while the DoD and VA are partnered in this process, there may be two separate disability ratings given for a service member. The DoD provides a rating that determines whether or not a service member is fit for duty and, if not, what type of separation is most appropriate. The VA provides a disability rating that is used to determine VA disability benefits.

TYPES AND CHARACTERIZATION OF SEPARATIONS

Each veteran receives a Report of Separation, commonly known as Form DD214. This form is issued by the Department of Defense and it outlines each veteran's condition of discharge. These conditions include information that is needed to verify a service member's eligibility for benefits, retirement, membership in veteran's organizations, and employment (www.dd214.us). Form DD214 also gives detailed information about the service member's condition of separation (explained below); specialized training and education; combat tours; foreign service and total credited service; and all military awards, decorations, medals, citations, and badges; and the last duty assignment and rank before separation. Military separations are categorized as either administrative or punitive.

Administrative   Administrative separations for enlisted service members, described in DoD Instruction 1332.14 (DoD, 2014d), are *uncharacterized* (the quality of service is not noted) or *characterized* (the quality of service is noted).

Uncharacterized separations include entry-level separations (those that occur before completing 180 days of service), void enlistments or inductions (e.g., without parental consent if under 17 years old, enlisted without the capacity to understand the significance of doing so including being intoxicated or insane or was a deserter from another military service), and being dropped from the rolls (may be used to release someone away without leave for 30 days or more, or found guilty by a civilian court and confined to Federal or state penitentiary or correctional institution) (Department of the Army, 2014, p. 33).

Characterized separations include honorable, general (under honorable conditions), and under other than honorable conditions.

An *Honorable* characterization, also referred to as an honorable discharge, is issued "when the quality of an enlisted Service member's service has met the standards of acceptable conduct and performance of duty for military personnel, or is otherwise so meritorious that any other characterization would be clearly inappropriate" (DoD, 2014d, p. 30).

A *General (Under Honorable Conditions)* discharge is issued "when the positive aspects of the enlisted Service member's conduct or performance of duty outweigh negative aspects of the enlisted Service member's conduct or performance of duty as documented in their service record" (DoD, 2014d, p. 30).

An *Under Other Than Honorable Conditions* characterization is issued when the Service member has had "a pattern of behavior" or has had "one or more acts or omissions that constitute a significant departure from the conduct expected of enlisted Service members of the Military Services" (DoD, 2014d, pp. 30–31).

The type of characterization, or discharge, is important as only an honorable discharge results in a veteran being eligible for all veteran benefits. For example, a General (Under Honorable Conditions) can restrict veterans from re-enlisting, being hired by veteran groups, or receiving GI Bill education benefits. A separation issued *Under Other Than Honorable Conditions* may result in a veteran being ineligible for all VA benefits.

Punitive   For Enlisted personnel, punitive separations include a Dishonorable Discharge as a result of a court-martial, and a Bad-Conduct Discharge issued Under Other Than Honorable Conditions. Commissioned Officers who are discharged as a result of a general court-martial receive a Dismissal notice (the equivalent to a Dishonorable Discharge for enlisted personnel). For those who are convicted in a court-martial as part of their Bad Conduct or Dishonorable Discharge, prison time in the military prison system may be part of the consequences and all VA benefits are lost with a criminal conviction.

SUPPORTS FOR TRANSITIONING OUT OF THE MILITARY

Active duty service members have several pathways to consider as they contemplate post-military life. Some service members may be facing pressure to separate from a variety of sources. For example, there may be family considerations for needing to make a lifestyle change (e.g., starting a family, family member illness, or loss), personal considerations (e.g., always viewed service as a pathway to adulthood and building job skills for returning to civilian life), periodic downsizing of the military force, meeting eligibility for retirement, or injuries incurred during service that limit or prevent continuation of service. This section describes programs that support service members through their transition out of the military.

Programs and pathways

The Transition Assistance Program (TAP) is a mandatory employment workshop to help service members prepare to enter the civilian labor market and is offered as both a three-day face-to-face format or as an online format. This curriculum is also available to veterans who have already transitioned out of the military and spouses of service members (Department of Labor, 2014). TAP is an interagency workshop coordinated by the Departments of Defense, Veterans Affairs, Transportation, and Labor and is part of the 2011 VOW to Hire Heroes Act, passed by Congress and signed into law by President Obama, which established several provisions to address the increasing unemployment rate of returning post 9/11 veterans (Democratic Policy and Communications Center, 2012). Attendees are coached on developing resumes and cover letters that translate their military experience into the civilian labor market, how to conduct a job search, and how to understand the current occupational and labor market. In addition, attendees receive updated information on VA benefits. For separating service members who have a service-connected disability, additional time and services are offered to help meet the unique needs their disability status may create.

The Post-9/11 GI Bill is the most current version of an educational benefit package and is specifically authorized for those who served in the U.S. military after 9/11.

Post-9/11 GI Bill

Since 1944, the Department of Veterans Affairs has sponsored an educational benefit package for veterans who have successfully completed an enlistment in the military service (U.S. Department of Veterans Affairs, 2013c). However, no educational benefit has been as comprehensive as the Post-9/11 GI Bill, which became available to veterans in 2009. Eligible service members can receive up to 36 months of educational benefits—tuition and fees, a monthly living allowance, and a stipend for books and supplies. Costs for tutorial assistance and reimbursement for any tests required for licensing and certification are also provided by the Post-9/11 GI Bill. All educational programs must be offered by an institution of higher learning approved by the VA. Approved training includes graduate and undergraduate degree programs and vocational or technical training.

An unprecedented feature of the new GI Bill is that qualified career service members can transfer their unused benefits to family members (Department of Veterans Affairs, 2013c). A service member can transfer the entire 36 months of benefits—if the member has used none—or up to the total remaining months of unused Post-9/11 GI Bill benefits. The service members can transfer the benefits to a spouse, to one or more children, or to any combination thereof.

COLLEGES AND UNIVERSITIES AS OPTIONS DURING AND AFTER SERVICE

Military veterans and students serving in the Reserve Component (i.e., National Guard, Reserves, and ROTC) have been present on many college and university campuses for decades as have their spouses, children, and parents. Active duty personnel have been pursuing degrees with universities that offer degree programs on military installations and now online. With the passage in 2008 of the Post-9/11 GI Bill, the number of veterans on college campuses, either the brick and mortar campus or the virtual campus, is expected to continue to increase in the coming years. With the transferability of the Post-9/11 GI Bill, the number of family members of veterans on campuses may also increase. This section notes the administrative services that can facilitate the transition to college or university life. It also highlights the experience of transitioning from being a service member to being a student, whether as a veteran or as a "military student" who is still serving in the Active or Reserve Component. Finally, it offers recommendations for creating welcoming classrooms and campuses.

On-Campus Services

Military-friendly institutions of higher learning typically are members of the **Servicemembers Opportunity Colleges** (SOC). To join SOC, the institution of higher learning must be listed in the Council for Higher Education Accreditation (CHEA) database as accredited; grant degrees and be accredited by an agency recognized by the U.S. Department of Education (DoE) or by CHEA; meet appropriate provisions of DoD Directives 1322.8 (*Voluntary Educational Programs for Military Personnel*) and 1322.25 (*Voluntary Education Programs*), and related service regulations if offering courses on military installations; be approved by the state's approving agency for veterans' benefits; agree to submit relevant data for the SOC Consortium Guide; not have an excessive student loan default rate as determined by the DoE; have an administrator who commits the institution or a subdivision of it to comply with and support SOC principles and criteria; and be approved as meeting the SOC principles and criteria (SOC, n.d.).

Likewise, many institutions of higher education adhere to the American Council on Education guidelines for credit evaluation recommendations. *ACE Military Guide to the*

Evaluation of Educational Experiences in the Armed Services is the reference book for evaluating learning acquired in the military for college credit. The first guide was published in 1946. Institutions, service members, and veterans can explore the guide by military training course to see the recommended number of credits (the guide is accessible online at http://militaryguides.acenet.edu).

More colleges and universities are establishing an office dedicated to serving military students and veterans and encouraging the development of military student and veteran organizations (Cook & Kim, 2009). The **Student Veterans of America** (SVA; a national organization for veterans on college and university campuses, see http://www.studentveterans.org) suggests that establishing a center for military students centralizes services and programs and provides easier access to information and assistance that would otherwise be spread among various campus offices. A physical center provides a location for camaraderie with peers, so they can support one another as they become more comfortable with campus life. Office staff who understand the potential physical and psychological health issues faced by some veterans and military students, academic preparation, military experience and training, drill requirements, and activation facilitate the transition from military life to campus life. Such policies, space, and understanding encourage retention (Garcia, 2009).

A center ideally would be staffed by a liaison or coordinator serving as the point of contact to coordinate services, make referrals, develop programs, address students' financial and enrollment processes and concerns, and advocate for military students. In addition, a veteran benefits certifying official would serve as the campus liaison with the VA and state education agency and assist veterans, military, and family members with required paperwork to access VA, state, and other benefits. Some institutions may be eligible for a VA work–study position for a student veteran, and a veteran in this position could assist staff members and provide support services and referrals for students (Garcia, 2009). The following Voices From the Frontline describes how one university established an office to serve military students and veterans.

Voices From the Frontline

VETERANS ARE A SPECIAL RESOURCE AND DESERVE SUPPORT AND ENCOURAGEMENT WHEN THEY SEEK HIGHER EDUCATION

I was an advisor to non-traditional students in 2006 when I recognized that an increasing number of Afghanistan and Iraq veterans were among our returning former students. Often, transcripts revealed incompletes or unapproved dropped courses, resulting in a failed semester and a dismal academic record. We sought to find a reason for the phenomenon. This was not an easy task as veterans were reluctant to report that they had responded to 9/11 by enlisting in the military or, if already in the service, had been immediately deployed to Afghanistan. Our surveys received few responses; however, personal interviews were more successful as veterans realized the university wanted to support veterans in their efforts to begin or continue their college education. By listening to veterans, we came to understand the challenges of re-entry and they realized the university cared about their success. Out of this, the Office of Military and Student Veteran Affairs was developed.

Based on our discussions with student veterans the office adopted two principal goals:

1. To assist veterans in their transition from military life to active citizenship in their communities and families.
2. To provide a supportive environment that enables reintegration and academic success.

We came to understand that vets not only transition to school but also return to civilian life. They do not just feel different: they feel strange. Not only are they set apart by age from the typical college student but their world view has been altered by their military experience. They have seen life from many perspectives. Veterans bring to academic life focus and commitment to priorities. It is important to help them apply their military skills and values to their current lives.

To create a supportive veteran environment, we needed support from all segments of the university and thus we reached out to the whole university community. We called on every possible university and external resource as well as veterans themselves. An oversight committee comprised of administrators, faculty, staff, students and community representatives was charged with the development and oversight of a caring community. Through these efforts, the office currently serves approximately 600 veterans and active military.

Veterans come to the office for two reasons:

1. To meet and enjoy fellow veterans in a comfortable environment.
2. To seek advice and support from staff.

Veterans have a lounge for their exclusive use. Staff members are available to address their concerns and needs. Besides a comfortable meeting place, many issues have been resolved through new and revised policies. Students have priority registration, spouses and children have tuition reimbursement, and there is an extended time for receipt of tuition. Veterans' health benefits can be used at the university clinic and helpful course adaptations address PTSD and other issues.

Making our university a good place for veterans is a gift we give for their service. They have enriched our community in return.

Gerry Schma
Founder and Retired Director of Western Michigan
University's Office of Military and Veterans Affairs

What Military Students and Veterans Bring to Campus

For some, joining the military is, to a small or large degree, a means to a college education. For others, transitioning out of the military prompts them to consider earning a college degree for the first time. Military undergraduates (i.e., student service members and veterans) as a group are older than traditional undergraduates, yet younger and more diverse than the larger group of veterans. In the 2007–2008 academic year, 85% of military undergraduates were age 24 and older, and they were more likely to be non-White. In the same year, 27% of military undergraduates were women (Radford, 2009).

Military students come to campus likely having lived in or been deployed to other countries. Students will have a variety of cross-cultural experiences—some positive, some negative, and some life-changing. In addition to first-hand experiences in other countries, most service personnel have been introduced to basic tenets of cultural sensitivity through training to develop skills about how to interact with others of differing values, religion, and language, which are critical to mission success (McFarland, 2005).

The perspectives they share in the classroom reflect their often wide-ranging life experiences and training. Those stationed at one of the permanent U.S. military installations outside of the United States for one or more tours may have acquired basic or advanced language skills in a second or third language. Many will have traveled extensively throughout Europe or Asia, visiting major cultural, religious, and national locations that they then study in history, geography, art appreciation, language, anthropology, design, music, engineering, and business courses.

Military students may have seen Renaissance masterpieces in the Louvre, gazed at the dome of the Pantheon, worshipped in Trier Cathedral, been groundlings at the reconstructed Globe Theatre, strolled through Hiroshima Peace Memorial Park, felt the cramped rooms of the Secret Annex, or viewed the modern architecture of Hong Kong. The Pyramids, the Great Barrier Reef, the Alps, the Greek Isles, Istanbul, Lisbon, or Mount Fuji could have been their weekend get-away destinations.

As veterans and service members transition to college or university, they bring these and many more experiences and dreams with them (see Box 6.2). A study of 25 veterans and National Guard and Reserve force members in college noted the self-awareness, maturity, and determination brought to campus by those who have experienced combat. They can also bring experiences of great loss, fear, and visible and invisible injury (Ackerman, DiRamio, & Garza Mitchell, 2009). While service members, they may have only known deployments to areas of conflict. Preliminary analyses of the first wave of data from a longitudinal study of 354 college students (i.e., 195 student veterans/active duty, 68 enrolled in a ROTC program, and 91 civilian students with no prior military service) indicated that veterans reported less stress, fewer psychological and somatic symptoms, and no differences in PTSD symptoms than the ROTC and civilian students (Whiteman & Barry, 2010). However, they did perceive less social support from university friends and greater role overload than the other two groups. Implications of this study include acknowledging that veteran and student service members form a unique subgroup among the college population. These students could potentially benefit from facilitation of formal and informal social support; encouragement to connect with faculty, advisors, and peers; and support as they balance multiple roles (Whiteman & Barry, 2010). Included below are additional ideas for student service members, veterans, military family members, faculty, and staff to ease the transition to campus.

BOX 6.2   TIPS FROM THE FRONTLINE

TRANSITIONING TO SCHOOL: SERVICE MEMBERS, VETERANS, AND FAMILY MEMBERS

- *Acknowledge that going back to school is a balancing act, particularly for those with families.* Pat Chandler notes, "It's different being in school when you have a family and bills. On Wednesday I have a class and have to leave right afterward to make sure my son gets to Cub Scouts on time. When my fellow students stay up until 2 AM finishing their paper, I've long ago gone to bed. I'm older. I get tired. And I have to get my kids up and off to school in the morning."
- *Find support from family and friends.* Encouragement or a few hours of uninterrupted time to study make a difference.
- *Allow time to get back into the education groove.* The rules and culture of higher education are different from the military and take time to learn until

they feel comfortable. Talk with faculty. Structure time so readings, papers, and projects are done on time.

- *Investigate programs and benefits for veterans.* Use the services of the military/veteran advocacy office, and talk with other veterans. If the institution does not have an office, seek out an administrator, faculty member, or advisor who listens and cares.
- *Look into and fill out military equivalency paperwork.* As Pat reflects, "Why should you need to pay for and take a physical education class if you've been in the military?"
- *Recognize possible stressors.* Transitioning to school may occur while still carrying out military duties if a member of the Reserve Component and/or while attending to visible or invisible injuries. These realities may add a layer of stress as self-perceptions change. Pat explains, "For me, it was an injury and evaluation leading to a medical discharge that has changed how I see myself."
- *If stressed, take action early.* Use assistance available to facilitate the transition to school. Seek guidance on study tips, managing stress, or dealing with an injury.

FACILITATING THE TRANSITION TO SCHOOL: WHAT STAFF AND FACULTY CAN DO

- *Listen and learn.* When talking with staff and faculty, Gerry Schma suggests, "Let veterans and families know you care and are committed. Do not judge. Do not feel you have to have the answers. When vets know you care and are supportive, they, like all of us, are more likely to share their needs and concerns."
- *Empower veterans and service members to seek support in achieving their success.* "Veterans don't expect you to solve their problems, but sometimes they need guidance and support as they do." Gerry concludes, "It boils down to respecting their experience and dignity."
- *Avoid letting the fact that you have not shared similar experiences interfere.* Gerry Schma explains, "When vets or families tell me, 'You can't understand,' I acknowledge, 'You're right, but I can listen.'"
- *Learn basic information about military life.* A professor may insist a student never miss a class session until they learn about the requirements and restraints on active duty and reservists. Be flexible in terms of due dates if they or loved ones are mobilized in the middle of a semester or term. Be aware that not every deployed service member has easy access to the Internet.
- *If veterans' family members stop by to talk, do so if possible.* If you are unable to meet, check in to determine if there is an immediate crisis. If so, use campus resources. If not, agree on a time to talk soon. Remember, your top priority is to serve veterans.
- *If veterans or student service members have difficulty with the course material or do not come to class, check in and offer to meet with them.* Let them know you have noticed their absence and offer to talk with them.
- *Involve the entire college or university community, including veterans and families.* A single office or advocate on campus cannot do it alone.

- *Provide guidance on maneuvering through military education benefits and other services.*
- *Publicize student services and local community services to veterans and student service members.* Ensure staff and faculty are familiar with the range of support services and how to access them.
- *Provide professional development to staff and faculty on relevant issues.* For example, train staff to meet the needs of students with brain injuries and physical disabilities.

Cook and Kim (2009), Patrick Chandler SFC (Retired), Gerry Schma

SUMMARY

- Scholarship on military families generally increases during times of military engagement and gradually decreases after actions come to a close.
- Due to the cyclical nature of research on military families, everyday mechanisms of resilience may be better understood within the service member population due to the extensive monitoring of information on their demographics, health, and performance than in the military family population.
- More knowledge about everyday resilience in military families would enhance our understanding of how families remain resilient or struggle with resilience when under the extreme stressors of military engagement.
- Young adults, whether in the civilian or military population, face similar developmental tasks related to gaining job skills and financial independence, establishing a household, forming adult friendships and romantic relationships, and making choices about parenthood.
- The military, as an organization, has made significant investments in material supports that foster positive personal and relational development, as well as support daily living needs, in spite of the typical risks inherent in military service.
- New service members complete both basic and advanced training and are expected to continue their skill development by attending technical and/or leadership schools.
- Differences in living allowances and other in-kind benefits between single and married active duty service members and relative job stability may foster an environment conducive to earlier marriage and parenthood, on average, than the civilian population.
- The Millennium Cohort Study is the most comprehensive research project ever undertaken by the DoD. This longitudinal study is already generating new knowledge of characteristics and experiences of military life that predict vulnerability and resilience in both active duty and selected reserve personnel. This study has recently included spouses to begin collecting data about couple dynamics and family resilience.
- Risk factors including problem drinking and other substance misuse, risk-taking and aggressive behaviors, disordered eating, and increased life/family stressors compromise individual health and readiness, as well as unit readiness. Many of these risk factors are thought to be common to late adolescence and young adulthood, which includes 45% of the Active Component and 33% of the Reserve Component personnel.
- High unit trust and cohesion, job training that includes psychological skill building in addition to technical skill building, positive perceptions of unit leaders, and

positive emotional connections with others act as protective factors for service members and foster resilience.

- Meaningful connections between military and civilian communities can facilitate better understandings of military stressors that affect behaviors, health, and relationships of all family members.

EXERCISES

1. This chapter highlighted several ways in which the developmental task of pursuing work and establishing a career are shaped by military service. What resources do persons who choose to work in the civilian sector rely upon to develop their professional lives?

2. Generally speaking, how important do you think financial and residential independence are in forming long-term romantic relationships and becoming a parent? What research literature would help you find out more about these choices in the civilian population?

3. Go to the Millennium Cohort Study website, at http://www.millenniumcohort. org/index.php, and select a few research publications to review. What are your chosen studies trying to learn more about? How do these studies add to useful knowledge about service members?

4. Interview two college students who are veterans or are serving in the National Guard or Reserves. Ask what recommendations they have for other veterans or service members who are transitioning to college. Ask what observations they have of college students with no military background and recommendations for working with classmates who do.

7

The Effects of War on Service Members

In Chapter 7, you will

- Meet Rick L. Campise, Colonel, U.S. Air Force, BSC Commander, 559th Medical Group.
- Learn about the physical and psychological impact of combat on service members.
- Develop an appreciation for the risks that service men and women take when they agree to defend the United States.
- Acquire information that you, as a helping professional working with military families, can apply to help family members deal with the effects of deployments on their loved ones.

Meet

**Rick L. Campise, Colonel, U.S. Air Force, BSC,
Commander, 559th Medical Group**

This excerpt is from a letter Colonel Campise wrote to his family on July 12, 2009 while in Iraq.

You may wonder, "Exactly what does a psychologist do in a deployed environment?" The duties vary depending upon the location and the number of other mental health staff present. I am the only mental health provider for 1200 Airmen and Soldiers, but there are also 30,000 Soldiers in the local area that might come see me rather than their own mental health providers. In addition, the military airport is a 10-minute walk away so sometimes one of the 100,000 people who pass through the airport each month finds their way to my office.

Throughout the week I visit units, sometimes just two and sometimes up to 10 a week. The average person is afraid to visit mental health and wouldn't come see me if their hair was on fire and I had the only water in camp. So I try to visit units and walk around, giving them a chance to see that I don't have horns, am relatively sane, and let them ask any questions about "their friend." I've done more counseling in units than in my office.

There is of course the obvious trauma associated with the real and potential loss of life and limb in a war environment. Perhaps on a previous deployment you were exposed to some horror that you successfully defended against but for some reason a recent event has brought it all out of the closet and the nightmares or flashbacks are weighing you down. Or during this deployment you might have watched the occupants of the vehicle in front of you die when an IED exploded and except for luck that could have been your vehicle.

You feel frightened you almost died and guilty that you lived. You may have even been flying an aircraft that almost crashed.

But a lot of what I see is a product of the sacrifices America's men and women make being deployed. You might see me because someone you trusted to take care of your affairs while you are fighting a war instead emptied your bank account; you have been deployed 3.5 of the last 5 years and no longer know your children; your all consuming stateside work schedule made you oblivious to the state of your marriage and you and your spouse are reflecting on things that need to change; your romantic partner wants to break-up; your romantic partner tells you if you don't come home right now they will break up; your romantic partner or a neighbor tells you your romantic partner is sleeping around; your grandmother or favorite aunt is dying but since they are not immediate family members you can't go home; your wife is having a baby and since it's a normal birth you can't go home. (The Army would let you go; but for the Air Force, it would have to be a problematic birth to go home.)

You might see me because you are in charge of people and really aren't very good at it. Or, you are a good leader that worries about their people and you are the person responsible for placing them in harm's way.

Maybe you suffer from "toxic leadership syndrome" and need some tips on how to survive a bad boss. Or perhaps you are on a new shift and want help resetting your biological clock by 10 hours so that you can sleep.

I lead tobacco cessation groups, a monthly workshop on how to study and a parenting forum. Every Tuesday morning and Wednesday afternoon I team up with the chaplain and give the "reunion briefing." Last week I started participating in "Right Start" briefings designed to prepare newly deployed people for their time in the sand. My role: give a 10-minute briefing on suicide prevention and how to take care of themselves and others. Also volunteer to work issues that affect all the mental health providers who are deployed and love doing that work.

INTRODUCTION

By the end of 2010, more than 2 million service members had been deployed to Afghanistan and Iraq in support of OEF, OIF, and OND since the terrorist attacks on the United States on September 11, 2001 (Office of the President of the United States, 2011). By the end of 2009, more than 793,000 of those service members had been deployed more than once with longer deployments and shorter breaks between deployments than in prior wars (Tan, 2009). The wars in Iraq and Afghanistan have exposed U.S. military personnel to life-threatening combat, hazardous duty, and dangerous environmental conditions. Many have returned home and have had to deal with severe physical injuries and permanent physical and/or neurological changes and limitations, psychological health problems, homelessness, and joblessness.

Environmental conditions and individual experiences such as poor or restricted diet, weather (e.g., extreme heat and arid conditions), poor or unfamiliar sleeping and living quarters, prolonged separations from family members, and the disruption of careers or educational goals (particularly for National Guard and Reserve service members) can add stress to the already challenging deployment experience (Litz, 2005) and can have negative implications for service members' psychological and physical well-being. Even the stress of not being able to deploy, when one is expected to, can be a stressor.

PHYSICAL EFFECTS OF WAR ON SERVICE MEMBERS

Although shrapnel from artillery bombs, mortars, and grenades were responsible for approximately 60% of the 9.7 million military deaths during World War I (Alexander, 2010), advanced battlefield medicine and improved protective combat gear have resulted in service members surviving severe wounds that would have been fatal in past wars. Many are alive because of these advances in battlefield medicine and protective equipment but are coming home with extensive physical injuries, such as missing limbs and head injuries.

By the May 2015, over 6,800 service members had died and over 52,000 had been wounded serving in Operations Enduring Freedom, Iraqi Freedom, and New Dawn (DMDC, 2015). Of those wounded, approximately 29% sustained injuries so severe as a result of direct combat action that they required medical air transportation to move them to a location where they could receive the appropriate level of medical treatment for their injuries. Medical air transports can also occur for nonhostile reasons (e.g., illness, disease, injuries).

The most frequent injuries and reasons for evacuation of service members from the OIF/OEF combat theaters from the beginning of 2004 to the end of 2007 were musculoskeletal and connective tissue injuries (24%), combat injuries (14%, some of which incurred during combat missions but were not caused by enemy fire; e.g., back pain and overuse injuries), neurological disorders (10%), psychiatric diagnoses (9%), and spinal pain (7%) (Cohen et al., 2010). However, the two "signature injuries" from these conflicts are TBI and PTSD (Department of Defense Task Force on Mental Health, 2007). Because of the prevalence of these conditions—up to 22% of returning veterans reported having experienced a TBI (Okie, 2005) and approximately 14% suffer from PTSD (Tanielian & Jaycox, 2008)—and the potentially chronic character of their symptoms, they have the potential for being long-term, challenging concerns for those working with military members, veterans, and their families.

Voices From the Frontline

STORY OF A WOUNDED WARRIOR

If you see that a person you know and love has a problem, say something. I was in the Marines and served in Fallujah and Ramadi, Iraq. On April 17, 2006, I was shot in both legs. A bullet went right through the right leg. Another blew out the knee and femoral artery in my left leg. I've had 16 operations and am now looking at a semi-constrained knee replacement.

I got addicted to painkillers, but I was never depressed enough that I thought about killing myself. That wasn't me. I was depressed knowing I couldn't be a police officer or play soccer ever again.

It took me 4 years to realize I needed help. I just completed the PTSD program at the Lyons VA in New Jersey where we had group therapy two times a week and individual therapy as well. Now I am participating in outpatient therapy at a VA clinic and at a Vet Center.

The most important thing for friends and families is to be supportive. There will be times we do not want to talk or be around anybody. Know it and respect it. Then there will be times we want to talk. So just be there and listen. Don't force it.

But don't walk on eggshells either. Be yourself around me. My friends never said anything like, "You have a problem with pain killers," but my family did. They said, "You are going to detox because we want our son back."

I got clear for a little bit. Then I fell and hurt myself. I started taking painkillers that a doctor prescribed. It wasn't as bad as before. This time I went in, got clean, and have stayed clean. I'm doing well now even though I'm in pain all the time.

I want to be me again. I know I'll never be that person, but I'll get as close as I possibly can. I want to get back to what made me happy before—helping people.

Michael Sarbu
Veteran

TRAUMATIC BRAIN INJURY

Approximately 1.7 million Americans suffer from **traumatic brain injuries** (TBI; a strike or jolt to the head or penetration of the head by an object, disrupting brain function) annually, making brain injuries a significant health concern in the United States. (Centers for Disease Control and Prevention, 2010). A TBI can affect language, emotions, behavior, and the ability to think and learn. It can also cause epilepsy and seizures and can increase the risk for Alzheimer's disease, Parkinson's disease (a disorder of the nervous system that affects movement), and other brain disorders that usually occur later in life. Falls (35%) and motor vehicle-traffic accidents (17%) are the leading causes of TBI in the general public. However, military service members deployed to combat zones are at high risk for experiencing TBIs as a result of bullets and blasts from improvised explosive devices (IEDs), bombs, land mines, mortar rounds, and rocket-propelled grenades (Defense and Veterans Brain Injury Center, 2009). Improved protective equipment is one major reason for the increased numbers of service members who survive TBIs in combat. Enhanced body armor and helmets protect service members from bullets, shrapnel, and flying debris; the injuries from these objects would have been fatal in previous wars. However, this new equipment cannot protect service members from the closed brain injuries and TBIs caused by the blasts of IED explosions (Okie, 2005; Warden, 2006).

Brain injuries are more common in the wars in Iraq and Afghanistan than in other recent wars involving U.S. Forces (Okie, 2005). Approximately 19% of service members returning from deployments reported that they had suffered a probable traumatic brain injury during their deployment (Tanielian & Jaycox, 2008). However, the prevalence of brain injuries among service members injured in Iraq and Afghanistan may be greater than 22%, because some injuries are not recognized and counted as TBIs until later in the diagnosis and treatment process (Okie, 2005). In 2011, 33,149 U.S. service members were diagnosed with a TBI (CDC, NIH, DoD, and VA Leadership Panel, 2013).

Johnson (2010) identifies the following five types of traumatic brain injuries (Johnson, 2010):

- Contusions (bruises of the brain).
- Hematomas (bleeding in the brain).
- Skull fractures (breaks—penetrations, cracks or dents—in the skull).
- Diffuse axonal injuries (tears in the small nerve fibers of the brain).
- Concussions (temporary brain injuries involving confusion, loss of memory, or loss of consciousness).

Many of these injuries are mild traumatic brain injuries (mTBIs), concussions, or injuries in which there is "loss of consciousness or altered mental status (e.g., dazed or confused)" (Hoge, McGurk, Thomas, Cox, Engel, & Castro, 2008, p. 453). The severity of traumatic brain injuries can range from "mild" (i.e., a change in mental status or consciousness for a brief period) to "severe" (i.e., an extended period of unconsciousness or amnesia for an extended period after the injury; Centers for Disease Control and Prevention, 2010). The three levels of severity of TBI—mild, moderate, and severe—are based on clinical factors, including the length of time of the loss of consciousness following the injury (CDC et al., 2013). Table 7.1 illustrates the classification of severity for non-penetrating TBIs used by the DoD and the VA.

The **Glasgow Coma Scale** (GCS) is another measurement tool used to determine the initial severity of brain injury (U.S. Department of Veterans Affairs, 2010). The GCS is a three-component scale that assigns a numeric value to an individual's ability to respond in three areas: to open his or her eyes, to respond verbally, and to respond through physical

TABLE 7.1   DoD/VA Severity Determination Factors for Non-penetrating TBI

	Mild	Moderate	Severe
MRI[a], CT[b] scan or other neuroimaging results	Normal	Normal or abnormal	
Duration of loss of consciousness	0–30 minutes	Over 30 minutes but less than 24 hours	24 hours or more
Duration of post-injury amnesia	Up to 1 day	More than 1 day but less than 7 days	7 days or more

[a] **Magnetic resonance imaging** uses a magnetic field and pulses of radio wave energy to produce images of the brain.
[b] **Computed tomography** uses computer-processed x-rays to construct images of the brain.
Source: Adapted from Table 2 (p. 18) CDC, NIH, DoD, and VA Leadership Panel (2013). *Report to Congress on traumatic brain injury in the United States: Understanding the public health problem among current and former military personnel.* New York: Centers for Disease Control and Prevention (CDC), the National Institutes of Health (NIH), the Department of Defense (DoD), and the Department of Veterans Affairs (VA).

movement (CDC et al., 2013). The GCS score indicates whether the individual has a "severe," "moderate," or "mild" brain injury. However, the GCS is influenced by intoxication, by other physical injuries, and by the length of time between the brain injury and the administration of the GCS and is not especially useful in the assessment of mild TBI (U.S. Department of Veterans Affairs, 2010).

Most cases of TBI in U.S. military personnel are mild TBI (CDC et al., 2013). Mild TBI is sometimes undetected or overlooked, especially when individuals have more life-threatening injuries. Since 2012 the DoD requires that every deployed service member who is injured or who was within 50 meters of a blast be screened, to reduce the occurrence of undetected TBIs. If the screening results indicate that the service member has suffered a TBI, the screening results are followed up with a comprehensive TBI evaluation. Evaluations should be conducted by TBI specialists who have the appropriate training and skills, such as a neurologist or a neuropsychiatrist who is trained in TBI assessment (U.S. Department of Veterans Affairs, 2010). The TBI evaluation should include identifying the cause of the patient's injury, assessing for neurological or behavioral symptoms, and a follow-up treatment plan to address the symptoms (CDC et al., 2013).

When a service member suffers a TBI, there are often accompanying physical/neurological, cognitive, psychological, and behavioral changes that can be long-lasting (Kushner, 1998; Vaishnavi, Rao, & Fann, 2009). Cognitive problems often include short-term memory problems, attention problems; difficulties planning, organizing, and strategizing; difficulties processing information; and language problems. Physical/neurological changes can include headaches, dizziness, balance and coordination problems, pain, low energy and fatigue, and problems sleeping. Psychological problems often include anxiety, depression, irritability, emotional volatility, blunted emotions (lack of range of emotion), and lack of empathy. Behavioral issues can include increased impulsivity, decreased inhibition, a lack of spontaneity, and apathy. The severity of these symptoms in mild TBI can range "from transient mild symptoms to ongoing disabling problems" (Kushner, 1998, p. 1617).

The individual's symptoms and recovery depend on the type of injury, the severity and location of the injury, how the injury occurred, other injuries sustained, pre-existing physical conditions, and psychosocial aspects (U.S. Department of Veterans Affairs, 2010). Rehabilitation services are generally provided through collaboration by specialists from different disciplines with close interaction between interdisciplinary team members and integration of each treatment component. Individuals who have sustained a TBI may require different types and levels of treatment and support for varying durations, possibly for the rest of their lives. Ideally, care is provided in the "least restrictive setting possible"

(p. 24). However, some individuals with severe TBI symptoms may require long-term care in assisted living facilities or nursing homes.

One of the primary medical and research challenges of the effects of combat is the overlap of TBI and psychological stress in terms of what kinds of trauma cause these conditions and their resulting symptoms. Many of the same kinds of traumatic combat events (e.g., blasts and impacts) can cause TBI psychological problems, or both. In addition, many of the symptoms are common to both of these conditions. In an examination of current research on the **chronic multi-symptom illness** (a constellation of health problems that do not clearly link to an exposure event and may have multiple, non-related health consequences) observed in many service members who deployed in the first Persian Gulf War, Friedl, Grate, and Proctor (2009) state that two pressing challenges facing the medical and research communities are the ability to distinguish between them and an understanding of the impact of their interaction on causing later psychiatric or neurological problems.

Return to Duty

Approximately 5%–6% of service members deployed in support of OIF/OEF are medically evacuated; of these, about one-third to one-fifth return to duty (Cohen et al., 2010). The conditions that most frequently prevent service members from returning to duty are combat injuries, psychiatric disorders, musculoskeletal or connective tissue (e.g., cartilage) disorders, and spinal pain. Service members with chest or abdominal pain, urinary and genital organ disorders, gastrointestinal disorders, and neoplasms (tumors or other abnormal tissue growths) are more likely to be returned to military duty.

Injured or ill service members receive medical and psychosocial screening; then appropriate treatment for their recovery is arranged (DoD, 2008b). Those who are unlikely to recover sufficiently to return to duty within 180 days are likely to be separated or retired from the service. The Military Department Wounded Warrior Programs, which are managed by each of the military services, track recovering service members as they undergo treatment, recovery, rehabilitation, and return to duty or separation or retirement and reintegration into the civilian community (DoD, 2008a). In December 2004, the DoD instituted a policy that allows active duty and reserve troops wounded on active duty to stay on active duty and work within their capabilities (Smith, 2006). Thus, if service members opt to remain on active or reserve duty, they are able to do so—provided that they can still complete their jobs or are approved for retraining into another job specialty. Growing numbers of wounded service members, including those severely wounded are choosing to continue their military service. Even severely wounded service members, with 30% or higher disability ratings, have applied to stay on active duty and have been approved (Miles, 2007). The DoD recognizes that these service members have specialized skills and leadership experience that they can continue to contribute to the military.

PSYCHOLOGICAL EFFECTS OF WAR ON SERVICE MEMBERS

Voices From the Frontline

PROVIDING MENTAL HEALTH SUPPORT IN THE FIELD

I was a combat stress prevention officer. Small teams of two to four of us would drive out with convoys to provide mental health support. Everyone has a breaking point and will need some help. Who knows what it is for any one person? How many IEDs?

We'd say something like, "We're just here to get you through this stressful time. Combat is stressful." We might talk about "loose ends at home," instead of saying,

"You have a problem with your marriage." Or maybe we'd say, "This is a time to talk about losing someone. For the next hour or two we can talk about this, and it's OK. Then it's over. We'll use no names." Soldiers felt it was helpful. When you frame it as having short-term stressors, people are more receptive.

A service member might lose a buddy in the Humvee next to them and need a few days to recover. That person would come to our Restoration Clinic. Hopefully in 72 hours they could go back to whatever they were doing, which might mean being up on the turret of Humvee the next day and maybe experiencing more loss. If someone was being transported to a restoration program they did it with a battle buddy. We did the combat stress clinic with a buddy. When it comes to the military, there aren't any loners out there.

Mostly people relied on each other for resilience, though we weren't using that word in 2005. You are in a shared, similar experience with other Soldiers, Airmen, Navy guys, Marines, civilian contractors. We're all in the same boat. We understood each other. As for my support, I looked to the chaplain and my fellow team members. The whole thing is that you take care of your fellow Soldiers.

Chris Sullins
Former Army Reserve Combat Stress Prevention Officer

The Continuum of Stress Reactions

Since the American Civil War, **combat stress reactions**—"expected, predictable, emotional, intellectual, physical, and/or behavioral reactions of service members who have been exposed to stressful events in combat" (Department of the Army, 2006b, p. Glossary-5)—have been observed and named. During the Civil War, they were called "soldier's heart" and "nostalgia." Since World War I, the U.S. military has been aware that these reactions were the psychological effects of combat on its members, and extreme reactions to combat stress were then called "shell shock" (Jones & Wessely, 2003). Initially, during World War II the same phenomenon was called a "nervous" reaction or "exhaustion." These terms were later changed to "battle fatigue," a term that only very recently was changed to "combat stress reaction," or CSR, the term currently accepted and used by all U.S. military branches (Department of the Army, 2006b).

The DoD recognizes that there is a continuum of CSRs, from adaptive (positive) stress reactions to maladaptive (negative) stress reactions (Department of the Army, 2006b). Combat stress includes all of the physical and psychological stresses that can result from exposure to all of the dangers and demands of combat—both positive and negative. "Focused stress is vital to survival and mission accomplishment" (p. 1–2). However, prolonged or extremely intense stress impairs the ability of service members to function effectively and can progress into disabling CSRs, which can include behavioral problems or psychological distress.

The DoD attempts to control the impact of combat stress on military members by "minimizing maladaptive stress reactions while promoting adaptive stress reactions, such as loyalty, selflessness, and acts of bravery" (Department of the Army, 2006b, p. viii). The DoD also attempts to prepare service members mentally and physically, through intense and frequent training, to endure the stressors of military life and combat. In some cases however, extreme stress can tax service members beyond their ability to cope with the stress. Examples include exposure to extremely traumatic events during combat, interpersonal conflicts with unit members that compromise the service member's support network, and concern about the welfare of family members and relationships back home. If not addressed, these reactions can lead to long-term psychological problems or to maladaptive behaviors that can threaten the well-being of service members.

Perceived Invincibility and Risk-Taking

Sometimes, one of the consequences of exposure to the violence and trauma of high-intensity combat is engaging in unsafe behavior and taking potentially dangerous risks. A study sponsored by the Walter Reed Army Institute of Research (Killgore et al., 2008) revealed that many of the soldiers who served in Iraq were engaging in risky behaviors after their return home. The specific risky behaviors examined in the study were related to alcohol use and to aggressive behaviors. These included increased frequency and amount of alcohol consumed, driving under the influence of alcohol, riding with someone who was under the influence of alcohol, yelling or shouting, threatening someone with physical violence, and destroying property. However, the researchers noted that high-risk behaviors among returning service members might include many other health-threatening or life-threatening activities. Thrill-seeking by engaging in dangerous recreational activities, driving too fast or recklessly, using illegal drugs or abusing prescription drugs, engaging in unsafe sexual practices, gambling, and smoking are behaviors that can adversely impact on the health and well-being of service members returning from combat. Although the findings were not specific to soldiers who had deployed, the U.S. Army reported a total of 146 deaths of active duty members related to high-risk behaviors in 2009, including 74 drug overdoses (Department of the Army, 2010). In fact, in 2009 more soldiers died as a result of high-risk behavior than died in combat. Killgore et al. (2008) suggest that one of the contributors to the phenomenon of increased risky behavior after deployment might be that "an individual's perceived threshold of invincibility" (p. 1112) is elevated after having witnessed and survived extremely dangerous and violent combat experiences.

Voices From the Frontline

HOME AGAIN

It takes a while to adapt back into civilian life. Life at home felt kind of dull. It took awhile for that feeling to diminish. I talked with other soldiers. They felt the same way.

Sometimes I'd stop and hesitate for a second on my way to work. I'd think, "I forgot my weapon" and then laugh at myself because I don't have a weapon. It's startling, and then you use humor to push it away.

Once walking down the street in the middle of Chicago, a garbage truck was letting down a dumpster and there was a big crashing sound. I stopped in my tracks. Another time, I saw a beat up car without a license. My heart started beating fast. My first thought: "It's an IED, a car bomb." My second thought: "In the middle of Chicago?"

There were many times I was scared in Iraq, but I never thought I'd die. A lot of other people have a much harder transition back than I did.

Ted Cravens
Army Reserve Combat Stress Prevention Officer

Psychological Health Problems

Combat deployments have exposed troops to extreme psychological stress and trauma that increase the risk for developing psychological health problems. The exposure to trauma can result in **posttraumatic stress**—a spectrum of reactions to a trauma (The Management of Post-traumatic Stress Working Group, 2010). Those who survive a trauma may only experience some of the reactions, while others may experience the entire spectrum. The first two reactions listed below are not diagnoses as defined by the *Diagnostic and Statistical Manual V* (DSM V) (American Psychiatric Association, 2013), the American Psychiatric Association's publication that lists mental health disorders).

Acute stress reaction is used to describe temporary symptoms (e.g., disorientation, agitation, anxiety, confusion) in response to a traumatic event. These symptoms usually disappear in hours or days.

Combat and operation stress refers to the physical, mental, and emotional symptoms (e.g., anxiety, hyperarousal, fatigue, depression, concentration problems) that extend beyond 4 days after a traumatic event.

According to the DSM V, PTSD is categorized as a trauma- and stressor-related disorder, a change from the DSM-IV that listed PTSD as an anxiety disorder. A PTSD diagnosis requires: exposure to actual or threatened death, serious injury, or sexual violation; and with symptoms that persist more than 1 month after the traumatic event resulting in impairment in functioning in one or more areas of life. Symptoms include reexperiencing the traumatic event, avoiding trauma-associated stimuli, changes in cognition and mood, and arousal and reactivity. It is important to note that symptoms can begin soon after the trauma or months later. Exposure includes experiencing a traumatic event, witnessing a traumatic event as it was being experienced by others, learning that a close friend or family member experienced a traumatic event, or experiencing repeated or extreme exposure to details of a traumatic event (usually experienced by professionals such as first responders, healthcare professionals). When symptoms last between 4 days and 1 month, the diagnosis is acute stress disorder. Table 7.2 lists possible PTSD symptoms. In addition to the direct or indirect experience of a traumatic event noted, a diagnosis of PTSD requires at least one re-experiencing and one avoiding symptom, at least two symptoms related to negative thoughts and mood, and at least two symptoms related to arousal.

PTSD is one of the most common psychological consequences of combat (Dedert et al., 2009; Hoge et al., 2004). Other common psychological health problems resulting from combat include major depression, alcohol abuse or dependence, and other anxiety disorders. The lifetime prevalence of PTSD is 6.8%, and the lifetime prevalence of depression is 16.6% in the general public (Kessler, Bergland, Demler, Jin, & Walters, 2005). About 14% of OEF and OIF veterans suffer from PTSD and 14% experience major depression (Tanielian & Jaycox, 2008). In fact, Hoge et al. (2004)

TABLE 7.2 Symptoms of Post-traumatic Stress Disorder

Re-experiencing	Avoiding	Negative Thoughts and Moods	Arousal
• Involuntary, repeated, intrusive memories • Nightmares • Flashbacks or other dissociative reactions • Intense or prolonged distress • Physiological reactivity	• Avoiding or trying to avoid distressing memories, feelings, or thoughts related to the traumatic event • Avoiding or trying to avoid reminders to the traumatic event	• Unable to recall an important detail of traumatic event • Persistent and distorted negative beliefs about self, others, and/or the world • Distorted thoughts of self-blame • Ongoing negative feelings such as guilt, horror, fear, shame, anger • Disinterest or engagement in important activities • Feeling detached or isolated from others • Unable to feel positive emotions such as love, satisfaction, happiness	• Irritability and anger • Recklessness, self-destructiveness • Hypervigilance • Easily startled • Poor concentration • Problems sleeping

Sources: American Psychiatric Association (2013). *Diagnostic and statistical manual of mental disorders, fifth edition.* Arlington, VA: Author.
American Psychiatric Association (2013b). *Posttraumatic stress disorder.* Retrieved November 22, 2014 from www.dsm5.org/Documents/PTSD%20Fact%20Sheet.pdf
U.S. Department of Veterans Affairs (2014). *DSM-5 criteria for PTSD.* Retrieved November 22, 2014 from www.ptsd.va.gov/professional/PTSD-overview/dsm5_criteria_ptsd.asp

found that approximately 17% of service members returning from combat duty in Iraq and Afghanistan screened positive for these psychological health disorders. Several years later, in a study of Army and Marine service members who completed a routine health screening form after returning from deployments in Iraq or Afghanistan, Hoge, Auchterloine, and Milliken (2006) found that 19% of service members who served in Iraq and 11% who served in Afghanistan reported having a psychological health problem. They reported problems with PTSD, depression, or other psychological health problems. The same study revealed that 35% of those who had served in Iraq sought psychological health services in the year after returning from the war. A recent study of the prevalence rates among returning veterans of PTSD or depression with serious functional impairment (Thomas et al., 2010) suggests that PTSD and depression cause a significant impairment in level of functioning for 8%–14% of returning veterans and some impairment for 23%–31%.

The rate of PTSD and other psychological health disorders among returning service members may be underdiagnosed. For example, the first participants in the Millennium Cohort Study were enrolled between 2001 and 2003. Of the 75,000 military members enrolled in the study, 2% of those who had deployed to combat zones reported symptoms of PTSD without reporting a diagnosis—over four times more than those who reported both symptoms and a diagnosis of PTSD (Smith, Wingard et al., 2009). The rate of PTSD may also be under-reported by corpsmen, medics, nurses, and doctors who do their job in theatre and under life-threatening conditions. These healthcare providers attend to patients, perhaps a seemingly endless number, with severe physical injuries and with injuries so extensive the patients are disabled or die. Healthcare providers may believe they need to be the strong ones or are the ones, due to their profession, who are protected from absorbing the stress of witnessing death, injury, and disability without harmful effect (Gibbons, Hickling, & Watts, 2011).

In studying data from the 2008 DoD Survey of Health Related Behaviors, researchers (Bray, Spira, Williams, & Lane, 2010) found that the prevalence of psychological health problems was greater for those service members who had experienced higher levels of combat exposure (e.g., exposure to more traumatic types of combat experiences or more instances of engaging in direct combat with the enemy; being exposed to mines, IEDs, or other explosions; seeing bodies or human remains; or having unit members who were casualties). Service members who had experienced higher levels of combat exposure reported higher levels of work and family stress, anxiety, symptoms of depression and PTSD, and more frequent thoughts of suicide. Other types of combat exposure have also been associated with PTSD symptoms. Exposure or perceived threats of exposure to biological/chemical agents, including having to don protective clothing and a mask when hearing alarms warning of the presence of biological/chemical agents increases the likelihood of developing PTSD symptoms (Smith, Wingard et al., 2009). Depression has also been found to develop more frequently in service members with high levels of combat exposure than for service members who have not deployed or those with less combat exposure during deployment (Wells et al., 2010).

Psychological health problems may also be more prevalent in Reserve Component service members following deployment. In a study of soldiers from four Active Components and two National Guard infantry brigade combat teams, active duty and National Guard soldiers reported similar rates of combat exposure during deployment and similar prevalence rates of PTSD and depression 3 months following deployment (Thomas et al., 2010). However, 12 months after returning from a deployment the prevalence rate of PTSD and depression, accompanied by an increase in aggressive behaviors and the misuse of alcohol, was significantly greater among National Guard soldiers. DoD and Army researchers believed the difference in prevalence rates at this point in the deployment cycle relates to readjustment to civilian life, lack of health care, or both. National Guard members return from deployment to their civilian lives, while active duty members continue to work with one another daily, perhaps providing needed social support. Also, National Guard members are entitled to free military medical coverage, including psychological health care, for 6 months after returning from a deployment. They must purchase the medical coverage after that time, which may not be financially feasible, or seek services at Veterans Affairs facilities whose locations may be at great distances.

Greenberg, Langston, and Jones (2008) identify the following additional indicators of current psychological problems or possible risk factors for service members developing PTSD or other psychological problems:

- Perception that they were out of control during the event.
- Perception that their life was threatened during the event.
- Blaming others for what happened.
- Shame/guilt about their behavior during the event.
- Experiencing acute stress following the event.
- Exposure to substantial stress since the event.
- Problems with day-to-day activities since the event.
- Involvement in previous traumatic events.
- Poor social support (family, friends, unit support).
- Drinking alcohol excessively to cope with stress.

Friedman (2004) is concerned that the reported prevalence of PTSD among service members returning from combat deployments will increase in the coming years. Friedman's assertion is supported by a study of Gulf War veterans (Wolfe, Erickson, Sharkansky, King, & King, 1999), which concluded that rates of PTSD increased over time. Friedman (2004) further states his belief that psychological problems will continue to increase over time despite the changing nature of the U.S. Armed Forces missions in Iraq and Afghanistan from a "campaign for liberation to an ongoing armed conflict with dissident combatants" (p. 76). Again, Friedman draws on evidence from research on past conflicts; this time from a study of the psychological impact of deployments to Somalia (Litz, Orsillo, Friedman, Ehlich, & Batres, 1997). The Somalia study suggests that service members who are involved in peacekeeping-type deployments in life-threatening conditions are at increased risk for PTSD.

In a 2010 survey of 911 soldiers and marines assigned to combat forces in Afghanistan, the rates of psychological problems among the participants was compared to similar groups of service members who had been surveyed while serving in support of OIF and OEF in 2005 and 2009. The results of the study indicated that the rates of acute stress were significantly higher in 2010 than in both 2005 and 2009 and that the overall rates of psychological problems (i.e., acute stress, depression, and anxiety) were significantly higher in 2010 than in 2005. Possible reasons suggested for the increase are that more service members had experienced multiple deployments and more had been exposed to higher levels of combat over the years. Thus, as long as the current deployments for U.S. service members remain dangerous and the number of service members who are deployed and exposed to traumatic events continues to rise, we can expect the prevalence of PTSD and other psychological problems to continue to increase. Friedman (2004) suggests that it may "be too early to assess the eventual magnitude of the mental health problems related to deployment to Operation Iraqi Freedom or Operation Enduring Freedom" (p. 76).

Some of the common psychological disorders associated with combat deployments and the associated symptoms are listed in Table 7.3.

TABLE 7.3   Symptoms of Common Psychological Disorders Associated with Combat Deployment

Depression	Anxiety	Stress Reactions	Substance Abuse
• Depressed mood (sadness or emptiness) • Reduced interest in activities • Sleep disturbances • Loss of energy or reduction in energy level • Difficulty concentrating, holding a conversation, paying attention, or making decisions • Suicidal thoughts or intentions	• Excessive anxiety and worry • Difficulty controlling the worry • Restlessness • Easily fatigued • Difficulty concentrating • Irritability • Muscle tension • Sleep disturbance	• Dissociative symptoms (numbing, detachment) • Reduction in awareness of surroundings • Reexperiencing of the trauma • Avoidance of trauma-associated stimuli • Significant anxiety • Irritability • Poor concentration • Difficulty sleeping • Restlessness	• Impairment in functioning • Recurrent use resulting in failure to fulfill major obligations at work, school, or home • Recurrent use in situations that are physically hazardous (e.g., driving while intoxicated) • Craving or a strong desire or urge to use a substance • Continued use despite significant social or interpersonal problems

Source: Information from the American Psychiatric Association. (2013). *Diagnostic and statistical manual of mental disorders* (5th ed.). Arlington, VA: American Psychiatric Publishing.

Overlap of TBI and PTSD

Although TBI is a neurological condition, not a psychiatric disorder, most individuals who have had a TBI also were exposed to an event that could also lead to PTSD—an event in which the person felt in danger of his/her life, helpless, and powerless. Many of these individuals will display symptoms of a stress reaction and may have a TBI and PTSD resulting from the same event(s). Some individuals with TBI may have had exposure to events leading to PTSD prior to or subsequent to the TBI. Psychological health problems may also result from the experience of living with the results of a TBI (e.g., losses in function, changed career prospects, changed family roles and goals). In addition, PTSD and TBI share many of the same symptoms; and other mental health problems, such as substance abuse problems, may be present in individuals with PTSD or TBI. The overlap of symptoms between TBI and PTSD can be seen in Table 7.4.

Moral Injury

Subsequent to the recent wars in Iraq and Afghanistan, clinicians and researchers have become increasingly concerned about the ethical and moral implications of war and the psychological and behavioral impact of these implications on service members and veterans (e.g., Litz, Stein, Delaney, Lebowitz, Nash, Silver, & Maguen, 2009). Service members are aware that some combat and operational missions may require them to do things that are discordant with their beliefs or moral code, such as killing (Drescher, Foy, Kelly, Leshner, Schutz & Litz, 2011). Even with this knowledge, however, their actual participation in these actions can sometimes cause service members to question their humanity. **Moral injury** is the concept used to describe the inner conflict service members experience when their behavior or the behavior of others—through action, inaction, or witnessing—conflict with their moral beliefs and expectations (Maguen & Litz, 2012). Actions that might result in moral injury include betrayal by leaders, peers, or trusted civilians; failure to uphold one's own moral principles; mistreating enemy combatants; destroying civilian property; sexual assault; and friendly fire.

TABLE 7.4   TBI and PTSD Symptom Similarities

Mild TBI	PTSD
Anxiety	Anxiety
Depressed mood	Depressed mood
Memory problem	Memory problems
Poor concentration	Poor concentration
Irritability	Irritability
Insomnia	Insomnia
Fatigue	Fatigue
Headaches	Intrusive thoughts
Dizziness	Avoidance behaviors
Noise & light intolerance	Emotional numbing

Source: Information from Kennedy, J. E., Jaffee, M. S., Leskin, G. A., Stokes, J. W., Leal, F. O., & Fitzpatrick, P. J. (2007). Posttraumatic stress disorder and posttraumatic stress disorder-like symptoms and mild traumatic brain injury. *Journal of Rehabilitation Research & Development, 44,* 895–920.

Moral injury can cause individuals to experience shame, guilt, anxiety about the consequence of the acts, or anger about the perceived betrayal of leaders or peers that caused the individual to be or to feel responsible for the discordant act. In an effort to further define and understand the construct of moral injury, Drescher et al. (2011) interviewed a variety of health-care and religious professionals who had experience with service members and veterans, including chaplains, psychological health providers, researchers, and policymakers. The researchers included questions about the signs and symptoms observed in veterans who seemed to suffer from moral injury. The researchers grouped the responses into the following categories:

- Social problems, including withdrawal, lack of concern for the effects of their behavior on others, inability to fit in, legal problems, disciplinary problems, and alienation from their children.
- Sense of betrayal and loss of trust.
- Spiritual issues and issues relating to human existence, including questioning morality, profound sorrow, loss of meaning to life, loss of caring, and feeling haunted.
- Psychological and social problems, including depression, anxiety, anger, denial, and difficulties with work.
- Self-deprecation, including loss of self-worth and feeling guilt, shame, self-loathing, and damaged.

Maguen and Litz (2012) suggest that there is overlap between the psychological concepts of PTSD and moral injury and that more research is needed to understand the unique aspects of each construct and how they are distinct consequences of war.

Suicide

One of the tragic consequences of psychological health problems among returning service members is that more and more service members are committing suicide. The suicide rate among U.S. military has historically been significantly lower than among civilians, which is approximately 19 per 100,000 people (Department of the Army, 2010). However, a larger number of service members than ever before are dying by suicide (Kuehn, 2009). Suicide rates began increasing in the military in 2004 (Department of the Army, 2010). Between 2001 and 2007, suicide rates in the Army and Marine Corps, "which have borne the majority of ground combat operations increased steadily," while the Navy and Air Force rates increased only slightly (p. 16). In 2008, the Army suicide rate surpassed the national average, reaching 20 per 100,000; and for the first time in 28 years, the suicide rate among military personnel is higher than that of a comparable civilian population (Kuehn, 2009). The DoD estimates that 2% of the Army attempted suicide in 2008 (DoD, 2008a). In 2009, 160 active duty soldiers committed suicide, making it the third highest cause of death among soldiers (Department of the Army, 2010). Of the suicides completed by active duty Army personnel in 2009, 96.9% were committed by male service members. A total of at least 334 service members (all services and active duty and reserve members combined) committed suicide in 2009 (Donnelly, 2010).

Psychological health disorders can increase the risk of suicide among those who suffer from these conditions (Kuehn, 2009). In addition, the 2007 Army Suicide Event Report found that "there was a significant relationship between suicide attempts and number of days deployed to OIF/OEF" (Suicide Risk Management & Surveillance Office, 2008, p. 2).

The Department of the Army (2010) report on suicide identified the following principal risk factors and stressors associated with suicidal behavior among soldiers:

- Relationship problems.
- Military or work stress (e.g., voluntary or involuntary separation from the Army, combat/dangerous work environment, and increased optempo).
- Legal problems, encounters with law enforcement personnel/systems, and military disciplinary or administrative actions.
- High-risk behaviors and medical conditions.

Stigma and Other Barriers to Care

Often, service members who need help with psychological problems after returning from a deployment do not seek help. One of the reasons that service members do not report psychological health problems upon their return from deployments is that they may not experience symptoms immediately. Even if they do experience symptoms, they may not be willing to report them. One reason is that they do not want the psychological health assessment and treatment process to delay the start of their postdeployment leave (vacation) and reunion with their families. Barriers to care can also include not understanding what kinds of treatment are available, not knowing how to access them, and not having adequate time to invest in obtaining treatment (Britt et al., 2008). Hoge et al. (2004) found that service members cited not knowing where to get treatment and not being able to get time off for treatment as barriers preventing them from accessing care for psychological health problems they were experiencing.

The continuing stigma of psychological health within the military is a larger deterrent to reporting problems and seeking assistance with psychological health problems; it is the most frequently cited barrier to care (Hoge et al., 2004). Of those service members who screened positive for psychological health disorders, "only 23 to 40 percent sought mental health care" (p. 13); they were twice as likely as those returning service members who screened negative for psychological problems to cite stigmatization as a main deterrent to seeking help. The Department of the Army (2010) has stated that stigma continues to be the leading deterrent to seeking help. However, based on a comparison between National Guard and active duty soldiers on the rate of use of psychological health services and the impact of stigma (Kim, Thomas, Wilk, Castro, & Hoge, 2010), Reserve Component service members appear to have fewer concerns about stigma and seek psychological health care more readily than active duty service members.

The impact of the stigma of psychological disorders takes several forms. Corrigan (2004) cites two types of stigma that can impede individuals from seeking psychological health care—public stigma (prejudice and discrimination against those with psychological disorders) and self-stigma (internalization of the public's biases against those with psychological illnesses).

Since military personnel are expected to function at a high level of performance at all times and to be dependable and steadfast, the impact of stigma may be more pronounced for military personnel than for civilians. Many service members are embarrassed or ashamed of having psychological problems, which they may view as a weakness. They may also be reluctant to admit that they need help for fear that they will be viewed as inferior, inadequate, and unable to complete their mission by their leaders, since this information is not kept confidential from their superiors.

Voices From the Frontline

MILITARY CULTURE AND MENTAL HEALTH

The military culture has always been that you don't stick your head up and ask for things. In the military you are dealing with a portion of the population that is the strongest and best adapted. They don't want to feel like they are draining the resources. They want to feel they are the resource.

Military culture wants support to be like a checklist. "Help me figure out what I need to do for myself. Give me the tools and let me move on with things."

In most cases, it is effective. If you run into a serious mental health issue, extra assistance is needed. It can be hard to ask for help when the checklist approach/culture doesn't work. At those times, we hope that a buddy intervenes and helps them ask for help.

Chris Sullins
Former Army Reserve Combat Stress Prevention Officer

In an exploration of the impact of officer leadership and unit cohesion (togetherness and bonding) on military personnel's propensity to seek psychological health care, Wright et al. (2009) found that lower stigma and barriers to care were associated with high officer leadership qualities and cohesion within their units. The researchers also noted that recently implemented training programs for military personnel and leaders have begun to address stigma and the importance of military leadership in changing attitudes about psychological health.

Alcohol and Substance Use/Abuse

Data from the 2008 DoD Survey of Health Related Behaviors suggest that service members who had greater levels of exposure to combat-related experiences were more likely to engage in health threatening behaviors (Bray, Spira, Williams, & Lane, 2010). They tended to smoke more, to increase the use of or become dependent on alcohol, or to use illicit substances. The National Survey on Drug Use and Health (Office of Applied Studies, 2005) compared the use of alcohol, the rate of driving under the influence of alcohol, and daily cigarette smoking among veterans and nonveterans in 2003. The results indicated a greater incidence of these behaviors among veterans than nonveterans. Approximately

57% of veterans used alcohol within the past month, 13% reported driving under the influence, and almost 19% reported smoking daily; nonveterans reported rates of approximately 51%, 12%, and 14%, respectively. Alcohol use, alcohol misuse, and alcohol-related high-risk behaviors are associated with increased rates of injury, automobile accidents, and psychological health problems. Both cigarette use and alcohol misuse are associated with numerous physical health problems.

OTHER CONSEQUENCES OF COMBAT DEPLOYMENTS ON SERVICE MEMBERS

Living Conditions and Environmental Stressors

One of the consequences of engaging in combat in overseas locations is the challenging change in living conditions and environments, which often creates additional stressors in an already stressful combat environment. In the case of recent U.S. military deployments to OIF and OEF, both the living conditions and the environment have added significant stress for service members. Poor living conditions can include crowding in camps or in sleeping quarters (e.g., tents); uncomfortable cots (portable folding beds); lack of privacy and personal space; constant noise from small-arms weapons (guns, rifles, and machine guns), larger artillery, and explosions; and lack of adequate shelter from bad weather. Means for good hygiene and sanitation can also be insufficient: latrines may be primitive, unavailable, or inadequately maintained; washing facilities may be communal and lack privacy; showers are often infrequent, not available, or cold; and clothes washing facilities or services may not be available. Harsh environmental conditions can include hot dry summers, with temperatures often reaching over 140°F, and relatively cold winters, with night temperatures that can drop below freezing; wind, blowing sand, and severe sandstorms; scorpions, snakes, camel spiders (solifugae, which are large, quick spiders that can bite if disturbed); and packs of feral dogs.

Voices From the Frontline

A NOTE HOME FROM IRAQ

We are getting dust storm after dust storm and temperatures between 110°F and 130°F every day now. The dust gets so thick that it looks like thick fog. The ground is so dry now that when a vehicle passes by, it leaves a huge cloud of dust that takes minutes to settle and leaves one tasting the dust and feeling it stick to sweat and lips, and burn one's eyes. The intense heat saps our energy quickly. It's easy to get dehydrated, and we have to work at getting enough water to drink. If I find myself getting headaches, feeling light-headed, feeling worn-out, and getting muscle aches, I get an extra bottle of water (1.5 L) and keep drinking until I have finished the bottle.

Angela Pereira
Colonel, U.S. Army, Retired

Environmental threats can include exposure to numerous chemicals and other substances. Exposure to these environmental stressors during the Gulf War included kerosene, diesel, and gasoline used in tent heaters, stoves, and generators (Committee on Gulf War and Health, 2008). These substances are still used in OEF and OIF. Other environmental stressors can include exposure to pesticides, depleted uranium, and numerous other substances that may not yet have been identified as environmental threats.

Many of these harsh living conditions and environmental stressors clearly pose a threat to the physical health of military service members who are deployed. Some are currently being studied to assess their impact on health. The Committee on Gulf War and Health (2008) has acknowledged, however, that these exposures are "psychologically stressful and physiologically challenging" (p. 39).

Joblessness and Homelessness

Although these are not problems common among active duty service members, joblessness and homelessness can be very real issues facing Reserve Component service members and veterans who have separated from the military who do not have the consistent pay that active duty members earn. Reserve Component service members often have difficulties maintaining a civilian career because of the requirement to go on active duty status whenever called upon by their reserve units. Reservists must be prepared to leave jobs, sometimes suddenly, and their employers must be prepared to let them go. This can severely disrupt the business for the employer and the career for the reservist.

The U.S. Department of Labor (2011) reported that the 2010 unemployment rate for veterans who served in the Armed Forces since September 2001 was over 11%. However, for young male veterans, ages 18–24, the unemployment rate was over 21%.

By analyzing data from the Department of Veterans Affairs and the Census Bureau, the Homelessness Research Institute at the National Alliance to End Homelessness (Cunningham, Henry, & Lyons, 2007) learned that, "Homeless veterans can be found in every state across the country and live in rural, suburban, and urban communities" (p. 3). This report suggests that, in part, the high rate of homelessness among veterans stems from a lack of affordable housing causing veterans to have to pay too much for rent and from the large numbers of veterans returning from combat with PTSD and TBI.

Traumatic Growth

Most research to date focuses on the negative consequences of deployment and exposure to combat-related trauma and the impact of those experiences on service members. However, recent interests in the role of resilience in overcoming hardship and trauma and in the contribution of exposure to trauma in the development of resilience in military members have led to greater attention to the potential for positive outcomes from exposure to combat-related trauma and hardship. Exposure to stress and involvement in traumatic events can lead to positive adaptation and growth. It can help one develop new perspectives on life and living and wisdom. Growth as a result of stress and trauma can include new perspectives on vulnerability and strength; positive changes in relationships; and philosophical, physical, and spiritual growth.

In a study on the possible beneficial effects of exposure to combat and combat-related trauma on Gulf War veterans (Maguen, Vogt, King, King, & Litz, 2006), researchers found that several factors contributed to positive postdeployment growth. They found that being in the National Guard or Reserves (versus active duty) and having experienced "perceived threat" (fear for safety and well-being) while deployed were associated with an increased appreciation of life. Adequate postdeployment social support (emotional and tangible help) was associated with an enhanced ability to relate to others, personal strength (the ability to handle difficulties), and posttraumatic growth (overall personal growth after experiencing a traumatic event). The results of the study also suggest that some ethnic minority service members might experience greater hope in "new possibilities" (establishing a new path for their lives) after a combat deployment.

Voices From the Frontline

A MESSAGE TO FAMILY AND FRIENDS AFTER AN INSURGENT ATTACK IN IRAQ

When the attack was over, 59 people, including 44 U.S. troops, had been wounded, some seriously, but none killed—by some miracle. Thirty-three of the wounded were the Marines who guard our perimeter. We are all grateful that they were here since four vehicle-borne IEDs came from various sides with Iraqi insurgents attempting to breach our perimeter. Even as other insurgents came through the holes they created, the Marines were there to shoot them.

I did a series of critical event debriefings with the Marine unit after the attack. It was the third time I had done intensive work with this group and they treated me like "part of the circle." I'll never forget or repeat some of the gruesome things they told me. They were very stoic about their experiences during the attack and used a lot of humor when describing what they saw and did. But they were also able to express their thoughts and feelings and listened carefully when I described possible responses to what they had experienced and warned them that they might have some difficulty dealing with what they lived through once they got home.

At the end, they left a signed book for me—*Being Happy*—a motivational book by Andrew Matthews.[*] In it they each wrote some messages: "We are well adjusted, despite the killing," "I'm OK ... really," and "I will not hurt anyone when I get home, I promise." I feel extremely proud that I was able to help them cope with what they experienced.

Angela Pereira
Colonel, U.S. Army, Retired

SUMMARY

- Combat deployment exposes U.S. military personnel to life-threatening combat, hazardous duty, and dangerous environmental conditions.
- Veterans often return with severe physical injuries and permanent physical and/or neurological changes and limitations, and psychological health problems.
- TBI and PTSD—the two "signature injuries" from the current conflicts—are prevalent among returning veterans; they present unique, long-term challenges to the military and civilian communities and are often missed or confused because of the sometimes hidden and overlapping symptoms characterized by these conditions.
- Other potential consequences of exposure to combat are engaging in unsafe behavior and taking potentially dangerous risks that threaten veterans' health or lives.
- Reserve Component service members and veterans who have separated from the military are increasingly facing joblessness and homelessness.
- Positive outcomes from exposure to combat-related trauma and hardship contribution of exposure to trauma include the development of resilience to positive adaptation and growth.

---

[*] Mathews, A. (1988). *Being happy*. New York: Price Stern Sloan.

EXERCISES

To further explore the physical and psychological effects of war on service members, answer the following questions:

1. What knowledge, skills, and sensitivities do you need to talk to someone who has been in combat about the physical and psychological effects of war on them?
2. Go to the Library of Congress Veterans History Project website at http://www. loc.gov/vets/about.html. Go to the digitalized collection and listen to two or three firsthand accounts of veterans' experiences during two different wars. Compare and contrast the impact of war on their lives.
3. Locate a copy of the Kessler et al. (2005) article on the prevalence of mental health disorders based on the results of a national survey. The article is listed in the references. Find the lifetime prevalence of PTSD in the general public according to the survey. How does this differ from the rate of PTSD in the military? What do you think will be the long-term societal consequences of combat-related PTSD?
4. Change your physical appearance in some way (e.g., use crutches or a wheelchair, wear a blindfold) for 2–3 hours of your normal daily routine to get a small glimpse of what it might be like to return home from war with a disfiguring scar or a physical injury. Write a short essay on your experience. What did you learn about yourself and others? What insights into the daily lives of wounded warriors did this experience provide?

8

The Effects of War on Families

In Chapter 8, you will

- Meet Benjamin Karney, PhD, a leading researcher at the University of California, Los Angeles, in the field of family science who studies change and stability in intimate relationships.
- Learn about recent and cutting edge research that helps us understand the ways in which war affects family systems and familial relationships.
- Learn how everyday assumptions about the role of stress in military families can be empirically tested.
- Be able to identify current gaps in our knowledge about military families and war.
- Acquire information about evidence-based programming designed to strengthen families.

Meet

Benjamin Karney, PhD, Social Psychologist

I have been studying marriage for 20 years. The research is pretty clear—the effect of stress on marriage is negative. When I had an opportunity to study military marriage, I thought, "This is going to be easy. We know military families are under stress, especially during wartime."

I am not in the military and I didn't have any friends in the military when I started this work. That didn't stop me from assuming divorce rates should be higher during wartime. Not only because of stressful deployments but because many people who join the military are young and I know young people have higher divorce rates.

All of this together, suggested to me, a scholar of marriage, that all I had to do was to document what was happening. As it turned out, I was in for a big surprise: In 2005, divorce rates were about where they had been in 1996. The data looked at divorce in all services starting 5 years before and after the start of the current conflicts. Though the stress and demand on families had increased greatly, the divorce rate hadn't.

I wondered, "What if we look only at people who were deployed—those people who were more likely to divorce?" We did another analysis comparing them to married civilians in the years from 2002 to 2005. We matched both groups by age, ethnicity, race, employment status, and education level. They were very similar except one group was in the military and one wasn't. The divorce rate among the civilians was higher.

I realized that I knew about marriage, but I didn't know military families. I had to step back and ask, "What did I miss?"

- *First, the military does a lot of things to take care of military families. It offers the best health care and child care in the United States. It provides a housing allowance. Separation pay. These benefits and others are protection against stress.*
- *Second, the stress of military families has a higher meaning that changes the way it is experienced. I met a young woman whose new husband signed up to redeploy. When I asked how she felt about that, she said, "I'm proud of him for serving our country." She told me that when he gets home they will have enough money to buy a house.*

Looking at the impact of war on marriage is complex. We don't know about how husbands and wives are communicating, how children are doing, and if people are feeling sad and lonely even when they are together. Just because we aren't seeing the negative effects now, doesn't mean they won't occur. The way families are reacting to stress may be changing over time. We're starting to see some of this with a rising suicide rate over the last few years.

The big lesson from my experience is to check your assumptions at the door. Keep listening to families and be open to what you might see and learn.

INTRODUCTION

There are approximately 4 million military-connected children in the U.S. with about half of this number currently living in an active duty or Guard and Reserve family and the remaining half who have a veteran parent (Lester & Flake, 2013). Over 1 million children and their families have experienced at least one military deployment since 2001 (MacDermid Wadsworth, 2010). The decade since 9/11 has created unique opportunities to examine how family life is impacted by a myriad of events within military service. Researchers are identifying particular kinds of wartime experiences in order to better understand differential connections to family, spousal, and children's stress and resiliency. Some of these experiences include distinguishing types of deployment experiences (e.g., combat and noncombat deployments, repeated deployments and extended deployments), deployment-related trauma and injury, extended use of Reserve Component service members, and separation from service into the civilian world.

Our understanding of the effects of war on families continues to evolve, with researchers from multiple disciplines adding to our knowledge. Researchers vary in their backgrounds; some are career military service members, some are career civilian employees within the military, some are faculty at universities and colleges throughout the United States, and some are consultants for independent research corporations.

This chapter discusses research focused on risk and resilience experienced in family systems and familial roles in relation to war and deployment experiences. Common family system relationships include those of the family of creation: spousal and parent-child. However, these are not the only family relationships. Service members often negotiate relationships with their own parents and siblings, as well as with extended family members; and parents of service members may also be involved in caregiving for their service member's children. Each of these relationships offer opportunities to better understand strengths and concerns for military family well-being. In turn, these findings also inform policies that are directed toward these families.

You may recall from Chapter 2 that our knowledge about military family relationships is guided, in part, by the definition of family member (dependent) used to identify those members who are enrolled in DEERS and have access to military-based services and supports. This definition influences which relationships are of primary importance to the military research community and also helps us identify the limits of our knowledge.

THE DEPLOYMENT–REINTEGRATION CYCLE AND FAMILY WELL-BEING

With the continuing increased optempo of service member deployments and activation of Reserve Component personnel to active war zones, research has identified stressful transitions families negotiate, as well as positive and negative effects of deployment for families, spousal relationships, and children. Several studies highlight deployment and pre-deployment related stressors (see, for example, Di Nola, 2008; Warner, Appenseller, Warner, & Greiger, 2009) while others focus more on changes and challenges in relational processes as the deployment cycle moves from one phase to the next (Faber et al., 2008). Research in the field of communication examines spousal patterns of communication with their deployed partner and use of community supports in coping with stressors and in relation to marital satisfaction (Joseph & Afifi, 2010). McNulty (2008) focuses on concerns and assumptions about family reintegration after deployment, and work by Sayers, Farrow, Ross, and Olsin (2009) highlights the role of family distress in service members who have been referred for a mental health evaluation upon return from deployed status. Several researchers have focused specifically on alcohol misuse of the service member and the risk of interpersonal violence with romantic partners (McCarroll, Fan, & Bell, 2009; Newby, Ursano, et al., 2005) and whether or not there is an increased risk for child abuse and neglect while a service member parent is deployed (Gibbs et al., 2007; Lincoln et al., 2008). Each of these areas of research helps us learn more about resilience processes and challenges for families and highlights areas that need further investigation.

Marital Stability

There is a common perception, as Benjamin Karney mentioned in his interview, that the stresses of the ongoing engagement in Iraq and Afghanistan must be linked with higher rates of marital distress and divorce in military marriages. Researchers at the RAND Corporation conducted a study of military marriages for the Office of the Secretary of Defense in 2007 (Karney & Crown, 2007). This detailed study of 10 years of military personnel records from FY 1996 to FY 2005 led researchers to note the following.

First, marital dissolution rates were similar in 1996 during a time when fewer demands were placed on the military and in 2005 during a time when the military was experiencing greater demands. Marital dissolution (including divorces, annulments, legal separations, and cases in the process of legal divorce) among active duty branches peaked in FY 1999 and hit a 5-year low in FY 2000. From 2000 to 2005, the rate of marital dissolution gradually increased in the Army, Air Force, and Marine Corps, to the point of being similar to the dissolution rate of 1996. The Navy showed a slightly different pattern. Marital dissolution increased after FY 2001 but then declined in FY 2004 and 2005 to a rate similar to 1996. Marital dissolution among the selected reserve showed similar patterns during this decade.

Second, enlisted personnel were at greater risk of divorce than officers. This difference was likely due to the older age of officers when marrying, as marriage at a younger age is related to an increased risk of divorce (Karney & Crown, 2007).

Third, female service members displayed a much higher risk of divorce than their male counterparts. Their greater likelihood of being married to another service member (48% of female active duty service personnel were in dual-military marriages compared with 12% of male service members) does not explain this increased risk of marital dissolution (Karney & Crown, 2007).

Fourth, deployment did not seem to increase the risk of divorce for those service members married after OEF or OIF began through FY 2005. Only for active Air Force enlisted personnel and officers did the risk of divorce increase with more days deployed during this time. This lack of influence on marital stability seems contrary to popular beliefs that separations, particularly separations in which the service member is at risk of injury or death, can stress a marriage so much that the couple divorces. This study was unable to analyze the relationship between marital dissolution and level of combat experienced during deployment. Also, this study could track only those who remained in the military during the study and tracked service personnel for only 4 years or less (those who married after OEF or OIF began, through FY 2005).

The Karney and Crown 2007 study is limited in examining data for military marriages between 1998 and 2005, spanning the years immediately before and into the first 4 years of our current engagements in the global war on terrorism (GWOT). As the post-9/11 engagement, with its high deployment cycle, has persisted now for another decade, it continues to be important to follow military and veteran families. Changes in risk for marriage instability and family dysfunction need to be assessed as they may be linked to multiple deployments and potential co-occurring risks of physical and psychological injury.

Negrusa and Negrusa (2012) reported effects of deployment for Army personnel that partially contradict the Karney and Crown (2007) study. Specifically, Negrusa and Negrusa, in their study of Army data from 1999 to 2008, found that length of time deployed was associated with an increase in the risk of divorce for enlisted Army personnel and that personnel who were PTSD symptomatic after a deployment were at an even higher risk for divorce. This study gives some insight into how cumulative effects of stress can contribute to increased risk for military family stability.

Other research also suggests that military combat increases the risk of marital dissolution. A **Mental Health Advisory Team** (MHAT-VI, 2009; a team established by the Office of the U.S. Army Surgeon General to examine behavioral health of service members and behavioral health care in OIF and OEF) reported that there has been a steady increase in the percent of junior enlisted soldiers (E-1 to E-4) in maneuver units (an Army or Marine Corps unit deployed in OIF) who indicated their intention to seek a separation or divorce, from 12.4% in 2003 to 21.9% in 2009. A similar trend was seen in their response to "I have a good marriage." In 2003, 79.2% agreed or strongly agreed with this statement but by 2009 only 57.8% did so. However, there has been no statistical change to indicate that the soldiers who reported these intentions actually followed through with separations or filing for divorce.

Additional research with veterans and with service personnel who remain in the military will be necessary to determine whether deployment, the number of days deployed, and combat experiences increase the risk of divorce in those who served in OEF and OIF (Karney & Crown, 2007).

Other researchers have noted that active duty personnel, who tend to marry earlier than their civilian counterparts, also divorce and remarry earlier than the civilian population (Adler-Baeder, Pittman, & Taylor, 2005). When coupled with the greater likelihood of becoming parents in their early 20s as compared to the civilian population, the trends of earlier divorce and remarriage indicate that many young military families may be comprised of single parents, blended families with stepparent and stepchild relations, and divorced service members with children who are nonresidential and with whom they may or may not have partial custody. You learned in Chapter 2 that military women are more likely to divorce than both their male counterparts and civilian women. Additionally, of children who live in single parent households in the United States, about 85% live with their biological mothers (U.S. Census Bureau, 2008) and military service women are almost three times as likely to be single parents as compared to male service members (DUSD, 2010). Thus, one area of research identified as a current priority focuses on single parent families, particularly custodial mothers who are service members and the ways in which deployment affects both their well-being and that of their children (Kelley, Doane, & Pearson, 2011).

Marital Satisfaction and Distress

A second, related research interest is that of marital satisfaction and distress for both service members and their spouses and how the quality of the relationship is connected to retention, readiness, and deployment experiences. Previous research has linked spousal commitment to military life with a service member's intention to remain in the service (Gade, Tiggle, & Schumm, 2003; Hosek et al., 2006), and the military has realized that family conflict and stress can have a negative impact on service member readiness and intention to remain in the service.

An emerging body of research is examining change and continuity in marital satisfaction through the deployment cycle in general and when the service member reports combat experiences, trauma, or injury during deployment (McCleland, Sutton, & Schumm, 2005; Renshaw, Rodrigues, & Jones, 2008). Both compromised physical and/or psychological health have been shown to increase the complexity in maintaining resilience at the individual and family levels. In Chapter 7, you learned about the prevalence of PTSD and depression in service members returning from deployment. You also learned that TBI has significant overlap of behavioral symptoms with PTSD.

Service members and veterans who are identified with any one or a combination of these health issues have been found to be at increased risk of marital distress (Fear et al., 2010; Hoge et al., 2004). Spouses of service members with PTSD, depression, or TBI are also at higher risk of developing psychological and marital distress themselves (Dekel, Solomon, & Bleich, 2005; Goff, Crow, Reisbig, Hamilton, 2007; Sayer et al., 2010) and may exhibit aspects of **caregiver burden** or **secondary traumatization** (Calhoun, Beckham, & Bosworth, 2002; Dekel et al., 2005; Dirkzwager, Bramsen, Ader, & van der Ploeg, 2005). Caregiver burden refers to the increased sense of responsibility and stress that a caregiver experiences in attending to the needs and welfare of another person. In the context of military families, service members who return with physical or psychological injuries may need increased assistance in completing daily activities and may have injuries that compromise their ability to resume a variety of familial roles, such as romantic partner, parent, son/daughter, or aunt/uncle. Secondary traumatization refers to the indirect exposure to trauma because of interactions with the traumatized person, which begins to affect the well-being of the persons around the individual. This indirect exposure to trauma can include spouses who are likely to be engaging with their service member partner in daily family life activities and renegotiating family roles, and children who are stepping back into parent–child roles after an extended absence and may be at different developmental levels than when the parent deployed. The transmission of secondary trauma to children has been described in World War II and Vietnam era research as **intergenerational trauma** as it indicates that the well-being of the parent can have a profound effect on the well-being of the child.

One area of this research has focused on spousal mental and physical health risks that can be linked to the deployment cycle experience of the at-home spouse (Warner et al., 2009). Army Combat Brigade Team (CBT) spouses participated in a cross-sectional study at the time that their service member spouses were deploying for a 15-month tour in Iraq. They were asked to identify deployment stressors and potential barriers to seeking care for themselves. Of the 295 spouses who participated, 43% met or exceeded the threshold level for moderate depression and about 20% reported that they had sought mental health care within the past year (including currently) or during their spouse's last deployment (Warner et al., 2009). The spouse sample was comprised of mostly females (96%), who had been married 5 or fewer years (49%), had one or more children (70%), and had at least some college education (74%). Their military spouses were mostly enlisted personnel (E-1 to E-4: 41%; E-5 to E-9: 45%).

The most frequently cited stressors for this group of spouses included safety of the deployed spouse (96%), feeling lonely (89%), raising a young child without spouse present (63%), having problems communicating with spouse (61%), and caring/raising/disciplining children with spouse absent (56%). Further, over half cited trying to balance work/family obligations as a stressor (Warner et al., 2009). These stressors link back to the family roles and relationships that are functionally altered with deployment: increased danger in the service member's daily work environment, less family member support in maintaining daily schedules, maintaining a spousal relationship, and having a partner to share caregiving responsibilities for children.

Warner et al. (2009) assessed the ranking of potential barriers to seeking mental health care after dividing the sample into two groups: nondepressed ($n = 177$) and depressed ($n = 128$). Overall, 85% of the sample agreed that they would be willing to seek mental health care if they or others thought they were having problems. However, those in the depressed group differed from the nondepressed group on several items indicating that there were several barriers to seeking that care: being seen as weak or feeling embarrassed, belief that their mental health could have an adverse effect on their spouse's career, belief that the military spouse would view them differently, worry that it could possibly hurt their own career, and depressed spouses were less likely to endorse taking medication to help than their nondepressed counterparts. The timing of this study must be taken into consideration. It was beneficial to gather the data at the time spouses were experiencing predeployment activities. These responses represented their current feelings and worries as their spouses readied for an extended combat deployment. However, the ability to complete at least one follow-up with the spouses could assess if either the stressors or perceived barriers to care changed once the deployment was underway and if there were changes in depressed status for the group. It is possible that future reports are forthcoming that will note changes over time.

Voices From the Frontline

"A COLONEL IN THE BACKYARD"

A colonel told me a story that shows war affects families, too. He took a unit to Afghanistan and lost several soldiers. When he got back, everyday he'd take a cup of coffee into the backyard and stand there, looking out into space. Every morning his wife would see him. She'd come out and say, "Honey, do you want to talk about it?" Every morning he would say, "No, I'm fine." Eventually they went to counseling where he was able to explain that he had to think about what happened in his own time and that when he had done that he'd talk to her about it. "She kept bugging me," he said. It can be hard to give someone space, to see your spouse in pain, especially when you are going through the transition, too and looking for encouragement, too.

Ginny Wescott, Certified Family Life Educator C.F.L.E.
Family Advocacy Program Prevention & Education Specialist for
Marine Corps and Army as well as long time military spouse

A current limitation to a broad understanding of marital satisfaction and distress in military families is that studies often only elicit information from one person, either the service member or the spouse. **Dyadic research**, where data is gathered from both members of a couple, is the typical method of studying shared and nonshared perceptions the couple has about their life and marriage although it can be more challenging—particularly with couples who are geographically separated for an extended period of time and who likely have unequal access to technology used for data collection (e.g., imagine being asked to use your weekly 30-minute window of technology access time in the chaplain's tent to complete an online survey about marital satisfaction while deployed with a combat support team instead of talking with your spouse and children). Thus while this type of data collection can inform us as to the degree to which couples share common and have unique concerns about their lives together and stressors that their family system faces with military life, the increased burden on a service member during the deployment cycle may make this type of research difficult to accomplish. Lastly, research on marital satisfaction and distress would also benefit from longitudinal study so that we can learn more about the process of building and maintaining marital satisfaction in the military context (Willerton, MacDermid Wadsworth, & Riggs, 2011).

Voices From the Frontline

A DUAL-MILITARY COUPLE: TRYING TO BE TOGETHER

Colonel Angela Pereira (retired) and her husband, Major Tony Vargas (retired), knew it would be difficult to be together because of their high ranks in different specialties: Angela is a social worker and Tony is a physician assistant (PA). They shared this time line of a family trying to be together.

1993–Summer 1994: Angela is assigned at Fort Jackson in Columbia, South Carolina, and Tony at Fort Stewart in Hinesville, Georgia. It is a 200-mile drive to be together on weekends.

Summer, 1994: Tony is assigned to Fort Jackson after they marry. He packs up and moves to South Carolina.

Before he completes a 3-week orientation, unpacks, or sees a single patient: Tony is sent to support a reserve unit for 6 months in Guantanamo Bay, Cuba.

Spring, 1995: Tony returns from Cuba.

Fall, 1995: Tony hears that he might be sent to Korea on a 1-year unaccompanied tour. Tony explains he wants to stay in Columbia to support Angela who is working on her doctorate. He is given no choice—or guarantee—that he would be assigned back to Fort Jackson after the year in Korea. After the time and effort of getting into the joint domicile program for married spouses, it could be 4 years before their assignments match up again.

1996: Tony retires with 20 years in the military. It is the only way he and Angela can be together. He returns to the same job as a civilian.

1998: Angela finishes her PhD and is assigned to Aberdeen Proving Ground, Maryland. Tony moves to Maryland with Angela and applies for PA positions in Maryland. They buy a house nearby, deciding they would eventually retire in Maryland.

2001: Angela is assigned to Germany. Tony applies for PA positions in Germany and, 3 months later, follows Angela to Germany.

2004: Angela returns from Germany and is sent to Fort Belvoir, Virginia. Tony follows in 5 months and moves back into their home in Maryland.

90 days later: Just after she signs a lease for an apartment in Virginia and before her car arrives from Germany, Angela is deployed to Iraq.

2005: Angela returns from Iraq and works at Fort Belvoir, VA. Tony works in Maryland. There are 2 more years of weekend commuting.

2007: Angela is assigned to Germany. Tony stays in their home in Maryland and keeps his job as a PA at a VA Medical Center.

2009: Angela retires and returns to Maryland. They can now be together.

Spousal Communication and Role Negotiation

Two small research studies have focused on relational processes couples use to share information during deployment (Joseph & Afifi, 2010) and negotiate family role expectations due to the deployment cycle (Gambardella, 2008). Both of these studies have the potential to be easily translated into practice. Two of the practical decisions at-home families have to make, often more than once, are if and when to disclose stressful information with their deployed family member and how to be flexible in adjusting expected family member roles and ways in which those roles are met after a return from deployment.

One consideration the at-home spouse or other family member may take into consideration is if sharing information about a stressful event would add to the stress of the deployed person (Hagedoorn, Kuijer, Buunk, DeJong, & Wobbes, 2000). For instance, stressful events at home could range from an adolescent being suspended from school to a natural disaster that damages the family home or a medical crisis of a close relative. Yet, the at-home family member may be hesitant to add to the burden of the deployed family member.

Joseph and Afifi (2010) specifically studied communication decisions wives made in regard to sharing stressful family information with their deployed husbands. They hypothesized that the wife's perceptions of her husband's danger/stress and expectations for how her husband would respond to the disclosure, as well as the wife's level of military community support, would predict whether to disclose or not. Using the concept of **communal coping**, the authors framed spousal disclosures of stressful events as consequences of two types of coping processes: appraisal of the situation (is an individual or group responsible for the problem) and action taken to solve the problem (is an individual or group responsible for taking action) (Joseph & Afifi, 2010). Communal coping acknowledges that individuals are nested within groups, such as marital dyads and family systems, and that the other members of the group are likely to be affected when one or more members are distressed (Lyons, Mickelson, Sullivan, & Coyne, 1998). A decision to **buffer** the deployed family member from stressful events would be a result of appraising a situation as being a group problem (such as a teenager's truancy from school affects the whole family) but deciding to take responsibility for solving individually ("I will meet with the school and decide the discipline for the youth and not worry my husband"). The authors caution that protective buffering is actually associated with decreases in marital satisfaction (Coyne & Smith, 1994) for both partners and increases in distress (Suls, Green, Rose, Loundsbury, & Gordon, 1997) for the bufferer, indicating that it is not a good long-term communication strategy for marital couples.

The results of this study indicated that wives did indeed buffer stressful events from home if they thought sharing would increase risks for their husbands' safety. However, if wives thought that their husbands would be supportive of the disclosure, wives were more likely to disclose, and having community support networks did not influence their decisions to disclose or buffer stressful information. The authors speculate that disclosure to one's deployed spouse served the function of keeping the deployed partner engaged with family life, even if the news was not positive and created stress for the service member (Joseph & Afifi, 2010).

The second study examined dyadic processes in military couples focused on helping military couples to identify role changes and challenges after deployment (Gambardella, 2008) with an aim to lower marital discord. This was a small clinical study with 10 couples who ranged in age from 21 to 47 years and who each sought out counseling to address concerns about couple conflict. Nine couples were active duty and one couple was in the Reserve Component. Six of the couples had been married 7 years or less, while the remaining four couples had been married between 14 and 21 years. Six of the service members had been in the military for more than 10 years and all had experienced at least one deployment, with the reservist reporting a high of six deployments.

The couples attended between 10 and 15 therapeutic sessions lasting 90 minutes each and, as part of the therapeutic work, each person identified their respective family roles predeployment, during deployment, and postdeployment and compared their perspectives for areas of agreement and disagreement (Gambardella, 2008). The therapist worked with the couples to renegotiate roles that each person identified as important, but in conflict. Each person kept a journal between counseling sessions to keep notes on instances when role change processes worked and when the couple needed to continue working on a particular stress point.

Six of the 10 couples reported an improvement in their relationships at the end of the therapeutic intervention. Gambardella (2008) noted that three of the four couples who did not show improvement had a deployment history of either a very long deployment (18 months) or multiple deployments for extended periods of time, indicating that the couples who spent the most time apart had the most difficulty in reentering existing roles or renegotiating those roles upon reunion. It may be that these three couples were challenged to maintain a close relationship that consistently built a shared perspective for important couple and familial goals. Flexibility to adapt to changes in the family system while maintaining a sense of stability has previously been identified as a common challenge military families face. Another group of clinicians refers to this process as the need to find a "new normal" for spousal roles and expectations (Lapp, Taft, Tollefson, Hoepner, Moore, & Divyak, 2010).

Voices From the Frontline

ANGELA'S HUSBAND TALKS ABOUT THE YEAR SHE WAS IN IRAQ

When Angela was in Iraq, the specialness of life was gone.

Angela left for Iraq with 3 weeks notice. What was most difficult for me was providing general emotional support. Even though I'd been in Iraq under combat, I was never in a situation like she was.

I could e-mail her but I couldn't call. So there were limits to how often we talked. To her credit, she called me as much as she could. I had to listen to very few words and try to understand what was really going on. I understand—you don't want to retell things because that means experiencing them again. Even years later, we haven't discussed things Angela might want to talk about but not relive.

Some of the roughest times were when it looked like she was coming home, then didn't because they wanted to keep someone there that they could count on. It wasn't just that I wanted to be with her. I wanted her to be out of there. I would have been happy knowing she was sent somewhere not so bad.

It was a pretty solitary life for me—and a long year. My mission was to make it through the year. We have a big house, in a fairly rural area. There weren't lots of people stopping by. I didn't receive any support from her new unit. So I stayed very busy doing things at work and with the house. I focused on tasks rather than the bigger picture. Angela helped out in that regard. Even from Iraq, she would call with honey-do lists.

It felt like it was backward to have my wife at war. I would have been more comfortable with me there knowing Angela was safe at home. Angela and I first met in Iraq. In a way it helped me—I saw that Angela could handle herself. She had soldier skills and could take care of herself.

On the other hand, I also knew that she would go out to places that others wouldn't because she thought it was the right thing to do. She would be careful but she'd take risks. That got her into trouble more than once—during the Gulf War and in OIF. Once during the Gulf War, she got caught outside the camp perimeter gates in a dust storm on her way back from helping a unit. Then, during OIF, she was walking around the Abu Ghraib prison compound, checking to see how soldiers were doing, and was trapped in the cross fire of an insurgent ambush.

I liked to add things to the boxes I sent to Angela. She'd put the basics together before she left. So I added some fun and frivolous stuff. I found these cotton pajamas with little monkeys and bananas. Then I saw some fuzzy cow slippers. I thought it would make her—and other people smile. I sent some dark chocolate made by Bomboys, a local candy maker. When I explained I was sending it to my wife in Iraq, they gave me a 10-pound block for half price. Those were just little touches. There wasn't a whole lot I could do, but I tried to do whatever I could for her.

Tony Vargas
Major, U.S. Army, Retired, Physician Assistant and Gulf War Veteran

Intimate Partner Violence

Acts of sexual aggression, including intimate partner violence and military sexual trauma, have serious legal, psychological, and relational ramifications for both the aggressor and the survivor. Research in this area does not fit easily into one level (individual/family) of analysis and discussion. One the one hand, we implicitly frame these topics at the individual level: aggressor, victim/survivor, and then focus therapeutic and preventive programs on individual behaviors with a one-on-one focus. On the other hand, these are experiences that are inherently relational, whether between two people who are intimate partners and family members, colleagues, or members of the larger community.

Voices From the Frontline

TURNING RESEARCH INTO POLICY

We started looking at how deployment affects family violence in 2003, early in the conflicts in Iraq and Afghanistan. The Army documents every incident of family violence worldwide. They provided us with data files, with no identifying information, on active duty families that experienced child maltreatment or partner abuse.

It is common sense that in times of enormous change and stress, some families doing fine will rise to the challenge and thrive. Others may crumble. Some already-fragile families may become even more so.

Our bottom-line conclusion was that the rate of child maltreatment increases when soldiers are deployed. At the same time that we did our study, Danielle Rentz, a doctoral student working with our team, did a study using different data and came up with similar findings.

Putting good numbers on what people out there working with families already know from their own experience is helpful. Our studies raised awareness of the issue for the Army and in the public.

One of the striking things about the military is that even though it is a big, complicated system, findings can become the operating policy of the system all over the world. Our findings were used to get more support to families during deployment, such as respite child care. As another example, the Army's Surgeon General directed all physicians in Army facilities to ask parents seeking primary care for themselves or their child(ren), "How are you doing?" Physicians were also instructed to screen for depression, which is related to child maltreatment, and, if it seemed indicated, to refer parents for support.

There are a lot of ways in which people can make a difference in the world. Some people have the skills, temperament, and training to work directly with military families. My training and temperament is to be a researcher. You hope to do good quality research but you don't have final say as to if your research changes policy and practice.

I've been fortunate to collaborate with people in the military who are learners. People who want to take what they can learn from the research and use it to improve the lives of families. They have the mechanisms in place to create and implement new programs and policies, although not always easily. Having no personal ties to the military, I'm constantly struck by the commitment and hard work of the people I've collaborated with.

In trying to support the families we studied, it is important to keep in mind that the larger body of data suggests that military families have many strengths and are highly resilient. Every military family has at least one adult who is employed in a structured environment. They have access to health insurance and social services that our many civilian families do not have.

You might assume repeated deployment adds to the issue, but that research hasn't been done yet. Now families are into their third, fourth, and fifth deployments. We'll see what the numbers have to tell us.

Deborah Gibbs, MSPH
Senior Health Analyst at RTI International

The subject of intimate partner violence has been the focus of several types of studies within the military community. Some researchers have approached this topic from the perspective of identifying individual level psychological disorders that have higher co-occurring rates with family problems, including domestic violence (DV) (Sayers et al., 2009). Other researchers have documented unique trends in rates of nonmutual and mutual DV incidents within military couples and the role alcohol plays in the prevalence of these incidents (McCarroll et al., 2009). Recent studies of service members who have experienced deployment for OIF and OEF have helped clarify our understanding of links between deployment to and traumatic experiences in a combat zone and incidence rates of intimate partner violence (Newby, Ursano, et al., 2005).

Sayers et al. (2009) found several interesting links between specific clinical conditions and prevalence of certain family problems in their sample of recently returned veterans who had been referred for a mental health evaluation by their primary care providers. The sample was comprised of 199 veterans from all branches of the armed forces and from the Active and Reserve Components. Each respondent had returned from deployment and then separated from service within 2 years of their referral, experiencing two major life transitions in a very short period of time. The most common clinical conditions and provisional diagnoses reported in the study included any depression, PTSD, generalized anxiety disorder, major depression, and at-risk alcohol use.

Sayers et al. found that over 75% of the married/partnered respondents reported at least one family readjustment issue with many of these same respondents stating that these concerns were ongoing, rather than one-time issues. Significant and somewhat surprising to the researchers was the high rate of self-reported mild to moderate levels of DV in the sample (53%), as self-reports of DV tend to be underreported by as much as 10% compared to reports made by both partners. The most commonly reported specific item within the domestic abuse questions was that the service member's partner was afraid of them (27.6%) with 4.4% reporting injury due to a DV incident. Higher rates of family reintegration struggles were associated with other co-occurring risks of depression and PTSD in this clinical sample, indicating that as the number of individual stressors and risks increases, there is a corresponding increase in the likelihood of poorer family functioning and relationship satisfaction.

McCarroll et al. (2009) reviewed data from 1998 to 2004 collected through the Army Central Registry for verified DV incidents (physical or emotional) that occurred within enlisted Army personnel spousal systems. These researchers were interested in identifying characteristics of the DV event, including whether an event was nonmutual (one aggressor, one victim) or mutual (each member of the couple listed as both aggressor and victim) and if alcohol was included as a factor in the event. Analyses indicated that overall incidence rates for both nonmutual and mutual incidents decreased significantly over this 6-year period (by 23% and 57%, respectively), that men and women were represented equally as victims in the mutual DV episodes but that women were significantly overrepresented as targets of DV in nonmutual episodes (72%), and that alcohol contributed to both aggressor and victim experiences. More severe violence in both types of incidents was associated with offender drinking and, while the overall incidence rates for both types of DV incidents decreased over the study period, that decrease did not hold true for rates where the offender was drinking. McCarroll et al. recommend that programs focusing on DV and alcohol misuse include material on the increased risk of interpersonal violence when alcohol is a factor.

With the ongoing military actions related to OIF/OEF/OND, as well as peacekeeping efforts and episodic disaster intervention both in the United States (such as the flooding in Memphis, Tennessee, in May 2010) and abroad (including the Haitian Earthquake in January 2010), deployment is a common aspect of present-day military life. Experiences during deployment with violence, loss, and threats to life and health have been shown to impact service member health and risk-taking behaviors. Previous research (McCarroll et al., 2000) found that risk of severe DV by Army soldiers was linked to length of deployment but that the overall *unique* contribution of deployment to DV rates was quite small. The most consistent risk factors for postdeployment DV in this study were prior history of DV, being young, and living off base. Another study of soldier reports of DV rates between 3 and 5 months after deployment found no support to indicate that deployment was related to DV (McCarroll et al., 2003). Newby and colleagues (2005) further contributed to our knowledge of how deployment may contribute to understanding rates of DV within the Army by examining spouse reported DV rates at 10 months past a specific deployment.

The emotional cycle of deployment is often described as having a "honeymoon" phase shortly after return, even though research has not shown this characterization to be common or consistent across families. However, family support professionals use the description of the emotional cycle of deployment to help families identify when the honeymoon phase recedes and the challenges of reintegrating into everyday family routines may begin.

One possible indicator of this change is a potential increase in spousal conflict and violence. Thus, studies examining postdeployment rates are usually very specific in defining the window of time postdeployment that was investigated. In their 2005 study, Newby and colleagues found that deployment was not a significant risk factor at 10 months past deployment. Instead, the significant risk factors for postdeployment DV were being younger and having a history of DV prior to deployment. This research group cautions that while the specific deployment in their studies (Bosnia, 6 months) did not have a unique or significant contribution to postdeployment DV rates, other aspects of military life not included in their studies, such as longer and repeated deployments, may have an effect on both spousal conflict and DV rates.

Different approaches to the study of interpersonal violence in military and veteran couples lead to different findings, which limits the ability to make any broad-sweeping summary statements. Sayers et al. (2009) found that DV was a common element in a clinical sample of veterans with deployment experiences and noted that mental health issues including depression and PTSD were likely to be present when DV was present. Newby and colleagues (2000, 2003, 2005) found little (2000) to no support (2003, 2005) for the hypothesis that a specific deployment was a significant factor in later DV rates at a large Army post. Through their study of substantiated DV incidents over a 6-year span, McCarroll et al. (2009) were able to show significant decreases in both nonmutual and mutual DV rates in the Army, unless alcohol was used by the aggressor. These varied findings contribute to our overall understanding of interpersonal violence and give support to prevention and intervention programs that are multifaceted (attending to more than one issue) and targeted to higher-risk groups.

The study of couple violence in the military is ripe for cross-disciplinary research. Current concepts used in family research with heterosexual couples distinguish between **situational couple violence**, **coercive controlling violence**, and **violent resistance** and posit that these different forms of intimate partner violence produce different consequences within family systems and need tailored prevention and intervention strategies (Johnson, 2009; Kelly & Johnson, 2008). Situational couple violence tends to be much more gender symmetrical (both men and women engage in violent action) and is linked with particular couple conflicts unique in the relationship of the couple while coercive controlling is primarily perpetrated by men and is based upon a motivation to dominate a spousal relationship through violent force and control. The term violent resistance describes the partner's actions (usually female) to resist against an attempt by a spousal partner to control her actions and opportunities. While the research cited in this section has included studies on mutual and nonmutual DV, connecting research in this area with the larger body of interpersonal violence research may help shape interventions and prevention programming to better address the needs of couples who experience different kinds of violence in their family system.

COMBAT-INJURED FAMILIES

Working with and learning from **combat-injured families** is yet another area of research linked with the current conflict and is still in its infancy. There is very little research published on these families at this time although there are ongoing studies. Combat-injured families are comprised of the spouses, children and stepchildren, parents, ex-spouses, siblings, and other extended relations of an injured service member. As you learned in Chapter 7, the most common type of physical injury in OIF/OEF/OND is musculoskeletal/connective tissue injury (Cohen et al., 2010), while the most common sources of injury are blasts and IEDs (Owens et al., 2008). Concussive blasts are also responsible for one of the signature injuries of this conflict: traumatic brain injury. Due to advances in both protective gear and medical treatment from emergency care to rehabilitation, service members in the current conflict are surviving devastating injuries yet face extensive recovery and rehabilitation needs (Gawande, 2004).

The **recovery trajectory**, or the process of recovery over time from illness or injury with expected advances, setbacks, and potential changes in abilities, is a concept used in the medical and rehabilitative fields. Cozza and Guimond (2011) outline the complexity that service members and their families face when a deployment-related injury occurs. The complexity of deployment-related injury and recovery is derived from extensive variability in several factors: Injuries vary widely in their severity and ability to heal to the satisfaction of the service member; the service member's family composition is likely complex with parents of the service member, spouses/significant others or ex-spouses, children who may range in developmental age and ability, family history and patterns, and siblings; and the medical treatment required can range from a few interventions to many months and years of rehabilitative and reconstructive work.

Family members face additional stressors once injury occurs, including logistical concerns (families are likely not located near the medical facility), negotiating complex healthcare decisions, meeting the needs of children to help them understand what has happened to their parent while trying to maintain a stable caregiving environment, negotiating potential conflicts between members of the family (such as parents of the service member and spouse/significant other) over care decisions, and working through ambiguous loss and grief due to facing the unknown as family and relational roles are challenged.

Family-Centered Care

Family-centered care is a concept currently evolving in the medical literature for combat-injured service members and veterans (Cozza, Holmes, & Van Ost, 2013). Severely injured service members in the current conflicts are likely to have multiple injuries (**polytraumatic injuries**) requiring extended medical and rehabilitative care at a specialized polytrauma center. Additionally, veterans may experience polytraumatic injury at any time after military service and be in need of similar care. There are currently five polytrauma rehabilitation centers (PRC) within the VA that provide comprehensive inpatient rehabilitation, with approximately 100 or so additional outpatient polytrauma programs (Wilder Schaaf, Kreutzer, Danish, Pickett, Rybarczyk, & Nichols, 2013). Scheduling multiple appointments across an array of medical care and rehabilitative professionals, potentially negotiating care across the DoD, VA, and civilian sectors, and, in many cases, juggling these demands from afar because the care facility is not local, in addition to managing daily family needs is a daunting set of tasks for every family.

Service members with less complex injuries may also require extended support for their recovery and all injured service members and their families can benefit from a family-centered focus in the rehabilitation and recovery process. Family-centered care recognizes that injuries and trauma experienced by the service member or veteran have effects on family system functioning and health (Cozza et al., 2013). Cozza and colleagues outline five strategies to provide instrumental and emotional support throughout the injury-recovery process. These strategies are described in detail in Chapter 13, a chapter that focuses on preparing professionals to work effectively with combat-injured families.

A recent, cross-sectional study established some baseline information for how well needs were met at one polytrauma rehabilitation center (Wilder Schaaf et al., 2013). Wilder Schaaf and colleagues found that military family experiences were similar to civilian family experiences with inpatient polytrauma care. Forty-four military family members, 48% parents, 34% spouses, 9% siblings, 2% adult children, and 7% not otherwise identified (who included other blood relations or unrelated persons who had power of attorney) completed the Family Needs Questionnaire (Kreutzer, 1988), a well-known instrument used to assess a family's perceived needs after brain injury. Each respondent had an inpatient, injured service member or veteran at the PRC at Hunter Holmes McQuire Department of Veterans Affairs Medical Center in Richmond, VA. Just under half of the injured personnel had sustained their injury during operations in Iraq or Afghanistan, while the remaining injuries were sustained while deployed to other sites or happened within the continental U.S. The mean age of injured personnel was 30 years and 97% were men. The most common injury was TBI (81%), which presented with multiple physical, cognitive, and/or emotional impairments.

Family members reported that health information was important or very important (100% endorsed this need) and that this need was most likely to be met during their injured family member's inpatient stay from 52%, to have information on the patient's rehabilitative or education progress to 83%, to have explanations from professionals given in terms I can understand. Family members also reported that needs that were most frequently not met related to emotional (e.g., help for preparing for the worst, help getting over my doubts and fears about the future) and instrumental support (e.g., to get a break from my problems and responsibility, to get enough rest or sleep).

Family Caregiving

Moderate or severe injury often means separation from the military for the service member and subsequent caregiving responsibilities for family members. Providing care for veterans who have been injured can bring substantial changes in family finances, structure, and dynamics. After initial hospitalization and institutional rehabilitation, most veterans' primary support and care shifts from institutional-based to home-based care. When a service member transitions to home-based care, family members may assume primary responsibility for assisting with daily living tasks. Caregivers may be spouses, significant others, parents, children, extended family members, and friends who are committed to sharing life with their service members and veterans. Caregivers can find their lives consumed by the numerous tasks and demands. They may spend hours each day providing personal care (e.g., bathing, dressing, feeding) to their loved one, orchestrating multiple doctor and rehabilitation appointments each week, completing and organizing necessary paperwork, and advocating on behalf of their loved one and themselves as they seek services.

A military caregivers' study conducted in 2013 by the RAND Corporation (Ramchand, Tanielian, Fisher, Vaughan, Trail, Epley, Voorhies, Robbins, Robinson, & Ghosh-Dastidar, 2014) estimated that there are 5.5 million military caregivers in the U.S. Nearly 20% (1.1 million) are caring for a post-9/11 veteran. While military caregivers of pre-9/11 veterans resemble civilian caregivers, post-9/11 caregivers are more likely to be: under the age of 30, caring for a veteran with a mental health or substance abuse condition, employed, nonwhite, and a veteran themselves. Fifty-three percent of post-9/11 caregivers did not use a network, that is, they did not use an individual or group to help with caregiving; however, they were more likely to use mental health resources and support services such as caregiving, education and training (e.g., classes, webinars, workbooks), online or in-person social support groups, and helping hand services (e.g., loans, legal guidance, transportation services).

Few studies have tracked the trajectory of families engaged in long-term caregiving as a result of military service-related injury. The Family and Caregiver Experience Study (Griffin, Friedemann-Sanchez, Jensen, Taylor, Gravely, Clothier, Simon, Bangerter, Pickett, Thors, Ceperich, Poole, & van Ryn, 2012) was designed to determine caregiver characteristics and type of care provided to OIF/OEF service members who had been discharged from one of five VA polytrauma rehabilitation centers to institutional or community (i.e., home) care between 2001 and 2009. Of the 1,045 patients, responses were received from 564 caregivers. Most caregivers were women (79%), under 60 years old (84%), the veteran's parent (62%) or spouse (32%), and married (77%). Fifty-five percent were working or in school; over two-thirds (70%) had individual incomes of less than $40,000 per year (Griffin et al., 2012).

Parents were more likely than spouses to be caregivers of OEF/OIF veterans with polytraumatic injuries. The tasks that caregivers performed in this study were the same whether the injuries had occurred 1 or 7 years previously. Caregiver tasks included helping with activities of daily life such as feeding, bathing, and toileting and with driving, cleaning, and management of money and medication. In addition, caregivers helped veterans with emotional issues (70%), health-care system navigation (54%), legal system (54%), and benefits (53%). Other tasks included: setting up medical appointments (44%), managing pain (36%), and helping with therapies (37%) or assistive devices (33%; Griffin et al., 2012).

Caregiving varied in intensity based on the veteran's needs, from high to low intensity. Nearly half of high-intensity caregivers spent 80 hours or more a week caregiving and another 15% provided 40–79 hours a week of care; a third reported sole responsibility for providing care. High intensity caregivers were more likely to report being socially isolated; 80% of them lived with the care recipient while 58% of moderate-intensity caregivers and 29% of low-intensity did so. Many caregivers also had other demanding roles: 41% of high-intensity, 60% of moderate intensity, and 58% of low-intensity caregivers engaged in paid employment or went to school. Nearly a third of high-intensity caregivers also cared for children under the age of 18 (Griffin et al., 2012).

A study of the economic impact of caregiving commissioned by the Joint Department of Defense and Department of Veterans Affairs Wounded, Ill, and Injured Senior Oversight Committee, found that 57% of caregivers provided at least 10 hours of care per week, 75% quit work or took time away from school or work, a third made new child care arrangements, and 11% changed housing or location. In addition, 37% had unmet financial obligations and 41% acquired new financial obligations. The percent of caregivers having financial obligations correlated with the hours of caregiving provided each week. Some caregivers lost their jobs if their time away from work exceeded that allowed by the Family Medical Leave Act. For some, losing a job also meant losing access to health insurance, such as parents of a service member (Christensen, Atkins, Baucom, & Yi, 2010).

Service Members and Spouses in Combat-Injured Families

Earlier in this chapter, the term *caregiver burden* was defined with a list of examples describing how it might operate in combat-injured military families. When a combat injury occurs, not only is there the immediate crisis of the injury, there is an ongoing need for couples to make adjustments related to injury-induced changes in physical and emotional health as well as to negotiate reintegration (Badr, Barker, & Milbury, 2011). Earlier research indicates that wives of wounded veterans report more distress than wives of noninjured veterans (Calhoun et al., 2002), which is congruent with the research described earlier in the chapter that wives of service members who are diagnosed with psychological trauma such as PTSD and depression also report higher distress than wives whose husbands do not have these additional psychological challenges (Dekel et al., 2005; Goff et al., 2007; Sayer et al., 2010).

What challenges are likely for the service member? Badr et al. (2011) caution that the type and severity of the injury will create different consequences and challenges for the service member and the spousal/romantic partner (see their chapter for a detailed overview of different injuries and their unique recovery challenges). Briefly, the service member may incur physical disfigurement such as burns and other injury scarring; partial or complete amputation of an injured limb; and limitations in mobility (ability to move in one's environment: e.g., stairs, depth perception, balance) and in dexterity (fine motor skills: e.g., writing, tying shoes, buttoning shirts, opening jars). As well, there may be hidden injury due to TBI that impacts sensory systems (vision, hearing, taste, smell, and touch), emotional regulation, short- and long-term memory, and body control. The service member is challenged with a potentially significant change in his or her capabilities, both physically and psychologically. These changes may, in turn, affect the service member's sense of identity and ability to fulfill family roles (Cozza & Guimond, 2011) such as being a provider, identifying with a career, being a romantic partner, being an adult son or daughter, and being a parent, uncle, or aunt.

Spousal partners are also faced with a significant amount of ambiguity as they wait, watch, and support their injured spouse. Again, depending on the injury and the expected level of recovery, spouses face pressure to keep the family going, often with increased stressors and conflict in being present for their spouse and being present for their children and other family members. Spouses and romantic partners also face the possibility that their injured spouse may be significantly changed because of the injury and may not be able to relate with them and other families members in the same ways as before an injury (e.g., not being able to practice soccer dribbles with a daughter, forgetting names or important family memories). If the injured spouse cannot resume or reshape expected spousal and familial roles, there is potential for increased marital conflict or distress.

Children in Combat-Injured Families

Parental emotional distress of the at-home parent and the injury of the deployed parent create a challenging caregiving environment for children that is linked to poor child outcomes (Beardslee & Wheelock, 1994), and stressful family environments have differential effects on children depending on their developmental age (Cozza & Guimond, 2011). The onset of a family crisis can trigger behaviors that are not usually experienced by individuals and families, some of which are categorized as **developmental regression**, particularly in very early childhood. Developmental regression describes an individual's inability to maintain developmental gains and revert back to earlier behaviors. For children experiencing crisis, this is often framed as the child seeking a safe and stable level of operating in the world that does not add to the stress of learning and making developmental gains. Examples of developmental regression triggered by increased stress or crisis in a family system include toddlers going back to self-soothing techniques (thumb sucking, needing a nightlight or comfort object like a blanket or stuffed animal) and regressing in toilet training. Older children may seek more reassurance about family life and decisions to participate in activities that take away from being with family (sports, scouting, special religious or school events).

Infants and toddlers look to their primary caregivers to gauge what is safe, to implement predicable routines that help them learn about the social and physical world around them, and to foster their ability to cope when distressing events occur (Fogel, 2010). When parents are not able to mirror effective coping or offer comfort, stability, and a sense of security, very young children pick up on the distress but have limited skills and experience in meeting extreme coping demands.

As children enter the preschool and early elementary years, the developmental phenomena of **magical thinking** (making incorrect assumptions about cause and effect: e.g., "If I wish hard enough my Daddy will be OK") paired with a limited **theory of mind** (a limit in the ability to understand things from another person's point of view: e.g., "Why is grandma happy that Daddy is going into surgery? Isn't surgery bad?") can shape their perceptions of their role(s) as a family member. Cozza and Guimond (2011) posit that normative developmental processes can lead a child to mistakenly assume responsibility for the stress in the family system (e.g., "Mommy left me with Grammy and Papa because she is mad at me") or for the injury to their parent (e.g., "I forgot to pray for Daddy's safety and that's why he got hurt").

School-age children and adolescents have more mature cognitive, emotional, and coping capabilities than younger children but still have anxiety over what they "should" do when a parent is injured and the family system is experiencing crisis. Older children and adolescents also look to the adults around them to assess the seriousness of the crisis and injury to the parent, as well as rely on their familial relationships to help mediate distress and keep their **sense of self** (how one views one's self and abilities; a self-definition of who one is) intact in the face of the crisis.

Factors that offer protection to children and parents in combat-injured families include previously established patterns of family routines and care and availability of extended support relationships of family and friends (Cozza & Guimond, 2011). Additionally, standard practices developed by the Child Life Council (the professional organization for child life specialists who have completed training and certification in working with medically fragile children and children in medical environments) focus on ways to foster effective coping for children facing medical crises and chronic illness. Child life specialists are skilled in parent education and serve as a liaison in helping families cope with the challenges of an injured or ill child. The professional organization has recently begun to expand areas of service to include traditional physician's offices, hospice facilities, child and youth camps for fragile children, and funeral homes (Child Life Council, 2010). A logical extension would be to include Child Life Services in military and VA hospitals and rehabilitation centers.

BEST PRACTICES

Communicating Injuries with Children and Youth

The Workgroup on Combat Injured Families (Cozza, 2009, as sited in Cozza et al., 2013) has developed a short set of guidelines to help children understand their parents' injuries:

1. Speak with children about the injury as soon as possible so that they do not have to worry and wonder without concrete knowledge over an extended period of time;
2. Adults need to share information in a calm and supportive manner, with developmentally appropriate language and, for younger children, using a doll or other prop may be useful in explaining the injury;
3. Tailor the information to the age of the child, including reassurance for care of the injured parent and care for the child, and more detailed information for older children who may voice particular questions about changes in the family system and their own responsibilities; and
4. Create a family context that encourages ongoing discussions and questions, allowing for flexibility in individual members' reactions, progress and setbacks in the healing process, and changes in interpersonal dynamics between members. (Cozza, et al., 2013, p. 318).

EVIDENCE-BASED PROGRAMMING TO HELP FAMILIES RECONNECT

Military and veteran families, regardless of injury, can benefit from programming that is designed to strengthen and improve family relationships, address traumatic experiences, and help families reconnect after deployments and other work-related parental absences. While Chapter 13 will discuss some therapeutic interventions that address traumatic experiences, we want to highlight four evidence-based programs that can be implemented to strengthen Active and Reserve Component families and veteran families. Three programs focus specifically on the parent–child relationship and the fourth focuses on marriage enhancement. As you may recall from Chapters 2 and 4, the largest age group of children in Active Component families are between birth and 5 years old and the largest group of children are ages 6 to 11 years old within the Reserve Component. In Chapters 3 and 6, you also learned that service members tend to marry at a younger age than their civilian counterparts, and that women service members have a higher risk of divorce than do male service members.

Frequent separations due to military commitments are a concern for both service member mission readiness and family readiness. Within the veteran population, the VA is mandated to address the needs of the veteran population; yet family members are only included in treatment plans if and when there is a specific connection to a veteran's identified treatment needs (*VHA Handbook 1010.01*, 2009). National Guard and Reserve families are geographically dispersed, living in civilian communities where military informed programming may be difficult to access (Murphy & Fairbank, 2013). These varying contexts can complicate program delivery across the military and veteran populations.

The programs described here have both initial and ongoing evaluations in order to assess how well they meet the needs of military and veteran families. As programs are continually being created and/or adapted for military families, you can check the current list of programs on the Clearinghouse for Military Family Readiness website to see which programs have been reviewed for their evidence base and potential to be useful for the military and veteran family populations.

FOCUS: Families OverComing Under Stress

FOCUS is a program that has been used with active duty and veteran families (Lester, Stein, Saltzman, Woodward, MacDermid Wadsworth, Milburn, ... & Beardslee, 2013; Lester, Saltzman, Woodward, Glover, Leskin, Bursch, ... & Beardslee, 2012). It is considered a preventive or universal intervention program, which means that all families are eligible to participate and do not need to meet eligibility criteria based on some level of risk. FOCUS is designed to improve family functioning and overall resiliency and reduce children's distress. Adaptations of FOCUS are currently under development and evaluation. These adaptations include a focus on wounded, injured, or ill service members and their families (FOCUS WW), FOCUS for couples (FOCUS CC), and families with young children (FOCUS EC) Leskin, 2010). Dr. Mogil describes this program's purpose and the process of designing and implementing FOCUS across different populations in the Best Practices box below.

BOX 8.1 BEST PRACTICES

A RESEARCHER TALKS ABOUT HIS WORK

PREP is a research-based divorce-prevention/marriage-strengthening program that Scott Stanley and I developed. We know from research that training about communication skills, intimacy, and conflict management has a positive impact on marriage satisfaction and reduces rates of violence and divorce. In PREP, we teach couples skills to strengthen and enhance their relationship before and during marriage.

We've worked with the military since 1989. Our work started with Navy chaplains who took our PREP training and now provide it for their service members. The word spread and today I'm proud to say that PREP has been adapted for the Army's Strong Bonds program. As you can imagine, battling inside the home is not good for people coping with battle outside the home. In the words of the Army, "Stronger relationships mean a stronger Army."

We have also developed Got Your Back, a curriculum designed to help single service members with skills for communication, conflict resolution, and making good choices in terms of partners. These are skills that soldiers can use in current and future relationships in their personal and professional lives.

Working with the military has been a highlight of my career. I am grateful to have the privilege to do my small part to help our country by supporting our soldiers and their families.

Our entry to collaborating with the military was our research and wanting to learn from the people working with soldiers and their families. Research can open many career paths. At our university, we have undergraduate and graduate students analyzing our data and publishing their findings. For example, one student is focusing on how relationships can impact soldiers' PTSD symptoms. If you enjoy trying to understand the story that data tell and know how to ask good questions, I suggest looking into teaming up with a researcher working in an area that interests you.

Howard Markman, PhD
Codirector, Center for Marital and Family Studies, University of Denver

ADAPT: After Deployment: Adaptive Parenting Tools

ADAPT (Gewirtz, Pinna, Hanson, & Brockberg, 2014) focuses on Reserve Component families. Families in the National Guard and Reserve face unique challenges to their functioning and readiness due to being geographically dispersed and often living far away from military communities. These families are embedded within the civilian fabric of the U.S. and may not know or have another military-connected family in their community. Resources and programming for family support that are located on military installations are not easily accessed or available to Reserve Component families.

ADAPT is a modification of a well-known evidence-based parenting intervention, the Parent Management Training—Oregon Model (PMTO)—and tailored for delivery to families who are geographically remote. ADAPT focuses specifically on reintegration after deployment and the parent–child relationship. The first implementation of ADAPT included both face-to-face meetings and web-based enhancements. Topics covered in the program include a range of positive parenting practices and specific tools to address parenting challenges faced by families who experience military separations, whether these are dual parent or single parent families. Similar to FOCUS, the ADAPT program is categorized as a universal prevention program and appropriate for all Reserve Component families.

PCIT: Parent–Child Interaction Therapy

The third parent-child program is PCIT (Eyberg, Bogg, & Algina, 1995) and is considered at least an indicated or secondary prevention program, which means that families need to meet eligibility criteria in order to participate in the program. The criteria for eligibility include an identified child behavioral problem in a child ages 2 to 7 years old (e.g., symptoms of Oppositional Defiant Disorder, Attention Deficit Hyperactivity, or Conduct Disorder). As with the other two programs described in this section, the service delivery is focused on the parent(s) and provides therapeutic support to the parent to increase positive interactions between a parent and child and to decrease a child's aggression and increase compliance. Parents and children are assessed as part of setting treatment goals.

PCIT has not yet, to our knowledge, been implemented with military or veteran specific populations; however, Pemberton, Cramer, Borrego, Jr., and Owen (2013) advocate for PCIT as a program that can be used in the veteran population and delivered through VA medical centers. They cite this program as an example of being able to meet a specific family member need (a child with behavioral challenges) through the VA system as part of the care plan for a veteran who is struggling with parenting. Pemberton and colleagues strongly suggest that program managers and developers need to find ways to work within the VA system to better address the family and parenting needs of veterans, particularly the newest veterans who tend to more closely resemble the demographics of the active duty population – under 30 years old and with young children. Programs such as PCIT work directly with the parents to address the needs of children and to strengthen the parent–child relationship.

FAMILIES OVERCOMING UNDER STRESS

The FOCUS project is a multiservices resiliency-building program for military families with children (Saltzman, 2010). FOCUS includes structured parent–children sessions designed to strengthen family resiliency skills such as goal setting, problem solving, regulating emotions, managing reminders of combat and deployment, communication, and mutual support (Saltzman, Lester, Beardslee, & Pynoos, 2008). The core components of FOCUS include family-level education on child development, the combat operational stress continuum, and trauma; an individualized family deployment timeline used to bridge misunderstandings, promote co-parenting, and connect skills to family members' experiences; and links to additional services and resources. FOCUS also provides workshops and community outreach; consultations with families and providers; and family checkups (Saltzman, 2010).

Evaluation of FOCUS has been ongoing. An analysis of 821 families who had used FOCUS revealed that 42% were self-referred. Other sources of referral included schools, military organizations, health and mental health providers, and chaplains. Children who attended reported significant positive increases in problem solving and emotional regulation. Parents reported significant improvement in children's prosocial behavior and reductions in children's problematic conduct and symptoms of anxiety and depression. In addition, parents reported significant decreases in their own symptoms of anxiety and depression. Families improved in the areas of problem solving, communication, affective responsiveness, behavior control, and roles (Saltzman, 2010).

Initiated by the Navy's Bureau of Medicine and Surgery (BUMED), in 2009 FOCUS was expanded to designated Air Force and Army installations. In addition, FOCUS is being adapted for couples (FOCUS C); wounded, injured, or ill service members and their families (FOCUS WW); and families with young children (FOCUS EC). These adaptations are undergoing pilot testing (Leskin, 2010).

Strong Bonds

The Strong Bonds program began as an Army marriage-enhancement program for couples in 1997. Because of the current frequency of deployments, the use of the Strong Bonds program has become more widespread and is used to assist couples and families in the process of reuniting after a deployment. It now also includes a series of new training modules: single soldiers, couples, families, predeployment, and redeployment. Chaplains facilitate Strong Bonds workshops, which take place in a weekend retreat format. Strong Bonds for couples is based on the Prevention and Relationship Enhancement Program (PREP) originally developed for civilian couples (Stanley, Blumberg, & Markman, 1999). Researchers are conducting a longitudinal study in which couples were assigned to either PREP for Strong Bonds or a control group (Allen & Markman, 2010). Initial results indicate that recent deployment was related to husbands' posttraumatic symptoms which, in turn, were related to marital functioning (Allen, Rhoades, Stanley, & Markman, 2010). Results also indicate that marital functioning may be improved by marriage education (Allen & Markman, 2010). At one year post intervention, approximately 6% of the control couples had divorced compared with approximately 2% of the Strong Bonds couples. Soldiers interested in participating in one of the Strong Bonds workshops can locate events at https://www.strongbonds.org.

UNDERSTUDIED RELATIONSHIPS AND DIRECTIONS FOR FUTURE RESEARCH

Military family research has primarily focused on spouses and children of the service member and understandably so. These relationships are directly affected by daily military life and cultural context because of the service member's work. Yet, not all spousal and parent–child relationships are equally represented in the literature, and there are other familial relationships that are not well understood. Little is known about sibling relationships of military children and the role they play in individual and family adjustment. Remarriages and blended families are not differentiated in the data that are reported by the individual

BOX 8.2   BEST PRACTICES

INVESTED IN MEETING THE NEEDS OF VETERANS AND THEIR FAMILIES

We believe parents want to do the right thing and, at the same time, they may not have the information and skills they need to make decisions about how to best support their children. The Families OverComing Under Stress (FOCUS) Program is a resiliency-building intervention for military and veteran families with children. Together family members each build their narrative then share and understand their story from all perspectives. Parents are set up to be the leaders of family conversations, to repair misunderstandings, and get their families back on trajectory after the numerous life challenges associated with wartime service and the changing circumstances not only during active duty, but also in the transition to veteran life.

There are four core elements to FOCUS:

1. A Family Psychological Health Check-in, a real-time assessment of individual and family strengths and risks.
2. Family-specific psychoeducation based on findings of the Family Psychological Health Check-in which may include information about responding to children at different stages of development, understanding symptoms and behaviors of diagnoses such as PTSD and TBI, and navigating systems of health and mental health care.
3. A family narrative timeline in which a Resilience Trainer supports parents and children to develop timelines of major events surrounding key transitions (e.g., deployment, moving, injuries) and then brings the family together to share individual perspectives and create a shared family narrative.
4. Teaching family-level resilience skills which include emotional regulation, problem-solving, communication, managing reminders of deployment, trauma or loss, and setting collaborative family goals.

We took great care in serving military families on active duty installations. Once we were comfortable that we were managing that effectively, we started serving veterans in Los Angeles, our backyard. It can be hard for vets to access high quality services so we have experimented with ways to respond to their needs.

We began with the basics of our model and adapted accordingly. For example, we asked ourselves, what would it mean to see couples without children? How can we use technology to do a real-time assessment to evaluate family functioning and assess the mental health needs of the adults and children? Would families like using an iPad rather than paper and pencil? How do we teach parents to scan their families for symptoms and know that their family needs help? We have come up with two primary ways to better support veteran families. First, we train community providers including pediatricians, dentists, mental health providers, and teachers about what a veteran family may be experiencing and what to look for when working with veteran families. We start by asking what information the providers include on their intake form. The LA unified school district began asking all families if the child is militarily connected: "Is anyone in your family a veteran?" This is an important step forward in being able to identify and respond to the needs of families.

Second, we are figuring out ways to deliver family care using technology to apply our model. When families live on an installation, it is not so hard for them to come to you. Trying to serve veterans living all over the LA basin is a different situation.

We began by teaching the FOCUS model to organizations including the LA County Department of Mental Health that are serving veterans and their families. We've also trained some Veterans Administration (VA) providers in a parenting version of FOCUS in which the veteran and his or her partner learn to do family FOCUS activities at home and then discuss the process and outcome during FOCUS sessions. This has had the benefit of introducing work with children and families to the VA where staff members who work skillfully with veterans do not always have a strong background in working with children or families.

We've also led parenting skill building groups at our VA in West LA and in Long Beach. Veterans seem to be open and like the group format and the focus on parenting and family resilience skills that includes communication, emotional regulation, and problem solving.

For example, we teach about communicating with a child at different developmental levels. How you talk to a 4-year-old is very different than how you talk with a teenager. A 4-year-old doesn't need or want and can't handle as much information as a teenager, for example about a parent's injury or substance abuse, illness or depression. Or in response to questions like, "Why do we have to keep moving?" or "Why is it so hard for you to hold down a job?"

When children ask questions, sometimes parents ignore them or gloss over the topic because they don't know what to say. Children learn that some topics are not to be talked about. One of the basic skills we teach parents to say is: "That's a good question. Let me think about it and get back to you." It is a simple parenting skill that reduces pressure and promotes conversation.

We encourage parents to ask their child, "What do you already know about _____? What have you heard? What do your friends say?" Then parents can clarify misunderstandings and extend knowledge. We talk about how to tell when a child is "filled up" with enough information. If a child keeps asking questions, keep going. If they stop, they have the information they need for now and may be back for more tomorrow or in a few days or weeks.

We are currently working with a group of female vets in transitional housing through U.S. Vets at the Villages at Cabrillo, many of whom are single mothers recovering from being homeless and for many, sexual abuse also. They are close enough to the VA to get services for themselves but are not yet ready (or able) to access services for their entire families so we visit them at home. We talk about how as parents, we see life through adult eyes and sometimes project from our own childhood experiences. We encourage mothers to think about what their child(ren) might be seeing, thinking, and feeling.

We have also been using technology. I'm from the old school and at first I quietly hoped it wouldn't work to meet with families via the Internet so that we would get back to sitting in the same room together. I was surprised and now am glad that we found it is effective to offer virtual home visits through Tele-focus, a virtual home visiting program that uses a secure videoconferencing platform. Families like it. They can work with us at a convenient time and without the hassle of travel.

Military and veteran families adapt to their situations and we had to do the same with our model. This is an important lesson for all veteran-serving organizations, we need to adapt or we will continue to see high levels of homelessness, PTSD, and suicide. We are invested in meeting the needs of veterans and their families.

Catherine Mogil, Psy.D
Director of Training, UCLA Nathanson Family Resilience Center, Los Angeles

branches or by the DoD. Marital stability and satisfaction in the Reserve Component have not been as well studied as those in the Active Component (Renshaw et. al., 2008). The transitions Reserve Component families negotiate as they move between civilian and active duty status may offer new insights into our understanding of military family resiliency. In particular, marital satisfaction, parent–child relations, and the strengths and challenges that their social networks and communities face in providing effective supports and resources are all topics that would benefit from further inquiry. Knowledge about other aspects of Reserve Component family life also lags behind research with Active Component families. For example, very little is known about divorce and remarriage rates, interpersonal violence, or child maltreatment that occurs when the service member is not activated.

Other romantic relationships are also understudied (MacDermid Wadsworth, 2010). Dating relationships and processes of couple formation are two areas with very little research although programs to enhance dating and mate selection skills and prepare for marriage (e.g., PREPARE/ENRICH) are offered to service members. Additionally, the DADT policy that had prohibited gay and lesbian service members from serving openly, in concert with the federal **Defense of Marriage Act** (DOMA: a federal act passed in 1996 that explicitly states that marriage at the federal level is only recognized if it occurs between one man and one woman and reaffirms that individual states are not compelled to recognize same-sex marriages that occurred in a different state), has also limited our understanding of romantic partnerships within this particular service member population (Defense of Marriage Act, 2011). Same-sex marriage has experienced a watershed moment since the first edition of this textbook. The number of states recognizing same-sex marriage increased from 6 to 34 at the time of our writing. Yet, it still remains difficult to identify same sex couples in national data sets and is not yet possible in the yearly DoD Demographic Reports. Given the broader U.S. context, romantic and long-term partnerships in this population are extremely difficult to study systematically and without adding to the potential risks of exposure for these service members (National Conference of State Legislatures, 2011). With the recent repeal of DADT and the evolving status of legal marriage and civil union within the United States, research that describes and identifies stress and resilience processes for same-sex military couples and families may not be too far off into the future.

Parents and siblings of service members are also not well represented in the family literature. Considering that just under half of the Active Component and just over half of the Reserve Component are single and that 66% of active duty personnel and 53% of the selected reserve are 30 years or younger (DASD, 2014), it is reasonable to assume that connections to parents and siblings are important in service members' lives as well as their children. Parents may also contribute to caregiving for grandchildren while their service member parent is deployed, and similarly aunts and uncles can be important family supports including acting as temporary parents. Prevalence of extended familial and **extrafamilial** (caregivers outside the family system) caregiving and the challenges and strengths of these caregiving environments are not known.

In addition, a small proportion of family members identified in DEERS is classified as a group of **adult dependents**. These are family members who are a parent, grandparent, former spouse, sibling, disabled older child, or any other individual who is claimed by the service member as a dependent (DASD, 2014). Among active duty families, in 2013, there were just under 11,000 individuals in this category in addition to more than 1.2 million children and more than 689,000 spouses. Among families of the selected reserve, there were almost 2,000 recognized adult dependents, more than 716,000 children, and more than 391,000 spouses enrolled in DEERS in 2013. The majority of individuals in the adult dependent category across both groups were older women: 37% of adult dependents of active duty were between 51 and 62 years with another 33% at age 63 years or more, and 53% of adult dependents of selected reserve members were 63 years and older. While the numbers are much smaller for the adult dependent category in both Active and Reserve Components, we do not know much about military service members and families who are caring for adults in their daily lives.

A specific emerging concern is that of suicide among military family members. Suicide prevention programming has increased over the last few years for both service member and veteran populations. Supplemental program materials often include pamphlets and online support for family members who may be concerned about their service member or veteran. However, very little is known about the prevalence of suicidal ideation and suicide among military and veteran family members. In the 2014 Military Family Lifestyle Survey (Blue Star Families, 2014), 13% of veteran respondents indicated they had thought about suicide in the past year, while 9% of active duty respondents and 8% of active duty spouses also reported suicidal ideation. Further, 2% of respondents reported their children had attempted or contemplated suicide. Of those active duty service members and spouses reporting suicidal ideation, over one-third in each group did not seek help from any identified support resource (38% and 34%, respectively). Another 28% of service members and 41% of spouses sought help from their family or friends. Service members in this survey sought professional counseling at higher rates than spouses (38% and 29%, respectively).

In response to specific requests from the Senate and House Arms Services Committees, the DoD Defense Suicide Prevention Office (DSPO) conducted a feasibility study to assess the potential for tracking DEERS identified family member suicide. Part of this study included identifying current systems and practices within each of the services (Garrick, 2013). The DSPO study also identified sources for data from other agencies, such as the Centers for Disease Control and Prevention and the National Center for Health Statistics, that could potentially be leveraged to help expand the ability of the DoD to track family member suicide across all four services.

Three small studies are beginning to expand our understanding of parents and their adult service member children: one from the perspective of male senior officers' concerns about their aging parents (Parker, Call, Dunkle, & Vaitkus, 2002), a second study from the perspective of parents' emotional processes, stressors, and supports when their adult child deployed to a combat zone (Crow & Myers-Bowman, 2011), and a third study from the perspective of Iraq and Afghanistan veterans who return and live with their parents (Worthen, Moos, & Ahern, 2012). These studies provide a beginning point for researchers and practitioners to think more systemically about extended family relationships in military families.

Parker et al. (2002) conducted their research with 277 senior-ranking male officers who attended the U.S. Army War College (USAWC) over the course of two summers. The vast majority of these participants were between 40 and 49 years (95%), were married (98%), and had at least one child still at home (93%), while relatively few (16%) reported that they have responsibility for caring for an elderly person. At the time of data collection, 40% had experienced at least one combat deployment and about 75% had experienced a deployment that lasted 12 months or longer.

Within this sample, aspects of military life created opportunities for stress in maintaining connections with their parents: high mobility with assignments far from their parents, potential limits in being able to communicate with one another on a regular basis, and lack of military housing suitable for bringing a frail parent into the family home. Some of the factors that were linked with increased worry about parents included previous illnesses of the parent(s), parental age, and if the service member had an angry temperament (Parker et al., 2002). Factors that helped ease officers' worry included having siblings (presumably to help share the care and concern for parents) and having a "parent care plan" so that if a medical crisis were to occur, the adult child(ren) would know the wishes of the parent in regard to medical decisions and care.

This study was not able to access the role of the military spouse in the parental caregiving process or address potential worry about parents-in-law. However, it does give some insight into family processes that are commonly identified as part of midlife and being in the "sandwich" generation of an extended family system.

The second study focused on parents of service members and their sources of concern and support as their adult child deployed to a combat zone (Crow & Myers-Bowman, 2011). This small, qualitative study elicited in-depth, written responses from 42 parents to a series of 10 open-ended questions. These questions were framed to let the parents "describe their feelings and experiences with their child's first deployment ... [those] whose children had deployed more than once were presented the same ten questions again with the focus on the most recent deployment rather than the first" (p. 170). Both mothers ($n = 33$) and fathers ($n = 9$) participated and had both sons ($n = 38$) and daughters ($n = 4$) who had deployed.

The most commonly reported responses to learning about their adult child's deployment included fear and worry, closely followed by anxiety and concern. While most of their emotional responses were focused on their adult child—fear for safety, concern for the types of danger he/she might be facing—some parents also indicated that their response extended to their adult child's spouse and children. Thus parents worried about their child and the family their child had created. Many parents reported these concerns with other, more positive responses. For example, parents also felt proud knowing what their children were about to do in service to their country and that they would be putting their skills to use, and confident that their children were capable of doing what they were being called to do.

Some of the functional stressors that parents reported included difficulties or inconsistency in being able to communicate with their deployed son or daughter and worry when planned communications were delayed. Additional communication difficulties were reported in trying to gain information from unit command, and one parent noted that she realized that her son's first priority for communication was going to be with his wife, not his mom. Along with difficulties in communication, parents often noted that both knowing what was happening and not knowing what was happening could be stressful. Some parents had either been service members themselves or been military spouses, and they noted that the experience of seeing their adult child deployed was a qualitatively different experience than being the service member or the spouse. One parent reported that since her son was single at the time, he came to her to complete his predeployment paperwork, including going over his funeral arrangements. Her feeling of helplessness and awareness that she could not protect her child highlighted a significant change in their parent–child relationship.

Many parents also identified that finding both informal and formal support was difficult (Crow & Myers-Bowman, 2011). When asked about coping techniques parents used to help with the stress of the deployment experience, the authors found that parents described far fewer details about their coping strategies than about their reactions and struggles. The most number of strategies reported was four, but the average was just under two strategies. Having friends who were against the war and living in a community that hosted events protesting military involvement increased feelings of isolation; not living near a military installation or having strong ties to other parents who also had children in the service were also difficult. The two most common sources of support were a sense of spirituality or having religious faith and having supportive friends and family members. Nearly a third reported that they used media outlets to try and stay updated, while a few stated that they actively avoided media reports as a way to lower their distress. One-fifth joined formal support groups and less than one-fifth stated that they actively sought out ways to maintain connection with their deployed child. Three of the parents responded that they had not found any useful coping strategies, which prolonged feelings of distress.

Parents reported a range of possible effects that their adult child's deployment had had in their own marital relationships. For about 40% of parents, the deployment had very little effect on the quality of their marital relationship. Another 40% reported that they thought this experience had brought them closer with their spouse. The remaining parents indicated that the experience increased emotional distance between themselves and their partners or had a mixed effect, both positive and negative. The parents who reported greater emotional distance often commented that their partner was not a source of support in coping with the stress of their child's deployment.

This study is one of the first to systematically draw in information about how parents of service members experience deployment. Though small, it has the potential to be very useful in guiding human service professionals to develop empathetic and supportive environments in a wide variety of communities and organizations. Many parents do not live in or near military communities and may not have easy access to military friendly support programs. Lay leaders in religious communities can identify ways of providing support to parents and extended family members; community counselors and family life educators can create programming that specifically meets needs of parents of service members and make connections with existing support programs.

As described in Chapter 10, the veteran population for the post-9/11 era comprises a significant number of young adults (49% who are 23–32 years old) and 32% who have never been married. Worthen, Moos and Ahern (2012) note that 27% of the young veteran population in California alone currently live with a parent, while an even greater number temporarily reside with parents after separation from military service. Among that state's young, single veteran population, almost half (49%) reside with their parents. In their interviews with young veterans, Worthen and colleagues focused on the veterans' separation from service experiences and reintegration into civilian life, including their family of origin. Participants in this study explained ways in which their parents provided instrumental support (e.g., helping them get back on their feet, providing a bridge until school or a new job started) and emotional support (e.g., getting caught up with each other, creating opportunities to have adult-to-adult conversations). Participants also described experiences of parents not being able to relate to deployment experiences.

Returning to live with parents after military service can also create challenges in redefining family roles and expectations. The veterans in this study described some of the points of contention in being treated like a kid (again) through issues such as use of money, time, and having a parent set a curfew. Conversely, some veterans noted that their parents shifted significant responsibility for family duties to them upon return, including relationship management and household functioning.

Veterans also noted how family members were often instrumental in identifying difficulties in transitioning back to civilian status and more serious mental health needs of their veteran. Family members also served as advocates for their adult veteran child in obtaining services for care. Worthen and colleagues (2012) recommend that family and veteran programs need to be extended to include parents of veterans and that such programming would benefit in using both broader family systems (Carter & McGoldrick, 2005) and family resilience (Walsh, 2002) frameworks.

A last area of research and writing that is missing from the military family literature is that of understanding the ways families grieve the loss of a military family member. While there are publications on families and children experiencing military death that are directed to the professional human service community (Cohen et al., 2006; Scott, 2010), studies that give voice to grieving experiences across familial relationships (parent of service member, sibling, spousal/romantic partner, and children) are not yet available. Listening to and representing the experiences of families who have lost a service member are important, however, and can contribute to a better understanding of how to support grieving families. We end this chapter with one mother's voice.

Voices From the Frontline

A MOTHER TALKS ABOUT LOSING HER SON

My mission is to be sure people remember that Daniel was here and made the ultimate sacrifice.

Daniel arrived in Ramadi, Iraq, early in July, 2005, and passed away September 28, 2005. He was killed with four other soldiers from the 109th Infantry Unit out of New Milford, Pennsylvania, when their vehicle was attacked.

Losing a child is the most devastating experience any parent could ever have. It's been 6 years, and the pain never goes away. At first grief overtakes you. But now there's a lot of pride too as I learn to appreciate who Daniel was, where he was, and what he did.

Daniel left two boys, and they were his world. Devin who was 3½ when Daniel died didn't smile for 6 months. He and Daniel had a special relationship. It's like he was attached to Dan's leg. If Dan went downstairs, Devin did, too. It amazes me how much he can remember. He's always saying, "Grandma, do you remember when Daddy and I...." I'm so glad he had time with Daniel even though it was cut short.

Kody was 17 months old. As he got older, he'd say: "Okay, Grandma, the next time I come, can we go to Heaven and get my dad? He's been gone long enough." I didn't know what to say to him. He doesn't say that any more. I think he knows his dad isn't coming back.

We are fortunate the boys live nearby and their mother, Kim, shares them with us. We share holidays and vacations. Every year we go to Washington, DC, together for Family United's celebration for Fallen Soldiers.

Right before Daniel left for Iraq, he wrote letters to Kim, the boys, and to my husband and me. Kim hung on to them and gave us our letter after he died. He told us how proud he was to serve whether or not we understood. He asked us to be sure his sons always remember him and to make them a part of the Arnold family.

Daniel was my son. I knew what kind of person he was. But I didn't understand his commitment to serving our country until I read his letter. It can be hard to understand, and I'm part of a military family. My husband served. So did my two sons. My son-in-law just got back from Kuwait. Whether they believe in war or not, each of them performed their duties. Without them we wouldn't have the freedoms we have. A lot of people don't think about that.

Did Daniel want to make the ultimate sacrifice? No. But he would if it would make someone's life better and our country safer for his boys. I don't know if I could make so deep a commitment, but I am glad there are people like Daniel who will.

Everyone handles grief in their own way. We've been offered counseling anytime we need it for the rest of our lives. For now, I told a counselor, "I lost my son. Unless you can take away my pain, this is something I have to learn how to deal with myself."

Even though it is painful, it helps to talk and for people to remember Daniel. Because Daniel was part of the National Guard and we are from a small community, our experience may have been different than in bigger places. Daniel's unit still considers us part of the family. We've been visited by everyone from the Adjutant General all the way down. I can see now why my son wanted to be part of this unit.

That September after Daniel died, we met personally with President Bush. We have received letters from the Governor, Senators, and people all around the world. A lady in Iowa made us a personalized quilt with photos and stories of Daniel. Two artists each painted a portrait of him. We even received a plaque from the Iraqi government thanking Daniel for his service. All these will be treasured and passed along to his sons one day.

Janet Arnold
Mother of Staff Sgt. Daniel L. Arnold (1977–2005)

SUMMARY

- Marital dissolution rates were similar in 1996 during a time of fewer demands placed on the military and in 2005 during a time when the military was experiencing greater demands. There is a worrisome trend of an increase in the number of junior enlisted from 2003 to 2009 who report their intention to seek a separation or a divorce and a decrease during the same time of the number who report being in a good marriage.
- Active Component personnel tend to marry earlier than their civilian counterparts and also divorce and remarry earlier than the civilian population.
- When coupled with the greater likelihood of becoming parents in their early 20s, the trends of earlier divorce and remarriage indicate that many young military families may be comprised of single parents, blended families with stepparent and stepchild relations, and divorced service members with children who are nonresidential and with whom they may or may not have partial custody.
- Service members and veterans who are identified with any one or a combination of TBI, PTSD, or depression are at increased risk of marital distress. Spouses of service members with PTSD, depression, or TBI are also at higher risk of developing psychological and marital distress themselves and may exhibit aspects of caregiver burden or secondary traumatization.
- Frequent and extended deployments may pose a significant challenge for couples to maintain a close relationship that consistently builds a shared perspective for important couple and familial goals.
- Research into the connections between DV and deployment shows limited and inconsistent links. More consistent risk factors for DV in military families are young age and having a history of DV prior to deployment.
- The complexity of deployment-related injury and recovery is dependent upon the extensive variability in several factors: injury severity and ability to heal; the service member's family composition, family history and patterns; and the medical treatment required.
- The type and severity of the injury will create different consequences and challenges for the service member and the roles they have within their family system (parent, adult child, romantic partner, sibling).
- Factors that offer protection to children and parents in combat-injured families include previously established patterns of family routines and care and availability of extended support relationships of family and friends.
- There are several areas of military family research that need attention: blended and same-sex families, National Guard and Reserve families, extended family relations in service members' lives, parents and siblings of service members, and the ways in which service member injury and death affect their family members.

EXERCISES

1. You have been asked to develop a community interest group for families who are caring for adult dependents at your installation. What would you need to know about your population before beginning the interest group? What resources do you think would be helpful as you build this interest group?

2. Examine the materials produced by the ZERO TO THREE organization for caring for very young children in military families who experience deployment, combat injury, and death (http://www.zerotothree.org/about-us/funded-projects/military-families/).

   a. What guidelines do these materials recommend to help young children process these stressors at a level that is developmentally appropriate for their age and cognitive and emotional abilities?

   b. How would you adapt and/or develop similar programs for elementary school age children or adolescents?

3. The research on DV in military families does not yet frame violence between couples using current terms of situational couple violence, coercive controlling, and violent resistance. Choose and read one of the studies on DV discussed in this chapter and then read Michael Johnson's work in describing the current terms (Johnson 2009; Kelly & Johnson, 2008 among other publications).

   a. How would the study you chose be changed if it were framed using these terms?

   b. What differences in conclusions and recommendations could you envision if the study were reframed to include these terms?

4. Combat-injured service members often face months of hospitalization and rehabilitation, and these facilities are not necessarily family or child friendly.

   a. What practical challenges do these facilities face in accommodating spouses, parents, and children?

   b. What practical recommendations would you offer to help minimize the stress of visits for children and other family members?

   c. Children's hospitals offer a different model of providing care and creating environments that lower stress levels for patients and families. What aspects of this model could be transferred to military and VA hospitals and rehabilitation centers?

5. Chapter 4 offers detailed information about children's experiences with deployment and the stressors their families and at-home parents face. What new connections can you make between the research on academic performance, well-being, and risks for maltreatment now that you have a better understanding of how war affects the important adults in their lives?

6. There are several areas of research with family members that need more attention. If you had the opportunity to design a study that gave voice to National Guard and Reserve families, siblings, parents, or same-sex partners, what would you include in your study and what method(s) and design(s) do you think would be most useful for your research and friendly to the families?

9

Women in the Military and Women Veterans

In Chapter, 9 you will

- Meet Captain Emily Spencer, U.S. Army, an active duty Explosives Ordnance Disposal Specialist, United States Military Academy instructor, wife of a service member, and mother.
- Learn about the changing role of women in the U.S. Armed Forces.
- Review important demographic and socioeconomic characteristics of women veterans.
- Gain insights into some of the concerns impacting women in the military and women veterans, including sexual assault, health issues, homelessness, and combat-related psychological disorders.
- Explore the evolving relationship between women veterans and the Department of Veterans Affairs.

Meet

CPT(P) Emily Spencer, U.S. Army

It is unique being in a field dominated by men, in an Army that is dominated by men.

I joined the military after 9/11. I was a freshman in college. I don't come from a military family and my parents were upset but I felt I needed to give back. I was commissioned through ROTC and went on active duty.

I started hearing about Explosive Ordnance Disposal (EOD). Improvised explosive devices (IEDs) were taking a lot of soldiers' lives. Qualified technicians were needed and I felt if I could help I would. People told me it was one of the hardest schools to get through. It sounded like a challenge and if there's a challenge out there I'm going to try it.

EOD is a unique job. Our work is to blow up or take other actions to eliminate the threat of an explosive device. In Baghdad there were lots of IEDs in our sector. We supported infantry guys and an armored unit. When troops found an IED they'd set up security around the area and call us.

We have a mission back in the States, too. When units go to ranges to train for deployment or readiness, they still use ordnances that can malfunction. In my last job, I was a commander of the disposal unit in the North Virginia area. Then I applied to teach at

West Point. To prepare for that assignment I completed a graduate degree. Now I teach at West Point.

It is unique being in a field dominated by men, in the Army that is dominated by men. In some of my units, I've become one of the guys; people said what they wanted, yet we trusted one another and felt comfortable opening up to one another. You form a tight knit relationship with those you deploy with. I see it as a strength to be a woman. I never felt at a disadvantage.

I have lots of sources of support. The military has my back with resources I could tap into. Personally I get more out of talking with people who are with me in a situation, especially during deployment. We'd all go back to our rooms to talk through and process what happened or what we are gearing up for. We all had good days and bad days. We had scary times. Sitting around the table helped.

My husband is my biggest support though. He's in my corner. I bounce my ideas and questions off of him to see if I am over-reacting. He's been in the military twice as long as I have. But even though he has more experience than I do, we both have our own strengths and weaknesses. He's Infantry. They sometimes see the world in black and white. I feel like I use him as a sounding board for technical stuff and procedures. I help him with the gray areas to give him different perspectives.

We have a 2 ½ year old and a 9 month old. I had assumed major caregiving responsibilities but now we share with my work beginning earlier now. My husband does the wake–up and school drop-offs; he's taken on a large brunt of the childcare since my schedule is more hectic. I take them to the doctor if one gets sick and for immunizations. When I had my son, I was in a command position. Even when I didn't have flexibility I wanted to be the one who was there. I'm a little obsessive about details.

My son knows mommy and daddy are in the Army. He has a little Army kit. We play with little soldiers. He's seen me in my uniform a few times. It's easier for me to change before I pick them up and come home. He sees my husband a lot in uniform. When we're playing soldiers, my husband reminds him that "mommy is in the military," too. When we're traveling and people say to my husband, "Thank you for your service," he always responds, "My wife is in the Army as well." Most people are surprised by that.

INTRODUCTION

Women's history in the U.S. Armed Forces is characterized by the perseverance of generations of women who braved a traditionally male-dominated establishment to participate in increasing numbers in the defense of our nation (U.S. Department of Veterans Affairs, 2011). Women have served in some capacity in every U.S. war (U.S. Department of Veterans Affairs, 2007), though not always in official capacities. The history of women serving with or in the U.S. military varies by service, and the expansion of their roles has evolved over time (Burrelli, 2013). Women were officially assigned as lighthouse keepers in the 1830s. In 1908, Congress created the Navy Nurse Corps. However, it was not until 1948 that Congress made women part of the military on a permanent basis. The 1948 Women's Armed Services Integration Act limited the number of women serving in the military to 2% of the enlisted corps and 10% of the officer corps. Yet, the proportion of the Armed Forces that was made up of women remained at less than 1% until 1973.

The women's rights movement of the 1960s and 1970s led to demands for equal rights and an increase in opportunities for women in all professional fields, including the military (Burrelli, 2013). Additionally, the end of the military draft and compulsory enlistment and the establishment of an all-volunteer military in 1973 contributed to challenges in recruiting and retaining qualified service members. The Defense Department began actively recruiting women to fill non-combat military occupations. Since then, women have gradually become an integral part of the military services (Burrelli, 1996). In 1972 women made up only 2% of the Armed Forces. By 1996, this had risen to over 12%, ranging from less than 5% of the Marine Corps to 16% of the Air Force. In 2013, over 355,000 women were members of the active duty and reserve components of the Armed Forces, comprising approximately 16% of the Armed Forces (Office of the Deputy Under Secretary of Defense, 2013). Women numbered 203,895 and accounted for 14.9% of the Active Duty force; they numbered 155,589 and represented 18.5% of the Reserve Component (Office of the Deputy Under Secretary of Defense, 2014).

Until recently women have been excluded from most combat jobs (Burrelli, 1996). Legislation known as the "Combat Exclusion Policy" prohibited women from serving in direct combat positions or in units (e.g., infantry, armor, artillery units) whose mission was combat or in support of combat missions (Keenan, 2008). The Persian Gulf War demonstrated the end of a clear delineation between a front line—the "dangerous" area of a combat zone where direct combat, hostile fire, and capture are likely to occur—and the "rear"—traditionally the "safe" area behind the front line where support personnel were located. Congress realized it had to acknowledge that all service members were now "at risk" for exposure to direct combat. Gradually, increasing numbers and types of positions became open to women.

In January 2013 the DoD eliminated restrictions on assigning women to combat units and positions and directed each of the services to integrate women into previously restricted occupations and units by January 1, 2016 (Dempsey & Panetta, 2013). The U.S. Special Operations Command and the service branches are also analyzing the impact of integrating women into elite Special Forces units (e.g., Navy Sea, Air, Land Teams; SEALs) that undertake atypical, sometimes covert and clandestine, missions often in austere and remote environments (Kelly, 2013).

The wars in Afghanistan and Iraq were the first combat operations in which a large number of women had repeated exposures to direct combat and multiple deployments. Over 200,000 military women deployed in support of OEF and OIF and served over 300,000 tours during those operations (DMDC, 2012). During these conflicts, women were still prohibited from serving in direct combat specialties or assigned to ground combat units. However, they served in all specialties except those that traditionally would have exposed them to direct engagement with the enemy through enemy fire, direct physical contact, or capture. They served in combat support specialties and units as truck drivers, pilots, medics, mechanics, military police, intelligence and civil affair personnel, explosive ordnance disposal, and numerous other specialties.

As the wars in Afghanistan and Iraq progressed, increasing numbers of women were serving in, around, and near hostile territory. They had a substantial role in supporting direct combat activities (Smith, Jacobson, Smith, Hooper, & Ryan, 2007), which means they were often co-located with military personnel directly engaged in combat. As in the Persian Gulf War, the locations and directions of attacks were unpredictable in the recent wars, and there was no clear distinction between the "front" line and "rear" areas—those areas which were relatively "dangerous" areas and "safe" areas in traditional wars. Women were exposed to direct fire and engagement with the enemy. Like male service members, they were subjected to ambushes, mortar and grenade attacks, and improvised explosive devices. They engaged in firefights, were captured and taken prisoner, and became casualties. They also handled corpses and body parts, witnessed and/or experienced severe injury or death, and were subjected to other traumatic events.

Since women were excluded from combat units and combat-specific occupations, they have not had the same exposure to death and injury as their male peers until recently. An analysis of Defense Manpower Data Center (DMDC, 2014b) and Congressional Research Service (Fischer, 2014) reports indicate that as of February 2014, 159 women were killed in the recent Global War on Terror (Operations Enduring Freedom, Iraqi Freedom, and New Dawn combined) compared to over 6,700 men whose lives were lost during these conflicts. These numbers represent a vastly greater percentage of deaths among men than women service members who served in these operations. Deaths among women service members accounted for just over 2% of the total deaths during these operations, while women constituted approximately 11% of the forces (DMDC, 2012). Since women are no longer excluded from combat units and combat-specific occupations due to the 2013 DoD elimination of those restrictions, in future wars their casualty numbers will likely more closely approximate those of their male peers.

The number of women veterans continues to grow, as do their needs. As of the end of fiscal year 2012, the number of women veterans in the U.S. was 1.6 million—approximately 8% of the total number of U.S. veterans (U.S. Department of Veterans Affairs, 2014b). The VA estimates that because of the increasing number of women entering and separating from the military, the longer life span of women, and the younger average age of women veterans compared to men veterans (U.S. Department of Veterans Affairs, 2007), the percentage of women making up the veteran population will increase to 12 by 2020 and will approach 20 by 2040 (U.S. Department of Veterans Affairs, 2013e).

With the recent increase in the number of women in the military and women veterans, the DoD and the DVA will be providing services to more women than in the past. Both the DoD and the DVA have been forced to develop and provide new services to meet women's needs and to examine how their programs and policies relate to their women members and to develop new programs and policies to address the needs of this population.

Voices From the Frontline

SERVING BY CHOICE

As far as we have come in the military it is still not viewed as a traditional role for women.

All of us choose the path we go down. I wear my combat boots and uniform to work every day. I'm an American citizen by choice and serve America by choice. My family and I came here as illegal immigrants. I remember going hungry in Mexico and sleeping on dirt floors, crossing the border and knowing we are doing something wrong. We didn't know the language and had only the clothes on our back. My mother said we will not go on welfare and we never did.

Being in the military is all I've really ever done. I was a single parent of a 3-month-old son after high school. Today I am a mother and a wife of a military man. We have four children. My son, the oldest, is active duty in the Air Force. He's deployed for 6 months. It's a proud and worrying time for me.

I've done deployments in Germany, Iraq, and Saudi Arabia. As a woman in a combat situation, you try to show how good you are. (So do the men.) As a female, you're not there to be coddled or babysat. I can't win an arm wrestle with a man but we can be comrades in arms. I have his back; he has mine.

I was wounded in a terrorist act—the Khobar Towers bombing, in Saudi Arabia—and was awarded a Purple Heart about 18 years ago. There are achievement medals you strive for. The Purple Heart is not one of those. That night we lost 19 people. Their last flight was in a metal casket. They never saw their medals. My scars, mental and physical, are still there. I gave my medal to my mother. She was very proud.

We have a Purple Heart license plate. People assume it is my husband's. If they get me on a sassy day, I say, "Do you understand that my combat boots are the same as his?" As far as we have come in the military, it is still not viewed as a traditional role for women.

Norma Gillette
Master Sergeant, Recruiting Office Supervisor, Michigan Army National Guard

SOME DEMOGRAPHIC AND SOCIOECONOMIC CHARACTERISTICS OF WOMEN VETERANS

The Department of Veterans Affairs' National Center for Veterans Analysis and Statistics used data from the U.S. Census Bureau 2012 American Community Survey to compare demographic and socioeconomic characteristics of women veterans with non-veteran women (U.S. Department of Veterans Affairs, 2014f). It also compared men and women veterans. These comparisons yielded the following general profile of women veterans:

- The average age of women veterans is 48.
- They tend to marry earlier than non-veteran women. About 33% of 17 to 24-year-old women veterans are married, compared with only 9% of non-veteran women of the same age. Twenty-five to 34-year-old veterans also marry at greater rates than non-veterans. However, at ages 35 and older, non-veteran women marry at higher rates.
- They are more likely to divorce—comparing 17-year-old and older veteran and non-veteran women by age groups, veterans are more likely than non-veterans to be divorced; in general, approximately 24% are divorced compared to 13% of non-veteran women.
- They are less likely to be married (47%) than men veterans (66%) but more likely to be divorced (23%) than men veterans (15%).
- A higher percentage completes a Bachelor's or advanced degree than non-veteran women.
- A higher percentage enrolls in college, completes some college, or completes a Bachelor's or advanced degree than veterans who are men.
- They are less likely than non-veteran women to be living in poverty (approximately 11% compared with 20%).
- They tend to live in households where the average household is higher than that of non-veteran women; the median income for households with women veterans is over $51,000, compared to $40,000 for households with non-veteran women.
- They are 5% more likely to have jobs in management and professional fields versus service occupations than non-veteran women; they are also more likely to hold jobs in management, professional fields, and offices (76%) than men veterans (59%).
- They are more likely to hold government positions at the federal, state, and local level than non-veteran women (37% compared to 17%).

CONCERNS IMPACTING WOMEN IN THE MILITARY AND WOMEN VETERANS

Since the military has just recently included women in significant numbers, many of their needs have not been routinely examined and consistently provided. Among these are sexual assault and sexual harassment; psychological health, reproductive health and other health issues; access to veterans benefits; and homelessness. The following sections address these topics in depth.

Sexual Assault and Sexual Harassment

The DoD acknowledges that sexual assault in the armed forces is a serious problem and has repeatedly pledged a "zero-tolerance" approach toward sexual assault (CBS News, 2014; Gleason, 2007; Hlad, 2012). However, the occurrence of sexual assault in the military has continued to escalate and is particularly problematic during periods of conflict. Both

men and women service members are at higher risk for sexual assault and sexual harassment in combat environments (Litz, 2005). However, women are the targets of sexual
assault and sexual harassment much more frequently than for men. To estimate the differences in the prevalence of sexual harassment and assault between men and women
reservists, Street, Stafford, Mahan, and Hendricks (2008) surveyed 3,946 former reservists (2,318 women and 1,628 males). They found that higher proportions of the women
reservists reported both sexual harassment (60% of women and 27.2% of males) and sexual
assault (13.1% of women 1.6% of men). While women are more likely to experience sexual
assault and sexual harassment while deployed, sexual assault and harassment impact negatively on the psychological well-being of both female and male service members (Kang,
Dalager, Mahan, & Ishii, 2005; Vogt, Pless, King, & King, 2005).

During the 1990–1991 Gulf War, women were over 16 times more likely to be the victim of sexual assault and 25 times more likely to experience sexual harassment than men
(Kang et al., 2005). One theory for this phenomenon is that women serving in job categories that have recently been opened to women may have a less developed social and peer
support network (Vogt et al., 2005). The military is predominantly a "male" culture and
women are still a numerical minority in the military, making it more difficult for women
to develop a protective social support network when working in jobs dominated by male
service members. They may, therefore, be at increased risk for being the targets of sexual
assault and harassment.

Estimates from studies on female service personnel during the Gulf War (1990–1991)
suggest that a minimum of 3% to over 7% of women experienced sexual assault and 24%
to 66% experienced sexual harassment (Committee on Gulf War and Health, 2008). For
men, the corresponding estimates were 0.2% for sexual assault and 0.6–8% for sexual
harassment.

The results of the Armed Forces 2002 Sexual Harassment Survey (Lipari &
Lancaster, 2003), which also included questions on sexual assault, revealed that the
rates of sexual assault for women in the military were 6% in 1995 and 3% in 2002; for
men, the rate for both years was 1%. The rates of reported sexual harassment for women
were 46% and 24% in 1995 and 2002, respectively, while the corresponding rates for
men were 8% and 3%. The Department of Defense (2004) reports that the rates of
sexual assault prior to the onset of, and during, the initial months of large deployments
in support of the Global War on Terror were 69.1 and 70.0 per 100,000 service members in 2002 and 2003, respectively. The number of sexual assaults reported in the
U.S. military area of operations that encompasses countries in the Middle East, North
Africa, and Central Asia, including Afghanistan and Iraq, rose from 24 in 2002 to 94
in 2003. These rates suggest that the incidence of sexual assault and sexual harassment
in the military is much lower during times when the United States is not engaged in
large-scale combat operations.

Data from OIF and OEF indicate that the incidence of sexual assault during deployments is significantly greater than when U.S. Forces are not deployed. Since the onset of
the recent wars, rates of sexual assault and sexual harassment have escalated sharply. The
Department of Defense Fiscal Year 2009 Annual Report on Sexual Assault in the Military
(2010) stated that the number of sexual assaults among service members deployed in Iraq
and Afghanistan was 26% higher in 2009 than in 2008, while the overall increase for
active duty service members (deployed or not deployed) was 8%.

More recent results indicate that these numbers have continued to soar. The DoD
recorded over 3,000 incidents of sexual assault in FY 2011 but estimates that the actual
number is probably closer to 19,000, because sexual assaults are very frequently not
reported (DACOWITS, 2013). During FY 2010, 21% of women and 3% of men in the
military reported being sexually harassed in the previous year.

In FY 2012, there were 3,374 reports of sexual assault involving victims and/or perpetrators who were service members (DoD, 2013b). In a DoD 2012 survey of active duty service members, 6.1% of women and 1.2% of men respondents reported that they had experienced "unwanted sexual contact" (sexual crimes involving any intentional sexual contact without consent) in the preceding 12 months. While the change in the rate of unwanted sexual contact for men was not statistically significant, there was a statistically significant increase of 4.4% over the number reported by women in 2010. Based on the 2012 survey, the Defense Manpower Data Center estimates that out of 1.4 million military active duty service members, 26,000 experienced unwanted sexual contact in the previous year. Among reserve component service members, 2.8% of women and 0.5% of men reported experiencing unwanted sexual contact in 2012 (Defense Manpower Data Center, 2013b and c). These rates did not represent statistically significant differences for reserve component women or men between the number of reported unwanted sexual contacts in 2008 and the number reported in 2012.

In an effort to control the military's current "sexual assault epidemic" (Tsai, 2013), Congress enacted a significant number of legislative changes in 2013 (One Hundred Twelfth Congress of the United States of America, 2013). The National Defense Authorization Act for Fiscal Year 2013 added the following provisions in an attempt to reduce the number of sexual assaults in the military:

- Separating military members who have been convicted of a sexual offense and prohibiting the recruitment of anyone with a sexual assault conviction.
- Requiring a review of **unrestricted sexual assault reports** (reports by victims of sexual assault who desire medical treatment, counseling, legal assistance, notification to command or law enforcement officials, and an official investigation of the crime) and the separation of anyone who reported a sexual assault from the military.
- Informing service members who reported a sexual assault and subsequently received disciplinary action or punishment of the options to have their military records changed.
- Improving data collection and reporting methods for incidents of sexual assault and harassment.
- Keeping or returning reserve component service members who are victims of sexual assault to active duty.
- Requiring all new commanders to receive training on sexual assault prevention, response, and policies.
- Adding personnel to enhance the DoD's ability to investigate and prosecute cases of sexual assault.
- Maintaining **restricted sexual assault reports** (the victim does not want the perpetrator prosecuted in order to maintain the victim's anonymity) made by service members for up to 50 years.
- Requiring each of the Armed Services to extensively publicize resources available for reporting and responding to sexual assaults, including telephone hotline phone numbers and Internet websites.

These provisions are intended to make service members who report sexual assaults less fearful of retaliation, make retaliation less likely, allow reserve component service members to be placed on active duty during an ongoing investigation or in order to testify in a sexual assault case (to allow access to the full range of services the DoD provides to sexual assault victims, including medical treatment for injuries and illness incurred from a sexual assault and counseling), and provide service members who have made a restricted report continued access to medical or psychological health services (Tsai, 2013)

However, as noted by the Defense Task Force on Sexual Assault in the Military Services (2009), in order for the DoD to improve its prevention and response to sexual assault, "culture change is essential" (p. 5) at all levels. The Task Force cited several features of military culture that influence sexual assault in the military. One aspect is during training—an essential element in creating a capable and ready military force. Military training is conducted in an environment where service members being trained view their trainers as absolute authority figures, creating a condition where power and authority can be abused; trainers have immense control over whether a trainee succeeds or fails and have complete oversight of the locations and actions of trainees. The trainer can potentially abuse his or her position to control the actions of trainees—in forcing them to submit to unwanted sexual contact, to yield in dismissing or minimizing the occurrence of a sexual assault, or to retract a report of sexual assault. This absolute power combined with the frequent lack of response to sexual assaults that occur during training give some **cadre** (experienced military professionals who train new recruits) a sense of invincibility and trainees the impression that the axiom "zero tolerance" for sexual assault is a hollow doctrine—an impression that can remain with them throughout their time in the military.

A second cultural aspect the Task Force (2009) identified as having an impact on the prevalence of sexual assault is that many younger military members "see binge drinking and casual sexual encounters as nothing more than social activities" (p. 8). The Task Force recommended that through the use of military training and the military chain of command, individuals from different social, cultural, and generational backgrounds can be socialized to embrace new standards and expectations, including trust, mutual respect, and commitment to other service members. Training can teach individual service members new norms that reject any violation of trust or mutual respect. The chain of command—the hierarchical system that provides order, accountability, and discipline in all military units—has the most profound impact on sexual assault prevention and response. Thus, in an attempt to reverse the military's sexual assault epidemic, Congress and the DoD are creating new military sexual assault legislation and ever stronger DoD directives holding unit commanders accountable for an authentic "zero tolerance" policy and ensuring that "victims of sexual assault are treated with dignity and respect" (The Associated Press, 2014, para. 7). Proposed legislation also provides legal counsel for victims of sexual assault, removes the statute of limitations for military trial of alleged perpetrators of sexual assault cases, and makes it a crime to retaliate against a victim reporting a sexual assault crime.

Street et al. (2008) found evidence that military sexual harassment and assault have major consequences for the psychological and physical health-care needs of veterans. In an analysis of the existing research on women veterans' health (Goldzweig, Balekian, Rolón, Yano, & Shekelle, 2006), the investigators learned that several studies found an association between sexual assault history and increased numbers of medical and psychiatric conditions, poorer health status, alcohol abuse, risky behaviors, and eating disorders. Both sexual harassment and sexual assault are associated with higher rates of PTSD, depression, somatic symptoms, and medical conditions (e.g., diabetes, hypertension, arthritis, cancer; Street et al., 2008). The VA warns that sexual assault and harassment during military service can cause the following problems, even many years later (U.S. Department of Veterans Affairs, 2013d):

- Disturbing memories or nightmares.
- Feeling vulnerable or unsafe.
- Depression.
- Numbness.
- Feeling isolated from others.
- Anger or irritability.

- Problems with alcohol or other drugs.
- Problems sleeping.

Voices From the Frontline

AT THE HANDS OF FELLOW SOLDIERS

Don't pretend it didn't happen . . . doesn't happen . . . won't happen again.

In 1980, I was 18 and I was raped by a fellow student who was in AIT [Advanced Individual Training; specialized training that teaches individuals the skills to perform a specific military occupation] with me. I was the only woman with 350 men in special electronic device repair training. I joined in January, graduated from Basic Training and went to AIT in October, and was assaulted in November.

I told the CQ [Charge of Quarters; an enlisted service member who handles administrative duties in the unit after normal duty hours] what happened. He said, "We'll call the Commander in the morning." I wanted to report it right away, but the CQ decided that it could wait until the next day. So, before PT the next day, I had to go tell the Commander. The Commander asked, "Are you sure it happened?" and "Are you sure you want to report it?" I still pressed charges. I have a strong constitution of right and wrong, black and white.

I was never taken to the hospital.

Between the incident and going to the court martial, I had to go to school with this person every day. I was told over and over that he has a family. I was told, "No one is going to believe you!" I was harassed by the military police investigator who constantly followed me and asked me, "Are you sure you want to report it?" "Did you know that he has a family?" "What were you wearing?" "Why were you drinking?" "How much did you drink?" "How promiscuous are you?"

He was acquitted because alcohol was involved. We had both been drinking. He was drunk and I was in my room sleeping when it happened, but I was at fault. After the trial, I left the courtroom and he drove past me and said, "I told you I would get away with it!"

I didn't get any counseling—not then and not any time while I was still in the Army. Since he was acquitted, the attitude was that it didn't happen. I was never asked about sexual assault until after I retired. I put it in a box my whole career and tried to ignore it.

I experienced constant, never-ending sexual harassment during most of my career, both from men in my unit and from others. In one assignment, when I arrived the First Sergeant told me, "You are new meat. That's what you are in this unit." He touched my face and I told him off, so he started to choke me. I was yelling for him to stop it, until other people pulled him off of me. I told the Commander what had happened. The Commander's response was, "Well, I heard that you like it rough!"

Once, my unit in Germany was in the field, and I was sleeping in my sleeping bag. Three guys jumped me and dragged me out into the mud. From that point on I started to sleep with a knife. I went days without sleeping. Other times, I was taped up and hung from a crane, I had my breast grabbed and asked if they were real, I was "dry-humped," and lots more . . . all by my fellow soldiers.

Being a woman in the military, you have to know who you are. Be strong and independent. I don't mean pay your own bills. I mean be aware of the fact that you are not safe in any situation—sleeping in your bed at night, walking across the field, in a combat situation. At any point in time the person who is supposed to be protecting you could be the person who is holding you down and hurting you. You are on edge 24 hours a day. There is no point when you can let your guard down. It is mentally, physically, and emotionally exhausting.

I was told that I needed to dress a certain way, never go anywhere alone, etc., so that I wouldn't be attacked by male soldiers. My father once read something that said about 85% of women in the military experience some kind of sexual harassment or assault while in the military. Even my father said, "What do you expect when you join an organization full of men?" It makes me so angry when I hear comments like that.

I'm messed up because this happened to me. But I am still standing. I never gave up. My message to others is this: Don't pretend it didn't happen . . . doesn't happen . . . won't happen again. I get counseling now, but it's hard for me. I still try to keep the Band-Aid on the wound. I keep my "body armor" on.

L. Hunter
Sergeant First Class, U.S. Army (Retired)

Intimate Partner Violence

Intimate partner violence (IPV; the use of physical and/or sexual violence to exercise control over a partner) is a national health concern (Black & Merrick, 2013; Tinney, 2014. However, while our knowledge of this form of violence has increased significantly in recent years, IPV's impact on military women and women veterans is a very recent subject of study. Using 2006 data from the Centers for Disease Control and Prevention researchers explored the associations between veteran status and lifetime exposure to intimate partner violence (Dichter, Cerulli, & Bossarte, 2011). They found that almost one-third of women veterans had experienced IPV victimization. Thirty-three percent of women veterans reported ever experiencing IPV, while 23.8% of non-veteran women reported exposure to IPV. The researchers also found a connection between IPV and depression, smoking, and heavy drinking. Analyzing interviews with over 1,400 active duty women conducted in 2010 (Black & Merrick, 2013), researchers at the Centers for Disease Control learned that the women who had been deployed within the 3-year period prior to the interviews were more likely to have experienced IPV than women who had not deployed during that period.

Dichter et al. (2011) suggest that in caring for women veterans and service members, providers must screen for this form of interpersonal violence and view IPV as a prevalent health issue that could result in chronic conditions, including chronic vascular disease and mental health disorders resulting from their trauma exposure.

Reproductive Health Care

Until 2014, reproductive health-care coverage for military women and for female family members of military men and women did not include abortions "except where the life of the mother would be endangered if the fetus were carried to term" (DACOWITS, 2013, p. 14). Department of Defense funds could not be used to cover abortions under any other circumstances. So, military women and female family members paid for abortions regardless of reason, including when pregnancy resulted from rape or incest. This constraint particularly impacted junior enlisted women who have some of the highest incidence rates of rape and are less likely to be financially able to pay for an abortion.

New legislation passed as part of the National Defense Authorization Act for Fiscal Year 2013 (One Hundred Twelfth Congress of the United States of America, 2013) now provides "military women the same coverage to which Medicaid recipients and prison inmates have been entitled" (Montgomery, 2014, para. 2). This change in policy is partly due to the DoD's increasing focus on military sexual assault and its response to sexual assault.

Other Health Issues Impacting Women in the Military and Women Veterans

Through interactions with military representatives, subject matter experts, and service members; literature reviews; and analyses of survey data and other available research; the Defense Advisory Committee on Women in the Services (DACOWITS, 2012) concluded that the health issues of women service members "are addressed inconsistently and not as effectively as they should be" (p. i). The committee suggested that the individual services and DoD do not collect and share information on women's health issues. The DACOWITS recommended that the DoD and the VA collaborate on conducting and collecting research and developing and sharing lessons learned and best practice methods.

Health of Deployed Service Women

Through a DoD briefing on the results of a study on the health issues of women in the 2 years following deployment, the DACOWITS (2013) learned that compared to women who had not deployed in support of OEF/OIF and men who had deployed in support of the operations, women who had deployed reported higher rates of several health conditions. The health conditions reported by women who had deployed included migraine headaches; back and neck problems; anxiety, depression, and other psychological health conditions; upper respiratory issues; and reproductive health issues.

The DACOWITS (2013) was concerned about the health of deployed women and barriers to women seeking medical care while deployed. The committee's concerns included women's fear of being stigmatized for seeking medical care in an operational field environment and their reservations regarding the ability of military health-care providers to diagnose and treat women's health issues competently and professionally:

> There is too often unwillingness on the part of deployed women to seek medical care because of fear that it will be seen as a weakness, lack of confidence in the training of medical staff to address health issues particular to women or a belief that medical personnel do not protect privacy or take women's health concerns seriously. (p. ii)

Other researchers have also found that military women in deployment settings often feel that military health-care providers are not adequately trained to deal with their medical issues and that they were not able to obtain the gynecologic care and supplies they needed while deployed (Steele & Yoder, 2013; Wilson & Nelson, 2012).

According to the DACOWITS (2013), specific issues paramount to women's health during deployments include training for military health personnel on diagnosing and treating deployed women, ensuring that the equipment and supplies required for women's health are readily available during deployments, the prevention of injuries through the development of combat gear designed specifically for women, and educating military women on maintaining their health while deployed. The committee recommended that military health-care providers receive training to increase their competence and confidence in treating women's health in an operational field environment while ensuring their privacy and encouraging them to seek treatment when necessary. The DACOWITS suggested that birth control supplies, emergency contraception, medication to treat vaginitis and urinary tract infections, self-diagnosis kits for urinary tract and vaginal infections, tampons, and sanitary napkins be available to health-care providers and women during deployments. The committee recommended that education for women before and during deployment include information on genitourinary hygiene practices, symptoms and treatment of vaginitis and urinary tract infections, birth control, menstrual cycle control, and stress management.

The DACOWITS (2012) recommended that supplies available to deployed women include urinary diversion devices (devices that allow women to urinate discreetly and safely). Such devices would reduce the prevalence of urinary tract infections and other health risks related to the genitourinary system, the most common health issues for deployed female service members (DACOWITS, 2007). Because of security and safety issues, a lack of privacy, unsanitary conditions, primitive or absent toilet facilities, difficult terrains, insects, and extreme climates, defecation and urination in field and combat environments are difficult for both men and women. However, due to anatomic differences in the genitourinary structures of men and women, a reduced ability to be discreet, and the need to remove clothing and heavy equipment each time they urinate, women face greater challenges with urination than men when deployed (Steele, 2013). To avert these challenges, deployed women have resorted to practices that increase the risk of vaginal and urinary tract infections and other gynecological problems (Steele, 2013; Trego, 2012). They include deliberately restricting the intake of fluids to avoid having to urinate; voluntarily holding urine for extended periods; using bottles, jars, plastic bags, cans or other objects to urinate into by squatting over them or holding them up to their bodies; and wearing multiple layers of perineal pads, sanitary napkins, or disposable incontinence briefs to absorb urine. These practices threaten the health of deployed women by increasing the chance of dehydration and by promoting the growth of bacterial and other microorganisms that can infect the urinary tract and lead to other health problems. Because health risks related to the genitourinary system are the most common health risks for deployed women, researchers are developing urinary diversion devices and studying their effectiveness in reducing the number of female urinary symptoms and urinary tract infections (Task Force Medical Afghanistan Public Affairs, 2013).

Menstruation management is another health concern for women in combat and field environments (Wilson & Nelson, 2012). The lack or paucity of personal hygiene and laundry facilities, the sometimes limited supply of tampons and sanitary napkins, and the inconvenience of and lack of privacy for changing tampons and pads led to many women using various methods to suppress their menstruation while in a combat theater. These methods varied from oral contraceptives and intrauterine devices to injections. However, for women who chose to suppress their menstruation, it was often difficult to get a year's supply of oral contraceptives from military medical facilities and some turned to non-military agencies, such as Planned Parenthood, to get their supplies.

In its 2012 Report the DACOWITS also expressed concern about the failure of the DoD to develop appropriate individual combat equipment for women. The committee asserted that because of the wearing of combat equipment designed specifically for men, women are developing injuries and experiencing pain in their hips, backs, and knees, as well as other injuries. The DACOWITS urged the military services to collaborate on developing and quickly distributing equipment designed and fitted to women's bodies.

Feedback from women who had been deployed indicates that health care and treatment of deployed women have improved (DACOWITS, 2013). Supplies and medication are more readily available; the number of women medical care personnel has increased; and psychological health treatment for deployed personnel has improved. However, health matters—such as genitourinary health, contraception management and menstrual cycle control, pain and musculoskeletal injuries, and psychological health—continue to be a problem for deployed women.

Women and Combat-Related Psychological Disorders

Like military men, military women are at risk for exposure to combat-related incidents and trauma, which have the potential to result in PTSD, other stress reactions, and other psychological health issues. In an overview of current research on the effects of combat-related stressors and deployment experiences on the physical and psychological health of military service women, Pierce (2010) states that we do not fully understand the effects on women in the military of multiple deployments and stressors not related to deployment. There are few studies of how women are affected psychologically by these experiences. The findings of the studies that do exist are mixed. Hoge, Castro, Messer, McGurk, Cotting, and Koffman (2004) reported that women have about the same risk as men of getting PTSD or other psychological health disorders when exposed to combat. To examine a possible gender difference Hoge, Clark, and Castro (2007) reviewed the existing research to identify possible differences among male and female Iraq war veterans and the development of PTSD and other psychological health disorders. They concluded that, at that time, there was no evidence of a significant difference in the likelihood of men and women developing PTSD or depression after serving in Iraq and that further research was warranted. However, other studies on veterans who served in prior wars (e.g., Perconte, Wilson, Pontius, Dietrick, & Spiro, 1993) suggest that women may develop higher levels of psychological health problems as a result of combat exposure. In a study on the prevalence of psychological health problems among Army soldiers and Marines after their return from deployment to Iraq or Afghanistan (Hoge, Auchterlonie, & Milliken, 2006), 23.6% of the women and 18.6% of the men in the study reported a mental health concern—a 1.3 to 1 ratio. These findings approximate the 2 to 1 ratio of women to men who suffer from PTSD in the general population (Kessler, Sonnega, Bromet, Hughes & Nelson, 1995). In spite of this, a comparison of women veterans and men veterans from the Vietnam and Gulf Wars suggests that when controlling for the level of combat exposure, men are three times more likely to be given a diagnosis of PTSD than their female counterparts (Pereira, 2002). This study also suggested that when the PTSD diagnosis is given to women, it is related to prior sexual assault, not combat-related trauma. This phenomenon may be due to cultural expectations that make it difficult for society, as a whole, and mental health practitioners, specifically, to recognize that women are exposed to combat and may subsequently develop psychological health disorders. Additionally, there is a tendency in the mental health profession to diagnose women with depression, anxiety, and borderline personality disorder instead of giving them a diagnosis of PTSD (Becker, 1994). Nevertheless, research indicates that women are more likely to experience trauma in the military, including **military sexual trauma** (MST; sexual trauma experienced during military service), and develop PTSD as a result (Street et al., 2008). Research also suggests that women veterans with PTSD are significantly more impaired in several areas than those without PTSD (Goldzweig et al., 2006). In general, women veterans with PTSD have poorer health status and physical functioning and more physical health symptoms, medical conditions, body pain, and somatization (psychological manifestations of physical problems). Although not specifically limited to women veterans who have deployed, research comparing suicide rates of women veterans and women non-veterans (McFarland, Kaplan, & Huguet, 2010) suggests that women veterans with psychological problems are more likely than women non-veterans to complete suicide.

The impact of deployments on the psychological health of military women may be related to the types of jobs they have. In a study on the effects of serving in combat-related occupations on the psychological health of women Navy and Marine Corps service members, researchers found that women in combat support occupations were less likely to be hospitalized for reasons related to psychological health than women in non-combat-related jobs (Lindstrom, Smith, Wells, Wang, Smith, Reed, et al., 2006). The researchers offered two possible explanations for their results. First, women serving in non-traditional combat-support occupations may be more afraid of stigma related to seeking help for psychological issues. Second, women working in non-traditional career fields may have developed more effective coping skills and, therefore, experience less stress in combat-related occupations.

Pierce (2010) asserted that research is needed to distinguish between the impact of stress of work-family conflict (when the needs of a job or career interfere with family life and the responsibility of raising children) and the impact of combat stressors on women in the military, in order to better assist women service members in preparing for deployment, returning home after deployment, and continuing their military careers. While the levels of work-life conflict have not been determined for the military population, 42% of employees in the general U.S. population have reported that their work and family life interfere with each other (Tang & MacDermid Wadsworth, 2010). In an initial study to determine the impact of work-family conflict and combat stress on the psychological well-being of military women, Pierce (2010) studied the relationship between work-family conflict and psychological well-being in Air Force women who had deployed to Iraq. She found that both higher work-family conflict and greater combat exposure were predictive of higher levels of depression, PTSD, and poorer emotional functioning. She suggests that while exposure to combat stressors is difficult to control for women who choose military jobs or careers, the stress of work-family conflict may be a target area for offering assistance to military women in an effort to reduce their overall stress.

In another attempt to differentiate the impact of different stressors on service members (Vogt, Pless, King, & King, 2005), researchers examined the impact of mission-related stress and interpersonal stress on men and women deployed in support of the 1990–1991 Gulf War. The results of the study suggest that both men and women were affected by both mission-related stress–"stressors that are specific to the deployment mission"–and interpersonal stress–"stress associated with social interactions and relationships during deployment" (p. 282), including family relationships. However, women reported that they had experienced more interpersonal stress than men, and interpersonal stress had a stronger impact on the psychological well-being of female veterans than on that of male veterans. Thus, the research suggests that women service members may benefit from help in coping with the stressors of work-family conflict and with interpersonal stress.

Voices From the Frontline

UNDERSTANDING MILITARY WOMEN THROUGH RESEARCH

There are more questions than answers when it comes to women in the military and mothers who are serving our country. We need a lot more research.

I am a developmental psychologist. Twenty years ago, I started focusing on women in the military. At that time I started noticing an increasing number of women on Navy ships. When a ship is out to sea—especially years ago before all of today's technology—it had to operate as its own town. Every ship had a different climate. Some were more favorable towards women than others. It all started with the CO. If he was supportive of women, his attitude cascaded throughout the ship and women were happier.

I studied single enlisted Navy mothers. Pre-deployment for single mothers is very difficult. My early research revealed that they were very concerned about how their children would do. Then, and even now, society is more comfortable with dads deploying. This isn't to say that dads don't feel sad or find it difficult. Young mothers, though, are less likely to have had experience with deployment; society's views about a woman leaving her children adds to the complexity.

Typically when fathers are deployed, mothers are home and continue children's routines. When single mothers are deployed, that isn't the case. Children may stay with an ex-spouse. About half the time they stay with the mother's mother. Because children are very young and their grandmothers rarely live nearby, many of these children may not know their grandmothers well. Other children stay with members of her extended family. It's my observation that children of single mothers are more likely than children of married couples to be uprooted and moved to a new place.

There are more transitions and adjustments for children and adults alike in single parent families.

There are more questions than answers when it comes to women in the military and mothers who are serving our country. We need a lot more research: How do women service members adjust? How do their partners adjust? Their children? How does life work in a dual career couple or when the woman is the service member? Where and how do women in the military meet their partners? At work? What does this imply for future research of dual military families?

We need to learn more about protective factors for women. A study we did in 2006 found that command support and friendships made a difference versus more traditional sources of support such as resources or counseling. In the Navy sailors and officers are on a ship for 6 to 7 months. The only thing they see is the water, the sky, and the people they work with.

There's been a lot of focus on PTSD. We also need to look at cumulative stress of deployment and moving every 2 or 3 years on women service members and their families, particularly as families move through different stages of development.

Michelle Kelley, PhD
Professor of Psychology, Old Dominion University

Women Veterans and Homelessness

Just as losing consistent pay is a risk factor for homelessness for anyone who loses a job, veterans are at risk for homelessness after leaving the military service. However, the likelihood of being homeless is greater for women veterans than men veterans or women nonveterans. In a study on the prevalence and risk of homelessness among veterans, Fargo et al. (2011) noted that veteran status was associated with a 47% increase in the risk of becoming homeless for men and a 97% increase for women. They also found that homeless veterans made up approximately 1% of the men who are veterans in the general population while 2% of women veterans in the general population are homeless. For women veterans, homelessness was highest among the cohort ranging from 18 to 29 years, with an increase in age associated with a decline in the risk of homelessness. The women veterans at greatest risk for homelessness were those women who were young and Black; this group had a 40% probability of homelessness when compared to the general population of the U.S. living below the poverty level and an overall 9% probability of homelessness when compared to the U.S. population as a whole. Women veterans who are homeless are also more likely than men to have minor children living with them (33% versus 8%; U.S. Government Accountability Office, 2011).

During a single night of data collection by the U.S. Department of Housing and Urban Development (2014) in January 2014, 578,424 people were homeless. Among these were 49,933 veterans, who accounted for over 11% of the homeless adults. Almost 10% (4,722) of the homeless veterans were women.

In a survey of homeless women, Gamache, Rosenheck, and Tessler (2003) found that in any age range, women veterans are two to four times more likely to be homeless than women who are not veterans. The cohort of women veterans aged 45 to 54 were most at risk for homelessness and were over four times more likely to be homeless than nonveteran women in the same age range. The Gamache et al. (2003) survey revealed that the proportion of veterans making up the population of homeless women was greater than the proportion of veterans among women who were not homeless. The researchers found these findings puzzling, since veterans generally have better personal and social support resources—stable families of origin, more education, current employment, present spouses or other significant persons, and access to VA benefits and service. Washington et al. (2010) assert that the risk factors for homelessness among women veterans have not been identified but acknowledge that military sexual trauma, unemployment, disability, poor health, and PTSD and other anxiety disorders are associated with homelessness in this population. They found that over 53.3% had experienced military sexual trauma. To understand why women veterans are more likely to be homeless than women who are not veterans, Gamache et al. (2003) studied the characteristics of their participants and found that they had the following risk factors for homelessness: low income, childhood abuse, PTSD and other psychiatric problems, substance abuse, and poor health. Reaching out to women veterans at risk for becoming homeless—because of psychological health issues, joblessness, substance abuse issues, and other conditions that place them at risk—is essential in reducing homelessness among women veterans.

WOMEN VETERANS AND THE DEPARTMENT OF VETERANS AFFAIRS

The significant role women have played in the defense of the U.S. and as members of the community of veterans is "sadly one not always acknowledged or appreciated" (U.S. Department of Veterans Affairs, 2007, p. 22). For much of U.S. history, women veterans have been "forgotten" and "invisible" (Willenz, 1983). In a survey of women veterans in California (Foster & Vince, 2009), participants cited the lack of respect and acknowledgment for their service as the primary challenge in their transition from service member to veteran status. They still do not receive the respect and demonstration of gratitude for their service in combat that their male cohorts are given. Both the nation as a whole and the Department of Veterans Affairs have been slow to acknowledge that women veterans have earned and deserve the same recognition and services as their male peers. Since the 1980s the VA has struggled with the need to provide appropriate, adequate, and accessible services to women veterans (U.S. Department of Veterans Affairs, 2011).

While women have officially been serving in the military since 1901, they were not considered qualified for veteran status and veteran benefits until after World War II (U.S. Department of Veterans Affairs, 2011). Even after having been granted veteran status, women still did not have equal access to VA benefits well into the 1980s. Women veterans who went to VA facilities for medical care did not receive complete physical examinations or gynecological care. They were not routinely and thoroughly informed of their benefits as veterans, and many were not even aware that they had access to VA services. Just like their male counterparts, female veterans' benefits can include financial compensation for service-related disabilities, pensions, education and training, health care, home mortgage loans, insurance, vocational training, and burial benefits (U.S. Department of Veterans Affairs, 2011). In general, women veterans use VA services and facilities less than men (Goldzweig et al., 2006). Female veterans are less likely to use VA health care than male veterans; and they are more likely to use only the health-care services and no other VA programs and services (U.S. Department of Veterans Affairs, 2011). Approximately 11% of women veterans use VA medical facilities for some or all of their health care, and women veterans account for only about 5% of all users at VA facilities (Goldzweig et al., 2006). The difference in the rate at which women use VA facilities may be partly because female veterans have health needs that differ from those of male veterans. These differences might be explained by dissimilar experiences while in the military, an increased prevalence of conditions in women (e.g., psychological health issues), varied manifestations of physical and psychological health conditions from those of men (e.g., an increased presence of emotional components in women), and other gender-specific issues (e.g., gynecologic and reproductive health). Some female veterans are also unwilling to seek services from the VA because of a perception that there is a partiality for male veterans in the VA system; some note experiencing sexual harassment in VA facilities

(Service Women's Action Network, 2012). Women veterans may find the VA inhospitable and feel ill-at-ease. Staffing shortages are resulting in inadequate numbers of women health-care providers. Residential and inpatient VA facilities are to have separate and secure accommodations for women; however, not all facilities are meeting this standard due to aging buildings. Moreover, 31% of medical centers and community-based outpatient centers have difficulty providing women and men who are seeking MST treatment the option of choosing the gender of their mental health-care provider (Disabled American Veterans, 2014).

However, some important recent developments in the VA have contributed to a shift toward increased use of VA services by women veterans. To correct their failure to adequately serve women veterans, and in recognition that many of the services required by women veterans and some of their issues are different from those of men, Congress and the Department of Veterans Affairs put several systems in place in the 1980s and 1990s (U.S. Department of Veterans Affairs, 2011). These included an Advisory Committee on Women Veterans to assess the needs of this population in terms of compensation for service-related injuries and illnesses, rehabilitation, health care, and outreach. The committee recommends improvements to programs and services to the VA and to Congress in a bi-annual report. Recommendations typically include changes to programs and policy, research, and other activities designed to improve services to women veterans. A Women Veterans' Program Office was established to address the specific concerns of women veterans, many of whom were not using the health-care services and readjustment programs available to them. A Center for Women Veterans was created to monitor the administration of health care, benefits, and programs for women. The center also endeavors to advocate for women veterans, to raise awareness of the needs of women veterans, to encourage societal recognition of their services and contributions, and to promote dignity and respect in the treatment of women veterans.

The Veterans Health Administration has also taken actions to improve the quality and access to health care for women veterans, including redesigning the health-care delivery system, providing comprehensive primary care from providers trained in women's health care, identifying women veterans' health-care needs, and compiling data to use for developing policy and planning programs for this population (U.S. Department of Veterans Affairs, 2011). Each VA medical center in the United States has a Women Veterans Coordinator who serves as the primary contact for women veterans and provides information on VA benefits for women veterans and their beneficiaries. Coordinators can help women veterans enter the VA system; assist them in filing claims for compensation and for military sexual trauma; and help them negotiate the often confusing, intimidating process of obtaining services. Each VA medical center also has a Women Veterans Program Manager who advocates for women veterans, advises them, and helps to coordinate all of the medical services a woman veteran might need. The Women Veterans Program Manager is the best person to help a woman veteran enter the VA medical system and receive the health-care services she needs, from routine care to specialized care, including reproductive health and psychological health. The VA has made much progress in its development of programs designed specifically for women veterans. As the VA continues to improve services for women, more women veterans will choose to enter the VA system to obtain benefits and health care.

RAISING THE GLASS CEILING

The military services, while traditionally male-dominated and initially limited in positions and advancement opportunities for women, now offer women challenges and opportunity in a wide spectrum of occupational specialties (Harris, Simutis, & Gantz, 2002). While historically not always the case, the DoD is making changes to provide women with equal opportunities for advancement and deliberate about identifying and quelling gender-based discrimination that would prevent or reduce promotion or leadership opportunities for women. The DoD (n.d.) provides the following examples of women who have risen to the highest ranks and the highest leadership positions:

- By the 1990s women flew jets and commanded bases and ships.
- In 1993 Sheila Widnall became the first woman appointed as Secretary of the Air Force.
- In 1999 Colonel Eileen Collins, an Air Force instructor and test pilot, was appointed as the first woman to command a National Aeronautics and Space Administration (NASA) Space Shuttle.
- In 2008 Army General Ann Dunwoody was the first woman in U.S. military history to earn a fourth star.
- In 2010 the Navy opened submarine positions to women.
- In 2011 Rear Admiral Raquel Bono became the first Hispanic woman to attain the Naval rank of rear admiral; she later became Chief of the Navy Medical Corps.
- On March 31, 2011 the first combat mission planned and flown entirely by women, was carried out in Afghanistan.
- In 2009 Michèle Flournoy was confirmed as the Under Secretary of Defense for Policy, the third-ranking official in the U.S. Department of Defense, and the highest-ranking woman in the history of the Pentagon.
- The numbers of women who held positions as generals and admirals numbered 68 women reserve component members in 2012 (Office of the Deputy Under Secretary of Defense, 2013) and 67 women active duty members at the end of 2013 (Defense Manpower Data Center, 2013d).

Army General Ann Dunwoody states that, "breaking barriers, shattering glass ceilings, brass ceilings, and rewriting history, is nothing new for the armed forces" (Lopez, 2009). The DoD (n.d.) professes that the opportunity for women to hold leadership positions in the military has never been better.

This increase in the number of women in military leadership positions is one indicator of an evolving military culture. Other indicators of change for women service members and veterans include developing military sexual assault legislation in Congress, holding commanding officers accountable for enacting the policy of "zero tolerance" of sexual assault and treating victims with respect and dignity, and establishing a Women Veteran Coordinator and Program Manager at each VA medical center. Women veterans' organizations and advocacy groups (e.g., Service Women's Action Network, n.d.; American Women Veterans Foundation, 2014) promote continued improvements, so that women service members can serve their country without discrimination and women veterans can receive the care and respect they have earned.

SUMMARY

- Women constitute a significant minority in the military, about 15%. The number of women veterans, currently 1.6 million, (8% of all veterans) continues to grow, as do their needs.
- Afghanistan and Iraq were the first combat operations in which a large number of women had repeated exposures to direct combat and multiple deployments.
- Female veterans differ from their male veteran counterparts and from female non-veterans in several ways; these differences are important to understand for programming and policy within the Veterans Health Administration and in civilian communities of care.

- Sexual assault and sexual harassment are serious issues and occur at significantly higher rates for women in the military. While the climate for accepting or tolerating these acts is now changing, survivors face significant challenges as they may be working with or under the command of the perpetrator and the reporting system can threaten continued employment.
- More research is needed to distinguish between the impact of stress of work-family conflict (when the needs of a job or career interfere with family life and the responsibility of raising children) and the impact of combat stressors on women in the military, in order to better assist women service members in preparing for deployment, returning home after deployment, and continuing their military careers.
- Each VA medical center in the U.S. now has a Women Veterans Coordinator who serves as the primary contact for women veterans and provides information on VA benefits for women veterans and their beneficiaries.

EXERCISES

1. If possible, interview a woman who has served or is currently serving as an active duty or reserve member of the military. Consider the following questions for your interview:
   a. What motivated her to join the military?
   b. What challenges has she faced while serving?
   c. What does she think about the 2013 DoD elimination of the Combat Exclusion Rule?
2. Although the Combat Exclusion Rule preventing women from serving in combat units and combat positions has been eliminated, the argument about women in combat is not over. For example, many U.S. citizens are still disturbed by photographs of women hugging their babies before deploying to combat. Write a short essay examining your thoughts and feelings about women going to war. Include why you think it is appropriate or why you do not think it is appropriate.
3. Locate a copy of *SERVICE: When Women Come Marching Home*, a documentary film about seven women veterans' transition from active duty to civilian lives, by Marcia Rock and Patricia Lee Stotter. If your library does not have a copy of the film, purchase and rental information is available at http://www.wmm.com/filmcatalog/pages/c843.shtml. After watching the film as a class or with a group of your classmates, discuss the themes of the film and your responses to the film.
4. How would you respond to a woman veteran who has revealed to you that she has experienced military sexual trauma?
5. The U.S. is one of a modest number of countries to review and revise policy regarding women serving in combat roles. Starting with the essays by Anna Mulrine (2013) and Max Fisher (2013), choose one or two other nations whose policies support women in combat roles. Try to find out what their military system is like compared to the U.S. For example, do personnel enlist or are they conscripted in to military service? How is "combat role" defined within their system? When were policy changes made to include women in these roles? Is there information about the process of making this change?
   http://news.nationalgeographic.com/news/2013/13/130125-women-combat-world-australia-israel-canada-norway/
   http://www.washingtonpost.com/blogs/worldviews/wp/2013/01/25/map-which-countries-allow-women-in-front-line-combat-roles/

10

Veterans and Families

In Chapter 10, you will

- Meet the Yeary family, a recently retired career Marine Corps family of four who share their perspectives on transitioning from military to civilian life: husband and father Lon Yeary, Colonel (Retired), wife and mother Julia, daughter Jackie, and son LA.
- Learn about the current veteran population, including the emerging population of veterans who have served since 2001.
- Learn about unique veteran and veteran family experiences within and between generations of combat.
- Increase your knowledge about the services offered by and the challenges facing the Department of Veterans Affairs.
- Explore how a range of veteran organizations advocate for and assist military families.

Meet

The Yeary Family, USMC Lon Yeary, (Colonel Ret.), Husband and Father

I graduated from the U.S. Naval Academy in 1978 and chose to go into the Marine Corps. Later I earned a masters' degree. I went to flight school and have worked in the military as a helicopter pilot, a flight instructor, Squadron Commander at Camp Pendleton and at Headquarters with the Marine Expeditionary Force. I've deployed to many places: Asia, Japan, and Korea. Never in combat.

My last 6 years in the military we moved off base to live outside of Chicago where I was Commanding Officer of the United States Military Entrance Processing Center at Great Lakes Naval Base outside of Chicago.

In the early 1980s I met my wife Julia. She's a social worker. We met when I went to a Family Service Center. She was part of the team helping to prepare a family briefing. I didn't have a family at the time. I thought, "Let's just get on the boat and go." Julia taught me we have to consider the whole family.

When you are in the military, you are part of a structured organization. You know who everyone is and their rank by their uniform. Missions are well defined. The military provides you with equipment, your pay, and medical benefits. You know if you are a

Colonel, the next step is a General. You have goals and boards to meet throughout your career. You either get promoted and perform or get out.

Throughout my career people told me: "Everyone out there in the civilian world is going to love you. You'll make lots of money." Well, I left the military in 2008. It was not a good time for the U.S. economy.

They sent me to an exit class for a couple of days where they tell you about writing a resume. I figured, "A resume will take 20 minutes to write. It'll be a piece of cake." It wasn't. They say you have to "dress for success." I never had to worry about going to a closet and picking out what to wear. Depending on the day, I'd either put on a flight suit or utilities. I realized I'd have to find a doctor, a dentist.

It was challenging and heart wrenching in some ways. I found myself walking back into a world I'd been out of 35 years, trying to get a job. A week out of the Marine Corps there I am sitting in my living room, working on the first resumé I ever wrote and filling out application forms.

You start to question "what's wrong with me?" How could I put 180 Marines and 12 helicopters on a boat to head to Afghanistan where people would be shooting at them and not find a job?

Searching for a job is another shock. Wearing my uniform, I drew immediate respect. Now I found myself walking into settings in a suit where people who were significantly younger than me are asking, "Tell me about your qualifications." I wanted to say, "Are you kidding me? I could run the whole damn place." ...

The change is also good. Our family had been moving around a lot. My daughter, Jackie, did lots of moving and bouncing around. Of course she also has friends in California, Virginia, and Wisconsin. My son who is 5 years younger can go to one high school in one community. He knows the same classmates, teachers, and coaches. There's something to be said for that.

Julia Yeary, MSW, Consultant with ZERO TO THREE Military Projects, Wife and Mother From top to bottom we are a military family. We see things through the lens of military culture. When we hear about conflicts in current events or the drawdown of the Department of Defense budget, we think: "What does that mean for our military family?" "What does it mean for potential stress on our military families?" "Will there be more deployments?"

There is pride in being a military family. I believe we are more conscious of our patriotism. When our kids hear the National Anthem playing, they immediately stand at attention, hands on their hearts. It has meaning to all of us about the sacrifice of others.

My children always went to schools with civilian and military children. In the morning school routine for a DODEA school, everyone stands for the Pledge of Allegiance and National Anthem. When we moved away from a military installation my daughter's homeroom teacher would not make kids stand. My daughter did. Other kids kept talking and doing what they were doing. I don't focus on what the others aren't doing and get upset, instead it makes me proud of my daughter. She expressed the values and beliefs I hoped she would have learned growing up in our family.

Our transition to the civilian world happened in stages. For me the hardest transition was when we moved off base to outside Chicago. Lon was still in the military but we were no longer surrounded by deploying families. I went from being super-involved to not knowing anyone at my husband's work. So I got involved in my children's schools.

By the time he had retired, 6 years later, I was adjusted. I think I also have the benefit that the work I do professionally is working with military families. It's something I think about all the time: How can we create a community, military and civilian, which focuses on fully supporting active duty service members and veterans? This book you are writing is a step in that direction.

My husband was a Colonel when he retired in 2008. The economy had tanked and he had to find a civilian job. His buddies who got out earlier had their pick of jobs. Not having a job waiting for him as he left the service was very hard.

There are so many little things people may not even think about in the transition from active duty to veteran. Things that are simple when you are used to them can be difficult. For example: What do you wear to work? At first my husband had only one suit. I had to talk him into getting others.

He had to cope with a whole different way of operating in the work place. Marines have this sense of a bigger-than-life mission and purpose. Everyone is on board and everyone works until the job is done. It's not the same in the civilian world.

In the civilian world things are much more process oriented. It was a shock for him. In the military my husband was in charge of moving people and equipment across the world. That was easier for him than when his office moved to a new building at work in the same parking lot. They had to have a month of talking with everyone involved and letting them express their feelings about the change before they could move everyone to the new building. My husband just didn't understand why this would be important.

When he comes home stressed, it is hard for the whole family. I'm a social worker and am glad I have my professional skills. I can see how families struggle.

He's been out now for 6 years and he's getting used to it. At the same time he says, "If I could put a uniform back on, I wouldn't hesitate. I'd do it in a heartbeat."

Jackie Yeary, Digital Outreach and Communications Coordinator at Ocean Conservancy, 23 years old, Daughter   My transition to civilian life happened gradually. I grew up living on base or near to a base. My dad was CO of a helicopter squadron. We lived far away from my grandparents but the young pilots would come over to celebrate holidays. The military was my extended family.

The first piece of the transition for me was not being so tied into the military world. When I was 11, we moved to Great Lake's Naval Base. It was my first time living off a Marine Base. We made friends but they weren't always part of the military.

I was a junior in high school when Dad retired. His first job required him to fly to DC on Monday and back home Friday. It caused a lot of tension for me. For example, I would have school plays, and was frustrated that he couldn't make it. Sometimes, if I got into trouble, he'd get upset—even if I had smoothed things over with my mom. He wasn't around to see how the situation had been resolved, and I often felt unfairly punished. [So, sometimes veterans still aren't around their families even after leaving the military.]

He didn't like his first job and found a new one in Madison, Wisconsin. My parents moved there 10 days before I left for college. Transitions are hard enough for college freshmen, but this made it even more difficult. When I went home for breaks, I was going home to a house that wasn't mine. I would see photos of my high school friends hanging out together, but they were too far away for me to visit frequently.

I know Dad is having trouble with transition. His dissatisfaction affects his moods and the family. He is trying to make the best of it but it is difficult and I know he gets frustrated. My dad is a very hard worker. He wants to do the best job he can. It's an attitude that led him to excel in the military world. He's had to deal with many people in the civilian world who don't pull their weight, but there is nothing he can do.

My dad is a private person. When I call him, even if it's only 10 minutes, I try to let him know that even though I'm far away, I am thinking about and care about him. We both like photography and I often send him photos and a note telling him about my latest projects.

My brother is now a freshmen in college. He's focused on friends and school. I don't think he has super strong memories of living on base. I think he and my parents have the usual teens-and-parents tension. When my dad has a bad day I don't think my brother attributes it to the transition.

Commitment and sacrifice are values instilled in me as a kid. I can't say if they come from the military or my parents, but it's probably a combination of the two. I have some understanding of the bond between people in the military so I know it must be difficult for my dad not to be part of it any longer.

LA Yeary, High School Student, Son   *There was definitely a transition. It's different to have my dad home consistently. I enjoy it. The first year he was commuting a lot but now we're all settled down as a family.*

When I was really young and dad was gone a lot, it was Christmas morning whenever he came in the door. Now that he comes in the door every night, we still treasure him. It's a gift to have some consistency—to have both your parents home. It's easier on my mom. It makes everything smoother.

I'm a go-with-the-flow person. I think having a military family teaches you to transition well. In the Marine Corps you move every 3 years. I didn't get the moving around my sister got. But still, the military teaches you to be adaptable. You learn to appreciate what you have now and to enjoy where you are going next.

Being part of a military family comes up early in new friendships, when you are getting to know someone and explaining your philosophy of life. Then your friendships move from there. My friends have been here their whole lives. They don't appreciate what they have here and are not as willing to explore something in new places.

I have two friends going to boot camp in San Diego after high school. I think it is partly my dad's influence. I'm considering joining the military but I want to go to college first and see how things work out. If I don't get a job, the military is a great option. You get leadership opportunities you can't get anywhere else.

INTRODUCTION

Nearly 9% of U.S. adults aged 17 and older, or approximately 21.3 million Americans, are veterans (National Center for Veterans Analysis and Statistics [NCVAS], 2014). While the number of family members of veterans is unknown, if we consider veterans' parents, partners, children, grandchildren, and extended family members, we can assume a substantial percentage of the American population is part of a veteran family (U.S. Department of Veteran Affairs, 2013a).

Because we have more data about veterans than their families, this chapter will address the lives of veteran families by exploring who veterans are, what unique risks they may face due to their military service, what challenges they face as they transition from the military to civilian life, and how they experience civilian life. Within each cohort described in the following pages, we pay special attention to an identified unique risk, consequence, or challenge of post-military life. These details help us better understand the personal, familial, social, historical, and medical ecologies experienced by veterans and their families. These special foci include experiences of prisoners of war, hospice and palliative care, homelessness, chronic multi-symptom illness, and veterans courts.

Annual reports produced by the National Center for Veterans Analysis and Statistics (NCVAS) are referred to for veteran specific information, such as that in Table 10.1. For data that focus on family life, we turn to the same national and representative data set used by NCVAS to extract variables that capture important information about veterans' lives, including household information, marital status, children in the household, employment, and disability status. The data set used for NCVAS reports and in our descriptions of veteran families in this chapter are derived from the American Community Survey (ACS) 2012 Data Set and all statistics for these groups were computed through the Integrated Public Use Microdata Series at the Minnesota Population Center, University of Minnesota

TABLE 10.1   Marital Status by Era of Veteran Population (FY 2012)

Marital Status		WWII	Korean Conflict	Vietnam	Pre-9/11	Post-9/11
				Era of Combat Experience		
Married	Men	58%	70%	71%	68%	55%
	Women	18%	36%	48%	54%	46%
Separated	Men	<1%	1%	2%	3%	4%
	Women	<1%	<1%	2%	3%	4%
Divorced	Men	5%	8%	17%	16%	11%
	Women	12%	16%	29%	26%	17%
Widowed	Men	34%	18%	5%	1%	<1%
	Women	64%	41%	11%	2%	1%
Never Married	Men	3%	3%	6%	12%	31%
	Women	5%	7%	10%	15%	33%

Source: Compiled from the Integrated Public Use Microdata Series. (2014). *American Community Survey, FY 2012.* Retrieved from www.usa.ipums.org/usa/.

(www.usa.ipums.org/usa/). The ACS is a continuous, annual national survey administered through the Bureau of the Census. The VA uses ACS data to determine how to allocate, develop, and maintain resources for educational, employment, and health-care programming to support the veteran population.

FIVE ERAS OF COMBAT VETERANS

Veterans alive today served during five conflict eras: World War II (WWII), the Korean Conflict, the Vietnam Era, Pre-9/11, and Post-9/11, which continues to the present time. For purposes of VA benefit administration, the Pre-9/11 era of service includes Gulf War I (August 2, 1990 to September 11, 2001) and multiple other deployments to conflict zones (Military Health History Pocket Card for Clinicians: Gulf War, 2013). Interspersed throughout these eras of conflict are stretches of peacetime service; approximately one quarter of both male and female veterans, the second largest veteran cohort for both sexes, report having served during peacetime only (NCVAS, 2014). Data from the 2012 ACS indicate that there are significant gender differences by cohort (see Figure 10.1). The largest cohort of living male veterans served in Vietnam, while the largest cohort of living female veterans served since 9/11 (U.S. Department of Veterans Affairs, 2014e).

Data from the 2012 ACS indicated that there were an estimated 21.3 million veterans, aged 17 years and older, living in the United States and Puerto Rico at that time. Of these, 1.6 million were women (NCVAS, 2014). The 2010 ACS data (U.S. Census Bureau, 2011) indicated that 1.3 million veterans (~ 17%) served in multiple wars, with the largest living cohort serving in two wars: Pre-9/11 to post-9/11 (n=837,000). Veterans who served in three wars (WWII, Korea, and Vietnam) numbered 54,000.

The median age of male veterans was 64 years while the median age of female veterans was 48 years (NCVAS, 2014). This age difference reflects both the 1948 action by Congress that officially made women part of the military on a permanent basis, and more recent changes in recruiting women after the 1973 shift to the all-volunteer force. Veterans as a group differ from their civilian counterparts along some specific economic measures of well-being. Both male and female veterans who were in full-time, year-round employment

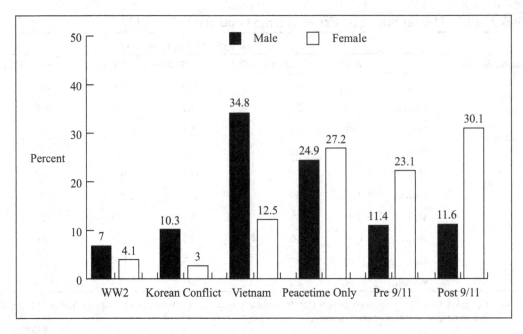

Figure 10.1   Era of service by gender. Period of service dates: peacetime only: January 1947 to June 1950, February 1955 to July 1964, and May 1975 to July 1990; Pre 9/11: August 1990 to August 2001; Post 9/11: September 2001 to present. (Veterans who served in multiple eras are included in the category of their most recent service).

Source: Data compiled from National Center for Veterans Analysis and Statistics, Department of Veterans Affairs (2014). Profile of veterans: 2012 Data from the American Community Survey. (p. 14.) Washington, DC: Author. Retrieved from National Center for Veterans Analysis and Statistics, Department of Veterans Affairs (2014). Profile of Veterans: 2012 Data from the American Community Survey. Washington, DC: Author.

had higher median earnings and personal income than their non-veteran counterparts. Veterans were also more likely to be insured than non-veterans.

As you learned in Chapter 2, the Department of Defense uses DEERS (Defense Enrollment Eligibility Reporting System) to define family members who meet criteria for military-based services and benefits. DEERS affords both researchers and practitioners the ability to identify military families and their needs, and determine whether these needs are similar to non-military families or unique to military life. The Department of Veterans Affairs (VA) does not use this same system nor does the VA keep track of family members with the same kind of attention and detail required to be able to provide for active duty and reserve families. However, the VA is responsible for the administration of veteran benefits, some of which are transferable to eligible family members, such as spouses, children, and survivors. Thus, data exist regarding usage of benefits by veterans and their eligible family members. These data will be described in the upcoming section on veteran benefits.

Marital status gives a basic foundation to understand the close relationships in which veterans today live. Table 10.1 shows the diversity of marital status for each cohort of combat veterans. In each era there are differences between male and female veterans regarding their relationship status, with men in each era more likely to report being married than their female counterparts and women reporting divorce and widowhood more than men. Consider the martial status of each cohort as you read information about veterans in each group below.

World War II Veterans and Families

Tom Brokaw, an American television journalist, coined the term "The Greatest Generation" to describe the men and women who served either in the military or on the home front for the U.S. during World War II (Brokaw, 1998). Sixteen million men and 350,000 women served in the U.S. military during WWII. This generation grew up during the Great Depression and the Dust Bowl, the most significant drought known to the country at that time.

In 2012, this cohort numbered 1,604,205 individuals (approximately 10% of the total who served in WWII), ranging from 81 years to 95 years or older. Thirteen percent of WWII veterans reported living with one of their children, but the data do not indicate why. For example, these households could represent veterans caring for a disabled adult child or could also represent a multigenerational household where a veteran parent has moved in with an independent adult child and potentially that adult child's spouse and children.

Approximately 14% of WWII veterans reported having some level of service-connected disability. It is not possible (from the ACS data) to know if these disabilities were directly related to WWII service or service in a subsequent conflict (e.g. Korean War), or sustained in a non-deployment setting. However, the Veterans' Health Administration (VHA) reports that the signature physical injuries of WWII included cold injury, such as hypothermia and frostbite; chemical warfare (e.g., mustard gas); chemical exposure in the workplace (e.g., asbestos, paints, industrial chemicals, DDT); and exposure to nuclear weapons and waste (both testing and cleanup) (Military Health History Pocket Card for Clinicians: World War II, 2013). This first generation of **atomic veterans** (veterans exposed to radiation while assigned to the Pacific Theatre during WWII or Korea or exposed to nuclear tests) included not only those working at U.S. test sites but also both men and women **prisoners of war** (**POWs:** military personnel who were captured by opposing military forces) in the Pacific theatre, who were used as labor in the cleanup of Nagasaki and Hiroshima. At the same time, WWII veterans were the first to benefit from the burgeoning development of antibiotics in the 1930s and other significant advances in medicine, including wound treatment and immunizations against highly contagious diseases that flourished on the battlefronts.

The men who were drafted for military service in WWII ranged in age from late adolescence to middle adulthood. At least one study has tested whether or not age at mobilization affected their work and family trajectories after the war (Hastings, 1991). Using data from the Stanford-Terman Longitudinal Study, which followed high ability children in California from 1922 through 1986, Hastings examined the life trajectories of over 800 men. He was particularly interested in the effects of a combination of life factors including age at mobilization, combat experience and rank, emotional health, and lifetime earnings. Hastings hypothesized that there were differential risks due to age. Using life course theory, he proposed that younger age could increase the likelihood of entering as an enlisted service member, serving in combat, and entering with less maturity for coping with the stressors of military life. However, one could also argue that younger age could indicate potential for greater flexibility in adapting to adverse experiences and opportunities for growth. Concomitantly, mid-life mobilization into WWII could have significant disruptive effects, in both work and family life, as men experienced extended and unanticipated absences from their careers and family roles. But, mid-life mobilization could have a protective aspect due to greater maturity and coping skills. Hastings' study found that age at mobilization in combination with officer rank was a significant protective factor in postwar mental health for both young and midlife aged men. This study also demonstrated that there was no significant relative earnings disadvantage linked to age of mobilization; rather, mental health after military service was a significant risk factor for lost earnings in the post-war lives of this population.

For decades now, WWII veterans and their families have been facing the challenges of aging, the long-term effects of injuries and exposures, and loss. Like Dr. LaRossa in his interview below, family members, including grandchildren and great-grandchildren, may wish they could know more about their veteran's military experiences while others will have had extensive conversations. Some, WWII veterans are beginning to share their memories with their families and others, as Margaret Von Steinen describes in Chapter 13.

Families of the WWII era may have suffered alone as their veteran battled undiagnosed or untreated PTSD or an mTBI, alcohol abuse, depression, or anxiety. As these veterans have aged into geriatric care and needs, sequelae from injuries and from traumatic experiences sustained as part of their service may manifest in new ways that impact daily life. Spouses and adult children and grandchildren may accompany their WWII veteran when seeking treatment in civilian or VA medical facilities. These family members may become active caregivers for their veteran as health declines. For example, the VA notes that WWII, Korean, and Vietnam era conflict veterans are susceptible to common diseases associated with aging: cardiovascular diseases, cancers, and dementias including Alzheimer's (Military Health History Pocket Card for Clinicians: World War II, 2013).

Spotlight on Research

WORLD WAR II IN THE LIVES OF FATHERS AND THEIR FAMILIES

World War II was a momentous event. It transformed the globe. I wanted to better understand what it meant and embarked on a study that culminated in **Of War and Men: World War II in the Lives of Fathers and Their Families** (University of Chicago Press, 2011).

Too often we have a tendency to simplify things and not appreciate complexities. Yet only by understanding the diversity of people's lives can we understand the meaning and impact of war. How do we as individuals open our eyes to this? Putting war in a historical perspective helps us to recognize and appreciate its myriad effects.

To understand these effects I pored through countless primary and secondary sources: letters, books, magazines, comic strips, old television shows, and boxes of records stored in places including the Library of Congress and National Archives. Historical work is like paleontology, putting together bone fragments to create a picture of an entire dinosaur. As I delved into questions, I continued to formulate new ones—even about my life.

People may assume that everyone benefitted from the economic boom of war. America was in the grips of the Great Depression and the war brought many men—and women—jobs. Yet we cannot understand the culture and conduct of fatherhood until we acknowledge that the impact of the war was not the same for everyone. African American men were not allowed to enlist at first. Japanese American men and their families were forced to leave their homes and were imprisoned, then later unable to return to jobs they had or to find new ones. When these men eventually were allowed to serve they served with distinction.

We refer to the 16 million American soldiers in World War II as part of the Greatest Generation and honor them. Yet each soldier was an individual with his or her own experience. The same is true for service members today. When a service member in fatigues comes up the escalator at the Atlanta airport people applaud. Yet each who is so honored has had his or her own experience in the military and may feel differently, and even ambivalently, about this public recognition.

My father served as an Air Corps radioman during World War II. When I was a boy, I asked him, "Did you ever kill anybody?" He and many others never answered this question. For some the idea of killing another was too horrible to think or talk about. Others may have been unwilling to say anything because they were ashamed to admit they had not seen combat and never fired a weapon.

When people talk about fathers in war, they frequently talk about the men who are serving and who are fathers. There is a tendency not to talk much about the fathers of the soldiers. There usually seems to be the assumption that the service member's mother is the one who needs to be nurtured and that the father's job is to nurture her. We should also recognize, however, the sadness that men felt and feel. This includes men who were so grief stricken that they had heart attacks and were debilitated by the loss of their child. It also includes men who, following the death of one son, marched another down to the recruiting office. As leaders of tomorrow, students need to appreciate that people caught in the throes of the same event can have very different experiences.

I wish my parents were alive when I began this work. It wasn't that I didn't ask them questions about World War II but that the questions were too narrow. By familiarizing ourselves with the complexities of history we can come up with questions and discoveries about our opportunities and struggles and about how we have become who we are.

Ralph LaRossa, PhD
Professor Emeritus of Sociology, Georgia State University

Prisoners of War (POWs)

Boehnlein and Sparr (1993) noted that there are well-documented, long-term psychological health effects for American former prisoners of war (POWs) who experienced imprisonment during WWII, Korea, and Vietnam. Identified psychological challenges include PTSD, interpersonal detachment, and difficulties in emotional expression. National holidays, such as Memorial Day, Veterans Day, and D-Day, as well as anniversary dates of capture and liberation can be triggers for anxiety and/or avoidance. Each of these issues can have adverse impacts on interpersonal and familial relationships. In describing the processes of change in their 2-year group therapy intervention with a small group of WWII ex-POWs, Boehnlein and Sparr reported that both the veterans and their spouses expressed an improved sense of well-being and social functioning, even though there continued to be clinically significant symptomatology 1 year into the treatment process. The authors give much discussion to working with older survivors who have been living with psychological injury for 45 to 50 years. In their closing remarks, the authors call on professionals in geriatric and VA treatment settings to be cognizant of potential, unspoken psychological needs of this population. Further, they express that it is never too late to intervene therapeutically to help older survivors resolve past trauma.

As part of the Veterans Health Initiative, the VHA developed a continuing education study module to assist clinicians and helping professionals in recognizing connections between POW experiences and potential long-term physical and psychological effects (Skelton, III, 2002). As you read earlier in this section, WWII veterans faced a variety of serious health risks as part of their service. Prisoners of war encountered additional injuries to physical and psychological health. There are differences by ex-POW group within the two main theatres of war in WWII and between eras of conflict. These differences are attributed to location of internment, length of internment, and whether or not the capturing military forces were acting on behalf of a government that had ratified and abided by the 1929 Geneva Prisoners of War Convention (www.icrc.org). This convention outlined expectations for the conditions under which POWs were held, including nutrition, housing, use as labor, visitation by the International Red Cross, and eventual repatriation.

WWII veterans who served in the Pacific Theatre have the highest mortality rate of any ex-POW group and this group also had the highest mortality rate while in captivity (37% vs. 1% in the European Theatre). This group includes the largest proportion of women veterans, mostly nurses, who were held as POWs for 4 years in the Philippines. WWII veterans who were POWs in the European Theatre were interned for a shorter period of time, on average, than those in the Pacific Theatre (less than 1 year versus 3 to 4 years, respectively).

World War II is not the only conflict in which there were POWs. Prior conflicts of the American Civil War and World War I, as well as the later conflicts of Korea, Vietnam, Gulf War I, and Post-9/11 have also resulted in varying numbers of service members being captured and interned as part of the conflict. POWs from the Korean Conflict had the second highest mortality rate while imprisoned (38%) and, as veterans, continue to have the second highest post-internment death rate among ex-POW cohorts. This group has a significantly higher percentage of service-connected disability, approximately 60%, compared with their non-POW Korean Conflict counterparts at 5%. Korean Conflict POWs comprised the youngest cohort with an average age of 23 when captured, and as a group they averaged just over 2 years in captivity. They experienced similar, extremely harsh treatment as WWII Pacific Theatre ex-POWS during their internment, partially due to the fact that Korea did not recognize the then recently updated 1946 Geneva Convention, Article III on the Treatment of Prisoners of War. Additionally, POWs of the Korean Conflict were the first to endure the extensive practice of brainwashing techniques in addition to extreme deprivation and physical abuse (Skelton, III, 2002).

Vietnam War POWs were the oldest, on average, at age of capture (30 years old), partially due to the ranks and specializations of a significant number of downed aviators. The average length of internment for this group is significantly longer than all previously described cohorts, with an average of 5 years. Reports of physical and psychological torture, including extended confinement in 4x4 foot cubes, are commonplace within this ex-POW cohort. As a result of their confinement, virtually all Vietnam War ex-POWs have service-connected disabilities and their levels of disability rating are higher overall as compared with their non-POW veteran colleagues.

American service members have also been captured during campaigns in both the Pre-9/11 and Post- 9/11 eras albeit at much reduced rates. Overall, former POWs have a higher mortality and morbidity rate when compared to their fellow veterans who were never captured.

Korean Conflict Veterans and Families

The Korean Conflict denotes the first major conflict for the U.S. in the Cold War Era and lasted from 1950 to 1953. The U.S. participation was part of a United Nations effort to stem the spread of Communist ideology and politics from the USSR to neighboring countries in Asia (Hickey, 1999). As this conflict began only 5 years after the end of World War II, many of the military tactics, weapons, and risks were similar across these two eras; 5.7 million Americans served during this war.

By 2012, there were slightly fewer than 2.3 million living veterans of the Korean Conflict, of which 98% were men. The age range of this cohort was 73 years to 95 years or older at the time of reporting. Over two-thirds of this cohort (68%) reported that they had married only once, with another 20% marrying twice, and these rates were similar for both male and female veterans. Overall, approximately 11% of all Korean Conflict veterans reported living with an adult child in their household, although that also differed by whether the veteran was male (11%) or female (16%).

Approximately 13% of Korean Conflict veterans reported some level of service-connected disability in 2012, among whom the largest reporting group (4%) identified having a fairly low disability rating of 10–20%. The signature injuries of the Korean Conflict are quite similar to those identified with WWII. Risks included exposures to Agent Orange (a chemical defoliation spray used to kill off heavy vegetation), other chemical agents, and nuclear weapons. Cold weather injuries accounted for the single largest non-battle injury (16%), largely due to a combination of an extremely harsh winter in 1950–51 and a lack of cold weather gear (Military Health History Pocket Card for Clinicians: Korean War, 2013).

Korean War era veterans and their families are also facing the challenges of aging, and those who sustained cold weather injuries during the war are at elevated risk of long-term consequences that can become more pronounced (Military Health History Pocket Card for Clinicians: Korean War, 2013). For example, nerve damage caused by such injuries can put veterans at higher risk for skin cancer in the previously affected areas and the damage to nerves can progress as other health factors emerge (e.g., aging, diabetes, arthritis, and cold sensitivity). In many cases, these comorbid factors can aggravate each other, leading to significant chronic health challenges.

Veterans as Caregivers

Although the descriptions of each era of combat veterans includes information on service-connected disabilities, most older veterans enjoy good health and have good medical care to help manage acute and chronic health issues. Veterans are important members of family systems and as such, may fulfill roles as caregivers for their own loved ones who experience both chronic and acute illnesses. The veterans' experiences in the military may offer protection against the stressors of caregiving. Using data collected in 2011 for the National Health and Resilience in Veterans Study, Monin, Levy, and Pietrzak (2014) found that approximately one in five veterans are serving as caregivers for family members. Their study aimed to add to the caregiving literature by examining whether or not veterans' combat exposure affected their perceptions of caregiving stress and if grandparenting, as a particular form of caregiving, was more rewarding than other types of caregiving. The sample in this study was overwhelmingly male (97%) and married (86%). Approximately 50% of veteran caregivers in this study reported caring for their spouse, with neighbors(s)/friend(s) and grandchildren as the next two most common groups receiving care (14% and 12%, respectively). Analyses showed that combat exposure was associated with lower caregiving strain in this population. Monin and colleagues connected this finding to a body of literature suggesting that earlier trauma or stress may facilitate greater resilience when facing later life stressors. They also suggest that further study of veterans who provide caregiving may expand our knowledge about combat-related resilience and **post-traumatic growth**, or positive personal changes from dealing with trauma and its effects (Tedeschi & McNally, 2011). Analyses also indicated that grandparenting was a particularly rewarding type of caregiving relative to other caregiving relationships, despite the increased physical demands of grandparenting care. Overall, the veteran caregiver population mirrored many characteristics of non-veteran caregivers in acknowledging the physical (39%) and emotional (53%) strain of this work, while still viewing the work of caregiving as rewarding (67%).

Vietnam War Veterans and Families

U.S. military involvement in Vietnam spanned from 1964 to 1973 and this particular conflict highlighted a significant change in war tactics from previous eras of warfare. The North Vietnamese leadership shifted their primary mode of military engagement from standard battlefield tactics to ambushes and short attacks within densely covered forests and swamps and high use of hidden land mines, booby-traps, and tunnels, also known as guerilla tactics. This shift created poorly defined fighting fronts and challenged traditional responses by U.S. military personnel. The Vietnam War is also significant in American history as this was a war that started off with strong support that declined drastically as U.S. casualties increased and taxes to support the war also increased without a corresponding sense of making progress toward success. Returning service members reported that they were not welcomed back and that their military service was equated with support for the increasingly unpopular war. The changing sentiment of the American public for this particular conflict included pressure to drop the draft system of military conscription. As you may recall from the first chapter, conscription into military service was used from 1792 through 1973. Ultimately, the Vietnam War is associated with the most significant shift in the organization of the U.S. military: the change to an all-volunteer force.

In 2012, there were 7.3 million living veterans who served in Vietnam, ranging in age from 52 to 94 years old. Approximately 3% (219,841) in this cohort are women. As with previous cohorts, there are significant differences in marital status for male and female Vietnam veterans. Seven percent of female Vietnam veterans live in households with at least one grandchild, while just over 4% of male veterans in this cohort share their household with a grandchild.

Most Vietnam era veterans (80%) do not report having a service-connected disability. Of those who do report having some level of disability, men and women are similar in percentages reporting a low-level disability rating (6.5% men, 5.8% women) and a high-level disability rating (6.5% men, 5.7% women). The signature injuries and risks for this cohort included exposure to chemicals such as Agent Orange and Napalm (a highly flammable petroleum product), skin infections complicated by prolonged exposure to high humidity, and malaria. As described in the section on Prisoners of War, U.S. personnel taken prisoner in the Vietnam War experienced the longest time in captivity and routinely received extremely harsh treatment. Almost all ex-POWs in this cohort have some level of service-connected disability. This is also the first conflict cohort to have exposure conditions recognized by the VA that can pose health risks for their children (Military Health History Pocket Card for Clinicians: Vietnam War, 2014). Specifically, exposure to Agent Orange is linked to higher incidences of spina bifida, a spinal cord malformation that occurs early during fetal development.

Homelessness

According to the National Coalition for Homeless Veterans (2014), approximately 12% of the overall homeless adult population are veterans, who account for 20% of all male homeless persons. Two thirds of homeless veterans served in the military for at least 3 years, and one third served in a war zone. While just over half of homeless veterans are 51 years or older and most of this group served in Vietnam, it is estimated that another 9% of homeless veterans are between the ages of 18 and 30 years. The majority of homeless veterans are men (92%). Multiple factors influence veteran homelessness, including lack of affordable housing, difficulty in securing livable income, and barriers to health care, and each play a significant part in contributing to the risk of homelessness. Veterans may have additional risk factors for experiencing homelessness, including lingering effects of post-traumatic stress and substance misuse, as well as struggling to transfer military occupational skills into the civilian workforce.

The VA has several initiatives to help address the challenges homeless veterans face in establishing safe living quarters, work, and healthcare (see http://www.va.gov/homeless/). These initiatives include a national call center staffed with trained counseling staff, transitional and supported housing, drop-in centers, compensated work therapy for disabled homeless veterans, and special outreach counselors who serve to help connect homeless veterans with their VA benefits. The overall rate of veteran homelessness declined substantially between 2009 and 2013, with an overall reduction of 24% (U.S. Department of Housing and Urban Development, 2014).

Pre-9/11 Gulf War Era Veterans and Families

The Pre-9/11 era of service includes Gulf War I and multiple other deployments to conflict zones. Gulf War I is also known as the First Gulf War, the Persian Gulf War or by its military actions, Operations Desert Shield and Desert Storm. The U.S. military was also involved in several other smaller conflicts, including actions as part of NATO and as support for multiple United Nations peacekeeping exercises. These short-term engagements included deployments and actions in Somalia, Haiti, and the Balkan Peninsula, or the Balkans—Bosnia-Herzegovina, Serbia, and Kosovo.

In 2012, the Pre-9/11 veteran cohort numbered approximately 3.9 million, 14% of whom were women. Of all veterans in this cohort who were married and whose spouse resided with them, slightly fewer than 80% reported having children in their household. Most of these families reported one child (23%), two children (29%), or three children (12%) in their households. Eighteen percent of these families reported having 1–2 children under the age of 5. Veterans of other marital statuses (married with spouse absent, separated, divorced, widowed, or never married/single) also reported having children in their households, although at much lower rates than the married with spouse present group.

The composition of those who served in Gulf War I was unique in many ways to all conflicts prior to this one. It is considered the first significant engagement of U.S. military personnel since the end of the Vietnam War in 1973 and the transition to an all-volunteer force. At the time of their deployment, this cohort of veterans was older and more ethnically diverse than any previous cohorts deployed in the 20th century. More members were women and all members were more likely to be parents than in previous cohorts. Additionally, this conflict represented the first significant activation of both the Reserves and National Guard to active duty (Veterans Health Initiative, 2011).

Gulf War I also signified a major shift in media coverage and technology (Ferrari, 2003). For the first time, there was real-time coverage and broadcasting from the war zone, by multiple outlets until an air raid on Baghdad destroyed the central telephone exchange. CNN was able to continue live broadcasts because they were using a different phone exchange. This live and ongoing coverage brought the war into the living rooms in a different way than previous war coverage. Previously, war coverage had been limited to digest reports on network news broadcasts, and in earlier eras, news reels at movie theatres and radio news updates. The Pentagon issued new rules of reporting owing to the CNN coverage such that mandated reporters had to be escorted by a military affairs officer at all times, all visits had to be approved in advance, and all stories and photographs also had to be approved in advance by military censors. The increase in censorship of information and close monitoring of journalists created a system of reporting that shaped a war narrative closely tied to official military policy. Independent reporting was extremely difficult, forcing journalists and photographers to either heed the new Pentagon rules or risk going out on their own without protection.

Chronic Multisymptom Illness

Although Gulf War I lasted less than one year, in its aftermath service members from the U.S., Canada, and Great Britain began reporting a range of health problems that were baffling to health-care providers. The variety of symptoms defied attempts to be organized into a concrete diagnosis or to be tied to a particular exposure event. For example, service members reported fatigue, headaches, joint pain, indigestion, insomnia, dizziness, respiratory disorders, and memory problems (Blanchard et al., 2006). While some service members began having health problems during deployment, more service members reported problems shortly after returning from deployment. This constellation of health problems is referred to in the military and veteran medical communities as **chronic multisymptom illness (CMI)** (Lange, McAndrew, Ashford, Reinhard, Peterson, & Helmer, 2013; Veterans Health Initiative, 2011). Although this medical challenge has been labeled in the media as Gulf War Syndrome, it is an inaccurate and misleading description. In fact, since the U.S. Civil War, there has been documentation of post-conflict increases in non-specific, multi-symptom illnesses for each major conflict and this documentation extends to other military forces since the late 1800s (Greenberg & Wessely, 2008).

While it has taken several years of searching for answers to and working with veterans who have CMI, the VA now "presumes that certain medically unexplained symptoms and illnesses are related to Gulf War service" (Military Health History Pocket Card for Clinicians: Gulf War, 2013). The VA has established a Gulf War Registry and Gulf War Veterans Helpline to document and track otherwise unexplained illnesses within this cohort.

Most members of this cohort of veterans are healthy; but those who report health problems within the parameters of CMI often highlight the challenges of living with a chronic, treatment resistant, and many times debilitating set of health issues. Within the ACS 2012 data set, fully 75% of Gulf War I veterans report no service-connected disability. Of the 25% who do report some level of service-connected disability, 9% report a lower level **disability rating** of 10–20% while 5% report a rating of 70% or greater. Unique health risks for the Pre-9/11 cohort of veterans include chemical weapon exposure, airborne pollution from open pit fires and bombed chemical plants, depleted uranium, immunizations, parasitic infections, and reproductive health issues (Military Health History Pocket Card for Clinicians: Gulf War, 2013).

Post-9/11 Veterans and Families

The newest veteran generation has served since September 2001. As a group, these veterans are younger, with higher rates of service for women than in any previous war era. Using 2012 ACS data for veterans aged between 18 and 55 years, 49% of Post-9/11 veterans ranged in age from 23 to 32 years old. Another 40% of Post-9/11 veterans were between the ages of 33 and 55 years old. The most common age of the Post-9/11 veteran group was 28 years (5.4%) for men and 29 years (6.2%) for women.

Of all the cohorts described in this chapter, the Post-9/11 men and women are the most similar in percentages reporting the range of marital statuses. Of those who were married and whose spouse resided with them, 69% reported having one to three children in their household. Those who were married but whose spouse was not present in the household were significantly less likely to have any children in their household (80%, no children; 18% one to three children). Post-9/11 veterans who identified as separated or divorced were most likely to report having no children in their household (73%), followed by having one child or two children (14% and 9%, respectively) living with them. However, these data only indicate children within the veteran's household, not children who might reside with an ex-spouse or other family member.

Eighteen percent of veterans in this data group reported some level of VA service-connected disability. The VHA guide for clinicians notes that there are several health risks for veterans who served in the Post-9/11 era (Military Health History Pocket Card for Clinicians: OIF/OEF, 2013, retrieved September 30, 2014). These include animal bites/rabies, blast injuries, sensory damage (e.g. vision, hearing), skin issues, reproductive health issues, parasitic and drug-resistant infections, TBI, and mTBI.

Veterans Courts

Veterans courts are a recent example of a community response to returning veterans with substance misuse or mental health issues that land them in the civilian legal system. The first veterans court was established in 2008 in Buffalo, NY and has served as a model for replication and refinement as the concept has spread across the U.S. (Russell, 2009). These courts are designed after drug treatment and mental health treatment courts, which offer alternatives to incarceration and include highly structured treatment plans to address the underlying problems. These types of alternative programs are part of a movement called "problem-solving justice" (Kravetz, 2012). As Judge Karen Khalil describes below, veterans must meet eligibility criteria to be placed in this diversion program and must maintain compliance with the court-ordered treatment plan.

While veterans courts are a recent development in the civilian legal system, there is a vigorous and ongoing set of discussions to shape the scope of what types of offenses and degree of severity (of substance abuse and/or mental health needs) courts can and should address. Most veterans courts limit the offenses to misdemeanors and non-violent felonies and do not try to address treatment for veterans with severe mental illness. Veteran mentors are an important part of the veteran court program. These mentors provide support to the veteran offender within the courtroom and throughout the judicial process (Moore, 2012). Training of mentors varies significantly at this point. Some suggestions for identifying court mentors include seeking mentors who have been successful in working through the veteran court system and who may have had to address their substance abuse or mental health challenges, as well as intentionally seeking female mentors to work with female offenders who enter the veteran court system. As this mentoring occurs within a specific legal context, explicit knowledge of when and how a mentor needs to report a potential violation of the program is important to work effectively within the intent of the program.

One of the current dialogues about the appropriateness of veterans courts concerns the intersection of intimate partner violence with mental health or substance use issues. Kravetz (2012) argues against adjudicating domestic violence/IPV cases with a mental health or substance use element through this alternative program, suggesting these courts do not have access to resources and professionals with expertise in both combat-related trauma and interpersonal violence and it may place the victim in a more precarious position within the justice system (e.g., Justice for whom? Victim or perpetrator?).

Voices From the Frontline

THE IMPORTANCE OF VETERANS' TREATMENT COURTS

The first veterans treatment courts in the country were started in Buffalo, New York; Tulsa, Oklahoma; and Santa Ana, California. Like the judges from these courts, I started recognizing a need for a veterans court in my community when faced with a few cases on my criminal docket involving veterans and active military personnel who were home on leave. The Seventeenth District Veterans Court program was dedicated in Redford Township, Michigan, in November, 2011, after months of research and planning. It was the fourth veterans court in the state at the time I began the program.

The Seventeenth District Veterans Court adheres to the Ten Key Components of Veterans Treatment Courts, which follows the U.S. Department of Justice guidelines for Drug Courts, with modifications for veterans. These principles are said to provide the foundation for a successful program. We have found this to be true and many of the veterans who have completed the rigorous probation sentence have said it has been the best thing that has happened in their lives.

While current statistics speak for themselves, we all know that veterans in our communities are facing alarming suicide rates, joblessness, homelessness, moral injury, post-traumatic stress injuries, and traumatic brain injuries. There are so many who have returned with life altering physical and emotional scars and the veterans are not the only persons being affected. The family members of these veterans also face the consequences of their service-related issues.

Our program, like many, is successfully providing treatment and compassion to those who have served our country and are struggling in the criminal justice system and often in other ways. We offer a unique collaboration between numerous agencies to provide the necessary assistance to our veteran participants and their families. The connection between the court and Veterans Administration helps provide veterans in the program with enhanced access to benefits they are entitled to as a result of their service to our country. Veteran mentors are assigned to the participants to give them an opportunity to connect to someone else who can serve as a friend or buddy. We even have utilized the services of a treatment dog which makes our court only the second in the country to do so.

This treatment court program also serves to protect the public, reduce participant contact with the criminal justice system, reduce the costs associated with criminal case processing and re-arrest, and introduces participants to an ongoing process of recovery.

Our program consists of four phases and is incentive laden. As participants progress through the program they are rewarded for their achievements. A graduation ceremony is held to honor the veterans who successfully fulfill the requirements of the program.

The men and women who serve in the United States Armed Forces have in many ways put their lives on the line for this country. In my opinion, it is our responsibility to embrace these wounded warriors, guide them toward recovery, and help them regain control of their lives. We are achieving that goal through this program.

The Honorable Karen Khalil, Presiding Judge
Seventeenth District Veterans Court, Redford Township, Michigan

Understanding Veterans Across Generations

As you can see, there are both common and unique characteristics between generations of veteran families. The era or eras in which one has served creates an important sociohistorical context for understanding roles and expectations of service members, their family members (particularly their romantic partners and children), and the role of community support for the conflict and peacekeeping efforts in which they were involved. Each era also has important distinguishing features that should affect our understanding of the physical and psychological challenges these veterans face. As war technology changed, so did the types of threats faced on the battlefields, frontlines, and auxiliary posts. Concomitantly, both life-saving medical innovations and our understanding of psychological threats, needs, and care have changed significantly in response to the life-changing experiences of war for service members and veterans.

The medical and psychological disciplines continue to evolve to better meet the needs of both these populations. Table 10.2 highlights the signature injuries, both physical and psychological, for American service members in all of the major conflicts beginning with the American Civil War through to the current post-9/11 era. The concepts that attempt to capture the distress service members experienced have evolved over time. As noted in the table, these concepts have, at times, been used to describe both elements of physical and psychological injury. Our current understanding of TBI and PTSD now take into account the potential overlap in symptomology that complicates accurate diagnoses and treatment. It is likely that these concepts will continue to evolve as we learn more about the interactive influences of psychological and physical trauma.

TABLE 10.2 Mass U.S. Military Mobilizations: Civil War through Post-9/11

Conflict Duration (U.S. Involvement)	American Civil War (1861–65)	World War I: The Great War (1917–18)	World War II (1941–45) AND Korean Conflict (1950–53)	Vietnam (1959/64–75)	Operation Desert Shield/ Storm (1990–91)	War in Afghanistan: OEF (2001–) / War in Iraq: OIF/OND (2003–11)
Documented signature or common physical injuries and health risks	• Amputations • Wound infection • Infectious diseases • Malnutrition	• Chemical weapon injuries: Mustard gas • Concussive head injuries	• Cold injury • Chemical warfare experiments • Nuclear weapon exposure[1]	• Herbicide and chemical weapon injuries[2],[3]– Agent Orange, Napalm • Hepatitis C • Malaria	• Chemical weapon exposure[4]. [5]– Open pit fires, bombed chemical plants, depleted uranium • Immunizations • Reproductive health issues	• IED/Blast injuries[6]; [7]–Amputations, groin, spinal, and sensory damage • mTBI • TBI
Documented signature or common psychological injuries and health risks	Melancholy nostalgia[8]	Combat neuroses[9]	Combat fatigue transitioning to use of term "Combat stress reaction"	Combat stress reaction	• PTSD • Depression • Anxiety	• PTSD • Depression • Anxiety disorders
Evolving concepts in helping literature	Soldier's heart (both physical and psychological usage)	Shell shock (both physical and psychological usage)	Shell shock (now more linked with psychological injury) Postconcussional syndrome (linked to blast proximity)	Post traumatic stress disorder (after 1980, when this entered the DSMIII)	• Post traumatic stress disorder • Chronic, multisymptom illness	• Polytrauma • Invisible wounds • Combat-affected families • Secondary trauma/ PTSD
Emerging and identified public health concerns				Veteran homelessness	Multi-symptom, Unexplained illness	• Moral injury • Military sexual trauma • Suicide • Veteran employment

1 Military Health History Pocket Card for Clinicians: World War II, downloaded 3/25/14 from: http://www.va.gov/oaa/pocketcard/worldwar.asp?p=6

2

3 Military Health History Pocket Card for Clinicians: Vietnam, downloaded 3/25/14 from: http://www.va.gov/oaa/pocketcard/vietnam.asp?p=3

4

5 Military Health History Pocket Card for Clinicians: Vietnam, downloaded 3/25/14 from: http://www.va.gov/oaa/pocketcard/vietnam.asp?p=2

6

7 Military Health History Pocket Card for Clinicians: OEF/OIF/OND, downloaded 3/25/14 from: http://www.va.gov/oaa/pocketcard/oefoif.asp?p=1

8 Dr. Matthew Friedman, downloaded 3/25/14 from: http://www.pbs.org/wgbh/pages/frontline/shows/heart/themes/shellshock.html

9 Jones, E., Fear, N. T., & Wessely, S. (2007). Shell shock and mild traumatic brain injury. American Journal of Psychiatry, 164, 1641-1645.

IMPLICATIONS OF RETIREMENT OR
SEPARATION FOR VETERAN FAMILIES

Separating from the military by completing a contract, resigning a commission, or retiring has implications for family members. Some service members choose to separate while others must leave due to downsizing or injury. Although we have less data and research on veteran family members, it is prudent to "recognize that we are at the beginning, not the end, of the post-war lifetimes for the new generation of veterans and their families" (MacDermid Wadsworth, 2013, p. 420).

Family members may have a range of emotions and even conflicting emotions when service members separate, such as sadness, relief, happiness, worry, and excitement. Even when chosen, separation due to retirement can mean adjustment for all family members, as illustrated by the Yeary family introduced at the beginning of this chapter. Separation typically brings decisions such as where to live and what type of employment or education to pursue. A partner, whose own employment opportunities may have been limited while a trailing spouse, may now choose to invest energy and time in employment or education (Burland & Lundquist, 2013).

Voices From the Frontline

IT CAN BE DEVASTATING IF JOBS ARE HARD TO FIND

We are going to see more and more military members transitioning out due to financial restraints. After 20 years of service, military members are eligible for a pension; unlike in the civilian world they don't have to wait until age 65. But now, because of downsizing, we are seeing people who intended to do their 20 years whose contracts are not being renewed. People who may have been on numerous deployments serving their country are being told they no longer have a job. The military might have been the only life they know as working adults. If they haven't put in their 20 years, when they leave the military, it's as if the gate closes behind them. They are still eligible for VA services but no longer have an income or housing and can no longer shop on base. It can be devastating if jobs are hard to find. Whenever we hear Congress talking about downsizing, that means people are losing their jobs.

People being asked to leave are often angry. There's denial and resentment. My husband retired from the Navy after 26 years. Even leaving on good terms and knowing it was coming, it was tough. He came home and packed up everything from the Navy. I knew he needed time.

Ginny Wescott, Certified Family Life Educator (C.F.L.E.)
*Family Advocacy Program Prevention & Education Specialist for
Marine Corps and Army as well as long time military spouse*

As you may recall from Chapter 6, each service branch has a Transition Assistance Program (TAP), a joint effort between the DoD, the VA, and the Department of Labor (DOL). Veterans and spouses can still access services (e.g., career coaching, job-search databases) for 180 days after separation or retirement. While 180 days (6 months) may seem like a nice window for transitioning from service member to veteran status, it is important to consider the magnitude of this change and the surrounding contexts in which the service member and their family experience this transition. Review the list of topics in Chapter 6 that are covered in the TAP workshop. Then, consider how these transition needs can differ for service members who may be experiencing involuntary separation due to injury or down-sizing. As the Yeary family told us at the beginning of this chapter, even planned separations and retirements can be stressful for an extended period of time. Each service member and each military family member experiences the complex transition to veteran status in multiple ways. Whether planned or unplanned, separation from military service is a significant shift in individual and family life.

CARING FOR WOUNDED AND AGING VETERANS

Family caregiving, hospice, and palliative care are three services among the potential socioemotional and healthcare services directed toward older adults and those who are facing serious, potentially terminal illnesses. In the U.S., we currently have three cohorts of veterans (i.e.: WWII, Korean Conflict, Vietnam War) who are aging into eldercare services. Additionally, veterans with life-threatening injuries or illnesses, regardless of age and whether or not these are related to their military service, may be in need of assistive or end of life care.

Separation due to injury brings additional challenges for family members who may take on caregiving roles. Injuries may call for only slight adjustment in the veteran's and family's life, whereas moderate or severe injury impacts family life extensively. The wars in Afghanistan and Iraq have resulted in over 52,000 service members who have been wounded in action (DoD, 2015). Visible injuries are easily noted by others, such as amputations or blindness; however, invisible injuries usually are not physically apparent but result in problems with cognitive, behavioral and social functioning such as traumatic brain injury (TBI), post-traumatic stress disorder (PTSD), and depression.

Reports of service members returning from combat indicate one-third experience TBI, PTSD, or depression (Cozza, Holmes, & Van Ost, 2013). Service members experience polytrauma when they have both a TBI and another injury such as burns, fractures, amputations, PTSD, and hearing or vision loss (Griffin et al., 2012). In addition, service members who experience visible injuries are also susceptible to PTSD and depression, and symptoms of invisible injuries may not be noticed until months after coming home (Cozza et al., 2013).

However, injury does not only occur during combat or in a war zone. For example, between 2000 and the end of 2013, over 290,000 service members were diagnosed with TBI; only 20% occurred during deployment (Defense and Veterans Brain Injury Center, 2014). The remaining 80% of TBI diagnoses in this time period occurred in non-deployed settings and were commonly attributed to motor vehicle crashes (both private and military), falls, recreation activities, and job-related training.

Similar to the aging non-veteran population, aging veterans are also likely to need care and supportive services when they experience limitations in their ability to accomplish daily living activities (e.g., personal care and grooming, cooking, laundry, driving) or when it becomes evident that the veteran is experiencing some form of dementia. Several studies indicate that there may be a need for special considerations in supporting family caregivers of veterans, whether the services are for daily living or dementia care. Two evidence-based programs focusing on these caregiving concerns have been piloted and evaluated in the veterans' health-care system. Both programs strive to coordinate care, education, and support across multiple healthcare providers and support services.

The Patient Aligned Care Teams (PACT) program focuses on providing veteran-centered primary care in the veteran's home environment, where assessments may identify additional needs for services within the home. Yet, not all veterans may be eligible for this primary care program and their needs for services may not be identified in a traditional office visit. Thus, in 2011, a Geriatric Assessment Program (GAP) was piloted to address the gap in service need identification and to better support veterans who need assistance with daily living. A third primary goal is to support the veterans' caregivers with a primary goal of reducing caregiver burden. GAP program services are administered by nurse practitioners, clinical social workers, and occupational therapists, each of which can detect "unresolved medical, social, safety, and environmental needs that cannot be detected during a primary care clinic visit" (Campbell, McCoy, Hoffman, & O'Neil, 2014, p. 59).

Partners in Dementia Care (PDC) is also a service coordination program that prioritizes concerns of veterans with dementia and their caregivers in coordinating both medical and non-medical needs (Bass, et al., 2013). Estimates are that over 300,000 veterans with dementia are receiving care through the VA health system. The PDC program is intended to support veteran families and, in particular, caregivers by strengthening the informal care network, providing health and caregiving information, coaching, and emotional support in addition to coordinating medical and nonmedical services. This program works to establish long-term relationships between the families and the care coordinators so that trust is a central feature of the relationship. When caregiving needs change over time, this trusted relationship between caregiver and coordinator can facilitate successful negotiation of potentially difficult dynamics. A matched intervention-comparison site evaluation of this program across five VA facilities found that those families who received the PDC program benefitted in several ways compared to a control group of families who received care as usual for their veteran with dementia. Most of the caregivers in this study were women (94%) while most veterans were men (98%), and most of these families had received an initial dementia diagnosis 2 to 4 years before the study. Bass and colleagues followed the families for 12 months and found that, by 6 months, the intervention group (those receiving PDC) reported fewer unmet needs, less of a sense of being trapped in their caregiving role, lower physical health strain, and lower depression than caregivers in the control group. In addition, the intervention group reported higher scores on positive outcomes of caregiver support use and the number of informal helpers available. There were additional effects for caregivers whose veteran was more severely impaired, indicating that the intervention was strongest for those families who had more difficult caregiving situations.

The VHA offers a range of geriatric and extended care services (*Guide to Long Term Care*, 2014), including hospice and palliative care. Hospice care originated in the U.S. in the 1970s as an in-home support primarily for patients with cancer but has expanded to include a wide range of serious/terminal diagnoses and now provides care in homes, hospitals, nursing care, and hospice residences (National Hospice and Palliative Care Organization, 2012). Veterans were identified as an underserved population, with hospice use rates of only 5% compared to a use rate of 22% by non-veteran Medicare enrollees. Thus, there have been several VA initiatives in the past two decades to better meet the end-of-life needs of the veteran population, beginning with the creation of a Hospice and Palliative Care Office in 2002–03. In 2009, the VHA created the Comprehensive End of Life Care initiative. This initiative funded an interdisciplinary palliative care team "at every VA medical center and established partnerships with community hospices in every state in the country" (Wachterman, Lipsitz, Simon, Lorenz, & Keating, 2014, p. 37). The partnerships with community hospices are important as the majority of veterans receive hospice care outside the VA system. These partnerships can facilitate better coordination of care and sharing of pertinent medical information, as well as provide support to family members during a difficult time. A recent research report referred to military service as an often hidden variable in aging research and one that may have specific impacts on family functioning and caregiver stress in older veteran families, including families facing end of life care (Holland, Currier, Kirkendall, Keene, & Luna, 2014). Strengthening VHA and community medical care connections may help make this variable more visible and, in turn, help tailor programming to veterans and their families.

As the VHA has expanded services to become a direct hospice and palliative care provider for veterans, a variety of wrap-around support programs for family members have been created. Among these is the inclusion of a grief/bereavement counselor as part of the support team (Flanagan-Kaminksy, 2013) and the development of a palliative volunteer program (Gerber, 2013). The Louis Stokes Cleveland VA Medical Center added the role of a grief counselor into their Home Hospice Program in 2004 (Flanagan-Kaminsky, 2013). The purpose of this support person is threefold and is enacted through regular home visits with the veteran and caregivers:

- To offer support to the veteran as he or she comes to term with their life-limiting illness (anticipatory mourning support).
- To extend support to the caregiver through separate visits.
- To offer bereavement support up to 13 months after the death of the veteran.

Not all veterans have family or other support and there are times when it is difficult for family to be present. The Minneapolis VA Health Care System developed their palliative volunteer program to provide extended support to hospice patients beyond paid personnel, who need to attend to multiple patients on the unit. The palliative volunteer program focuses on providing veteran-centered companionship and comfort to veterans who are in the end stage of life and admitted to a VA inpatient hospice and palliative care unit (Gerber, 2013). Using standards developed by the National Consensus Project for Quality Palliative Care and their own VA Voluntary Services, and with input from other VA facilities utilizing palliative care volunteers, the Minneapolis system developed two volunteer positions: volunteers who came in on a regularly scheduled basis as compassionate companions, and volunteers who provided a comforting presence for dying veterans as needed.

Caregivers and Veterans Omnibus Health Services Act of 2010 (S. 1963).

The Caregivers and Veterans Omnibus Health Services Act was signed into law in May 2010. This law provides assistance to caregivers of veterans injured in the line of duty or training on or after September 11, 2001 and in need of personal care services, and it improves provision of health care to veterans, including women veterans and veterans living in rural areas. Under this law, family caregivers have access to respite care, mental health services, medical care, a monthly personal caregiver stipend, and training in order to provide care. A recent report by the Government Accounting Office (2014) indicated that the number of caregiver applications and approvals has greatly exceeded the Veteran Health Administration's (VHA) expectations. The VHA projected 4,000 caregivers to be approved for services; however, as of May 2014, approximately 35,000 applications had been submitted and over 15,000 caregivers were approved. The GAO recommended that the VHA reassess and restructure the Family Caregiver Program to meet the needs of caregivers.

The law also requires training and certification of mental health-care providers of the Department of Veterans Affairs to deliver services for sexual trauma and post-traumatic stress disorder. Another provision of the law is establishment of peer outreach and support services and readjustment counseling and services for veterans who served in Operation Enduring Freedom and Operation Iraqi Freedom, particularly those from the National Guard and Reserves. In addition, for 3 years following the return of the veterans from Operation Enduring Freedom and Operation Iraqi Freedom, their immediate family members will have access to services (e.g., education, counseling) pertaining to veterans' readjustment to civilian life, recovery of veterans from injuries or illness incurred during the deployment, and family readjustment to the return of veterans. Among additional provisions, the law also authorizes the Department of Veterans Affairs to carry out demonstration projects to examine ways to expand the care of veterans in rural areas (Caregivers and Veterans Omnibus Health Services Act of 2010, Pub. L. No. 111-163, 124 Stat. 1130, 2010).

ORGANIZATIONS

Describing all of the civilian organizations and programs available for military families and veterans is not possible in a textbook of this size. For example, the Office of the Secretary of Veterans Affairs maintains a list of Veterans Service Organizations (VSO). Over 200 organizations are listed, including Departments of Veterans Affairs for each state, the District of Columbia, and territories (see http://www1.va.gov/vso/). Rather than offering an exhaustive list, we want to introduce some of the key organizations and their programs. Many of their websites contain links to other organizations that you can use to discover other services and resources.

The following section begins with an overview of the Department of Veterans Affairs, a department of the U.S. federal government U.S. Department of Veterans Affiairs, 2014c) We then look at examples of civilian organizations that serve military families exclusively and those that serve military families among other constituents, and examples of collaborations between civilian organizations and the DoD. This chapter ends with a list of interest, hobby, and affinity groups that have chosen to demonstrate their appreciation for military service personnel and families. Many citizens interested in "giving back" to military families and veterans have found ways to do so through these groups or through the organizations listed in this chapter.

The Department of Veterans Affairs

Beginning with the Continental Congress of 1776 that provided pensions for soldiers who were disabled, benefits for veterans and their families have grown. Following the Revolutionary War, states and local communities provided some medical and hospital care to veterans. In 1811, the federal government authorized the first domiciliary and medical facility and in subsequent years benefits and pensions were expanded and included widows and dependants. Following the Civil War, states established veterans' homes to provide medical and hospital treatment. As the U.S. entered WWI in 1917, Congress enacted programs for disability compensation, insurance for military members and veterans, and rehabilitation services. These services were administered by three Federal agencies: the Veterans Bureau, the Bureau of Pensions of the Interior Department, and the National Home for Disabled Volunteer Soldiers. In 1930 these services were consolidated into the Veterans Administration. The National Cemetery System, minus Arlington National Cemetery, was placed under the Veterans Administration in 1973. In 1989, the Department of Veterans Affairs, commonly referred to as "the VA," was made a cabinet-level position. The VA has three units: the Veterans Benefits Administration, the Veterans Health Administration, and the National Cemetery Administration (U.S. Department of Veterans Affairs, n.d.). Each is described in more detail below (U.S. Department of Veterans Affairs, 2013b).

Eligibility for most VA benefits requires discharge from active military service under other than dishonorable conditions. Reservists and National Guard members may qualify for VA benefits if they were called to active duty for reasons other than training only by federal order and served the full time ordered. Prior to separating from active duty or post-deployment for Reservists and National Guard, military members apply for enrollment (U.S. Department of Veterans Affairs, 2010).

The Veterans Health Administration   The Veterans Health Administration (VHA) operates more than 1,400 facilities where health services are provided. Facilities include hospitals, community-based outpatient clinics, community living centers (i.e., nursing homes), **domiciliaries**, and readjustment counseling centers. As the largest integrated health-care system, it provides care to 5.5 million veterans annually (U.S. Department of Veterans Affairs, 2011a).

The VHA is responsible for providing care and support for disabled veterans. When applying for enrollment for VA health care, each veteran is assigned to a priority group. The highest priority goes to veterans with disabilities who have a rating of 50% or more and/or veterans determined to be unemployable because of service-connected conditions. The lowest priority goes to those veterans with no service-connected disabilities. Veterans discharged on or after January 28, 2003 are eligible for enhanced priority for 5 years under a "combat veteran" designation (U.S. Department of Veterans Affairs, 2010). Recent innovations including the use of telehealth programs provide some services to veterans in their homes or at a local clinic.

Medical Centers, Domiciliaries, and Outpatient Clinics. Over 150 medical centers provide a range of services, including surgery, critical care, mental health services, pharmacies, physical therapy, and specialty areas (e.g., neurology, oncology, dental, prosthetics). Each medical center has an OEF/OIF Care Management Team that coordinates a patient's care. The 35 VHA domiciliaries provide residential care for veterans with medical, psychiatric, educational, vocational, or social challenges. Over 800 community-based outpatient clinics provide outpatient medical and health and wellness services (U.S. Department of Veterans Affairs, 2011a).

Vet Centers. Unlike other VHA benefits, Vet Centers are open to all veterans who served in a combat theatre or anywhere during times of armed hostilities and to their family members (see http://www.vetcenter.va.gov). Congress established Vet Centers in 1979 to serve Vietnam veterans with readjustment challenges. Since then services have been added and extended. The nearly 300 community-based Vet Centers offer individual and group counseling; family therapy related to military issues; sexual trauma and harassment counseling; employment and substance abuse assessment and referral; screening and referral for medical issues (e.g., TBI, PTSD, depression); and outreach and education. Bereavement counseling is available to parents, spouses, and children of service members, including Reservists and National Guard, who die while on duty. Services at the Vet Centers are free. Mobile Vet Centers in the lower 48 states serve locations with no local Vet Center. Housed in RV-type vehicles, the Mobile Vet Centers enable staff to offer the same services as are found at the stationary Vet Center (U.S. Department of Veterans Affairs, 2011b).

The National Cemetery Administration   The National Cemetery Administration is responsible for national and state veterans' cemeteries, the headstones, markers, and presidential memorial certificates. Burial in a national cemetery is available for: service members on active duty who die; veterans discharged under conditions other than dishonorable and who served for 24 continuous months or for the full time called for active duty; and members of the reservists component eligible for retirement pay or who die while training, hospitalized, or undergoing treatment for medical conditions incurred during service (U.S. Department of Veterans Affairs, 2010).

The Veterans Benefits Administration   The Veterans Benefits Administration (VBA) is responsible for managing education benefits (e.g., the Post-9/11 GI Bill, the

Montgomery Bill), disability compensation, pensions, burial allowances, vocational rehabilitation, home loans, life insurance, and survivors' benefits (U.S. Department of Veterans Affairs, 2010).

Since 1944, the Department of Veterans Affairs has sponsored an educational benefit package for veterans who have successfully completed an enlistment in the military service. However, no educational benefit has been as comprehensive as the Post-9/11 GI Bill, which became available to veterans in 2009. The new GI Bill® is authorized for qualified active duty and reserve component service members who served in the U.S. military after September 10, 2001. Eligible service members can receive up to 36 months of educational benefits—tuition and fees, a monthly living allowance, and a stipend for books and supplies. Costs for tutorial assistance and reimbursement for any tests required for licensing and certification are also provided by the Post-9/11 GI Bill. All educational programs must be offered by an institution of higher learning approved by Veterans Affairs. Approved training includes graduate and undergraduate degree programs and vocational or technical training (U.S. Department of Veterans Affairs, 2015).

An unprecedented feature of the new GI Bill is that qualified career service members can transfer their unused benefits to family members (Department of Veterans Affairs, 2009). A service member can transfer the entire 36 months of benefits—if the member has used none—or up to the total remaining months of unused Post-9/11 GI Bill benefits. The service members can transfer the benefits to a spouse, to one or more children, or to any combination thereof. Spouses and children of service members who died in the line of duty may access the Marine Gunnery Sergeant John David Fry Scholarship that provides tuition costs, a stipend for books and supplies, and a monthly housing allowance. The Survivors' and Dependents' Education Assistance Program provides a monthly allowance for full-time training to eligible dependants of veterans who died on active duty or as a result of military service or who were permanently and totally disabled. The VA reports that 25% of those using VA education benefits are non-veterans (Department of Veterans Affairs, 2013c).

Recent Critiques of the VA   The Veterans Health Administration has experienced a series of critiques in recent years centered on increasing access to benefits, management of disability compensation claims, provision of services to veterans, and homelessness of veterans. In response, the VA initiated an electronic claims process through the Veterans Benefits Management System in order to reduce the number of days to review veteran disability claims. A quarter of a million Vietnam-era cases were added to the review process in 2011 as a result of a court decision (Leal, 2014). Even though the number of backlogged claims decreased nearly 50% from March 2013 to March 2014, over 300,000 cases remained. By April of 2014, it became glaringly apparent to the American public that VHA scheduling practices were terribly flawed. Veterans and veterans' advocacy groups had complained for years about delays in making initial and follow-up appointments and instances of poor quality of care (Pearson, 2014). Whistleblowers and family members who lost loved ones spoke up and media reports of veterans dying while waiting for a medical appointment through the Phoenix VA Health Care System (PVAHCS) hit newscasts, newspapers, and blogs in January 2014. For nearly a decade, reports by the VA Office of Inspector General (OIG) and the General Accounting Office (GAO) had noted the need to improve "collecting, trending, and analyzing clinical data ... [regarding] wait times, scheduling practices, data integrity concerns, and the lack of physician and nurse staffing standards" (OIG, 2014b, p. 90).

The OIG undertook an investigation of the PVAHCS based on allegations first made through the OIG hotline. The VA Secretary and the Chairman of the HVAC requested

OIG expand its investigation following an April 9, 2014 House Veteran Affairs Committee meeting on VA medical care and patient deaths (OIG, 2014a). The investigators found that that while 1,400 veterans waiting for an appointment were on an official electronic wait list, over 3,500 veterans were not; they were on unofficial paper wait lists meaning they were "at risk of never obtaining their requested or necessary appointments" (p. ii). While the OIG investigators did not conclude veterans died because of lack of timely care from the Phoenix VA, they did conclude that some patients did not receive appropriate "follow-up, coordination, quality and continuity of care" (OIG, 2014b, p. ii). The failure to link deaths directly to lack of timely care was criticized by whistleblower Dr. Sam Foote, a former VA physician who provided testimony to the House Veterans' Affairs Committee. He asserted that the report "minimize[s] the damage done and the culpability of those involved by stating that none of the deaths can be conclusively tied to treatment delays" (CSPAN, 2014, 0:26).

Because of subsequent allegations of similar manipulation of wait times occurring at other VA health-care sites, the VA OIG Office of Investigations opened up 93 additional investigations, in coordination with the Department of Justice and the Federal Bureau of Investigation. Although a majority of these investigations were ongoing at the time this second edition was being revised, the OIG had confirmed that wait time manipulation was pervasive throughout the VHA. The OIG investigators wrote that they will report to Federal prosecutors any "confirm[ed] potential criminal violations," and, "if prosecution is declined," the OIG investigators will give the documented results to the VA for action (OIG, 2014b, p. iv).

The OIG (2014b) investigation resulted in 24 recommendations to which the VHA concurred and began taking action with the goal of completing all recommendations by September 2015. Fourteen recommendations focused on practices of the Phoenix VA and 11 on VHA practices nationwide. Recommendations included:

- "Take immediate action to ensure the Phoenix VA Health Care System reviews and provides appropriate health care to all veterans identified as being on unofficial wait lists. . .
- Initiate a nationwide review of veterans on wait lists to ensure that veterans are seen in an appropriate time, given their clinical condition. . .
- Require facilities to perform internal routine quality assurance reviews of scheduling accuracy of randomly selected appointments and schedulers. . .
- Selectively monitor calls from veterans to schedulers and then incorporate lessons learned into training or performance plans. . .
- Conduct a review of the Veterans Health Administration's Ethics Program to ensure the Program's operational effectiveness, integrity, and accountability. . .
- Ensure data representing VA's national performance are validated by an internal group that has direct access to the Under Secretary for Health" (pp. 123–131).

In August 2014, President Obama signed into law H.R. 3230, the Veterans' Access, Choice, and Accountability Act of 2014. This act was a bi-partisan effort primarily to address problems revealed by the OIG investigation. The goals of this 16.3 billion measure include reducing wait time for appointments through key initiatives. "Veteran choice" cards allow those facing long wait times or who live 40 miles from the nearest VA facility to seek medical services from non-VA doctors. The VA will hire 10,000 additional medical clinicians to increase the number of appointments, and will add 27 new VA medical facilities. The measure also bestows greater authority on the VA Secretary to fire senior VA employees for mismanagement or poor performance. The measure also expands treatment and counseling for veterans who experienced military sexual trauma while on inactive duty training, extends from 2014 to 2017 the Assisted Living-Traumatic

Brain Injury Pilot Program, and expands the Marine Gunnery Sergeant John David Fry Scholarship to include spouses as well as children.

Veteran Organizations

Veterans Service Organizations (VSOs) include those that: 1) are Congressionally chartered and recognized by the VA for the purposes of assisting veterans with their claims to the VA and 2) those that are not. The VA's Directory of VSOs lists both types. The first type are non-profit with a national range of scope, and have been in existence for at least 3 years (Office of the Secretary of Veterans Affairs, 2013). Both types are interested in representing American veterans.

We have chosen to list a few organizations below to illustrate some of the most visible or newest veterans groups. They advocate for veterans and their families at a national level and often provide local community services. Membership in these groups is restricted to veterans although most offer a way for non-veterans to be affiliated. Some VSOs offer veterans assistance with preparing and filing claims to the VA.

American Legion: http://www.legion.org
Iraq and Afghanistan Veterans of America (IAVA): http://iava.org
Service Women's Action Network (SWAN): http://servicewomen.org
Veterans of Foreign Wars (VFW): http://www.vfw.org

SUMMARY

- Veterans comprise almost 9% of our total population in the United States and span multiple generations from young adults to our oldest old. They reside in urban, suburban, and rural areas throughout the U.S.
- Veterans' military experiences have been varied from peacetime only to serving in multiple conflicts, being conscripted into military service or having a choice to join.
- Research on veterans indicates that their military service has lasting impact on their lives and those of their families, both positive and negative.
- Government and private organizations work to provide care and support to veterans and their families in multiple, sometimes complex contexts.
- There are particular concerns unique to the veteran population due to their potential exposure to danger and trauma; we are learning more about multiple pathways of resilience and post-traumatic growth because of their lives.

EXERCISES

1. The veterans of WWII are often called "The Greatest Generation." You may have a family member who served as part of this generation. You can research the war experiences of an individual WWII veteran through the National WWII Museum in New Orleans. Whether the service member made it home after the war or was lost on one of the many battlefields, this museum offers guidance on how to conduct an in depth search for those who served during this conflict. Go to: http://www.nationalww2museum.org/honor/research-a-veteran.html
2. Do a search of your local community to find out where the closest VA medical services are located. What is available for veterans in your community? Is there transport for facilities that are more distant?

3. Which veterans' organizations are present in your community (town, county)? Find out what these organizations offer and the population they serve.
4. Is there a student veteran population at your campus, perhaps a local chapter of the Student Veterans of America (SVA) or the Iraq and Afghanistan Veterans of America (IAVA)? Connect with members of these groups to learn about their services and outreach to veteran and military student populations.
5. Dive into the veteran and veteran family data for your community or state by accessing data from the ongoing American Community Survey and using the online IPUMS tool available through the Integrated Public Use Microdata Series at the Minnesota Population Center at University of Minnesota (www.usa.ipums.org/usa/). Online guides and web-based basic data extrapolation tools are available to the public.

11

Policies and Programs that Support Military Families

In Chapter 11, you will

- Meet Jonathan Douglas, Major, U.S. Marine Corps, Retired; a prior Branch Head at Personal and Family Readiness Division, Headquarters, Marine Corps.
- Learn about the different ways that the Department of Defense (DoD) ensures that Active and Reserve Component families from all branches of the military are supported as they respond to the challenges associated with being military families.
- Consider the laws and policies that respond to unique situations faced by military members and their families.
- Learn how the DoD is attempting to change the military view of psychological health and to encourage military members and their families to seek psychological health care when they need.
- Review the programs that the DoD has developed in response to the increased challenges and stress that military families experience as a result of the sustained U.S. military involvement in numerous military operations around the world.

Meet

Lieutenant Colonel Jonathan Douglas, U.S. Marine Corps (Retired) and prior Branch Head at HQ, Marine Corps, Personal and Family Readiness Division

I joined the Marines in 1983. Back then, your family was not considered part of the military. The attitude was, "that's your baggage." There were limited programs available and no focus on children of different ages.

I was a helicopter pilot. That's all I wanted to do. Eighteen years later, I found myself running all of these programs for families. In part I chose this assignment because of location. It was this or a 2-hour commute. I ended up loving the work. Everything we did day-by-day supported Marines and/or their families including spouses, children, parents, extended family, and others that our Marines and Sailors designated.

I had a staff of 14. All but two were civilian. Their professions included counselor, recreation directors, health educator, physical education teacher, and nurse. I oversaw many programs, including suicide prevention, recreation departments, and aquatics programs in 54 swimming pools across the world.

We ran a Single Marines Program. We aligned with sororities and fraternities so we could get ideas and learn how to serve 18–26 year olds. Think about college kids going off to school, not knowing how to do their laundry. Some of the new recruits were in the same position but unlike their peers in college, they had to be neatly dressed and at work at 6:30 AM. I never thought about anyone in the Marines trying to arrange for a concert tour to play close to an installation, but that's the kind of thing we did.

Our work could have immediate impact on somone's life. Say we had money on hand to start a new program. Within 30 days it would be up and running. Thirty days later we'd know if it was working and if there were changes to make, we could make them.

We worked with the civilian community when we could. For example, say we were underfunded for youth football at an installation. We'd build a connection with a team and tell families, "This team outside the gate will give you a good rate and be glad to see your child."

The military is a great way of life if done right. We're not perfect at it but now we see how important family programs are. People just don't join the military. They come with a family or often get one soon after they join. Families are part of the infrastructure. If doing something is possible, you are happy to try to figure how. Something as simple as turning two racketball courts into child care so moms can exercise and get a little time for themselves, can make someone's life better.

INTRODUCTION

When families are cared for and doing well in the military community, service members are more likely to stay in the military and to concentrate on their jobs when deployed or away from their families. Civilians who know that their families will be taken care of are more likely to join the military. Therefore, as a matter of recruitment and retention, DoD has developed an extensive infrastructure with the sole purpose of assisting families with military specific issues like moving to a new installation or having a loved one go off to war to managing a wide variety of problems that can occur in any family. Some of the programs are voluntary programs for military families; others are mandated by the service member's chain of command. Some programs provide information or are intended to make life more convenient for military families while others are there to provide basic necessities for the family.

The DoD offers many services and programs for military families, but historically these services have often been more plentiful and accessible for active duty families. While service members who are on active duty usually live near or on military installations, members of the National Guard, Reservists, and veterans and their families live across the United States in communities that may have limited access to DoD programs and services. As the role of reservists has become more prominent and the needs of their families have become more salient, some programs have been expanded and others developed specifically for the Reserve Component.

In recognition of the demands placed on Army soldiers and families due to deployments to war zones and in other military operations, such as humanitarian missions, the Army has declared its gratitude and commitment through "The Army Family Covenant" (U.S. Army Installation Management Command, 2010), a unique contract and promise to provide Army families with accessible and high-quality support programs and services:

BEST PRACTICES

THE ARMY FAMILY COVENANT: KEEPING THE PROMISE

- We recognize the commitment and increasing sacrifices that our Families are making every day.
- We recognize the strength of our Soldiers comes from the strength of their Families.
- We are committed to providing Soldiers and Families a Quality of Life that is commensurate with their service.
- We are committed to providing our Families a strong, supportive environment where they can thrive.
- We are committed to building a partnership with Army Families that enhances their strength and resilience.
- We are committed to improving Family readiness by:
  - Standardizing and funding existing Family programs and services.
  - Increasing accessibility and quality of healthcare.
  - Improving Soldier and Family housing.
  - Ensuring excellence in schools, youth services, and child care.
  - Expanding education and employment opportunities for Family members.

(U.S. Army Installation Management Command, 2010)

You are reading this book because you are interested in helping military and veteran families. One of the ways that you can assist military families is acquiring a basic understanding of programs and policies in place to help them. A large percentage of military families do not know or have accurate knowledge of available benefits and services, due in part to "the plethora of resources that are offered by a complicated patchwork comprising DoD, the services, civilian support agencies, and state government" (MacDermid et al., 2008, p. 19). Understanding the kinds of programs that are available to military and veteran families will help you assist them to access the appropriate programs to meet their needs. This chapter will introduce you to some of the long-standing and new programs, policies, and attitudes adopted by the DoD in its attempt to honor its commitment to military families.

MILITARY INFRASTRUCTURE

Among the active duty, National Guard, and Reserves there are approximately 3 million military family members who are part of the United States Armed Forces community (DASD, 2014). The DoD is responsible for programs and policies that support these family members. The Active and Reserve Components each have a senior civil service assistant and advisor to the Secretary of Defense who is responsible for creating and managing these programs and policies. For active duty families, it is the Deputy Under Secretary of Defense for Military Community and Family Policy. For Reserve Component families, it is the Assistant Secretary of Defense for Reserve Affairs. The DoD family support infrastructure includes a mixture of service members, civil service employees, and contractors who work together but often have different roles in developing and managing the programs and policies that support military families.

Deputy Under Secretary of Defense for Military Community and Family Policy

The Office of the Deputy Under Secretary of Defense for Military Community and Family Policy is responsible for establishing and maintaining all military community programs and policies for active duty service members and their families (Department of Defense, 2012b). It is responsible for policy, advocacy, and oversight of all quality of life issues; family and casualty assistance; morale, welfare, and recreation programs; the Military OneSource website; the DoD Education Activity; and the DoD's commissary (similar to a grocery store) and exchange (similar to a department store) services.

Assistant Secretary of Defense for Reserve Affairs

The Assistant Secretary of Defense for Reserve Affairs is the principal staff assistant and advisor to the Secretary of Defense on all matters involving members of the Reserve Components of the United States Armed Forces, including the Army and Air National Guards and all reserve components of the Army, Navy, Marine Corps, Air Force, and Coast Guard (Office of the Assistant Secretary of Defense for Reserve Affairs, 2010b). To ensure that all Reserve Component members and families receive the support they need through appropriate policies and programs, the Office of the Assistant Secretary of Defense for Reserve Affairs and the DoD Office of Family Policy formed a strategic partnership (Office of the Assistant Secretary of Defense for Reserve Affairs, 2010a). This partnership and commitment to provide exceptional quality of life programs for the Reserve Component is part of the DoD's commitment to make sure reservists and their families are not left behind in the effort to provide quality family support programs across the entire military force.

POLICIES THAT SUPPORT MILITARY FAMILIES

This section reviews policies and organizations available to protect and serve military personnel and their families.

Strengthening Our Military Families

In January 2011, President Barack Obama announced a presidential initiative, Strengthening Our Military Families, to support military families through a coordinated Federal approach that directs Cabinet secretaries and heads of agencies to focus on four priorities central to the lives of military families ("Strengthening Our Military Families," 2011). The goals of this unified approach are to:

- "Enhance the well-being and psychological health of the military family.
- Ensure excellence in military children's education and their development.
- Develop career and educational opportunities for military spouses,... [and].
- Increase child care availability and quality for the Armed Forces" ("Strengthening Our Military Families," 2011, pp. 2–3).

The goals of this presidential initiative reflect the research on and feedback from military families and service members about the challenges that most affect them. Efforts noted in the initiative, some of which are already in progress, include improving and expanding mental health preventive services and treatment at the community level, training school staff on the educational needs of military children, increasing employment opportunities in careers in Federal government and public workforce for military spouses, and increasing access to child care.

National Defense Authorization Act

The **National Defense Authorization Act** is a federal law that is passed by Congress every year to grant the Department of Defense, including Active and Reserve Components, funds to operate and specific guidance on how to spend those funds. The law is a way for Congress and the U.S. President to ensure that the DoD is accomplishing goals that are set by Congress and to closely control how American tax dollars are spent on national defense. The law specifies the number of military personnel and equipment types and numbers that each branch of the service should have as well as other activities that the services should be engaged in (e.g., the types of aircraft that the Air Force should have, the requirement to purchase new body armor for service members to wear when deployed, how much and what types of research and testing will occur).

The National Defense Authorization Act also ensures the well-being of military members and their families. For example, the National Defense Authorization Act for Fiscal Year 2010 included a pilot program that allows the DoD to reimburse federal agencies for the costs of hiring a military spouse as an intern; a revised plan for implementing the services' sexual assault prevention and response policies; a requirement that the services report to Congress on the effects of domestic violence on military families; and a mandate to assess the impact of deployment on children of military members.

The Family and Medical Leave Act

The **Family and Medical Leave Act (FMLA)** of 1993 offers eligible employees of covered employers job-protected, unpaid leave of up to 12 workweeks for the care of seriously ill family members, to attend to their own serious health condition, or upon the birth or adoption of a child. FMLA applies to all public agencies (i.e., state, local, and federal employers), schools, and private-sector employers with 50 or more employees. Employees are eligible for FMLA when they have worked for the employer for 12 months, worked at least 1,250 hours the previous year, and work in a location where at least 50 employees are employed in a 75-mile radius. Family members are defined as parent, spouse, daughter, or son. Employers are required to maintain pre-existing group health-care coverage for employees on FMLA leave and to "reinstate [them] to the same or an equivalent job with equivalent employment benefits, pay, and other terms and conditions of employment" (Family Medical Leave Act Regulations, 2007, p. 35550).

The National Defense Authorization Act for Fiscal Year 2008 amended the FMLA to include military family leave entitlements, and the National Defense Authorization Act for Fiscal Year 2010 expanded these entitlements. The first entitlement allows eligible employees to take up to 12 weeks of job-protected leave for any "qualifying exigency" due to the active duty or call to active duty of a spouse, parent, daughter, or son. Qualifying exigencies include situations related to notification of deployment on short notice (7 days or fewer); military service-related activities such as family support programs and informational sessions; child-related responsibilities such as arranging child care or schooling; financial and legal arrangements related to the military member's absence; counseling sessions; up to 5 days of leave to be with a military member on short-term leave during deployment; post-deployment activities (e.g., arrival ceremonies, reintegration briefings) and other official military programs for a period of 90 days after completion of active duty status; issues related to the death of the service member; and any other employer-employee agreed upon event (U.S. Department of Labor, 2010).

The second military family leave entitlement is the military caregiver leave. This entitlement allows an eligible employee up to 26 workweeks of unpaid leave within a single 12-month period to care for a service member with a serious illness or injury. The employee must be the spouse, parent, daughter, son, or next of kin of the service member. A covered service member is a veteran within 5 years of seeking medical help or a current member of the Armed Forces, including the National Guard and Reserves, who is in outpatient status undergoing medical treatment, recuperation, or therapy or is on the temporary retired list because of a serious illness or injury incurred or aggravated while on active duty (U.S. Department of Labor, 2010).

FMLA leave can be taken as a block or intermittently. Employees should try to schedule medical treatments to cause the least disruption to the employer's operation (U.S. Department of Labor, 2010). The Wage and Hour Division of the Department of Labor investigates complaints (see http://www.dol.gov/whd).

Uniformed Services Employment and Reemployment Rights Act (USERRA)

The **Uniformed Services Employment and Reemployment Rights Act (USERRA)**, administered by the Veterans Employment and Training Services in the U.S. Department of Labor, prohibits employers from discriminating on the basis of an employee's consideration of joining the military or an employee's current or past military service. It applies to all private and public sector employers in the U.S. regardless of size, including foreign companies with locations in the U.S., its territories, or its possessions. USERRA also protects re-employment rights for returning service members. They must be re-employed in the original or equivalent position (i.e., similar seniority, status, and pay) and are entitled to increases in benefits or seniority that would have occurred if they had not done military service. Once back from military service, an employer cannot fire a service member without cause within 180 days of re-employment if the military service was between 31 and 180 days, or within 1 year of re-employment if the military service was over 180 days (U.S. Department of Labor, 2009).

Service members returning to work after 30 days or fewer of military service must report back for the next regularly scheduled work period, allowing for travel. If the service period was 31 to 180 days, service members submit an application of re-employment with the employer no later than 14 days after completing their military duties. If the service period was 181 days or more, service members submit an application of re-employment within 90 days. Service members hospitalized for or convalescing from injury or illness incurred or aggravated during service have 2 years to report to the pre-service employer. In general, the cumulative time in service cannot exceed 5 years while employed by the employer although there are exceptions (U.S. Department of Labor, 2009). Service members who believe their USERRA rights are being violated may obtain assistance by contacting the Employer Support of the Guard and Reserve (ESGR; www.esgr.org).

COMPREHENSIVE DEPARTMENT OF DEFENSE RESOURCES FOR MILITARY FAMILIES

The following resources are the results of DoD's attempts to provide easy access to information and referral sources for programs and policies available to military members and their families. They are excellent starting points for finding information to help military families with whom you may be working. The first, military family assistance centers, are one-stop service and support centers for military members and families. The second, Military OneSource, provides online information, services, and resources for service members and family members.

Military Family Assistance Centers

The active components of each branch of the military service have family assistance centers that house many of the family programs you will learn about in this chapter. Each branch has its own name for its family support centers: Army Community Service Centers; Marine Corps Marine and Family Service Centers; Navy Fleet and Family

Support Centers; Air Force Airmen and Family Readiness Centers; and Coast Guard Work-Life Centers (*Air Force Times*, 2010). For all services, these are one-stop centers for military members and their families to go to find information, obtain assistance, enroll in programs, and become volunteers in their communities. Family centers usually provide outreach services for families in remote or isolated areas. The centers also serve mobilized National Guard and reserve members, DoD civilians, and military retirees.

Typical family center programs include the following:

- Counseling and crisis assistance.
- Deployment and mobilization support services.
- Family advocacy programs.
- Financial management.
- Employment assistance.
- Information and referrals.
- Outreach programs.
- Parenting, stress management, and life skills education.
- Relocation assistance.
- New parent-support programs.
- Special-needs family member assistance programs.

The National Guard Family Program has staff members in each state and in four territories serving Air and Army National Guard and their families. Each state has a program director and one or more additional staff: Airman and Family Readiness Program Manager, Family Readiness Support Assistant, Family Assistance Specialists, or Child and Youth Program Coordinator (see www.jointservicessupport.org). While each state is different with regard to its family programs, many states also have standing Family Assistance Centers, which provide services to National Guard families (for examples, see www.ndguard.ngb.army.mil/family/support/familyassistancecenter/Pages/default.aspx; www.il.ngb.army.mil/family/fac/facmain.aspx; and www.al.ngb.army.mil/Resources/sfss/fac/default.aspx). The state National Guard headquarters can also activate a Family Assistance Center when a unit is mobilized.

In addition, as part of a Joint Family Support Assistance program, military and family life counselors provide non-medical counseling and referrals to Reserve Component families; they address relationships, parenting, loss, and adjustment issues. Likewise, child and youth behavioral counselors locate resources for children and youth and can provide counseling and education in the area of children's development, behaviors, separation, and anxiety. Since 2008, these counselors deliver "mobile family support and services" to those families located far from military installations (see www.militaryonesource.mil/deployment/joint-family-support-assistance-program).

Army Reserve family support programs include six family support centers, called Army Strong Community Centers, located in areas far from military installations. These centers are located in Connecticut, New York, North Carolina, Michigan, Oregon, and Pennsylvania. They support members of all branches of the military, veterans, retirees, and their families. Army, Navy, Marine Corps, and Air Force Reserve families can also access services and support online through their respective family programs and through Military OneSource (see https://www.arfp.org/programs.html#programtwo).

Voices From the Frontline

SERVICES FOR SAME-SEX PARTNERS
The military is moving in the right direction

As an advocate for families, I'm very excited about the repeal of Don't Ask-Don't Tell. Now we can offer services to same-sex partners. It's becoming the norm. It used to be that if a couple was seeking counseling or if there was a domestic violence incident we had to refer same-sex partners to services in town because they didn't have a military ID card. Now they have access to those services. The mindset is changing and the military is moving in the right direction.

Ginny Wescott, Certified Family Life Educator (C.F.L.E.)
Family Advocacy Program Prevention & Education Specialist for
Marine Corps and Army as well as long-time military spouse

Military OneSource

Military OneSource provides information and resources on an array of topics that impact on military life (see http://militaryonesource.mil/). Trained MOS consultants are available 24 hours a day, 7 days a week by phone, online, or via email to provide information and referrals and to offer personalized support to active duty, Guard, and Reserve members and their families at no charge. Military OneSource programs include:

- Individual, marital, and family counseling.
- Strategies and resources on dealing with stress.
- Financial counseling.
- Child-care planning and referrals.
- Parenting issues.
- Deployment and reintegration support.
- Spouse employment assistance.
- Education and relocation assistance.
- Information on local resources and recreational opportunities.
- Assistance in using the online, virtual DoD morale, welfare, and recreation library to download books, write a resumé, or take practice college entrance exams.
- Wounded warrior information and referrals on veterans' affairs (VA) benefits, health-care services, and military facilities.

Short-term, problem-focused counseling sessions on life issues are also available. These sessions can be provided in person, via telephone, or online. This service is designed to address a variety of issues, such as improving relationships at home and at work, marital issues, normal grief and loss issues, and adjusting to life changes and challenges. Military members who are more comfortable going outside the military community for counseling services can choose this option for issues that do not require more extensive mental health care from the military medical care system. They can receive up to 12 free counseling sessions through Military OneSource.

ADDITIONAL RESOURCES FOR MILITARY FAMILIES IN DISTRESS

The following two resources, military chaplains and military aid and charity organizations, are important sources of support and assistance for individuals and families in distress or in need of immediate counseling or aid.

Military Chaplains

Military chaplains have accompanied the U.S. military worldwide for over 200 years. Chaplains are qualified clergy who are ordained by their individual religious denomination or faith group prior to joining the military. As personal staff officers, chaplains advise commanders on upholding the free exercise rights of religion, unit morale, and ethics (U.S. Army Chaplain Corps). Chaplains provide religious services and ceremonies and assist military members and their families with faith issues; personal issues, such as stress; redeployment and reunion issues; and moral and ethical concerns. Many times chaplains are the first source of support for military personnel outside of their chains of command, because they are easy to access. In this case, chaplains can counsel personnel or make appropriate referrals to social service agencies or other appropriate organizations that can help military members with their issue. Many have further training and certification in counseling fields, such as marriage and family therapy, and can provide those services as well. Chaplains in the Active and Reserve Components offer workshops and retreats for couples (e.g., the Army's Strong Bonds, the Navy's PREP, and the Air Force's Marriage Care) and individuals (e.g., the Navy's Personal Resiliency Retreat).

Chaplains provide care to service personnel and their family members regardless of faith beliefs. As a matter of professional obligation chaplains hold all information shared with them in confidence, unless the service or family members give permission for a chaplain to disclose their identity and/or the content of the communication. This confidential communication covers both oral and written disclosures and extends beyond the end of a counseling relationship and death of the person who disclosed. Commanders must honor and support this confidential communication. Not adhering to this policy of confidentiality can lead to loss of chaplain credentials and/or action noted in the Uniform Code of Military Justice or the Military Personnel Manual (e.g., Department of the Navy, 2008).

Because of the policy of confidentiality granted and adhered to by chaplains, service members often seek them out when they need to talk. Chaplains will guide persons to the resources needed and will not leave individuals alone when they or others are at risk.

Military Aid and Charity Organizations

Several types of emergency and charitable associations and organizations serve military members and their families. While they are not DoD-sponsored programs, they are heavily supported by military members and are considered extremely important "safety nets" for military members and families. Military members are strongly encouraged to contribute to these organizations and willingly do so, as they provide a mechanism for military members to "care for their own." Each branch of the service relies on a charitable organization to assist its members. They are the Army Emergency Relief (AER), the Air Force Aid Society (AFAS), and the Navy-Marine Corps Relief Society (NMCRS). These organizations are private, non-profit organizations; however, they have close ties to the DoD, are largely funded through service-specific fund drives, and rely on command or installation personnel to distribute funds to military members in need. They provide emergency assistance, emergency grants and loans, advocacy services, counseling services, and other emergency and support services for active duty and Reserve Component members and their families. The service branches' emergency relief organizations have a cross-servicing agreement, so that personnel who are not located near an installation of their own branch can request help through the emergency relief offices of the other organizations.

Each military branch's emergency and charitable organization was created differently and in response to varied needs, emphasizes diverse needs, provides slightly different types of assistance, and is accessed differently. Service members should be encouraged to consult their Military Family Assistance Center (discussed previously in this chapter) for information on what services their branch provides and how to access those services.

SPECIAL PROGRAMS FOR IDENTIFIED
OR POTENTIAL PROBLEMS

Two of the following programs are mandated programs designed to identify and assist families requiring special services. The third program, the New Parent Support Program, is intended to strengthen families, so that they are less likely to be at risk for child abuse or neglect.

Exceptional Family Member Program

The DoD's Exceptional Family Member Program (EFMP), called Special Needs Identification and Assignment Coordination in the Air Force, requires service members to identify family members with special medical or educational needs and helps those families obtain required services (Department of Defense, 2010g). The family members are enrolled in the program and the services they require are documented. The documentation includes requirements for special educational needs and specialty medical services. In decisions about the military member's future assignments, special family needs are heavily considered and attempts are made to match the family needs with military assignments and communities that can support those needs. This process ensures those families have access to necessary services, wherever they are assigned. The EFMP helps families connect with medical and educational programs with the goals of increasing family self-sufficiency and improving family self-advocacy skills.

Responses to the online Blue Star Families' 2014 Military Family Lifestyle Survey, conducted in February and March 2014 with more than 6,000 respondents, indicated that 21% of the respondents had a family member enrolled in the EFMP. The top four conditions reported in the survey were autism, developmental delay, speech or language impairment, and mental health disorder. Between 58% and 73% of respondents with a family member enrolled in the EFMP indicated that they experienced the following challenges to continuity of care when moving: finding vocational services, doctors, early intervention services for infant/toddlers, and Individualized Education Plan (IEP) services; receiving SSI/SSDI (69%); accessing respite services; getting educational accommodations; and accessing community and state-based support programs, such as Medicaid.

Family Advocacy Program

Changing to an all-volunteer force has resulted in higher numbers of service members who are married and have children. Since the number of military families has grown, so has the awareness of potential spouse and child abuse and neglect in the military services. The stressors of military life, including deployments, separations, frequent moves, and distance from extended family and friends has also been associated with an increased risk and incidence of abuse. A University of North Carolina at Chapel Hill study (Rentz, Marshall, Loomis, Casteel, Martin, & Gibbs, 2007) showed that prior to October 2002, the rate of abuse and neglect was slightly higher among non-military families when compared to military families. However, between October 2002 and June 2003, after the U.S. started sending larger numbers of troops to Afghanistan and Iraq, the rates of abuse and neglect in military families increased substantially while the rates for non-military families remained stable. The average number of incidents of child abuse in military families doubled. In fact, the rate of child abuse in military families increased by about 30% for each percent increase in the number of military members leaving for or returning from deployments.

The DoD Family Advocacy Program (FAP) is a coordinated effort to prevent, identify, report, and treat all aspects of domestic abuse and violence. It is a command support program for identifying and helping military families who are at risk for or impacted by issues of domestic abuse or violence, such as child abuse or neglect and spouse or partner abuse. The FAP provides policy and program guidance to assist each military branch of the FAP, which has staff at each installation where families are assigned. These Army, Air Force, and Navy FAPs (the Marine Corps families receive services from the Navy FAP) provide local outreach, prevention, and intervention. They provide a wide range of services and programs in order to address the specific needs of families.

The FAP tries to prevent or stop domestic abuse by educating service members and families about domestic abuse; identifying and assisting families experiencing domestic abuse; providing support and counseling services to victims of abuse; and providing treatment and discipline for abusers.

The FAP staff members work with military commanders and leaders, law enforcement personnel, the medical community, family support personnel, victim advocates, and military chaplains to assist families involved in domestic abuse. They also coordinate staff with civilian organizations and agencies in communities where service members and their families live to provide a community response to family and intimate partner abuse and to ensure that military families get the help they need to recover from and prevent further domestic abuse. Intervention includes safety planning, counseling, educational programs, advocacy, and other services. For more information go to http://www.militaryonesource.mil/abuse?content_id=266706.

New Parent Support Program

The New Parent Support Program (NPSP) offers primary prevention for young families as well as intensive services for those at risk for abuse or neglect. Focused on expectant and new parents, services include information on child development and positive parenting skills, parent/infant groups and sibling groups, and a lending program (DoD, 2014c).

In an evaluation study, surveys from 821 program users, both active duty and family members, from 22 NPSP locations across the Navy were analyzed (Kelley, Schwerin, Farrar, & Lane, 2007). A majority of users reported that the program was better or much better than expected. Over 75% of program users reported that the program helped them quite a bit or a great deal with coping with parenting stress appropriately, with improving their parenting skills, and with feeling a greater sense of community. Over 90% of users who attended the parenting classes or received home visits agreed or strongly agreed that the program demonstrated concern for and contributed to the health and safety of sailors and families, and that it contributed to their quality of life; 62% of those who attended parenting classes and 72% who received home visits indicated that the program helped them to concentrate at work; and over 70% of users agreed or strongly agreed that it contributed to readiness. However, a majority neither agreed nor disagreed that it contributed to their decision to remain in the Navy.

PROGRAMS DESIGNED TO HELP FAMILIES DEAL WITH DEPLOYMENTS AND THEIR CONSEQUENCES

The following programs are available to family members during times when their service member is preparing to deploy, while he or she is gone, and when he or she returns from a deployment.

Deployment Cycle Programs

Pre-deployment programs are common across the services. Deployment programming was common in some services prior to September 11, 2001, especially in the Navy, where sailors have always been away from families for long periods of time. Now in all of the services, families are invited to presentations on financial, legal, emotional, and relationship preparation for separation. The family support centers typically offer a presentation for couples and another for parents and children. These presentations may occur in the evening or over a weekend, and at the family support center or through a command (i.e., the families are invited to a deployment readiness briefing at the unit's location, for example, aboard the ship). Some of the Navy's Fleet and Family Support Centers may also conduct command-requested Return and Reunion programs for service members onboard ships as they transit back to the homeport (Blaisure & Arnold-Mann, 1992).

The Navy offers a weekend Returning Warrior Workshop (RWW) for individual augmentees (i.e., service members who are temporarily assigned to another command, deploy with the new command, and return to their parent command upon completion of the deployment) and their guest. The RWW is offered through the Navy's five Reserve Component Commands and is open to active duty and reserve members. The guest may include a spouse, a significant other (e.g., boyfriend or girlfriend), or a family member (e.g., sister, brother). The RWW is offered so sailors and their loved one can reconnect and learn how best to support one another during the reintegration phase (see https://navyreserve. navy.mil/Pages/Returning_Warrior_Workshop.aspx).

<hr>

Voices From the Frontline

BUILDING CONNECTIONS

Some of our best family support programs . . . naturally emerged among families.

It's common for people today to think, or say, "Just give me a pill and I can get better." It's true for civilians and for people in the military. But it doesn't work that way. People need other people to support them but today everyone is so busy it is hard to find the time to get together. Having a one-on-one support network is hard. Life moves fast. Sometimes the technology that is supposed to be enhancing communication between us gets in the way. Many people don't know how to connect. But that doesn't change the need. Some of our best family support programs today come from what naturally emerged among families. For example, Key Wives and ombudsmen volunteer spouses who support other spouses.

Evonne Carawan, Director, Personnel Readiness and Community Support,
Office of the Deputy Assistant Secretary of the Navy (Military Personnel Policy)

<hr>

Family Readiness Groups and Navy Family Ombudsman Program

The Family Readiness Group (FRG), also called the Key Volunteer Network in the Marine Corps, is one of the most important programs for supporting family members while individual service members or units deploy. Providing support for family members allows deployed service members to focus on their mission without unnecessary worry about their families. The FRG is a command-sponsored organization made up of service members, civilian employees, and family member volunteers (Office of the Assistant Secretary of Defense for Reserve Affairs, 2007). Its purpose is to provide a structure and forum for service members and their families to provide social and emotional support and outreach services, and to distribute information to each other. The FRG is a vital organization for helping maintain family member morale and for helping families resolve problems.

Family readiness group activities might include voluntary telephone rosters, or "trees" with family member contact information, in case of emergencies or to relate important information; deployment-related (before, during, or after a unit goes to a combat zone) or mobilization-related (Reserve Component units called to active duty for deployment or training) information briefings/meetings; newsletters with information on unit missions, self-help programs and services, benefits and entitlements, and events; free or low cost social activities for spouses and/or families (Department of the Army, 2000).

In addition to the FRG program, the Navy also has a Family Ombudsman program as part of its family support system. The Navy Family Ombudsman program provides support to Navy families during times of deployment and when units are home. Like FRG volunteers, Navy ombudsmen are volunteers and spouses who wear no uniform and hold no rank, but are key members of the command support team DoD. All Navy commands, including Navy Reserve commands, have a command-appointed ombudsman. Navy Reserve Ombudsmen are fully trained to assist both activated and non-activated Navy Reserve families. They serve as information links between command leadership and Navy families. They are official command representatives and points of contact for all family members associated with the command, including spouses, parents, and extended family members (Command, Navy Instalations Command, n.d.).

Voices From the Frontline

BUILDING A SOCIAL AND EMOTIONAL SUPPORT NETWORK
Family Readiness Support helps people know that they . . . are not alone.

Family Readiness Support helps people know that they are connected to the resources and support. They are not alone. Our goal is to build a social and emotional support network that happens more naturally on military installations. We provide deployment and reunion briefings, help family members understand the Unit's mission, and provide information and referrals. My work takes me all over the state working with 11 Family Readiness Groups, one for each armory that has soldiers serving in the 86th Infantry Brigade Combat Team. We also reach out to the other states that are part of the Brigade (seven plus small groups from other states who have sought to join the mission).

The chain of concern is supposed to work like this:

- We have developed telephone trees headed by volunteer trained callers who check in with families once a month. If families have questions or the furnace breaks, this person is their first point of contact. Families know they are not alone.
- Callers then report back to the Telephone Tree Coordinator, who is supervised by the Family Readiness Group Leader. To maintain confidentiality, info passed up the chain may describe a situation but not name a person unless permission is given or if it is an emergency.
- The Telephone Tree callers let the Coordinator know of any issues that need to be addressed. Sometimes those come to me but more often go directly to the Family Assistance Center, the "one stop shop" for issues: TRICARE, finances, legal, whatever it may be. We also remind families of the other services available to them: a Military Family Life Consultant who works with families and children and visits school and educates the educators about the unique challenges of military children; the youth coordinator who oversees programs and camps for military children; a psychologist; Military OneSource; and outreach specialists who work with veterans and their families.
- Every family receives a From the Home Front newsletter that continues to list the resources available as well as upcoming support groups and other events.

Being military family members helps my co-worker and me reach other military families. We understand what they are experiencing and can respond to some of their needs. For example, the Family Readiness Program has offered programs called Beyond the Yellow Ribbon, which are pre-mobilization programs for soldiers and families, during mobilization for the families, and post-mobilization at 30 and 60 days for the soldier and family. A mid-deployment event was aimed at supporting the families (this we planned and a Yellow Ribbon Brief that lasted a whole day). We wanted to give people time to relax a little, to talk with each other, and to ask questions. It's hard to take in information when so much is changing in your life. When my family members were deployed the first time, the brief lasted only three hours. I'm smart, but it took me a year after the briefing to realize that I was covered by TRICARE, the military health insurance. I don't want that to happen to other family members.

Barbara Purinton
Vermont National Guard Family Readiness Support Assistant;
Wife and Mother of Soldiers Serving in Afghanistan

The Rear Detachment

Whenever there is a deployment of a military unit to combat or to another military operation, a group of military members of that unit is selected to remain at the home installation. This group is called the "rear detachment." In the past the rear detachment was often made up of individuals who had medical conditions, family issues, or other reasons that prevented them from deploying. However, senior military leaders learned that the rear detachment personnel played a vital part in the success of a deployed unit's mission. More and more unit commanders are selecting their most competent and dedicated personnel to make up the rear detachment.

The rear detachment is responsible for all of the personnel and equipment that remain at the unit's home installation (Office of the Assistant Secretary of Defense for Reserve Affairs, 2010). One of the main responsibilities of the rear detachment is to coordinate closely with family readiness staff (paid staff members who work directly for the unit commander) and volunteers (usually military spouses who act as leaders and advocates for the collective families of the unit) to ensure that the families of military members who deploy are well-informed and well cared for. The rear detachment, the deployed portion of the unit, and the family readiness staff and volunteers must have a good working relationship and an open exchange of information in order to have a good family readiness program (i.e., a means to disseminate information to families, address their concerns, and involve them in the unit). A good family readiness program keeps the morale and well-being of its families high during the deployment by using social activities, the Internet (a unit website and email), newsletters, teleconferences, telephone trees, and the use of toll-free phone numbers to engage families (Office of the Assistant Secretary of Defense for Reserve Affairs, 2007).

Wounded Warrior Programs

Each branch of the military has programs for wounded, injured, and ill service members and their families: the U.S. Army Wounded Warrior Program (AW2), the Air Force Wounded Warrior Program (AFW2), the Marine Corps Wounded Warrior Regiment (WWR), and the Navy Safe Harbor (which also provides assistance to wounded, injured, or ill Coast Guard members and their families).

These Wounded Warrior Programs provide assistance and advocacy for severely wounded, ill, and injured service members and their families (U.S. Army Medical

Department, Army Wounded Warrior Program, 2010a; U.S. Air Force, 2010; Navy Personnel Command, 2010; U.S. Marine Corps, 2010). Services include providing support and advice about medical treatment and rehabilitation and help during the transition back into the military service or into the civilian community. The programs help military and family members access federal, state, and civilian programs that often require beneficiaries to negotiate difficult systems to access. These include medical, financial, educational, employment, and legal programs; assistance with retirement or transition to civilian life; individual and family counseling; and information about benefits to which they are entitled.

Voices From the Frontline

CREATING NEW SERVICES

It's not a mystery as to how new services are created

The military is very responsive given its size. In my appointed role as Deputy Assistant Secretary of the Navy for Force Support and Families in the first Bush Administration, I had oversight of all quality of life issues for the Navy and Marine Corps for the Secretary of the Navy. My job was to develop and implement policy for Navy and Marine Corps quality of life programs including medical care, military housing, family support, and child development centers.

It's not a mystery as to how new services are created. To create family support programs I went out to commands and listened to families. It takes listening to understand what people in different places need. What works for Naval Air Station Jacksonville is not necessarily the right thing for Naval Air Station San Diego.

We used to meet regularly with family support groups like the National Military Family Association, a private non-profit organization that works to improve the quality of life for military families, that let us know what supports they saw were needed. I'd share what I saw. Sometimes the military could provide a needed service. Sometimes military support civilian organizations could provide services we couldn't.

It helps you reach more families any time you can sit at the table, tell people what you need, see what they can provide using their personnel and, in return, give them visibility.

Marianne "Mimi" Blackburn Drew
Rear Admiral, U.S. Navy (Retired)

PROGRAMS AND POLICIES DESIGNED TO SUPPORT NATIONAL GUARD AND RESERVE MEMBERS AND THEIR FAMILIES

In 2010, the Department of Defense aligned several programs designed specifically to provide support to National Guard and Reserve military members and their families under a new directorate. The newly created Family and Employer Programs & Policy directorate falls under the Office of the Assistant Secretary of Defense for Reserve Affairs and includes the Yellow Ribbon Program, Employer Support of the Guard and Reserve (ESGR) program, and Individual and Family Support Policy. While not a Family and Employer Programs & Policy program, the Joint Family Support Assistance Program also exists to provide services to National Guard and Reserve members and their families. Through these programs, the DoD hopes to better meet the needs of Reserve Component service members and their families and to provide them with more information and greater access to resources.

Voices From the Frontline

ADVOCATING FOR FAMILIES

Families have become a priority of command and leadership

I'm an advocate for military families. My job is to support their overall readiness and well-being, so that they can be constantly ready for a deployment. We're a purple service—meaning that I support any military family. We currently have 998 Air Guardsman on base and about 1,000 families. I'm on call 24 hours a day. If a family has a deployment-related need, I will provide direct service. For other issues, I am like a resource and referral agency and help guide people to services they need.

Part of my job is to bring awareness of family needs to senior leaders on base. I go to all the major meetings so I can be aware of what is happening and see how families might be affected. I also reach out to the broader community. I educate people about the military as I build relationships with organizations and agencies so that I can help our families connect with resources.

Guard and Reserve families don't always identify themselves as military families until deployment is upon them. They are trying to adjust and get to know the military culture as they deal with deployment without the same support network that active duty families get. National Guard and Reserve children and families often feel alone. They are flooded with media and may hear frightening or negative things about the war on the news, from teachers, classmates, and even from people in the grocery store. When you are on active duty and live on an installation, most people are careful about what they say and your community buffers you from negativity.

My role as family advocate was not created until 2001. Prior to that we did not have a full time position for family support in the Air National Guard. There was no funding for family programs. Services were provided by family members and volunteers.

The shift toward supporting families started before 9/11 but it increased in speed afterwards. Leaders learned that the members of the Guard were not so quick to respond if they felt their families were in peril. Since then, families have become a priority of command and leadership—it's good to see. The military culture now is "Mission first, but family always."

Robin Berry
Airman & Family Readiness Manager, 110th Air Wing,
Michigan Air National Guard

Department of Defense Yellow Ribbon Reintegration Program

The Yellow Ribbon Program was developed by the DoD specifically to provide assistance and support to National Guard and Reserve military members and their families (see www.yellowribbon.mil). The program provides services, information, and referrals to Reserve Component members and families before, during, and after they are called to active duty and eases the process of transitioning to active duty during mobilization and back to civilian life during demobilization. It also helps Reserve Component members and their families connect with local resources before, during, and after deployments.

The program uses comprehensive outreach methods to reach Reserve Component members and families in even the most isolated locations. Yellow Ribbon activities can include informational presentations (e.g., coping with deployment), family social activities, and reunion events. Events usually occur on one or two weekend days during which presentations on topics such as health care, education and training, and financial and legal benefits are given. Staff from DoD and civilian organizations (e.g., Military OneSource,

Military Family Life Consultants, the Red Cross) provide information about their services and answer questions. The Yellow Ribbon Program also provides referrals to DoD and other government agencies (e.g., Veterans Affairs) and civilian programs.

Employer Support of the Guard and Reserve

The Employer Support of the Guard and Reserve (ESGR) was established by the DoD in 1972, because the DoD recognizes that civilian employers are crucial in supporting the large numbers of reservists who defend the nation (Employer Support of the Guard and Reserve, 2009). Employers must comply with existing employment laws that protect the rights of those who hold civilian jobs while also serving in the Reserve Component. The ESGR's mission is to enhance cooperation and understanding between Reserve Component members and their civilian employers, to encourage employer support for reserve members, and to help resolve conflicts arising as a result of an employee/military member's military commitment. The ESGR accomplishes this by increasing civilian employers' awareness of applicable laws governing reservists called to active duty and their civilian job status, recognizing exceptional support by civilian employers, and resolving conflicts between employers and service members when they arise. Through an extensive network of volunteers, the ESGR provides services throughout the U.S. and its territories.

Individual and Family Support Policy

The Office of the Assistant Secretary of Defense for Reserve Affairs' (2010b) Individual and Family Support (IFS) Policy program is to strengthen family support programs, policies, and partnerships with civilian agencies. The IFS guides DoD policies and partnerships in support of Reserve Component members and their families.

Joint Family Support Assistance Program

In 2007 Congress authorized the DoD to develop a Joint Family Support Assistance Program (JFSAP) for National Guard and Reserve members and their families. While the newly created Family and Employer Programs & Policy directorate does not include the Joint Family Support Assistance Program, the JFSAP also exists to provide services solely to National Guard and Reserve members and their families. The primary goal of the program is to provide high-quality services to those families who are located in areas where there are no military installations from which they could receive support and services. The JFSAP reaches out to isolated military families.

The JFSAP has been available in all states and U.S. territories since September 2008 and provides ongoing support to Reserve Component families during the full deployment cycle—before, during, and after deployments. It also provides mobile and community-based support services, including information and referral, financial assistance, child care, outreach by the military grocery and department stores, transition assistance, recreational programs, and counseling services. The services are delivered by federal, state, and local government organizations and by non-profit agencies, with the JFSAP coordinating the provision of these services. The following are the DoD's goals for the JFSAP (Managed Health Network Government Services, 2010a):

- Create a "high-tech, high touch" web-enabled community to connect military families with each other and with supportive resources 24/7.
- Increase availability of resources for family members.
- Increase awareness of active/guard/reserve members and families of existing services.

- Inform leadership and service providers about the range of available programs and services, and how they may be accessed.
- Provide child development resources and referral services.
- Sponsor volunteers and family support professionals.
- Assess the need for enhanced support.
- Integrate services and programs into a comprehensive delivery system that responds to members and families at all stages of the deployment cycle.

Voices From the Frontline

THE JOINT FAMILY SUPPORT ASSISTANCE PROGRAM

We support families by building on what state family support programs already know and do

The Joint Family Support Assistance Program (JFSAP) was launched in 2008 by the DoD Military Community & Family Policy (MC&FP) program. Its creation was in response to a congressional mandate to provide mobile family support and services for Guard, Reserve, and active-duty families whose access to support was challenging because they live away from installations.

JFSAP was visionary. Congress said to augment, not replace services. We took this to mean build community capacity. Rather than create separate programs, we went to State Family Program Directors and said, "We are here to augment your needs." Every state now has a JFASP team of four people: one Military and Family Life Counselor (MFLC); one Child and Youth Behavioral MFLC; one Military OneSource Consultant; and one additional position chosen by the state (most choose a Personal Financial Counselor).

This partnership approach has been invaluable. Every state is unique. Family Program Directors have been out there for years. They know their community, their service members, the geography, and local culture. Because they didn't have many resources for so long, they became creative problem solvers and thinkers. We went out to offer them support but it didn't take long before we were asking, "What can we learn from them?"

There's a shift occurring from thinking about Family Centers as bricks and mortar and a collection of programs to seeing them as service delivery systems. This is vital. Over the last 10 years, money has been flowing for the creation of services. Now commanders, families, and professionals are saying there is too much out there and it's confusing.

We have to look at the connections between programs always being grounded in who families are and what they need. We need to think carefully about the services we provide and why, and then assess our effectiveness.

Families will be in communities for their whole lives. Communities are going to be left supporting service members and their families with challenges due to multiple deployments to combat theatres long after funding is diverted elsewhere. It is going to take coordination and collaboration between health and human services agencies, non-profit and for-profit organizations, and state and local agencies to integrate services to promote military family readiness and resiliency in a sustained and ongoing way.

Gerry Carlon, LCSW,
Senior Policy Analyst, Office of the Deputy
Assistant Secretary, Defense

HEALTH CARE

The following programs are the DoD's ways to ensure that military members and their family members are able to access health care that is at least as high in quality and availability as that afforded to civilian families.

The Military Health System

The DoD Military Health System (MHS) is an enormous organization that includes the Office of the Assistant Secretary of Defense for Health Affairs and the medical departments of the Army, Navy, Marine Corps, Air Force, and Coast Guard (MHS, 2010b). It provides the oversight for all military medical programs, including medical education, research, and the provision of medical care for all beneficiaries (i.e., military members and their families, retirees, and eligible DoD civilians and their families). The MHS is responsible for medical care during all military operations, natural disasters, and humanitarian missions with which the U.S. military is involved.

The MHS works together to ensure that medical care is available to service members worldwide. The Army, Air Force, and Navy (also responsible for medical care to the Marine Corps) each have medical departments that operate hospitals, health clinics, and dental clinics on installations throughout the world. They also have mobile hospitals and clinics that are set up where military operations are taking place and are responsible for ensuring that every beneficiary receives the best possible care—either through local MHS facilities or through an MHS facility in another location or in a civilian facility.

TRICARE

TRICARE is the DoD's regionally managed health-care program that provides medical and dental care services for active duty service members, activated Reserve Component members, retired members of the uniformed services, their families, survivors, and other DoD beneficiaries of military benefits (MHS, 2010a).

While the military services have their own health-care systems, the primary mission of those organizations is to support military operations, which sometimes reduces the ability of the military health-care system to provide all of the medical and dental care that military members and their families require. To provide better access and high quality service to all beneficiaries, TRICARE brings together the health-care resources of the military branches with medical facilities—the Army, Navy, and Air Force—and supplements them with civilian health-care networks and professionals, including civilian health-care providers, hospitals, and pharmacies (TRICARE Management Activity, 2010a). The Marine Corps has no separate medical facilities; it obtains its medical support from the Navy and from the civilian networks that participate in TRICARE.

Members of the Reserve Component and their family members are eligible for different TRICARE benefits depending on their status (TRICARE Management Activity, 2010a). Generally, Reserve Component family members are eligible for medical and dental care through TRICARE when certain qualifying conditions exist: The reserve military member is a member of the Selected Reserve; is serving on active duty for a period of more than 30 consecutive days; is medically retired due to a service-connected injury, illness, or disease that occurred in the line of duty; completes 20 years of qualifying active duty service, reaches age 60, and starts receiving retired pay; or dies on active duty or due to a medical condition incurred or aggravated while on active duty. Family members are covered under TRICARE for additional periods—up to 90 days before the member reports to active duty and up to 180 days following release from active duty—if the Reserve Component member is on active duty for more than 30 days.

Psychological Health

As the United States' involvement in military operations continues in frequency and intensity, psychological health is a growing issue among the military and military family members. The DoD has responded by encouraging military members and their families to seek psychological health care promptly. The DoD is actively attempting to reduce stigma against psychological health treatment, to encourage military leaders to be aware of and support military and family members who might need psychological health care, and to improve the quality of and access to psychological health care.

Psychological health care is available through most health clinics and is provided by highly trained and licensed military and civilian providers. Often however, the availability of psychological health care is limited, so family members are often referred to civilian providers in the local communities through TRICARE. TRICARE covers outpatient and inpatient psychological health care for military members or family members when it is medically or psychologically necessary, as determined by a health-care referral (TRICARE Management Activity, 2010b). A consultation is written by the health-care provider for therapy or for hospitalization. The local military health-care facility can approve and renew the authorization to go to a civilian provider for a limited number of therapy sessions.

PROGRAMS THAT REFLECT A NEW VIEW OF PSYCHOLOGICAL HEALTH

Traditionally, the U.S. Armed Forces trained its troops by focusing on physical strength and endurance along with skill development. This physical and job-skill training, along with a strong spiritual belief, were seen as the attributes that would keep service men and women strong in combat and while carrying out other military operations. In recent years, however, the DoD has begun to develop a new attitude about the importance of psychological health as part of military fitness and readiness. It now uses a comprehensive mind-body-spirit model of strength and fitness. This new incorporation of psychological health in the DoD and its focus on the holistic—psychological, physical, social, and spiritual—health of military members and their families is the basis of the programs listed below.

Defense Centers of Excellence for Psychological Health and Traumatic Brain Injury

The Defense Centers of Excellence for Psychological Health and Traumatic Brain Injury (DCoE) was created in 2007 to address the needs of the growing numbers of service members and families who are challenged with psychological health issues and TBI (DCoE, 2010a). The DCoE develops standards for preventing, identifying, and treating psychological health and TBI in the U.S. military forces. The DCoE works closely with the DoD medical and research communities and senior leaders, the Department of Veterans Affairs, civilian and military clinical experts and researchers, and academic institutions. The DCoE takes the best practice models from this collaborative network and helps service members and families deal with psychological health and TBI issues through the most advanced treatment methods, education, and outreach programs. It also evaluates and monitors programs that prevent, identify, and treat psychological health and traumatic brain injury.

The DCoE also works to reduce the stigma that prevents many service members and families from getting treatment for psychological health (DCoE, 2010a). Through its "Real Warriors Campaign," the DCoE promotes resilience, recovery, and the reintegration of returning service members and their families. The campaign includes printed educational materials, an interactive Internet site, and media outreach featuring stories of real service members who have successfully been treated for psychological health issues.

Post-Deployment Health Reassessment

Every service member who deploys is given a health screening before and after every deployment. Any health issues identified at that time are then further assessed and treated. However, because many service members do not want any identified problems or treatment to delay their deployment or their return home after the deployment, the DoD developed an additional screening—the Post-Deployment Reassessment Health Assessment (PDRHA)—which is administered 90 to 180 days after returning from deployment (Force Health Protection & Readiness Policy & Programs, 2007).

The first priority for many service members after deployment is to get home to their families and to return to a more normal life. It is common and normal for them to think that their health and emotions will return to what is normal for them after they have spent some time in a more stable, home environment. But many deployment-related health and psychological problems may not be apparent until 3 to 6 months after a deployment, when service members have had time to readjust and recognize how deployment affected their health and emotional well-being (Force Health Protection & Readiness Policy & Programs, 2007). The goal of the PDRHA is to identify and begin treating any health and emotional issues before they become chronic problems. Psychological issues are especially critical to identify and treat early; therefore, the PDRHA includes specific questions on emotional well-being and on any traumatic experiences that might have occurred during the deployment.

It is every commander's responsibility to ensure that all service members, active duty and reserve, complete the PDRHA (Force Health Protection & Readiness Policy & Programs, 2007). The assessment includes a medical screening questionnaire, education, and follow-up health assessment and treatment for any identified health and psychological health issues. After completing the questionnaire, service members speak with a health-care provider individually to review their responses. Together the service member and the health-care provider determine if follow-up evaluation and treatment are necessary. Often, a mental health provider is available at the screening site as well. Depending on how the process is set up, every service member might be screened by a mental health provider or this might take place only for service members with a psychological health concern.

Families often worry that deployments affect their loved one's health, and completing the PDRHA can reduce their concern by assuring them that any health issues the service member might have will be addressed. To ensure that this occurs, family members can encourage their loved one to disclose any emotional or physical problems they are having.

Resilience Training

The Army's Resilience Training program—also called "Battlemind Training," the original name for the program—is the Army's mental health resilience training system (United States Army Medical Department, Resilience Training, 2010b). As you learned t in Chapter 5, resilience is the ability to cope with and recover quickly and effectively from difficult experiences or situations. The Army's resiliency program stems from a new attitude about the importance of psychological health as part of a comprehensive mind-body-spirit view of strength and fitness. Resilience Training supports the new DoD focus on the physical, spiritual, emotional, family, and social health of military members and their families by encouraging self-awareness, a strong mind, and psychological well-being. The program comprises an integrated series of modules specifically designed to correspond with the potential stressors that service members and their families might encounter at various points in their lives and military careers.

The Army Resilience Training program provides education about psychological health and self-awareness presentations and discussions to soldiers and their family members throughout their careers (beginning with entry-level training, during continuing military education, and at other key points during their careers) and throughout the deployment cycle (before, during, and after deployments). The training provides a developmental approach to mental health skill building timed to the specific phases of the soldier's career and deployment cycle. The program also provides specific resiliency training to leaders and medical and psychological health-care providers, so that they can encourage resiliency and identify soldiers and family members who may need additional assistance to deal with difficult issues in their lives.

Training for soldiers is intended to help soldiers recognize evidence of stress in themselves and in their fellow soldiers, develop healthy ways to reduce the effects of stress, deal with hardship effectively, reduce stigma about seeking help for psychological issues, and increase their ability to face the psychological impact of combat and other military operations (United States Army Medical Department, Resilience Training, 2010b). The U.S. Army's Mental Health Advisory Team (Mental Health Advisory Team [MHAT] V, 2008) found that soldiers who received resiliency training before deployment reported fewer mental health problems than those who did not. Training for family members is available for spouses, children, siblings, and parents of soldiers. Family resilience training addresses how to deal with family issues that are common during a deployment, such as coping personally, helping children cope, staying connected, and normal reactions that can occur during separation and reunion.

RESPECT-MIL

In an effort to reduce stigma-related barriers to seeking psychological health care in the military, the United States Department of Defense's Deployment Health Clinical Center designed RESPECT-Mil. RESPECT-Mil stands for Re-Engineering Systems of Primary Care Treatment in the Military; however, it is known simply as RESPECT-Mil (DoD Deployment Health Clinical Center, RESPECT-Mil, 2010b). It is a program based in the military health-care system that takes advantage of the fact that service members are seen frequently by general practice or family physicians. Often, psychological health concerns are first discussed by service members in health-care clinics where they are less afraid of stigma and where physical complaints seen often have a psychological component. RESPECT-Mil teaches these physicians and other medical staff members who support the program to screen, assess, and treat active duty soldiers with post-traumatic stress disorder (PTSD) and depression.

The program encourages routine and consistent screening for these psychological problems through the use of questionnaires that are filled out by the soldier and assessment tools that are filled out by the health-care provider (DoD Deployment Health Clinical Center, RESPECT-Mil, 2010b). These screening tools help to identify when a soldier may be suffering from depression or PTSD. Soldiers who have symptoms of depression or PTSD are also screened to determine if they are at risk for suicide. Other elements of the program include educating patients about depression/PTSD and treatment options and encouraging patients to be more involved in their care. Treatment could include medication, counseling with a RESPECT-Mil psychological health-care provider, or a combination of the two.

The U.S. Army Medical Command has implemented RESPECT-Mil for active duty soldiers or National Guard and Reserve soldiers while they are on active duty status in many of the Army's primary care facilities. A study of the program (Engel et al., 2008) concluded that RESPECT-Mil is a feasible program that is safe and accepted by military health practitioners and patients and that the psychological health of participants often improved. The DoD is planning to implement the program for the other branches of the military as well.

Military Family Life Consultants

In 2004 the DoD established the Military Family Life Consultant (MFLC) program to provide short-term, situational, problem-solving counseling services for issues that do not require more extensive psychological health care (Managed Health Network Government Services, Military & Family Life Consultant (MFLC) Program, 2010b). MFLC counselors are Masters or PhD level, licensed, and credentialed counselors; usually psychologists, social workers, or other mental health professionals. They provide up to 12 sessions of counseling per person, per issue for issues such as anger management, stress and coping skills, parenting, communication, couple and family relationships, deployment, separation and reunion, loss and grief, work-related issues, and other military-life related topics. The MFLCs can provide crisis intervention and can help identify appropriate resources and services for issues requiring psychological health services through the military health-care system. They can also provide group psycho-educational presentations on deployment, mobilization (Reserve Component units or individuals being called to active duty), communication, stress management, and grief and loss to units and family member groups.

The MFLC program is a good option for service members and their families who are uncomfortable going to their medical treatment facilities for counseling services; since MFLCs provide confidential services, unless there is any indication of child or domestic abuse or threat of harm to self or others. Since MFLC counselors can travel to remote and distant locations to provide services to military families, this program is also extremely important for Reservist and National Guard families who often live hundreds of miles from a military installation. The MFLC program is available to all military services within the continental United States; Alaska; Hawaii; Europe; and the Pacific.

Military Pathways®

Military Pathways®—formerly called the Mental Health Self-Assessment Program—is a DoD mental health and alcohol screening program for service members and military families (DoD Deployment Health Clinical Center, 2010a). Individuals can complete a screening questionnaire anonymously online, by phone, or in person at education and awareness events held on military installations and National Guard and Reserve units. Separate screening questionnaires are available for depression, alcohol use, anxiety, PTSD, and **bipolar disorder** (characterized by mood swings that range from depression to feeling euphoric and energetic). Results are provided at the completion of the assessment, with a list of resources and respective contact information.

EDUCATION, CHILD CARE, AND YOUTH PROGRAMS

One of the most challenging issues facing military members is providing consistency in child care, a quality education for their children, and regular after school and summer activities in spite of the frequency with which they are required to move to new communities. The following programs can be found on U.S. military installations throughout the world; they ensure that the children in military families can enroll in a school and be at approximately the same educational level as their new classmates, they can quickly join children the same age in extra-curricular or after school activities, or they can be started in a safe, affordable child-care program.

Department of Defense Education Activity

Most of the 1.2 million children of military service members attend civilian—private or public—schools in the communities where they live or are home-schooled (Department of Defense Education Activity, 2014b). More than half (58%) attend public schools, and approximately 9% attend private schools (Blue Star Families, 2013). Over 78,000 children of active duty military and DoD civilians attend one of 181 accredited schools located on military installations (Department of Defense Education Activity, 2014b). These schools are managed by the DODEA, a DoD organization that falls under the direction of the Undersecretary of Defense for Personnel and Readiness and the Deputy Under Secretary of Defense for Military Community and Family Policy. The DODEA consists of two separate school systems: the DoD Dependents Schools (DODDS) overseas (located in Europe, Guam, and the Pacific), and the DoD Domestic Dependent Elementary and Secondary Schools (DDESS) in the United States.

Family members of military personnel face unique challenges during the course of their education (Department of Defense Education Activity, 2010). For example, they usually move much more frequently than students whose parents are civilians. They are also subjected to the additional stress of having parents that could be or have been deployed to combat or are absent for long periods for other military requirements. Students also frequently are in countries where they do not speak the language and/or are unfamiliar with the local customs and culture. The DODEA schools provide students with a standardized curriculum that makes it easier for students of military families to move from school to school, particularly from a domestic school to an overseas school or vice versa. The DODEA schools provide resources and support to help students deal with the stress of frequent moves and other stressors that come with being a military family member. Of the 23% of the family members surveyed as part of the Blue Star Families Military Family Lifestyle Survey (2014) who reported having a child in a DODEA school at one time, 77% were satisfied the DODEA schools and 48% believed that their DODEA education prepared their children very well for advancement to higher grade levels.

The DoD also provides resources to civilian schools attended by military family members, so that even those students who are not in a location with a DoD school can receive help dealing with the challenges of being a student in a military family (Department of Defense Education Activity, 2010). In October 2009, the DODEA granted $56 million to public schools throughout the nation that serve military children, for improving the education for military students and for providing professional development for educators in schools that serve military students.

Voices From the Frontline

TEACHING MILITARY CHILDREN
We teach children about how to deal with stress

I'm an art teacher in Sicily working with children from kindergarten through the fifth grade. I also teach fourth grade social studies, science, and health. We have 373 children in our elementary school. They score above national standards on Terra Nova, the standardized tests that the military gives. They always score above stateside education standards. Our children are world travelers. I think this is one of the reasons we don't have bigotry in our schools.

In some ways, stress is lower for our children than for many in the U.S. Each has one family member employed, all have a home and all have food.

In other ways stress is higher, especially with today's repeated deployments. I find children often imagine the worst when their parents are deployed. Added to that, they have no control over when their parents come home and leave again.

In the school, we have a deployment support group for kids. We teach children how to deal with stress. We do breathing exercises, and counting. We all learn to take time-outs when we need a little break from the group. We visit parents at work so children can see all the equipment parents have to keep themselves safe. We use humor and try to put as much joy in our lives as possible.

Every time a child comes to art class, I greet them at the door. I look them in the eye and they have to smile before they come into the classroom. For that one moment of the day, they can get beyond the hard things in their lives.

Lately there have been leaking pipes in my classroom. I'm using them to show children that I'm not superhuman, that things get to me but I can handle them. Military children living overseas don't have the chance to see how Grandma or other close family members and friends respond when things happen. Here, I'm one of their models.

Outside of school, our base is a community. We all shop at the same store and go to the same movie theatre. I meet parents at the commissary who ask me questions they would ask their mother or sister if they were home. Though it's sometimes hard when everyone knows everything about you, the closeness we have is supportive.

The average age of DODEA teachers is mid-fifties. We're an educated work force. Over three-quarters of our staff have masters degrees. A few are teaching overseas as a second career. Some of us are at a time of big change in life such as a divorce. Some, like me, chose this work because we love to travel. It's not for everyone. You aren't with your family. To work for DODEA, you have to be the kind of person who can take initiative and take care of yourself out in the middle of nowhere.

Francie Hammond
Teacher with DODEA

Child Care and Youth Activity Programs

Military service entails many deployments and separations, frequent moves, long working-hours, and changing schedules. These hardships often create a need for child care for the military family. Another factor increasing the need for child care is the fact that military spouses often work outside the home or attend educational programs to attain higher degrees. Additionally, the number of families where both parents are military members and the number of single-parent military members have increased (Military Advantage, 2010). For many military families child care plays a vital role in their being able to continue to contribute to the military service. In fact, service members are required to have Family Care Plans in place, as they are expected to put their military mission ahead of all personal needs. In order for military members to contribute to the military to this extent, they must be assured that their children are safe and thriving, while they are being cared for by people outside the family. Yet, finding child care can be very challenging in many of the areas where military families are assigned.

The DoD mandates, reviews, and creates programs for child care and youth activities in order to provide the best possible programs for military families. The DoD programs include the Child Development Program, Youth Activities, Family Child Care, School-Age Care, and child care resource and referral (Department of Defense, 2014b). The DoD provides subsidy funding to most military Child Development Centers and Family Child Care (FCC) providers (certified child-care providers who care for children in their own homes). Those centers and individuals can, thereby, charge lower fees to the families. The FCC providers may receive subsidies in monetary form or through other means, such as by receiving training required in order for them to be certified as an FCC provider. The DoD subsidies often makes child-care costs for the military family lower than in the civilian community. In addition, because of the high standards for child-care center accreditation and for individual provider certification, the quality of child care often exceeds that received by non-military families.

The DoD operates approximately 800 child development centers in 300 locations throughout the world (Department of Defense, 2010a). These centers care for approximately 200,000 military and DoD civilian children each day. Most centers provide full-day, part-day, and hourly care for children from the age of 6 weeks to 12 years old. The centers are usually open during the normal work week, but installation commanders can decide to extend center hours to meet the work and deployment needs and schedules of their population.

The Family Child Care program meets the needs of those families who want their children to be cared for in a home environment or whose schedules are not conducive to using child-care centers (Department of Defense, 2010a). The FCC program provides lists of installation-certified providers who provide in-home child care. These providers often provide overnight or longer child care, when needed.

The DoD child-care and youth program also includes the School Age Care program (SAC; Department of Defense, 2010a). The SAC program provides structured before and after school and summer and holiday child care for children aged 6–12 years old. Social and recreational programs for children over 12 are provided by youth and teen programs sponsored by military youth services and community centers found on larger military installations.

OTHER QUALITY OF LIFE PROGRAMS AND SERVICES

The following programs and services are overseen by the Under Secretary of Defense for Personnel and Readiness. They are designed to improve quality of life for military members and their families.

Commissaries and Exchanges

The Defense Commissary Agency (DeCA) operates tax-free grocery stores on military installations throughout the world. These military grocery stores, called "commissaries," are reserved for use by military beneficiaries only. Military families and other beneficiaries are able to purchase the same kinds of items they can at civilian grocery stores, but at significant savings. Groceries are sold to patrons at the same cost that DeCA pays for them, plus only a 5% surcharge; and patrons pay no taxes on the groceries (Defense Commissary Agency, 2010). By using this military benefit, military families can purchase their groceries at an average of 30% less money than they would spend for the same groceries in civilian grocery stores.

Exchange services—the Army and Air Force Exchange Service (AAFES), Navy Exchange (NEX), and the Marine Corps Exchange (MCX)—are similar to civilian department stores (Department of Defense, 2014h). They provide merchandise and services to active duty, guard and reserve members, military retirees, and their families at competitively low prices. Exchanges save military families approximately 20% compared with civilian low cost department stores. When military members and families deploy to combat, overseas, or remote locations around the world, exchanges quickly set up shopping and service facilities to bring them products, making it easier and more affordable to obtain items that they require or that will make their lives more comfortable. Exchange services are also designed to give money back to military communities by generating money that helps support morale, welfare, and recreation (MWR) programs.

Morale, Welfare, and Recreation (MWR) Programs

The DoD knows that in order to attract and keep quality service members, it must provide a quality of life at least as full and satisfying as that of civilians. A large part of that is the opportunity to participate in recreation programs. Military recreational programs and services are managed very similarly by each service, but are known by different names: Army Morale, Welfare and Recreation; Marine Corps Community Services; Navy Morale, Welfare, and Recreation; U.S. Air Force Services; and Coast Guard Morale, Well-Being, and Recreation (Department of Defense, 2010).

The Morale, Welfare, and Recreation (MWR) programs in each of the military branches provide a large variety of recreational programs, both on and off the installation, to service members and their families. Most MWR programs fit into several major categories: fitness and sports centers and activities, library and information services, recreational/art skill development programs, travel and vacations, and programs specifically designed for single service members (Office of the Under Secretary of Defense for Personnel and Readiness, 2009a). These programs are operated by civilians with military oversight. They provide service members with the opportunity to relax, promote fitness and esprit de corps, promote a strong sense of military community, and result in a higher quality of life for all members of the military community. About 45 different programs fall under MWR; however, not all installations offer every MWR program or service. These programs are essential for keeping up the morale of military personnel and their families.

SUMMARY

- The DoD family support infrastructure is made up of service members, civil service employees, and contractors who develop and manage the programs and policies that support military families.
- Military family assistant centers house many of the family programs that provide key support to military families.
- Family Readiness Groups, the Navy Family Ombudsman Program, and the "rear detachment" help families deal with deployments.
- Wounded warrior programs provide assistance and advocacy for severely wounded, ill, and injured service members and their families.
- The Department of Defense Yellow Ribbon Reintegration Program, the Individual and Family Support Policy, and the Joint Family Support Assistance Program are new policies and programs designed to support National Guard and reserve members and their families.
- Health care, including psychological care, is provided by the Military Health System and TRICARE.
- The DoD now uses a comprehensive mind-body-spirit model of strength and fitness and is encouraging a new attitude about the importance of psychological health as part of military fitness and readiness.
- Defense Centers of Excellence for Psychological Health and Traumatic Brain Injury, Post-Deployment Health Reassessment, Resilience Training, RESPECT-Mil, Military Family Life Consultants, and Military Pathways® are programs that provide military members and their families with alternative methods to learn about psychological health needs and to obtain assistance when they need it.

EXERCISES

To further explore the types of policies and programs available to military families, answer the following questions:

1. What do you think are the most important programs that the DoD offers military families? Why?

2. Can you think of any problem you may have personally encountered in your life that might have been easier to deal with if you would have had the resources described in this chapter available to you? Which resources would have been particularly helpful?

3. What policies or programs described in this chapter would you refer a military family member to for each of the following problems or issues? (Some issues may be addressed by more than one program or policy.)
   - A child who is having problems reading in school.
   - A military member and his or her spouse are arguing a lot and think they need help with their marriage.
   - A spouse who is new to the military and doesn't know where to go to learn about the resources on his or her installation.
   - The wife of a military member who is afraid of her husband because he has hit her on several occasions.
   - A child who is having problems adjusting to the deployment of a parent.
   - A military member and his or her spouse are having problems understanding each other after he or she returned from combat.
   - Parents of an active duty service member who returned from deployment are worried about their son's angry outbursts and withdrawn behavior.

4. Why do you think it would be particularly difficult for service members and their families to seek help with psychological problems? Can you think of any time in your life when you could have used help dealing with an emotional or psychological problem? Did you seek help? Why or why not?

5. Think about how you would approach a military family member you think could be helped by one of the DoD programs or policies, but they have not asked for your help. How would you let them know about it? What would you say to them?

6. Read more about one of the policies described in this chapter. If possible, talk with someone who benefitted from the policy.

7. How important is it that the DoD continues to develop new programs for military members and their families? Why?

12

Civilian Organizations that
Support Military Families

In Chapter 12, you will

- Meet Dr. Shelley MacDermid Wadsworth, Director of the Military Family Research Institute at Purdue University.
- Discover how civilian organizations advocate for, assist, and increase our knowledge about military families.
- Learn about civilian programs that assist military families to thrive in the face of unique challenges, including deployments.
- Gain insight into how collaborative efforts can improve life for military families.

Meet

Shelley MacDermid Wadsworth, PhD, Director of the Military Family Research Institute at Purdue University

Work-family issues have been a focus of my work for a long time. One day in 1999, a colleague at Purdue called to ask me to write a proposal with him to study military families with a work-family focus. We applied and were awarded the grant. That was the start of my education about the military and the Military Family Research Institute (MFRI). We were given a crash course about the military from people who live it, and also a rare opportunity to think about all the branches of service at once.

Learning about military families, I learnt about myself, my assumptions and stereotypes. I had always thought that people who joined the military instead of going to college didn't set a priority on education. The reality is people in the military go to extraordinary efforts to deepen their education.

I thought military people might be attracted to violent jobs. Instead, I discovered that military life is about discipline, judgment and staying calm. It is not seen as acceptable to lose control and inflict unnecessary damage whether on a mission or at home. While service members are expected to never leave someone behind and to pursue the mission using their last drop of energy, it is always under this umbrella of discipline.

I was once sent a photo of a marketplace in Baghdad right after a bomb went off. Everyone is running away except for a U.S. service member who is running towards the spot where the explosion took place. If someone walked into my office with a gun, I would hide behind my desk. A service member would be prepared to go toward the gun if necessary. It's humbling to work with and on behalf of people who would literally die for me.

Initially, we were solely a research organization. Later, we received funding to expand our mission to include programs and outreach on behalf of service members, families, and veterans. So we're now also working to figure out what innovations we can create and resources we can leverage to create positive change.

Our research projects are varied. For example, a few years ago, we were asked by DoD to prepare a literature review about risk and resilience. We posted it on our website, and it has turned out to be influential. A highly placed military official told me that it changed her thinking about how families should be supported.

When the Family Medical Leave Act (FMLA) was revised, we were asked for input about how to structure the law. MFRI is quoted twice. We made a difference—maybe a small difference but one that influenced many families.

We have been bringing researchers together from around the U.S. and the world to share their work about military families. Their work has led to several published books. These too will add to our efforts to help people learn about military families and to create a future workforce to support military families.

At MFRI we consider ourselves engaged scholars. It is our responsibility as researchers to do work that practitioners will find useful, just as practitioners have a responsibility to continue learning about and applying research to their practice. Together we can ensure that the state of our knowledge and our programs and policies are as responsive to families as possible.

INTRODUCTION

Supporting service members, veterans, and their families can be considered a societal responsibility (Tick, 2005). One way to carry out this responsibility is by building community capacity to support families of military members and veterans. In addition to the Department of Defense and the Department of Veteran Affairs, civilian organizations and partnerships reviewed here are sharing the responsibility for the welfare of the military community and enhancing the competence of practitioners who serve military families.

Community capacity includes assuming a *"shared responsibility* for the general welfare of the community and its members and *collective competence*, demonstrating an ability to take advantage of opportunities for addressing community needs and for confronting situations that threaten the safety and well-being of community members" (Huebner, Mancini, Bowen, & Orthner, 2009, p. 219, emphasis in original). The community capacity approach perspective suggests that formal and informal networks generate social capital that leads to families positively adapting to stressors (Mancini, Bowen, & Martin, 2005).

When applied to the military, formal networks include military leadership and military and civilian organizations and agencies. Informal networks include those personal relationships formed voluntarily, such as relationships neighbors, friends, and work colleagues. Huebner and colleagues (2009) argue that one function of formal supports is to grow informal networks. For example, two spouses may meet at a pre-deployment briefing and develop a friendship that includes sharing emotional support and practical help such as providing child care for one another during the deployment.

This chapter will introduce some of the key policies, organizations, and examples of programs available for military families at national and state levels. Many of their websites contain links to other organizations that you can use to discover other services and resources. This chapter also reviews the formal civilian networks that are constructed through policies and organizations created to support military personnel and their families. As you read about these policies, organizations, and initiatives, imagine how they also assist families in growing their informal networks of support.

ORGANIZATIONS CREATED TO SERVE MILITARY FAMILIES AND SERVICE MEMBERS

National Military Family Association

The National Military Family Association, formed in 1969 as the Military Wives Association, advocates for benefits and programs that support military families and teaches military family members to advocate for their families (see Box 12.1). The association is often called to speak before Congress on behalf of military families. It has three prominent programs: Military Family of the Year, Operation Purple camps, and educational scholarships for military spouses (http://www.militaryfamily.org).

Each year, the association chooses one family from each of the uniformed branches (i.e., Army, Navy, Marine Corps, Air Force, Coast Guard, National Oceanic and Atmospheric Administration, and US Public Health Service) to represent that branch. From these seven families, one family is named the Military Family of the Year.

In 2004, NMFA began Operation Purple camps for military children from all branches of the uniformed services, including National Guard and Reserve. **Purple** indicates an activity that includes all branches. Priority is given to children dealing with a parental deployment. Camps are offered every summer in multiple locations throughout the U.S., including national parks. Additional camps include leadership camps for 15 to 17 year olds, family retreats, and wounded active duty or medically retired service members and their families (http://www.militaryfamily.org).

BOX 12.1   BEST PRACTICES

NATIONAL MILITARY FAMILY ASSOCIATION

We know we can make a difference.

The National Military Family Association is more than 40 years old. We don't take government funding. Instead we have a lot of backing from concerned citizens, foundations, and corporations. This backing has allowed us to expand as the need for services grow. Grounded in our knowledge of, research about, and commitment to military families, we develop services in different ways:

- **We listen and respond to families.** For instance, we developed our Operation Purple® Program by asking families what they needed. Early in the war, spouses told us, "We're fine. Help us help our kids." The first summer 1,000 kids came to one of our overnight camps and connected with other kids from military families and experienced activities that helped them deal with their parents' deployment. In the program's 8 years, we have sent almost 45,000 kids for free to camp. We've also started family retreats in National Parks to help families come back together after the service member's return from deployment. We also hold special family retreats for wounded warriors and their families.
- **We educate members of Congress.** Because of the massive call-ups of Guard and Reserve, every member of Congress now has military families in their district and is concerned about military personnel and family issues we had always been working on. Members call us asking, "What can I do to help?"
- **We build on existing community initiatives.** Most military families live in civilian communities and not on military installations. Their children

attend community schools, military spouses work for civilian employers, they attend places of worship in the community, and they may seek medical care from civilian health-care providers. Military families need the support of their communities. We work with many organizations, such as camping programs or community groups, to enhance support for military families.

- **We guide people who want to support military families but don't know how.** We created resources on our website (www.militaryfamily.org) and publications to help people who want to help military families. Our 10 Things Military Kids and Military Teens Want You to Know toolkits and our Finding Common Ground Community toolkits give people concrete ideas about how to help military families and their children. Some ways are really simple. If your kid is on a soccer team with a kid from a military family, offer to car pool. Organize members of your place of worship to send care packages.

Because so many organizations and individuals are developing ways to help military families, we emphasize the need to evaluate and collaborate more to be more effective and to sustain support over the long term. We have to work smart. When troops start coming home, will people think, "The war is over" and turn their attention to something else? We need to build a sustainable support structure, so we can continue to be flexible and meet the needs of military families.

Joyce Wessel Raezer
Executive Director, National Military Family Association

Military Family Research Institute at Purdue University

Celebrating its 15th year in 2015, the Military Family Research Institute (MFRI) at Purdue University conducts research on military families, designs and implements outreach activities, and builds partnerships within civilian and military communities. The idea for this textbook emerged from the leadership of MFRI and is an example of MFRI's mission to "extend and strengthen" the ability of people and organizations to understand and support military families. MFRI's research projects have focused on children and youth; military families, particularly National Guard and Reserve families; and public health and family support. MFRI offers consultation to postsecondary institutions to strengthen their support of student service members and veterans, and assistance to student veteran organizations as they become established on college campuses. In collaboration with the Center for Deployment Psychology (http://www.deploymentpsych.org/) and others, MFRI developed Star Behavioral Health Providers (SBHP), a system for training civilian behavioral health specialists in military culture, challenges associated with military service, and clinical skills. Accompanying the training is an online resource for military families to locate trained providers knowledgeable about military life. First started in Indiana, SBHP now includes Michigan, Georgia, and California and expanded to include Ohio and South Carolina in 2013 (see http://www.starproviders.org/).

Other initiatives include a joint effort with the Departments of Defense and Agriculture and the NMFA, to develop an 11-issue publication, *How to Help Military and Veteran Families*, for community audiences (e.g., employers, child-care providers, faith-based communities, teachers, first responders), available online at MFRI, Military OneSource, and USDA's Cooperative Extension. Through MFRI's Community Mobilization Grant Program

Indiana communities can access monetary grants to expand and improve services to military families at a local level (www.mfri.purdue.edu).

American Red Cross

One of the primary missions of the American Red Cross is to provide assistance to victims of wars and natural disasters. The Red Cross will send emergency communications to military members stationed anywhere. Messages are delivered 24 hours a day, 7 days a week throughout the year. The Red Cross sends factual and verified descriptions of the emergency through the military chain of command, and unit commanders rely on such verification of emergencies when deciding whether emergency leave is possible. Families have to provide details about the emergency situation (e.g., the name of the individual who is ill or who has died, the family relationship, and the contact information for the hospital or funeral home) and information about their service member. To facilitate timely contact families must be prepared to give the service member's full name and military address, social security number or date of birth, rank and rating, branch of service, unit name, and if deployed, the name of the home unit.

Along with military aid societies, the Red Cross provides financial assistance to eligible active duty and retired military personnel, their dependants, and widows of retired military personnel. The Red Cross Casualty Travel Assistance Program provides for transportation for two immediate family members to attend a memorial or funeral service for a military member killed in a combat zone or to go to the bedside of a service member wounded in a combat zone. As in other conflicts, the Red Cross maintains canteens in Iraq and Afghanistan where service members can relax, make phone calls, use email, watch a video, or chat with one of the workers or other service members (http://www.redcross.org).

Blue Star and Gold Star Organizations

Beginning in World War I, small "service flags" were hung in the front windows of homes of service members. The home's service flag had a blue star for each member of the family who was in military service. The blue star was changed to a gold star if the military member died. From this practice emerged the terms *blue star mother* and *gold star mother* and the formation of organizations recognizing those families.

American Gold Star Mothers, Inc. (http://www.goldstarmoms.com) was incorporated as a non-profit organization in 1929. Members provide comfort to one another, volunteer at hospitals for veterans, and offer support to veterans and their families. They participate in national holidays that recognize veterans and service in the military.

Gold Star Wives, Inc. (http://www.goldstarwives.org) was formed after World War II, and today is open to widows and widowers of service members who die on active duty or due to a military-related cause. Members provide support to one another, participate in national memorial services, and volunteer at VA medical centers and in their local communities.

The beginnings of Blue Star Mothers of America, Incorporated trace back to World War II (http://www.bluestarmothers.org). Members volunteer at VA hospitals or clinics, send care packages to troops, assist other veteran organizations, and promote patriotism.

Blue Star Families (http://bluestarfam.org) was started in 2008 to advocate for military families with policy makers and connect citizens and military families. Programs include distributing books to libraries on military installations; offering an online survey for military families to indicate their concerns; and assisting civilians through Operation Appreciation to communicate their gratitude to military families.

Founded in 2005, Military Families United is a coalition of Gold Star and Blue Star families (http://www.militaryfamiliesunited.org). It hosts Gold Star Family luncheons where families who have lost a service member may meet one another; a database of service members who died since World War II; and other projects.

Tragedy Assistance Program for Survivors

Started by the wife of an Army officer after her husband died in a military plane crash, Tragedy Assistance Program for Survivors (TAPS) is a non-profit organization that serves the needs of families whose service member has died. The organization's cornerstone program is the peer support network staffed by volunteers who are at least 1 year beyond the death of their military member and who have attended TAPS peer-mentor training. TAPS also offers crisis response professionals by phone 24 hours a day, assistance with understanding military benefits, a quarterly magazine, a guide for survivors, and online chats and webinars. Survivor Seminars provide social support and education about grief and traumatic loss, and Good Grief Camps for children teach coping skills and build social support (http://www.taps.org).

Military Child Education Coalition

The Military Child Education Coalition (MCEC) is a non-profit organization that promotes quality education for military children who may experience multiple transitions as they change schools during a parent's military career. MCEC works with military installations and schools that serve military children to provide information for families with school-age children. It offers access to school requirements for each state, the DODEA, and Washington, DC. MCEC offers workshops for parents so they can advocate for quality education for their children, and materials that address how deploying parents can stay involved in their children's education, how parents can encourage development of literacy skills, and how parents and other family members can support learning prior to a child entering school. It also sponsors military student peer-to-peer programs to help students transitioning to and from schools. It offers educational materials for communities and schools to raise awareness of the military culture and ideas on how they can support military children (http://www.militarychild.org).

National Resource Directory for Military and Veteran Communities

The National Resource Directory is a website for ill, injured, or wounded service members, veterans, family members, and their supporters. The directory includes military and civilian resources and services available at national, state, and local levels to assist with recovery, rehabilitation, and reintegration into the community. Included are veteran service and benefit organizations, non-profit and community agencies, universities, and professional organizations. Glossaries provide definitions of terms used by DoD, the VA, the Department of Labor, TRICARE, and mental health and long-term care settings (www.nationalresourcedirectory.gov).

ASSISTING MILITARY MEMBERS AND THEIR FAMILIES TO REINTEGRATE AND REUNITE

The following programs are designed to help military members with issues related to continuing their lives successfully after deploying and to help military families reunite after a long and difficult separation.

Operation Healthy Reunions

Operation Healthy Reunions is sponsored by Mental Health America (formerly known as the National Mental Health Association), a community-based non-profit agency committed to improving the psychological health of everyone who lives in the U.S. (Mental Health America, 2010b). Operation Healthy Reunions was developed to improve the psychological health of military members and families after their return from deployments (Mental Health America, 2010a). Its goal is to facilitate a healthy reunion among military couples and families. The program provides education on reuniting with spouses and children after a deployment, coping with war and the psychological health problems that can result from the war experience (i.e., depression and PTSD). Often, Operation Healthy Reunions staff members and volunteers provide psychological health services in military families' local communities free or at low cost to the family. Many of Mental Health America's over 320 nationwide affiliates provide some or all of the following additional services to military families:

- Confidential evaluations and treatment by professional mental health providers.
- Case management (coordination of treatment).
- Support groups.
- Symptom recognition and management classes.
- Couples and family counseling.
- Advocacy.

Voices From the Frontline

NEW SUPPORTS FOR FAMILIES

Today families are getting more support with homecoming.

In late 2005, there were no family reintegration programs. My return home was quick. My family had some idea I was coming back in November. They didn't know exactly when until 48 hours before I came back. Our unit came into Fort Benning. We did our out-processing, each of us got a plane ticket and scattered in all different directions.

The system is so large it is difficult to navigate. I got that airplane ticket home and there I was—the little guy in the big system . . . on my own. Today families are getting more support with homecoming. They don't have to have to navigate this complex time totally alone.

Chris Sullins
Former Army Reserve Combat Stress Prevention Officer

Heroes to Hometowns

The American Legion—a non-profit veterans' mutual help organization—sponsors Heroes to Hometowns (H2H), the only nationwide transition-assistance program for severely wounded veterans injured in the global war on terrorism (American Legion, 2010). The focus of H2H is to provide prompt and easily accessed services and benefits to service members who cannot remain in the military because of their injuries. In order to facilitate services and avoid duplicating services, H2H has established networks at the national, state, and local community levels that can coordinate government and civilian resources. The H2H program offers a support network and coordinated resources for individual service members and their families.

The H2H helps transitional service members and their families deal with aspects of leaving the military service. Services range from psychological support to practical assistance and can include such services as help with paying bills, adapting vehicles and homes to accommodate physical limitations, transportation to medical care, and a referral to the United States Paralympics Military Division (a division of the U.S. Olympic Committee that promotes an international sport event for athletes with physical disabilities every 4 years).

Homes for Our Troops

Homes for Our Troops is a national non-profit organization founded in 2004 to provide homes for service members who have come home from combat deployments since September 11, 2001 with serious disabilities and injuries (Homes for Our Troops, 2009). Homes for Our Troops raises money, building materials, and professional labor through donations. They also coordinate the building of homes that provide disabled service members with greater independence and the maximum freedom of movement allowed by their injuries. Homes for Our Troops works with the VA to ensure that the homes are provided at no cost to all veterans, including military members still serving. Veterans and service members who are eligible can receive a grant from Veterans Affairs specially adapted housing. If the grant is insufficient for the building of a home for the veteran's needs, Homes for Our Troops will cover all costs not covered by the grant.

Intrepid Fallen Heroes Fund and National Intrepid Center of Excellence

In June 2010 the Intrepid Fallen Heroes Fund opened the new, state-of-the-art National Intrepid Center of Excellence (NICoE) as a research, diagnosis, and treatment center for service members and veterans with Traumatic Brain Injury (TBI) and psychological health conditions (Defense Centers of Excellence, 2010c). The NICoE is located on a Navy installation in Bethesda, Maryland, next to the new Walter Reed National Military Medical Center. It has close access to the Uniformed Services University, the National Institutes of Health, and the Veterans Health Administration.

The Intrepid Fallen Heroes Fund was originally established in 2000 to provide financial support for family members of military personnel killed in the line of duty (Intrepid Fallen Heroes Fund, 2010). It receives its funds through fundraising and contributions. After September 11, 2001 and the beginning of the war on terrorism, the fund was expanded to help meet the growing numbers of families with financial hardships as a result of losing their military family member. In 2003 the fund officially became an independent non-profit organization; it continued to provide monetary gifts to military families needing financial assistance. In 2005 the U.S. government substantially increased the benefits to families who lost a loved one due to military duty, and the Fund turned its efforts to helping service members who have been critically injured in the performance of their duty.

The NICoE is equipped with the most advanced diagnosis and treatment equipment and facilities (Intrepid Sea Air & Space Museum, 2008). It will share state-of-the-art screening, diagnosis, and treatment methods with the military and VA hospitals and with medical facilities throughout the U.S. Long-term follow-up care will be part of each client's care plan, ensuring that when service members separate from the military, they continue to receive the treatment they need. The NICoE is also co-located with two 21-room Fisher Houses to accommodate the families of service members and veterans receiving services at the NICoE. Fisher Houses provide accommodation to families of military patients at no charge, similar to civilian Ronald McDonald Houses providing a temporary home for families with a hospitalized child. You will learn more about the Fisher House Foundation in the following section.

Fisher House Foundation

The not-for-profit Fisher House Foundation constructs houses with 8 to 21 suites where military family members may stay while their service member is hospitalized for injury, illness, or disease. The 64 Fisher Houses are located on military installations with a major medical center and VA medical centers. The Foundation donates the houses to the U.S. government, and secretaries of the military departments and the VA operate and maintain the houses. Stays at a Fisher House are free to military families.

Between 1990 and 2013, over 200,000 military families stayed at a Fisher House. In 2013, the average length of stay for a family whose service member had experienced a combat-related injury was 45–60 days. Over 22,000 families stayed at a Fisher House that year, saving those families $35 million in lodging, food, and transportation costs. The Fisher House Foundation also supports three other programs: Hero Miles, which has provided 50,000 airline tickets to service members and their families; Newman's Own Award, a grant program that supports other military charities; and Scholarships for Military Children, which has provided 7,000 military children and spouses with $11,000,000 in scholarships ("Fisher House Facts," n.d.).

Operation: Military Kids

Operation: Military Kids (OMK) is a partnership of Army Child, Youth and School Services (CYS) and the 4-H National Headquarters of the U.S. Department of Agriculture to support National Guard and Army Reserve children. OMK has six goals: to create local networks of support for military children during deployment; to provide educational, social and recreational programs through local community organizations near where children live; to support military children as they cope with stress related to combat deployments; to collaborate with schools so teachers and staff are prepared to support military children; to educate the public on the deployment cycle and its implications for families; and to connect Guard and Reserve families with OMK's partner programs offered by 4-H Clubs, the American Legion, Boys and Girls Clubs of America, and other organizations (Oram, n.d.). In 2013, over 105,739 military youth participated in activities conducted by OMK Teams in 49 states and the District of Columbia (Operation: Military Kids, n.d.).

OMK uses several programs to achieve its goals. Ready! Set! Go! Training provides community members and groups with training about the experiences and military children, military culture, and deployment so that they can be better prepared to work effectively with military children. Speak Out for Military Kids (SOMK) is a means by which military and non-military youth educate local communities about military children and deployment, and encourage support of military youth in local communities. Mobile Technology Lab travels to community locations so military children can use digital cameras, scanners, video and photo editing software, and webpage design programs to enhance their technology skills (www.operationmilitarykids.org).

Sesame Workshop

In 2006, Sesame Workshop began addressing military family issues with its English and Spanish versions of Talk, Listen, Connect programs for children and adults (see Box 12.2). Separate programs address deployment, homecoming, changes brought about by injuries to a service member, and grieving the death of a service member. Each of these programs includes video segments for adults and for children, materials for download, activities for children and families, and links to other organizations. In the Family Connections section of the Sesame Street website, families can create their own online family network where members can post messages, artwork, and photos and record video

BOX 12.2   BEST PRACTICES

SESAME WORKSHOP SUPPORTS MILITARY FAMILIES

Our goal is to give parents words they can use to help children share their feelings during these difficult times.

One morning in 2005, on his train ride to work, Gary Knell, President and CEO of Sesame Workshop, saw a newspaper article about challenges facing military families. He called me saying, "There's a problem here. We need to understand military families and their children."

We know about the Muppets and media. So we brought together experts about military children to help us understand what they were experiencing and how we could help. We learned there were 800,000 preschoolers in active duty and National Guard and Reserve families. Support materials for them existed but they were antiquated and not in "kid-speak."

It was the start of an amazing journey for all of us as we began developing resources to help children and their adults talk about changes in their lives when a parent goes away, comes back changed visibly or invisibly, and when a parent dies. You can find many of them at http://www.sesameworkshop.org/initiatives/emotion/tlc.

It is comforting to children—and their parents—to hear Elmo speaking about what they are experiencing as the 3½ year old he is. When people can talk together, they are not alone and life feels more manageable. When children in military families are doing well, their parents can focus on their work.

We've been received well at all levels up to Admiral Mullen. I think it is important to see that an organization like ours, outside the military, cares about military families. We are continuing to assess what the needs are, with the goal of reaching out to other members of children's support community including extended family members, doctors, and teachers. Military families are going to need support for a long time as service members return home changed to families that have changed.

When we started this work, I did not know one person in the military. It has changed my perspective on life. Learning about military families' bravery, loyalty and dedication to our country has made me a better mother, wife, and friend. I feel blessed to have had the opportunity to oversee this work.

Lynn Chwatsky
Assistant Vice President, Outreach Initiative and Partners, Sesame Workshop

messages. Sesame Street, in collaboration with the USO, also tours a Muppet show as part of the Talk, Listen, Connect initiative.

Studies conducted on the Talk, Listen, Connect programs (i.e., deployment, multiple deployments and homecoming, and changes due to injuries) indicated that program materials were widely appealing, understandable, and relevant. Military parents and those caring for military children reported the materials changed the way they helped children cope with deployment and parental injury and increased their level of comfort in doing so. They cited increased communication with children and encouraging children to ask more questions. A majority of parents and caregivers reported the information presented was "very" or "extremely" helpful (Burton & MacDermid Wadsworth, 2011; Chawla & MacDermid Wadsworth, 2011).

ZERO TO THREE

ZERO TO THREE, a non-profit organization, provides information, support, and training to parents, professionals, and policy makers on the health and development of infants and toddlers. ZERO TO THREE has developed materials to help the parents, caregivers, and professionals who are providing care to the more than 500,000 children born to military families during the Iraq and Afghanistan wars (ZERO TO THREE: National Center for Infants, Toddlers and Families, 2014). As noted in Box 12.1, these resources were developed to address the challenges of military life, from deployment and relocation to the trauma, grief, and loss that are experienced by some military families. Materials can be ordered at no charge through Military OneSource at www.militaryonesource.com.

BOX 12.3   BEST PRACTICES

Trust and relationships deepen and families and children grow even stronger.

Children under three sense and absorb what is happening around them. We want to be the voice of the baby and toddler to help families and professionals see and understand the child's perspective and behavior so they can decide how best to respond. Parents have a lot on their plates—even on the best of days. When a family is dealing with separation during deployment, homecoming, an injury (seen or unseen) or a transition to civilian life it is even more difficult to provide the safe base young children need to feel secure and thrive.

We want anyone working with families of babies and toddlers to have information they need, from the home visitor, to the pediatrician, to the person at the front desk of a child-care setting or health clinic. Think for a minute about a mom whose partner has been deployed for the last 3 months. She's exhausted and her toddler's shoe has been lost on the way to child care. Put yourself in her place. How does she feel when the person at the desk greets her with criticism, whether in a look or words? What if that same person says, "Toddlers are always wiggling around when you try to get their shoes on; it can be so hard getting them out the door sometimes. What can I do to help? Shall I go look in your car?" When you are helpful to a family, you are helpful to their young child.

One of our first forays in working with the military community was soon after 9/11. We had developed a brochure called Little Listeners in recognition that 9/11 was a national trauma and that all families were affected, which meant babies and toddlers would be impacted, too.

We started thinking about the additional implications for military families and tried to be mindful about their unique lens. Not only were they contending with 9/11, but they were also dealing with not knowing how their families might be affected in terms of increased OPTEMPO and deployment. We decided to adapt Little Listeners so that it was more tailored to military families' needs and experiences.

At Fort Riley we convened The Little Listeners Committee of interdisciplinary professionals, who work with families. Together we developed training and materials they could use to spread the word so that all of their colleagues on the installation had information they needed to support families with children under three. Because military families are so busy and have so much information coming at them, we realized, the simpler the better. Our strategy became offering "easily digestible nuggets" of information through parent flyers in the commissaries, pediatrician's offices, and other places that families typically go.

In our first years, we also developed materials for families and professionals about topics such as deployment, homecoming, and managing on the home front. We also wrote a number of children's books. Over time, to respond to the realities military families were dealing with, we developed materials for families experiencing their service members' physical injuries and unseen injuries such as TBI, PTSD and depression. We also wrote about what a young child might experience and ways to respond when a parent dies. Most of our resources for parents and professionals are downloadable at http://www.zerotothree.org/about-us/funded-projects/military-families/. And the majority of our children's books are available through Military OneSource at http://www.militaryonesource.mil/.

More recently we have been responding to families transitioning out of service. The military has gone such a long way from the days of "If we had wanted you to have a wife, we would have issued you one." It has built out an incredible infrastructure of family services including home visiting, early care and education, and early intervention services.

When families transition out, they must deal with the loss of these services even as they deal with a shift in identity as an individual and as a family. Veteran families are also losing their social support system at a time they need it most. If a family is dealing with the residue of a physical or emotional injury of their service member, life is even more complex.

Veteran families are going to be relying on their surrounding communities. How do we help build community capacity to respond to them? Just knowing to ask, "Have you or a family member ever served?" can be a powerful first step in identifying, engaging, and supporting a family who has transitioned out of service. We have adapted materials and training to include the voices of veterans and their families. Guides for professionals and veteran families can be downloaded on our website and we're searching for funding to be able to distribute hard copies more widely.

As part of our ongoing effort to be responsive, we've also adapted our training: Coming Together Around Veteran Families™. Most recently we have been developing a parenting app that reflects military and veteran family perspective and video podcasts, 2–3 minutes long that will provide virtual "digestible nuggets" of information.

Military and veteran families are resilient. When we can help family members think about what their youngest children experience, they can then use this information to make decisions about how to respond. As a result, trust and relationships deepen and families and children grow even stronger.

Dorinda Silver Williams, PhD, LCSW-C, ACSW
Director, Military Family Projects, ZERO TO THREE

COLLABORATIVE ENDEAVORS TO PROVIDE SERVICES FOR MILITARY FAMILIES

Civilian organizations are partnering with the Active and Reserve Components of the Armed Forces to develop and offer programs, services and resources to military families. Collaborative efforts occur at the national, state, and community levels; and between government agencies, universities, and non-profit organizations. The following are examples of these collaborations and of the resulting services and programs in support of military families.

United States Department of Agriculture (USDA) and Land-Grant Universities

The DoD has partnered with the USDA, land-grant universities, and the Extension Service to conduct research and offer education and extension programs for military personnel and their families (U.S. Department of Agriculture & Department of Defense Partnership, 2010). Each state has been granted land by the federal government to establish a **land-grant university** to make education more accessible to the working class and to teach agriculture, engineering, sciences, and military tactics; to conduct research; and to provide Extension Services (Washington State University Extension, 2009). The Extension Service, also referred to as the Cooperative Extension Service, is part of the USDA. Extension Services are offered in each state through the state's land-grant university. The goal of Extension Services is to "reach out" and "extend" research-based information and education to the state's citizens (USDA, 2011).

The partnerships among the DoD, USDA, Extension Services, and land-grant universities are many; we will focus on a few here. To learn about others, go to partnership webpage (http://militaryfamilies.extension.org/mission).

The Clearinghouse for Military Family Readiness is housed at Pennsylvania State University. Its purpose is to disseminate scientifically based information about military family readiness, including evidence-based programs; to offer guidance to professionals who work with military families, youth, and children; and to create a virtual library of research on Exceptional Family Member Program Support and best practices on how best to support families.

The Clearinghouse reviews programs for their evidence base to support their intended outcomes and continued effects for the individuals, families, and communities targeted by the program. By establishing a rigorous and systematic review process, the Clearinghouse is able to produce concise and unbiased fact sheets about programs that military partners may be considering for use with their populations. The Continuum of Evidence outlines the criteria for vetting programs along the spectrum of Effective to Ineffective, taking into consideration research design, sustained effects beyond program intervention, independent replication of a program evaluation, significant effects, practical significance of findings, appropriate measurement and use of assessment tools, and both attrition and representativeness of the participant population.

Programs can have their placement on the Continuum changed over time due to new peer-reviewed research that further supports or refines previous outcomes, that extends knowledge of sustained effects, or that is conducted by an independent evaluator (one who is not the program developer and has no conflicts of interest). Placement status of a program does not extend to adaptations of that program, unless the adaptation shows the same outcomes and sustained effects utilizing a shortened intervention time.

The Military Extension Internship Program is housed at Purdue University. Interested college students apply for internships at child and youth development programs on military installations. Program staff conduct initial training in military culture and family life prior to the interns leaving for their placements. Amy Schott, Internship Coordinator, describes the program in more detail in *Best Practices*. In *Voices From the Frontline*, Laura Peterson describes her experience in the Military Extension Internship Program.

Voices From the Frontline

FORMER INTERN SHARES HER EXPERIENCES

Thinking about doing an internship? Do it. During my internship I worked with the Navy Child, and Youth Programs (CYP). I gained personal friendships and professional colleagues, and I applied what I learnt from classes and textbooks about children and families to the program.

Thanks to my internship I am now the Training and Curriculum Specialist at Naval Support Activity, Annapolis. I provide annual required training for staff in our child development center, youth center, and child development homes. The military is a strong community. I'm big on creating community in our programs, too. I believe in collaborating with families and invite them into our programs.

Children in military families do face stressors. How the stressors impact them depends on the child, the family, and the supports available. Civilian children experience stress as well; however, they may not have access to the supports they need. If we give children support, they can be resilient whether they are part of a military or civilian family.

Laura Peterson
Training and Curriculum Specialist at Naval Support Activity, Annapolis

---

BOX 12.4   BEST PRACTICES

INTERNSHIP OPPORTUNITIES FOR COLLEGE STUDENTS

There are many benefits for students.

I coordinate the Military Extension Internship Program at Purdue Extension Service for college students and recent graduates who want to learn about hands-on work with youth and child-care programs and program management. We recruit nationwide and look for people with a commitment to the field. The program is a collaboration between the Department of Defense and the Cooperative Extension Service.

Our interns typically have an academic background in family studies, education, sports and recreation, or management. Some of them are members of military families or soon-to-become members. Others know nothing about the military when they first apply. They live and work on military installations around the world for 10 weeks to 6 months. They are compensated with a stipend or an hourly wage, depending on the military branch.

There are many benefits for students. The military's child-care programs are accredited and people working in them know what they are doing. Students have amazing opportunities such as planning a curriculum or a big event for a program. They develop a sense of self as a professional. Being an intern is a tremendous opportunity to network, not within a single center but with other interns and education and recreation programs around the world.

To get everyone off to a solid start, we have a 5-day orientation where we bring together interns, supervisors, points of contact with the Armed Services and experts on military families. Interns learn about our program guidelines, military culture and military children, youth, and families. We take them to an installation for the day. It is comforting for people with no experience with the military. I think what surprises people the most is that even though the military has a clear hierarchy, they can be creative, have fun with children they work with and have the opportunity to grow as a professional.

Anyone who is interested in being an intern must be ready to work hard. These are challenging positions. The people who work with the interns are very busy, so interns need to be able to take the initiative at times; however, there is also lots of support. People at these programs love their jobs. I tell our interns, "You are walking into a supportive community of people who are committed to each other and to the children and families they serve."

Amy Schott
Internship Coordinator, Cooperative Extension Service, Purdue University

Interstate Compact on Educational Opportunities for Military Children

The Interstate Compact on Educational Opportunities for Military Children is an agreement among states on how to handle educational issues that often vary across states, such as enrollment, placement, eligibility, and graduation requirements (Council of State Governments, 2008). The compact was drafted by the **Council of State Governments** (a non-profit, non-partisan organization for state governments) in response to guidance provided by an advisory group convened in 2006 and in cooperation with the DoD to examine the educational needs of military children resulting from parental deployment and relocation. The compact was developed to avoid educational inconsistencies across states. For example, a child who begins kindergarten in one state may be denied enrollment in kindergarten in another state 4 months later when the family relocates. Or a child in a gifted and talented program may be barred from placement in an equivalent program in a new school. At times, military children who transfer schools find themselves repeating or missing courses (e.g., Algebra I, U.S. History) or course work, or barred from participating in extra-curricular activities due to missing deadlines for tryouts. The Interstate Compact on Educational Opportunities for Military Children provides guidance to school personnel to recognize and appropriately address these unfortunate situations.

Both sending schools (i.e., a school the military child is leaving) and receiving schools (i.e., a school the military child will be attending) have responsibilities. The sending school must prepare educational records for parents to take to the new (i.e., receiving) school, and provide and verify information sought by a receiving school. The receiving school must enroll a student based on the unofficial records pending validation by official records and must request official records; allow students 30 days to obtain the required immunizations; and allow students, regardless of age, to continue in kindergarten or first grade or enroll a student at the next highest grade if the prerequisite grade was completed. The receiving school is also to place students in courses (e.g., honors, technical, advanced placement) and programs (e.g., gifted and talented, English as a Second Language) based on those at the sending school, and recognize the current Individualized Education Program (IEP) and make reasonable accommodations and modifications to address needs of students with disabilities. Receiving schools should show flexibility in waiving prerequisites or preconditions of courses or programs and facilitate a student's inclusion in extracurricular activities regardless of deadlines. If a waiver is not given for specific course requirements completed satisfactorily at another school, the receiving school is to provide coursework so graduation may occur on time. If students, transferring at the beginning or during their senior year, are ineligible to graduate from the receiving school, they are to receive a diploma from the sending school if graduation requirements of that school are met. In addition, the receiving school is to accept exit requirements or exams required for graduation from the sending state, national achievement tests, or alternative testing. Students are to be granted additional excused absences to visit a parent or legal guardian who will be deploying, or is on leave or returning from combat deployment (Council of State Governments, 2008). Finally, receiving schools are to recognize a special power of attorney or guardianship for actions requiring parental consent; not charge tuition for a military child placed with a non-custodial parent or other person acting in loco parentis who lives in the school jurisdiction other than the custodial parent; and allow a child residing with a non-custodial parent or other in loco parentis to continue to attend the school enrolled in while residing with the custodial parent.

If parents encounter difficulty in transferring their children from one school to another, they can contact the National Military Family Association or the Military Child Education Coalition for guidance about the compact and ideas for advocating on behalf of their children (Council of State Governments, 2008). In August 2014 New York became the 50th state to adopt the interstate compact to facilitate a smoother transition for military children as they transfer schools and experience a parent's combat-related deployment (Military Interstate Children's Compact Commission, 2014).

State-Level Collaborations with Universities

The past decade has seen the formation of several partnerships between the Reserve Component and universities within states. Four examples are given here to illustrate how such collaborations are resulting in services to Active and Reserve Component families. As Bob Short describes in Voices From the Frontline, these services are needed.

The Buddy-to-Buddy program is a collaboration between the University of Michigan, Michigan State University, and Michigan Army National Guard leaders. This peer-to-peer program trains soldiers selected by the command to be a buddy who initiates regular contact with an assigned group of MI ARNG soldiers returning from deployment. During "check in" calls, a buddy normalizes getting help when necessary, conveys knowledge of resources and referrals, and maintains contact when a soldier seeks help. Second level buddies are trained more extensively in motivational interviewing and civilian and military resources; they staff the National Guard Armories during drill weekends (Greden, Valentine, Springer, Blow, Gorman, Dalack, Marcus, & Kees, 2010).

Voices From the Frontline

BUDDY-TO-BUDDY

One of the most rewarding things I've done in my life.

Buddy-to-Buddy was developed at the University of Michigan in partnership with the Army National Guard in Michigan, and faculty from the Veterans Administration Health System and Michigan State University. When deployments started, leaders recognized that National Guard troops who came home and scattered to the winds in small communities would be isolated from the Army and each other. They would need support.

One of the great ironies I run into all the time with young veterans is that they are very quick to help when they see other people in danger. If someone is in trouble they are there. They have learned to be strong, independent, and self-sufficient.

I tell young veterans that I was the same way when I came home. I figured if I had survived war, I could handle anything that comes at me. I also say I've lived long enough now to know that everyone has or can benefit from a helping hand and accepting that is a sign of strength, not a weakness.

A big part of what we do is to reach out and listen. Coming home, veterans feel disconnected. They are different people than when they left home. Sometimes they are reluctant to tell their stories. We say, "If you are interested in telling me, I'd like to hear your story."

To become a volunteer, a veteran has to present her or himself well and be able to learn new skills. We have 120 volunteers and assign them to units close to their homes. They go to monthly drills and get to know people. We tell volunteers not to expect people to line up and share their deepest experiences. It takes time to be viewed as trustworthy.

About 50% of our volunteers are Vietnam vets like me. We are retired and have time. We remember how it felt to come home and feel like a fish out of water. Close to a third of our volunteers are post-9/11 vets. Many of them have received assistance from vets in our program and now want to help others. The rest are in between.

We go to events like veteran job fairs to make our services known. We have made connections with the Veterans Administration (VA), clinics, and hospitals in Michigan so that they can refer vets to us and we can refer vets to them as needed.

Veterans have a bond across generations. We've all served in the uniform and many of us in war. It's not putting down people who haven't served and their desire to try to understand. It's just that serving is a unique experience.

Half of our training is devoted to communication skills. We talk about how to listen, to pause, to ask for permission to take notes and how to offer advice. It is very different to ask someone, "May I offer an idea or two?" rather than present a list of steps to be taken.

We also teach our volunteers about confidentiality. It is key to building trust. We make it clear that we do not report back to chain of command with two exceptions: when a veteran is thinking about or actually hurting themselves or someone else.

We tell volunteers that the program isn't about them. It is about the young veterans. Ironically though, at some point, many of our volunteers admit they are benefitting more than the person they are helping. There's a quote about PTSD: "It's not what we get but what we give that heals us." It applies here, too.

Vets tend to realize we are not going to judge them. A young veteran may have been in rotten situations and done rough things up to and including killing people. Sometimes that is even more difficult to deal with after the fact. Often veterans are afraid of getting a reaction of disgust from family members. We accept them and let them know that whatever they had to do, we understand.

I think people come out of war not knowing how they feel. So many years later, being part of a writing group has helped me get in touch with feelings I didn't know I had. Buddy-to-Buddy is about the power of reaching out to young veterans, listening and connecting. Many times you almost see the light bulbs setting off in their heads: "I need to stop drinking," "We need to see a marriage counselor." People hear themselves for the first time. Being seen by someone else lets you see yourself.

Here are two stories about the power of listening:

Several months ago, I was in a barbershop having my hair cut. The woman cutting my hair asked what I did. I told her about Buddy-to-Buddy. She was quiet. A few minutes later, she told me that her brother could use help. He'd fought in the two battles of Fallujah. He was drinking and living in his father's basement.

He called me a few weeks later. He walked in shuffling, head down. He had fought both battles of Fallujah. He talked about how we had taken Fallujah, then lost it to the Iraqi insurgency and had to take it again. "I'm angry and don't know why," he said. I told him I was the same when I came home from Vietnam. We shared a few laughs and a few tears. I could see him sitting up straighter. He slammed his fist on the table hard, taking me by surprise. "You know what I need," he said. "I need to work with other vets like you." After that one hour conversation and a cup of coffee, he moved out of the basement and he and his father have started a small business.

In October, the mother of another Iraq vet called me. She told me her son had broken his neck in Iraq, he was full of anger and wouldn't talk to her. I said, "If you can get him to call me, we'll talk."

In December I called back and left a phone message for her. She let her son listen to it. He called me at a time I wasn't there to pick up the phone and left a very angry message and (his mother later told me) had jumped in his truck and driven off. I called him back and we arranged to meet.

Two volunteers and I met him for coffee. He was angry about how he had been treated. He said he'd been pushed out of the Army and had no trust in the Veterans'

Administration (VA). One of the volunteers offered to help him connect to a patient advocate we know at the VA.

In March I saw in the local news that this young vet had been killed. He'd rolled his pick-up truck over one night. A few hours later the phone rang. It was his mother. I expected her to be angry but she wasn't. She told me she was absolutely sure he hadn't committed suicide. He'd gotten into the VA and was looking forward to getting a job and a dog. He had regained his soul before he died. He had stopped sleeping with a loaded gun. They had long talks together. She was calling to say, "thank you."

The people we select as volunteers are sincere. They know the value of someone reaching out a hand that pulls you up, not down. Many of them learned from not having or taking a hand.

This is one of the most rewarding things I've done in my life.

Bob Short, MS, MBA
Former Director of Training and Western Michigan Regional Coordinator
Buddy-to-Buddy Volunteer Veteran Program

Deployment programming for the Michigan Army National Guard (MI ARNG) resulted from a partnership that developed between the MI ARNG and faculty from Michigan State University and the University of Michigan Medical School. Programming at predeployment and reintegration 2-day events include educational presentations about stress reactions, TBI, and military and civilian community resources; and sessions in which service members and family members speak about their deployment experiences. Lessons learnt from this partnership include the importance of integrating two cultures, military and university, which differ in management structure and expectations about research and program development (Dalack et al., 2010).

Essential Life Skills for Military Families is a program designed specifically for Reserve Component members to strengthen relationship and practical skills. Supported by funding from the U.S. Department of Health and Human Services and the Administration for Children and Families, East Carolina. University faculty, North Carolina National Guard family support leaders, and Cooperative Extension agents worked together to design the curriculum (Carroll, Robinson, Orthner, Matthews, & Smith-Rotabi, 2008). A key feature of this program is that it creates a community-level partnership between a civilian support organization and the National Guard and Military Reserves (Huebner et al., 2009). The 8-hour, evidence-based curriculum addresses unexpected challenges, financial matters, legal issues, and family resilience (see http://www.militaryfamily lifeskills.org/).

Passport Toward Success is a reintegration program for military children and youth aged 5 to 17, offered at Indiana National Guard Yellow Ribbon events 60 days after a unit returns from deployment (Wilson, Wilkum, Chernichky, MacDermid Wadswoth, & Broniarczyk, 2011). Staff from the Military Family Research Institute at Purdue University developed the program which is delivered by trained facilitators and community volunteers, thereby building the local community's understanding of military children (Huebner et al., 2009). Informed by models of family resilience (e.g., Walsh, 2003c) the program promotes skill development and family processes in such areas as sharing emotions, perceiving and receiving social support, and communication. Grouped by ages, children visit three "islands" (i.e., feelings, relaxation, and communication). Evaluation of the program in its initial 2 years showed, among other findings, that a majority of youth who participated in the program reported acquiring new ideas about resiliency skills. Youth who reported more stress related to deployment and reunion evaluated the program as especially beneficial (Wilson et al., 2011).

CONTINUING EDUCATION FOR CIVILIAN PROFESSIONALS

In addition to becoming familiar with the polices, services, programs, and resources covered in Chapters 11 and 12 and throughout this book, you may wish to continue learning more about military and veteran families and to develop specific clinical skills if you are a mental health provider or in graduate training to become one. Courses on military family life are offered at many universities. Some of these may offer a certificate or a concentration in military families. Regional or statewide trainings sponsored by professional associations may offer workshops (Waliski, Kirchner, Shue, & Bokony, 2012). Other avenues for continuing education and training include webinars, multiple-day trainings, and learning communities. Explore the options offered by a range of centers:

- The Center for Deployment Psychology (http://www.deploymentpsych.org/psychological-training): offers online training in military culture competence, combat stress on families and children; clinical issues and treatments; self-assessment exercises; a Speakers Bureau; a week-long course for couple and family therapists, licensed professional counselors, psychiatrists, psychologists, and social workers on behavioral health concerns of service members, veterans, and their families. It also provides training for the Star Behavioral Health Providers program to increase the number of mental health professionals in local communities who have the knowledge and skills to treat service members, veterans, and their families.
- Defense Centers of Excellence for Psychological Heath & Traumatic Brain Injury (http://www.dcoe.mil/Training.aspx) offers monthly webinars on topics pertaining to psychological health and traumatic brain injury.
- Defense and Veterans Brain Injury Center (http://dvbic.dcoe.mil/online-education) offers webinars on TBI.
- The National Center for PTSD (http://www.ptsd.va.gov/professional/continuing_ed/index.asp) offers online education on topics related to trauma and PTSD.
- The National Child Traumatic Stress Network (http://learn.nctsn.org) offers continuing education on Psychological First Aid, child trauma, and military families; and a military families learning community.
- Massachusetts General Hospital (http://mghcme.org/page/from_the_war_zone_to_the_home_front) offers online education for health-care professionals on many topics, including military culture, trauma and treatment, and family challenges.

SUMMARY

- Civilian organizations are partnering with the Active and Reserve Components to develop and offer programs, services, and resources to military families.
- Programs designed to provide care for military members who have been injured and to help their families include Wounded Warrior Programs, Heroes to Hometowns, Homes for Our Troops, the Intrepid Fallen Heroes Fund, and the National Intrepid Center of Excellence.
- Partnership programs sponsored by the DoD, the USDA, Extension Services, and land-grant universities include the Clearinghouse on Military Family Readiness and the Military Extension Internship Program.
- Examples of partnerships between the Reserve Component and various universities to provide services to active duty and Reserve Component families include

Buddy-to-Buddy, deployment programming for the Michigan Army National Guard, Essential Life Skills for Military Families, and Passport Toward Success.

EXERCISES

To further explore the types of organizations and programs that serve military families, answer the following questions:

1. Edward Tick, a psychotherapist who has worked with hundreds of veterans with post-traumatic stress disorder, stated, "[t]he moral responsibility for a war must ultimately fall not upon the common soldiers who fought it but upon the nation and its leaders who created it ... The social group must not only witness the stories of its warriors; it must also accept responsibility for their deeds during war and their condition afterward" (Tick, 2005, p. 236). Consider the following questions:

   • To what degree are citizens of a nation responsible for the actions of its political leaders? For its military?
   • To what degree do you agree with Tick's view that the members of society that send someone to war must accept responsibility for the deeds committed during that war and for the well-being of military members upon return from that war?
   • To what degree do programs such as the ones reviewed in this chapter demonstrate our society taking responsibility for the well-being of its service members and their families? What else, if anything, needs to be done to fulfill this responsibility?

2. Go online and learn more about the history of an organization that supports military families. If possible, interview a member from a local chapter of that organization about why she or he joined the group.

3. What programs are available in your community that assist wounded warriors' transition to civilian life?

4. Go to the Clearinghouse for Military Family Readiness website and see what types of programs have been identified to help families, spouses, and children cope with stress and support healthy development. How many of these programs have been used specifically within a military population? What is each program's placement on the Continuum of Evidence? What other factors are on the fact sheets that would help a program manager decide whether or not to invest in a particular program? http://www.militaryfamilies.psu.edu/programs

13

Involving Families in Systems and Strategies of Care

In Chapter 13, you will

- Meet Dr. Shirley Glynn, Clinical Research Psychologist, Manager, VA Family Services National Evidence-based Clinician Training Program and Research Psychologist, and Co-Director, UCLA Welcome Back Veterans Family Resilience Center.
- Gain insight into family-focused systems of care.
- Discover phases of a family-focused injury recovery trajectory and family-centered strategies to use when working with combat-injured families.
- Consider principles of care to use when working with injured service members and their families.
- Review treatment approaches to TBI and PTSD.
- Learn about supporting military families who are engaged in caregiving or are grieving the death of their service member.

Meet

Shirley M. Glynn, PhD, Clinical Research Psychologist; Manager, VA Family Services National Evidence-Based Clinician Training Program; and Research Psychologist Co-Director, UCLA Welcome Back Veterans Family Resilience Center

Expanding Family-Centered Care For Veterans

My job at the Veteran's Administration (VA) is overseeing national training in evidence-based family therapies in mental health services. The VA has been challenged with cultivating more family-centered care for mental health disorders. To shift the culture, we are disseminating four evidence-based behavioral family treatments: behavioral family therapy for psychiatric disorders (Mueser & Glynn, 1999); behavioral couples therapy for substance abuse (O'Farrell & Fals-Stewart, 2006); integrative behavioral couples therapy for marital distress (Christensen et al., 2010); and cognitive-behavioral conjoint therapy for PTSD (Monson & Fredman, 2012). We are also using the Consumer Centered Family Consultation model from the Rochester Family Institute (see http://www.nysfamilyinstitute. org/fiepr-research/).

Part of our work is helping the professionals find their stance with regard to veterans and their loved ones: to consider not only what to say and do but how to be. We are encouraging a much more collaborative stance with veterans and families. Recovery should be personal and consumer-driven. Sometimes clinicians use their knowledge as self-protection and to create distance from families. Many times they would be more effective if they could just be there and listen and offer consultation and support as needed.

Becoming a good listener is often easier said than done. The VA hires and treats a lot of veterans. I am not a veteran. I can't assume I have the same experience as the people I work with or make assumptions about what their experience has been. I cannot do this for those I treat either. I have to be curious about their experiencies. If you keep your curiosity alive and are nonjudgmental you can listen, you can develop empathy for the other person. You can be real and hopeful. By adopting this attitude, you can also help veterans seeking treatment see that they can relate to non-veterans, which will be essential to their successful reintegration into the community.

I wanted to be a clinician and work with families in part because I think my family did not get help with mental health issues when we needed it after some difficulties my relatives had. Twenty-five years ago, I went to the VA to do research on family interventions. I could see the need that veterans had for family support and began researching that area. Today when I'm teaching, I tell people: "Social support is important. The vast majority of the people in the world including those with mental health challenges, want someone to call when they get a bad medical diagnosis or win the lottery, and our job is to shore up those relationships so they have someone to call."

INTRODUCTION

In previous chapters you learned about features and challenges of military life, theories of stress and resilience, the effects of war on service personnel and family members, and support provided by military and civilian communities to military and veteran families. In this chapter we consider injury recovery, psychological first aid, PTSD and TBI treatment, caregiving, and death of a service member. First, we will begin with the importance of family-focused systems of care.

TOWARD FAMILY-FOCUSED SYSTEMS OF CARE

As noted throughout this book, military service has implications for family members, and family life and support are integral to service members' and veterans' well-being. For example, spouses experience disruptions in employment and lower earnings, children experience both benefits and challenges of military family life (Hosek & MacDermid Wadsworth, 2013), and parents of service members worry about their adult service member's safety and well-being (Crow & Myers-Bowman, 2011). Family support during deployment is a protective factor against PTSD (Gewirtz, Polusny, DeGarmo, Khaylis, & Erbes, 2010), stressors at home may increase the risk of posttraumatic stress symptoms (Interian, Kline, Janal, Glynn, & Losonczy, 2014), and single OEF/OIF veterans appreciate parental emotional and instrumental support during the transition to civilian life (Worthen, Moos, & Ahern, 2012).

The interdependence among service members, veterans, and their family members, immediate and extended, highlights the relevance of a systemic perspective when developing services (MacDermid Wadsworth, Lester, Marini, Cozza, Sornborger, Strouse, & Beardslee, 2013). A systems perspective already provides a basis for many preventive programs in use with military and veteran families, including ADAPT, FOCUS, FOCUS-CI, Passport Toward Success, and Strong Bonds. Workshops, counseling, and services offered by military family support centers, and online information and guidance provided by

Military Onesource recognize both the role family members play in supporting service members and the challenges that come with a military life. At the community level, many of the organizations also noted in Chapter 12 (e.g., Military Child Education Coalition, Sesame Workshop) do likewise.

While many programs and services apply a family systems perspective, more work is needed to integrate family-centered approaches into therapeutic treatment and into more organizations that touch the lives of these families, particularly veteran families (MacDermid Wadsworth et al., 2013). The next section describes a family-centered approach applied to caring for combat-injured service members.

Combat-Injury Recovery Process

When service members receive one or more combat injuries, visible or invisible, or become ill, their families enter a medical world for which they may be unprepared. As noted in Chapter 8, practitioners can help families navigate this journey. To assist in this navigation, researchers investigating the impact of service members' combat injuries on families (Cozza et al., 2010) and clinicians have developed a family-focused injury recovery trajectory framework and family-centered intervention strategies to guide their work with families impacted by service members' combat injuries (Cozza, Holmes, & Van Ost, 2013; Cozza et al., 2010; Holmes, Rauch, & Cozza, 2013). The trajectory and strategies are described below. They are followed by a summary of principles of care that provide guidance to civilian as well as military medical and human service providers (Cozza, 2009b).

Phases   A family-focused injury recovery trajectory is conceptualized as having four phases: acute care, medical stabilization, transition to outpatient care, and long-term rehabilitation and recovery (Cozza, Holmes, & Van Ost, 2013; Holmes, Rauch, & Cozza, 2013). The *acute care phase* begins where the injury occurred (e.g., battlefield, aboard ship) and near-by combat hospitals and Naval hospital ships. The focus is to save and sustain life. During this time, as families are notified and receive updates back home, children may overhear information and sense or see and hear the distress and uncertainty of adults. Older children may begin to assume caretaking tasks such as watching younger siblings or doing household chores while a parent is busy with phone calls or is at the hospital.

The second phase, *medical stabilization*, occurs at major medical facilities where medical and/or surgical care is given. A spouse, parent, or friend may relocate to be with the service member. For families with service members with complex injuries, the stay may be quite lengthy and may mean losing a job if the stay goes beyond the Family and Medical Leave Act's 12 weeks of allowed time off the job. This phase can mean a long hospitalization with multiple surgeries or medical procedures and a service member's status can fluctuate (e.g., from critical to serious to fair to serious), adding to the distress of family members.

During this second phase, family roles and routines change as one or more members relocate or spend substantial time at the hospital. Children may accompany their parent in a temporary relocation or remain with a family member or friend. Their daily lives are disrupted. They may visit the hospital once or frequently where they may be exposed to sights of injured people for which they are unprepared. Even if they do not visit their hospitalized parent, children can become frightened and extremely worried by the emotions of their parent or caregiver at home, what they overhear, and what they imagine their injured parent enduring. Children may regress in behavior, become more dependent, or become more aggressive. Older children may do more caregiving and household tasks or disengage from family members.

The third phase is *transition to outpatient care* and begins before the service member is discharged from the hospital. Plans are made for outpatient rehabilitation services, transfer to local doctors, follow-up appointments, financial needs, transportation, and use of community resources. During this phase families may feel overwhelmed as it becomes apparent that they will likely be taking on responsibilities and new roles.

The fourth phase, *rehabilitation and recovery*, occurs as families and service members transition home or to new communities. They will have to establish relationships with a new set of medical and health-care providers and adjust to new routines, expectations, functioning, and roles. Children will now experience family life that centers more around the injured parent's needs. If the family has moved, children will have new schools, peers, and neighbors to adjust to.

Family-Centered Intervention Strategies

Five family-centered intervention strategies for injured service members and their families are being used by practitioners to "promote family equilibrium and resilience under the stress of combat injury and its sequelae" (Cozza et al., 2013, p. 315). These strategies are education, family care management, emotion regulation skills, injury communication, and optimism and future hopefulness (Cozza et al., 2013; Holmes et al., 2013).

Education. The first intervention is education, including education about the injury, its impact, and expected recovery process. Family members enter a confusing world, practically and emotionally, when a service member is injured. It is helpful for them to know that feeling confused and sensing their world is now in chaos is typical and the chaos can be thought of as phases. Likening recovery as a journey with some possible re-hospitalizations and surgeries can offer some predictability and a sense of hope. Families often benefit from talking with other families experiencing similar situations, similar journeys (Cozza et al., 2013).

Education also includes guiding adult family members as they consider developmentally appropriate information to share with children and whether they should come to the hospital, arrangements for children's care, and practical matters related to an extended stay, such as finances, travel, housing. Practitioners may address individual concerns and conflict among family members. They also help the family plan the transition to outpatient care and facilitate problem-solving and acceptance of a new family life. As the recovery process unfolds, family members need education on diagnoses, medical terminology, expected outcomes, and community supports. Family members, especially children, need guidance and reassurance that the injured family member's changed behavior is due to the injury and not their fault or an indication of lack of love or commitment to the partner, child, or family. Children should be protected from taking on responsibilities that hinder their development academically and emotionally (Cozza et al., 2013).

Family Care Management. Family care management (FCM) focuses on developing a plan that considers both medical and psychosocial factors related to the injury and develops connections among health-care, mental health, and community resources. The coordination of and access to services offers predictability and encourages a calmer atmosphere in the home, facilitating more effective family functioning. Families can increase or decrease services as they are needed, and they have someone to go to if they have concerns about services. FCM may include exploring potential problems that might cause stress in family relationships such as substance abuse or mental health problems (Cozza et al., 2013).

Emotion Regulation Skills. Teaching families stress reduction techniques, including being aware of their own emotional states and what precipitates them, is important. Family members can learn to identify feelings and then share them constructively with others and learn to plan for the time of day or situations that prompt discomfort. Positive self-talk, taking breaks, identifying realistic expectations, and prioritizing can lead to more calmness internally and in the home. Family members may become upset or distressed when "triggered" by a memory or a situation (e.g., a child becomes upset when a parent is unexpectedly absent due to running late or an unforeseen appointment). Family members can identify these possible situations and make a plan, including not taking a service member's behavior personally and prompting use of calming techniques. Family members can also identify activities that the family all can enjoy in order to promote cohesiveness (Cozza et al., 2013).

Injury Communication. Central to providing quality care to families of an injured service member is communication. **Injury communication** is an important process to understand, and the accompanying skills are key to successfully supporting families. Injury communication is a process of "effective communication about injury-related topics and information both within the family and with others in civilian and military communities" (Cozza & Guimond, 2011, p. 271). Injury communication begins with the notification of the family about injury of the service member and continues throughout the treatment process and rehabilitation. The goal throughout this process is to promote injury recovery and family function and health (Cozza, 2009b).

Effective injury communication facilitates developing a shared understanding of the injury and its consequences, including the impact on the service member and her or his functioning, family members, and family roles, routines, and goals. Injury communication takes into account family members' capacity to understand and to use the information provided (Cozza & Guimond, 2009).

It is helpful to think about injury communication across relationships, developmental ages, and time. Sharing information about an injury and its implications for family life occurs with the person injured, as well as with a partner, parents, children, extended family members, health-care providers, friends, other supportive people (e.g., chaplains, priests, pastors, community resources). Injury communication occurs between and among these people, and the ease with which one person speaks to another may differ. For example, parents able to speak with their son or daughter who is injured about the injury may find it difficult to talk with their grandchild, or a spouse able to explain the injury to an elementary school-age child may falter when explaining it to a teenager (Cozza & Guimond, 2011).

Effective injury communication requires an approach sensitive to a person's developmental and cognitive abilities. Young children who easily gauge the emotional environment require simple yet straightforward descriptions of what has happened to a parent, a sibling, a grandparent, or whoever was injured (Cozza & Guimond, 2011).

Injury communication occurs across time. The information family members want and need to know immediately upon notification of injury to their service member differs from the information they and the service member will need to know for successful participation in treatment. A transition back home will require yet other information, for example how to negotiate community resources or how to respond to strangers' questions about the injury (Cozza et al., 2013).

Optimism and Future Hopefulness. The injury recovery journey includes grieving for what once was and at some point developing hope about the future (Cozza et al., 2013). It can be helpful to introduce the concept of ambiguous loss (a concept described in Chapter 6) as families may need support adapting to the loss of a person as he or she once was. Living and caring for someone with TBI or PTSD can be experienced as an ambiguous loss as the person may be physically but not psychologically present or not psychologically present in the same way as before the injury (Boss, 2006). This stressor of ambiguity can become unmanageable and immobilizing, and therefore, traumatizing to family members. However, family members can experience the stressor of ambiguity, although chronic, as manageable (Boss, 2006). While self-care techniques are important, Boss (2006) argues that they are not enough when loss is an ambiguous one. Recognition of an ambiguous loss and the ambiguities it brings (e.g., now both a spouse and a caregiver, uncertain what each day will bring) are important in making the loss manageable.

Boss (2006) reminds us that while resilience is more common than we might think, learning to live well with ambivalence takes work. Practitioners can encourage families on this journey by recognizing how family members are coping well and exploring any changes they wish to make. For example, families can better accept a changed future by becoming skilled at managing daily life and finding a purpose in or meaning to their situation. Likewise, hope can develop when family members are connected to trusted family and friends, they advocate for themselves and their injured family member, and they share positive interactions and experiences. Accepting an imperfect situation requires flexibility in expectations of self and others and permission to enjoy life. Family members can also acknowledge that they may differ in their readiness to set goals and future plans. Part of managing daily life may include family members setting goals all can ascribe to and pacing themselves as they seek to reach those goals (Boss, 2006; Cozza et al., 2013).

Principles of Care The Workgroup on Intervention with Combat Injured Families developed principles of care to guide human service professionals as they assist military families (Cozza, 2009b). These principles of care can guide the work of not only military but civilian professionals, providers, organizations, and communities as they offer appropriate care and services to military and veteran families (Gutierrez & Brenner, 2009; Thomas, Wilk, Riviere, McGurk, Castro, & Hoge, 2010). These principles are summarized in Box 13.1.

BOX 13.1 BEST PRACTICES

CARING FOR FAMILIES OF SERVICE MEMBERS WITH VISIBLE AND INVISIBLE COMBAT INJURIES (COZZA, 2009B)

When providing care and services to families of those injured, military and civilian providers, professionals, organizations, and communities:

- Apply principles of psychological first aid, that is, attend to families' safety and comfort, give information and practical assistance, and connect families to community resources in order to encourage recovery.
- Provide family-focused medical care for the injured by relieving family distress, supporting parental functions and parenting effectiveness, and providing guidance on how to talk with children about combat injuries.
- Reinforce the resilience of families and address possible problems that require further help and support.
- Offer effective injury communication that is timely, contains appropriate and accurate information, and addresses family members' anxiety and sustains hope, from the time of notification through rehabilitation.
- Tailor services and care to the family's changing needs through treatment and rehabilitation, recognizing the family's strengths and anticipating future needs.
- Understand that children's responses vary by age and gender and recognize how distress, need for care, and ability to communicate vary by age.
- Reach beyond professional boundaries to foster collaboration and coordination of services among the family, and military and civilian health-care resources and treatment.
- Respect the traditions of military families and a family's background (e.g., culture, language, composition, ethnicity, and religion).
- Help families to access care and address barriers to service, including educating communities about the needs of families.
- Be knowledgeable about and provide educational materials that address challenges faced by families.

PROVIDING CARE AND TREATMENT

In this section we look at the provision of care and treatment to those who have experienced a traumatic event and who experience the effects of another's physical or psychological injury or injuries. We will address individual and family treatment for TBI and PTSD, including military sexual trauma. Evidence-based practice guidelines on post-deployment health, mild traumatic brain injury (mTBI), and mental health issues (e.g., PTSD, depression, substance use) are found at a VA/DoD website (http://www.healthquality.va.gov/index.asp). Clinical practice guidelines are tools to inform practitioners' decision making when working with a client or patient who is experiencing physical or psychological health problems. Recommendations in the practice guidelines are based on a critical review of epidemiological, diagnostic, prognostic, and treatment studies (The Management of Concussion/mTBI Working Group, 2009).

This section begins with a model for helping others immediately following a traumatic event. Then treatment information for service members with a TBI or PTSD and their family members is addressed. This section ends with a discussion on caregiving.

Psychological First Aid (PFA)

Psychological First Aid (PFA) is a way of helping children, adolescents, adults, and families immediately following a traumatic event to "reduce distress, assist with current needs, and promote adaptive functioning, not to elicit details of traumatic experiences and losses" (Brymer et al., 2006, p. 8). This model does not assume that experiencing a traumatic

---

BOX 13.2   BEST PRACTICES

CORE ACTIONS OF PSYCHOLOGICAL FIRST AID (BRYMER ET AL., 2006. P. 19, USED WITH PERMISSION)

- Contact and Engagement: To respond to contacts initiated by survivors, or to initiate contacts in a non-intrusive, compassionate, and helpful manner.
- Safety and Comfort: To enhance immediate and ongoing safety, and provide physical and emotional comfort.
- Stabilization: To calm and orient emotionally overwhelmed or disoriented survivors (if needed).
- Information Gathering: To identify immediate needs and concerns, gather additional information, and tailor Psychological First Aid interventions.
- Practical Assistance: To offer practical help to survivors in addressing immediate needs and concerns.
- Connection with Social Supports: To help establish brief or ongoing contacts with primary support persons and other sources of support, including family members, friends, and community helping resources.
- Information on Coping: To provide information about stress reactions and coping to reduce distress and promote adaptive functioning.
- Linkage with Collaborative Services: To link survivors with available services needed at the time or in the future.

Source: Information compiled from Brymer, M., Jacobs, A., Layne, C., Pynoos, R., Ruzek, J., Steinberg, A., Vernberg, E., & Watson, P. (2006). *Psychological first aid: Field operations guide* (2nd edn). National Child Traumatic Stress Network and National Center for PTSD. Retrieved from http://www.nctsn.org/content/psychological-first-aid. With permission.

event will automatically result in mental health problems or persistent difficulties. Rather, it assumes that persons will exhibit a range of early behavioral, physical, psychological, and spiritual reactions. Some of these reactions may interfere with effective coping; PFA may help survivors positively manage distress and assist in recovery.

PFA is based on five evidence-informed intervention principles recommended by an international panel of experts who study and treat those exposed to disaster and mass violence studies (Hobfoll et al., 2007). These principles are offered to guide and inform prevention and early to mid-term intervention efforts following traumatic events. These principles are to promote: "1) a sense of safety, 2) calming, 3) a sense of self- and community efficacy, 4) connectedness, and 5) hope" (Hobfoll et al., 2007, p. 284). From these five principles emerge the core PFA actions that trained PFA workers perform; these actions are listed in Box 13.2.

Panel members included representatives of the American Red Cross, the National Center for Posttraumatic Stress Disorder, the National Child Traumatic Stress Network, the Center for the Study of Traumatic Stress, and other organizations. Many organizations have incorporated these principles into their programs and publications (Benedek & Fullerton, 2007). PFA is used in a variety of settings by a variety of helping professionals, including first responders, emergency health-care workers, school crisis response teams, and those who work in disaster relief organizations (Brymer et al., 2006). Just as we can learn and apply basic first aid procedures in response to physical trauma (e.g., CPR, techniques to stop bleeding, insure optimal body temperature, prevent infection), we can learn to apply first aid procedures after psychological trauma. Learning basic *physical* first aid means we can try to stop blood loss while we wait for an ambulance, or clean and apply antibacterial medication to a cut rather than making a doctor's appointment. Likewise, tools to promote *psychological* wellness can be applied immediately after experiencing a highly stressful situation or a traumatic event. Just as non-medical personnel may administer first aid for a physical trauma, PFA is designed to be administered by non-mental health-care professionals who have received appropriate training in order to protect and promote psychological health and well-being (Brymer et al., 2006).

Military and civilian mental health and family support professionals, chaplains, and medical personnel are also using PFA when responding to the psychosocial needs of others who have experienced a traumatic event (Nash, Westphal, Watson, & Lits, 2010). Using PFA procedures, the Navy and Marine Corps implemented the Combat and Operational Stress First Aid (COSFA) to guide early interventions with individuals who have experienced a traumatic event; it is expected to be adapted for use with Navy and Marine Corps families (Nash et al., 2010).

Civilians may obtain training in PFA online (go to http://www.nctsn.org/content/psychological-first-aid and follow links to register) or from state organizations (e.g., department of human services) and local chapters of the American Red Cross (which also has a training specifically on coping with deployments). Before seeking training in PFA, consider your comfort level with working with highly distressed individuals in a variety of backgrounds and unpredictable settings, being assigned non-mental health related tasks (e.g., serving meals, cleaning the floor), collaborating with professionals from diverse fields, and providing support to individuals with diverse backgrounds (e.g., ethnicity, culture, religion, developmental levels). Also consider whether your health and responsibilities at work and with family allow you to be away should you decide to volunteer or work with an agency that sends PFA workers to disaster areas for a period of time (Brymer et al., 2006).

Traumatic Brain Injury

The optimal treatment of TBI requires tailored coordination of care for the unique needs of each service member or veteran (Jafee et al., 2009). Service members with TBI may receive care in a variety of healthcare settings, in particular if they are eventually discharged from the military. Throughout their treatment they receive care at military treatment facilities, the VA, and civilian health-care systems. TBI, particularly moderate and severe TBI, affects cognitive abilities such as understanding and negotiating complex situations, language comprehension, memory, concentration, and judgment. These cognitive effects may translate into missing appointments, failure to take medications, and an inability to drive or take public transportation. TBI can also result in negative behavioral symptoms such as aggression, outbursts, irritability, and disinhibition resulting in confusion, discomfort or fear in others, including treatment providers unfamiliar with TBI (Jafee et al., 2009).

Some persons with moderate or severe TBI may be unable to live independently. Consequently, family members become caregivers, advocates, and managers to insure service members and veterans with TBI receive the care they need. The vital role played by family members in treatment was acknowledged by the Management of Concussion/mTBI Working Group (2009) that noted "early education of patients and their families is the best available treatment for concussion/mTBI and for preventing/reducing the development of persistent symptoms" (p. vi).

During treatment and recovery, doctors, nurses, and other professionals look to the caregiver for feedback on how the service member is progressing as injuries can differ from person to person and so treatment effects can differ. Ideally, care is family-centered, that is, the service member, family, and medical personnel work as a team.

Voices From the Frontline

BOX 13.3   A CAREGIVER'S REFLECTIONS

On July 8th of 2010, my husband of 32½ years fell 8 feet down a trap door, landing on a concrete floor. He sustained serious head injuries and was in a coma for four weeks. Although his TBI was not from military combat, he is retired from the U.S. Air Force so the VA figures prominently in his rehabilitation. Here's what I am learning as a caregiver that might be useful to pass on to others:

- **Ask questions**. Ask all medical and rehabilitation staff until you receive the information you seek. No questions are stupid, because your life has been altered forever.
- **Use resources**. Search for others who have experienced what you have. For a few weeks I avoided the Internet, terrified of what I'd find. But knowledge is power, so ask medical staff for recommendations. Useful sites: the Defense and Veterans Brain Injury Center at www.dvbic.org, the Centers for Disease Control and Prevention at www.cdc.gov/TraumaticBrainInjury/index.html, an initiative from the Office of the Surgeon General at www.traumaticbrain-injuryatoz.org, and the Brain Injury Association at www.biausa.org.
- **Advocate**. Doing what I have needed to do means I'm a stronger, more confident, and more empowered advocate. Before, some situations would have had me quivering in my shoes. No more. When dealing with health insurance companies, the VA, or an employer I have followed this advice: be polite, be pleasant, but be persistent. Someone may try to discourage you, especially if you're a woman. Speak to the supervisor. Say, "This is unacceptable." But don't go looking for a fight. Pick your battles; save energy for what matters. Your family member doesn't have a private room? Unless a roommate is disrupting recovery and rehabilitation, let it go.
- **Each TBI is different**. Doctors, websites, and books describe what you MAY expect and what MAY happen. But persons progress at their own rate and have different deficits, depending on the area of the brain injured.

- **Use what the military and DoD offer**. The VA has a Polytrauma System of Care for TBI rehabilitation. Had I known earlier, I would have made every effort to get my husband placed there sooner; his progress would have been faster and better. The VA has pilot programs your loved one may qualify for, military liaisons who will work on a plan of care, and psychologists who stand ready to support you. In my experience most civilian social workers only know about local facilities in their county and not about VA resources. If using a civilian facility, visit many and choose one acceptable to YOU. If it doesn't participate with your health insurer, ask why. Perhaps it can be changed. It never, ever, hurts to ask!

- **Now is not the time to rock the "I'm independent, I can handle anything, and I'm proud of it" attitude**. Because the fact is, no, you really can't. If you're lucky, family will help. Many friends will be thrilled to help, and you'll be surprised and touched. Consider friends' strengths and use them: computers, electronics, medical, financial, and home repair. Some can take in the mail and keep an eye on the house. Some listen. Friends prop me up and dust me off when I fall, and gently shove me forward with their words and their confidence in me when I sometimes have none, and give me the strength to continue to cope. Saints and martyrs are boring; don't join that club!

- **Some friends will disappear.** My social life has taken a hit, and it makes me very sad. A few friends continue to include me and I'm grateful.

- **Make multiple copies of your loved one's Durable Power of Attorney and Medical Power of Attorney**. You'll need them for banks, financial companies, hospitals, and other institutions. If you don't have these documents, get an attorney to guide you. Use any legal help offered through the military.

- **Look for coping mechanisms, ways to help deal with what is and to let go of what was**. I continue to look. There are days I can take anything thrown at me. Other days, I cry more tears than I ever thought possible. I'm angry my husband injured himself. Then there's frustration, sadness, grief, depression, and embarrassment. I'm tired of taking care of all the problems. I have trouble focusing sometimes and staying on task.

- **I miss having someone love me**. My friends are absolutely wonderful, but they don't kiss me goodnight. I miss my husband before I'm even out of the parking lot of the facility where he's living and cry for the first few miles. My head spins: Will he ever be able to come back home to live? Will he need supervision?

- **Well-meaning persons say puzzling things.** For instance:
  - "Maybe this was a sign that your husband needed to slow down." Really? Sustaining a TBI is a radical way to do it.
  - "Take care of yourself and stay strong so you can take care of your husband." Seriously? How about the concept of taking care of me, because I'm worthy of it on my own, and because I'm a decent, valuable human being, worthy of staying healthy, strong and sane for ME?

- **I'm a married widow who can't "move on."** I grieve for the life after retirement we looked forward to. My hope is someday we have a semblance of that life. As my husband's colleague told me, "Watching a person with a TBI heal and progress is like watching white paint dry." He's right. I can't commit to certain things; I can't plan too far ahead. Our lives are in limbo.

- **I don't know how much of my husband will come back**. Because of his TBI, my husband has become unable to show his usual love and affection. Some has come back, but it's different. When he says mean things to me, my brain tells me it's the TBI. My heart, however, can't seem to remember and it hurts. It hurts a lot.

- **It's normal to grieve for the person who was.** Part of me will always grieve for the husband I knew, the best friend I've lived with and loved for over 30 years. A different version of that person has appeared. I'm hoping, with time, more of the person I knew will come back. It's happened some already; I pray it will continue.

Glyni Fenn
Wife and Advocate

As Glyni Fenn notes, human service professionals must know civilian, DoD, and VA resources inside and outside of their area, region, or state in order to best serve service members, veterans, and their families. A number of professionals can be involved in the care of service members and veterans with TBI. Point of contact case management team members can include: a primary care manager who provides clinical care and refers to specialists; a nurse or nurse practitioner medical care case manager at the military treatment facility or VA Polytrauma Center; a non-medical care manager to help with the disability systems and transitions between health-care systems (e.g., from the DoD to the VA); the DoD recovery care coordinator (for mild to serious TBI) or the DoD/VA Federal recovery care coordinator (for severe to catastrophic TBI) to coordinate medical personnel, Wounded Warrior program staff, federal health care teams, and community resources; the Defense and Veterans Brain Injury Center regional care coordinator to insure care from injury to rehabilitation to re-entry; and the TRICARE managed care support case managers to coordinate care within the TRICARE system. For service members their non-medical case manager is called one of the following depending upon the branch of service: the Army Wounded Warrior Case Manager; the Wounded Warrior Program Case Manager (Air Force); the Navy Safe Harbor Program Case Manager; and the Wounded Warrior Regiment Case Manager (Marine Corps). For veterans, their non-medical case manager may be called the OEF/OIF Program Manager Liaison, the Transition Patient Advocate, or the VA Liaison (Center for Excellence in Medical Multimedia, 2011).

Studies of military families with a service member with a TBI are limited, so we need to consider what has been learned from studies of civilian families. These studies have highlighted the relationship between family members' positive coping and the injured person's process of recovery. In addition, family members (e.g., parents, spouses, and siblings) report assuming care for the injured loved one out of love, deep compassion, and an ethical responsibility (Jumisko, Lexell, & Soberberg, 2007).

Research over the past 30 years indicates that family members experience a great deal of stress, even a decade or more post-injury. Families with young children, financial problems, and minimal social support are more vulnerable to stress. The injured person's cognitive, emotional, and behavioral problems are experienced as more problematic for family members than physical problems. The stress associated with the unrelenting task of being their loved one's champion and primary caregiver in cases of moderate and severe TBI may result in depression, anxiety, and other stress reactions. As a result, marital or relationship partners may seek divorce or relationship dissolution (Verhaeghe, Defloor, & Grydonck, 2005).

Family members' coping strategies may be considered adaptive (e.g., accomplishing important tasks, identifying new roles, seeking social support) or maladaptive (e.g., using alcohol or medication as means of denial or escape). Coping strategies are influenced by the severity of the injury. For example, family members may be more likely to withdraw from social contact if their loved one's behavior is socially inappropriate.

BOX 13.4   BEST PRACTICES

"WE TRY TO SUPPORT EACH FAMILY MEMBER IN DEVELOPING EMPATHY FOR THE OTHER"

It is important for providers to know that most of the veterans and families we see are dealing with concurrent mental and physical health issues. Because right now there is not a strong evidence-based family intervention for traumatic brain injury (TBI), our preference has been to tailor each intervention to the individual and family experiencing TBI and resulting issues such as inhibition or disinhibition. We talk about how do you to compensate for the lack of initiative, withdrawal and memory deficits, or for impulsivity and anger.

The toughest problems most veterans and families face in the transition to civilian life is that they have to get their lives together: finding a place to live, finding a job or go to school, paying their bills, and parenting their children. If the veteran has impairment of functioning, if he or she is irritable or impulsive, if it is hard to get up and get going in the morning, all of these tasks are more difficult.

There are often relationship issues. As clinicians, we think about "how do you support a partner who never bargained for dealing with these service-related deficits and a new reality?" In a partner relationship most of us expect reciprocity and when these impairments arise, the partner often has to compensate and often do "more of the heavy lifting." Only about half of the people who served in Iraq and Afghanistan were married so we also have to think about parents or other family members who are supporting a veteran.

Many veterans, including those with TBI, have bad headaches and trouble with hearing caused by an improvised explosive device (IED) exploding near them and remaining in the country for months after. They may have muscular and skeletal pain from carrying backpacks and other gear. They don't feel good. They can't do everyday things like picking up their child. The question then becomes, "what else can you do to play and show you care? Sit down on the floor with her? Play a game?" We have to help veterans manage these kinds of day-to-day obstacles.

In our family treatment programs we integrate a general framework that includes (a) good education about TBI in laymen's terms; (b) helping family members improve their communication, for example by being brief and using "I statements"; and (c) teaching people a systemic way to problem solve challenges collaboratively.

We try to support each family member in developing empathy for the other. There are two ways you can talk about TBI. You can say, "If you have TBI you have problems a, b and c." Or you can get people to talk together about how they feel and draw the symptoms and experiences out through a guided conversation. If people have goodwill they can develop empathy. I think, for example, about a vet who hears a family member say it is hard to handle the bills on her own, but stating it in a non-judgmental, non-blaming way. That may be a new perspective for him. Understanding another's perspective can lead to change in behavior. Identifying and working towards a shared goal allows family members to work as partners and to work with their therapist as a partner.

Shirley M. Glynn, PhD
Clinical Research Psychologist Manager, VA Family Services National
Evidence-Based Clinician Training Program and Research Psychologist
Co-Director,
UCLA Welcome Back Veterans Family Resilience Center

Family members often find receiving social support and assuming important roles previously undertaken by the loved one can reduce the experience of stress (Verhaeghe et al., 2005). While families learn more effective ways to cope over time, educational information and social support can enhance their coping. Family members want clear and accurate information about TBI; details about treatment plans, prognosis, course of recovery, and possible worse and best scenarios; and strategies on how to care for their loved one (Griffin, Friedemann-Sánchez, Hall, Phelan, & van Ryn, 2009).

TBI may be accompanied by other injuries (e.g., damage to tissue, bones, eyes; chronic pain; PTSD), requiring intensive hospital stays and rehabilitation. Long-term treatment of these polytraumas may result in emotional strain for families. Families support their loved one through a long course of medical treatment and rehabilitation; interact with the bureaucracy of the DoD and VA; and spend significant amounts of time away from their homes and/or daily lives as they participate in their loved one's care. In addition, those with polytrauma due to combat, versus veterans suffering an injury after separating from the military, tend to be in the early years of marriage and tend to have young children. VA clinicians have used both the theory of ambiguous loss and medical family therapy employing cognitive-behavioral, narrative, and family systems approaches to support these families (Collins & Kennedy, 2008).

In the beginning of this chapter, Dr. Shirley Glynn addresses important points for providers and clinicians to keep in mind when working with veterans with a TBI and their families. The current approach is to tailor treatment to each veteran and family because effects of a TBI differ from veteran to veteran and mental health issues often accompany the TBI. The general framework guiding treatment is to provide a solid education about TBI in terms the veteran and family members understand, to help families improve their communication, and to teach families a system to problem-solve challenges collaboratively.

A family-focused treatment initiated in recent years for those with a TBI and their family members includes **multifamily group treatment**. This treatment is a combination of individual sessions, education workshop, and group sessions. Content includes information about TBI, family and relationship issues, problem-solving cognitive difficulties, self-identity issues, family responses and adjustment, and coping strategies for families (Perlick et al., 2011). In Voices From the Frontline, Dr. Perlick describes the results of a pilot study of Multifamily Group Treatment for Veterans with TBI (Perlick et al., 2013; Straits-Troster, 2013).

Voices From the Frontline

FAMILIES, VETERANS, AND TBI

Studies have estimated that 22 to 35% of service members wounded during OEF/OIF have combat-related traumatic brain injury (TBI), making TBI the signature injury for those serving in Afghanistan and Iraq. A TBI not only affects those injured but also their families, particularly as it can take up to 2 years for a diagnosis. TBIs can negatively affect memory and executive functioning, resulting in family conflict, caregiver burden, and child distress. Additionally, some veterans experience a TBI and PTSD; both injuries can affect areas of the brain integral to emotion regulation.

Many families lack information about TBIs, and clinicians lack evidence-based treatments to offer families. In response, colleagues and I are studying Multifamily Group Treatment for Veterans with TBI, an adaptation of an evidence-based multifamily group treatment for serious mental illness. At this point in our journey we have conducted a pilot study that showed benefits for veterans and family members. Our 9-month trial consisted of two to three individual family sessions, an educational workshop about TBI, and bimonthly multifamily problem-solving sessions across 6 months that focused on compensatory strategies, emotional regulation, and communication skills.

Results are promising. Veterans decreased in anger expression and had gains in social support and occupational activity. Caregivers reported decreased burden in caregiving and improvement in coping. In follow-up focus group interviews, veterans and family members reported that this treatment provided "eye-opening awareness" about TBI. Until then they had been told that a veteran had a TBI but not what to expect and how to adapt.

Recognizing that others were dealing with this type of injury was transforming for veterans and spouses. In the presence of others with a TBI, veterans felt safer to talk about their difficulties and explain how they compensated for deficits and tried to manage stress. Spouses who were struggling with their veteran returning from deployment a different person found understanding in the group. Sharing common struggles reduced veterans' and spouses' isolation. They shared ideas for coping with such situations as memory deficits, and they learned communication strategies that promoted understanding and compassion. Veterans gained awareness of the overlap between TBI and PTSD and how both can affect others in their lives; family members reported understanding TBI and PTSD better increased their patience. Friendships developed outside of the group, providing continuing social support.

Veterans with mild TBI and their families face challenges. We found these young families eager for services; they wanted to learn how to rebuild their lives. Some of the veterans considered the multifamily group an indication of the VA's commitment to them. We also found that knowledge about veterans and military culture, and experience working with groups and families made providing treatment easier for clinicians. Our next steps include conducting a larger scale study and writing a manual that includes communication training because TBI interferes with communication. These veterans and families are inspiring; we are grateful for their participation in research that can lead to better services for veterans and their families.

Deborah A. Perlick, PhD
Associate Professor of Psychiatry
Icahn School of Medicine at Mount Sinai
Associate Director for Family Intervention Research,
U.S. Department of Veterans Affairs, Mental Illness Research, Education
and Clinical Center (MIRECC)
Veterans Affairs Integrated Service Network 3

J.J. Peters *VA Medical Center*

As part of the National Defense Authorization Act of 2007, Congress mandated the development of a specific family caregiver curriculum for those providing care to a service member or veteran with TBI. A result of this mandate is the curriculum *Traumatic Brain Injury: A Guide for Caregivers of Service Members and Veterans.* Useful for both family members and those who work with them, the curriculum is found on the website, *Traumatic Brain Injury: The Journey Back Home* (www. traumaticbraininjuryatoz.org), a collaborative effort between the Defense Health Board and the Center of Excellence for Medical Multimedia (2011; an initiative from the Office of the Surgeon General).

The *Journey Back Home* website contains videos, interactive features, and materials for those with TBI and for family caregivers. The "Caregiver's Journey" portion of the website contains videos of caregivers describing their journeys, illustrating common reactions of family members and service members and the tasks they face. A video series of family caregiver meetings with a social worker cover topics such as managing the physical and cognitive effects of TBI, problem solving, advocating, taking care of self, helping children cope, addressing family needs, transitioning home, obtaining help with caregiving, addressing everyday issues, moving forward, and having hope. These sessions parallel content found in the caregiver guide available for download. The guide covers an introduction to TBI, the effects of TBI and how to help, becoming a caregiver, and navigating services and benefits. Templates can also be downloaded to help with recording notes on: physical, cognitive, behavioral and communication effects; family needs; children; legal matters; problem solving; and progress on recovery. Other materials available for download include worksheets, assessments, and descriptions of TRICARE and the VA systems. TBI survivors, experienced caregivers, treatment experts, and a family caregiver advisory board developed the materials ("Traumatic Brain Injury," 2010).

Post-traumatic Stress Disorder

In this section we review some of the therapeutic treatments for individuals diagnosed with PTSD. Then we consider the implications of PTSD for family members and support available for them. As Dr. Laura Meis, assistant professor at the University of Minnesota, explains, some approaches bring family members into the PTSD treatment whereas other approaches integrate PTSD into family groups and couples' therapy. Both approaches to helping veterans and their families are covered.

Voices From the Frontline

FAMILY MEMBERS ARE EAGER TO SUPPORT THEIR VETERANS IN TREATMENT

The mental health and family support fields still have much to learn about how to effectively work with families of veterans who have PTSD. Mostly clinicians are trying to integrate family into support groups and couples therapy. Our work looks at how to integrate families into traditionally individual-focused treatments for PTSD and the barriers to doing so.

How people at home talk and think about a veteran's treatment can make a big difference. Treatment for PTSD may include weekly sessions for up to 4 months and daily homework. When you ask someone to do this without the support of a family member, it can be hard to stick with it.

Think, for example, about veterans whose homework is to listen to their account of a traumatic event that they audio taped during a session with a clinician. A veteran takes the tape recorder into a room, closes the door, and comes out an hour later tense and on alert. Later that night she or he has horrible nightmares. A spouse or partner who is on board can be prepared for this, be supportive, and reinforce the idea that recounting memories of traumatic events can be helpful so that the memories are less linked to fear and avoidance.

Involving families doesn't mean that veterans have to share their memories, something many veterans are concerned about. Many do not want to burden family members with their stories. Our focus is on partner-assisted treatment in which the spouse is a coach who supports the treatment process, not a witness to the veteran's recall of experiences, unless that is what the veteran wants.

Currently we are collecting data about how a significant other or spouse influences the impact of treatment. My hope is that we will eventually develop a tiered approach that will include developing a manual with specific ways to include families and providing guidance to clinicians about how to reach out to families to find out what veterans want and to articulate how family involvement influences treatment.

Our survey findings, the quantitative aspect of our research, already reveal that family members are eager to support their veterans in treatment. Once a veteran nominates a support person we have an 80% response rate, which is extremely high for mailed survey research.

We are learning through interviews, the qualitative piece of our work, that those in support roles have very little knowledge about what is going on in their veteran's treatment. At the same time they are eager to tell about how their veteran is suffering and coping at home and to learn how they can be involved.

With regard to advice for clinicians working with veterans and families, I have personal opinions. Whether the data will bear them out has yet to be determined but I offer them as points to consider:

- *What* you say and *how* matters. From the beginning, clinicians have to articulate and clarify different roles a family member can play, for example, that of a coach or witness. This needs to happen in the context of a conversation. Veterans are often ambivalent about involving a family member but if the reasons why are articulated clearly and clinicians encourage it, veterans tell us they are willing to consider and even embrace the idea.
- Take an individualized approach. In some cases, the support person is most effective as a coach. In others, a family member who begins in a coaching role may end up assuming the role of witness if the veteran decides to share stories of trauma-related experiences. In others, the support person may provide well-intentioned help that is contrary to the goals of therapy, like encouraging the veteran to avoid distressing memories or tasks. It is important to make sure that a family member is involved in a way that is meaningful for both the veteran and the family member.
- Be willing to consider if and how working with families fits into your own practice. Although you may not be trained to do family therapy, you may be comfortable doing assessment at a basic level.
- We need more data on engaging children in age appropriate ways. Parents with PTSD are more likely to have problems with anger and aggressive behavior than parents without PTSD. Parenting behavior and the environment of the entire household is affected by PTSD. There is certainly a period of time when children are old enough so that it may be helpful for them to know more about what is going on, such as that mom or dad is getting help and ways in which the family can rally around a parent who is having a rough day.
- The health-care system is frequently not as flexible as would be preferable in allowing clinicians to account for their time when they take extra steps to involve family in veterans' care. It takes time to identify appropriate family members, reach out, and include them in care. It would benefit everyone if the health-care system could find a better way to reward clinicians for their extra initiative.

Involving families can help veterans remain in treatment and make the most out of the care they receive. As a mental health professional, finding creative ways to educate, support, and integrate family into care can be enormously rewarding. I hope, through my research, to motivate others to make meaningful family involvement in veterans' treatment for PTSD the standard of care rather than the exception.

Laura Meis, PhD
*Assistant Professor, Department of Medicine, University of Minnesota
Core Investigator, Center for Chronic Disease Outcomes Research,
Minneapolis Veterans Affairs Health Care System*

Treatments for Post-traumatic Stress

Post-traumatic stress is considered to be a spectrum of reactions to a trauma: acute stress reactions, combat-operation stress reactions, acute stress disorder, and PTSD (Management of Post-Traumatic Stress Working Group, 2010). Those who survive a trauma may only experience some of the reactions while others may experience the entire spectrum (the spectrum is described in Chapter 7). The goal is early intervention to increase the likelihood of preventing more severe stress reactions such as PTSD.

Service members who exhibit acute stress reactions or combat-operational stress reactions should be accessed and provided PFA and care of basic physical needs. Additional interventions may be warranted, such as psychotherapy and facilitation of spiritual and social support (The Management of Post-Traumatic Stress Working Group, 2010).

For those who are diagnosed with PTSD, treatment may consist of some or all of the following: evidence-based psychotherapy, medication, treatment of a concurrent substance use disorder, alternative care options (e.g., hypnosis to help manage pain, anxiety, or nightmares), management of specific pain, family therapy, and social and spiritual support. Relaxation techniques may help those who are physically tense or hyper-reactive. Imagery rehearsal therapy (i.e., imagining in a relaxed state more pleasant and positive images in place of a nightmare) may reduce nightmares and difficulties related to sleeping (Management of Post-Traumatic Stress Working Group, 2010).

VA/DoD clinical guidelines strongly recommend the use of evidence-based practices in screening, therapeutic treatments, and medications. Recognizing PTSD early allows treatment to begin quickly, resulting in less impairment and less time suffering (Management of Post-Traumatic Stress Working Group, 2010). These treatments are briefly described below. For more information on treatments for PTSD and related topics access the VA's continuing education series for community providers (www.mentalhealth.va.gov/communityproviders).

Cognitive therapy (CT) techniques are widely used in the treatment of PTSD. Studies confirm its effectiveness in reducing symptoms of the disorder. CT includes teaching clients about symptoms of PTSD, identifying thoughts and feelings associated with the trauma, identifying and challenging dysfunctional beliefs about the trauma (e.g., "I should have been able to … during the event," "I should have known...") that give rise to or sustain PTSD symptoms, and replacing these beliefs with more logical, functional, and reality-based beliefs. CT techniques often are combined with techniques from other treatments, as in cognitive processing therapy that includes CT and exposure therapy. (Management of Post-Traumatic Stress Working Group, 2010).

Prolonged exposure (PE) therapy is a form of cognitive behavioral therapy that includes psychoeducation (e.g., learning about trauma reactions, PTSD, and symptoms) and deliberately re-experiencing the traumatic event repeatedly, until one has gained control over the physical and emotional response caused by the reminders. Specifically, an in vivo exposure has the person physically being exposed to safe but feared stimuli that trigger PTSD symptoms, from stimuli that cause fewer and less severe symptoms to those that cause the most disturbing responses. For example, a veteran who avoids crowds because it triggers the memory and feelings of being in one when an IED exploded, may be asked to first watch a crowd from a distance, then walk toward a small crowd, then stand and talk with someone near a crowd, then walk through a crowd. Each step is repeated until it can be experienced with low emotional or physiological responses, and then the next step is approached. Imaginal exposure includes imagining the trauma and describing its physical and emotional details with a therapist in order to gain more control over feelings and thoughts about the trauma. Written exposure includes writing about the traumatic event and then reading what is written to the therapist. Treatment usually spans eight to 15 sessions (Committee on Treatment of Posttraumatic Stress Disorder, 2008; Management of Post-Traumatic Stress Working Group, 2010).

A VA study on the effectiveness of prolonged exposure therapy for veterans with PSTD suggests that PE reduces the symptoms of both PTSD and depression (Eftekhari et al., 2013). The study included 1,931 veterans from all wars. It included men and women and combat-related PTSD and non-combat-related PTSD. The percentage of veterans with symptoms of PTSD decreased from 87% before PE treatment to 46% after PE treatment. Even though PE is not used specifically for the treatment of depression, participants in the study also experienced a reduction of depression symptoms. Of those veterans who completed the PE treatment program, depression symptoms were reduced from an average of almost 30% to less than 19%. Based on their results, the researchers suggest that PE is an effective treatment of PTSD for both men and women veterans, for veterans from different eras, and for PTSD related to various types of trauma.

Like prolonged exposure, **stress inoculation training (SIT)** is a form of cognitive behavioral therapy. It is a structured, overlapping three-phase process that encourages individuals to use their existing coping skills and teaches them new stress management skills (Meichenbaum, 1996). In the first phase, clients learn about stress, its prevalence, and how to see perceived threats as problems to solve; to identify their stressors and stress reactions; and to identify which stressors can be eliminated or reduced and which will require existing or new coping skills to manage.

The second phase focuses on the development and practice of coping skills that may include emotion regulation, controlled breathing and relaxation, assertiveness training, positive self-talk, thought stopping, emotional regulation, self-soothing, interpersonal communication skills training, stress-reducing activities, using social support systems, and acceptance. Clients then practice these skills through role-play, by visualizing a distressing situation, or when experiencing an actual situation.

During the final phase of SIT, application and follow through, clients apply their coping skills while experiencing increasing levels of stressors through imagery and behavioral rehearsal, modeling, role playing, and in vivo exposure to situations of increasing stress, as a form of inoculation or developing a resistance to stress. SIT is typically conducted in 8 to 12 sessions or over a 3 to 12 month time period (Management of Post-Traumatic Stress Working Group, 2010; Meichenbaum, 1996).

While several studies on the effectiveness of SIT confirm that it reduces the symptoms of PTSD more than supportive counseling or no treatment, PE reduces a broader range of PTSD symptoms and produces greater treatment gains (Rauch & Foa, n.d.). Thus, it may be a better initial choice for the treatment of PTSD.

Eye movement desensitization and reprocessing (EMDR) uses memories of the traumatic event in combination with information processing and rapid, rhythmic eye movements to divert the client's attention from the physical and emotional responses to the trauma. It has been used successfully with combat veterans and is considered by some researchers as a first-line treatment for PTSD in veterans (Silver, Rogers, & Russell, 2008).

An EMDR treatment session can last up to 90 minutes, and treatment occurs in eight phases (EMDR Institute, 2011). The therapist moves his or her fingers back and forth in front of the client's face (alternatively, hand or toe tapping or musical tones are used). The client follows the hand motions with his or her eyes while recalling a traumatic event and experiencing the emotional and physical feelings the memories evoke. EMDR is based on the belief that negative emotions are reduced by the rapid eye movement by allowing the client to recall traumatic events while distracting them from the debilitating effects of reliving the trauma. With repeated sessions the client gradually remembers the trauma but is not overcome by the memory and is able to link the memory with more adaptive feelings and responses. DoD and VA clinical practice guidelines have recommended EMDR for treating PTSD in veterans (Department of Veterans Affairs and Department of Defense, 2010), and the American Psychiatric Association suggests that EMDR may be helpful for individuals who cannot talk about their traumatic experiences (American Psychiatric

Association, 2004). A review of research conducted on the effectiveness of EMDR, including seven meta-analyses conducted since 1998, concluded that EMDR is an efficacious treatment for PTSD (Spates & Rubin, 2012). However, it is important to note that one meta-analysis study reported that EMDR is more efficacious with civilians than combat veterans (see Bisson, 2007). Spates and Rubin (2012) suggest further research on the use of additional procedures, such as homework and additional sessions, with combat veterans to address this disparity.

Treatment for Sexual Trauma

Sexual assault is a type of trauma, so veterans who have experienced sexual trauma while in the military receive the treatment appropriate for the psychological condition that results from the trauma (U.S. Department of Veterans Affairs, 2014a). While depression, anxiety, and substance abuse are common responses to sexual assault, PTSD is the most common psychological health diagnosis associated with sexual assault in the military (U.S. Department of Veterans Affairs, 2012). Therefore, many of the treatment methods used by both the DOD and the VA for military sexual assault are the same as for PTSD. The VA also has individual and group therapy, outpatient, inpatient, and residential treatment programs specifically for veterans who have experienced sexual trauma (U.S. Department of Veterans Affairs, 2014a). These often include separate programs for men and women. Individual and group therapy for sexual trauma is also available through community-based Vet Centers.

Family Interventions

Most service members, including those who experience combat, do not develop post-traumatic stress disorder (PTSD). However, when it does occur, PTSD has implications for the family members as well as the service personnel. Family members become extremely concerned when they see their loved one exhibiting symptoms of PTSD: re-experiencing the trauma (e.g., flashbacks, nightmares, exaggerated emotions and physical actions), avoiding contact and engaging in emotional numbing (e.g., loss of interest, detached, restricted emotion), and showing increased arousal (e.g., difficulty sleeping, outbursts of anger, hypervigilance, exaggerated startle response). They may feel afraid, unsure how to help, and worried about the person's safety (Management of Post-traumatic Stress Working Group, 2010).

In response to family members' need for guidance on how to intervene, the VA initiated two services. Make the Connection website (http://maketheconnection.net) provides information on symptoms (e.g., relationship problems), conditions (e.g., PRSD, depression), and links to VA services. The website can be personalized for family members, veterans, clinicians, and reserve and active components. Veterans can personalize the site further by era served and service branch. Through Coaching Into Care (www.mirecc.va.gov/coaching) family members can receive coaching by phone on how to talk with their veteran about their concerns and help and treatment that are available.

Effects of PTSD on Families   Research on couples and families from previous wars and across multiple countries has documented the effects of PTSD not only on the service members and veterans but also on family relationships. Wives have reported feeling tense, anxious, depressed, lonely, confused, and burdened by caregiving (Dekel, Goldblatt, Keidar, Solomon, & Polliack, 2005). Couples in which a trauma-exposed veteran has PTSD are at a greater risk of relationship distress, violence, and divorce than those couples who do not. Severe PTSD symptoms, particularly emotional numbing, negatively affect marital adjustment for both male and female veterans (Dekel & Monson, 2010). Families may

experience rigidity in functioning, violence, low cohesion, and high conflict; may scape-goat the person with PTSD; and may restrict intimacy, self-expression, and personal open-ness (Dekel et al., 2005).

Researchers and clinicians are attempting to identify the mechanisms by which stress reactions, including PTSD, are transmitted from a traumatized person to another person. The process is not clearly understood, but evidence exists that suggests multiple mecha-nisms probably contribute (Dekel & Monson, 2010).

One mechanism by which stress reactions are transmitted may be the empathy felt by the caregiver for the trauma survivor. This empathy may encourage over-identification with the survivor to the point of assuming the survivor's stress reactions. Second, perceived burden and chronic stress of caregiving on emotional and physical health, social life, and financial well-being may lead to stress reactions. Third, adaptation to traumatic stress may depend upon the interaction of individual functioning, couple functioning (e.g., nurtur-ance, communication, conflict), and previous unresolved stress (Dekel & Monson, 2010).

Fourth, behaviors (e.g., not expressing emotions, limited self disclosure) that are used to avoid situations, memories, or emotions related to the trauma can be detrimental to relationship satisfaction. Cognitive processes (e.g., interpreting other's behaviors nega-tively) can also maintain relationship and family difficulties. They may have shattered assumptions about safety and difficulty understanding the behavior of the person with PTSD. Finally, living with a traumatized person may be experienced as an ambiguous loss in which the person is physically but not psychologically present. If the ambiguity becomes immobilizing, it can lead to stress reactions (Dekel & Monson, 2010).

Treatment Options for Families   When compared to the focus placed on individual treatment for PTSD, discussion of treatment and support of family caregivers has been minimal. Until recently, most treatment options have been primarily geared toward the individual with PTSD and emerged from the goal of helping the person with PTSD by decreasing relationship stress or increasing family support of the trauma survivor (Dekel & Solomon, 2007). For example, family members, typically partners, can be included in individual sessions with their loved one or group education sessions with other families.

However, it is becoming clear that the effects of PTSD on families call for a more sys-temic approach to care and treatment (Erbes, Polusny, MacDermid, & Compton, 2008). Evidence suggests including a partner in treatment can benefit the partner and relation-ship functioning, and improve PTSD symptoms (Monson, Fredman, & Adair, 2008).

As noted earlier by Dr. Shirley Glynn, the VA is expanding treatment to include fam-ily therapy for veterans with a mental health disorder, and couples' therapy for veterans with substance abuse problems or marital distress. This expansion includes application of behavioral models adapted to the specific disorder, including PTSD.

One way that family members and loved ones can be included in PTSD treatment is with **cognitive-behavioral conjoint therapy (CBCT)**. CBCT is psychotherapy that is based on the principles of cognitive-behavioral therapy and that includes both the indi-vidual diagnosed with PTSD and his or her intimate partner in the therapy sessions.

The goal of CBCT is to address PTSD and the relationship issues that may accompany it. Monson and Freedman (2012) have developed a three-phased treatment protocol of 15 sessions. They discuss PTSD as a "disorder of impeded recovery," meaning that over time most people exposed to a traumatic event will experience a lessening of symptoms and "recover" without intervention (p. 11). The acronym RESUME reflects the three phrases of treatment: rationale for treatment and education about PTSD and relation-ships; satisfaction enhancement and undermining avoidance; and making meaning of the trauma and end of therapy. Training is available for psychotherapists.

To determine if including partners in PTSD therapy would improve the partners' mental health, researchers (Shnaider, Pukay-Martin, Fredman, Macdonald, & Monson, 2014) studied the effects of CBCT on 40 couples that included one partner who had been diagnosed with PTSD. Half of the couples participated in 15 therapy sessions, while the other 20 did not receive treatment. The researchers found no statistically significant differences between the psychological functioning of the two groups at the end of the treatment period. However, when examining individual outcomes on the partners of those with PTSD who had exhibited psychological distress prior to treatment, they found significant improvement and no worsening of those partners' levels of psychological functioning. The researchers concluded that CBCT may be beneficial for the partners of individuals with PTSD who are experiencing distress.

In acknowledgement of the need of services for veterans and for family members, the VA is training its clinicians in Behavioral Family Therapy and Multifamily Group Psychoeducation, both evidence-based interventions (Makin-Byrd, Gifford, McCutcheon, & Glynn, 2011). Veterans with PTSD most likely will welcome such family participation in treatment. In one study, a majority of veterans who were receiving PTSD treatment considered PTSD to be a source of family stress, wanted their families to be more involved in their PTSD treatment, and wanted guidance on how to communicate with their family members (Batten et al., 2009).

Family members have indicated wanting assistance directly for their own sake and not just as a caregiver for someone else. They want help with reducing their stress levels, and prefer a partners-only group, cultural and leisure activities to counteract feelings of isolation, and individual therapy for themselves (Lyons, 2007). In addition, support for family members needs to extend beyond an initial diagnosis of PTSD to acknowledge life cycle changes, stages of PTSD, and the strengths family members bring to their caregiving. Barriers to participation (e.g., child care, transportation, objections of service member or veteran) need to be lowered (Dekel & Solomon, 2007).

Resources for Family Members Multiple sources of information about stress responses and PTSD have recently been developed for family members. The VA has materials for download, including explanations of PTSD, descriptions of treatment options, and video discussion of stress responses in women (http://www.ptsd.va.gov/public/index.asp). For those who wish for more in-depth information, a free online course, PTSD 101, can be found at http://www.ptsd.va.gov/professional/ptsd101/ptsd-101.asp. The Defense Centers of Excellence for Psychological Health and Traumatic Brain Injury (DCoE) launched the *Real Warriors Campaign* to reduce stigma about seeking psychological services, and encourage awareness and helping-seeking behaviors (www.realwarriors.net). Families are part of this campaign. Through the website they are provided information on how to support their service member and care for themselves. Recommendations include taking time for oneself, using clear communication, maintaining healthy habits, being positive and patient, asking for help, and seeking services.

In response to a mandate by Congress, the www.afterdeployment.org website was developed to address problems and concerns experienced by service members and their families following deployment. The website offers assessments, online workshops, videos, and links to more information including a blog on PTSD and Pentagon Channel videos on service members overcoming PTSD.

The DoD and the nonprofit organization Screening for Mental Health® launched Military Pathways, a screening program for family members and service personnel in both the active duty and reserve components. These anonymous mental health and alcohol self-assessments are found at http://mentalhealthscreening.org/programs/military.

TECHNOLOGICAL ADVANCEMENTS

In our lifetimes, we may witness technological changes that could bring about what now seems like inconceivable changes in the fields of medicine and psychological health. Artificial intelligence technology might be connected, through surgical implants or through external sensors, directly to the brain (Luxton, 2013). Currently, nonmedical uses of similar technology are found in programs that control robots and provide virtual reality entertainment. Future applications might include artificial intelligence that can "restore neurological functions following a stroke, traumatic brain injury (TBI), or other organic disorders" (http://t2health.dcoe.mil/news/create-news-articles-5). This section introduces three recent technological advances that are currently in use by the DoD and/or the VA: telehealth, mobile telephone applications, and virtual reality.

Telehealth

Telehealth technology, also called telemedicine, is health care that relies on recent technological developments to serve populations that are not geographically located near facilities that could provide the health care they require (Institute of Medicine, 2012). It can also extend the reach of scarce resources and provide a greater number of individuals who are spread over a wider geographical area access to specialized medical knowledge and skills. Telehealth relies primarily on the Internet and includes videoconferencing, streaming media, and wireless communications. Both private and public sectors continue to develop telehealth programs and technologies. However, issues of reimbursement, licensure, and costs are barriers to the use of these technologies.

The VA, a national leader in telehealth, uses it to reduce costs, increase quality, and improve access to care (Darkins, 2012). The VA uses three key methods of telehealth: home telehealth, store and forward telehealth, and clinical video telehealth. Home telehealth is provided primarily through video and mobile devices for the treatment of veterans with long-term chronic conditions, for acute care, and for health promotion and prevention. The number of VA patients who receive home telehealth has grown steadily between 2008 and 2011. In fiscal year 2011, over 65,000 veterans received home telehealth.

Store and forward technology is the electronic transmission of medical information, including digital images (e.g., X-rays, magnetic resonance images, and photos) documents, and pre-recorded videos (e.g., video clips of medical examinations) usually via electronic mail (Institute of Medicine, 2012). This transmission of medical information usually takes place between medical professionals to facilitate making diagnoses and for providing medical consultations when face-to-face contact or live video are not possible or not necessary.

Clinical video telehealth is the use of videoconferencing for real-time consultations between healthcare providers and patients or between providers at different locations, such as VA medical centers and VA outpatient clinics, reducing travel (Darkins, 2012). The VA uses video telehealth primarily for psychological health services and for consultations with medical specialists (e.g., audiologists, cardiologists, and neurologists).

Using the three types of telehealth, the VA provided care for over 380,000 veterans in 2011 (Darkins, 2012). Over 6,700 of those veterans were seen for psychological health care via home telehealth. When reviewing records of over 98,600 veterans who received home telehealth service for psychological treatment between 2006 and 2010, the VA found that there was a 25% reduction in hospitalizations for psychological reasons among those veterans.

Darkins (2012) states that the greatest barrier the VA has encountered in its efforts to provide telehealth services to veterans is the lack of providers who are trained in the use of telehealth. He cites two reasons for this shortfall; telemedicine is not included in training programs for healthcare providers and there are no outside resources to train providers in telehealth.

Mobile Phone Applications

As the psychological health community incorporates new technology into its work with clients, mobile phone applications are increasingly used to give clients additional tools for understanding and managing their symptoms. Two examples of such applications are *PTSD Coach* and *Virtual Hope Box*. *PTSD Coach* was developed by the VA National Center for PTSD in partnership with the DoD National Center for Telehealth and Technology (T2). This application uses cognitive-behavioral techniques to help clients manage PTSD symptoms. The findings of research with veterans who used the *PTSD Coach* application suggested that the veterans found the application helpful (Kuhn et al., 2014). They reported that it helped them manage their symptoms, feel more able do something about their symptoms, and find practical solutions to their problems. A tool contained in the application, called "Take a Time Out," provides a five-minute countdown with suggestions for calming down during the time-out (U.S. Department of Veterans Affairs, 2014a).

Virtual Hope Box, developed by T2, contains six major sections: "Remind Me," "Distract Me," "Inspire Me," "Relax Me," "Coping Tools," and "Support Contacts." It is designed to help clients cope with stress through positive activity planning, distraction tools, and relaxation exercises, including guided imagery, controlled breathing, and muscle relaxation. The user can add family photos, videos, recorded messages from loved ones, inspirational quotes, and soothing music to the application. T2 has developed additional mobile applications and has endorsed others developed for use with military clients. Detailed descriptions of *PTSD Coach*, *Virtual Hope Box*, and other mobile applications are available on the T2 website at http://www.t2.health.mil/products/mobile-apps.

Virtual Reality

Earlier in this chapter, you learnt about exposure therapy as a treatment method for PTSD for individuals who have suffered a trauma. Recall that exposure therapy involves re-living the traumatic event, while working with a therapist to reduce the negative responses—emotions and thoughts—about the trauma. An individual's re-experiencing of the trauma can be activated through exposure to trauma-related stimuli (e.g., sights, sounds, or smells) that remind the individual of the event and bring back their feelings and thoughts about the event. Visual and auditory memories can be simulated by using virtual reality programs. The sights and sounds in virtual reality scenes can be customized to resemble the individual's memories of the traumatic event (Conaboy, 2013). Scenes can include details based on the veteran's memories—a view of the desert sky, the vibration of a vehicle seat, the explosion of a car bomb, and even the smells of an Arabic market place—can be programmed into the scene. Because of its ability to help veterans remember the details of a traumatic event and re-experience their emotions during the event, some therapists are now using virtual reality exposure therapy to help veterans process the trauma they have lived through and to help reduce their PTSD symptoms.

CARING FOR INJURED SERVICE MEMBERS AND VETERANS

One clear lesson emerging from OIF and OEF is that providing quality care for injured service members and veterans requires providing quality care for their families. Family members who are caregivers may experience stress reactions as they confront loneliness, worry, injury of their loved one, and loss. Stressed caregivers have had a sense of the world as just, and connections, identities, beliefs about themselves and others, and relationships are disrupted (Boss, 2006; Cozza, 2009b; Dekel & Monson, 2010). It is easy for caregivers to use most of their energy and time providing physical and emotional care to their loved one and being the advocate for the individual and family.

When working with families, practitioners should encourage and facilitate self-care for caregivers in order to prevent burnout. Caregivers may benefit from exercise, good nutrition, adequate sleep, regular and extended time away from caregiving, social support including someone who will listen who is nonjudgmental, accepting emotional reactions as normal, valuing their own needs and interests, prioritizing what is important (including their own well-being, and letting other time and energy demands fall off the list (Dekel et al., 2005).

Caregivers may benefit from formal and informal supports. Family caregivers can go online for resources and information through the VA (http://www.caregiver.va.gov). Also, as noted in Chapter 10, the Caregivers and Veterans Omnibus Health Services Act of 2010 provides eligible family caregivers of post-9/11 veterans with access to practical and emotional support: training on caregiving, respite care, mental health services, and a monthly personal caregiver stipend. Some primary caregivers may also be eligible for medical care coverage. Family caregivers can go online for information on applying (http://www.caregiver.va.gov).

Most commonly a spouse or a parent will be the daily caregiver and advocate. Yet all family members—spouses, parents, partners, siblings, adult children, aunts, and uncles—can serve as champions for their injured service member, working on behalf of their loved one. Primary caregivers function best if surrounded by a cadre of family members, friends, neighbors, and others who can provide practical support (e.g., respite care, child care, help with household chores or repairs) and social/emotional support (e.g., listening, friendship, trips to the movies, a meal out). Social support protects against negative stress reactions following a trauma (Brewin, Andrews, & Valentine, 2000). Those who work with military and veteran families can prompt caregivers not only to accept such support but to actively develop it.

DEATH OF SERVICE MEMBERS: FAMILY RESPONSES AND RESOURCES

Voices From the Frontline

A WIFE TALKS ABOUT THE DEATH OF HER HUSBAND

Surviving military families live out the Ultimate Sacrifice of their loved ones each and every day.

My husband, a Navy pilot, was killed when the helicopter he was flying exploded in mid-air. None of the seven crewmen onboard survived. As a military wife-made-widow, I searched for resources to understand the chaos of emotion, thought, and feeling which was brewing within me, and found no written resource in the civilian sector that adequately described the complexity of military loss. My home-grown survival group of military widows and widowers was able to identify with the criteria for Traumatic Grief, as originally presented by Holly Prigerson, et al. (1999) to a limited degree. Yet, these criteria fell short of defining either the full depth of a military death in the line of duty in times of peace or war, or our complicated reactions to this death.

Most military deaths are traumatic and the remains are often unviewable, comingled or non-recoverable. Many military deaths occur in hostile theaters of operation, on deployments, and in off-sight training exercises, making the scene of the death unreachable to surviving family members. Suicides by military service members are often disenfranchised, resulting in deprived grief and recognition in the surviving families. Surviving spouses and dependent children usually live at a duty station, placing them great distances from family and friends. Surviving parents are dispersed throughout the country, and most often lack the connection or availability to military installations. In our post September 11th environment, military deaths are publicized in the media, yet often reduced to a 30-second sound-bite, which is perceived as minimizing the loss in the eyes of surviving family members.

Service to country and commitment to duty further complicates a military death. Common symbols of our country, such as the American flag, become powerful reminders of a military death to a loved one.

It's safe to say surviving military families live out the Ultimate Sacrifice of their loved ones each and every day, in big and small ways that go unnoticed or unacknowledged. It takes years for a surviving military family to fully accept the reality of their profound loss.

Joanne Steen
Co-author of Military Widow: A Survival Guide

As noted in Chapter 8, little research exists on military families who have experienced the death of a service member. However, personal accounts such as that written by Joanne Steen and research on loss from literature on civilians suggests multiple points to consider when working with families whose service member has died.

First, resilience is more common than not, and most individuals adapt to a loss without professional intervention or grief counseling (Bonanno, 2004); however, understanding the process of grief can help individuals cope with a loss (Bonanno & Mancini, 2008; Bonanno et al., 2002). Second, yearning for the one who has died is a predominant emotion during the time when grieving is more intense (Shear & Mulhare, 2008). Third, individuals and families differ in grief responses and length of time to accept a death to the point of thinking of the loss and experiencing the reminders of the person without overwhelming distress (Bonanno et al., 2002).

Fourth, rather than seeing bereavement as a process through stages, researchers are considering the "states" of bereavement (Prigerson & Maciejewski, 2005/6) and are looking at factors that may help or hinder a process of recovery (Wright, Burrell, Schroeder, & Thomas, 2006). In Western societies, bereaved persons typically experience **acute grief** during which time she or he yearns for the loved one daily, feels deep sadness, struggles with the finality of the loss, is preoccupied with memories and thoughts of the loved one, and has diminished interest in ongoing life (Shear & Mulhare, 2008). Acute grief typically becomes **integrated grief** in which bereaved persons comprehend the death, are not preoccupied by thoughts and memories, and have interest in life.

Fifth, evidence from studies of bereaved civilian spouses indicates that sudden and traumatic loss, such as from combat or military service in general, may be associated with continuing distress years after the loss (Wright et al., 2006). They may experience **complicated grief** in which they experience prolonged yearning and other symptoms such as disbelief or bitterness over the loss, numbness, a sense that life is empty, and an inability to move forward with plans (Bonanno, Rennicke & Dekel, 2005; Prigerson & Maciejewski, 2005). They may feel guilty about not preventing the death or suffering, believe it is wrong to enjoy life when the loved one cannot, and feel angry or disappointed with others or with the unfairness of life. At the same time, they may avoid reminders that the loved one is dead. Persons experiencing complicated grief may experience depression, PTSD or both; may engage in reckless behaviors; may have sleep disruptions; and may have thoughts of suicide (Shear & Mulhare, 2008).

Those who experience complicated grief may benefit from cognitive and behavioral therapy (Bonanno et al., 2002). Modified interpersonal psychotherapy, based on attachment theory and using strategies from cognitive behavioral therapy for PTSD has been initially tested with promising results for those who stayed in the treatment (Shear & Mulhare, 2008).

In addition to individual therapy, other intervention strategies have been proposed for coping with a traumatic loss because they promote adaptive processes associated with family resilience: belief systems, organizational patterns, and communication (Walsh, 2007). These key processes of family resilience were introduced in Chapter 5.

Applied to grieving families, belief systems that promote family resilience include arriving at a meaning for the loss that brings comfort. The military's ceremonial recognition and rituals convey honor of and respect for those who die while carrying out their duties. This public acknowledgement of sacrifice of a military member's life in selfless service to others and showing reverence, respect, and gratitude to family members offer specific ways for families to ascribe meaning to their loss (Wright et al., 2006). However, it must be recognized that families or individual family members may differ in the extent to which they find such public rituals helpful. Some family members may see rituals as something to endure while others see them as a source of comfort (Steen & Asaro, 2006).

Organizational patterns such as the use of formal and informal supports is another key process in promoting adjustment to a traumatic loss. Support can come from military leaders when they formally acknowledge the contributions of those who have died, and through the assistance of the Army's Casualty Assistance Officer, the Navy or Marine Corps Casualty Assistance Calls Officer, or the Air Force Casualty Assistance Representative. Military family groups and friends can provide critical emotional and practical support initially and subsequently (Wright et al., 2006).

Self-help books such as Steen and Asaro's (2006) *Military Widow: A Survival Guide*, and the organizations, Gold Star Mothers, Gold Star Wives, Military Families United, and Tragedy Assistance Program for Survivors offer compassion and guidance on practical and emotional matters.

Human service professionals can assist family members to: identify additional sources of formal support (e.g., religious groups, child and youth programs, self-help groups, and health-care providers) and informal support (e.g., colleagues at work, church members, neighbors); and examine ways to locate such support, such as initiating conversations, self-disclosure, becoming involved in a group or club, and volunteering (Huebner, Mancini, Bowen, & Orthner, 2009; Mancini, Bowen, & Martin, 2005).

When grieving, open communication and productive problem-solving processes can also encourage positive coping by families. Families benefit from clear and consistent messages about the death of their service member; however, they often need patience as information can be delayed as details are verified (Steen & Asaro, 2006). Additionally, they can benefit from recognizing that individuals within the same family may express their grief differently and that there is no "right" way to grieve (Bonanno, 2004).

Months into their bereavement, military families may sense a change in their relationship with their loved one's unit or with the military in general. While the military "takes care of its own" with casualty assistance, funeral rituals, and initial daily contact by unit and/or family readiness group members, families may feel bewildered when the telephone calls and visits taper off and when they realize military functions such as promotions or holiday parties pass by without an invitation. They may feel abandoned by the military. However, unit life moves on as individuals transfer and deployments occur (Steen & Asaro, 2006). While they might not be involved in the day-to-day life of their loved one's last unit, families may continue a connection with the military through participation in local or national events that recognize their loved one's service and sacrifice and in military rituals on national holidays.

Steen and Asaro (2006) acknowledge that going through grief is not pain-free and it encompasses all aspects of life. They encourage those who have lost a loved one to talk with those who will listen and acknowledge grief. They suggest learning more about grieving the death of a military service member and emphasize, "the life skills you developed as a military [family] will help you cope with military bereavement" (p. 14).

Empirical and clinical studies of military families over the past 70 years have added to our knowledge of family functioning during stressful situations such as war and following traumatic events such as injury and death (MacDermid Wadsworth, 2010). Those who work in military and civilian communities can support military families by using resilience-related practices that promote positive coping strategies.

SUMMARY

- Family-centered approaches to treatment are being developed for combat-injured families. Treatments for veterans diagnosed with TBI and/or PTSD are including family members and caregivers.
- Psychological First Aid (PFA) is a way of helping children, adolescents, adults, and families immediately following a traumatic event.
- TBI treatment requires tailored coordination of care for the unique needs of each service member. Many cognitive-behavioral treatments for PTSD are available.
- PTSD has implications for the family members as well as the service personnel. Family members of service members diagnosed with a TBI and/or PTSD may benefit from participating in multifamily group treatment, behavioral family therapy, or cognitive-behavioral conjoint treatment, and using online resources.
- Caregivers can benefit from self-care and use of formal and informal supports.
- Little research exists on bereaved military families. However, research on civilians indicates most bereaved persons experience acute grief and eventually integrated grief. Traumatic loss appears to increase the possibility of complicated grief in which the bereaved experience prolonged yearning and other symptoms.

EXERCISES

1. Prepare a 15-minute presentation for colleagues on campus or at work on one of the following: injury communication, PFA, one of the evidence-based treatments for PTSD, how to support families with a member who has a TBI (consider the differences between mild, moderate, and severe TBI), how to support caregivers, or how to support those in grief. Use the information presented in this chapter as a springboard to additional information and resources.
2. Imagine parents of a veteran came to you, worried that their daughter or son was not sleeping and was angry and irritable most of the time. They don't know what to do and they ask for ideas. Outline what you would say to them, including the resources you would recommend. Spend time studying the resources in this chapter and elsewhere in this book before outlining your response.
3. Role-play a situation in which a service member (active duty or reservist) describes symptoms typical of post-traumatic stress but does not want to get help because only "the weak" have problems. What would you do and say? What resources could the two of you explore together?
4. If you are a civilian mental health clinician or in training and a service member comes to you with PTSD symptoms, what intervention would you offer? Do you

need additional training to offer that intervention? If so, identify ways you can obtain that training.

5. Identify evidence-based couple-based interventions for military and veteran couples and intimate partner violence, depression, substance abuse disorders, infidelity, PTSD, and TBI. Examine the evidence of its efficacy and effectiveness, guidelines for treatment, and factors to consider when applying the intervention to military and veteran couples.

6. Using the resources noted in this book, locate one or more online videos of military family caregivers. What surprised you? What tips would you pass on to other caregivers?

14

Serving Military Families

In Chapter 14, you will

- Meet Ashley Armand, a senior majoring in family studies, and Stephen Fountain, a graduate student, who are working with or plan to work with veterans, service members, and their families.
- Consider some of your beliefs and attitudes about working with families.
- Examine career paths that lead to serving military families.
- Consider the importance of compassion satisfaction and compassion fatigue.
- Discover practices and ways to promote self-care to encourage compassion satisfaction.
- Identify the settings where you might apply what you learn in this book.

Meet

Ashley Armand, Senior, Family Studies Student

I took a military family life course as a stepping stone to working with military families. I want to work with military families whose service member has a TBI. I have learned that a TBI can change who people are and how they act. My goal is to work in an organization that studies and treats TBI. A TBI places a great deal of stress on families, and I want to focus on how we can best support them. If there are enough people out there who support military families, their issues will become normal in our society. Military families will be better off. All families will be better off.

Stephen Fountain, Graduate Student in Student Affairs

I have a lot of military in my extended family. My grandfather served in the Korean War and was promoted to Colonel. It couldn't have been easy, especially because of all he had to go through being black. My uncle and half-sister have served, too. The course on family life and the military allowed me to better understand things about my family and myself. Learning about what people in the military may endure helps me understand why some may be hesitant to speak about their experiences. However, if those of us in a helping profession demonstrate we are compassionate and trustworthy, veterans may confide in us if they need support. For example, I heard about a veteran who slept with a gun under his pillow and a knife under his bed because he felt he needed those things to protect his life. He found faculty and staff on campus to support his adjustment and is successfully completing his degree.

*My Master's degree will be in education with a focus on student affairs and develop-
ment. I currently work with student organizations on campus. Insights from this class are
helping me today and will help me with my career in the future to better understand what
veterans experience in the college setting.*

INTRODUCTION

As Ashley Armand and Stephen Fountain, you may be in school studying and planning
for a career working with service members and military families. Or you may have an
established career and find you have the opportunity to work with military families.
Whether you are working in a military or civilian setting, you are likely to meet and
have the opportunity to learn from and support military and veteran families. Ginny
Wescott, CFLE, who you first met in Chapter 3 says that "knowing the military culture
and being informed about military services can allow any helping professional to support active duty, Guard or Reserve, veteran service member and/or family that they
encounter in any setting or capacity." She points out that, "with downsizing there are
going to be many more former service members and families living out in communities." Ginny also highlights the importance of bridge building between civilian and
military services for families. In her words, it will "make services for families stronger
on both sides of the gate."

In prior chapters, you were introduced to numerous military and civilian agencies and
organizations that serve military families. You read results from many studies on military
families and read about policies that recognize the opportunities and challenges of military family life. It is now your turn to take this information with you on your own career
path or in your future work with service members and military families.

In this chapter, we invite you to consider some of your beliefs and attitudes about
working with families. Reflecting on your professional stance is vitally important because
it impacts relationships you build and ultimately your effectiveness. We then examine some of the obvious and not-so-obvious careers that offer a way to serve military
families, either directly or indirectly. These career paths are illustrated through stories
shared by working professionals. You may be surprised about the myriad ways you can
apply your knowledge of military families. In addition, we note the paths to take if you
wish to work directly with military families by describing the federal and contract paths
and listing online job search sites. Finally, we emphasize the satisfaction that comes with
working with military families and ideas for maintaining this satisfaction as you continue
in your career.

Your Beliefs and Attitudes About Working with Families

No matter your role and the skills and knowledge you bring to your work with military
families, how you are is as important as what you say and do. As Shelley, a co-author of
this book, once advised Amy: "You know what you know. It will take all of us to support
military families. So don't hesitate to bring what you do best to the table."

The more aware you are of the beliefs and attitudes that lay at the foundation of your
practice, the more clearly you will be able to see and make decisions about how best to
respond to family members as unique individuals, and the more effective you will be in
serving military families.

Throughout this book, many people have shared their insights, lessons learned, and
wisdom about serving military families. In this section we highlight the stories shared by
four of them and encourage you to go back and reread what they have said. As you consider
their beliefs and attitudes, we invite you to reflect upon those you hold as a future or current family support practitioner.

You may find similarities or differences between your approach to your work and theirs. You may even discover an idea that causes you to question or consider a shift in your view of your work and yourself as a helping professional.

What is your stance as a professional? To help the VA take a more family-centered approach, Shirley Glynn, PhD explains that "Part of our work is helping the professionals find their stance… to consider not only what to say and do but *how to be*. We are encouraging a much more collaborative stance with veterans and families. Recovery should be personal… sometimes clinicians use their knowledge as self-protection and to create distance from families. Many times they would be more effective if they could just be there and listen and offer consultation and support as needed." *What do you see as the link between being there, listening, and effectiveness in working with a family?*

What does it mean to help a family? Colonel Charles Engel, MPH, MD talks about broadening our sense of what it means to help. He says, "We have to be creative and open to options, working with everyone starting where they are." Dr. Engel shares the insight that, "We also need to think about how we define success. If someone feels better about who they are by engaging in a leisure time activity, we've had a big impact. If a family moves from not functioning to functioning, we've had a big impact." *How do you measure "success" in working with a family?*

How do you make a difference? Kathleen Marin, Director of Installation Services, U.S. Army Office of the Assistant Chief of Staff for Installation Management, and Dee Geise, Chief, Soldier & Family Readiness, U.S. Army Office of the Assistant Chief of Staff for Installation Management talk about how interactions matter, for example the words and actions of the person distributing pots and pans to new families on base. What you say and do matters. *What is something you have recently said or done that made a positive difference to a family?*

How do you view families? Froma Walsh, MSW, PhD, Co-director, Chicago Center for Family Health, University of Chicago shares the story from her childhood and how "hard times" led to her resilience. She reminds us, "It is important to see families not as damaged, but as challenged by adversity, with the potential to repair and rebuild their lives." *What are examples of signs showing a family's "potential to repair and rebuild" that you might see?*

THE MANY PATHS TO SERVING MILITARY FAMILIES

There are many paths that allow us to serve military families. No matter what path you take, expect the unexpected in your work. You may find yourself traveling to a military installation in a country you never imagined visiting, or being lowered down to the deck of a ship from a helicopter to give presentations to sailors on their way home from a deployment. You may discover renewed excitement and satisfaction in work you have been doing for more than 25 years as you and a military family celebrate their resilience. Or find yourself humbled and inspired by a child who draws a picture of herself and her mommy holding hands across an ocean. Like many of the people you have met in this book, you may find yourself questioning your assumptions about the military and gaining new insights into what is meant by resilience, commitment, and honor. As you serve military families, you will likely find that your life, too, is being enriched.

The Researcher Path

Deborah Gibbs, MSPH and Senior Health Analyst at RTI International, shares the path she took to working in support of military families:

"I think that the key to finding satisfying work is in making a match between an issue that you care about and your skills and temperament. I can imagine the process working in reverse, that is, someone who starts with their skills, then finds the issue on which they'll use those skills. And then, of course, you hope that such work is available and reasonably compensated!

"Child welfare and issues affecting vulnerable women and families are such issues for me. I've done some direct service work, enough to know that I wasn't particularly good at it. The tasks that I was drawn to involved synthesizing information and answering interesting questions. I became a researcher and am now focusing some of my work on military families.

"There are trade-offs to make when choosing a career: knowing that you made a difference in one person's life, versus hoping to make a difference in a lot of lives; and working face to face or remotely from the people affected. These are just two examples of the choices we make."

The Writing Path

Margaret von Steinen
Communications Officer
Haenicke Institute for Global Education
Western Michigan University

A few years ago, I went to a presentation by Mark Salzman (an award-winning novelist and non-fiction writer) who runs writing groups with teen felons. He talked about how writing helped them understand the reasons they ended up incarcerated had to do with how they grew up. I wanted to do something similar and started looking for possibilities.

I have an MFA in Creative Writing and have been leading a writing group of veterans at Portage District Library that hosts us. We have four World War II veterans, three Korean veterans, three Vietnam veterans, and an Afghanistan veteran. One gentleman has been in the group since our first session in 2009. The retired vets have time to write, and some write outside of the group, too. New veterans are generally harder to attract because they are too busy going to college and raising families.

We meet for 1½ hours two times a month. We start by talking a little about what's been happening since we last met. Then I give a trigger word(s) as a writing prompt. For example: your helmet, boot camp, a hand grenade, shade, returning home. They write for 10 minutes. Then share what they wrote and we have an open discussion in which they often compare and contrast their experiences.

Everyone takes their writing in their own direction. For example, one person might talk about taking a bullet in his helmet, another about eating a meal from his. One night the prompt was "mess hall." A few wrote funny things. One man wrote about how hard it was to see children who lived close to the base going through the garbage for food as their mothers waited a short distance away in the woods.

They were each very young adults and went through a rite of passage in the military in a combat situation. That's too important a part of life to forget about: the friends you made, the things you learned that served you well the rest of your life. I want to help them see the value of their experiences, as well as what made it difficult.

It is not the guts and gore that they want to share but the life-changing experiences that they had as a young person growing up. Military life often means lots of time sitting—on base or in a trough you dug—waiting and thinking.

Most people imagine that I get together with these guys every 2 weeks and that they share horrible stories of grueling combat and we cry. We've had our moments but there are a lot more nods, smiles, and laughter.

Members of the group come to trust that I am providing a forum and believe they benefit from conversations with each other. I am friendly but firm. If someone starts going off on a tangent, I put the brakes on and we turn to the writing. I remind them that this isn't a group for us to work out problems. Its purpose is to record military experiences for their own benefit, for their families, and for the community at large for those who wish to participate in readings or seek publishing. There is safety in this.

One member, a World War II veteran, joined the group after a long summer vacation with his grandchildren. His grandson had asked, "Granddad, you were in World War II, right?" The veteran started talking. Two hours later he was surprised to note that he was still talking and his grandson was still listening. He saw an ad for the group in the fall and jumped in.

Sometimes writing helps people own their memories. One night the prompt was: "Write about the last night before you headed overseas." One gentleman, Don, wrote about having trouble getting to sleep in the barracks. Another Marine in his unit who knew Don had a good voice called out as they were all tossing and turning, "Don, sing us some songs." He did. Though he couldn't recall what he sang, we could tell a light had come on revealing a new good memory. Then he told us, with a big smile on his face, "Margaret, I have not thought about that since it happened nearly 70 years ago."

I'm starting now to get involved with veterans working at the university. We decided that one way to honor people who have served our country to is let them share something they have written about their service. So we're going to invite people to submit entries for a Veteran's Day reading. We'll see where that might lead.

Here are some things to think about for people who might want to begin a group like this:

- Experience as a writer is not needed—for the group leader or participants.
- Use prompts to guide the content of the writing and conversation. Many combat veterans would like to share their experiences and many civilians would like to hear about them. But no one wants to answer a question like, "How many people did you kill?"
- Encourage participants to keep their writing and mementos from war in one place and to let someone know where it is stored. A doctor who served in World War II once wrote about a scarf he had received from home and how he wore it during a cold winter. I invited him to bring it in next time we met and he did. If he had kept it all these years, it must have meant lots to him and I believe it will mean lots to his family years from now.

If we are going to send people to war, we need to be open to their stories when they come home and encourage them to share their stories. It is not fair to send them away and pretend it never happened. We have to let veterans know there are people who are willing and want to listen. Our interest in their stories is proof that we, as civilians of the nation they fought for, are with them in solidarity.

The Video Producer Path

Kristin Westbrook, Creative Director, Science Applications International Corporation (SAIC), explains how she began her work supporting service members and their families. "We use video to engage reluctant audiences in the military. We are training what people want to hear about least of all: casualty notification and assistance, sexual assault prevention, and suicide prevention.

"We totally stumbled on this work. I had worked with an ad agency before that produced high-level national TV commercials. My husband, Wayne, a member of our team, is a cinematographer. He's brilliant at lensing, that is the use of lenses in filming. He understands light.

"The Air Force Academy rape scandal in 2003 put us all to the test. Congress demanded that the Air Force tell Congress what they were going to do to change the culture. The Air Force wanted a top-notch course with a dramatic scenario; as luck would have it, the division of SAIC supporting this customer was on the same floor as our division and knew our work.

"Recently we've been focusing on suicide prevention. Suicide is a mystery that may never be solved. Everyone working in this field is a pioneer, trying to figure this out. We've been talking with lots of families who have honored us by sharing their stories. Each talks about how service members who kill themselves 'unplug' or 'disconnect'; the challenge is trying to reach them.

"This work gives us a chance to serve. Working with military families, we are part of something bigger. It's an amazing feeling. Military families are inspiring. The deep respect that I now have for people in the military came gradually. Not because it wasn't deserved from the people I met right off the bat. It's that I came from a parallel peacenik universe.

"I guess that's the beauty of life—making new connections and relationships. Thanks to service members, their families, and this experience, I feel like I'm just hitting my stride as a producer and I will do whatever I can to support them."

The Veteran Supporting Other Veterans Path

Perhaps you are a veteran who wants to support other veterans. This desire may lead you to apply for a job in higher education, as it did for Welby Alcantara, Veterans Affairs Coordinator, City College of New York, who describes, "Coming back to the civilian world you can feel like an immigrant who doesn't speak the language or know the culture. You spend months being trained so that when you hit combat, you do what you have to do without a pause. Thinking is minimal.

"After being told where to go, what to eat, who your friends are, and what to do, you get out and even choosing what socks to put on can be an issue. When you are in Iraq or Afghanistan, you have a rifle or sidearm right there. You feel empowered. When you come back, you don't feel safe.

"Veterans are coming back stressed out. They need help. Their families need help, too. The ones who speak up are doing OK. It's the quiet ones who won't share some of their pain. They are the ones I fear for.

"That's why lots of us are leading and taking part in many new programs today. We know if we don't do something, lots of other vets are going to fall through the cracks. I don't see my work with vets who are students as a job. It's like they are my brothers and sisters. When I help another vet, it is like helping myself.

"Vietnam vets are stepping up, too. They are taking the watch cap and doing the right thing. They see a younger version of themselves and are determined that the way they were treated when they returned home is not going to happen again. That's why you have all those people at the airports to welcome people home. It means a whole lot."

Welby Alcantara's assistant, Aarian Oliver, who is also a veteran, adds, "Most vets and their families didn't know what they were getting into when they joined the military. I was a medic. Depression was a big thing for service members and their spouses. We'd have many on base who were 'frequent flyers' to the ERs for treatment.

"People who were in the military know what others experience. That's why we can and want to support one another. It doesn't mean that if you weren't in the military you can't be effective. But for us … we're a family. When I see these new student vets come in, it's like Welby and I are their granddads."

The Family Member to Family Readiness Manager Path

As Robin Berry, who you met in Chapter 11, explains, "I'm a military spouse and the mother of a son. My now former husband deployed two times. Our family's experience has turned out to be helpful in my work today. It gave me some understanding into what other military families might be experiencing and prompted me to think about what extended family members and community members might experience as they support or try to support military families.

"When my husband deployed in 2003, we found that a lot of people did not know how to respond to us. It's not a surprise. We were the only military family that any of us knew. But it was a challenge. Everyone in our family started helping out. My brother-in-law took over caring for the pool, a job my husband usually did. We felt that everyone was helping so much we were reluctant to ask for more help when it was really needed.

"Yet, some close friends stopped asking me to go bowling or play cards because they thought it would be a burden for me to have to make child care arrangements. We had always done these activities as couples, and it was awkward now that I was on my own.

"I had to change jobs, so I was not working evenings and weekends and could be home with our son. That left me in a new work situation with new colleagues who did not know me or my family situation.

"At church, the sermons said we should all be at peace. I agree with that, but they made it sound like going to war is a really bad thing. When you have someone in your family deployed, you do not want to hear that. So we felt isolated from church.

"After working as an Airman and Family Readiness Manager for nearly 10 years, I believe that most of the support and resources military families need is relationship-based. I learned early on that family members and service members had to be able to trust me. Going to work with military families and/or those who support them requires knowing the military culture or being open to learning about it. Only then can we adapt what we know from our own experiences and education to support military families."

The Educator Path

Into the foreseeable future, there will be a need for coordinated and sustainable services to support military families. With this need in mind, Karen Blaisure, one of the coauthors of this book, created a course titled *Family Life and the Military* where she teaches. "Within a few years of 9/11 and the deployment of large numbers of Reserve Component members, it was evident that our family studies and child and family development undergraduate and graduate students would need to understand the experiences of military families. We began offering a one-credit weekend course that developed after a few years into a three-credit course. Along with studying issues of relocation, spouse employment, and education of children, we want students to learn about the impact of deployment and combat deployment on family life. We want our graduates prepared to interact sensitively and practically with military families in their current work and in their future careers in child development, social service, and education. We also wanted to highlight job opportunities for working primarily with military families."

Hearing Karen's presentation about the course at a conference, Tara Saathoff-Wells, another coauthor of this book, created a similar course, *Military Family Life*, at her university. As she explains, "I felt students needed a safe space to address academic issues, personal issues, and career issues related to the military. They needed a place they could explore their feelings about the war, about the troops, about things they see in the media, and about experiences they may have or hear about with family members or friends in the military.

"Also, we had a lot of students expressing interest in working with military families as career options. They were given websites to explore and that's about it. I wanted them to have more. This course gives students a chance to explore career options in the civilian and military worlds."

Alisha Cederberg enrolled in the course on family life and the military for both personal and professional reasons. Alisha, a graduate student and financial services specialist recounts, "My husband was in the Air Force for 2 years. It's been frustrating for him getting others to accept that his years of service counted for something. The class has given me a framework to understand more of what he is experiencing as well as what veterans and military spouses I work with on campus experience. I think of one student whose wife was deployed. Now a single parent, he thought he'd have to withdraw from school. We talked about ways he might be able to organize his time so that he could take a course online, continue to get financial aid, and not totally stop attending the university."

SUPPORTING MILITARY FAMILIES IN YOUR COMMUNITY

> In every community, every day, we can find concrete ways to show our military families respect and gratitude …. You don't have to come from a military family, have a base in your community, or be an expert in military issues to make a difference. Every American can do something.
>
> **Michelle Obama and Jill Biden (2010)**

You may encounter civilians who wonder what they can do to show their appreciation and support for military families. Supporting the services provided by the organizations noted in other chapters is one way to show appreciation. Joining a group or participating in their service projects are other ways, as is joining military family members who are sending boxes to their loved one.

Voices From the Frontline

REFLECTIONS FROM A WIFE AND MOM

My husband and daughter are both soldiers currently deployed. Last time they were in two different countries. Caitlin ended up on the border of Kuwait and Iraq—one of 60 women in a 600-person deployment. Charlie was a chaplain in Ramadi, Iraq.

This time they are both at Bagram Airfield Base in Afghanistan. With flat rate boxes, I can put stuff in the same box for both of them. The box I'm packing today is a bunch of stuff Caitlin put aside before she left for training.

I send odds and ends. Charlie needed vitamins and tea. I forward their magazines. Send snacks. I just sent Charlie a cap from North Hero, Vermont. It's sunny over there.

They are on a 5-year rotation. Having gone through deployment before, you know you can do it. Last time when people asked, "Are you OK?" I would need to admit, "No, I'm not." This time I thought I really needed to be working with the military families to make it through this. So, in January 2008, I started working as a Family Readiness Support Assistant. Supporting other families helps me.

Barbara Purinton
Military Wife, Mother, Family Readiness Support Assistant

Since 9/11, numerous groups have formed for the purpose of finding a way to contribute or to support those who are acting on behalf of the United States. Many of these groups have chosen projects to demonstrate their support for service members and their families. To find these groups, talk with others in your community. Check on the Internet.

You will find organizations small and large, local and national that support military families with activities including:

- Quilt making.
- Sewing pillowcases.
- Adopt a soldier/unit/platoon programs.
- Remodeling of homes for wounded warriors.
- After-school and summer activities for children of military families.
- Putting together and sending of care packages.
- Purchasing calling cards troops can use to call home.
- Writing and sending thank you cards and poems.
- Providing motorcycle escorts at funerals.

Examples of occasional or unexpected interactions with military families are endless. They may be as simple as being a K-12 teacher where a child in your classroom has a parent who is a member of the Reserve Component and has been called up for deployment overseas. Perhaps that child's family is the only family in town undergoing activation and deployment. You may participate in programs such as Big Brothers/Big Sisters and be a "big" for a child with a deployed parent. For others, you may live and work near a large installation where the cycle of deployment is part of everyday life, and you can see ways in which the larger community adapts to the changes with large numbers of people entering and leaving on different assignments.

Here are other suggestions of how you might support military family members from some of the people you have met in this book:

- *"Be respectful, not intimidated by uniforms and jargon.* Always remember where military families come from and what they care about: the same places and things as you and your family," *Joyce Wessel Raezer, Executive Director, National Military Family Association.*
- *"Say, 'Thank you!' when you see a service member or military family.* As civilians we can choose our beliefs and actions about war. Our soldiers don't have a choice. They lifted their right hand and said they will support and defend our country and they have to go. We as family have no choice either," *Sabrina Behari, Military Family Member.*
- *"Ask, 'What can I do to support you?'* Don't go out looking to solve a big problem or to do therapy. Something as simple as inviting an at-home parent for a cup of coffee while your kids play together or taking a child to soccer practice every Thursday afternoon can be a life-preserver and make all the difference," *Chris Sullins, former Army Reserve, Combat Stress Prevention Officer.*
- *"Find a way to listen.* Not being in the military may not be a hindrance. You just have to be open to get to know someone and discover how to make a connection," *Ted Cravens, Army Reserve Combat Stress Prevention Officer.*
- *"Know there are things you may not know—or will ever know.* They say you can't understand someone until you walk a mile in their shoes. Sometimes service members and families have unique experiences and we can't follow their footsteps. That doesn't mean you can't be there for them," *Rhonda Thomlinson, Military Family Member.*
- *"Be familiar with resources available to military families.* This knowledge allows you to be able to help families connect to services in your community. At the same time, these resources can also help you learn more about the military and military families," *Rick Campise, Col, USAF, BSC, Commander, 559th Medical Group.*

- *"Make it clear to your representative in Congress that supporting the military is important. We require a standing military to keep our country free and that costs money. Service members are not paid a lot for what they do," Marianne Blackburn "Mimi" Drew, Rear Admiral (LH), USN (Retired).*

One final thought about supporting military families: there is nothing too small you can do to support a service or family member. As we were working on this book in the home of coauthor Colonel Angela Pereira and her husband Major Tony Vargas, coauthor Shelley MacDermid Wadsworth explained that her mother was working with a group of other women to make small cloth bags that would be filled with toiletries and sent to troops overseas. Hearing that, Angela said, "I think I have some of those. They were sent to us in Abu Ghraib." She ran upstairs and returned with three small bags. "I still treasure these little cloth bags someone sent to us in Iraq," she explained. "They were like gold. There was a central location where things sent to us were put. You could go through and find what you needed. I found these there. They held small bottles of care products like shampoo and conditioner. Hair conditioner in desert conditions is an amazing thing. But more than that, there was heart in these bags. They are pretty and so different from the world I was in." Years later, the memories caused her eyes to fill with tears as she continued, "They were made with love. Someone was saying, 'We know you are out there. We care about you.'"

CAREERS

Some of you may want to pursue career options within the military community. One option is to join a branch of the military and specialize in your training and education as a human services or health-care professional, such as a social worker, a psychologist, physical therapist, or a nurse. If you have already graduated from college, you may investigate the option of Officer's Candidate School as a way to join the Active or Reserve Component.

There are civilian options as well. Civilians who work in DoD or one of the service branches may be hired as government employees, and their pay follows a set pay scale. A government position requiring someone with a bachelor's degree would likely be listed as a General Schedule (GS) grade of 7 or 9. A position that requires a master's degree in a mental health profession would likely be a GS-11 grade. The base pay scale for GS positions can be found online (U.S. Office of Personnel Management, n.d.). The DoDEA hires civilian employees for many jobs on and off military installations, in many career fields including teachers.

For-profit companies and not-for-profit organizations also hire civilians to fill social service or behavioral health positions needed by the military. These companies or organizations are typically awarded a contract with the DoD for a set number of years, and they hire employees to carry out the required work of the contract. It is common to have military personnel, GS workers, and contractors working together on military installations.

A number of human service organizations and agencies exist in each of the service branches and their titles may be slightly different across branches. These positions may be GS or contract positions and include such titles as family life consultants; family life and education specialists; work/life consultants; social services support specialists; child development center directors and staff; substance abuse counselors; domestic violence counselors; early childhood, primary, secondary and/or special educator within the DoD school system; relocation specialists; new parent support home visitors; medical social workers; family therapists; child and youth program specialists; recreation staff; and guidance counselors.

The Veterans Health Administration also hires professionals in medical and behavioral health. Vet Centers are staffed by mental health professionals such as social workers and psychologists and have recently established marriage and family therapy positions.

Job postings for civilians can be found on the list of websites that follows. It is recommended that you check these sites regularly as positions may only be open for a short time. Follow application directions carefully to ensure that your application is processed correctly and for the positions in which you are interested.

- Jobs are listed at https//www.usajobs.gov by government agency and area of focus, and it includes links for DoDEA, and the Departments of the Army, Navy, and Air Force.
- The following organizations hire contractors to serve in various capacities; information on their hiring processes is available on their individual websites. Contracts are awarded for a set number of years at the conclusion of which the contracts are put up for bid again. The same or another organization may be awarded the contract.
  - MHN Government Services (www.mhngs.com)
  - Zeiders (http://zeiders.com/)
- Positions for military spouses are listed by military installation or job search category at http://jobsearch.spouse.military.com.

PROMOTING COMPASSION SATISFACTION

As the professionals in this chapter and throughout this book confirm, most individuals who work with and on behalf of military families find their work highly satisfying. In general, such satisfaction is common among helping professionals. The term **compassion satisfaction** refers to this type of powerful satisfaction, fulfillment, and joy of helping others and seeing small and large transformations in their lives (Radey & Figley, 2007).

The work of helping others, however, is not without its own stress. Ochberg (n.d.) described the process as follows:

> We do our job and we do it well and we feel gratified—even blessed. [We ...] hear the story told with such intensity, or we hear similar stories so often, or we have the gift and curse of extreme empathy and we suffer .... We tire ... we aren't ourselves ... from too much caring and too little self-caring. (para. 2, 5)

Military and civilian helping professionals from medicine, family support, behavioral and social health, and faith communities may experience the process described by Ochberg (Besterman-Dahan, Barnett, Hickling, Elnitsky, Lind, Skvoretz, & Antinori, 2012; Steward, 2009). Other professionals and volunteers who work with, study, and support service members may also experience stress (Bride & Figley, 2009).

Compassion stress is used to refer to a natural outcome of experiencing another's suffering, great or small, and wanting to relieve it. Signs of compassion stress include feelings of confusion, helplessness, and isolation (Figley, 1995). To reduce the likelihood of experiencing compassion stress, it is important that helping professionals practice positive self-care, adopt a positive attitude, and avail themselves of resources that can help mitigate the stress.

However, prolonged exposure to compassion stress can lead to **compassion fatigue** that is a state of short-term "exhaustion and dysfunction, biologically, physiologically, and emotionally" (Figley, 1995, p. 2). Prior unresolved trauma, uncontrolled work stressors, poor self-care, and work dissatisfaction can contribute to the experience of compassion fatigue (Figley, 1995).

Compassion fatigue differs from **burnout** (i.e., feeling long-term exhaustion, a decreased interest in work, and dissatisfaction with the work environment) in that the former includes the aspect of caregiving in the context of another person's experience of trauma (Bride & Figley, 2009). The effects of compassion fatigue may mirror the effects of being directly exposed to a traumatic event: distressing emotions, functional impairment, hyperarousal, avoiding reminders of the trauma, and intrusive thoughts and images of the trauma, including nightmares (Bride & Figley, 2009).

Radey and Figley (2007) proposed a conceptual model to explain how compassion satisfaction develops among helping professionals. First, we respond to the situation with the right amount of assistance that is neither too little nor too much. Second, expressing gratefulness, appreciation, and liking helps us to see more possible ways to respond effectively to a situation: "positivity widens the range of thoughts and actions (e.g., play, explore, cooperate, interact, greet) and generates greater flexibility and innovation" in contrast to expressing negativity that limits creative solutions (Radey & Figley, 2007, p. 209).

The next component in this model of how compassion satisfaction develops is **self-care**, that is taking action to be healthy through such steps as exercise, proper nutrition, self-reflection, interaction with family and friends, and taking time away from work. Organizations are important in promoting self-care of employees and can do so by providing a welcoming and warm environment in which to work; supervision, adequate benefits, and staff training; and limiting and diversifying caseloads (Radey & Figley, 2007).

This model suggests that combined with a caring workplace, the use of wise judgment, positivity, and self-care will result in helpers experiencing compassion satisfaction. Compassion satisfaction is shown by high morale and delivering high-quality services (Radey & Figley, 2007). Compassion satisfaction adds to positive fulfillment and encourages us to flourish as we provide "care within an optimal range that connotes goodness, flexibility, learning, growth, and resilience in the face of work demands. Flourishing caregivers provide highly competent and compassionate care while retaining high morale and work satisfaction" (Radey & Figley, 2007, p. 208).

In Box 14.1, we include suggestions for increasing the likelihood of experiencing compassion satisfaction when working with individuals and families who have experienced traumatic events. These suggestions, which are organized into categories developed by Radey and Figley (2007), include ideas offered and recommended by others. You and your colleagues may wish to add other suggestions to this list. It is particularly important to implement these suggestions when first noticing signs of compassion stress, in order to lessen the possibility of the stress developing into compassion fatigue.

Finally, the Green Cross Academy of Traumatology (n.d.) has recognized the importance of self-care. Members of this international nonprofit organization are mostly licensed mental health-care providers who provide crisis and trauma counseling, assessment, and referral following a traumatic event. They also offer education, training, and consultation about responding to traumatized individuals and families. This organization emphasizes the centrality of self-care in provision of competent assistance. Members are required to abide by standards of self-care as part of ethical practice and acknowledgement of a universal right to wellness (http:// www.greencross.org).

Military families look to knowledgeable, compassionate, and competent professionals for guidance during times of challenge and for direction in enjoying and maximizing the benefits of military life. As you complete your education, seek training, and begin or continue working, consider the importance of doing all you can to encourage positive attitudes, the use of resources, and self-care for yourself and for your colleagues. In so doing, you also benefit those you serve: military and veterans families.

BOX 14.1   BEST PRACTICES

**PROMOTING COMPASSION SATISFACTION AND
PREVENTING COMPASSION FATIGUE**

Increase or Maintain a Positive Attitude Toward Clients and Toward Life

- Practice gratitude (e.g., begin and end each day noting something to be grateful for).
- Express appreciation to others for who they are or what they have done.
- Express enthusiasm.
- Remember receiving another's compassion.
- Focus on the good being done.
- Accept that one person cannot fix everything.
- Reinforce others for taking care of themselves.

Increase Resources to Manage Stress

- Connect concepts and skills learned in the classroom with "real life".
- Take continuing education courses.
- Know personal limits, set boundaries, and say "no" when it is possible.
- Seek mentoring.
- Talk with someone you trust.
- Normalize reaching out for help.
- Add touches to the workplace, so it is more comfortable and soothing (e.g., comfortable chair, calming photographs or mementos).
- Participate in a nonwork activity that recharges and energizes.
- Visit places that nourish one's soul.
- Accept the love of a pet, the song of a bird, the beauty of a flower.

Increase Self-Care

- Set and meet personal goals to increase or maintain self-care (e.g., proper nutrition, exercise, meditation).
- Reflect on quality of care provided to clients and level of self-care at that time.
- Obtain adequate rest and sleep, follow healthy eating guides, exercise, meditate.
- Drink water to avoid dehydration.
- Take short breaks during work and practice deep breathing.
- Notice when hungry, angry, lonely, or tired and respond appropriately.
- Avoid alcohol, nonprescription medications, smoking, sugar, and caffeine.
- Spend time with family and friends who restore rather than deplete energy.
- Participate in or begin team meetings that provide opportunity to give and receive social support.

Compiled from Boss (2006), Brymer et al. (2006), Hirsch and Engel (2008), Radey and Figley (2007), and U.S. Department of Veterans Affairs (2010b).

SUMMARY

- Serving military families will take us all. Being aware of the beliefs and attitudes you bring to working with families will allow you to see and make the best decisions possible about how best to respond to and support families.
- There are many career paths that offer a way to serve military families, either directly or indirectly. Researchers, writers, video producers, family members, veterans, education specialist, and many other professionals have all found applications for their skills that benefit military members and families.
- Civilians can show their appreciation and support for military families by supporting organizations that serve military families, joining groups formed to support or honor military families or participating in their service projects, and showing respect and appreciation in daily encounters with military members and families.
- There are many options for pursuing a career within the military community: joining a branch of the military and specializing as a human services or healthcare professional, as a government employee in a helping profession, or as an employee of a private company or organization that has been awarded a contract with the DoD to provide civilians to fill social service or behavioral health positions needed by the military.
- Job postings for civilians who want to work as a government employee can be found on the websites of the individual organizations and agencies that provide services to military families.
- Most individuals who support and care for military families find their work satisfying, and they experience compassion satisfaction. However, helping others and experiencing another's suffering can be emotionally challenging and can lead to compassion stress, which, if not addressed, can result in compassion fatigue, that is, short-term physical and emotional exhaustion and dysfunction.
- To enhance their compassion satisfaction and deliver high quality services, helping professionals can judge the appropriate response to another's situation to avoid overresponding or underresponding, express positivity, practice self-care, and develop or find a caring workplace.

EXERCISES

1. Record three beliefs about working with families that are central to your current or future practice so that overtime you can review them to see if and how they may have shifted.

2. Using one of the online job search sites listed in this chapter, identify at least one position for which you qualify or will qualify based on your education, training, and experience. Study the basic requirements, and the knowledge, skills, and abilities necessary for each job. Prepare the required application materials for one of the positions.
3. Research the titles for human services professionals in each of the service branches.
4. Brainstorm how workers in a range of careers could encounter military families. How would they know someone comes from a military family? What might they do to invite military family members to identify themselves?
5. Develop attainable self-care goals that include at least one of each of the following components: exercise, better nutrition, self-reflection (e.g., meditation, prayer), interaction with family and friends, and taking time away from work on a regular basis.

Acronyms

AAFES Army and Air Force Exchange Service
ACU Army Combat Uniform
AER Army Emergency Relief
AFAS Air Force Aid Society
AFQT Armed Forces Qualifying Test
AFSC Air Force Specialty Codes
AFW2 Air Force Wounded Warrior Program
AW2 Army Wounded Warrior Program
AWOL Absent Without Leave
BUMED U.S. Navy's Bureau of Medicine and Surgery
CACO Casualty Assistance Calls Officer
CAO Casualty Assistance Officer
CAR Casualty Assistance Representative
CDCs Child Development Centers
CHEA Council for Higher Education Accreditation
CNO Casualty Notification Officer
CO Commanding Officer
CONUS Within the continental or contiguous United States
COSC Combat Operational Stress Control
COSFA Combat and Operational Stress First Aid
CSF Comprehensive Soldier Fitness
DADT Don't Ask, Don't Tell
DCoE Defense Centers of Excellence for Psychological Health and Traumatic Brain Injury
DDESS Department of Defense Domestic Dependent Elementary and Secondary Schools
DeCA Defense Commissary Agency
DEERS Defense Enrollment and Eligibility Reporting System
DoD Department of Defense
DoDDS Department of Defense Dependents Schools
DoDEA Department of Defense Education Activity
DSM Diagnostic and Statistical Manual of Mental Disorders
DUSD/MCFP Office of the Deputy Under Secretary of Defense (Military Community and Family Policy)
EFMP Exceptional Family Member Program
EMDR Eye movement desensitization and reprocessing
ESGR Employer Support of the Guard and Reserve
FAP Family Advocacy Program
FCC Family Child Care
FMLA Family and Medical Leave Act
FOB Forward Operating Base
FOCUS Families OverComing Under Stress
FRG Family Readiness Group
GAT Global Assessment Tool
GS General Schedule
H2H Heroes to Hometowns

HA/DR   Humanitarian Assistance/Disaster Response
IA   Individual Augmentee(s)
IAVA   Iraq and Afghanistan Veterans of America
IBA   Interceptor Body Armor
IED   Improvised Explosive Device
JFSAP   Joint Family Support Assistance Program
KIA   Killed in Action
MCEC   Military Child Education Coalition
MCM   Manual for Courts-Martial
MCX   Marine Corps Exchange
MEDEVAC or MEDIVAC   Medical Evacuation
MFLC   Military and Family Life Counselor
MFRI   Military Family Research Institute at Purdue University
MHAT   Mental Health Advisory Team
MIA   Missing in Action
MOS   Military Occupational Specialty
MOS   Military OneSource
mTBI   Mild Traumatic Brain Injury
MWR   Morale, Welfare and Recreation
NEC   Navy Enlisted Classification system
NEX   Navy Exchange
NICoE   National Intrepid Center of Excellence
NMCRS   Navy-Marine Corps Relief Society
NPSP   New Parent Support Program
OCONUS   Outside of the continental or contiguous United States
OEF   Operation Enduring Freedom
OIF   Operation Iraqi Freedom
OMK   Operation: Military Kids
OND   Operation New Dawn
OPTEMPO   Operational Tempo
PCS   Permanent Change of Station
PDHRA   Post-Deployment Health Reassessment
PFA   Psychological First Aid
POW   Prisoner of War
PREP   Prevention and Relationship Enhancement Program
PTSD   Posttraumatic Stress Disorder
PX or BX   Post Exchange or Base Exchange
RESPECT-Mil   Re-Engineering Systems of Primary Care Treatment in the
   Military
ROTC   Reserve Officer Training Corps
RWW   Returning Warrior Workshop
SAC   School-Age Care Programs
SAIC   Science Applications International Corporation
SIT   Stress Inoculation Therapy
SOC   Service Member's Opportunity College
SOMK   Speak Out for Military Kids
SVA   Student Veterans of America
SWAN   Service Women's Action Network
TAPS   Tragedy Assistance Program for Survivors
TBI   Traumatic Brain Injury
TDY or TAD   Temporary Duty
UCMJ   Uniform Code of Military Justice

USAFRICOM U.S. Africa Command
USCENTCOM or CENTCOM U.S. Central Command
USDA U.S. Department of Agriculture
USERRA Uniformed Services Employment and Reemployment Rights Act
USEUCOM U.S. European Command
USJFCOM U.S. Joint Forces Command
USNORTHCOM U.S. Northern Command
USPACOM U.S. Pacific Command
USSOCOM U.S. Special Operations Command
USSOUTHCOM U.S. Southern Command
USSTRATCOM U.S. Strategic Command
USTRANSCOM U.S. Transportation Command
VA Department of Veterans Affairs
VBA Veterans Benefits Administration
VETS Veterans Employment and Training Services
VFW Veterans of Foreign Wars
VHA Veterans Health Administration
WWR Marine Corps Wounded Warrior Regiment

Glossary

Accessions: Individuals accepted into the military, also called recruits.

Accompanied tour: A military assignment to an overseas location that includes the service member's family.

Active Component: The portion of the U.S. military forces comprised of full-time active duty members in the Army, Navy, Marine Corps, and Air Force.

Acute grief: During bereavement, the process of yearning for the loved one daily, feeling deep sadness, struggling with the finality of the loss, being preoccupied with memories and thoughts of the loved one, and having diminished interest in ongoing life.

Acute stress disorder: Symptoms that begin within 4 weeks of exposure to a traumatic event and last up to 1 month; an individual may exhibit anxiety and have impaired functioning in one area of life (e.g., work, family); symptoms may include reexperiencing the trauma (through dreams, flashbacks, reoccurring thoughts), avoiding stimuli (e.g., locations, smells, sounds, people) that may be reminders of the event, detachment from others, and emotional numbing.

Acute stress reaction: Temporary symptoms in response to a traumatic event (e.g., disorientation, agitation, anxiety, confusion) that usually disappear in hours or days.

Acute stressor: A short-term stressful event or situation (e.g., a child having difficulties with a friend).

Adaptive coping strategies: Approaches used by families to stabilize and maintain balance in the family system that promote individual growth and development and improve family functioning.

Adult dependents: Family members who are a parent, grandparent, former spouse, sibling, disabled older child, or any other individual who is claimed by the service member as a dependent.

Advanced Individual Training (AIT): Specialized training that teaches individuals the skills to perform a specific military occupation.

Allowance: A set dollar amount that is paid to service members in addition to their basic monthly pay that is designed to at least partially compensate for the costs of items considered necessary for the service member.

Ambiguous loss: Loss characterized by lack of closure or clear understanding of the extent of the loss (e.g., there is no verification of a loved one's death or no certainty that he or she will return or be the same as he or she used to be); boundary ambiguity may be experienced as an ambiguous loss.

Ambiguous loss theory: Part of the work in family stress theory that focuses specifically on understanding family events/crises that are not always resolvable, which mean that families face the challenges of finding meaning in their circumstances and being able to live and grow despite ongoing ambiguity, being resilient in the face of uncertainty.

Ambiguous stressor: A stressor characterized by limits to knowing what happened and/or what the outcomes might be.

Applicants: Individuals who apply to enter the military.

Armed Forces of the United States: All of the components of the Army, Navy, Air Force, Marine Corps, and Coast Guard when it augments the Navy.

Atomic veterans: Veterans exposed to radiation while assigned to the Pacific Theatre during WWII or Korea, including prisoners of war, and veterans exposed as part of nuclear testing.

Base: The Air Force and Navy term for a military installation.

Baseline data: In research, data provided at a beginning point in a research project or by compiling the results of several studies so that future data collected can be compared to beginning data to assess change and continuity.

Battle Rattle: Military slang for protective armor used in combat; also referred to as IBA or Interceptor Body Armor.

Being stressed: The state of someone who experiences tension created by a mismatch in his or her abilities and/or resources to meet the demands of a situation.

Beneficiary: Someone eligible to use or access a military-related benefit, such as shopping at stores on a military installation or accessing TRICARE health-care coverage.

Bipolar disorder: A psychological health disorder characterized by mood swings that range from depression to feeling euphoric and energetic.

Boundary ambiguity: An unclear perception of who is in and who is out of the family, created by having a family member "present" physically but not psychologically or present psychologically but not physically.

Buffer: In spousal communication processes, appraising a situation as being a group problem but deciding to take responsibility for solving it individually, instead of as a couple.

Burnout: A state of long-term exhaustion, a decreased interest in work, and dissatisfaction with the work environment.

Cadre: Experienced military professionals who train new recruits.

Camp: The Marine Corps term for a military installation.

Caregiver burden: The increased sense of responsibility and stress that a caregiver experiences in attending to the needs and welfare of another person.

Caregivers and Veterans Omnibus Health Services Act: A federal law that provides assistance to caregivers of veterans injured in the line of duty or training on or after September 11, 2001.

Casualties: Individuals who have died or have been wounded while serving.

Casualty Assistance Calls Officer: A Navy or Marine Corps representative who notifies a service member's designated next of kin when there is a death of a sailor or marine, provides information, and assists the family with funeral or memorial services, filing paperwork for benefits and entitlements, and relocation.

Casualty Assistance Officer: An Army representative who provides information and assists the family with funeral or memorial services, filing paperwork for benefits and entitlements, and relocation when there is a death of a soldier.

Casualty Assistance Representative: An Air Force Corps representative who notifies a service member's designated next of kin when there is a death of an airman, provides information, and assists the family with funeral or memorial services, filing paperwork for benefits and entitlements, and relocation.

Casualty Notification Officer: An Army representative, often accompanied by a military chaplain and/or organization commander, who notifies a service member's designated next of kin when there is a death of a soldier.

Chain of command: The highly structured line of authority and responsibility, which designates who is in charge of what and whom and along which orders are passed.

Charge of Quarters (CQ): An enlisted service member who handles administrative duties in the unit after normal duty hours.

Chief of Staff: The most senior ranking officer of a branch of the military service, who is responsible for the readiness of personnel, among numerous other responsibilities.

Child development centers: Facilities found on most military installations that provide daytime, business day child care for infants to 5-year-olds.

Chronic multisymptom illness: A constellation of health problems that do not clearly link to an exposure event and may have multiple, non-related health consequences.

Chronic stressor: A stressful longer-term event or situation (e.g., an ongoing health issue).

Cognitive-based therapy: In the treatment of PTSD, cognitive-based therapy includes learning about symptoms of PTSD, identifying thoughts and feelings associated with the trauma, identifying and challenging dysfunctional beliefs about the trauma, and replacing these beliefs with more logical, functional, and reality-based beliefs.

Cognitive-behavioral conjoint therapy (CBCT): Psychotherapy based on the principles of cognitive-behavioral therapy that includes both the individual in treatment and his or her intimate partner.

Cohorts: In research, a cohort consists of new enrollees who join the study at the same time where the research design calls for multiple points of new enrollments.

Combat and operation stress: The physical, mental, and emotional symptoms (e.g., anxiety, hyperarousal, fatigue, depression, concentration problems) that extend beyond 4 days after a traumatic event.

Combat Operational Stress Control: An overarching principle that guides military leaders as they develop regulations and policies on how to address the physical, cognitive, emotional, and/or behavioral stress symptoms that service members experience as a result of combat or other military operations and to keep stress within an acceptable range; policies and programs emphasize enhancing resilience and performance through prevention and early interventions with individuals and families who experience psychological injury.

Combat operational stress reactions: The physical, cognitive, emotional, and/or behavioral stress symptoms as a result of combat or as a result of other operations; these reactions may be experienced for just a few hours or days or may persist for weeks, months, or longer.

Combat stress reactions: The expected reactions of service members who have experienced stressful events while in combat, including emotional, intellectual, physical, and/or behavioral reactions.

Combat-injured families: The spouses, children and stepchildren, parents, ex-spouses, siblings, and other extended relations of an injured service member.

Commissary: Tax-free grocery stores located on military installations and reserved for use by military beneficiaries.

Communal coping: When appraisal of a problem and actions taken to resolve the problem are seen as group responsibilities, communal coping acknowledges that individuals are nested within groups, such as marital dyads and family systems, and that the other members of the group are likely to be affected when one or more members are distressed.

Community capacity: The collective ability of a community to address community needs and to confront situations that threaten the safety and well-being of community members.

Compassion fatigue: A state of short-term physical, physiological, and emotional exhaustion that can result after a prolonged period of experiencing other's suffering; prior unresolved trauma, uncontrolled work stressors, poor self-care, and work dissatisfaction can contribute to the experience of compassion fatigue.

Compassion satisfaction: The satisfaction, fulfillment, and joy of helping others and seeing small and large transformations in their lives that is common among helping professionals.

Compassion stress: A natural outcome of experiencing another's suffering, great or small, and wanting to relieve it; signs of compassion stress include feelings of confusion, helplessness, and isolation.

Complicated grief: During bereavement, the process during which the bereaved experience prolonged yearning and other symptoms such as disbelief or bitterness over the loss, numbness, a sense that life is empty, and an inability to move forward with plans.

Composite Life Cycle Model: A conceptual model used by the U.S. Army to illustrate how events and transitions in three areas of a soldier's life (i.e., unit, personal work, and family) relate to each other across time, family development, and career milestones.

Comprehensive Soldier Fitness: A strength-based program rooted in positive psychology and designed to enhance soldier, family, and civilian worker resilience and performance through a confidential personal assessment, online training, and unit training.

Compromising: Making family and individual efforts to achieve balance within a new community.

Conservation of resources: A theory used to understand ways that people seek out, invest, and protect resources they find valuable in coping with stressful events; it postulates that people invest in resources that they perceive to be valuable and useful, which are in turn shaped by family, community, and culture; when resources are lost or threatened, stress results and people will try to conserve (maintain) the resources they have.

Consolidating: When a family unit and its individual members unite in their group efforts and support individual efforts to make modifications to the family's operating system so that the family can better cope with stressors.

Constituents: In research, people and organizations that can benefit from the knowledge gained, as well as any sponsors of the research.

Coping: A variety of efforts to overcome challenges or difficulties.

Core concept: A principle that guides military leaders as they develop regulations and policies and that sets standards and expectations that leaders are to support.

Council of State Governments: A nonprofit, nonpartisan organization for state governments.

Cross-sectional: In research, studies designed to collect data from a group at a single point in time.

Cumulative stressor: A stressful event or situation that contributes to the current situation, creating a pileup of stressors.

Defense Enrollment and Eligibility Reporting System: A program that verifies those who are eligible for military-based services and benefits; each eligible person is enrolled into this system so that he or she can be identified as a family member or legal dependent when interacting with the military community.

Defense of Marriage Act: A federal act passed in 1996 that explicitly states that marriage at the federal level is only recognized if it occurs between one man and one woman and reaffirms that individual states are not compelled to recognize same-sex marriages that occurred in a different state.

Deficits model: A family development model based on identifying the factors families lack that are associated with unhealthy development.

Demilitarized Zone: A buffer zone between North Korea and South Korea.

Department of Defense: The federal department tasked with national security and supervising the U.S. Armed Forces.

Department of Veterans Affairs: A U.S. presidential cabinet-level position comprised of the Veterans Benefits Administration, the Veterans Health Administration, and the National Cemetery Administration, which provide medical care and other federal benefits to eligible veterans and their family members.

Deployment: The movement of military forces, equipment, and logistical support to an area of military operations.

Developmental regression: The inability to maintain developmental gains and revert back to earlier behaviors, particularly in very early childhood.

Diagnostic and Statistical Manual: The American Psychiatric Association's publication that lists mental health disorders and their symptoms.

Disability rating: A rating assessment that reflects the severity of one or more disabling conditions. The rating is intended to reflect how much the impairment(s) impact the veteran's ability to work.

Don't Ask, Don't Tell: DoD Directive 1304.26, a federal law prohibiting gays and lesbians from serving in the U.S. Armed Forces; under this directive, the military could not ask recruits about their sexual orientation and military members were not obligated to disclose if they were gay or lesbian because that knowledge would be grounds for their discharge from the military.

Dual-military marriages: Marriages in which a military member in one branch of service is married to a military member in the same or different branch of service.

Dyadic research: Research in which data is gathered from both members of a couple; a typical method of studying shared and nonshared perceptions the couple has about their life and marriage.

Emotional cycle of deployment model: An evolving six-stage model highlighting structural and emotional issues that families may encounter before, during, and after deployment.

Emotion-focused coping: Individual cognitive and behavioral strategies used to regulate one's distress.

Endstrength: The total number of military personnel required by the Armed Forces or a branch of the Armed Forces, taking into account recruitment, retention, death, and retirements and other separations.

Exchange: A shopping facility on a military installation that provides durable goods, merchandise, and services for military beneficiaries, including restaurants and businesses such as hair salons; large exchanges are similar to civilian department stores.

Explicit norm: An overtly stated expectation; in the military, an explicit norm is wearing a uniform on duty, while in a family an explicit norm may be a set bedtime for children.

Exposure therapy: In the treatment of PTSD, a model that includes psychoeducation (e.g., learning about trauma reactions, PTSD, and symptoms) and exposure to the trauma-related stimuli; in vivo exposure to a feared stimulus is used to gradually reduce the symptoms that are triggered by the stimulus by keeping the person safe and teaching him or her to use relaxation techniques to reduce the impact of the stimulus.

External locus of control: An individual's generalized expectations that they have little or no control over events that are affecting them.

Extrafamilial: Outside the family system.

Eye movement desensitization and reprocessing: In the treatment of PTSD, a model used to desensitize clients to the trauma-related memories that cause them distress by encouraging the recall of images and resulting emotions, identifying alternate understandings of the trauma experience, and challenging clients to consider these other understandings; the goal is to disable the distressing memories that trigger the symptoms.

Family and Medical Leave Act: A federal law that offers eligible employees of covered employers job-protected, unpaid leave of up to 12 workweeks for care of seriously ill family members, to attend to their own serious health condition, or upon the birth or adoption of a child.

Family Care Plan: A firm arrangement for the care of children during deployment, including a determination of who will care for the member's child or children during deployment and other absences; arrangements to provide financial, medical, and logistical support for the children's well-being; name and consent to the plan of any noncustodial parent who will not be the caregiver during the service member's absence; and designation of a temporary caregiver in case of incapacity or death of the service member while permanent custody is established.

Family child care providers or child development providers (Navy): Individuals certified to provide child care to children from infancy to 12 years of age in their homes on military installations; family child care homes may offer daytime, evening, nighttime, and weekend hours.

Family coherence: Satisfaction with interpersonal connections and dynamics among family members.

Family of creation: The family system created through partnering and/or parenting.

Family resilience framework: An expanded model of family resilience that examines key processes involved in family resiliency and resources that families draw upon to help manage and reduce stress and cultivate resiliency and positive growth, including family belief systems, family organizational patterns, and family communication processes.

Family separation allowance: Payment made to service members who are required to be away from their permanent duty station for more than 30 continuous days.

Family stress: An upset in the equilibrium, or steady state, of a family, which requires that the family makes adjustments in order to maintain or regain a sense of coherence.

Family stress theory: A body of theoretical work that describes family system experiences of crises (both normative and nonnormative) and the ways in which the family identifies resources, challenges, and strengths in coping strategies and coordinates efforts to maintain or regain coherence and resilience.

Family-of-origin relationships: Relationships with parents or siblings or others with whom one grew up.

First-time birthrate: A statistic calculated as the number of births of a first child per 1000 women, ages 15–44 in the civilian population.

Gearing up: Preparing personnel and gear for deployment by issuing personal gear and equipment, obtaining and preparing uniforms, going to medical appointments, completing legal and financial paperwork, participating in any additional unit or individual training, and preparing unit equipment for transportation.

General stress and coping theory: Principles used to explain and/or understand internal aspects of coping (cognitions and emotions).

Generalize: In research, to be able to apply what is learned from the study to everyone all the time.

Glasgow Coma Scale (GCS): A measurement tool used to determine the initial severity of brain injury based on an individual's ability to open his or her eyes, to respond verbally, and to respond through physical movement.

Gulf War I: The term used for U.S. military operations in the Persian Gulf from 1990–1991, also known as Operation Desert Storm or the Persian Gulf War.

Hardiness: A personality trait that allows an individual to cope with stress and catastrophe effectively.

Implicit norm: An implied expectation; in the military an implicit norm is showing respect for all military service members and veterans, while in a family an implicit norm is how affection is shown.

Inactive National Guard: National Guard personnel who are required to muster only once a year with their unit.

Indicated preventive interventions: Resilience programming targeted toward individuals who are exhibiting early signs of distress or loss of functioning.

Individual augmentee: A service member who is temporarily assigned to another command, deploys with the new command, and returns to his or her parent command upon completion of the deployment.

Individual Ready Reserve: Personnel who have served as active duty or in the selected reserve and still have time remaining on their military service obligation.

Individuals-nested in families-nested in social settings: An ecological model that centers individuals within their family and larger social settings (neighborhood, religious setting, school/work) and highlights how individuals need meaningful connections with others in order to access and build resources for healthy living.

Injury communication: Providing and delivering information related to the injury to families and to the impact on family members' capacity to understand and use the information provided.

Integrated grief: During bereavement, the process during which bereaved persons comprehend the death, are not preoccupied by thoughts and memories, and have interest in life.

Interfacing: When a family and its individual members interact with or operate within the larger social contexts of work, community, and school groups.

Intergenerational trauma: The transmission of secondary trauma to children.

Interstate Compact on Educational Opportunities for Military Children: An agreement among states on how to handle educational issues that often vary across states, such as enrollment, placement, eligibility, and graduation requirements.

Intimate partner violence (IPV): The use of physical, psychological, and/or sexual violence to exercise control over a partner.

Intimate terrorism: Violence usually perpetrated by men and based upon a motivation to dominate a spousal relationship through violent force and control.

Joint Chiefs of Staff: The senior officers of their respective services who are military advisors to the President, the Secretary of Defense, and the National Security Council.

Judicial due process: Due process of law; the principle that the government must respect all of the legal rights that are owed to a person, including witnesses, a jury, a pretrial hearing, formal notification of the charges, free legal representation, and a speedy trial.

Land navigation: Using a map and compass to travel from one place to another.

Land-grant university: A university established in each state on land granted to the state by the federal government to make education more accessible to the working class and to teach agriculture, engineering, sciences, and military tactics; to conduct research; and to provide extension services.

Longitudinal: In research, a term describing studies that collect data at multiple points in time, allowing researchers to follow people over time.

Magical thinking: Making incorrect assumptions about cause and effect (e.g., "If I wish hard enough, my Daddy will be OK.").

Meaning-focused coping: Individual cognitive and behavioral strategies used to reframe and give different meaning to a stressful event or situation.

Mental Health Advisory Team: A research team established by the Office of the U.S. Army Surgeon General to examine behavioral health of service members and behavioral health care in OIF and OEF.

Military brat, Air Force brat, Army brat, Navy brat, or Marine Corps brat: A positive and affectionate term claimed by military children to refer to themselves and others growing up in the military.

Military departments: The Department of the Army, the Department of the Navy (which includes the Marine Corps), and the Department of the Air Force; each is responsible for organizing, training, and equipping its personnel.

Military installations: Facilities owned or leased and operated by the military.

Military operational specialty: An assigned military job or occupation.

Military sexual trauma: Sexual trauma experienced while in active service.

Moral injury: The inner conflict service members experience when their behavior or the behavior of others conflict with their moral beliefs and expectations.

Motivation to serve: Reasons for serving in the military.

National Cemetery Administration: A branch of the VA responsible for national and state veterans' cemeteries, as well as headstones, markers, and presidential memorial certificates.

National Defense Authorization Act: A federal law that is passed by Congress every year to grant the Department of Defense funds to operate and specific guidance on how to spend those funds.

Neural plasticity: Flexibility in the development of neural connections that responds to early experiences and deprivations, starting the lifelong process of "tailoring" the brain to the person with all his or her personal, social, and environmental experiences.

Nonnormative stressors: Family life stressors that do not occur to most families and are unexpected (e.g., a child with a terminal illness); nonnormative stressors unique to military families are the injury or death of a family service member by friendly fire or missing in action.

Nonvolitional stressor: A stressful event or situation that is imposed upon the person/family (not wanted or chosen).

Normative stressors: Family life stressors that occur for most families and at expected times, such as life cycle transitions (e.g., birth of a child, death of an aged grandparent) and developmental changes (e.g., children going to school).

Norms: Expectations about how to act in a situation; can be explicitly stated or implicitly understood.

Operation Enduring Freedom: U.S. military actions in Afghanistan that began in October 2001.

Operation Iraqi Freedom: U.S. military actions in Iraq that began in March 2003 and ended in August 2010, when the name for continuing operations was changed to Operation New Dawn.

Operation New Dawn: U.S. military action in Iraq that began in September 2010.

Operational tempo or optempo: The frequency and intensity of military operations or missions.

Overall birthrate: A statistic calculated as the total number of births per 1000 women, ages 15–44 in the civilian population, which includes first, second, third, and all subsequent births.

Parental efficacy: Parents' availability and effectiveness in caring for their children.

Permanent Change of Station: A relocation of a service member's work affiliation from one unit or duty station to another; service members may request their duty preference but the assignment is determined by the needs of the branch of service.

Personally Procured Transportation Move: A "do it yourself" move (versus a government arranged move).

Pileup of stressors: An occurrence of overlapping demands on an individual, family, or other system.

Post: The Army term for a military installation.

Posttraumatic stress: A spectrum of emotional, physical, and behavioral reactions to a trauma, many of which may not be experienced by an individual exposed to trauma.

Posttraumatic stress disorder: An anxiety disorder that may occur following a traumatic event (e.g., threat of death, threat of death of another, or threat of physical, sexual, or psychological integrity) with symptoms that persist more than 1 month after the traumatic event.

Prisoner of War (POW): Military personnel captured by opposing military forces.

Problem-solving coping: Individual cognitive and behavioral strategies used to address the problem creating a stressful event or situation.

Propensity to serve: Interest or plans to serve in the military.

Prospective: In research, studies that start in the present and continue into the future to see what experiences are linked to physical and psychological health outcomes late in life.

Protective factors: Skills and resources that individuals and families can draw upon to help them cope with adversity.

Psychobiological stress research: Research that integrates neurobiological research with psychosocial research to include physiological measures of stress, such as cortisol, serotonin, and dopamine levels; autonomic response systems, including respiration and perspiration rates and eye dilation; and MRI brain scans, as well as self-reports on stressful events and circumstances.

Psychological First Aid: A way of helping children, adolescents, adults, and families immediately following a traumatic event to help reduce their stress level, ensure that their current needs are met, and encourage adaptive functioning.

Public stigma: Prejudice and discrimination against those with psychological disorders.

Purple: A term indicating that an activity or a program includes all branches of the U.S. Armed Forces.

Rank: An achieved military status, representing a level of responsibility and attainment of knowledge, expertise, and leadership skills.

Ready Reserve: One of the three components of the Reserve Component that includes the selected reserve, the Individual Ready Reserve, and the Inactive National Guard.

Rear detachment: Military personnel who remain at the home installation when there is a deployment of the unit to combat or to another military operation.

Recovery trajectory: The process of recovery over time from illness or injury with expected advances, setbacks, and potential changes in abilities; a concept used in the medical and rehabilitative fields.

Reserve Component: The portion of the U.S. military forces comprised of the Ready Reserve, Standby Reserve, and Retired Reserve.

Resilience: A process of positive adaptation and growth after experiencing an adverse event/circumstance; resilience can be measured by several outcome indicators and is influenced by a blend of risk and protective factors.

Resilience continuum: An evidence-based model that describes indicators of psychological health for individuals, families, and commands and refocuses responsibility for promoting psychosocial health on everyone in the system.

Restricted sexual assault report: A report by a military victim of sexual assault who does not want the perpetrator prosecuted in order to maintain the victim's anonymity.

Restructuring: Making modifications to the family's current operating system in the areas of roles, family rules, patterns of interaction and communication, and goals so that the family can cope with stressors.

Retired Reserve: One of the three components of the Reserve Component that includes those reserve officers and enlisted who receive retired pay or are eligible for retired pay but are not 60 years old or over, not members of the Ready or Standby Reserves, and have not chosen to be discharged.

Risky behaviors: Actions that heighten threats to an individual's health, safety, or emotional well-being, including alcohol and other drug misuse, disordered eating, increased risk-taking, and both sexual and nonsexual aggression.

Roles: A group of norms that govern a situation; similar to "parts" played by actors on stage or in a movie.

School-age care programs: Before and after-school programs located on many military installations that provide activities and supervision of school-age children of military families.

Scope: In research, how broad a research question is and how widely it can be generalized (applied to populations outside of participants who have been included in the study).

Secondary traumatization: The indirect exposure to trauma due to interactions with the traumatized person that begins to affect the well-being of the persons around the individual.

Secretary of Defense: A presidential cabinet member who oversees national security agencies and the Department of the Army, the Department of the Air Force, and the Department of the Navy (which includes the Marine Corps).

Selected preventive intervention: Resilience programming targeted toward those who may be at higher risk for developing distress or loss of functioning.

Selected reserve: Reservists in the Army, Navy, Marine Corps, Air Force, and Coast Guard, and members of each state's Air and Army National Guard.

Self-care: Actions taken to be physically and emotionally healthy through such steps as exercise, proper nutrition, self-reflection, interaction with family and friends, and taking time away from work.

Self-efficacy: The extent to which persons believe that they can meet a goal or expectation.

Self-stigma: Internalization of the public's biases against those with psychological illnesses.

Sense of self: How one views one's self and abilities; a self-definition of who one is.

Separation: A term often used by family members to refer to time apart from their service member; spouses may also use the word to indicate a break in a romantic relationship.

Separation from the military: Being released from active duty, discharged from military obligations, and transferred to the reserves or retired list.

Service-connected disability: A disability (illness or injury) determined by the VA to have occurred or been aggravated during military service.

Shoppettes: Convenience stores located on military installations and reserved for use by military beneficiaries.

Situational couple violence: Couple violence that tends to be much more gender symmetrical (both men and women engage in violent action) and is linked with particular couple conflicts unique in the relationship of the couple.

Squad tactics: Strategies used by a small unit of service members to achieve a goal.

Standby Reserve: One of the three components of the Reserve Component that includes personnel temporarily not in the Ready Reserves due to a hardship or disability or due to being designated as having civilian employment critical to national security.

Stigma: In psychological health, negative associations about psychological health disorders or the treatment of psychological health problems, and/or the belief that there are negative connotations associated with having a psychological health problem.

Strengths-based model: A family development model that identifies and builds on families' existing strengths to encourage healthy development.

Stress: Both a process and a state of being brought about when a person's appraisal of a situation or context results in a judgment of a mismatch in his or her abilities and/or resources to meet the demands of the situation.

Stress inoculation training (SIT): A form of cognitive behavioral therapy that encourages individuals to use their existing coping skills and teaches them new stress management skills.

Synergizing: Coordinating all family system and individual member's efforts to consolidate various change efforts within the family system.

Theory of mind: A limit in the ability to understand things from another person's point of view.

"Total" institution: An organization or a company that rewards and promotes based on performance and that has complete influence in an individual's daily experiences on and off the job.

Traumatic brain injury: A blow or jolt to the head or penetration of the head by an object, disrupting brain function.

Unaccompanied tour: An assignment to an overseas location where the family is not authorized to travel with and remain with the service member because the assignment area is deemed to be politically unstable, dangerous, or lacking in support services for families.

Unified Command Plan: An annual review with possible modification of the mission or jurisdiction of the Unified Commands.

Unified Commands: Two or more military departments working under a single commander to conduct operations in support of a continuing defense or combat mission in a region or an ongoing functional mission; there are currently six unified combatant commands with specific missions in regions throughout the world.

Uniform Code of Military Justice: Part of the U.S. Code of law that regulates the conduct of personnel in the uniformed services.

Uniformed Services: The Army, Navy, Marine Corps, Air Force, Coast Guard, Public Health Service Commissioned Corps, and the National Oceanic and Atmospheric Administration's Commissioned Officer Corps; the first five are Armed Services, and the last two are Noncombatant Uniformed Services.

Uniformed Services Employment and Reemployment Rights Act: A federal law that prohibits employers from discriminating on the basis of an employee's consideration of joining the military or an employee's current or past military service.

Universal preventive interventions: Resilience programming targeted toward all military families.

Unrestricted sexual assault report: A report by a military victim of sexual assault who desires medical treatment, counseling, legal assistance, notification to command or law enforcement officials, and an official investigation of the crime.

Vet Centers: Counseling facilities open to all veterans who served in a combat theatre or anywhere during times of armed hostilities and to their family members; they offer individual and group counseling, family therapy related to military issues, sexual trauma counseling, employment and substance abuse assessment and referral, screening and referral for medical issues, and outreach and education.

Veterans Benefits Administration: A branch of the VA responsible for managing education benefits, disability compensation, pensions, burial allowances, vocational rehabilitation, home loans, life insurance, and survivors' benefits for eligible veterans and their families.

Veterans courts: A recent addition to the U.S. courts system, these courts are designed after drug treatment and mental health treatment courts, which offer alternatives to incarceration and include highly structured treatment plans to address the underlying problems to the veteran population.

Veterans Health Administration: An integrated health-care system that provides medical care to eligible veterans and includes hospitals, community-based outpatient clinics, community living centers, long-term care facilities, and readjustment counseling centers.

Violent resistance: The partner's (usually female) actions to resist against an attempt by a spousal partner to control her actions and opportunities.

Volitional stressor: A stressful event or situation that was wanted or chosen (such as taking steps to change one's marital status).

Warrant officer: A military member who is designated an officer through a warrant (a specific authorization) as opposed to an officer who is designated through a commission; usually, warrant officers are technical experts or specialists with a specific set of skills.

References

Ackerman, R., DiRamio, D., & Garza Mitchell, R. L. (2009). Transitions: Combat veterans as college students. In R. Ackerman & D. DiRamio (Eds.), *Creating a veteran-friendly campus: Strategies for transition and success* (pp. 5–14). San Francisco, CA: Jossey-Bass.

Adler, A. B., & Dolan, C. A. (2006). Military hardiness as a buffer of psychological health on return from deployment. *Military Medicine, 171,* 93–98.

Adler-Baeder, F., Pittman, J. F., & Taylor, L. (2005). The prevalence of marital transitions in military families. *Journal of Divorce and Remarriage, 44,* 91–106.

Air Force Aid Society (2010). *Air Force Aid Society: The official charity of the U.S. Air Force.* Retrieved September 9, 2010 from http://www.afas.org.

Air Force Times (2010). Family centers. Retrieved August 24, 2010 from http://www.airforcetimes.com/benefits/family_resources/online_hbml10_milfam_familycenters/.

Alexander, C. (2010, September). *The shock of war.* Retrieved from http://www.smithsonianmag.com/history/the-shock-of-war-55376701/.

Allen, E., & Markman, H. (2010). *Marital functioning and intervention for U.S. Army couples.* Presented at the 2010 International Research Symposium on Military Families, Indianapolis, IN.

Allen, E. S., Rhoades, G. K., Stanley, S. M., & Markman, H. J. (2010). Hitting home: Relationships between recent deployment, posttraumatic stress symptoms, and marital functioning for army couples. *Journal of Family Psychology, 24,* 280–288.

American Psychiatric Association (2000). *Diagnostic and Statistical Manual of Mental Disorders, Fourth Edition, Text Revision (DSM-IV-TR).* Arlington, VA: Author.

American Psychiatric Association (2004). *Practice guideline for the treatment of patients with acute stress disorder and post-traumatic stress disorder.* Arlington, VA: American Psychiatric Association Practice Guidelines.

American Psychiatric Association (2013). *Diagnostic and statistical manual of mental disorders* (5th ed.). Arlington, VA: American Psychiatric Publishing.

American Red Cross (2011). *A brief history of the American Red Cross.* Retrieved from http://www.red-cross .org/museum/history/brief.asp.

American Women Veterans Foundation (2014). *About AWV.* Retrieved from http://americanwomenveterans.org/home/mission/

Ames, G. M., & Cunradi, C. (2004). Alcohol use and preventing alcohol-related problems among young adults in the military. *Alcohol Research in Health, 28,* 252–257.

Army Emergency Relief (2002). *Helping the Army take care of its own.* Retrieved November 30, 2011 from http://www.aerhq.org.

Aronson, R. (2005). The soldier's heart (R. Aronson, Director). In D. Fanning (Executive Producer), *Frontline.* Boston: WGBH.

Assistant Secretary of Defense (2014). Department of Defense (DoD) child development program fee ranges for school year (SY) 2014–15. Retrieved from https://www.myarmyonesource.com/ChildYouthandSchoolServices/InformationforParents/Cyss_Fees.aspx

Astore, W. (2012, January 24). *America, arms-dealer to the world.* Retrieved from http://www.salon.com/2012/01/24/america_arms_dealer_to_the_world/

Badr, H., Barker, T. M., & Milbury, K. (2011). Couples' psychosocial adaptation to combat wounds and injuries. In S. MacDermid Wadsworth & D. Riggs (Eds.), *Risk and resilience in U.S. military families* (pp. 213–233). New York, NY: Springer Science.

Barker, L. H., & Berry, K. (2009). Developmental issues impacting military families with young children during single and multiple deployments. *Military Medicine, 174,* 1033–1040.

Bass, D. M., Judge, K. S., Snow, A. L., Wilson, N. L., Morgan, R., Looman, W. J., . . . Kunik, M. E. (2013). Caregiver outcomes of partners in dementia care: Effect of a care coordination program for veterans with dementia and their family members and friends. *Journal of the American Geriatric Society, 61,* 1377–1386.

Bathalon, G. P., McGraw, S. M., Sharp, M. A., Williamson, D. A., Young, A. J., & Friedl, K. E. (2006). The effect of proposed improvements to the Army Weight Control Program on female soldiers. *Military Medicine, 171,* 800–805.

Batten, S. V., Drapalski, A. L., Decker, M. L., DeViva, J. C., Morris, L. J., Mann, M. A., & Dixon, L. B. (2009). Veteran interest in family involvement in PTSD treatment. *Psychological Services, 6,* 184–189.

Beardslee, W. R., & Wheelock, I. (1994). Children of parents with affective disorders: Empirical findings and clinical implications. In W. R. Reynolds & H. F. Johnston (Eds.), *Handbook of depression in children and adolescents* (pp. 463–479). New York, NY: Plenum.

Becker, D. (1994). Sex bias in the diagnosis of borderline personality disorder and posttraumatic stress disorder. *Professional Psychology Research and Practice, 25,* 55–61.

Beekley, M. D., Byrne, R., Yavorek, T., Kidd, K., Wolff, J., & Johnson, M. (2009). Incidence, prevalence, and risk of eating disorder behaviors in military academy cadets. *Military Medicine, 174,* 637–640.

Bell, N. S., Amoroso, P. J., Yore, M. M., Smith, G. S., & Jones, B. H. (2000). Self-reported risk-taking behaviors and hospitalization for motor vehicle injury among active duty Army personnel. *American Journal of Preventative Medicine, 18,* 85–95.

Benedek, D. M., & Fullerton, C. S. (2007). Translating five essential elements into programs and practice: Commentary on "Five essential elements of immediate and mid-term mass trauma intervention: Empirical evidence" by Hobfoll, Watson et al. *Psychiatry, 70,* 345–349.

Besterman-Dahan, K., Barnett, S., Hickling, E., Elnitsky, C., Lind, J., Skvoretz, J., & Antinori, N. (2012). Bearing the burden: Deployment stress among Army National Guard chaplains. *Journal of Health Care Chaplaincy, 18,* 151–168.

Betz, G., & Thorngren, J. M. (2006). Ambiguous loss and the family grieving process. *The Family Journal: Counseling and Therapy for Couples and Families, 14,* 359–365.

Bicksler, B. A., & Nolan, L. G. (2009). *Recruiting an all-volunteer force: The need for sustained investment in recruiting resources—An update.* Arlington, VA: Strategic Analysis. Retrieved from the Department of Defense Personnel and Readiness website: http://prhome.defense.gov/Portals/52/Documents/RFM/MPP/Accession%20Policy/docs/Bicksler%20Recruiting%20Paper%202009.pdf

Black, M. C., & Merrick, M. T. (2013). *Prevalence of intimate partner violence, sexual violence, and stalking among active duty women and wives of active duty men: Comparisons with women in the U. S. general population, 2010* (Technical Report). Atlanta, Georgia: Centers for Disease Control and Prevention.

Blaisure, K. R., & Arnold-Mann, J. (1992). Return and reunion: A psychoeducational program aboard U.S. Navy ships. *Family Relations, 41,* 178–185.

Blanchard, M. S., Eisen, S. A., Alpern, R., Karlinsky, J., Toomey, R., Reda, D. J., . . . Kang, H. K. (2006). Chronic Multisymptom Illness Complex in Gulf War I veterans 10 years later. *American Journal of Epidemiology, (163),* 66–75.

Blue Star Families in collaboration with Institute for Veterans and Military Families (2014). *2014 Military lifestyle survey: Comprehensive report.* Retrieved from https://www.bluestarfam.org/resources/2014-military-family-lifestyle-survey.

Boehnlein, J. K., & Sparr, L. F. (1993). Group therapy with WWII ex-POWs: Long-term posttraumatic adjustment in a geriatric population. *American Journal of Psychotherapy, 47,* 273–282.

Bonanno, G. A. (2004). Loss, trauma, and human resilience: Have we underestimated the human capacity to thrive after extremely aversive events? *American Psychologist, 59,* 20–28.

Bonanno, G. A., & Mancini, A. D. (2008). The human capacity to thrive in the face of potential trauma. *Pediatrics, 121,* 369–375.

Bonnano, G. A., Mancini, A. D., Horton, J. L., Powell, T. M., LeardMann, C. A., Boyko, E. J., et al., for the Millennium Cohort Study Team (2012). Trajectories of trauma symptoms and resilience in deployed US military service members: Prospective cohort study. *British Journal of Psychiatry, 200,* 317–323.

Bonanno, G. A., Rennicke, V., & Dekel, S. (2005). Self-enhancement among high-exposure survivors of the September 11th terrorist attach: Resilience or social maladjustment? *Journal of Personality and Social Psychology, 88,* 984–998.

Bonanno, G. A., Wortman, C. B., Lehman, D. R., Tweed, R. G., Haring, M., Sonnega, J., . . . Nesse, R. M. (2002). Resilience to loss and chronic grief: A prospective study from preloss to 18-months postloss. *Journal of Personality and Social Psychology, 83,* 1150–1164.

Booth, B., Segal, M. W., Bell, D. B., with Martin, J. A., Ender, M. G., Rohall, D. E., & Nelson, J. (2007). *What we know about Army families: 2007 update.* Retrieved from the U.S. Army Morale, Welfare, and Recreation website: http://www.army.mil/cfsc/research.htm.

Boss, P. (1987). Family stress. In M. B. Sussman & S. K. Steinmetz (Eds.), *Handbook of marriage and the family* (pp. 695–723). New York, NY: Plenum Press.

Boss, P. (2001). Definitions: A guide to family stress theory. In P. Boss (Ed.), *Family stress management* (2nd ed., pp. 39–70). Thousand Oaks, CA: Sage.

Boss, P. (2006). *Loss, trauma, and resilience: Therapeutic work with ambiguous loss.* New York, NY: W. W. Norton.

Boss, P. (2007). Ambiguous loss theory: Challenges for scholars and practitioners. *Family Relations, 56,* 105–111.

Bowen, G. L., Mancini, J. A., Martin, J. A., Ware, W. B., & Nelson, J. P. (2003). Promoting the adaptation of military families: An empirical test of a community practice model. *Family Relations, 52,* 33–44.

Boyce, W. T., & Chesterman, E. (1990). Life events, social support and cardiovascular reactivity in adolescence. *Journal of Developmental and Behavioral Pediatrics, 11,* 105–111.

Boyko, E. J., Jacobson, I. J., Smith, B., Ryan, M. A. K., Hooper, T. I., Amoroso, P. J., . . . Smith, T. C. for the Millennium Cohort Study Team (2010). Risk of diabetes in U.S. military service members in relation to combat deployment and mental health. *Diabetes Care, 33,* 1771–1777.

Bray, R. M., Spira, J. L., Williams, J., & Lane, M. E. (2010). Substance use and mental health issues among single service members: Findings from the 2008 DoD survey of health related behaviors. In *Proceedings from 2010 International Research Symposium on Military families.* Indianapolis, IN: RTI International.

Brewin, C. R., Andrews, B., & Valentine, J. D. (2000). Meta-analysis of risk factors for posttraumatic stress disorder in trauma-exposed adults. *Journal of Consulting Clinical Psychology, 68,* 748–766.

Bride, B. E., & Figley, C. R. (2009). Secondary trauma and military veteran caregivers. *Smith College Studies in Social Work, 79,* 314–329.

Britt, T. W., Davison, J., Bliese, P. D., & Castro, C. A. (2004). How leaders can influence the impact that stressors have on soldiers. *Military Medicine, 169,* 541–545.

Britt, T. W., Greene-Shortridge, T. M., Brink, S., Nguyen, Q. B., Rath, J., Cox, A. L., . . . Castro, C. A. (2008). Perceived stigma and barriers to care for psychological treatment: Implications for reactions to stressors in different contexts. *Journal of Social and Clinical Psychology, 27,* 317–335.

Brokaw, T. (1998). *The greatest generation.* New York: Random House.

Bruner, E. F. (2005). *Military forces: What is the appropriate size for the United States?* CRS Report RS21754. Washington, DC: Congressional Research Service, Library of Congress.

Brymer, M., Jacobs, A., Layne, C., Pynoos, R., Ruzek J., Steinberg, A., . . . Watson, P. (2006). *Psychological first aid: Field operations guide* (2nd ed.). National Child Traumatic Stress Network and National Center for PTSD. Retrieved from the National Center for PTSD website: http://www.ptsd.va.gov/professional/manuals/psych-first-aid.asp.

Bureau of Medicine & Surgery, Deployment Health Directorate (2008). *Operational stress control: Conserving the force.* Retrieved from the Navy and Marine Corps Public Health Center website: http://www.nmcphc .med.navy.mil/healthy_living/psychological_health/stress_management/operandcombatstress.aspx.

Burland, D., & Lundquist, J. H. (2013). The best years of our lives: Military service and family relationships – a life-course perspective. In J. M. Wilmoth & A. S. London (Eds), *Life-course perspectives on military service* (pp. 165–184). New York, NY: Routledge.

Burrell, L. M. (2006). Moving military families: The impact of relocation on family well-being, employment, and commitment to the military. In C. A. Castro, A. B. Adler, & T. W. Britt (Eds.), *Military life: The psychology of serving in peace and combat: The military family* (Vol. 3, pp. 39–63). Westport, CT: Praeger Security International.

Burrell, L. M., Adams, G. A., Durand, D. B., & Castro, C. A. (2006). The impact of military lifestyle demands on well-being, Army, and family outcomes. *Armed Forces & Society, 33,* 43–58.

Burrelli, D. F. (1996). *Women in the Armed Forces.* CRS Issue Brief 92008. Washington DC: Congressional Research Service, Library of Congress.

Burrelli, D. F. (2013). *Women in combat: Issues for Congress.* Washington D.C.: Congressional Research Service, Library of Congress. Retrieved from http://www.fas.org/sgp/crs/natsec/R42075.pdf

Burton, T. E., & MacDermid Wadsworth, S. (2011, May). *Evaluation of a multimedia intervention for children and families facing multiple military deployments.* Presented at the Annual Convention of the American Psychological Society, Washington, DC.

Calhoun, P. S., Beckham, J. C., & Bosworth, H. B. (2002). Caregiver burden and psychological distress in partners of veterans with chronic posttraumatic stress disorder. *Journal of Traumatic Stress, 15,* 205–212.

Campbell, C. L., McCoy, S., Hoffman, N., & O'Neil, P. (2014). Decreasing role strain for caregivers of Veterans with dependence in performing activities of daily living. *Health and Social Work, 39,* 55–62.

Caregivers and Veterans Omnibus Health Services Act of 2010, Pub. L. No. 111–163, 124 Stat. 1130 (2010).

Carlton, J. R., Manos, G. H., & Van Slyke, J. A. (2005). Anxiety and abnormal eating behaviors associated with cyclical readiness testing in a Naval hospital active duty population. *Military Medicine, 170,* 663–667.

Carroll, E. B., Robinson, L. C., Orthner, D., Matthews, W., & Smith-Rotabi, K. (2008). Essential life skills for military families: Mobilizing the cooperative extension system in NC. *Journal of Family and Consumer Sciences, 100,* 52–57.

Carter, E. A., & McGoldrick, M. (Eds.) (2005). *The expanded family life cycle: Individual, family, and social perspectives.* Pearson Allyn & Bacon: New York.

Casey, G. W., Jr. (2011). Comprehensive soldier fitness: A vision for psychological resilience in the U.S. Army. *American Psychologist, 66,* 1–3.

Castaneda, L. W., & Harrell, M. C. (2008). Spouse employment: A grounded theory approach to experiences and perceptions. *Armed Forces and Society, 34,* 389–412.

Castaneda, L. W., Harrell, M. C., Varda, D. M., Hall, K. C., Beckett, M. K., & Stern, S. (2008). *Deployment experiences of Guard and Reserve families: Implications for support and retention.* Santa Monica, CA: RAND Corporation.

CBS News (2014, March 6). Military sexual assault bills set for Senate votes. *CBSNews.com.* Retrieved from http://www.cbsnews.com/news/military-sexual-assault-bills-set-for-senate-votes

CDC, NIH, DoD, and VA Leadership Panel (2013). *Report to Congress on Traumatic Brain Injury in the United States: Understanding the public health problem among current and former military personnel.* Centers for Disease Control and Prevention (CDC), the National Institutes of Health (NIH), the Department of Defense (DoD), and the Department of Veterans Affairs (VA).

Cederbaum, J. A., Gilreath, T. D., Benbenishty, R., Astor, R. A., Pineda, D., DePedro, K. T., . . . Attuel, H. (2014). Well-being and suicide ideation of secondary school students from military families. *Journal of Adolescent Health, 54,* 672–677.

Center of Excellence for Medical Multimedia (2011). *Traumatic brain injury: A guide for caregivers of service members and veterans.* Retrieved from http://www.traumaticbraininjuryatoz.org/Caregivers-Journey.aspx.

Centers for Disease Control and Prevention (2010). *Facts about traumatic brain injury.* Retrieved September 29, 2010 from the BrainLine.org website: http://www.brainline.org/content/2008/07/facts-about-traumatic-brain-injury.html.

Chambers, J. W., II. (1999). Conscription. In J. W. Chambers, II, F. Anderson, L. Eden, J. T. Glatthaar, R. H. Spector, & G. K. Piehler (Eds.), *The Oxford Companion to American military history* (pp. 180–182). New York, NY: Oxford University Press.

Chandra, A., Martin, L. T., Hawkins, S. A., & Richardson, A. (2010). The impact of parental deployment on child social and emotional functioning: Perspectives of school staff. *Journal of Adolescent Health, 46,* 218–223.

Chandra, A., Lara-Cinisomo, S., Jaycox, L. H., Tanielian, Han, B., Burns, R. M., & Ruder, T. (2011). *Views from the homefront: The experiences of youth and spouses from military families* (Technical Report). Santa Monica, CA: RAND Corporation.

Charney, D. S. (2004). Psychobiological mechanisms of resilience and vulnerability: Implications for successful adaptation to extreme stress. *American Journal of Psychiatry, 161,* 195–216.

Chartrand, M. M., Frank, D. A., White, L. F., & Shope, T. R. (2008). Effect of parents' wartime deployment on the behavior of young children in military families. *Archives of Pediatrics and Adolescent Medicine, 162,* 1009–1014.

Chawla, N., & MacDermid Wadsworth, S. (2011, May). *A multimedia intervention for families of wounded veterans: A randomized study.* Presented at the Annual Convention of the American Psychological Society, Washington, DC.

Child Life Council (2010). *Child Life Council Fact Sheet.* Retrieved from http://www.childlife.org/About/

Christensen, A., Atkins, D. C., Baucom, B., & Yi, J. (2010). Marital status and satisfaction five years following a randomized clinical trial comparing traditional versus integrative behavioral couple therapy. *Journal of Consulting and Clinical Psychology, 78,* 225–235.

Christensen, E., Hill, C., Netzer, P., Farr, D., Schaefer, E., & McMahon, J. (2009). *Economic impact on caregivers of the seriously wounded, ill, and injured.* Alexandria, VA: CAN. Retrieved from http://www.cna.org/research/2009/economic-impact-caregivers-seriously-wounded-ill.

Christenson, W., Taggart, A. D., & Messner-Zidell, S. (2009). *Ready, willing, and unable to serve.* Retrieved from the Mission: Readiness website: http://cdn.missionreadiness.org/NATEE1109.pdf.

Cohen, J. A., Mannarino, A. P., Gibson, L. E., Cozza, S. J., Brymer, M. J., & Murray, L. (2006). Interventions for children and adolescents following disasters. In E. C. Ritchie, P. J. Watson, & M. J. Friedman (Eds.), *Interventions following mass violence and disasters* (pp. 227–256). New York: Guilford.

Cohen, S. P., Brown, C., Kurihara, C., Plunkett, A., Nguyen, C., & Strassels, S. A. (2010). Diagnosis and factors associated with medical evacuation and return to duty for service members participating in Operation Iraqi Freedom or Operation Enduring Freedom: A propsective cohort study. *The Lancet, 375,* 301–309.

Collins, R. C., & Kennedy, M. C. (2008). Serving families who have served: Providing family therapy and support in interdisciplinary polytrauma rehabilitation. *Journal of Clinical Psychology, 64,* 993–1003.

Combat Operational Stress Control (2007). *COSC continuum & decision matrix.* Retrieved from http://www.marforres.marines.mil/GeneralSpecialStaff/COSC/StressContinuumandDecisionMatrix.aspx.

Command, Navy Installations Command. (n.d.). Ombudsman Program (Overview). Retrieved May 25, 2015 from http://www.cnic.navy.mil/ffr/family_readiness/fleet_and_family_support_program/ombudsman_program_overview.html.

Commander, Navy Region Mid Atlantic (n.d.). Child development homes. Retrieved December 7, 2011 from http://www.cnic.navy.mil/CNRMA/FleetFamilyReadiness/SupportServices/Families/ChildYouthPrograms/ChildDevelopmentHomes/index.htm.

Committee on Gulf War and Health (2008). *Gulf War and health: Physiologic, psychologic, and psychosocial effects of deployment-related stress* (Vol. 6). Washington, DC: The National Academies Press.

Committee on the Initial Assessment of Readjustment Needs of Military Personnel, Veterans, and Their Families; Board on the Health of Selected Populations; Institute of Medicine (2010). *Returning home from Iraq and Afghanistan: Preliminary assessment of readjustment needs of veterans, service members, and their families.* Washington, DC: National Academies Press. Retrieved from http://www.nap.edu/catalog/12812.html.

Committee on Treatment of Posttraumatic Stress Disorder (2008). *Treatment of posttraumatic stress disorder: An assessment of the evidence.* Washington, DC: The National Academies Press.

Conaboy, C. (2013). Virtual reality, real help for veterans. *The Boston Globe.* Retrieved from http://www.bostonglobe.com/lifestyle/health-wellness/2013/09/15/virtual-reality-helps-veterans-with-ptsd/iM2o9DV3OdbzBCp4FJB01O/story.html.

Confidential Communications to Navy Chaplains Fact Sheet. (2013, May). Retrieved May 22, 2015 from http://www.chaplain.navy.mil

Congressional Budget Office (2011). *Analysis of Federal Civilian and Military Compensation.* Retrieved from http://www.cbo.gov/publication/22002.

Cook, B. J., & Kim, Y. (2009). *From soldier to student: Easing the transition of service members on campus.* Washington, DC: American Council on Education. Retrieved from http://www.acenet.edu/news-room/Pages/From-Soldier-to-Student.aspx.

Cooper, J. (1999). Militia and National Guard. In J. W. Chambers, II, F. Anderson, L. Eden, J. T. Glatthaar, R. H. Spector, & G. K. Piehler (Eds.), *The Oxford companion to American Military History* (pp. 440–443). New York, NY: Oxford University Press.

Cornum, R., Matthews, M. D., & Seligman, M. E. P. (2011). Comprehensive soldier fitness: Building resilience in a challenging institutional context. *American Psychologist, 66,* 4–9.

Corrigan, P. (2004). How stigma interferes with mental health care. *American Psychologist, 59,* 614–625.

Council of State Governments (2008). *Interstate compact on educational opportunity for military children: Legislative resource kit.* Retrieved from http://www.csg.org/knowledgecenter/docs/ncic/RESOURCEKIT-January2008final.pdf.

Coyne, J. C., & Smith, D. A. F. (1994). Couples coping with a myocardial infarction: Contextual perspective on patient self-efficacy. *Journal of Family Psychology, 8,* 43–54.

Cozza, S. J. (2009a, September). *Military children and families: Supporting health and managing risk.* Presented at the DoD Joint Family Readiness Conference, Chicago, IL.

Cozza, S. J. (Ed.). (2009b). *Proceedings of the workgroup on intervention with combat injured families, December 11–12, 2007.* Bethesda, MD: Center for the Study of Traumatic Stress.

Cozza, S. J., Chun, R. S., & Polo, J. A. (2005). Military families and children during operation Iraqi Freedom. *Psychiatric Quarterly, 76,* 371–342.

Cozza, S. J., & Guimond, J. M. (2011). Working with combat-injured families through the recovery trajectory. In S. MacDermid Wadsworth & D. Riggs (Eds.), *Risk and resilience in U.S. military families* (pp. 259–277). New York, NY: Springer Science.

Cozza, S. J., Guimond, J. M., McKibben, J. B. A., Chun, R. S., Arata-Maiers, T. L., Schneider, B., . . . Ursano, R. J. (2010). Combat-injured service members and their families: The relationship of child distress and spouse-perceived family distress and disruption. *Journal of Traumatic Stress, 23,* 112–115.

Cozza, S. J., Holmes, A. K., & Van Ost, S. L. (2013). Family-centered care for military and veteran families affected by combat injury. *Clinical Child and Family Psychology Review, 16,* 311–321.

Cozza, S. J., & Lerner, R. M. (2013). Military children and families: Introducing the issue. *The Future of Children, 23,* 3–11. Retrieved from http://futureofchildren.org/futureofchildren/publications/journals/journal_details/index.xml?journalid=80.

Crow, J. R., & Myers-Bowman, K. S. (2011). "A fear like I've never felt": Experiences of parents whose adult children deployed to combat zones. *Marriage and Family Review, 47,* 164–195.

CSPAN. (2014, September 17). *Phoenix VA medical director Dr. Sam Foote on whistleblower actions.* [Video file.] Retrieved from http://www.c-span.org/video/?c4508975/former-phoenix-va-medical-director-dr-sam-foote-whistleblower-actions.

Cunningham, M., Henry, M., & Lyons, W. (2007). *Vital mission: Ending homelessness among veterans.* Washington, DC: National Alliance to End Homelessness, Homelessness Research Institute.

Dalack, G. W., Blow, A. J., Valenstein, M., Gorman, L., Spinner, J., Marcus, S., . . . Lagrou, R. (2010). Working together to meet the needs of Army National Guard soldiers: An academic-military partnership. *Psychiatric Services, 61,* 1069–1071.

Daniel, L. (2010, September 2). *Military child development centers rates change.* The Dolphin. Retrieved from http://www.dolphin-news.com/.

Darkins, A. (2012). Experiences of the VA and HIS: U.S. Department of Veterans Affairs. In *Institute of Medicine, The role of telehealth in an evolving health care environment: Workshop summary* (pp. 99–104). Washington, DC: National Academy of Sciences.

Davis, M. C., Leucken, L., & Lemery-Chalfant, K. (2009). Resilience in common life: Introduction to the special issue. *Journal of Personality, 77,* 1637–1644.

de Burgh, H., White, C., Fear, N., & Iversen, A. (2011). The impact of deployment to Iraq or Afghanistan on partners and wives of military personnel. *International Review of Psychiatry, 23,* 192–200.

Dedert, E. A., Green, K. T., Calhoun, P. S., Yoash-Gantz, R., Taber, K. H., Mumford, M. M., . . . Beckham, J. C. (2009). Association of trauma exposure with psychiatric morbidity in military veterans who have served since September 11, 2001. *Journal of Psychiatric Research, 43,* 830–836.

Defense and Veterans Brain Injury Center. (2014). DoD worldwide numbers for TBI. Retrieved from http://dvbic.dcoe.mil/dod-worldwide-numbers-tbi.

Defense and Veterans Brain Injury Center. (DVBIC) and the TBI Family Caregiver Advisory Panel (2010). *Traumatic brain injury: A guide for caregivers of service members and veterans.* Retrieved from http://www.traumaticbraininjuryatoz.org.

Defense Centers of Excellence. (2010a). *The Defense Centers of Excellence for Psychological Health and Traumatic Brain Injury.* Retrieved October 8, 2010 from http://www.dcoe.health.mil.

Defense Centers of Excellence. (2010b). *How we do it: Promoting resilience, recovery, and reintegration.* Retrieved December 7, 2011 from http://www.dcoe.health.mil/HowWeDoIt.aspx.

Defense Centers of Excellence. (2010c). *National Intrepid Center of Excellence (NICoE).* Retrieved October 25, 2010 from http://www.dcoe.health.mil/ComponentCenters/NICoE.aspx.

Defense Centers of Excellence. (n.d.). *DCoE resilence continuum.* Retrieved from http://www.dcoe.mil/content/Navigation/Images/Resilience_Continuum_FINAL.pdf.

Defense Commissary Agency. (2010). *The Defense Commissary Agency: About us.* Retrieved November 30, 2011 from http://www.commissaries.com.

Defense Department Advisory Committee on Women in the Services. (2008). *Defense Department Advisory Committee on Women in the Services (DACOWITS) 2007 report.* Retrieved from http://dacowits.defense.gov/Portals/48/Documents/Reports/2007/Annual%20Report/dacowits2007report.pdf.

Defense Department Advisory Committee on Women in the Services. (2013). *Defense Department Advisory Committee on Women in the Services (DACOWITS) 2012 report.* Retrieved from http://dacowits.defense.gov/Portals/48/Documents/Reports/2012/Annual%20Report/dacowits2012report.pdf

Defense Finance and Accounting Service. (2012). *Types of retirement.* Retrieved from http://www.dfas.mil/retiredmilitary/plan/retirement-types.html.

Defense Manpower Data Center. (2009). *2008 survey of active duty spouses: Tabulations of responses* (Report No. 2008-041). Arlington, VA: Author. Retrieved from the Department of Defense

Personnel and Readiness website: http://prhome.defense.gov/MCFP/docs/2008%20Military%20 Spouse%20Survey.pdf.

Defense Manpower Data Center. (2012). *Data Request System for Military Personnel*. Retrieved from https://www.dmdc.osd.mil/drs/.

Defense Manpower Data Center (2013a). *2012 survey of active duty spouses: Tabulation of responses* (DMDC Report No. 2013-017). Alexandria, VA. Retrieved from http://www.militaryonesource.mil/footer?content_id=279101.

Defense Manpower Data Center. (2013b). *2012 workplace and gender relations survey of active duty members (Survey Note No. 2013-007)*. Arlington, VA: DMDC. Retrieved from http://www.sapr.mil/public/docs/research/2012_Workplace_and_Gender_Relations_Survey_of_Active_Duty_Members-Survey_Note_and_Briefing.pdf.

Defense Manpower Data Center. (2013c). *2012 workplace and gender relations survey of reserve component members (Survey Note No. 2013-002)*. Arlington, VA: DMDC. Retrieved from http://www.sapr.mil/public/docs/research/2012_Workplace_and_Gender_Relations_Survey_of_Reserve_Component_Members-Survey_Note_and_Briefing.pdf.

Defense Manpower Data Center. (2013d). *Table of active duty females by rank/grade and service*. Arlington, VA: DMDC. Retrieved from https://www.dmdc.osd.mil/appj/dwp/reports.do?category=reports&subCat=milActDutReg.

Defense Manpower Data Center. (2014a). *Active duty military strength report for September 30, 2014*. Retrieved from https://www.dmdc.osd.mil/appj/dwp/dwp_reports.jsp.

Defense Manpower Data Center. (2014b). *Data request system for military personnel*. Retrieved from https://www.dmdc.osd.mil/dcas/pages/casualties.xhtml.

Defense of Marriage Act. (2011). Retrieved from http://www.freedomtomarry.org/states/entry/c/doma.

Dekel, R., & Monson, C. M. (2010). Military-related post-traumatic stress disorder and family relations: Current knowledge and future directions. *Aggression and Violent Behavior, 15*, 303–309.

Dekel, R., & Solomon, Z. (2007). Secondary traumatization among wives of war veterans with PTSD. In C. R. Figley & W. P. Nash (Eds.), *Combat stress injury: Theory, research, and management* (pp. 137–157). New York, NY: Routledge.

Dekel, R., Goldblatt, H., Keidar, M., Solomon, Z., & Polliack, M. (2005). Being a wife of a veteran with posttraumatic stress disorder. *Family Relations, 54*, 24–36.

Dekel, R., Solomon, Z., & Bleich, A. (2005). Emotional distress and marital adjustment of caregivers: Contribution of level of impairment and appraised burden. *Anxiety, Stress, and Coping, 18*, 71–82.

Democratic Policy and Communications Center. (2012). *VOW to Hire Heroes Act*. Retrieved from http://veterans.house.gov/vow.

Department of Defense. (2004). *Task force report on care for victims of sexual assault*. Washington, DC: Author.

Department of Defense. (2008a). *The foundations of care, management and transition support for recovering service members and their families*. Washington, DC: Author.

Department of Defense. (2008b). *Report to Congress on the comprehensive policy improvements to the care, management and transition of recovering service members (NDAA Section 1611 and 1615)*. Washington, DC: Author. Retrieved from http://prhome.defense.gov/Portals/52/Documents/WCP%20Documents/09-16-08_1900_Final_Report_to_Congress_-_1611_and_1615.pdf.

Department of Defense. (2009). *DoD 101: An introductory overview of the Department of Defense*. Retrieved from http://www.defenselink.mil/pubs/dod101/dod101.html.

Department of Defense. (2011). *Unified Command Plan*. Retrieved from http://www.defense.gov/ucc/.

Department of Defense. (2013a). *Department of Defense annual report on sexual assault in the military*. Washington, DC: Department of Defense.

Department of Defense. (2013b). *Department of Defense Instruction 1332.30: Separation of regular and reserve commissioned officers*. Retrieved from http://www.dtic.mil/whs/directives/corres/pdf/133230p.pdf.

Department of Defense. (2014a). *A survivor's guide to benefits: Taking care of our own families*. Washington, DC: Author. Retrieved from http://www.militaryonesource.mil/f?P=MOS2:SEARCH:O::::P10_SEARCH:a%20Survivor%27s%20guide.

Department of Defense. (2014b). *An overview of children and youth programs*. Retrieved November 20, 2014 from the Military OneSource website: http://www.militaryonesource.mil/cyt?content_id=267586.

Department of Defense. (2014f). *New parent support program: Overview.* Retrieved November 20, 2014 from the Military OneSource website: http://www.militaryonesource.mil/parenting?content_id=266691.

Department of Defense. (2014g). *The Exceptional Family Member Program.* Retrieved November 20, 2014 from the Military OneSource website: http://www.militaryonesource.mil/efmp/overview?content_id=269174.

Department of Defense. (2014d). *Department of Defense Instruction 1332.14: Enlisted administrative separations.* Retrieved from http://www.dtic.mil/whs/directives/corres/pdf/133214p.pdf

Department of Defense. (2014e). *Estimated impacts of sequestration-level funding.* Retrieved from http://comptroller.defense.gov/budgetmaterials/budget2015.aspx#summary.

Department of Defense. (2014h). *Understanding and using your military exchange.* Retrieved November 20, 2014 from the Military OneSource website: http://www.militaryonesource.mil/shopping?content_id=268514.

Department of Defense. (2014c). *Annual report to the Congressional Defense Committees on the plans for the Department of Defense for the support of military family readiness: Fiscal year 2013.* Ref ID: 4-CA6A13F. Retrieved from http://www.militaryonesource.mil/footer?content_id=267470.

Department of Defense. (2015, May 20). *Operation Iraqi Freedom, Operation New Dawn, Operation Enduring Freedom, and Operation Inherent Resolve: U.S. casualty status.* Retrieved from www.defense.gov/news/casualty.pdf.

Department of Defense. (n.d.). *Women in defense of our nation.* Retrieved from http://www.armyg1.army.mil/EO/docs/DoD_Women_Factsheet.pdf.

Department of Defense. (2012b). Organizational of the Department of Defense (DoD). Retrieved from http://www.defense.gov/orgchart/.

Department of Defense Education Activity. (2010a). *About DoDEA.* Retrieved November 30, 2011 from http://www.dodea.edu.

Department of Defense Education Activity. (2010b). *DoDEA announces 2010 SAT results.* Retrieved November 30, 2014 from http://www.dodea.edu/newsroom/pressreleases/20100920.cfm.

Department of Defense Education Activity. (2010c). *DoDEA students continue positive performance on the TerraNova 3 multiple assessments.* Retrieved from http://www.dodea.edu/newsroom/pressreleases/09282010.cfm.

Department of Defense Educational Activity. (2015). Assistance to local educational agencies for Defense dependents' education (update). Alexandria, VA: Author. Retrieved May 21, 2015 from http://www.dodea.edu/Partnership/latestReports.cfm.

Department of Defense Education Activity. (2014a). *DoDEA announces SAT ® results.* Retrieved from http://www.dodea.edu/newsroom/pressreleases/20141007.cfm.

Department of Defense Educational Activity. (2014b). *Official facts, figures, and demographics: School year 2014-15.* Retrieved from http://www.dodea.edu/aboutDoDEA/today.cfm.

Department of Defense Task Force on Mental Health. (2007). *An achievable vision: Report of the Department of Defense task force on mental health.* Falls Church, VA: Defense Health Board.

Department of Defense-State Liaison Office. (2010). *The interstate compact on educational opportunities for military children: An overview.* Retrieved from http://www.mic3.net/pages/resources/resources.aspx.

Department of Labor. (2014). *Transition Assistance Program (TAP) Information.* Retrieved from http://www.dol.gov/vets/programs/tap/

Department of the Army. (2000). *Family readiness handbook* (USARC Regulation 608-1). Fort McPherson, GA: Department of the Army.

Department of the Army. (2006a). *Army regulation 614-100: Officer assignment policies, details, and transfers.* Washington, DC: Author.

Department of the Army. (2006b). *Combat and operational stress control* (Field manual No. 4-02.51). Washington, DC: Author.

Department of the Army. (2009). *Army regulation 614-200: Enlisted assignments and utilization management.* Washington, DC: Author.

Department of the Army. (2010). *Health promotion, risk reduction and suicide prevention report.* Washington, DC: Author.

Department of the Army. (2014). *Enlisted administrative separations (Army Regulation 135-178).* Washington, DC: Author. Retrieved from http://www.apd.army.mil/pdffiles/r135_178.pdf.

Department of the Navy. (2008). *SECNAV Instruction 1730.9: Confidential communications to chaplains.* Retrieved from http://doni.daps.dla.mil/SECNAV.aspx.

Department of Veterans Affairs. (2009). *Welcome to the GI bill web site.* Retrieved October 5, 2010 from http://www.benefits.va.gov/gibill/post911_gibill.asp.

Department of Veterans Affairs and Department of Defense. (2010). *VA/DoD clinical practice guideline for the management of post-traumatic stress*. Washington, DC.

Deployment Health Clinical Center. (2010a). *Military Pathways®*. Retrieved October 8, 2010 from http://mentalhealthscreening.org/programs/military.

Deployment Health Clinical Center. (2010b). *RESPECT-Mil*. Retrieved October 8, 2010 from http://www.pdhealth.mil/respect-mil/index1.asp.

Deployment Health Clinical Center. (n.d.). *Definition of deployment*. Retrieved from http://www.pdhealth.mil/ guidelines/annoC.asp.

Di Nola, G. M. (2008). Stressors afflicting families during deployment. *Military Medicine, 173*, v–vii.

Dichter, M. E., Cerulli, C., & Bossarte, R. M. (2011). Intimate partner violence victimization among women veterans and associated heart health risks. *Women's Health Issues, 21*, 190–194.

Dirkzwager, A. J. E., Bramsen, I., Ader, H., & van der Ploeg, H. M. (2005). Secondary traumatization in partners and parents of Dutch peacekeeping soldiers. *Journal of Family Psychology, 19*, 217–226.

Disabled American Veterans. (2014). *Women veterans: The long journey home*. Cold Spring, KY: Author. Retrieved from http://www.dav.org/women-veterans-study/.

Dobreva-Martinova, T. Villeneuve, M., Strickland, L., & Matheson, K. (2002). Occupational role stress in the Canadian forces: Its association with individual and organizational well-being. *Canadian Journal of Behavioral Sciences, 34*, 111–121.

Donnelly, J. (2010). *Rising military suicides*. Retrieved August 16, 2010 from the Congress.org website: http://www.congress .org/news/2009/11/25/rising_military_suicides.

Dorvil, M. J., & Pflieger, J. C. (2014, June). *2012 survey of active duty spouses: Spouse military support, deployment, reintegration, PCS moves, child well-being, education and employment, and spouse well-being*. Retrieved from http://www.militaryonesource.mil/footer?content_id=267470.

Drescher, K. D., Foy, D. W., Kelly, C., Leshner, A., Schutz, K., & Litz, B. (2011). An exploration of the viability and usefulness of the construct of moral injury in war veterans. *Traumatology, 17*, 8–13.

Drummet, A. R., Coleman, M., & Cable, S. (2003). Military families under stress: Implications for family life education. *Family Relations, 52*, 279–287.

Duckworth, J. (2003). The military culture. *Family Therapy Magazine, 2*(4), 12–17.

Duncan, P. M., Garcia, A. C., Frankowski, B. L., Carey, P. A., Kallock, E. A., Dixon, R. D., & Shaw, J. S. (2007). Inspiring healthy adolescent choices: A rationale for and guide to strength promotion in primary care. *Journal of Adolescent Health, 41*, 525–535.

Educator's Guide to the Military Child During Deployment. (n.d.). Retrieved December 4, 2011 from http://www2.ed.gov/about/offices/list/os/homefront/homefront.pdf

Eftekhari, A., Ruzek, J. I., Crowley, J. J., Rosen, C. S., Greenbaum, M. A., & Karlin, B. E. (2013). Effectiveness of national implementation of Prolonged Exposure Therapy in Veterans Affairs care. *JAMA Psychiatry, 70*, 949–955.

EMDR Institute, Inc. (2011). *What is EMDR?* Retrieved from http://www.emdr.com/general-information/what-is-emdr.html.

Employer Support of the Guard and Reserve. (2009). *About ESGR*. Retrieved November 30, 2011 from http://esgr.org/site/AboutUs.aspx.

Ender, M. (2006). Voices from the backseat: Demands of growing up in military families. In T. W. Britt, A. B. Adler, & C. A. Castro (Eds.), *Military life: The psychology of serving in peace and combat: The military family* (Vol. 3, pp. 138–166). Westport, CT: Praeger Security International.

Ender, M. G. (Ed.) (2002). *Military brats and other global nomads: Growing up in organization families*. Westport, CT: Praeger Security International.

Engel, C. C., Oxman, T., Yamamoto, C., Gould, D., Barry, S., Stewart, P., . . . Dietrich, A. J. (2008). RESPECT-Mil: Feasibility of a systems-level collaborative care approach to depression and post-traumatic stess disorder in military primary care. *Military Medicine, 173*, 935–940.

Engel, R. C., Gallagher, L. B., & Lyle, D. S. (2010). Military deployments and children's academic achievement: Evidence from Department of Defense education activity schools. *Economics of Education Review, 29*, 7–82.

Erbes, C. R., Meis, L. A., Polusny, M. A., & Arbisi, P. A. (2012). Psychiatric distress among spouses of National Guard soldiers prior to combat deployment. *Mental Health in Family Medicine, 9*, 161–169.

Erbes, C. R., Polusny, M. A., MacDermid, S., & Compton, J. S. (2008). Couple therapy with combat veterans and their partners. *Journal of Clinical Psychology, 64*, 972–983.

Eyberg, S. Boggs, S., & Algina, J. (1995). Parent-child interaction therapy: A psychosocial model for the treatment of young children with conduct problem behaviors and their families. *Psychopharmacology Bulletin, 3*, 83–91.

Faber, A. J., Willerton, E., Clymer, S. R., MacDermid, S. M., & Weiss, H. M. (2008). Ambiguous absence, ambiguous presence: A qualitative study of military reserve families in wartime. *Journal of Family Psychology, 22,* 222–230.

Family Medical Leave Act Regulations: A Report on the Department of Labor's Request for Information; Proposed Rule, 72 Fed. Reg. 35550 (2007).

Fargo, J., Metraux, S., Byrne, T., Munley, E., Montgomery, A. E., Jones, H., Sheldon, G., & Culhane, D. (2011). *Prevalence and risk of homelessness among U.S. veterans: A multisite investigation.* Washington, DC: U.S. Department of Veterans Affairs National Center on Homelessness among Veterans. Retrieved from http://www.va.gov/HOMELESS/docs/Prevalence_Study.pdf.

Fear, N. T., Jones, M., Murphy, D., Hull, L., Iversen, A. C., Coker, B., . . . Wesslely, S. (2010). What are the consequences of deployment to Iraq and Afghanistan on the mental health of the UK armed forces? A cohort study. *Lancet, 375,* 1783–1797.

Ferrari, M. (2003). *Reporting America at war: An oral history.* New York, NY: Hyperion.

Ferrier-Auerbach, A. G., Kehle, S. M., Erbes, C. R., Arbisi, P. A., Thuras, P., & Polusny, M. A. (2009). Predictors of alcohol use prior to deployment in National Guard soldiers. *Addictive Behaviors, 34,* 625–631.

Figley, C. R. (Ed.) (1995). *Compassion fatigue: Coping with secondary traumatic stress disorder in those who treat the traumatized.* New York, NY: Brunner/Mazel.

Figley, C. R., & McCubbin, H. I. (Eds.) (1983). *Stress and the family: Coping with catastrophe* (Vol. 2). New York, NY: Brunner/Mazel.

Finkel, L. B., Kelley, M. L., & Ashby, J. (2003). Geographic mobility, family, and maternal variables as related to the psychosocial adjustment of military children. *Military Medicine, 168,* 1019–1024.

Fischer, H. (2014). *A guide to U.S. military casualty statistics: Operation New Dawn, Operation Iraqi Freedom, and Operation Enduring Freedom.* Washington DC: Congressional Research Service, Library of Congress.

Fisher House Facts (n.d.) Retrieved December 7, 2011 from http://www.fisherhouse.org/about/.

Flake, E. M., Davis, B. E., Johnson, P. L., & Middleton, L. S. (2009). The psychosocial effects of deployment on military children. *Journal of Developmental and Behavioral Pediatrics 30,* 271–278.

Flanagan-Kaminsky, D. (2013). Intentional anticipatory mourning, caregiver and bereavement support program for terminally ill Veterans, their families, and caregivers in the VA Contract Home Hospice Program. *Omega, 67,* 69–77.

Fogel, A. (2010). *Infancy: Infant, family, & society* (5th ed.). Cornwall-on-Hudson, NY: Sloan Publishing.

Folkman, S., & Moskowitz, J. T. (2007). Positive affect and meaning-focused coping during significant psychological stress. In M. Hewstone, H. A. W. Schut, J. B. F. De Wit, K. Van Den Bos, & M. S. Stroebe (Eds.), *The scope of social psychology: Theories and applications. Essays in honor of Wolfgang Stroebe* (pp. 193–208). New York, NY: Psychology Press.

Force Health Protection & Readiness Policy & Programs (2007). *The post-deployment health reassessment: Safeguarding the health of those who protect us.* Retrieved from http://fhp.osd.mil/pdhrainfo.

Foster, L. K. & Vince, S. (2009). *California's women veterans: The challenges and needs of those who served.* Sacramento, CA: California Research Bureau, California State Library. Retrieved from http://www.library.ca.gov/crb/09/09-009.pdf.

Friedl, K. E., Grate, S. J., & Proctor, S. P. (2009). Neuropsychological issues in military deployments: Lessons observed in the DoD Gulf War Illnesses research program. *Military Medicine, 174,* 335–346.

Friedman, M. J. (2004). Acknowledging the psychiatric cost of war. *New England Journal of Medicine, 351,* 75–77.

Gade, P. A., Tiggle, R. B., & Schumm, W. R. (2003). The measurement and consequences of military organizational commitment in soldiers and spouses. *Military Psychology, 15,* 191–207.

Gamache, G., Rosenheck, R., & Tessler, R. (2003). Overrepresentation of women veterans among homeless women. *American Journal of Public Health, 93,* 1132–1136.

Gambardella, L. C. (2008). Role-exit theory and marital discord following extended military deployment. *Perspectives in Psychiatric Care, 44,* 169–174.

Garber, A. K., Boyer, C. G., Pollack, L, M., Chang, Y. J., & Shafer, M. (2008). Body mass index and disordered eating behaviors are associated with weight dissatisfaction in adolescent and young adult female military recruits. *Military Medicine, 173,* 138–145.

Garcia, R. (2009). *Veteran center handbook for student veterans.* Retrieved from http://www.studentveterans .org/resourcelibrary.

Garrick, J. (2013). *Suicide and military families: A report on the feasibility of tracking deaths by suicide among military family members*. Washington DC: Defense Suicide Prevention Office. Retrieved from http://i.cdn.turner.com/cnn/2014/images/02/05/final_report.pdf.

Gates, G. (2010). *Lesbian, gay, and bisexual men and women in the US military: Updated estimates.* Retrieved from the Williams Institute Military Issues Studies at UCLA School of Law website: http://williamsinstitute.law.ucla.edu/wp-content/uploads/Gates-GLBmilitaryUpdate-May-20101.pdf.

Gawande, A. (2004). Casualties of war: Military care for the wounded from Iraq and Afghanistan. *New England Journal of Medicine, 351*, 2471–2475.

Gerber, P. S. (2013). Last watch: Developing an inpatient palliative volunteer program for U.S. veterans in Hospice. *Omega, 67*, 87–95.

Gewirtz, A. H., Pinna, K. L., Hanson, S. K., & Brockberg, D. (2014). Promoting parenting to support reintegration military families: After Deployment, Adaptive Parenting Tools. *Psychological Services, 1*, 31–40.

Gewirtz, A. H., Erbes, C. R., Polusny, M. A., Forgatch, M. A., & DeGarmo, D. S. (2011). Helping military families through the deployment process: Strategies to support parenting. *Professional Psychology: Research and Practice, 42*, 56–62.

Gewirtz, A. H., Polusny, M. A., DeGarmo, D. S., Khaylis, A., & Erbes, C. R. (2010). Posttraumatic stress symptoms among National Guard soldiers deployed to Iraq: Associations with parenting behaviors and couple adjustment. *Journal of Consulting and Clinical Psychology, 78*, 599–610.

Gibbons, S. W., Hickling, E. J., & Watts, D. D. (2012). Combat stressors and post-traumatic stress in deployed military healthcare professionals: An integrative review. *Journal of Advanced Nursing, 68*, 3–21.

Gibbs, D. A., Martin, S. L., Kupper, L. L., & Johnson, R. E. (2007). Child maltreatment in enlisted soldiers' families during combat-related deployments. *Journal of the American Medical Association, 298*, 528–535.

Gleason, C. L. (2007, April 4). Officials emphasize zero tolerance of sexual assault. *American Forces Press Service*. Retrieved from http://www.defense.gov/news/newsarticle.aspx?id=32693.

Global Security (2005). *Marine divisions.* Retrieved from http://www.globalsecurity.org/military/agency/usmc/mardiv.htm.

Goff, B. S. N., Crow, J., Reisbig, A. M. J., & Hamilton, S. (2007). The impact of individual trauma symptoms of deployed soldiers on relationship satisfaction. *Journal of Family Psychology, 21*, 344–353.

Goffman, E. (1959). *The presentation of self in everyday life.* New York, NY: Doubleday.

Goldenring, H., & Cohen, E. (1988). Getting into adolescents' heads. *Contemporary Pediatrics, 5*, 75–90.

Goldstein, J. & Kenney, C. (2001). Marriage delayed or foregone? New cohort forecasts of first marriage for US women. *American Sociological Review, 66*, 506–519.

Goldzweig, C. L., Balekian, T. M., Rolón, C., Yano, E. M., & Shekelle, P. G. (2006). The state of women veterans' health research: Results of a systematic literature review. *Journal of General Internal Medicine, 21*, S82–S92.

Goodenough, W. (1981). *Culture, language, society.* Menlo Park, CA: Benjamin Cummings Publishing.

Goodspeed, M. H. (2003). *U.S. Navy: A military history.* Washington Navy Yard, DC: Navy Historical Foundation.

Gorman, G. H., Eide, M., & Hisle-Gorman, E. (2010). Wartime military deployment and increased pediatric mental and behavioral health complaints. *Pediatrics, 126*, 1058–1066.

Gorman, L. A., Fitzgerald, H. E., & Blow, A. J. (2010). Parental combat injury and early child development: A conceptual model for differentiating effects of visible and invisible injuries. *Psychiatric Quarterly, 81*, 1–21.

Graham, I. (2010, July 30). *DoD childcare fees will soon change.* Retrieved from the DoD Live website: http://www.dodlive.mil/index.php/2010/07/dod-childcare-fees-will-soon-change/.

Granado, N. S., Smith, T. C., Swanson, G. M., Harris, R. B., Shahar, E., Smith, B., . . . Ryan, M. A. K. for the Millennium Cohort Study Team (2009). Newly reported hypertension after military combat deployment in a large population-based study. *Hypertension, 54*, 966–973.

Greden, J. F., Valenstein, M., Spinner, J., Blow, A., Gorman, L. A., Dalack, G. W., Marcus, S., & Kees, M. (2010). Buddy-to-buddy, a citizen soldier peer support program to counteract stigma, PTSD, depression, and suicide. *Annals of the New York Academy of Sciences, 1208*, 90–97.

Green Cross Academy of Traumatology. (n.d.). *Standards of care: Standards of self care guidelines.* Retrieved from http://www.greencross.org/standards.html.

Greenberg, N., & Wessely, S. (2008). Gulf War Syndrome: An emerging threat or a piece of history? *Emerging Health Threats Journal, (1)*. doi: 10.3134/ehtj.08.010 [online.]

Greenberg, N., Langston, V., & Jones, N. (2008). Trauma Risk Management (TRiM) in the UK Armed Forces. *Journal of the Royal Army Medical Corps, 154,* 123–126.

Griffin, J. M., Friedemann-Sánchez, G., Hall, C., Phelan, S., & van Ryn, M. (2009). Families of patients with polytrauma: Understanding the evidence and charting a new research agenda. *Journal of Rehabilitation Research and Development, 46,* 879–892.

Griffin, J. M., Friedemann-Sánchez, G., Jensen, A. C., Taylor, B. C., Gravely, A., Clothier, B., . . . van Ryn, M. (2012). The invisible side of war: Families caring for U. S. service members with traumatic brain injuries and polytrauma. *Journal of Head Trauma Rehabilitation, 27,* 3–13.

Griffith, J. (2005). The Army National Guard soldier in post-9/11 operations: Perceptions of being prepared for mobilization, deployment, and combat. *Journal of Political and Military Sociology, 33,* 161–178.

Griffith, J. (2008). Institutional motives for serving in the U.S. Army National Guard: Implications for recruitment, retention, and readiness. *Armed Forces & Society, 34,* 230–258.

Griffith, J. (2009). After 9/11 what kind of reserve soldier? Considerations given to emerging demands, organizational orientation, and individual commitment. *Armed Forces & Society, 35,* 214–240.

Gutierrez, P. M., & Brenner, L. A. (2009). Helping military personnel and recent veterans manage stress reactions. *Journal of Mental Health Counseling, 31,* 95–100.

Hagedoorn, M., Kuijer, R., Buunk, B., DeJong, G., & Wobbes, T. (2000). Marital satisfaction in patients with cancer: Does support from intimate partners benefit those who need it the most? *Health Psychology, 19,* 274–282.

Haglund, M. E. M., Nedstadt, P. S., Cooper, N. S., Southwick, S. M., & Charney, D. S. (2007). Psychobiological mechanisms of resilience: Relevance to prevention and treatment of stress-related psychopathology. *Development and Psychopathology, 19,* 889–920.

Hamilton, B. E., Martin, J. A., & Ventura, S. J. (2010). *Births: Preliminary data for 2009.* National Vital Statistics Reports, 59 (3). DHHS Publication No. (PHS) 2011–1120. Retrieved from the Centers for Disease Control and Prevention website: http://www.cdc.gov/nchs/nvss/birth_products.htm.

Hansen, F. R. (2000). *American history teacher's book of lists.* San Francisco, CA: Jossey-Bass. Retrieved from http://www.teachervision.fen.com/us-history/resource/5669.html.

Hardy, L., Arthur, C. A., Jones, G., Shariff, A., Munnoch, K., Isaacs, I., & Allsopp, A. J. (2010). The relationship between transformational leadership behaviors, psychological, and training outcomes in elite military recruits. *The Leadership Quarterly, 21,* 20–32.

Harrell, M. C., Lim, N., Castaneda, L. W., & Golinelle, D. (2005). *Working around the military: Challenges to military spouse employment and education.* Santa Monica, CA: RAND Corporation. Retrieved from http://www.rand.org/pubs/monographs/MG196.html.

Harris, B. C., Simutis, Z. M., & Gantz, M. M. (2002). *Women in the U.S. Army: An annotated bibliography.* Special Report 48. Alexandria, VA: U.S. Army Research Institute for the Behavioral and Social Sciences. Retrieved from http://www.awm.lee.army.mil/pdfs_docs/WomenInTheArmy-Bibliography.pdf.

Harrison, J., & Vannest, K. J. (2008). Educators supporting families in times of crisis: Military reserve deployments. *Preventing School Failure, 52*(4), 17–23.

Hastings, T. J. (1991). The Stanford-Terman study revisited: Postwar emotional health of World War II veterans. *Military Psychology, 3,* 201–214.

Headquarters, Department of the Army. (2006). *Combat and operational stress control* [Field manual 4-02.51 (FM 8-51)]. Washington, DC: Author. Retrieved from http://www.fas.org/irp/doddir/army/fm4-02-51.pdf.

Heubner, A. J., Mancini, J. A., Bowen, G. L., & Orthner, D. K. (2009). Shadowed by war: Building community capacity to support military families. *Family Relations, 58,* 216–228.

Hickey, M. (1999). *The Korean War: The West Confronts Communism, 1950-1953.* Woodstock, NY: The Overlook Press.

Hill, R. (1949). *Families under stress: Adjustment to the crises of war separation and reunion.* New York, NY: Harper & Brothers.

Hill, R. (1958). Generic features of families under stress. *Social Casework, 49,* 139–150.

Hirsch, M. D., & Engel, E. J. (2013). *Coping with compassion fatigue.* Retrieved from the Military OneSource website: http://www.militaryonesource.mil/wounded-warrior?content_id=268677.

Hlad, J. (2012, April 16). Panetta touts 'zero tolerance' for sexual assault. *Stars and Stripes.* Retrieved from http://www.stripes.com/news/panetta-touts-zero-tolerance-for-sexual-assault-1.174631.

Hobfoll, S. E. (1989). Conservation of resources: A new attempt at conceptualizing stress. *American Psychologist, 44,* 513–524.

Hobfoll, S. E. (1998). *Stress, culture and community: The psychology and philosophy of stress.* New York, NY: Plenum Press.

Hobfoll, S. E., Dunahoo, C. A., & Monnier, J. (1995). Conservation of resources and traumatic stress. In J. R. Freedy & S. E. Hobfoll (Eds.), *Traumatic stress: From theory to practice* (pp. 29–47). New York, NY: Plenum Press.

Hobfoll, S. E., Horsey, K. J., & Lamoureux, B. E. (2009). Resiliency and resource loss in times of terrorism and disaster: Lessons learned for children and families and those left untaught. In D. Brom, R. Pat-Horenczyk, & J. D. Ford (Eds.), *Treating traumatized children: Risk, resilience, and recovery* (pp. 150–163). New York, NY: Routledge/Taylor & Francis.

Hobfoll, S. E., Watson, P., Bell, C. C., Bryant, R. A., Brymer, M. J., Friedman, M. J., . . . Ursano, R. J. (2007). Five essential elements of immediate and mid-term mass trauma intervention: Empirical evidence. *Psychiatry, 40,* 283–315.

Hogan, P. F. & Seifert, R. F. (2010). Marriage and the military: Evidence that those who serve marry earlier and divorce earlier. *Armed Forces & Society, 36,* 420–438.

Hoge, C. W., Auchterlonie, J. L., & Milliken, C. S. (2006). Mental health problems, use of mental health services, and attrition from military service after returning from deployment to Iraq or Afghanistan. *Journal of the American Medical Association, 295,* 1023–1032.

Hoge, C. W., Clark, J. C., & Castro, C. A. (2007). Commentary: Women in combat and the risk of posttraumatic stress disorder and depression. *International Journal of Epidemiology, 36,* 327–329.

Hoge, C. W., Castro, C. A., Messer, S. C., McGurk, D., Cotting, D. I., & Koffman, R. L. (2004). Combat duty in Iraq and Afghanistan, mental health problems and barriers to care. *New England Journal of Medicine, 351,* 13–22.

Hoge, C. W., McGurk, D., Thomas, J. L., Cox, A. L., Engel, C. C., & Castro, C. A. (2008). Mild traumatic brain injury in U.S. soldiers returning from Iraq. *New England Journal of Medicine, 358,* 453–463.

Holland, J. M., Currier, J. M., Kirkendall, A., Keene, J. R., & Luna, N. (2014). Sadness, anxiety, and experiences with emotional support among veteran and non-veteran patients and their families at the end of life. *Journal of Palliative Medicine, 17,* 708–711.

Holmes, A. K., Rauch, P. K., & Cozza, S. J. (2013). When a parent is injured or killed in action. *The Future of Children, 23,* 143–162. Retrieved from http://futureofchildren.org/futureofchildren/publications/journals/journal_details/index.xml?journalid=80.

Homes for Our Troops I (2009). *Homes for Our Troops: Building specially adapted homes for our severly injured veterans.* Retrieved from http://www.homesforourtroops.org.

Hooper, T. I., Debaky, S. F., Bellis, K. S., Kang, H. K., Cowan, D. N., Lincoln, A. E., & Gackstetter, G. D. (2006). Understanding the effect of deployment on the risk of fatal motor vehicle crashes: A nested case-control study of fatalities in Gulf War era veterans, 1991–1995. *Accident Analysis and Prevention, 38,* 518–525.

Hosek, J., & MacDermid Wadsworth, S. (2013). Economic conditions of military families. *The Future of Children, 23,* 41–59. Retrieved from http://futureofchildren.org/futureofchildren/publications/journals/journal_details/index.xml?journalid=80.

Hosek, J., Kavanagh, J., & Miller, L. (2006). *How deployments affect service members.* Santa Monica, CA: RAND Corporation. Retrieved from http://www.rand.org/pubs/monographs/MG432.html.

Huebner, A. J., & Mancini, J. A. (2005). *Adjustments among adolescents in military families when a parent is deployed.* Final report to the Military Family Research Institute and Department of Defense Quality of Life Office. Retrieved from the Military Family Research Institute website: https://www.mfri.purdue.edu/resources/public/reports/Adjustments%20Among%20Adolescents.pdf.

Huebner, A. J., Mancini, J. A., Bowen, G. L., & Orthner, D. K. (2009). Shadowed by war: Building community capacity to support military families. *Family Relations, 58,* 216–228.

Huebner, A. J., Mancini, J. A., Wilcox, R. M., Grass, S. R., & Grass, G. A. (2007). Exploring uncertainty and ambiguous loss. *Family Relations, 56,* 112–122.

Hutchinson, J. W., Greene, J. P., & Hanson, S. L. (2008). Evaluating active duty risk-taking: Military home, education, activity, drugs, sex, suicide, and safety method. *Military Medicine, 173,* 1164–1167.

Institute of Medicine. (2010). *Returning home from Iraq and Afghanistan: Preliminary assessment of the readjustment needs of veterans, service members, and their families.* Washington, DC: The National Academies Press. Retrieved from http://www.nap.edu/catalog/12812.html.

Institute of Medicine. (2012). *The role of telehealth in an evolving health care environment: Workshop summary.* Washington, D.C.: National Academy of Sciences.

Interian, A., Kline, A., Janal M., Glynn, S., & Losonczy, M. (2014). Multiple deployments and combat trauma: Do homefront stressors increase the risk for posttraumatic stress symptoms? *Journal of Traumatic Stress, 27*, 90–97.

Intrepid Fallen Heroes Fund. (2010). *Intrepid fallen heroes fund—About IFHF.* Retrieved from http://www.fallenheroesfund.org/About-IFHF.aspx

Intrepid Sea, Air & Space Museum. (2008). *National Intrepid Center of Excellence officially dedicated at National Naval Medical Center.* Retrieved from http://www.intrepidmuseum.org/LatestNews/June-2010/National-Intrepid-Center-of-Excellence-Officially-.aspx.

Jacobson, I. G., Ryan, M. A. K., Hooper, T. I., Smith, T. C., Amoroso, P. J., Boyko, E. J., . . . Bell, N. S. for the Millennium Cohort Study Team (2008). Alcohol use and alcohol-related problems before and after military combat deployment. *Journal of the American Medical Association, 300*, 663–675.

Jacobson, I. G., Smith, T. C., Smith, B., Keel, P. K., Amoroso, P. J., Wells, T. S., . . . Ryan, M. A. K. for the Millennium Cohort Study Team (2009). Disordered eating and weight changes after deployment: Longitudinal assessment of a large U.S. military cohort. *American Journal of Epidemiology, 169*, 415–427.

Jafee, M. S., Helmick, K. M., Girard, P. D., Meyer, K. S., Dinegar, K., & George, K. (2009). Acute clinical care and care coordination for traumatic brain injury within the Department of Defense. *Journal of Rehabilitation Research and Development, 46*, 655–666.

Johnson, J. (2010, August). Brain injury info. *Military Officer*, 46.

Johnson, M. (2009). Differentiating among types of domestic violence: Implications for healthy marriages. In E. H. Peters & C. M. Kamp Dush (Eds.), *Marriage and family: Perspectives and complexities* (pp. 281–297). New York, NY: Columbia University Press.

Joint Chiefs of Staff. (n.d.). *Joint Chiefs of Staff.* Retrieved from http://www.jcs.mil/.

Joint Mental Health Advisory Team 7. (2011). *Joint Mental Health Advisory Team 7 (J-MHAT 7) Operation Enduring Freedom 2010 Afghanistan,* report. Falls Church, VA: Office of The Surgeon General of the Army.

Joint Service Committee on Military Justice. (2008). *Manual for courts-martial, United States.* Washington, DC: Department of Defense.

Jones, E., & Wessely, S. (2003). "Forward psychiatry" in the military: Its origins and effectiveness. *Journal of Traumatic Stress, 16*, 411–419.

Jones, E., Fear, N. T., & Wessely, S. (2007). Shell shock and mild traumatic brain injury. *American Journal of Psychiatry, 164*, 1641–1645.

Joseph, A. L., & Afifi, T. D. (2010). Military wives' stressful disclosures to their deployed husbands: The role of protective buffering. *Journal of Applied Communication Research, 38*, 412–434.

Jumisko, E., Lexell, J., & Soderberg, S. (2007). Living with moderate or severe traumatic brain injury: The meaning of family members' experiences. *Journal of Family Nursing, 13*, 353–369.

Kang, H., Dalager, N., Mahan, C., & Ishii, E. (2005). The role of sexual assault on the risk of PTSD among Gulf War veterans. *Annals of Epidemiology, 15*, 191–195.

Karney, B. R., & Crown, J. S. (2007). *Families under stress: An assessment of data, theory, and research on marriage and divorce in the military.* Santa Monica, CA: RAND Corporation. Retrieved from http://www.rand.org/pubs/monographs/MG599.html.

Karney, B. R. & Crown, J. S. (2011). Does deployment keep military marriages together or break them apart? Evidence from Afghanistan and Irag. In S. MacDermid Wadsworth & D. Riggs (Eds.), *Risk and resilience in U.S. military families* (pp. 23–45). New York, NY: Springer.

Keenan, J. O. (2008). The DoD Combat Exclusion Policy: Time for a change? In M. M. Putko & D. V. Johnson (Eds.), *Women in combat compendium,* (pp. 21–25). Retrieved from the U.S. Army War College Strategic Studies Institute website: http://www.strategicstudiesinstitute.army.mil/pdffiles/pub830.pdf.

Kelley, M. L., Doane, A. N., & Pearson, M. R. (2011). Single military mothers in the new millennium: Stresses, supports, and effects of deployment. In S. MacDermid Wadsworth & D. Riggs (Eds.), *Risk and resilience in U.S. military families* (pp. 343–363). New York, NY: Springer Science.

Kelley, M. L., Schwerin, M. J., Farrar, K. L., & Lane, M. E. (2007). A participant evaluation of the U.S. Navy Parent Support Program. *Journal of Family Violence, 21*, 301–310.

Kelly, J. (2013, June 18). *Elimination of 1994 direct ground combat definition and assignment rule.* Retrieved from the Navy Office of Information Navy Live website: http://navylive.dodlive.mil/2013/06/18/elimination-of-1994-direct-ground-combat-definition-and-assignment-rule.

Kelly, J., & Johnson, M. P. (2008). Differentiation among types of intimate partner violence: Research update and implications for interventions. *Family Court Review, 46*, 476–499.

Kelty, R. Kleykamp, M. & Segal, D. R. (2010). The military and the transition to adulthood. *The Future of Children, 20,* 181–207.

Kennedy, J. E., Jaffee, M. S., Leskin, G. A., Stokes, J. W., Leal, F. O., & Fitzpatrick, P. J. (2007). Posttraumatic stress disorder and posttraumatic stress disorder-like symptoms and mild traumatic brain injury. *Journal of Rehabilitation Research & Development, 44,* 895–920.

Kessler, R. C., Sonnega, A., Bromet, E., Hughes, M., & Nelson, C. B. (1995). Posttraumatic stress disorder in the National Comorbidity Study. *Archives of General Psychiatry, 52,* 1048–1060.

Kessler, R. C., Berglund, P., Demler, O., Jin, R., Merikangas, K. R., & Walters, E. E. (2005). Lifetime prevalence and age-of-onset distributions of DSM-IV disorders in the National Comorbidity Survey Replication. *Archives of General Psychiatry, 62,* 593–602.

Khoshaba, D. M., & Maddi, S. R. (1999). Early experiences in hardiness development. *Consulting Psychology Journal, 51,* 106–116.

Killgore, W. D., Cotting, D. I., Thomas, J. L., Cox, A. L., McGurk, D., Vo, A. H., . . . Hoge, C. W. (2008). Post-combat invincibility: Violent combat experiences are associated with increased risk-taking propensity following deployment. *Journal of Psychiatric Research, 42,* 1112–1121.

Kim, P. Y., Thomas, J. L., Wilk, J. E., Castro, C. A., & Hoge, C. W. (2010). Stigma, barriers to care, and use of mental health services among active duty and National Guard soldiers after combat. *Psychiatric Services, 61,* 582–588.

Klesges, R. C., Haddock, C. K., Lando, H., & Talcott, G. W. (1999). Efficacy of forced smoking cessation and an adjunctive behavioral treatment on long-term smoking rates. *Journal of Consulting and Clinical Psychology, 67,* 952–958.

Knox, J., & Price, D. H. (1999). Total force and the new American military family: Implications for social work practice. *Families in Society, 80,* 128–136.

Kolb, L. J., Hoffman, M., & Blakeley, K. (2014). *A user's guide to the fiscal year 2015 defense budget.* Washington, DC: Center for American Progress. Retrieved from http://www.americanprogress.org/issues/security/report/2014/04/24/88516/a-users-guide-to-the-fiscal-year-2015-defense-budget/

Kravetz, P. (2012). Way off base: An argument against intimate partner violence cases in Veterans Treatment Courts. *Veterans Law Review, 4,* 162–205.

Kreutzer, J. S. (1988). *Family Needs Questionnaire.* Medical College of Virginia: Richmond, VA.

Kuehn, B. M. (2009). Soldier suicide rates continue to rise: Military, scientists work to stem the tide. *Journal of the American Medical Association, 299,* 1111–1113.

Kuhn, E., Greene, C., Hoffman, J., Nguyen T., Wald L., Schmidt, J. . . . Ruzek, J. (2014). Preliminary evaluation of PTSD Coach, a smartphone app for post-traumatic stress symptoms. *Military Medicine, 179,* 12–18.

Kushner, D. (1998). Mild traumatic brain injury: Toward understanding manifestations and treatment. *Archives of Internal Medicine, 158,* 1617–1624.

Landau, J., & Hissett, J. (2008). Mild traumatic brain injury: Impact on identity and ambiguous loss in the family. *Family, Systems, & Health, 26,* 69–85.

Lapp, C. A., Taft, L. B., Tollefson, T., Hoepner, A., Moore, K., & Divyak, K. (2010). Stress and coping on the home front: Guard and Reserve spouses searching for a new normal. *Journal of Family Nursing, 16,* 45–67.

Lauder, T. D., & Campbell, C. S. (2001). Abnormal eating behaviors in female Reserve Officer Training Corps cadets. *Military Medicine, 166,* 264–268.

Lauder, T. D., Williams, M. V., Campbell, C. S., Davis, G., Sherman, R., & Pulos, E. (1999). The female athlete triad: Prevalence in military women. *Military Medicine, 164,* 630–635.

Laurence, J. (2006). Poultry and patriotism: Attitudes toward the U.S. military. In T. W. Britt, A. B. Adler, & C. A. Castro (Eds.), *Military life: The psychology of serving in peace and combat: Military culture* (Vol. 4, pp. 211–228). Westport, CT: Praeger Security International.

Lavee, Y., McCubbin, H. I., & Olson, D. H. (1987). The effect of stressful life events and transitions on family functioning and well-being. *Journal of Marriage and the Family, 49,* 857–873.

Lazarus, R. S., & Folkman, S. (1984). *Stress, appraisal, and coping.* New York, NY: Springer.

Leal, R. (2014, April 1). Disability claims backlog reduced by 44 percent since peaking one year ago [Web log post]. Retrieved from http://www.blogs.va.gov/VAntage/13577/disability-claims-backlog-reduced-by-44-percent-since-peaking-one-year-ago/.

Leskin, G. A. (2010). *FOCUS project: Program adaptations.* Presented at the Navy and Marine Corps Combat & Operational Stress Control Conference 2010, San Diego, CA.

Lester, P., & Flake, E. (2013). How wartime military service affects children and families. *The Future of Children, 23,* 121–141. Retrieved from http://futureofchildren.org/futureofchildren/publications/journals/journal_details/index.xml?journalid=80.

Lester, P., Leskin, G., Woodward, K., Saltzman, W., Nash, W., Mogil, C., . . . Beardslee, W. (2011). Wartime deployment and military children: Applying prevention science to enhance family resilience. In S. MacDermid Wadsworth & D. Riggs (Eds.), *Risk and resilience in U.S. military families* (pp. 149–173). New York, NY: Springer.

Lester, P., Mogil, C., Saltzman, W., Woodward, K., Nash, W., Leskin, G., . . . Beardslee, W. (2011). Families overcoming under stress: Implementing family-centered prevention for military families facing wartime deployments and combat operational stress. *Military Medicine, 176,* 19–25.

Lester, P., Peterson, K., Reeves, J., Knauss, L., Glover, D., Mogil, C., . . . Beardslee, W. (2010). The long war and parental combat deployment: Effects on military children and at-home spouses. *Journal of the American Academy of Child & Adolescent Psychiatry, 49,* 310–320.

Lester, P., Saltzman, W. R., Woodward, K., Glover, D., Leskin, G. A., Bursch, B., . . . Beardslee, W. (2012). Evaluation of a family-centered prevention intervention for military children and families facing wartime deployments. *American Journal of Public Health, Supplement 1,* S48–S54.

Lester, P., Stein, J. A., Saltzman, W., Woodward, K., MacDermid Wadsworth, S., Milburn, N., . . . Beardslee, W. (2013). Psychological health of military children: Longitudinal evaluation of a family-centered prevention program to enhance family resilience. *Military Medicine, 178,* 838–845.

Library of Congress. (2009). *Uniform Code of Military Justice legislative history.* Retrieved from http://www.loc .gov/rr/frd/Military_Law/UCMJ_LHP.html.

Lincoln, A., Swift, E., & Shorteno-Fraser, M. (2008). Psychological adjustment and treatment of children and families with parents deployed in military combat. *Journal of Clinical Psychology, 84,* 984–992.

Lindstrom, K. E., Smith, T. C., Wells, T. S., Wang, L. Z., Smith, B., Reed, R. J., . . . Ryan, M. A. (2006). The mental health of U.S. military women in combat support occupations. *Journal of Women's Health, 15,* 162–172.

Lipari, R. N., & Lancaster, A. R. (2003). *Armed Forces 2002 sexual harassment survey* (DMDC report No. 2003-026). Arlington, VA: Defense Manpower Data Center.

Little, R. D., & Hisnanick, J. J. (2007). The earnings of tied-migrant military husbands. *Armed Forces and Society, 33,* 547–570.

Litz, B. T. (2005). *A brief primer on the mental health impact of the wars in Afghanistan and Iraq: A National Center for PTSD fact sheet.* Boston, MA: National Center for PTSD.

Litz, B. T., Orsillo, S. M., Friedman, M., Ehlich, P., & Batres, A. (1997). Posttraumatic stress disorder associated with peacekeeping duty in Somalia for U.S. military personnel. *American Journal of Psychiatry, 154,* 179–184.

Litz, B. T., Stein, N., Delaney, E., Lebowitz, L., Nash, W. P., Silva, C., & Maguen, S. (2009). Moral injury and moral repair in war veterans: A preliminary model and intervention strategy. *Clinical Psychology Review, 29,* 695–706.

Logan, K. V. (1987). The emotional cycle of deployment. *U.S. Naval Proceedings, 113,* 43–47.

Lopez, C. T. (2009, February 9). *Female flag officers honor first woman four-star.* Retrieved from the U.S. Army website: http://www.army.mil/article/16632/female-flag-officers-honor-first-woman-four-star/.

Lundquist, J. H. (2004). When race makes no difference: Marriage and the military. *Social Forces, 83,* 731–757.

Lundquist, J. H. (2006). The Black-White gap in marital dissolution among young adults: What can a counterfactual scenario tell us? *Social Problems, 53,* 421–441.

Lundquist, J. H. (2008). Ethnic and gender satisfaction in the military: The effect of a meritocratic institution. *American Sociological Review, 73,* 477–496.

Lundquist, J. H., & Smith, H. L. (2005). Family formation among women in the U.S. military: Evidence from the NLSY. *Journal of Marriage and Family, 67,* 1–13.

Luthar, S. S. (2006). Resilience in development: A synthesis of research across five decades. In D. C. Cicchetti (Ed.), *Developmental psychopathology: Risk, disorder, and adaptation* (2nd ed., Vol. 3, pp. 739–795). Hoboken, NJ: John Wiley and Sons.

Luxton, D. (2013). AI cognitive enhancements: Implications for psychological health. *National Center for Telehealth & Technology.* Retrieved from http://t2health.dcoe.mil/news/create-news-articles-5.

Lyle, D. S. (2006). Using military deployments and job assignments to estimate the effect of parental absences and household relocations on children's academic achievement. *Journal of Labor Economics, 24,* 319–350.

Lyons, J. A. (2007). The returning warrior: Advice for families and friends. In C. R. Figley & W. P. Nash (Eds.), *Combat stress injury: Theory, research, and management* (pp. 311–324). New York, NY: Routledge.

Lyons, R. F., Mickelson, K. D., Sullivan, M. J. L., & Coyne, J. C. (1998). Coping as a communal process. *Journal of Social and Personal Relationships, 15,* 579–605.

MacDermid Wadsworth, S. (2013). Understanding and supporting the resilience of a new generation of combat-exposed military families and their children. *Clinical Child and Family Psychology Review, 16*, 415–420.

MacDermid Wadsworth, S. M. (2010). Family risk and resilience in the context of war and terrorism. *Journal of Marriage and Family, 72*, 537–556.

MacDermid Wadsworth, S. M., & Southwell, K. (2011). Military families: Extreme work and extreme 'work-family.' *The Annals of the American Academy of Political and Social Science, 638*, 163–183.

MacDermid Wadsworth, S., Lester, P., Marini, C., Cozza, S., Sornborger, J., Strouse, T., & Beardslee, W. (2013a). Approaching family-focused systems of care for military and veteran families. *Military Behavioral Health, 1*, 31–40.

MacDermid Wadsworth, S., Pagnan, C., & Seidel, A. (2010, November). *Coming home after war: A longitudinal study of U.S. reservists and their families.* Paper presented at the Annual Conference of the National Council on Family Relations, Minneapolis, MN.

MacDermid, S. M., Samper, R., Schwarz, R., Nishida, J., & Nyaronga, D. (2008). *Understanding and promoting resilience in military families.* West Lafayette, IN: Military Family Research Institute.

MacDermid, S. M., Weiss, H. M., Green, S. G., & Schwarz, R. L. (2007). *Military members on the move.* West Lafayette, IN: Military Family Research Institute.

Maddi, S. R., Kahn, S., & Maddi, K. L. (1998). The effectiveness of hardiness training. *Consulting Psychology Journal, 50*, 78–86.

Maguen, S. & Litz, B. (2012). Moral injury in veterans of war. *PTSD Research Quarterly, 23*, 1–6. White River Junction, VT: National Center for Post-Traumatic Stress Disorder. Retrieved from http://www.ncptsd.va.gov.

Maguen, S., Vogt, D. S., King, L. A., King, D. W., & Litz, B. T. (2006). Posttraumatic growth among Gulf War I veterans: The predictive role of deployment-related experiences and background characteristics. *Journal of Loss and Trauma, 11*, 373–388.

Makin-Byrd, K., Gifford, E., McCutcheon, S., & Glynn, S. (2011). Family and couples treatment for newly returning veterans. *Professional Psychology: Research and Practice, 42*, 47–55.

Malia, J. A. (2006). Basic concepts and models of family stress. *Stress, Trauma, and Crisis, 9*, 141–160.

Managed Health Network Government Services (2010a). *MFLC Joint Family Support Assistance Program (JFSAP).* Retrieved from https://www.mhngs.com/app/programsandservices/jfsap.content.

Managed Health Network Government Services (2010b). *Military & Family Life Consultant (MFLC) program.* Retrieved from https://www.mhngs.com/app/programsandservices/mflc_program.content.

Mancini, J. A., Bowen, G. L., & Martin, J. A. (2005). Community social organization: A conceptual linchpin in examining families in the context of communities. *Family Relations, 54*, 570–582.

Marshall, T. C., Jr. (2011, July 22). Obama commends military for handling of law's repeal. *American Forces Press Service.* Retrieved from the Department of Defense website: http://www.defense.gov/news/newsarticle.aspx?id=64781.

Martin, J. A., & McClure, P. (2000). Today's active duty military family: The evolving challenges on military family life. In J. A. Martin, L. N. Rosen, & L. R. Sparacino (Eds.), *The military family: A practice guide for human service providers* (pp. 3–23). Westport, CT: Praeger Security International.

Martin, J. A., Rosen, L. N., & Sparacino, L. R. (2000). *The military family: A practice guide for human service providers.* Westport, CT: Praeger Security International.

Martinez, G. M., Chandra, A., Abma, J. C., Jones, J., & Mosher, W. D. (2002). Fertility, contraception, and fatherhood: Data on men and women from Cycle 6 (2002) of the National Survey of Family Growth. National Center for Health Statistics. *Vital Health Stat 23*(26). Retrieved from http://www.cdc.gov/nchs/data/series/sr_23/sr23_026.pdf.

Mathews, T. J., & Hamilton, B. E. (2009). *Delayed childbearing: More women are having their first child later in life. NCHS Data Brief, 21.* National Center for Health Statistics. Retrieved from the Centers for Disease Control and Prevention website: http://www.cdc.gov/nchs/data/databriefs/db21.pdf.

Maury, R. & Stone, B. (2014). *Military spouse employment report.* Retrieved from Institute for Veterans and Military Families website http://vets.syr.edu/?s=military+spouse+employment+report.

McCarroll, J. E., Fan, Z., & Bell, N. S. (2009). Alcohol use in non-mutual and mutual domestic violence in the U.S. Army: 1998–2004. *Violence and Victims, 24*, 364–379.

McCarroll, J. E., Fan, Z., Newby, J. H., & Ursano, R. J. (2008). Trends in U.S. Army child maltreatment reports: 1990–2004. *Child Abuse Review, 17*, 108–118.

McCarroll, J. E., Ursano, R. J., Liu, X., Thayer, L. E., Newby, J. H., Norwood, A. E., & Fullerton, C. S. (2000). Deployment and the probability of spousal aggression by U.S. army soldiers. *Military Medicine, 165*, 41–44.

McCarroll, J. E., Ursano, R. J., Newby, J. H., Liu, X., Fullerton, C. S., Norwood, A. E., & Osuch, E. A. (2003). Domestic violence and deployment in U.S. Army soldiers. *Journal of Nervous and Mental Disease, 191,* 3–9.

McCleland, K. C., Sutton, G. W., & Schumm, W. R. (2005). Marital satisfaction before and after deployments associated with the Global War on Terror. *Psychological Reports, 103,* 836–844.

McCubbin, H. I., & Patterson, J. M. (1983a). The family stress process: The Double ABCx model of adjustment and adaptation. In H. L. McCubbin, M. B. Sussman, & J. M. Patterson (Eds.), *Advances and development in family stress theory and research* (pp. 7–37). New York, NY: Haworth.

McCubbin, H. I., & Patterson, J. M. (1983b). Family transitions: Adaptation to stress. In H.I. McCubbin & C.R. Figley (Eds.), *Stress and the family: Coping with normative transitions* (Vol. 1, pp. 5–25). New York, NY: Brunner/Mazel.

McCubbin, H. I., Joy, C. B., Cauble, A. E., Comeau, J. K., Patterson, J. M., & Needle, R. H. (1980). Family stress and coping: A decade review. *Marriage and Family, 42,* 125–141.

McFarland, B. H., Kaplan, M. S., & Huguet, N. (2010). Self-inflicted deaths among women with U.S. military service: A hidden epidemic? *Psychiatric Services, 61,* 1177.

McFarland, M. (2005). Military cultural education. *Military Review, 85(2),* 62–69.

McFarlane, A. C. (2009). Military deployment: The impact on children and family adjustment and the need for care. *Current Opinion in Psychiatry, 22,* 369–373.

McLagan, M. & Sommers, D. (2008). Lioness (M. McLagan & D. Sommers, Directors). In S. J. Fifer (Executive Producer), *Independent Lens.* San Francisco: ITVS.

McMichael, W. H. (2008). *DoD approves more accompanied tours in Korea.* Retrieved from http://www .armytimes.com/news/2008/12/military_korea_assignments_121008w/.

McNally, R. J. (1999). EMDR and mesmerism: A comparative historical analysis. *Journal of Anxiety Disorders, 13,* 225–236.

McNulty, P. A. F. (2008). Reunification: The silent war of families and returning troops. *Federal Practitioner, 25(10),* 15–20.

Meichenbaum, D. (1996). Stress inoculation training for coping with stressors. *The Clinical Psychologist, 49,* 4–7.

Mental Health Advisory Team V. (2008). *Mental Health Advisory Team (MHAT) V Report.* U.S. Army Surgeon General. U.S. Army Medical Department.

Mental Health Advisory Team VI. (2009). *Operation Iraqi Freedom 07-09.* Retrieved from the U.S. Army Medical Department website: http://armymedicine.mil/Documents/MHAT-VI-OIF_ EXSUM.pdf.

Mental Health America. (2010a). *Military Mental Health.* Retrieved from the Mental Health America website: http://www.mentalhealthamerica.net/military-mental-health.

Mental Health America. (2010b). *Welcome to Mental Health America.* Retrieved from http://www.men-talhealthamerica.net.

Miles, D. (2007, July 13). *Severely wounded troops find meaningful ways to continue serving.* Retrieved November 30, 2011 from the Department of Defense website: http://www.defense.gov/news/ newsarticle.aspx?id=46714.

Military Advantage. (2014). *Military child care.* Retrieved November 20, 2014 from the Military.com website: http://www.military.com/benefits/resources/family-support/child-care.

Military Compensation and Retirement Modernization Commission. (2014). *About.* Retrieved from http://www.mcrmc.gov/index.php/about.

Military Interstate Children's Compact Commission (2011, November 8). MIC3: Month of the military family letter. Retrieved November 21, 2011 from http://www.mic3.net/documents/2014MonthofM ilitaryChildletter-Berg.pdf.

Military Interstate Children's Compact Commission. (2014). New York makes 50! [Press Release]. Retrieved from http://mic3.net/.

Military OneSource. (2014). *Spouse education and career opportunities fact sheet.* Retrieved from http:// www.militaryonesource.mil/seco.

Monin, J. K., Levy, B. R., & Pietrzak, R. H. (2014). From serving in the military to serving loved ones: Unique experiences of older veteran caregivers. *American Journal for Geriatric Psychiatry, 22,* 570–579.

Monson, C. M., & Fredman, S. J. (2012). *Cognitive-behavioral conjoint therapy for PTSD: Harnessing the healing power of relationships.* New York, NY: Guilford.

Monson, C. M., Fredman, S. J., & Adair, K. C. (2008). Cognitive-behavioral conjoint therapy for post-traumatic stress disorder: Application to Operation Enduring and Iraqi Freedom veterans. *Journal of Clinical Psychology, 64,* 958–971.

Montgomery, N. (2014, February 24). Will abortion law change help female troops? *Stars and Stripes.* Retrieved from http://www.stripes.com/news/will-abortion-law-change-help-female-troops-1.209513.

Moore, B. A., & Reger, G. M. (2007). Historical and contemporary perspectives of combat stress and the Army combat stress control team. In. C. R. Figley & W. P. Nash (Eds.), *Combat stress injury: Theory, research, and management* (pp. 161–181). New York, NY: Routledge.

Moore, E. C. (2012). A mentor in combat veterans court: Observations and challenges. *Future Trends in State Courts, 2012,* 38–43.

Morris, A. S., & Age, T. R. (2009). Adjustment among youth in military families: The protective roles of effortful control and maternal social support. *Journal of Applied Developmental Psychology, 30,* 695–707.

Morse, J. (2006). *The new emotional cycles of deployment.* Retrieved from the Force Health Protection & Readiness Policy & Programs website: http://deploymenthealthlibrary.fhp.osd.mil.

Mrazek, P. J., & Haggerty, R. J. (Eds.). (1994). *Reducing risks for mental disorders: Frontiers for preventive intervention research.* Washington, DC: National Academy of Sciences.

Mueser, K. T., & Glynn, S. M. (1999). *Behavioral family therapy for psychiatric disorders, 2nd ed.* Oakland, CA: New Harbinger.

Murphy, R. A., & Fairbank, J. A. (2013). Implementation and dissemination of military informed and evidence-based interventions for community dwelling military families. *Clinical Child and Family Psychology Review, 16,* 348–364.

Naimi, T. S., Brewer, R. D., Mokdad, A., Denny, C., Serdula, M. K., & Marks, J. S. (2003). Binge drinking among U.S. adults. *Journal of the American Medical Association, 289,* 70–75.

Nash, W. P., Westphal, R. J., Watson, P. J., & Litz, B. T. (2011). Combat and operational stress first aid: Responder training manual. Washington, DC: U.S. Navy, Bureau of Medicine and Surgery.

National Center for Veterans Analysis and Statistics. (2014). *Profile of veterans: 2012: Data from the American Community Survey.* Retrieved from http://www.va.gov/vetdata/docs/SpecialReports/Profile_of_Veterans_2012.pdf.

National Center for Veterans Analysis and Statistics, Department of Veterans Affairs. (2011). *America's women veterans: Military service history and VA benefit utilization statistics.* Retrieved from http://va.gov/vetdata/docs/SpecialReports/Final_Womens_Report_3_2_12_v_7.pdf.

National Center for Veterans Analysis and Statistics, Department of Veterans Affairs. (2013). *Profile of Veterans: 2011 Data from the American Community Survey.* Washington, DC: Author.

National Child Traumatic Stress Network. (2008a). *Traumatic grief in military children: Information for families.* Los Angeles, CA & Durham, NC: National Center for Child Traumatic Stress. Retrieved from http://www.nctsn.org/nccts/nav.do?pid=ctr_top_military.

National Child Traumatic Stress Network. (2008b). *Traumatic grief in military children: Information for medical providers.* Los Angeles, CA & Durham, NC: National Center for Child Traumatic Stress. Retrieved from http://www.nctsn.org/nccts/nav.do?pid=ctr_top_military.

National Child Traumatic Stress Network, Secondary Traumatic Stress Committee. (2011). *Secondary traumatic stress: A fact sheet for child-serving professionals.* Los Angeles, CA, and Durham, NC: National Center for Child Traumatic Stress. Retrieved from http://www.nctsn.org/resources/topics/secondary-traumatic-stress.

National Conference of State Legislatures. (2014). Retrieved November 20, 2014 from http://www.ncsl.org/research/human-services/same-sex-marriage-laws.aspx

National Defense Authorization Act for Fiscal Year 2010. Pub. L. No. 111-84, 123 Stat. 2190 (2009).

National Defense Authorization Act of 2008, Pub. L. No. 110-181, 532 (2008).

National Guard. (2009) *About the National Guard.* Retrieved from http://www.nationalguard.com.

National Healthy Marriage Resource Center. (2010). *Marriage and divorce in the National Guard and Reserves: A fact sheet.* Retrieved from http://www.healthymarriageinfo.org/resource-detail/index. aspx?rid=3132

National Highway Traffic Safety Association. (2010). *2009 Traffic safety facts: A compilation of motor vehicle crash data from the fatality reporting system and the general estimates system.* Retrieved from http://www-nrd.nhtsa.dot.gov/cats/listpublications.aspx?Id=E&ShowBy=DocType.

National Hospice and Palliative Care Organization. (2012). *NHPCO facts and figures: Hospice care in America.* Alexandria, VA: NHPCO.

National Military Family Association. (2006). *Report on the cycles of deployment: An analysis of survey responses from April–September, 2005.* Alexandria, VA: Author. Retrieved from http://www.militaryfamily.org/assets/pdf/NMFACyclesofDeployment9.pdf.

National Military Family Association. (2007). *Education & the military spouse: The long road to success*. Alexandria, VA: Author. Retrieved from http://www.militaryfamily.org/assets/pdf/Spouse_Education_Report_FINAL.pdf.

National Military Family Association. (2010). *We serve, too: A toolkit about military teens*. Retrieved from http://www.militaryfamily.org/publications/teen-toolkit/.

National Security Council. (n.d.). Retrieved from the White House website: http://www.whitehouse.gov/administration/eop/nsc.

Naval Inspector General. (n.d.). *Administrative separation*. Retrieved from http://www.public.navy.mil/bupers-npc/career/reservepersonnelmgmt/enlisted/Pages/ADSEP.aspx.

Navy Personnel Command. (2010). *Navy safe harbor foundation*. Retrieved from http://www.safeharborfoundation.org.

Navy Personnel Command. (n.d.). *Deployment support program: Desk guide*. Retrieved from http://www.public.navy.mil/surfor/cds9/Documents/CDS9_Deployment_Support_Program_Desk_Guide.pdf.

Navy-Marine Corps Relief Society. (2010). *Navy-Marine Corps Relief Society*. Retrieved November 30, 2011 from http://www.nmcrs.org

Negrusa, B., & Negrusa, S. (2012). *Home front: Post-deployment mental health and divorces*. Working Paper: RAND Center for Military Health Policy Research: Arlington, VA.

Newby, J. H., McCarroll, J. E., Ursano, R. J., Fan, Z., Shigemura, J., & Tucker-Harris, Y. (2005). Positive and negative consequences of a military deployment. *Military Medicine, 170,* 815–819.

Newby, J. H., Ursano, R. J., McCarroll, J. E., Liu, X., Fullerton, C. S., & Norwood, A. E. (2005). Post deployment domestic violence by U.S. Army soldiers. *Military Medicine, 170,* 643–647.

O'Farrell, T. J., & Fals-Steward, W. (2006). *Behavioral couples therapy for alcoholism and drug abuse*. New York, NY: Guilford.

Obama, M., & Biden, J. (2010, September 3). Michelle Obama, Jill Biden: The troops need us. *USA Today*. Retrieved from http://www.usatoday.com/news/opinion/forum/2010-09-03-column03_ST3_N.htm.

Ochberg, F. M. (n.d.). *When helping hurts*. Retrieved from the Gift From Within website: http://www.giftfromwithin.org/html/helping.html.

Office of Applied Studies. (2005, November 10). *Alcohol use and alcohol-related risk behaviors among veterans*. Retrieved August 17, 2010 from the Substance Abuse and Mental Health Services Administration website: http://www.oas.samhsa.gov/2k5/vetsAlc/vetsAlc.htm#link_group_1.

Office of the Assistant Secretary of Defense for Reserve Affairs. (2005). *Reserve component categories of the reserve components of the Armed Forces*. Washington, DC: Author. Retrieved from http://ra.defense.gov/documents/publications/RC101%20Handbook-updated%2020%20Sep%2005.pdf.

Office of the Assistant Secretary of Defense for Reserve Affairs. (2007). *Commander's family readiness toolkit*. Washington, DC: Author.

Office of the Assistant Secretary of Defense for Reserve Affairs. (2010a). *Family readiness*. Retrieved December 7, 2011 from Office of the Assistant Secretary of Defense—Reserve Affairs website: http://ra.defense.gov/programs/fepp/family.html.

Office of the Assistant Secretary of Defense for Reserve Affairs. (2010b). *Guard and reserve family readiness programs toolkit*. Retrieved August 27, 2010 from http://ra.defense.gov/documents/toolkit/Commanders%20Toolkit%200328.pdf.

Office of the Assistant Secretary of Defense for Reserve Affairs. (2010c). *Office of the Assistant Secretary of Defense—Reserve Affairs*. Retrieved August 24, 2010 from http://ra.defense.gov/.

Office of the Deputy Assistant Secretary of Defense, Military Community and Family Policy. (2015). *Military Family life project: Active duty spouse study*. Washington, DC: Defense Manpower Data Center. Retrieved May 20, 2015 from http://www.militaryonesource.mil/MilFamSterdam

Office of the Deputy Assistant Secretary of Defense, Military Community and Family Policy. (2014). *2013 demographics: Profile of the military community*. Washington, DC: Author. Retrieved from http://www.militaryonesource.mil/footer?content_id=279104.

Office of the Deputy Under Secretary of Defense, Military Community and Family Policy. (2013). *2012 Demographics: Profile of the military community*. Washington, DC: Author. Retrieved from http://www.militaryonesource.mil/12038/MOS/Reports/2012_Demographics_Report.pdf.

Office of the Law Revision Counsel. (2008). *Uniform Code of Military Justice*. United States Code. Washington, DC: Author.

Office of the President of the United States. (2011). *Strengthening our military families*. Washington, DC: The White House.

Office of the Secretary of Defense Sexual Assault Prevention and Response Office. (2010). *Department of Defense fiscal year 2009 annual report on sexual assault in the military.* Arlington, VA: United States Department of Defense.

Office of the Under Secretary of Defense. (2014). United States Department of Defense fiscal year 2015 budget request: Overview. Retrieved from http://comptroller.defense.gov/budgetmaterials/budget2015.aspx#summary.

Office of the Under Secretary of Defense, Personnel and Readiness. (n.d.). Population representation in the military services: Fiscal year 2011 report. Retrieved from http://prhome.defense.gov/RFM/MPP/AP/POPREP

Office of the Under Secretary of Defense, Personnel and Readiness. (n.d.). *Population representation in the military services: Fiscal year 2009 report.* Retrieved from http://prhome.defense.gov/MPP/ACCESSION%20POLICY/poprep.aspx.

Office of the Under Secretary of Defense, Personnel and Readiness. (2009a). *Military Morale, Welfare, and Recreation (MWR) programs* (DoD Instruction 1015.10). Washington, DC: Author.

Office of the Under Secretary of Defense, Personnel and Readiness. (2009b). *Monthly basic pay table for 2009.* Retrieved from http://militarypay.defense.gov/pay/bp/01_activeduty.html.

Office of Warrior Care Policy. (2014). *2014 Wounded, ill, and injured compensation and benefits handbook.* Alexandria, VA: OWCP. Retrieved from http://warriorcare.dodlive.mil/files/2011/11/Compensation-and-Benefits-Handbook-May-2014.pdf.

Okie, S. (2005). Traumatic brain injury in the war zone. *New England Journal of Medicine, 352,* 2043–2047.

One Hundred Twelfth Congress of the United States of America. (2013). *National Defense Authorization Act for Fiscal Year 2013.* Washington, DC: U.S. Government Printing Office. Retrieved from http://www.treasury.gov/resource-center/sanctions/Programs/Documents/pl112_239.pdf.

Oram. (n.d.). *Operation: Military kids hero packs.* Retrieved from the 4_H Military Partnerships website: http://www.4-hmilitarypartnerships.org/DesktopDefault.aspx?tabid=130.

Orthner, D. K. (2002). *SAF IV survey report: Relocation adjustment among Army civilian spouses.* Prepared for the U.S. Army Community and Family Support Center. Chapel Hill, NC: University of North Carolina.

Orthner, D. K., & Rose, R. (2009). Work separation demands and spouse psychological well-being. *Family Relations, 58,* 392–403.

Oswald, R. F., & Sternberg, M. M. (2014). Lesbian, gay, and bisexual military families: Visible but legally marginalized. In S. MacDermid Wadsworth & D. S. Riggs (Eds.), *Military deployment and its consequences for families* (pp.133–147). New York, NY: Springer.

Owens, B. D., Kragh, J. F., Jr., Wenke, J. C., Macaitis, J., Wade, C. E., & Holcome, J. B., (2008). Combat wounds in Operation Iraqi Freedom and Operation Enduring Freedom. *Journal of Trauma, 64,* 295–299.

Ozbay, F., Johnson, D. C., Dimoulas, E., Morgan III, C. A., Charney, D. S., & Southwick, S. (2007). Social support and resilience to stress: From neurobiology to clinical practice. *Psychiatry, 4,* 35–40.

Panetta, L. & Dempsey, M. (2013, January 24). *Elimination of the 1994 Direct Ground Combat Definition and Assignment Rule.* Memorandum. Retrieved from http://www.defense.gov/news/WISRJointMemo.pdf.

Parcell, E. S., & Maguire, K. C. (2014). Turning points and trajectories in military deployment. *Journal of Family Communication, 14,* 129–148.

Park, N. (2011). Military children and families: Strengths and challenges during peace and war. *American Psychologist, 66,* 65–72.

Parker, M. W., Call, V. R. A., Dunkle, R., & Vaitkus, M. (2002). "Out of Sight" but not "Out of Mind": Parent contact and worry among senior ranking male officers in the military who live long distances from parents. *Military Psychology, 14,* 257–277.

Parrish, K. (2010, December 22). Cheers, applause accompany "Don't Ask" repeal signing. *The American Forces Press Service.* Retrieved from the Department of Defense website: http://www.defense.gov/news/newsarticle.aspx?id=62216.

Parsons, T., & Bales, R. F. (1956). *Family socialization and interaction process.* Abingdon, UK: Routledge.

Pearson, M. (2014, May 30). *The VA's troubled history.* Retrieved May 30, 2014 from http://www.cnn.com/2014/05/23/politics/va-scandals-timeline/index.html?iid=article_sidebar.

Pellerin, C. (2011, January 7). Gates outlines "Don't Ask" repeal process. *American Forces Press Service.* Retrieved from the Department of Defense website: http://www.defense.gov/news/newsarticle.aspx?id=62370.

Pemberton, J. R., Cramer, T. L., Borrego Jr., J., & Owen, R. R. (2013). Kids at the VA? A call for evidence-based parenting interventions for returning veterans. *Psychological Services, 10*, 194–202.

Perconte, S. T., Wilson, A. T., Pontius, E. B., Deitrick, A. L., & Spiro, K. J. (1993). Psychological and war stress symptoms among deployed and non-deployed reservists following the Persian Gulf War. *Military Medicine, 158*, 516–521.

Pereira, A., (2002). Combat stress and the diagnosis of PTSD in women and men veterans. *Military Medicine, 167*, 23–27.

Perlick, D. A., Straits-Tröster, K., Dyck, D. G., Norell, D. M., Strauss, J. L., Henderson, C., . . . Cristian, A. (2011). Multifamily group treatment for veterans with traumatic brain injury. *Professional Psychology: Research and Practice, 42*, 70–78.

Perri, T. J. (2008). The economics of U.S. civil war conscription. *American Law and Economics Review, 10*, 424–454.

Peterson, C., Park, N., & Castro, C. A. (2011). Assessment for the U.S. Army Comprehensive Soldier Fitness Program: The global assessment tool. *American Psychologist, 66*, 10–18.

Pflanz, S. & Sonnek, S. (2002). Work stress in the military: Prevalence, causes, and relationship to emotional health. *Military Medicine, 162*, 643–648.

Pierce, P. F. (2010). Work-family conflict among deployed military women. *Proceedings from 2010 International Research Symposium of Military Families.* Indianapolis, IN: The University of Michigan Institute for Social Research.

Pierce, P. F. (2010, April). Work-family conflict among deployed military women. Invited presentation at the 2010 *International Research Symposium of the Military Family.* Research Institute at Purdue, Indianapolis, IN.

Pietrzak, R. H., Johnson, D. C., Goldstein, M. B., Malley, J. C., Rivers, A. J., Morgan, C. A., & Southwick, S. M. (2009). Psychological resilience and postdeployment social support protect against traumatic stress and depressive symptoms in soldiers returning from Operations Enduring Freedom and Iraqi Freedom. *Depression and Anxiety, 26*, 745–751.

Pietrzak, R. H., Johnson, D. C., Goldstein, M. B., Malley, J. C., Rivers, A. J., Morgan, C. A., & Southwick, S. M. (2010). Psychosocial buffers of traumatic stress, depressive symptoms, and psychosocial difficulties in veterans of Operations Iraqi Freedom and Enduring Freedom: The role of resilience, unit support, and postdeployment social support. *Journal of Affective Disorders, 120*, 188–192.

Pincus, S. H., House, R., Christenson, J., & Adler, L. E. (2001). The emotional cycle of deployment: A military family perspective. *Army Medical Department Journal, 4/5/6*, 15–23.

Pollock, D. C., & Van Reken, R. E. (2001). *Third culture kids: The experience of growing up among worlds.* Yarmouth, ME: Intercultural Press.

Polusny, N. A., Erbes, C. R., Murdoch, M., Arbisi, P. A., Thuras, P., & Rath, M. B. (2011). Prospective risk factors for new-onset post-traumatic stress disorder in National Guard soldiers deployed to Iraq. *Psychological Medicine, 41*, 687–698.

Pomper, K., Blank, H., Duff Campbell, N., & Schulman, K. (2005). *Be all that we can be: Lessons from the military for improving our nation's child care system.* Washington, DC: National Women's Law Center. Retrieved from http://www.nwlc.org/resource/be-all-we-can-be-lessons-military-improving-our-nations-child-care-system-2004-follow.

Prigerson, H. G., & Maciejewski, P. K. (2005). A call for sound empirical testing and evaluation of criteria for complicated grief proposed for DSM-V. *Omega, 52*, 9–19.

Prigerson, H. G., Shear, M. K., Jacobs, S. C., Maciejewski, P. K., Davidson, J. R., Rosenheck, R., . . . Zisook, S. (1999). Consensus criteria for traumatic grief. A preliminary empirical test. *British Journal of Psychiatry, 174*, 67–73.

Radey, M., & Figley, C. R. (2007). The socialpsychology of compassion. *Clinical Social Work, 35*, 207–214.

Radford, A. W. (2009). *Military service members and veterans in higher education: What the new GI Bill may mean for postsecondary institutions.* Washington, DC: American Council on Education. Retrieved from http://www.acenet.edu/news-room/Pages/Military-Service-Members-and-Veterans-in-Higher-Education-What-the-New-GI-Bill-May-Mean-for-Postsecondary-Institutions-.aspx.

Ramchand, R., Tanielian, T., Fisher, M. P., Vaughan, C. A., Trail, T. E., Epley, C., . . . Ghosh-Dastidar, B. (2014). *Hidden heroes: America's military caregivers.* Santa Monica, CA: RAND Corporation. Retrieved from http://www.rand.org/content/dam/rand/pubs/research_reports/RR400/RR499/RAND_RR499.pdf.

Ramsberger, P. F., LeGree, P. & Mills, L. (2003). Evaluation of the Buddy Team Assignment Program. United *States Army Research Institute for the Behavioral and Social Sciences.* Alexandria, VA.

Rauch, S. A. M., & Foa, E. B. (n.d.). *Stress Inoculation Training (SIT) for Posttraumatic Stress Disorder (PTSD).* Retrieved from http://www.therapyadvisor.com

Reivich, K. J., Seligman, M. E. P., & McBride, S. (2011). Master resilience training in the U.S. Army. *American Psychologist, 66,* 25–34.

Renshaw, K. D., Rodrigues, C. S., & Jones, D. H. (2008). Psychological symptoms and marital satisfaction in spouses of Operation Iraqi Freedom veterans: Relationships with spouses' perceptions of veterans' experiences and symptoms. *Journal of Family Psychology, 22,* 586–594.

Rentz, E. E., Marshall, S. W., Loomis, D., Casteel, C., Martin, S. L., & Gibbs, D. A. (2007). Effect of deployment on the occurrence of child maltreatment in military and nonmilitary families. *American Journal of Epidemiology, 165,* 1199–1206.

Riddle, J. R., Smith, T. C., Smith, B., Corbeil, T. E., Engel, C. C., Wells, T. S., . . . Blazer, D. for the Millennium Cohort Study Team (2007). Millennium Cohort: The 2001–2003 baseline prevalence of mental disorders in the U.S. military. *Journal of Clinical Epidemiology, 60,* 192–201.

Robinson, M. E., Teyhen, D. S., Wu, S. S., Dugan, J. L., Wright, A. C., Childs, J. D., . . . George, S. Z. (2009). Mental health symptoms in combat medic training: A longitudinal examination. *Military medicine, 174,* 572–577.

Rock, M., & Stotter, P. L. (2012). *SERVICE: When women come marching home* [Motion picture]. United States: Women Make Movies. (Available at http://www.wmm.com).

Roff, P. (2009, May 28). *Congress must help military vote [web log message].* U.S. News and World Report. Retrieved from http://www.usnews.com/blogs/peter-roff/2009/05/28/congress-must-help-military-vote.html.

Rosen, A., Walter, G., Casey, D., & Hocking, B. (2000). Combating psychiatric stigma: An overview of contemporary initiatives. *Australasian Psychiatry, 8,* 19–26.

Rosen, L. N., Durand, D. B., & Martin, J. A. (2000). Wartime stress and family adaptation. In J. A. Martin, L. N. Rosen, & L. R. Sparacino (Eds.), *The military family: A practice guide for human service providers* (pp. 123–138). Westport, CT: Praeger Security International.

Rowe, E. L., Gradus, J. L., Pineles, S. L., Batten, S. V., & Davison, E. H. (2009). Military sexual trauma in treatment-seeking women veterans. *Military Psychology, 21,* 387–395.

Ruscio, A. M., Weathers, F. W., King, L. A., & King, D. W. (2002). Male war-zone veterans' perceived relationships with their children: The importance of emotional numbing. *Journal of Traumatic Stress, 15,* 351–357.

Russell, R. T. (2009). Veterans treatment courts developing throughout the nation. *Future Trends in State Courts, 2009,* 130–133.

Saltzman, W. (2010). *FOCUS project: Program overview and outcomes.* Presented at the Navy and Marine Corps Combat & Operational Stress Control Conference 2010, San Diego, CA.

Saltzman, W., Lester, P., Beardslee, W., & Pynoos, R. (2008). *FOCUS project for military families: Training manual.* Retrieved from the Health Affairs website: http://content.healthaffairs.org/content/24/2/499 .full.html.

Sampson, R. (1995). Unemployment and imbalanced sex ratios: Race-specific consequences for family structure and crime. In M. B. Tucker & C. Mitchell-Kernan (Eds.), *The decline in marriage among African Americans: Causes, consequences, and policy implications* (pp. 229–254). Thousand Oaks, CA: Sage.

Sanchez, R. P., Bray, R. M., Vincus, A. A., & Bann, C. M. (2004). Active duty and reserve/guard personnel of U.S. military. *Military Psychology, 16,* 19–35.

Sandweiss, D. A., Slymen, D. J., LeardMann, C. A., Smith, B., White, M. R., Boyko, E. J., . . . Smith, T. C. for the Millennium Cohort Study Team (2011). The effects of preinjury psychiatric status and injury severity on postdeployment posttraumatic stress disorder. *Archives of General Psychiatry, 68,* 496–504 .

Sayer, N. A., Noorbaloochi, S., Frazier, P., Carlson, K. F., Gravely, A., & Murdoch, M. (2010). Reintegration problems and treatment preferences among recent veterans: New directions for trauma research. *Psychiatric Services, 61,* 589–597.

Sayers, S. L., Farrow, V. A., Ross, J., & Oslin, D. W. (2009). Family problems among recently returned military veterans referred for a mental health problem. *Journal of Clinical Psychiatry, 70,* 163–170.

Scott, D. L. (2010). War-related deaths in the family. In N. B. Webb (Ed.), *Helping bereaved children: A handbook for practitioners* (3rd ed.) (pp. 147–164). New York, NY: Guildford Press.

Seelig, A. D., Jacobson, I. J., Smith, B., Hooper, T. I., Boyko, E. J., Gackstetter, G. D., . . . Smith, T. C. for the Millennium Cohort Study Team (2010) Sleep patterns before, during, and after deployment to Iraq and Afghanistan. *Sleep, 33,* 1615–1622.

Segal, D. R., & Segal, M. W. (2004). America's military population. *Population Bulletin,* 59(4). Washington, DC: Population Reference Bureau.

Segal, J. (1973). Therapeutic considerations in planning the return of American POWs to Continental United States. *Military Medicine, 138(2),* 73–77.

Segal, M. W. (1986). The military and the family as greedy institutions. *Armed Forces & Society, 13,* 9–38.

Selective Service System. (2009). *Who must register.* Retrieved from http://www.sss.gov/FSwho.htm.

Serafino, N. M. (2004). *Peacekeeping and related stability operations: Issues of U.S. military involvement.* Washington, DC: Congressional Research Service, Library of Congress.

Service Women's Action Network. (2012). *Homeless women veterans: The facts.* New York: Service Women's Action Network. Retrieved from http://servicewomen.org/wp-content/uploads/2012/10/Final-HWV-Fact-Sheet-10.4.12.pdf.

Service Women's Action Network. (n.d.). *About.* Retrieved from http://servicewomen.org/#homehome.

Servicemembers Opportunity Colleges. (n.d.). *Military bill of rights.* Retrieved November 30, 2011 from http://www.soc.aascu.org/socconsortium/PublicationsSOC.html.

Servicemembers Opportunity Colleges. (n.d.). *SOC consortium guide 2009–2011* (Vol. 1). Washington, DC: Author. Retrieved from http://www.soc.aascu.org/socconsortium/PublicationsSOC.html.

Shear, M. K., & Mulhare, E. (2008). Complicated grief. *Psychiatric Annals, 38,* 662–670.

Sheppard, S. C., Malatras, J. W., & Israel, A. C. (2010). The impact of deployment on U.S. military families. *American Psychologist, 65,* 599–609.

Shnaider, P., Pukay-Martin, N. D., Fredman, S. J., Macdonald, A., & Monson, C. M. (2014). Effects of cognitive–behavioral conjoint therapy for PTSD on partners' psychological functioning. *Journal of Traumatic Stress, 27,* 129–136.

Silver, S. M., Rogers, S., & Russell, M. (2008). Eye movement desensitization and reprocessing (EMDR) in the treatment of war veterans. *Journal of Clinical Psychology, 64,* 947–957.

Singer, P. W. (March–April 2005). Outsourcing war. *Foreign Affairs, 84,* 119–132.

Skelton, III, W. P. (2002). *American Ex-Prisoners of War.* Veterans Health Initiative: Department of Veterans Affairs, Employee Education System. Retrieved from http://www.publichealth.va.gov/docs/vhi/pow.pdf.

Smith B., Wong, C. A., Smith, T. C., Boyko, E. J., Gackstetter, G. D., & Ryan, M. A. K. for the Millennium Cohort Study Team (2009). Newly reported respiratory symptoms and conditions among military personnel deployed to Iraq and Afghanistan: A prospective population-based study. *American Journal of Epidemiology, 170,* 1433–1442.

Smith, B., Ryan, M. A. K., Wingard, D. L., Patterson, T. L., Slymen, D. J., & Macera, C. A. for the Millennium Cohort Study Team (2008). Cigarette smoking and military deployment: A prospective evaluation. *American Journal of Preventive Medicine, 35,* 539–546.

Smith, L. K., & Sarkar, M. (2008). *Making quality child care possible: Lessons learned from NACCRRA's military partnership.* Arlington, VA: National Association of Child Care Resources & Referral Agencies. Retrieved from http://www.naccrra.org/publications/naccrra-publications/publications/LesnsLrnd%20Rprt-m2.pdf.

Smith, S. D. (2006, August 31). *Military coordinates effort to help wounded troops return to work.* Retrieved November 30, 2011 from the Department of Defense website: http://www.defense.gov/News/NewsArticle.aspx?ID=660.

Smith, T. C., Jacobson, I. G., Smith, B., Hooper, T. I., & Ryan, M. A. (2007). Validation of occupation and prevalence of exposures in Millennium Cohort Study. *International Journal of Environmental Health Research, 17,* 271–284.

Smith, T. C., Wingard, D. L., Ryan, M. A. K., Kritz-Silverstein, D., Slymen, D. J., & Sallis, J. F. for the Millennium Cohort Study Team (2008). Prior assault and posttraumatic stress disorder after combat deployment. *Epidemiology, 19,* 505–512.

Smith, T. C., Wingard, D. L., Ryan, M. A., Kritz-Silverstein, D., Slymen, D. J., & Sallis, J. F. (2009). PTSD prevalence, associated exposures, and functional health outcomes in a large, population-based military cohort. *Public Health Reports, 124,* 90–102.

Solomon, Z., Zur-Noah, S., Horesh, D., Zerach, G., & Keinan, G. (2008). The contribution of stressful life events throughout the life cycle to combat-induced psychopathology. *Journal of Traumatic Stress, 21,* 318–325.

Stahre, M. A., Brewer, R. D., Fonseca, V. P., & Naimi, T. S. (2009). Binge drinking among active duty military personnel. *American Journal of Preventative Medicine, 36,* 208–217.

Stanley, S. M., Blumberg, S. L., & Markman, H. J. (1999). Helping couples fight for their marriages: The PREP approach. In R. Berger & M. Hannah (Eds.), *Handbook of preventive approaches in couple therapy* (pp. 279–303). New York, NY: Brunner/Mazel.

Steele, N. & Yoder, L. H. (2013). Military women's urinary patterns, practices, and complications in deployment settings. *Urologic Nursing, 33,* 61–71.

Steen, J. M., & Asaro, M. R. (2006). *Military widow: A survival guide.* Annapolis, MD: Naval Institute Press.

Stewart, D. (2009). Casualties of war: Compassion fatigue and health care providers. *Medsurg Nursing, 18,* 91–94.

Street, A., Stafford, J., Mahan, C., & Hendricks, A. (2008). Sexual harassment and assault experienced by reservists during military service: Prevalence and health correlates. *Journal of Rehabilitation Research & Development, 45,* 409–420.

Strengthening Our Military Families. (2011). Washington, DC: The White House. Retrieved from the Department of Defense website: http://www.defense.gov/home/features/2011/0111_initiative/Strengthening_our_Military_January_2011.pdf.

Suicide Risk Management & Surveillance Office. (2008). *Army Suicide Event Report (ASER): Calendar year 2007.* Tacoma, WA: Army Behavioral Health Technology Office.

Suls, J., Green, P., Rose, G., Loundsbury, P., & Gordon, E. (1997). Hiding worries from one's spouse: Associations between coping via protective buffering and distress in male post-myocardial infarction patients and their wives. *Journal of Behavioral Medicine, 20,* 333–349.

Sussman, N. (2006). In session with Dennis S. Charney, M. D.: Resilience to stress. *Primary Psychiatry, 13,* 39–41.

Tan, M. (2009, December 20). A million soldiers deployed since 9/11. *Army Times.* Retrieved May 20, 2010, from http://www.armytimes.com/news/2009/12/army_deployments_121809w/.

Tang, C. Y., & MacDermid Wadsworth, S. (2010). *Time and workplace flexibility.* New York, NY: Families and Work.

Tanielian, T., & Jaycox, L. H. (Eds.) (2008). *Invisible wounds of war: Psychological and cognitive injuries, their consequences, and services to assist recovery.* Santa Monica, CA: RAND Corporation.

Task Force Medical Afghanistan Public Affairs. (2013, April 4). *Army researches small device to reduce female UTIs.* Retrieved from the U.S. Army website: http://www.army.mil/article/100247/Army_researches_small_device_to_reduce_female_UTIs/.

Taylor, A. (2014, May 21). MAP: The U.S. military currently has troops in these African countries. *The Washington Post.* Retrieved July 20, 2014 from http://www.washingtonpost.com/blogs/worldviews/wp/2014/05/21/map-the-u-s-currently-has-troops-in-these-african-countries/.

Teachman, J. D., & Tedrow, L. (2008). Divorce, race and military service: More than equal pay and equal opportunity. *Journal of Marriage and Family, 70,* 1030–1044.

Tedeschi, R. G., & McNally, R. J. (2011). Can we facilitate positive posttraumatic growth in combat veterans? *American Psychologist, 66,* 19–24.

Tejada-Vera, B., & Sutton, P. D. (2010). Births, marriages, divorces, and deaths: Provisional data for 2009. *National Vital Statistics Reports* (Vol. 58, No. 25). Hyattsville, MD: National Center for Health Statistics.

The American Legion. (2010). *Heroes to hometowns.* Retrieved from The American Legion: http://www.legion.org/heroes.

The Associated Press. (2014, March 11). *Senate OKs bill to combat military sexual assault.* Retrieved from http://bigstory.ap.org/article/new-senate-bill-combat-military-sexual-assaults.

The Management of Concussion/mTBI Working Group. (2009). *VA/DoD clinical practice guideline for management of concussion/mild traumatic brain injury.* Retrieved from the Department of Veteran's Affairs website: http://www.healthquality.va.gov/.

The Management of Post-traumatic Stress Working Group. (2010). *The VA/DoD clinical practice guideline for the management of post-traumatic stress: VA/DoD evidence based practice.* Retrieved from the Department of Veteran's Affairs website: http://www.healthquality.va.gov/Post_Deployment_Health_PDH.asp.

The Military Health System. (2010a). *Health care in the MHS.* Retrieved November 30, 2011 from http://www.health.mil/About_MHS/Health_Care_in_the_MHS.aspx.

The Military Health System. (2010b). *The military health system: Frequently asked questions.* Retrieved November 30, 2011 from http://www.health.mil/About_MHS/FAQs.aspx.

Theiss, J. A., & Knobloch, L. K. (2014). Relationship turbulence and the post-deployment transition: Self, partner, and relationship focused turbulence. *Communication Research, 41,* 27–51.

Thomas, J. L., Adler, A. B., Wittels, P., Ennes, R., & Johannes, B. (2004). Comparing elite soldiers' perceptions of psychological and physical demands during military training. *Military Medicine, 169,* 526–530.

Thomas, J. L., Wilk, J. E., Riviere, L. A., McGurk, D., Castro, C. A., & Hoge, C. W. (2010). Prevalence of mental health problems and functional impairment among active component and National Guard soldiers 3 and 12 months following combat in Iraq. *Archives of General Psychiatry, 67,* 614–623.

Tick, E. (2005). *War and the soul*. Wheaton, IL: Quest Books.

Tollefson, T. T. (2008). Supporting spouses during a military deployment. *Family & Community Health: The Journal of Health Promotion & Maintenance, 31*, 281–286.

Trego, L.L. (2012). Prevention is the key to maintaining gynecologic health during deployment. *Journal of Obstetric, Gynecologic, & Neonatal Nursing, 41*, 283–292.

TRICARE Management Activity. (2010a). *National Guard and reserve members and their families.* Retrieved November 20, 2014 from http://www.tricare.mil/~/media/Files/TRICARE/Publications/FactSheets/Choices_NGR_FS.pdf.

TRICARE Management Activity. (2010b). *TRICARE behavioral health care services.* Retrieved November 30, 2011 from http://www.tricare.mil/~/media/Files/TRICARE/Publications/FactSheets/BHC_FS.pdf.

TRICARE Management Activity. (2010c). *TRICARE welcome.* Retrieved November 30, 2011 from http://www.tricare.mil/Welcome.aspx.

Tsai, J. (2013, February 24). Congress taking aim at military sexual assaults. *Stars and Stripes.* Retrieved from http://www.stripes.com/news/congress-taking-aim-at-military-sexual-assaults-1.209512.

Tyler, M. (2002). The military teenager in Europe: Perspectives for health care providers. In M. Ender (Ed.), *Military brats and other global nomads: Growing up in organization families* (pp. 25–34). Westport, CT: Praeger Security International.

U.S. Army Chaplain Corps. (2015). History of one Chaplain Corps. Retrieved May 22, 2015 from http://chapnet.chaplaincorpsnet/?page_id-658

U.S. Air Force. (2010). *Air Force wounded warrior.* Retrieved from http://www.woundedwarrior.af.mil/.

U.S. Air Force. (n.d.). *Air Force mission.* Retrieved Decemeber 7, 2011 from http://www.af.mil/main/welcome .asp.

U.S. Army. (2010). *Health promotion risk reduction suicide prevention report 2010.* Retrieved from http://usarmy.vo.llnwd.net/e1/HPRRSP/HP-RR-SPReport2010_v00.pdf.

U.S. Army. (n.d.). *The Army values.* Retrieved December 7, 2011 from http://www.army.mil/values/.

U.S. Army Garrison Baumholder. (2008). *Baumholder Directive 420-1: Military quarters handbook.* Baumholder, Germany: U.S. Army Garrison.

U.S. Army Human Resources Command. (2010). *Frequently asked questions.* Retrieved from https://www.hrc .army.mil/site/Active/TAGD/CMAOC/CMAOCPages/cmaocfaq.htm#8.

U.S. Army Installation Management Command. (2010). *The Army family covenant: Keeping the promise.* Retrieved from http://www.imcom.army.mil/hq/afc.

U.S. Army Medical Department. (2010a). *Army wounded warrior program.* Retrieved from http://www.aw2.army.mil/.

U.S. Army Medical Department. (2010b). *Resilience training.* Retrieved from https://www.resilience.army.mil.

U.S. Census Bureau. (2008). *Table FG6. One-parent unmarried family groups with own children under 18 by marital status of parents: 2008.* Retrieved from http://www.census.gov/population/www/socdemo/hh-fam/cps2008.html.

U.S. Census Bureau. (2009). *A compass for understanding and using American Community Survey data: What PUMS Data users need to know.* Washington, DC: U.S. Government Printing Office:. Retrieved from http://www.census.gov/acs/www/Downloads/handbooks/ACSPUMS.pdf

U.S. Census Bureau. (2011). *How do we know? A snapshot of our nation's veterans.* Retrieved from http://www.census.gov/how/infographics/veterans.html.

U.S. Census Bureau. (n.d.). *U.S. and world population clock.* Retrieved from https://www.census.gov/popclock/.

U.S. Census Bureau, Current Population Survey. (2010). *Annual Social and Economic Supplement. Table PINC-04.* Retrieved from http://www.census.gov/hhes/www/cpstables/032010/perinc/new04_001.htm.

U.S. Coast Guard. (2010). *Missions.* Retrieved from http://www.uscg.mil/top/missions.

U.S. Department of Agriculture & Department of Defense Partnership. (2010). *Extension and military collaboration.* Retrieved from http://militaryfamilies.extension.org/mission/.

U.S. Department of Agriculture. (2011). Extension. Retrieved November 23, 2011 from http://www.csrees.usda.gov/qlinks/extension.html.

U.S. Department of Labor. (2009). *Uniformed services employment and reemployment rights act of 1994: Fiscal year 2008 annual report to congress.* Washington, DC: Author. Retrieved from http://www.dol.gov/vets/programs/userra/main.htm.

U.S. Department of Labor. (2010, February). *Fact sheet #28A: The family and medical leave act: Military family leave entitlements.* Washington, DC: Author. http://www.dol.gov/whd/fmla/finalrule.htm.

U.S. Department of Labor, Bureau of Labor Statistics. (2011). *Employment situation of veterans: 2010.* Washington, DC: Author. Retrieved December 6, 2011 from http://www.bls.gov/news.release/vet.nr0.htm.

U.S. Department of Housing and Urban Development. (2014). *The 2013 Annual Homeless Assessment Report (AHAR) to Congress.* Retrieved from https://www.hudexchange.info/resources/documents/AHAR-2014-Part1.pdf.

U.S. Department of Veterans Affairs. (2014b). *DSM-5 criteria for PTSD.* Retrieved from http://www.ptsd.va.gov/professional/PTSD-overview/dsm5_criteria_ptsd.asp.

U.S. Department of Veterans Affairs. (2014c). FY 2014-2020 strategic plan. Retrieved from http://www.va.gov/op3/docs/StrategicPlanning/VA2014-2020strategicPlan.PDF.

U.S. Department of Veterans Affairs. (2013a). *America's wars.* Washington, DC: Author. Retrieved from http://www.va.gov/opa/publications/factsheets/fs_americas_wars.pdf.

U.S. Department of Veterans Affairs. (2007). *Women veterans: Past, present and future.* Washington, DC: Department of Veterans Affairs Office of Policy and Planning.

U.S. Department of Veterans Affairs. (2010). *Traumatic brain injury.* Washington, DC: Employee Education System. Retrieved from http://www.publichealth.va.gov/docs/vhi/traumatic-brain-injury-vhi.pdf.

U.S. Department of Veterans Affairs. (2011). *America's women veterans: Military service history and VA benefit utilization statistics.* Washington, DC: National Center for Veterans Analysis and Statistics. Retrieved from http://www.va.gov/vetdata/docs/SpecialReports/Final_Womens_Report_3_2_12_v_7.pdf.

U.S. Department of Veterans Affairs. (2012). *Disability compensation for personal assault or military sexual trauma (MST).* Retrieved from http://www.benefits.va.gov/BENEFITS/factsheets/service-connected/MST.pdf.

U.S. Department of Veterans Affairs. (2013b). *2013 Performance and accountability report.* Retrieved April 6, 2014 from http://www.va.gov/budget/docs/report/2013-VAPAR_FullWeb.pdf

U.S. Department of Veterans Affairs. (2013c). *Education and training.* Retrieved November 19, 2014 from http://www.benefits.va.gov/gibill/education_programs.asp

U.S. Department of Veterans Affairs. (2013d). *Military sexual trauma.* Washington, DC: U.S. Department of Veterans Affairs. Retrieved from http://www.womenshealth.va.gov/WOMENSHEALTH/trauma.asp

U.S. Department of Veterans Affairs. (2013e). *Veteran population projections: FY2010 to FY2040.* Washington, DC: Department of Veterans Affairs Office of the Actuary. Retrieved from http://www.va.gov/vetdata/docs/quickfacts/Population_slideshow.pdf.

U.S. Department of Veterans Affairs. (2014a). *About VA Mental Health: Special Programs – Military Sexual Trauma Services.* Retrieved from http://www.mentalhealth.va.gov/VAMentalHealthGroup.asp.

U.S. Department of Veterans Affairs. (2014d). *Mobile app: PTSD Coach.* National Center for PTSD. Retrieved from http://www.ptsd.va.gov/public/materials/apps/PTSDCoach.asp.

U.S. Department of Veterans Affairs. (2014e). *Profile of veterans: 2013.* Washington, DC: National Center for Veterans Analysis and Statistics. Retrieved from http://www.va.gov/vetdata/docs/SpecialReports/Profile_of_Veterans_2013.pdf.

U.S. Department of Veterans Affairs. (2014f). *Profile of women veterans: 2012.* Washington, DC: National Center for Veterans Analysis and Statistics. Retrieved from http://www.va.gov/vetdata/docs/SpecialReports/Women_Veteran_Profile_2012.pdf

U.S. Department of Veterans Affairs and Department of Defense. (2010). *VA/DoD Clinical Practice Guideline for the Management of Post-Traumatic Stress.* Washington, DC.

U.S. Department of Veterans Affairs, Office of the Actuary. (2011). *Veteran Population Projection Model.* Retrieved from http://www.va.gov/vetdata/docs/Quickfacts/Homepage_slideshow_09_30_13.pdf.

U.S. Department of Veterans Affairs, Women Veterans Task Force. (2012, May 1). *2012 report: Strategies for serving our women veterans.* [Draft for public comment.] Retrieved from http://www.va.gov/opa/publications/Draft_2012_Women-Veterans_StrategicPlan.pdf.

U.S. Department of Veterans Affairs. (2010a). *Federal benefits for veterans, dependents and survivors: 2010 edition.* Washington, DC: U.S. Government Printing Office. Retrieved from http://www.va.gov/opa/publications/benefits_book.asp.

U.S. Department of Veterans Affairs. (2010b). *Working with trauma survivors: What workers need to know.* Retrieved from http://www.ptsd.va.gov/professional/pages/working-with-trauma-survivors.asp.

U.S. Department of Veterans Affairs. (2011a). *FY 2012 budget submission: Summary volume, volume 1 of 4.* Washington, DC: Author Retrieved from http://www.va.gov/budget/products.asp.

U.S. Department of Veterans Affairs. (2011b). *Vet Centers*. Retrieved from http://www.vetcenter.va.gov/index.asp.

U.S. Department of Veterans Affairs. (n.d.). *VA history in brief*. Washington, DC: Author. Retrieved from http://www.va.gov/opa/publications/archives/docs/history_in_brief.pdf.

U.S. Government Accountability Office. (2011). *Homeless women veterans: Actions needed to ensure safe and appropriate housing*. GAO-12-182. Washington, DC: U.S. Government Accountability Office. Retrieved from http://www.gao.gov/assets/590/587334.pdf.

U.S. Marine Corps. (2010). *Wounded warrior regiment*. Retrieved from http://www.woundedwarrior-regiment.org.

U.S. Marine Corps. (n.d.-a). *Combat operational stress continuum for families*. Retrieved August 27, 2010 from http://www.usmc-mccs.org/cosc/coscContMatrixFamily.cfm?sid=ml&smid=6&ssmid=2.

U.S. Marine Corps. (n.d.-b). *The values that define a marine*. Retrieved December 7, 2011 from http://www.marines.com/main/index/making_marines/culture/traditions/core_values.

U.S. Navy. (n.d.-a). *The stress continuum*. Retrieved December 7, 2011 from http://www.nmcphc.med.navy.mil/downloads/stress/stress_continuum_trifold.pdf.

U.S. Navy. (n.d.-b). *The United States Navy: Honor, courage, commitment*. Retrieved December 7, 2011 from http://www.navy.mil/navydata/navy_legacy_hr.asp?id=193.

U.S. Office of Personnel Management. (n.d.). *Salaries and wages*. Retrieved from http://www.opm.gov/oca/11tables/index.asp.

United Nations (1995). *Mission readiness and stress management*. New York, NY: Office of Human Resources Management. Retrieved from http://www.un.org/Depts/OHRM/stress.htm.

United States v. Windsor, 570 U.S. (2013). Docket No. 12-307.

VA Office of Inspector General. (2012). *Homeless incidence and risk factors for becoming homeless in Veterans*. Retrieved November 2, 2014 from http://www.va.gov/oig/pubs/VAOIG-11-03428-173.pdf.

VA Office of Inspector General. (2014a). *Interim report: Review of patient wait times, scheduling practices, and alleged patient deaths at the Phoenix Health Care System*. Retrieved September 26, 2014 from http://www.va.gov/oig/pubs/VAOIG-14-02603-178.pdf.

VA Office of Inspector General. (2014b). *Veterans Health Administration: Review of alleged patient deaths, patient wait times, and scheduling practices at the Phoenix VA Health Care System*. Retrieved September 25, 2014 from http://www.va.gov/oig/apps/info/OversightReports.aspx?RPP=10&RS=2.

Vaishnavi, S., Rao, V., & Fann, J. R. (2009). Neuropsychiatric problems after traumatic brain injury: Unraveling the silent epidemic. *Psychosomatics, 50,* 198–205.

Verhaeghe, S., Defloor, T., & Grydonck, M. (2005). Stress and coping among families of patients with traumatic brain injury: A review of the literature. *Journal of Clinical Nursing, 14,* 1004–1012.

Veterans' Access, Choice, and Accountability Act of 2014, Pub. L. No. 113-146. Retrieved from https://www.congress.gov/bill/113th-congress/house-bill/3230/text.

Veterans Health Administration (Department of Veterans Affairs). (2009). *VHA Handbook 1010.01: Care management of Operation Enduring Freedom (OEF) and Operation Iraqi Freedom (OIF) veterans*. Retrieved from http://www.va.gov/vhapublications/ViewPublication.asp?pub_ID=2093.

Veterans Health Initiative. (2011). *Caring for Gulf War I veterans*. Department of Veterans Affairs, Employee Education System. Retrieved from http://www.publichealth.va.gov/docs/vhi/caring-for-gulf-war-veterans-vhi.pdf.

Vogt, D. S., Pless, A. P., King, L. A., & King, D. W. (2005). Deployment stressors, gender, and mental health outcomes among Gulf War I veterans. *Journal of Traumatic Stress, 18,* 272–284.

Vythilingam, M. (2010, May 20). *Combat operational stress control (COSC): An integral part of force health protection*. Presented at the Naval Center Combat and Operational Stress Control Conference 2010. Retrieved from http://www.med.navy.mil/sites/nmcsd/nccosc/coscConference/Pages/2010/coscConference2010MediaDay3.aspx.

Wachterman, M. W., Lipsitz, S. R., Simon, S. R., Lorenz, K. A., & Keating, N. L. (2014). Patterns of Hospice care among military veterans and non-veterans. *Journal of Pain and Symptom Management, 48,* 36–44.

Walker, A. J. (1985). Reconceptualizing family stress. *Journal of Marriage and the Family, 47,* 827–837.

Wallace, A. E., Sheehan, E. P., & Young-Xu, Y. (2009). Women, alcohol, and the military: Cultural changes and reductions in later alcohol problems among female veterans. *Journal of Women's Health, 18,* 1347–1353.

Walmart Facts. (2014). Retrieved November 23, 2014 from http://news.walmart.com/walmart-facts/.

Walsh, F. (2002). A family resilience framework: Innovative practice applications. *Family Relations, 51,* 130–137.

Walsh, F. (2003a). Changing families in a changing world: Reconstructing family normality. In F. Walsh (Ed.), *Normal family processes: Growing diversity and complexity* (pp. 3–26). New York, NY: Guildford Press.

Walsh, F. (2003b). Clinical views of family normality, health, and dysfunction: From deficit to strengths perspective. In F. Walsh (Ed.), *Normal family processes: Growing diversity and complexity* (pp. 27–57). New York, NY: Guildford Press.

Walsh, F. (2003c). Family resilience: A framework for clinical practice. *Family Process, 42,* 1–18.

Walsh, F. (2007). Traumatic loss and major disasters: Strengthening family and community resilience. *Family Process, 46,* 207–227.

Warden, D. (2006). Military TBI during the Iraq and Afghanistan wars. *Journal of Head Trauma Rehabilitation, 21,* 398–402.

Warner, C. H., Appenseller, G. N., Warner, C. M., & Greiger, T. (2009). Psychological effects of deployments on military families. *Psychiatric Annals, 39,* 56–63.

Washington State University Extension. (2009). *What is a land-grant college?* Retrieved from http://ext. wsu .edu/documents/landgrant.pdf.

Washington, D. L., Yano, E. M., McGuire, J., Hines, V., Lee, M., & Gelberg, L. (2010). Risk factors for homelessness among women veterans. *Journal of Health Care for the Poor and Underserved, 21,* 81–91.

Watkins, S. J., & Sherk, J. (2008). *Who serves in the U.S. military? The demographics of enlisted troops and officers.* Retrieved from the Heritage Foundation website: http://www.heritage.org/research/reports/2008/08/who-serves-in-the-us-military-the-demographics-of-enlisted-troops-and-officers.

Weber, E. G., & Weber, D. K. (2005). Geographic relocation frequency, resilience, and military adolescent behavior. *Military Medicine, 170,* 638–642.

Wells, T. S., LeardMann, C. A., Fortuna, S. O., Smith, B., Smith, T. C., Ryan, M. A., . . . Blazer, D. (2010). A prospective study of depression following combat deployment in support of the wars in Iraq and Afghanistan. *American Journal of Public Health, 100,* 90–99.

Werner, M. J., Walker, L. S., & Greene, J. W. (1994). Screening for problem drinking among college freshmen. *Journal of Adolescent Health, 15,* 303–310.

Wertsch, M. E. (1991). *Military brats: Legacies of childhood inside the fortress.* New York, NY: Harmony Books.

Westat. (2010). *National survey of veterans, active duty service members, demobilized National Guard and Reserve members, family members, and surviving spouses: Final report.* Rockville, MD: Author. Retrieved from http://www.va.gov/vetdata/docs/SurveysAndStudies/NVSSurveyFinalWeightedReport.pdf.

Westat. (2010). *Support to the DoD comprehensive review working group analyzing the impact of repealing "Don't Ask, Don't Tell": Findings from the surveys* (Vol. 1). Rockville, MD: Author. Retrieved from the Department of Defense website: http://www.defense.gov/home/features/2010/0610_gatesdadt/.

Westphal, R. J. & Woodward, K. R. (2010). Family fitness. *Military Medicine, 175,* 97–102.

Whiteman, S., & Barry, A. E. (2010, April). *Operation diploma: Profiles of student veterans attending college.* Presented at the Military Family Research Institute's 2010 International Research Symposium on Military Families, Indianapolis, IN.

Wiens, T., W., & Boss, P. (2006). Maintaining family resiliency before, during, and after military separations. In C. A. Castro, A. B. Adler, & T. W. Britt (Eds.), *Military life: The psychology of serving in peace and combat: The military family* (Vol. 3, pp. 13–38). Westport, CT: Praeger Security International.

Wilder Schaaf, K. P., Kreutzer, J. S., Danish, S. J., Pickett, T. C., Rybarczyk, B. D., & Nichols, M. G. (2013). Evaluating the needs of military and veterans' families in a polytrauma setting. *Rehabilitation Psychology, 58,* 106–110.

Willenz, J. A. (1983). *Women veterans: America's forgotten heroines.* New York, NY: Continuum Publishing Company.

Willerton, E., MacDermid Wadsworth, S., & Riggs, D. (2011). Introduction: Military families under stress: What we know and what we need to know. In S. MacDermid Wadsworth & D. Riggs (Eds.), *Risk and resilience in U.S. military families* (pp. 1–20). New York, NY: Springer.

Willerton, E., Samper, R., & MacDermid, S. M. (2008). *Support for casualty assistance officers.* Purdue University: Military Family Research Institute. Retrieved from http://www.mfri.purdue.edu/content.asp?tid=2&id=8.

Willerton, E., Schwarz, R. L., MacDermid Wadsworth, S. M., & Oglesby, M. S. (2011, August). Military fathers' perspectives on involvement. *Journal of Family Psychology, 25,* 521–530.

Williams, J., Jones, S. B., Pemberton, M. R., Bray, R. M., Brown, J. M., & Vandermaas-Peeler, R. (2010). Measurement invariance of alcohol use motivations in junior military personnel at risk for depression or anxiety. *Addictive Behaviors, 35,* 441–451.

Wilsnack, S. C., & Wilsnack, R. W. (1995). Drinking and problem drinking in U.S. women: Patterns and recent trends. *Recent Developments in Alcoholism, 12,* 29–60.

Wilson, C. & Nelson, J. P. (2012). Exploring the patterns, practices, and experiences of military women who managed genitourinary symptoms in deployed settings. *Journal of Obstetric, Gynecologic, & Neonatal Nursing, 41,* 293–302.

Wilson, S. R., Wilkum, K., Chernichky, S. M., MacDermid Wadsworth, S. M., & Broniarczyk, K. M. (2011). Passport toward success: Description and evaluation of a program designed to help children and families reconnect after a military deployment. *Journal of Applied Communication Research, 39,* 223–249.

Wolfe, J., Erickson, D. J., Sharkansky, E. J., King, D. W., & King, L. A. (1999). Course and predictors of posttraumatic stress disorder among Gulf War veterans: A prospective analysis. *Journal of Consulting and Clinical Psychology, 67,* 520–528.

Woodruff, S. I., Conway, T. L., & Edwards, C. C. (2000). Increasing response rates to a smoking survey for U.S. Navy enlisted women. *Evaluation and the Health Professions, 23,* 172–181.

Woodruff, T., Kelty, T., & Segal, D. R. (2006). Propensity to serve and motivation to enlist among American combat soldiers. *Armed Forces & Society, 32,* 353–366.

Worthen, M., Moos, R., & Ahern, J. (2012). Iraq and Afghanistan veterans' experiences living with their parents after separation from the military. *Contemporary Family Therapy, 34,* 362–375.

Wright, K. M., Burrell, L. M., Schroeder, E. D., & Thomas, J. L. (2006). Military spouses: Coping with the fear and the reality of service member injury and death. In C. A. Castro, A. B. Adler, & T. W. Britt (Eds.), *Military life: The psychology of serving in peace and combat: The military family* (Vol. 3, pp. 64–90). Westport, CT: Praeger Security International.

Wright, K. M., Cabrera, O. A., Bliese, P. D., Adler, A. B., Hoge, C. W., & Castro, C. A. (2009). Stigma and barriers to care in soldiers postcombat. *Psychological Services, 6,* 108–116.

Zellman, G. L., Gates, S. M., Moini, J. S., & Suttorp, M. (2009). Meeting family and military needs through military child care. *Armed Forces & Society, 35,* 437–459.

ZERO TO THREE. (2009). *Honoring our babies and toddlers: Supporting young children affected by a military parent's deployment, injury or death.* Washington, DC: Author.

ZERO TO THREE. (2011). *Coming Together Around Military Families®.* Retrieved from http://www.zerotothree.org/about-us/funded-projects/military-families/.

Zvonkovic, A. M., Solomon, C. R., Humble, A. M., & Manoogian, M. (2005). Family work and relationships: Lessons from families of men whose jobs require travel. *Family Relations, 54,* 411–422.

Author Index

A

Abma, J. C., 137
Ackerman, R., 156
Adair, K. C., 326
Adams, G. A., 53
Ader, H., 185
Adler, A. B., 60, 147, 175
Adler-Baeder, F., 184
Adler, L. E., 60, 147
Afifi, T., 183, 188
Age, T. R., 90, 94
Ahern, J., 205, 206, 308
Alcantara, W., 238, 340
Aldwin, 103
Alexander, C., 162
Algina, J., 200
Allen, E. S., 201
Ames, G. M., 143
Amoroso, P. J., 146
Andrews, B., 330
Antinori, N., 345
Appenseller, G. N., 183
Arbisi, P. A., 60
Armand, A., 335
Arnold, Janet, 208–209
Arnold-Mann, J., 18, 270
Asaro, M. R., 332, 333
Ashby, J., 75
Astor, R. A., 90
Atkins, D. C., 196
Attuel, H., 90
Auchterlonie, J. L., 170, 223

B

Badr, H., 196
Balekian, T. M., 218
Bales, R. F., 50
Bann, C. M., 28
Barker, L. H., 88
Barker, T. M., 196
Barnett, S., 345
Barry, A. E., 156
Bass, D. M., 250
Bathalon, G. P., 145
Batres, A., 171
Batten, S. V., 146, 327
Baucom, B., 196
Beardslee, W., 84, 93, 197, 199, 200, 201, 308
Becker, d., 223
Beckham, J. C., 169, 185
Beekley, M. D., 145
Beharie, S., 59
Bell, D. B., 53, 146, 183
Bell, N. S., 93, 146, 183
Benbenishly, R., 90
Benedek, D. M., 314

Berglund, P., 169
Berry, K., 88
Berry, Robin, 274, 341
Besterman-Dahan, K., 345
Bicksler, B. A., 29
Black, M. C., 220
Blaisure, K. R., 18, 91–92, 270, 341–342
Blakeley, K., 6
Blank, H., 79
Blazer, D., 143, 145, 170
Bleich, A., 185
Bliese, P. D., 148, 175
Blow, A. J., 94, 95, 302
Blumberg, S. L., 201
Boehnlein, J. K., 239
Boggs, S., 200
Bonanno, G. A., 142, 331, 332
Booth, B., 53, 54, 62, 63, 65, 67
Borrego, Jr., J., 200
Boss, P., 18, 61, 62, 63, 66, 69, 74, 75, 102, 104, 106, 107, 114, 118, 119, 120, 311–312, 330, 347
Bossarte, R. M., 220
Bostian-Kentes, Ariana, 42–46
Bosworth, H. B., 185
Bottrick, Stephanie, 42–46
Bowen, G. L., 51, 52, 131, 288, 332
Boyce, W. T., 111
Boyer, C. G., 145
Boyko, E. J., 142
Bramsen, I., 185
Bray, R. M., 28, 143, 170, 175, 175
Brenner, L. A., 312
Brewer, R. D., 143
Brewin, C. R., 330
Bride, B. E., 245, 346
Brink, S., 174
Britt, T. W., 148, 174
Brockberg, D., 200
Brokaw, T., 237
Bromet, E., 223
Broniarczyk, K. M., 304
Brown, C., 163, 166, 193, 207
Bruner, E. F., 5, 6
Brymer, M. J., 207, 313, 314, 347
Burrell, L. M., 15, 53, 68, 331, 332
Burrelli, D. F., 212, 213
Burton, T. E., 296
Buunk, B., 188
Byrne, T. 225

C

Cable, S., 63
Cabrera, O. A., 148, 175
Calhoun, P. S., 185, 169, 196
Call, V. R. A., 205
Campbell, C. S., 145, 250
Campise, R. L., 84, 161–162, 343

Subject Index

A

ABCx Model, 113–118, 127
Academics, deployment on children, 84–85
Accessions, 25
Accompanied tours, 18, 40–41
ACE Military Guide to the Evaluation of Educational Experiences in the Armed Services, 153–154
Active Component, 132, 158, 353
  alcohol use, 143
  family interventions, 264, 325
  marital patterns, 135–136, 140, 198, 204, 209
  members, 5
  mental health, 170
  respondents, 25, 27–28
  social support, 148
  transitions to retirement, 149
Active duty, 53–55
  lesbian, gay and bisexual service members, 42–44
  personnel, 24, 29–30, 34
Acute grief, 331
Acute stress disorder, 169, 323
Acute stress reaction, 169, 323
Adaptive coping strategies, 116–117
Adolescents, in combat-injured families, 197
Adult dependent category, 204–205
AER, *see* Army Emergency Relief
AFAS, *see* Air Force Aid Society
African American men and women, 26, 32, 33, 39, 81, 136, 238
Air Force, 3–40
Air Force Academy, 340
Air Force Aid Society (AFAS), 267
Air National Guard, 55, 66, 66, 74, 80, 262
Alcohol
  misuse, 143–145, 175–176
  and substance use/abuse, 141–142, 144, 175, 245
Allowances, 133–134, 135, 137, 138, 254
All-volunteer force, 3, 4, 5, 14, 15, 21, 242
  need to be family friendly, 18, 50, 131, 235, 268
  recruitment and retention, 25, 27, 52, 132, 212, 235
Ambiguous loss, 61–62, 118, 102
Ambiguous loss theory, 118–119, 127
American Red Cross, 291
Anxiety disorder, 68, 169, 191, 226
Applicants, 25
Aptitude, 25–26
Armed Forces of the United States, 5–8
Armed Forces Qualifying Test (AFQT), 25–26
Armed Forces Sexual Harassment Survey, 216–218
Armed Services YMCA, 122
Army Emergency Relief (AER), 267
Army Family Covenant, 126–127, 260–261
Army National Guard, 43, 55–56, 60–69
Army, Navy, Air Force, and Marine Corps Reserves, 55–56
Army Resilience Training program, 280

B

Baseline data from the Millennium Cohort Study, 142–147
Basic Allowance for Housing (BAH), 134
Battle Buddies, 132
Battlemind Training, 279–280
Behavioral problems, in children, 85
Beneficiary, 14–15
Bereavement, 94–96, 207–209, 251, 330–333
Binge drinking, 143–144
Bipolar disorder, 281
Blue Star Organizations, 291–292
Boss's taxonomy of stressor characteristics, 104, 114
Boundary ambiguity, 61–62, 64
Buddy-to-Buddy program, 302–304
Buffer stressful information, 188
Burnout, 100, 330, 346

C

Care, principles of, 312
Careers, 344–345
Caregivers, 195–196, 204, 241
Caregiver burden, 185, 196, 250, 319
Caregivers and Veterans Omnibus Health Services Act of 2010, 251
Casualties, 68–69
Casualty Assistance Calls Officer (CACO), 68–69
Casualty Assistance Officer (CAO), 68–69
Casualty Assistance Representative (CAR), 68–69
Casualty Notification Officer (CNO), 68–69
CBT, *see* Cognitive-based therapy; Combat Brigade Team
Chain of command, 3–4, 11–14
Chaplains, 266–267, 311, 313–314
  rank, 14
  roles, 52, 68, 127, 139, 162, 167, 173
  training, 41, 199
Charity organizations, 266, 267
Chief of Staff, 4
Child care, 51, 56, 74, 78–83, 283–284
Child development centers (CDCs), 19, 50, 79, 134, 273, 283, 284
Children in DoDEA schools, 74, 81, 282–283
Chronic multi-symptom illness (CMI), 166, 243, 244
Civilian organizations, 252, 287–288, 305–6
  assistance to reintegrate, 292–298
  collaborative endeavors, 298–305
  continuing education, 305
  created to serve service members and their families, 289–292
Clearinghouse for Military Family Readiness, 109, 124, 198–199
Coercive controlling violence, 193